'This is the book somatic psychotherapy and psychotherapy in general has been waiting for! With clear and incisive analysis, Geuter convincingly argues why the subjective body must be included in all psychotherapy modalities. He provides a very clear philosophical and conceptual analysis of the need for all psychotherapy to embrace relational, emotional, embodied and enactive human experience, rather than biology, as the basis of understanding for clinical theory and practice. This professional tour de force, covering an incredibly broad range of the historical and contemporary professional and broader humanistic and philosophical literature, is a "must read" for all in the psychotherapy and related helping professions.'

Jeff Barlow, BA, BEd, MEd, *Somatic Psychotherapist, supervisor and trainer; founding director, Australian College of Contemporary Somatic Psychotherapy*

'Dr. Geuter offers us an intensely erudite yet delightfully readable survey of the contemporary field of body psychotherapy. His perspectives are refreshingly thoughtful and provide an interesting "take" on the current state of these vitally important modes of healing practice. This book will help to advance the field significantly'.

Barnaby B. Barratt, PhD, DHS, *Director of doctoral studies in Bodymind Healing at the Parkmore Institute, Parkmore (Johannesburg), South Africa; author of* The Emergence of Somatic Psychology and Bodymind Therapy

'This is an excellent book which transcends but values the differences between schools and is a masterly foundation for body psychotherapy as a mainstream of psychotherapy.'

David Boadella, PhD (Hon), *Founder of Biosynthesis; founding president and honorary member of the European Association for Body Psychotherapy* (†)

'Ulfried Geuter's theory of body psychotherapy takes up the current developments of embodiment research as well as body phenomenology and integrates them into a comprehensive and convincing conception. An indispensable foundational work for all who are theoretically and practically involved in this field'.

Thomas Fuchs, MD, *Karl-Jaspers-Professor for Philosophical Foundations of Psychiatry and Psychotherapy; director of the section "Phenomenological Psychopathology and Psychotherapy", Psychiatric Clinic, University of Heidelberg, Germany; chair of the German Society for Phenomenological Anthropology, Psychiatry and Psychotherapy*

'Ulfried Geuter has written a comprehensive book that will be greatly welcomed in the field of body psychotherapy, where rather than distinctions between body and psyche, the interpretive framework centers on whole living-experiencing subjects in relation to their world. It's an important attempt to theoretically unify a variety of practical approaches, "beyond the schools", while allowing for the legitimacy of a diversity of practices, that, at the same time, does justice to subjective experiences of both therapists and patients. Geuter importantly integrates the new insights of embodied and relational-intersubjective cognitive science with the essential practices of body psychotherapy in ways that are revelatory for both the science and the practice'.

Shaun Gallagher, PhD, D Phil (Hon), *Professor, Lillian and Morrie Moss Chair of Excellence in Philosophy at the University of Memphis, USA; Professorial Fellow at SOLA, University of Wollongong, Australia; co-editor-in-chief of* Phenomenology and the Cognitive Sciences *and co-editor of* The Oxford Handbook of 4E Cognition

'Geuter succeeds in tracing the theoretical and methodological diversity of body psychotherapies back to a few general psychological basic principles of perception, body experience, memory, affect, development, defence and communication. Upon reading this book, the fog clears and a clear view of the complex matter is revealed. The easily readable presentation is aided by a good didactic treatment of the material, with many case studies and methodical therapeutical hints. There is currently no other book that brings this valuable and comprehensive psychotherapeutic approach to the reader in such a systematic, clear and understandable way'.

Dirk Revenstorf, PhD, *Professor Emeritus for Clinical Psychology, University of Tuebingen, Germany, and Universidad de las Americas, Puebla, Mexico; co-founder of the German-Chinese Society for Psychotherapy; director of the Milton-Erickson-Academy for Clinical Hypnosis, Tuebingen; co-director of the European Academy for Couple Therapy, Mallorca, Spain*

'Geuter's remarkable textbook is one of the most significant milestones in the development of the field of body psychotherapy. Laying out clearly the theoretical paradigm of experiential, enacted and relational principles of body-oriented psychological interventions in clinical practice, this book outlines how body psychotherapy distinguishes itself from traditional talking therapies in theory and practice. About 100 years after Wilhem Reich laid the foundation for body psychotherapy, Geuter's book demonstrates how advances in cognitive sciences and psychology have been utilised to develop body psychotherapy into a distinct modality in the wider psychotherapy landscape. A must-read for all scholars of psychotherapy, and practitioners from all psychotherapy branches will benefit greatly from numerous practical examples that help illustrating the theoretical concepts'.

Frank Röhricht, MD, *Professor, Medical Director Research &*
Innovation at East London NHS Foundation Trust; Consultant
Psychiatrist and Body Psychotherapist; Honorary Professor of
Psychiatry at Queen Mary University of London

'At last, a book that is capable of bringing together the various traditions and schools of body psychotherapy, recognizing it not only as a branch of psychoanalysis, but appreciating body psychotherapy as something created in its own right, a complex synthesis of scientific and philosophical discourses, at once familiar and innovative. This book introduces a coherent theory without losing the richness of complexity and gives body psychotherapists a solid foundation'.

Maurizio Stupiggia, PhD, *Professor at the Department*
of Clinical Sciences – Faculty of Medicine and Surgery,
University of Milan, Italy; co-founder of the International
School of Biosystemic and of the Bio-Integral Institute of Body
Psychotherapy in Tokyo

'This book offers a clear and comprehensive account of body psychotherapy theory. It explores the significance of embodiment from a "lived body" context, which makes it a rich resource for the development of embodied research. The English translation is a rich addition to existing embodiment literature, and is an invaluable tool for students, faculty and clinicians in all psychological coursework'.

Jennifer Frank Tantia, PhD, BC-DMT, *Somatic*
Psychotherapist, private practice, New York; co-editor of The
Routledge International Handbook on Embodied Perspectives
in Psychotherapy *and editor of* The Art and Science of
Embodied Research Design: Concepts, Methods and Cases

Body Psychotherapy

This book introduces body psychotherapy as one of the essential approaches in psychotherapy, reflecting the increasing integration of the body into clinical mental health practice.

The book offers an entirely new view on body psychotherapy based upon advanced research on embodiment, memory, emotion regulation, developmental psychology and body communication and an experiential and relational understanding of psychotherapy. Accordingly, the author grounds the theory of body psychotherapy on the theoretical approach of enactivism, which regards experience as arising from meaningful living interaction with others and their environment. The book, fortified with clinical examples, shows the distinctiveness of body psychotherapy as compared with a traditional talking therapy approach. It also convincingly demonstrates that each form of psychotherapy should consider body experiences.

This text will be a comprehensive foundation for psychotherapists of every orientation, scholars of the humanities and students and especially those wishing to integrate embodied experience into their understanding of their patients.

Ulfried Geuter is a body psychotherapist and psychoanalyst who works in his own practice in Berlin. He taught body psychotherapy as a lecturer at the Free University of Berlin from 1995–2003 and as an honorary professor at the University of Marburg from 2010–2023 and is a training analyst, supervisor and lecturer in postgraduate psychotherapeutic training programs. He runs the Institute for Advanced Training in Body Psychotherapy in Berlin and is the author of *The Professionalization of Psychology in Nazi Germany*, 1992.

Body Psychotherapy

A Theoretical Foundation for Clinical Practice

Ulfried Geuter

Translated by Elizabeth Marshall

Routledge
Taylor & Francis Group

LONDON AND NEW YORK

Designed cover image: © Lydia Olbrich-Geuter

First published in English 2024
by Routledge
4 Park Square, Milton Park, Abingdon, Oxon OX14 4RN

and by Routledge
605 Third Avenue, New York, NY 10158

Routledge is an imprint of the Taylor & Francis Group, an informa business

© 2024 Ulfried Geuter

First German edition published by © Springer-Verlag Berlin Heidelberg, 2015
Translation from the German language edition:
Körperpsychotherapie; Grundriss einer Theorie für die klinische Praxis
by Ulfried Geuter, edition: 2
Copyright © Springer-Verlag Berlin Heidelberg, 2023
This edition has been translated and published under license from
Springer-Verlag GmbH, DE, part of Springer Nature.
Springer-Verlag GmbH, DE, part of Springer Nature takes no responsibility and shall not be made liable for the accuracy of the translation.

Library of Congress Cataloging-in-Publication Data
Names: Geuter, Ulfried, 1950- author. | Marshall, Elizabeth (Translator), translator.
Title: Body psychotherapy: a theoretical foundation for clinical practice/Ulfried Geuter;
translated by Elizabeth Marshall.
Other titles: Körperpsychotherapie. English
Description: First English edition. | Abingdon, Oxon; New York, NY: Routledge, 2024. |
"First German edition published by © Springer-Verlag Berlin Heidelberg, 2015.
Translation from the German language edition Körperpsychotherapie;
Grundriss einer Theorie für die klinische Praxis by Ulfried Geuter, edition: 2,
Copyright © Springer-Verlag Berlin Heidelberg, 2022"– galley. |
Includes bibliographical references and index.
Identifiers: LCCN 2023018867 (print) | LCCN 2023018868 (ebook) |
ISBN 9781032010465 (hardback) | ISBN 9781032010458 (paperback) |
ISBN 9781003176893 (ebook)
Subjects: LCSH: Mind and body therapies. | Psychotherapy–Methodology.
Classification: LCC RC489.M53 G4813 2024 (print) | LCC RC489.M53 (ebook) |
DDC 616.89/14–dc23/eng/20230623
LC record available at https://lccn.loc.gov/2023018867
LC ebook record available at https://lccn.loc.gov/2023018868

ISBN: 9781032010465 (hbk)
ISBN: 9781032010458 (pbk)
ISBN: 9781003176893 (ebk)

DOI: 10.4324/9781003176893

Typeset in Minion Pro
by Deanta Global Publishing Services, Chennai, India

Contents

Preface

Ulfried Geuter
Translated by Elizabeth Marshall

'Big things have small beginnings', says the protagonist in the film *Lawrence of Arabia*. Right from the start at the first congress in 1998, the members of the German Association for Body Psychotherapy (DGK) felt a need to work on developing a common ground for all the various body psychotherapeutic schools. I was asked to undertake this work and carried the idea around with me for a while. For a long time, I thought I would write a report of about 50 pages and that would be it. In the end this book grew out of that.

The first edition was published in German in 2015. I am very pleased that it is now appearing in English and will thus reach a larger audience. The translation follows the second revised edition published in German in 2023.

From 1998 it took a while until the time was ripe to actually write this book. It was still the era of the various schools, each eager to distinguish and develop themselves, rather than to bring their ideas into our field as a whole. And I was so busy with other things in my own life that I had no time for the project. However, over the years, both these things changed. I also needed those years to clarify my own thoughts on the scientific foundation of body psychotherapy. Simultaneously, interest in it was increasing on the part of psychotherapy in general, and a great deal of literature was published which I could evaluate for this book.

Due to my own experience, my interest was always in body psychotherapy as a whole and not in any particular school. At the end of the 1970s, I was working with a bodywork teacher, who had me lying with my spine along a broomstick, long before I heard about experiential therapies. Later on, when I at least had heard of Elsa Gindler, the grandmother of many experiential approaches, I found out that my teacher had been a student of Gindler's assistant Sophie Ludwig. Then I took part in groups run by an actual Gindler student, Frieda Goralewski. The atmosphere in the basement of a villa in Berlin was that of a select community, under the spell of Goralewski's perceptive eye. People spoke quietly and moved about with care. Gindler's was a world of women looking to the inside.

I had encountered another world in the student movement before – one of rebellion and the liberation of lust. I read pirate copies of Wilhelm Reich's books, bought in smoke-filled student pubs, where we philosophised about whether free love would revolutionise society. Years later, in the rooms of a therapist collective in Berlin Kreuzberg, I took part in my first Reichian therapy group. The atmosphere was proactive and confrontative. Having practised fine perceptiveness with Goralewski, here I experienced painfully how I almost suffocated at birth. The world of Reichian body psychotherapy encouraged powerful, cathartic and rebellious feelings. We looked to the inside so as to let it all hang out. And just like the social movement that promoted it, this kind of body psychotherapy remained for a long time non-conformist, creative and sceptical about the sciences.

However, even as both the gentle and the rebellious methods of body psychotherapy saw themselves as outsiders in relation to the established schools of psychoanalysis and behavioural psychotherapy, whose respective dogmas dominated the field of psychotherapy, they nevertheless developed their own dogmas. Many people who had an idea, charisma or both founded their own schools and offered trainings. Nobody bothered much about scientific thinking.

In those days, we learned through our own experience. The schools were built on experiential knowledge. This is a great treasure. However if we want to teach these experiences and bring them into the psychotherapeutic discourse, then we have to relate them to science and expose them to critical reflection. Thus body psychotherapy today has the task of clarifying the theoretical and conceptual foundation of its work in order to provide it with a scientific basis, whilst honouring the innovative achievements of its founders and preserving their legacy. This book is my contribution to this work.

When I was a student 50 years ago, psychology did not know feeling and experiencing human beings, but only perception, thinking, learning, motivation. As I was starting to research this book about 20 years ago, this had changed somewhat, but humans were not yet regarded as bodily experiencing beings. If psychotherapy was interested at all in the body, it was always only about the brain. Today, however, embodied psychology is becoming mainstream. In psychotherapy too, people are realising that here living, embodied subjects are communicating with each other.

I present body psychotherapy as an experiential and relational therapy approach. I base this on the systemic notion of life; on the intersubjective understanding of psychotherapy; on phenomenology, which in philosophy has highlighted the significance of the body for experience; and on enactivism. More recently there has been a profusion of publications on this theoretical approach, stemming from theories of the embodied mind, which see psychological processes as part of the living interaction of a person with others and their environment, the body as a mindful body which creates meaning and mental disorders as processes in the relationship of a person to all that constitutes their life. I have endeavoured to take this literature into account. However, as a practising psychotherapist, it is difficult for me to follow scientific discussions comprehensively parallel to my work.

Several monographs on body psychotherapy, published since I wrote the first edition, draw on ideas similar to mine, as Cornell (2015), Kern (2014), Rolef Ben-Shahar (2014), Totton (2015) and Westland (2015); so do many articles in *The Handbook of Body Psychotherapy & Somatic Psychology* by Marlock, Weiss, Young and Soth (2015) and in the *Handbook of Embodied Perspectives in Psychotherapy* by Payne, Koch, Tantia and Fuchs (2019).

In contrast to these more recent works, many European body psychotherapists still base their ideas mainly on the work of Wilhelm Reich and his successors. Reich's legacy indeed continues to be fertile soil for the development of body psychotherapy. However the foundations of a house for our time should be built on a theory of embodied subjectivity and intersubjectivity, which were not available in Reich's time. If we stand too long on the shoulders of giants, we will find it difficult to forge our own path. My own path I describe in this book.

Originally my idea was to depict both the theoretical basis and the principles of practice in one book. This proved to be impossible. It became clear during writing that both subjects needed their own elaboration, so that I decided to confine this book to the theoretical outline. I deal with the principles of practice and treatment techniques in body psychotherapy, indications and contraindications, the therapeutic relationship, mechanisms of change and the findings of research on the effectiveness of psychotherapy extensively in my book *The Practice of Body Psychotherapy*, published in German in 2019.

My book has developed during practical work with adult patients in individual settings. While it was evolving, I often wrote down what was happening in a therapy session, and I use these sketches to illustrate the approach of body psychotherapy. I take the liberty of guiding the reader from scientific theory to practical work and back again. The focus of my own experience means that this book deals with out-patient work in body psychotherapy with individual patients and not group therapy. Working with children is also not covered.

The book is addressed to psychotherapists of every orientation and to students training in the profession. However it is also meant for other professionals, such as dance and movement therapists, physiotherapists or occupational therapists, who encounter aspects of body psychotherapy in their work. And it is addressed to body psychotherapists themselves, who are often only familiar with the concepts of the one particular school where they were trained. People from outside the profession wanting to learn about body psychotherapy will find this book quite specialised.

My training as a psychotherapist started with client-centred psychotherapy. For a long time I also flirted with the idea of training as a psychoanalyst. However I knew that the institute I had chosen had for years concealed documents from the German Institute for Psychological Research and Psychotherapy from the Nazi period, which had long been thought lost. This was the reason I could only study there at a later date, after a more critical generation had taken charge. In my body psychotherapy training, as I cried deeply about the fate of one of my grandfathers during the Nazi period, I realised that with Ken Speyer I had chosen for my first teacher an anarchist Jewish American – a good match. With him it was possible to get in touch with the shadow. The most important thing I learnt in the training with him and Clover Southwell was not to be afraid of anything that comes up in therapy, however heavy it is. Body psychotherapy can induce disturbing feelings and irritating states, and as therapists, we must be able to hold the patients there. In training we experienced all this. I am extremely grateful for everything I learned about body psychotherapeutic work from Ken Speyer, Clover Southwell, David Boadella, Ebbah Boyesen and Wolf Buentig, and later in workshops with Gerda Boyesen, Alexander Lowen, Mike Noack, Bettina Schroeter, Herbert Meyer, Bernd Eiden, Helga Engel and John Pierrakos. I also learnt a lot about body experience from my ballet teacher Jacques Barkey and my Shiatsu and Jin Shin Do therapist Inge Berlin.

It was a long road from those experiences to this book. I am grateful to the German Association for Body Psychotherapy (DGK) and their chairperson of many years, my friend Manfred Thielen. He was faithful to the project of this book over many years and never wavered in his support, even when I thought I could never manage it. As senior editor of the publishing company Springer, Monika Radecki promoted and encouraged the project. She was always patient and lent me her support when the work turned out differently than I had expected. And she also supported my work on the second edition and gave me space to revise the text. Joanne Forshaw and Grace McDonnell of Routledge supported the project from the first idea for an English language publication in 2017 through to finalisation and were always available when I had questions. I am very grateful to them both.

Many of the ideas presented here developed out of discussions with a large number of colleagues. Frank Roehricht and Norbert Schrauth encouraged and supported the work on this book from beginning to end. Their suggestions, ideas and commentaries enriched many parts of the manuscript, and their support as colleagues and friends sustained me throughout. Thomas Harms read the whole first version of the manuscript, completed in 2011, and made time for a long discussion about its basic concept. David Boadella, George Downing and Irmingard Staeuble read the complete first version and gave me important advice. Irmingard helped especially with the structure, with the form of the introduction and with the historical chapter; George wrote pages of remarks on all the chapters, which I bore in mind for the rewrite. Angela von Arnim, Werner Eberwein, Sabine Koch, Juergen Kriz, Alexandre Métraux, Johannes Reichmayr, Dirk Revenstorf and Benajir Wolf supplied critical feedback on individual chapters, which helped improve the book. Other colleagues, too numerous to mention by name, drew my attention to relevant publications and provided their papers. My wife Lydia read parts of the first and all of the second version of the manuscript and pointed out what was still obtuse. And my brother Raimund read the whole thing and eliminated the linguistic mistakes. Henry Ibeka helped with the technical problems on the computer. I heartily thank all of them.

While preparing the second edition, Marek Szczepánski challenged my thinking by discussing my theoretical foundations, and Sheila Butler, Lidy Evertsen and Sofia Petridou discussed with me in depth the meaning of the systems view of life for our field. Frank Roehricht gave important suggestions as to the reworking of all chapters. He and Nina Papadopoulos helped me to prepare the extensive documentation that the publishers, Routledge, needed for the book proposal. Josephine Kirschner and Courtenay Young helped to find original citations in English publications that I had quoted in translation for the German edition. Kelly Lynch advised me on some aspects of the historical chapter, Frank Roehricht with clarifying which technical terms in English correspond to those used in the German text; George Downing gave some late advice. I am very grateful to them all for their assistance.

Over the years I have read, heard and experienced so much that I cannot always be sure where my ideas come from. If therefore I have depicted something without acknowledging the source, this is not because I am deliberately ignoring them; much more it is because this idea has become such a part of my own thinking that I can no longer locate its origin. Please forgive me for this. I bear responsibility for any mistakes that may be found in this book.

For the English edition I have slightly altered the text. Some passages relating specifically to German-speaking countries or to discussions limited to them have been deleted. I have replaced many German references with English ones and reworked the bibliography to better suit those reading the text in English. However in many cases the book still does rely on German sources. Also we have retained some of the characteristics of the German, for example in using the noun 'patient' instead of 'client'. In much of psychotherapy, this is common here. Because of its Latin root, the word 'patient' also means the one who suffers. For the English-speaking world, 'client' would perhaps have been more suitable, but we decided in this case to follow the German text.

In the wake of the discussion about gender pronouns, we have used 'they' and 'their' throughout, unless the gender is specifically stated.

Elizabeth Marshall took on the laborious task of translation despite the fact that the funds were by no means sufficient to cover the costs of the work. I am very grateful to her. She translated chapter for chapter parallel to my reworking of the text for the second edition. Even when over time I had amendments to the text already translated, she accepted all my wishes, true to the motto 'If a job's worth doing, it's worth doing well'. She made it possible for the book to appear in English.

Both the German and the European Association of Body Psychotherapy have supported my work financially. I am very grateful to them. The translation was made possible through the financial support of the Wilhelm Reich Foundation (WRF), the European Association for Body Psychotherapy (EABP) and the German Association for Body Psychotherapy (DGK). Here I would like to thank above all Lidy Evertsen who, after the dissolution of the WRF, decided with the support of Elisabeth de Lange and Erik Jarlnaes to allocate the money left in the foundation to translate this book. Likewise the board of the EABP and its president Carmen Joanne Ablack and Manfred Thielen as chairperson of the DGK at the relevant time deserve my gratitude. They and later Vladimir Pozharashki as treasurer of the EABP and Stefan Ide as chair of the DGK were very cooperative in realising this project.

In conclusion, I would like to thank those people from whom I have learnt most: my patients. They made it possible for me to learn from our experiences together and showed me what was helpful and what not. Those patients whose sessions are described here have given their permission. Two of them were untraceable, but I have changed all identifying information so they remain anonymous.

My wife Lydia and sons Jonathan and Joschua often had to take a backseat when I was immersed in my early work on this book. Now our sons are older and have gone their own ways, and only my wife had to continue to endure my work on the revision and the translation. They are the source of my deep contentedness with my life from the heart; this also gives me the strength for an intellectual endeavour like this book.

Berlin, 24 January, 2023
Ulfried Geuter

1

Introduction

Body psychotherapy is one of the major approaches of psychotherapy. It unites **three historical traditions** within itself. The first originated in **critical psychoanalysis**, which views psychological problems as being the result of the internalisation of deficient or harmful experiences. From this tradition, connected to the early work of Wilhelm Reich, we can assign body psychotherapy to the broad spectrum of depth psychology (Marlock, 2015b; Roehricht, 2021). As with other psychodynamic approaches, the focus of interest is the patient's inner life, the consideration of unconscious and repressed motives and conflicts of desire and defence, and also of transference in treatment. Body psychotherapy has this in common with Gestalt therapy, which developed out of the same tradition, so that they can be regarded as siblings.

A second tradition of body psychotherapy has its roots in **body education** and in bodywork methods developed out of **reform gymnastics**. From these and from expressive dance emerged an attentive and mindful form of therapeutic work with the body. In this tradition, body psychotherapy was primarily concerned with the perception and exploration of the body in breathing, posture and movement. Based on this we can view body psychotherapy as a phenomenological approach, since it focusses on what a patient experiences when sensing and becoming aware of themselves (D Johnson, 2015; Marlock, 2015a).

From the 1960s onwards, a third tradition of experiential body psychotherapy developed through the **human potential movement** and **humanistic psychotherapy**. In this tradition the focus is on the here and now, as in Gestalt therapy, and on utilising in treatment the patient's embodied experience in relation to the world as the source of meaning and sense (cf. Kepner, 1993; Yontef & Schulz, 2016). In their understanding, the psychotherapeutic process depends upon the patient experiencing themselves through feeling and sensing within a helpful therapeutic relationship (Marlock, 2010, p. 53). In this respect we can classify body psychotherapy with Elliott et al. (2013) as a sub-approach of the broader spectrum of the humanistic-experiential psychotherapies. Experiential approaches such as client-centred psychotherapy or Emotion-Focused Therapy emphasise experiencing (Gendlin, 1961) and understand psychological processes as tangible bodily processes (Waibel et al., 2009, p. 6). They also have in common the orientation towards the patient's growth, an idea that C.G. Jung advocated and that is characteristic of humanistic psychology (Eberwein, 2009).

All three above-mentioned traditions of body psychotherapy aim to facilitate the self-regulation of psychophysical and emotional processes and of human behaviour (Carroll, 2009).

Body psychotherapy however does have some special features which distinguish it from other psychotherapeutic approaches. Theory and practice are always related to the

DOI: 10.4324/9781003176893-1

human body and the somatic experience of self. The life of the psyche is seen as grounded in embodied experiences (Acolin, 2019; Barratt, 2010, p. 19). The body is 'the actual place where experiencing takes place, where feelings and moods become perceptible, and where differentiations between different emotional states … are made' (Weiss, 2015, p. 421). This is why body psychotherapy utilises body experience as the fundamental source of the experience of the self (Geuter, 2016; Roehricht, 2000, p. 26). Processes of body awareness, bodily expression or bodily interaction are included in treatment on principle.

Theoretically, body psychotherapy sees the human being as a unity of body and mind, not just objectively but also as a subjective experiential entity. Experience occurs simultaneously both bodily and mentally. Body and mind are seen as aspects of the whole human being, who lives life as an actor in interaction with the world of objects and of other human beings. We can call this the **holistic view of humanity** of body psychotherapy. We can distinguish between physiological and psychological processes, but as aspects of life processes they are at the same time one entity. Body psychotherapy treatment attends to both psychological and somatic processes as well as verbal and embodied interactions. Alongside verbal interaction, we utilise methods of working with and on the body. Its distinctive history, holistic understanding of human existence and own practice style set body psychotherapy apart from other approaches and constitute its therapeutic identity (Rolef Ben-Shahar, 2014, p. 74). In particular, the broad spectrum of treatment methods and techniques marks it out in a clinical context as a distinct approach (Geuter, 2004, p. 106). They include:

- Body awareness.
- Perception and regulation of the breathing.
- Clarification of the meaning of bodily experience.
- Facilitation of bodily expression and the affect language of the body.
- Somato-psychological regulation of dysregulated emotional processes.
- Exploration of so-called enactments in action dialogue.
- Working with somatic resonance and bodily interaction.
- Exploration and transformation of affect motor patterns.
- Stabilisation, reinvigoration, bordering or soothing through grounding and holding.
- Activation and harmonisation of psychophysical processes including the psychophysiological level of stress regulation.
- Development of resources whose potential can be sensed in the body.

Totton (2003) begins his introduction to body psychotherapy by describing various sessions:

- In one, based on the patient's sensations and the images connected to them, a therapist explores with him his headache and its possible symbolic meaning.
- In another session, when having touched her throat with her hand, a patient experiences a bout of coughing and a growling roar, she encourages the patient to let these autonomous body reactions just happen.
- In a third, she works with mirroring the patient's movements and from there to discovering their meaning.

These are all possibilities of body psychotherapeutic work. A body psychotherapist can however just be present, 'showing interest, concern, delight and supporting the client to self-regulate through rest or interaction' (Carroll, 2005, p. 20).

Hitherto body psychotherapy has developed largely in the form of various **schools**. The diversity of these schools – such as bioenergetics, biodynamics, biosynthesis, Bodynamic International, Hakomi, Somatic Experiencing, Focusing, Body-Mind Centering, Dance Therapy, Integrative Body and Movement Therapy, Functional Relaxation or Concentrative Movement Therapy and many more smaller ones – constitutes even today an important potential for further development and creativity.

However this also entails a conceptual multiplicity and heterogeneity (Roehricht, 2000, p. 15), which until now has impeded a comprehensive theoretical improvement of the field as a whole, as well as the integration of the various schools. In the *Handbook of body psychotherapy and somatic psychology*, Marlock and Weiss (2015, p. 8) speak of a 'plurality of different presumptions and positions that, in some cases, are difficult to reconcile with each other.'

Many schools were based on the teachings of a 'master', as Seewald (1991) referred to equivalent teachings in motology. They possess a rich informal knowledge, communicated in a master–student relationship within a training group, but limited by the focus only on their own ideas and therapeutic techniques, with hardly any reference to scientific research. To establish a foundation for a general body psychotherapy, we have to find a position beyond the schools.

The lack of a common theoretical basis and a common terminology is not altogether due to the diversity of the schools but also to the fact that there is no comprehensive psychological theory the subject of which is the human being as experiencing themselves as mind and body. Even in scientific subdisciplines such as embodied cognitive science, where currently they are developing the most promising approaches to a theory of embodied subjectivity, there is no general agreement on concepts and ideas (Di Paolo & Thompson, 2014) – on, for example, what we mean by conscious or non-conscious (Legrand, 2007, p. 577).

Some schools endeavoured to reach a clarification of terminology, particularly Hakomi (Weiss et al., 2015), Functional Relaxation (von Arnim et al., 2022), Integrative Movement Therapy (Petzold, 2003), Integrative Body Psychotherapy (Kaul & Fischer, 2016) and Dance Therapy (Trautmann-Voigt & Voigt, 2009). However probably the most important scientific task for body psychotherapy is still to define its conceptual and theoretical framework and to establish a common language (Totton, 2003, p. 138; 2002a, p. 202). It is time to bring these heterogenous traditions together and develop a coherent general theory, compatible with models in core scientific disciplines, which at the same time does justice to the subjective processes of experience that we are dealing with in psychotherapy.

This book is dedicated to that task. It offers a theoretical foundation for body psychotherapy above and beyond the schools, but in which their insights and experiential knowledge are still preserved. It positions body psychotherapy in the field of scientific research and provides it with a basis within this research. Furthermore, it aims to demonstrate that basically no psychotherapeutic approach can ignore the body and bodily interaction, since all experience and all behaviour is mediated consciously or unconsciously through the body (Noë, 2021, p. 960; Revenstorf, 2013, p. 178).

Psychotherapy is itself not a basic scientific discipline, but belongs like medicine to the healing professions. Thus it relies on practice experience and the insights and models of various scientific fields. These are the disciplines I think are most relevant for body psychotherapy (cf. Roehricht, 2009, p. 139):

- Theories of embodied mind and experience.
- Theories of body and self experience.
- Embodiment research.
- Theories of memory.

- Theories of emotions.
- Developmental psychology.
- Research on the body in interaction.
- Various aspects of physiological and neuroscientific theories.

I will discuss all these in this book. All the same I do not regard neuroscience as a discipline which can provide a scientific foundation for experiential body psychotherapy. Nonetheless, neuroscientific research findings and models can inspire the development of a theory and help us to better understand some mental disorders (Egle et al., 2020). However, we cannot develop psychotherapeutic interventions on that basis.

As psychotherapists we need additional insights, for example about psychopathology or people's life situation. In the context of this book, however, I deal only with theories from those fields that we need for a theory of the practice of body psychotherapy.

This book provides a rough outline of such a theory, as a guideline along which we can establish clinical practice. I am myself a practising psychotherapist and so I understand this basic outline in the sense of what Kurt Lewin has said: nothing is as practical as a good theory, but nothing develops a theory as well as good practice. In a second book I have taken on the task of incorporating the dazzling array of methods and techniques developed by the schools from clinical experience into a general system of principles of body psychotherapeutic practice and of describing this in detail (Geuter, 2019).

The book is intended to provide those psychotherapists and members of other professions interested in the field of therapeutic work with the body a theoretical understanding of body psychotherapy. It also aims at showing those with a general interest in psychotherapy that every psychotherapeutic approach can profit from an awareness of the body and of body experience.

1.1 BODY PSYCHOTHERAPY AS AN EXPERIENTIAL APPROACH

Body psychotherapy is often classified as belonging to other major paradigms of psychotherapy. Totton (2002, p. 7) describes it as a third way between humanistic psychotherapy and psychoanalysis; Eiden (2009) sees it as based equally on Reich's energy model and on humanistic principles; Eberwein (2009) and Thielen (2014) see it as a branch of the tree of humanistic psychotherapy. Downing (1996) affiliates his approach with psychoanalytical object relations theory. Voigt and Trautmann-Voigt (2001) define depth psychology-based Body and Dance Therapy as an extension of traditional psychoanalysis. Rolef Ben-Shahar (2014, p. 75), on the other hand, understands body psychotherapy as a 'unique therapeutic modality'. Barratt (2010, p. 21) even sees in bodymind therapy the future of psychotherapy as a whole.

Personally I used to see the place of body psychotherapy as at the interface between a basic psychodynamic orientation and a humanistic one (Geuter, 2006, p. 118). In this book, however, I suggest understanding it as an **experiential** and at the same time **relational psychotherapy approach**, which like no other in the field of psychotherapy does justice to current philosophical theories of embodied mind and enactivism (Di Paolo & Thompson, 2014; Hutto & Myin, 2013; M Johnson, 2007; Thompson, 2010). In relation to the basic major orientations of psychotherapy, I see my own stance as being mostly connected to the paradigm of humanistic psychotherapy and to an intersubjective, psychodynamic psychotherapy.

In my view the **fundamental idea** of body psychotherapy is of the **holistic nature of human experience**. If we start with experience, we will inevitably end up with the body. Experience always includes vegetative, motor and cognitive processes, permeated and defined by emotions and intentions. Affects shape these inner states in which self experience and its underlay of body experience takes place. They in their turn are formed by a person's biographical experiences, which create patterns or schemas in which they view the world and behave towards it. Such affect motor schemas (Downing, 1996) also form the disposition for mental disorders. They are deeply connected to bodily processes. When a person feels healthy and vigorous or depressive, anxious, panicky, excitable, confused, disorientated, instable, skittish, desperate, hyper-aggressive or remote-controlled, they experience this deep in their posture, breathing, muscle tension or gut feeling. And that is also where they will experience healing.

Body psychotherapy is a way of changing patterns which cause suffering, by opening up access to new patterns by way of embodied experience. Since we can usually change sensorimotor processes voluntarily, working with the body is a powerful means of loosening up ingrained patterns and thus demonstrating the difference between them and potential new experiences.

Many people were fascinated by body psychotherapy as it flourished after the 1970s; this was exactly because of their experiences of change on a deeper level, of vitality, vigour, lust, connection to the body or openness towards other people or towards nature. A scientific theory of body psychotherapy must also take this dimension of experience into account.

However in my opinion this does not mean that we need a biological theory of the body for a theory of psychotherapeutic treatment. In this I differ from Heller's (2012) fundamentals of body psychotherapy. Heller focuses on the concept of the organism. He sees five biological systems – the nervous system and the circulatory, respiratory, hormonal and immune systems – as the basic regulatory mechanisms, which connect the four dimensions of the organism, namely body and gravity, metabolic regulation, behaviour and interaction and the psyche and social integration (Heller, 2012, p. 12). In his system of organismic dimensions, psychotherapy is a treatment in the dimension of the psyche, 'body-work' one in the dimension of the body and gravity, behavioural therapy one in the dimension of behaviour. Body psychotherapy uses methods in all four dimensions (p. 20). Organismic therapies would therefore be aimed at 'the great regulatory systems of the organism' (Heller, 2012, p. 517; cf. p. 552).

When I use the **concept of the organism**, I understand it as being systemic, as does Rogers (1959). Here I do not use it as a key concept because it leans towards looking at human beings through a natural scientific lens. We can describe the human being as striving towards a regulative harmony in the organism. However from a humanistic point of view, we would describe them as striving for meaning in life. Meaningfulness tends to be determined by basic biological regulatory systems only when they are severely out of balance, for example when we are gravely ill.

According to enactive philosophy (Chapter 5), psychological experience arises through the interaction of the individual with their environment. 'The experience is owned by each of our organisms and by no other' (Damasio, 2012, p. 157), and we can only understand it by means of our life processes.

My aim is to liberate body psychotherapy from a theoretical foundation in a biological theory of the organism and locate it in that of a psychological theory based on experience. Thus my starting point is the **human being as experiencing subject** in relation to the world. I look at vegetative or motor processes from the point of view of how a person experiences themselves in those processes and on those levels. As psychotherapists, we view the body not as does a biologist, an immunologist, an internist or a pharmacologist, but from a psychological perspective as to how a person lives in their body and how they experience the world in and with it. 'Subjects are animate, bodily, experiencing persons who live in a meaningful world' (De Jaegher, 2018, p. 453). Fuchs (2020c, p. 14) calls this **concept of humanity** a humanism of the living, embodied mind.

A theory of body psychotherapy thus has to deal with how human experience, behaviour and personal interaction appear on a bodily level, how these are all shaped on that level and how this can manifest in a disposition to psychological suffering. As body psychotherapists we influence organic processes, but we do this through working with affect motor patterns of experience and behaviour and transforming them. Similarly Aposhyan (2004, p. 6) defines body psychotherapy as follows: 'Somatic psychology can be most simply defined as including all psychological approaches that focus significantly on the role of the body.'

Unlike other psychotherapy approaches, body psychotherapy works on all levels of experience, particularly on that of body experience. Its starting point is work with embodied awareness 'of the stream of arising subjective experiences in the body' (Westland, 2019, p. 256). It combines working with self-narration, what people express verbally about themselves, with embodied core processes of emotional experiencing, of memory or of early affect motor schemas and attachment styles.

I do not use the concept of the core as does Pierrakos (1987) as a centre of primary energy and love, nor in Fosha's (2001) sense of a core state of connection with oneself, and not in the cognitive sense of the core material of central memory, beliefs and images, as does Kurtz (1990, 2015). Here, the term **core processes** refers to bodily felt, procedurally memorised, basic regulatory patterns or strategies of experience and behaviour, which appear on the cognitive, affective, imaginative, sensory, motor or vegetative level. Therefore I will go into the significance of a bodily experienced core self in the chapter on body experience, that of emotional-procedural memory in the chapter on memory, that of core affects in the chapter on emotions and that of the forming of basic affect motor regulation in the chapter on development.

The experiential perspective is characteristic of the approaches of humanistic psychotherapy, such as Emotion-Focused Therapy, client-centred psychotherapy or Gestalt therapy. We also encounter it in behavioural therapy and in psychoanalysis. Whereas in a standard textbook of behavioural therapy published in 2009 the patient's experience is not once mentioned (Margraf & Schneider, 2009), the third wave of behavioural therapy, centred on mindfulness, sees itself as experiential (Hayes, 2004). Acceptance and Commitment Therapy explicitly regards itself as an experiential approach aiming at promoting the observation of self-experience and attentiveness for the moment as a characteristic of psychological flexibility (Hayes, 2004), with the aim of promoting the observation of self experience and attentiveness for the moment as a characteristic of psychological flexibility. All this however is eminently of the body.

Early on in psychoanalysis, Rank (1926) described the direct affective experience in the session as being the essential agent of therapy. However it was not until Rogers that this was taken seriously (Kramer, 2019). In recent years, Stern (2004) took up the idea from Gestalt therapy of working in contact with the present in the therapeutic setting, as does Plassmann (2021), who regards the restoring of emotional contact to the self as being a central task of psychotherapeutic transformation.

1.2 THE BODY IN THE WIDER FIELD OF PSYCHOTHERAPY

For a long time, body psychotherapy was generally ignored in psychology and psychotherapy. Also the body was commonly just blanked out. In Grawe's (2007) consistency theory, for example, the human being is without a body. Here needs are satisfied or frustrated, noticed or not, if approach schemas allow or avoidance schemas do not, but all within the sphere of a bodiless psyche. The fact that attachment is experienced and learned in the body, that control and coping skills are connected to motor function, emotional appraisal to bodily sensations and avoidance to a bodily turning away or isolation has no place in this theory.

In treatment, many psychotherapists traditionally have difficulties with the body. When for example Fiedler (2000, pp. 170–1) writes about borderline patients who experienced sexual violence, that body and mind are not to be separated when working through these experiences, this remains an idea and has no tangible consequences. In practice, Fiedler only talks about verbal treatment, although he calls his approach 'Integrative Psychotherapy'. When he notices that traumatised patients often cannot verbalise their experiences and inner states, he comes to the conclusion that we should construct a 'metacognitive' space so as to maintain an awareness of the wholeness of the person (Fiedler, 2000, p. 173). Wholeness, however, can only be maintained when it has been felt and experienced.

In psychoanalysis, Plassmann (2019) focuses on emotional regulation, but does not include regulation through the body. He speaks of co-regulation, but according to him only the patient's attention-regulating mental apparatus makes contact with the therapist; meanwhile the attention of the therapist moves back and forth between hearing and thinking (Plassmann, 2021, p. 101). As body psychotherapists, we additionally turn to our breathing, our bodily sensations and our motor impulses.

In the treatment of in-patients, the significance of working with the body has long been recognised. In many psychosomatic clinics in Germany, body psychotherapy is an established method within a multi-modal treatment concept (Huber et al., 2005, p. 70; Mueller-Braunschweig & Stiller, 2010, p. VI). A combination of experiential, reflective and routine exercises is in many cases standard (Bolm, 2015, p. 111). A survey of psychosomatic clinics in Germany showed that in 46% of these clinics, body psychotherapy is a regular component of the psychotherapeutic process; in a further 41% it is used occasionally (Braun, 2015). The author estimates that in this way about 200,000 patients a year come into contact with body psychotherapy. It is also becoming increasingly important in psychiatric clinics, especially as a treatment for the negative symptoms in schizophrenia (Roehricht & Priebe, 2006). The 'National Institute for Clinical Excellence', which in the UK is responsible for therapy evaluation, in 2008 recommended body psychotherapy for such patients (NICE, 2008). In the meantime, a 'clinical body psychotherapy' (Roehricht, 2002) has been developed also for out-patients.

Another impetus towards body psychotherapy comes from trauma therapy, which was boosted by the recognition of post-traumatic stress disorder as a diagnosis in 1980. Traumatic memories are stored pre-cognitively so that they are not verbally accessible (van der Kolk et al., 1996). Traumatic experiences remain in the body as chronic over-arousal for example, which is managed by shutting down (van der Kolk, 2014). Thus the task is to help the patient with the regulation of basic psychophysiological arousal. Trauma therapy became one of the main focuses of body psychotherapy along with the therapy of body experience disorders, functional disorders and psychoses.

In professional circles, body psychotherapy has increasingly become a subject of inter-est. The years when it was seen as a wild, marginal therapy belong to the past (Staunton, 2002; Totton, 2002a). Hartley points out that 'The discipline of body psychotherapy within the UK has moved from the margins of the psychotherapeutic profession to an established position within it' (2009a, p. 1). Meinlschmidt and Tegethoof (2017) see in the rediscovery of the body and of movement one of several trends currently found in all psychotherapy approaches. In the research field of *embodied cognition* too there is a call for a holistic conceptualisation of *body* and *mind* in all psychotherapeutic approaches (Leitan & Murray, 2014).

Psychodynamic and behavioural therapists are debating paying more attention to the body in psychotherapy (Anderson, 2008; Riskind et al., 2021; Sulz, 2015; Wiener, 1999). In client-centred (Kern, 2014; Femald, 2000) and in systemic therapy there is also a discus-sion about the link to body psychotherapy (Baxa et al., 2002; Wienands, 2014). Particularly mindfulness-based therapy approaches emphasise the importance of conscious body experience for psychotherapy and now regard awareness of bodily changes as generating transformation (Segal et al., 2012; Weiss et al., 2010; Williams et al., 2007). Contemporary psychotherapy, however, still views the body mainly as a location and a carrier of informa-tion about psychological events (e.g. Remmel et al., 2006) and has not yet assigned it a place in theory and treatment worthy of its potential (Klopstech, 2009).

These new developments raise the question of whether every psychotherapy approach should pay attention to bodily experience and processes, since it opens up an additional dimension for the understanding of the patient (Sulz et al., 2005, p. X). Perhaps body psychotherapy should be absorbed into a general psychotherapy which integrates various therapeutic approaches? By virtue of its integrative potential, Gassmann (2010, p. 344) would establish body psychotherapy as an integral component of such a psychotherapy. Wehowsky (2006, p. 189) too maintains that it is capable of being integrated into all psy-chotherapeutic approaches and is thus able to find its place within a general psychother-apy. Is it therefore still appropriate to emphasise body psychotherapy as an approach in its own right?

Psychotherapy nowadays seeks integration. It aligns itself with post-modern thinking, which rejects truths and sees opposites as complementing one another (Eiden, 2009, p. 17). Fiedler (2000, p. 56) remarks that psychotherapy approaches confined to a specific school have need of complementary relationships to one another, since they have different empha-ses and, due to their one-sidedness, differ in their perspectives. However a complementary relationship is not integration. Perhaps we need to sharpen the one-sidedness and empha-sise the special features, so that the various approaches can develop to their full potential, which they can then contribute to psychotherapy in general. Teams generally increase their productivity when members are allowed to unfold their individual talents.

In my view, body psychotherapy, as a proven psychotherapeutic approach, contributes something to the whole field of psychotherapy that other methods have not taken into account. No single approach can cover the whole field alone. Thus body psychotherapy should first of all figure out what its own theoretical basis and its focus in treatment is, before it can be integrated into the plurality of possible and necessary treatment forms.

1.3 THE BODY TURN IN SCIENCE

The recent interest in the body in psychotherapy is happening in the context of various developments in other scientific fields, especially in cognitive sciences, neuroscience, embodiment research, emotion research and infant and attachment research. In the last few years there has been a development that in philosophy, anthropology, sociology and political science is known as the *somatic turn, corporeal turn* or *body turn* (Busch, 2020; Csordas, 1990; Gugutzer, 2006; Schroer, 2005a; Sheets-Johnstone, 2009). The body has not only been discovered as an object of research; it is also being systematically integrated into the concept of sociality, as for example in the question of the bodily habitus described by Bourdieu (1984), which produces fine social distinctions.

Since the 1990s, the concept of **embodiment** has found its way into the discourse of sociology and the humanities. Here the themes are the performativity of the body, meaning how the body is used as a means of self-portrayal, or the body as a medium for habit or as a carrier of symbols, but also the felt body as the site of embodied experience. However the body is usually seen as a single body. Body contact is rarely a scientific subject (Schmidt & Schetsche, 2012a). Lately the embodiment concept is being used in psychology, psychiatry and psychotherapy (de Haan, 2020; Glenberg, 2010; Hauke & Kritikos, 2018; Koch, 2011; Krueger, 2019; Leuzinger-Bohleber et al., 2013; Robinson & Thomas, 2021; Spremberg, 2018; Tschacher & Storch, 2012). In body psychotherapy, embodiment has become one of the basic concepts (Aposhyan, 2004, p. 52; Roehricht et al., 2014; Shaw, 2003, pp. 32–8; Sletvold, 2014; Totton, 2015) and its meaning here is that of being at home in a living body (Rolef Ben-Shahar, 2014, p. 93).

The concept of embodiment plays an especially important role in **cognitive science** (Gallagher, 2021; Gangopadhyay, 2013). The theory of **embodied mind** starts from the assumption that the relationship of the body to the world, both as perceiver and as actor, establishes categories for the development of concepts, that conscious subjective perception of the world is connected to the inner perception of the body and that the phenomenal field of consciousness and experience are formed through a person's momentary bodily state (Adams, 2010; De Preester, 2007; Gallagher, 2005; Gibbs, 2006). One version of this theory, **enactivism**, believes that with the concept of the embodied mind it has resolved the cartesian dualistic separation of the mental and physical world, which is ultimately based on Plato (Hutto, 2011; Stewart et al., 2010; Velmans, 2007). According to numerous empiric studies, movement and bodily expression determine mental representations of the environment and of other people (Niedenthal et al., 2005, 2005a). This supports the basic idea of body psychotherapy of regarding human beings as body-mind subjects in a personal and material environment.

Research findings in the **neurosciences** also support the idea that mental processes are mediated by emotions, which in turn are experienced through somatic signals. Damasio (1994) sees emotions as changes in bodily states. According to his theory, the perception of feelings is linked to the ability to perceive the body. Neuroscientists point out that interoceptive perceptions are the basis of our moods and emotional states (Craig, 2002). These studies are consistent with the strategy of body psychotherapy of accessing psychological experience through bodily self-perception and of realising affects through their sensorimotor components if they exist split off from or fragmented in the body (Carroll, 2005, p. 27).

Neuroscientists emphasise that the experience of subjectivity is accompanied by changes in bodily states, which the subject has before, during and after a certain perception, and that these states are stored together with images and thoughts from significant life situations in the episodic memory (Ansermet & Magistretti, 2007). This indicates that autobiographical memory is an embodied memory and can be activated through the bodily states linked to the relevant events, a fact which body psychotherapy can turn to account.

Last but not least, in the last few decades **infant and attachment research** has shown convincingly that a baby acquires initial interaction experiences in a bodily affective dialogue with the mother or the father, which leads to the first generalised representations, which are mainly stored in the procedural memory (Stern, 1985). Recent ideas about human development thus tend towards brain-mind-body concepts (Schore, 2003). The experiences, stored preverbally, appear in therapy in the form of affect motor strategies, as patterns of stress regulation, attachment, implicit relational knowledge or as so-called 'enactments', that is to say as interactive scenes that are initially unconscious and can be explored through body language dialogue.

Body psychotherapy in the universities

Institutionally, body psychotherapy is connected to science through master's degree courses especially in the Anglo-American cultures. In the USA it is taught at four universities as 'somatic psychology':

- California Institute of Integral Studies, San Francisco.
- Pacific Graduate Institute, Santa Barbara.
- Naropa University, Boulder.
- John F. Kennedy University, Pleasant Hill (Wolf, 2010).

Other universities offer master's degree courses in dance and movement therapies in the USA as well as in Scotland (Queen Margaret in Edinburgh) and in five English universities. There are also university courses in dance and movement therapy in Argentina, South Korea, Australia and Israel as well as in several European countries (Payne et al., 2019, pp. 407–13). The Parkmore Institute in Johannesburg, South Africa offers a body psychotherapeutic Ph.D. in bodymind healing.

In England there is a master's degree course in body psychotherapy at the Anglia Ruskin University in Cambridge. In several European countries, psychotherapy is a post-graduate course at state recognised non-university institutes. In Switzerland, four body psychotherapeutic training institutes are accredited by the state, while in Italy two state-recognised institutes are connected to universities:

- Scuola di Specializzazione in Psicoterapia Biosistemica in Bologna
- Scuola Europea di Psicoterapia Funzionale in Naples, which offers a master's degree in cooperation with the local university.

In Austria, the University of Innsbruck established a guest professorship for body centred psychotherapy in 1996. In Germany, the University of Marburg established a specialisation in body psychotherapy as part of the master's degree course in motology in 2010. In Turkey, Maltepe university in Istanbul started offering a master in clinical psychology with a body psychotherapy certificate in 2018.

In this book I aim to connect body psychotherapy to these scientific developments. This has already happened for some areas such as infant research (Downing, 1996; Geissler, 2007; Trautmann-Voigt & Voigt, 1996) and for non-verbal communication (Heller, 2012; Trautmann-Voigt & Voigt, 2009). Fogel (2009) links in a profound manner theories of self-perception with psychophysiological and neuroscientific research. Body psychotherapy has the potential to integrate the findings of the relevant research, as it probably chimes more easily with it than do other psychotherapy approaches. Basically research tends to support the idea that psychotherapy methods which do not include the body should explain their attitude in the face of modern psychological and neuroscientific research results, and not the other way around.

1.4 THE INTERSUBJECTIVE TURN TOWARDS A
RELATIONAL BODY PSYCHOTHERAPY

Next to the body turn we can also detect an 'intersubjective turn' (De Jaegher, 2018) in various scientific fields, particularly in research on social cognition and social understanding (Di Paolo & De Jaegher, 2015). De Jaegher et al. (2017) speak of an interactive-experiential turn, in which the experience-oriented and intersubjective perspectives merge.

Recent Gestalt therapy has emphasised both these points of view (Staemmler, 2017; Wegscheider, 2020; Yontef, 1993). In psychoanalysis too there has been talk of an intersubjective turn for quite some time (Altmeyer & Thomae, 2006; Gerhardt et al., 2000; Gerhardt & Sweetnam, 2001). Kuchuck (2021) talks about a relational revolution, initiated by attachment research. Here it is not just about the significance of the therapeutic relationship for successful therapy, which is now recognised by all psychotherapy approaches (Horvath et al., 2011). It is about a different basic understanding of therapeutic work **within the** relationship. If relational psychoanalysis had made clear how much relationship experiences shape the inner world and how the therapist must be seen as the co-creator of their re-enactment (Wachtel, 2014), now the emphasis is on the significance of real interaction in the session for therapeutic change (Slavin & Rahmani, 2016).

This interactional perspective has recently found its way into body psychotherapy (Cornell, 2015; Rolef Ben-Shahar, 2014; Sletvold, 2014; Soth, 2019; Totton, 2015; White, 2014; Young, 2012). Per this understanding, the core of psychotherapy consists not of methods or techniques, but of a mutual process of experience. As part of this turn, intersubjective approaches in psychoanalysis take into account implicit bodily knowledge (Broschmann & Fuchs, 2020).

Human beings as subjects experience themselves in relation to what and who is around them (McGann et al., 2013). Subjects are not monads; rather they experience themselves in the world and in interaction with it. Gendlin (2016) speaks of 'interaction first'. Subjectivity develops in a shared environment (McGann, 2014), experiences find in relationships their 'relational home' (Staunton, 2008).

However, intersubjectivity means more than just interaction. It means that people exist in a *being with* other people (Marcel, 1976). We often experience emotions and intentions in a primal intersubjectivity, in which we understand each other (De Jaegher, 2015; Gallagher & Hutto, 2008). Understanding is not just a cognitive-affective occurrence, but also intercorporeal (Gallese, 2013; Merleau-Ponty, 1994, p. 194). People not only have an embodied mind and a mindful body; they share their embodied existence with each other (Fusaroli et al., 2012).

In therapy, patients can also find meaning for themselves and regulate their emotions alone. The intersubjective view is not a radical interactionism (De Jaegher & Di Paolo, 2013). But when someone enters psychotherapy, they enter into a process in which inner transformation occurs in a being together. In psychotherapy the embodied awareness I spoke of in Section 1.1 is a shared awareness. Here intersubjectivity means that two subjects, who each see themselves as a subject different from and yet still in relation to the other, are co-creating meaning (Yontef, 1993). According to the relational view, the therapist comes in as another human being and not just as a holding presence. This also shifts the focus onto embodied paraverbal communication (Donovan et al., 2017, p. 7). Garcia and Di Paolo (2018) speak of an *embodied coordination* space, in which participatory sense-making takes place. In the last few years more empirical research has been done on how relationships are constituted through body communication taking place in this space (Atzil-Slonim & Tschacher, 2019; Section 14.2).

This relational view of psychotherapy is not self-evident in body psychotherapy. Traditionally, the therapeutic relationship has been seen here as the therapist being the expert in making the patient conscious of their repressed affects and hidden resources with the help of bodily techniques (Geuter, 2019, p. 398). Body psychotherapeutic treatment, however, should not take place in a relationship in which an expert knows what is good for the other person, but in a subject–subject relationship (Rolef Ben-Shahar, 2014, p. XXVI). Only someone who approaches another person as a subject can learn anything significant about them. As therapists, we are not technicians but explorers (Boadella, 2019, p. 292).

Sometimes the use of bodily techniques has been depicted as characteristic of body psychotherapy (Heller, 2012, p. 1). Being in a relationship means however liberating oneself from fixed therapeutic stances and styles (Soth, 2019, p. 300). In a **relational body psychotherapy**, attention is not focused on interventions, but rather on a sensitive relating, in which the therapist uses their own body awareness as a central means for deciding what treatment is appropriate. In psychoanalysis, Plassmann (2019) calls this process-resonance. Boadella expresses it rather more poetically when he says: 'I am sensing you sensing yourself and sensing you while you are sensing me' (2019, p. 293).

Treatment develops on the basis of what the patient reveals in the resonant process of being together (Totton, 2019). Westland (2015, p. 6) and Totton (2015, 2020) call this **embodied relating**. Appel-Opper (2018) speaks of an inter-bodily togetherness, Sletvold (2014) of an 'embodied intersubjectivity' and Roehricht (2015) of an 'embodied and embedded relational psychotherapy', since we treat the person in their own life world.

> Our therapeutic work is a kind of meditation on what is happening in the interactions between ourselves and the one who has come to us for help with some kind of problem.
>
> (Boadella, 2019, p. 292)

Even some body therapists such as Feldenkrais teachers or Shiatsu therapists view their work these days as part of a relational process in which the practitioner is constantly adjusting the treatment on the basis of their resonance in the feedback loop; they speak of mutual incorporation or embodied interaction (Kimmel et al., 2015).

Relational, experience-oriented body psychotherapy is a communicative process between two subjects, which supports understanding and change by using the body's experiences to access self experience in a spirit of cooperation. This includes bodily communication and exploration. Totton and Priestman (2012) describe embodiment and relationship as two halves of a whole. I believe it to be the task of body psychotherapy, in practice as in theory, to link the aspect of the embodiment of psychological life with that of intersubjectivity.

1.5 BODY AND SOCIETY

The body turn in science is connected to a social and cultural reassessment of the body. On the one hand there is a growing awareness of how human diversity reveals itself in the body and what traces discrimination inflicts upon it (D Johnson, 2018; R Johnson, 2015, 2019). On the other hand, the body has increasingly gained significance as a reference point for the self, since other reference points for orientation are on the wane. Amid the general demand for flexibility, identity is becoming ever more fluid (Sennett, 2000) and virtual worlds allow us to construct various versions of self (Buongiorno, 2019).

Furthermore our competitive society demands from many people that they be entre-preneurs of the self and that they optimise the body as a resource (Broeckling, 2015). Since lifelong, fixed-role allocation in the working world and in the private sphere are becoming rare, each one of us must find out for ourselves what is appropriate for us. The question 'what do I want?' is replacing 'what are my skills?' and forces us to explore our own needs. This, however, calls for a sensing awareness of the body. The body becomes the scene where we find for ourselves meaning, support and orientation in life (Baumann, 2000) and where the modern tenet of the 'experience society' (Schulze, 2005), of not just living your life but experiencing, it is realised (Gugutzer, 2004, p. 37). And, when in burnout and depression the ability to act dwindles, it becomes the scene of exhaustion in the face of the task of constantly having to find oneself, to invent oneself (Ehrenberg, 2010).

At the same time, the connection to oneself is also disappearing in society. The upgrading and repression of the body go hand in hand. Bette (1989) sees in the turn towards the body a response to its disappearance. He calls this a paradox of modern times. We can observe the tension between these two processes from the end of the 19th century, when the body was displaced by technical means of transport and communi-cation. This led to a first wave of awareness of the sensed and lived body in the body culture movement of the time. We can see a second wave in the wake of a similar surge of modernisation and sensualisation since the 1970s, which proclaimed the liberation of the body (Chapter 3).

The internet and virtual social media further promote this distancing of the body from communication, since we can often no longer touch the world we are relating to (Buongiorno, 2019). At the same time, the modern cult of the body enacts what we have lost in a narcissistic or histrionic reaction (cf. Winterhoff-Spurk, 2005). As a defence against emptiness, the body becomes a project, a medium to produce identity through outward appearances. Instead of feeling the body, liberating it and making it our home, we strive to optimise it (von Arnim, 2017). Self-optimisation is the new social imperative (Straub, 2019). Lifelogging and self-tracking are testimony to this. Other evidence for this is the increase in plastic surgery in Germany three times over between 1990 and 2008 – 'self-presentation with scalpel' (Borkenhagen, 2011). In the USA, the number of female breast lifts rose by 108% between 2000 and 2018 and breast enlargements by 48%, while cosmetic surgeries for the chin, eyelid, forehead or ear decreased (ASPS, 2018). Non-surgical aes-thetic modifications of the body are increasing. Through fitness machines, yoga, Pilates, Feldenkrais or Tai Chi, many people try to achieve a body image corresponding to the beauty ideals prevalent in this milieu (Weiher, 2012, p. 78). In this case, these forms of movement are not aimed at finding out what suits the body, but at coping with the loss of living naturally with one's own given body. Focusing on one's body through any of these methods can assuage feelings of insecurity (Weiher, 2012, pp. 153–5) and body shame, which the dominant culture in the West engenders.

These developments are reflected in psychotherapy. At the beginning of the 20th cen-tury, the first impulses for the development of body psychotherapy came from the body culture movement, and then in the 1970s it flourished again in the new body and move-ment boom. In experiential groups people tried to rediscover their lost body sensibility (Kamper & Wulf, 1982, p. 10). Blomeyer (1981) observed that in an age of dwindling rela-tionships, body awareness is used to counteract anxiety and feelings of emptiness, since only in the body do people experience life. Nowadays, psychotherapy responds both to the need for a sensing, reflective encounter with one's self and to the trend for the opti-misation of the body, for example with biofeedback, autosuggestion, self-management or power meditation.

Body and history

The body we are dealing with in body psychotherapy is always one formed by history. The cultural formation of the human being finds its way into the natural body. In his studies on the process of civilisation, Elias (2000) impressively demonstrated how the constraints of living together in society lead to an apparatus of psychological and affect motor self-restraints. Psychoanalysis declared those areas of the psyche that are most repressed in this process, sexuality and aggression, to be drives, possibly because they drew great power out of their socially enforced suppression. Thus the focus of psychotherapy for Freud and Reich was to render these repressed drives conscious and to rescue them from suppression. Today, however, many patients need more impulse control, self-control and orientation (Maurer, 2010, p. 4).

Not only bodily and emotional expression are determined to a great degree by culture and within it by the various social classes. Symptoms too are changing. For example, anorexia has been a new body experience disorder in Western societies since the 19th century, as unlike the fasting of earlier times, the refusal to eat is motivated by a revolt against the beauty ideal (Habermas, 1994). Bulimia, however, was first described in the 1930s and 1940s. Habermas (1990) calls it a culture-bound syndrome, which arose through a change in the way we deal with food and with the body. Legrand (2010) sees anorexia as a self-objectification of the body that we can also recognise in the widespread phenomenon of self-harming behaviour. Reich (1973) linked psychosomatic symptoms to suppressed sexuality, as was usual at the time, and not with issues relevant today such as nutrition and the maltreatment of the body.

In addition the therapeutic relationship develops in the context of body images, in which sex, gender, skin colour and cultural background all affect the interaction.

1.6 STRUCTURE OF THE BOOK

In Chapter 2 I first propose a definition of body psychotherapy. Then, in a discussion of the often-used concept of the living body, I give my reasons for staying with the concept of body psychotherapy. Chapter 3 covers the history of body psychotherapy. Here I will describe how its different directions developed in the context of various social movements. Since I present body psychotherapy as an experiential psychotherapy approach, I will discuss its connection to the philosophy of life in its early history, neglected in the literature until now, on the one hand and its origins in the human potential movement on the other. I have described the history of the conceptual development of body psychotherapy and the various schools in more depth elsewhere (Geuter, 2000a, 2004a, 2015), so I will leave it out here. However in Chapter 4, I will describe the basic ideas of the body psychotherapeutic schools on which the general theory is grounded.

My own theoretical outline begins in Chapter 5, where I explain my view of the basic paradigms of body psychotherapy and integrate it into the philosophy of embodied mind and enactivism and into a theory of experience. In so doing I emphasise the experiencing subject as the central reference point of body psychotherapy. Chapter 6 deals with the theme of how self experience comes about, how it is grounded in body experience and how this can be disturbed. Here I explain the significance for psychotherapy of sensing through the inner senses and I introduce a body psychotherapeutic understanding of the concept of self. I also introduce a model of the three levels of experience and show how the breathing connects them. In Chapter 7, I discuss several aspects of the connection between the experiencing body and the physical body of natural science, with special reference to the autonomic nervous system. Here I also reason that the practice of body psychotherapy cannot be based either on neuroscientific theories or on a scientific energy model.

Chapter 5 through 7 deal with my basic understanding of body psychotherapy, and Chapter 8 through 10 with its foundations in general psychology.

Chapter 8 looks at empirical embodiment research and depicts how the cognitive and emotional evaluation of situations is linked to body postures and emotional states. Chapter 9 deals with the theory of memory. Memories that are important in psychotherapy are deeply connected to body experience and are stored in the emotional-procedural memory as embodied memories, which are accessible through body experience in therapy. In Chapter 10, I present a body-based theory of emotions, which sees them as appraisals based on the body. This chapter makes it clear that the emotional sense of pleasure and unpleasure, of arousal and calm and of emotions such as anxiety, sadness, anger, disgust, joy, pride or shame are all connected to bodily processes and bodily self-perception. Starting from two models of emotional processes, I show the various clinical tasks of a body-oriented psychotherapy, working with the perception and regulation of dysfunctional affective experience.

Chapter 11 formulates several basic ideas of a psychological theory of the development of the infant and early imprinting. Self experience develops in early, body-based interactive experiences, which form the underlying patterns of experience and coping strategies. As a result, affect motor schemas develop, in which condensed experiences live on in the present. I discuss the theory of these affect motor schemas in Chapter 12. Life experiences in early childhood are also inscribed as bodily patterns corresponding to patterns of behaviour, especially when a desire–defence conflict arises, mobilising both acute and chronic forms of bodily defence. Chapter 13 deals with this topic.

In Chapter 14 I will discuss the interaction of body with body and its significance in psychotherapy, a topic Heller (2012) places great emphasis for body psychotherapy. To understand this body-based relating in therapy, we need to understand bodily communication in the therapeutic dyad. Therefore I present research findings on interaction in facial expressions and gestures or the importance of the voice and show the significance of the body language dialogue between therapist and patient. In Chapter 15 I discuss the special issue of transference and therapeutic work with the aid of somatic resonance.

Chapter 16 shows how in body psychotherapy there is a special form of understanding based on the fact that meaning is created directly through experience. Finally Chapter 17 is given over to the concept of self-regulation, which is the ability to regulate a dysfunctional or dysregulated emotionality alone or with the help of others and is one of the higher objectives of therapeutic treatment.

I have written the chapters so that they can each be read individually. This is why some ideas appear in several chapters. The reader wishing to study specific themes more concerned with clinical practice can begin with Chapter 8. Perhaps they will then become curious about what is in the more general, theoretical Chapters 5 through 7. The reader who has no interest in the history of body psychotherapy can leave out Chapter 3 and start with Chapter 4 or 5. It is also possible to pick out a single chapter of interest and just read the one. For easier navigation I have provided a short description of the contents at the beginning of each chapter.

My aim with this book is not only to promote a theoretical understanding of body psychotherapy, but to encourage the creative practice of therapy. Nowadays, regrettably, psychotherapy is increasingly subject to demands for schematic, empirically validated techniques applied to specific disorders. This kind of psychotherapy is not concerned with treating human beings with specific disorders, but rather disorders connected to human beings. Psychotherapy as an interpersonal praxis (Richter, 2019), a dialogical process between two specific people or in a group of specific people, formed by what these people bring to the interaction, is in danger of being lost. Psychotherapy rests on the creativity of the therapist on the basis of their knowledge and life experience, in their concrete relationship to the specific human being they encounter.

Yalom asserts that 'psychotherapy is both an art and a science' (1995, p. XIV; cf. Hofmann &Weinberger, 2007, p. XVII). We learn the art through practice. Artists only get better when they practice their art. Psychotherapy is also based on skills that we learn by working on them. Young and Heller (2000) think that we cannot therefore regard psychotherapy as a distinct scientific discipline. However, good psychotherapy practice needs a basis in scientific knowledge. The art of psychotherapy consists of a therapist being of help to the individual patient on the basis of their knowledge, both scientific knowledge and knowledge of the social and cultural life context of their patients in general.

> When the therapist knows what she is doing and why, she is less apt to make mistakes. Theory is more useful than techniques, as techniques can fail, but theory rarely lets you down.
>
> (Rothschild, 2000, p. 65)

2

Towards a definition of body psychotherapy

In addition to the concept of body psychotherapy in the relevant literature, several other concepts are used:

- Body-oriented psychotherapy (Müller-Braunschweig & Stiller, 2010; Roehricht, 2000, 2009).
- Body-centred psychotherapy (Kuenzler et al., 2010; Kurtz, 1990).
- Sensorimotor psychotherapy (Ogden et al., 2006).
- Somatic psychotherapy (Tantia, 2019; Weiss et al., 2015).
- Body-mind psychotherapy (Aposhyan, 2004).
- Bodymind therapy (Barratt, 2010).

Barratt (2010) understands bodymind therapy as the applied branch of the academic discipline of *somatic psychology*, as body psychotherapy is referred to in the USA in academia. D. H. Johnson (2018) includes in the notion of *somatics* both body psychotherapy as well as the body therapies. Payne et al. (2019a) use *embodied psychotherapy* as a generic term for all dance, movement and body psychotherapeutic approaches.

Totton (2003, p. 26) suggested the concept of *holistic psychotherapy*. Today he (2015) calls it *body psychotherapy*. Next to this last term, Brown (1990) also uses *Organismic Psychotherapy*.

I prefer the term *body psychotherapy* for three reasons:

1. Of all the various concepts, this is the most internationally established. Leading professional societies such as the European Association for Body Psychotherapy and the United States Association for Body Psychotherapy use it, whereas the Australian professional body, disbanded in 2016, called itself the Australian Somatic Psychotherapy Association (Meyer, 2019). It is customary in other languages too: *Kroppspsykoterapi* in Swedish, *kroppsterapi* in Norwegian, *psicoterapia corporea* in Italian, *psicoterapia corporal* in Spanish and Portuguese, *psychothérapie corporelle* in French. In Dutch they call it *lichaamsgeoriënteerde* or *lichaamsgerichte psychotherapie*, where *lichaam* is the word for the anatomical body as opposed to *lijf* for the lived body.
2. The concept of body psychotherapy gives expression to the fact that we treat patients with bodily and psychological means, whereas notions such as body-centred or body-oriented psychotherapy make no distinction between the means and the object of treatment.

DOI: 10.4324/9781003176893-2

3. In the German literature, phenomenologically oriented psychotherapists in particular prefer the term *Leib* as a notion for the subjectively experienced body, for which in English the concept of the *lived body, subject body* or even *soma* are used, as distinguished from the body as object. This is why some authors speak of *lived body therapy, Leibtherapie* (Petzold, 2009). However I can see no advantage in using the concept of lived body therapy instead of body psychotherapy, as long as we are clear that the body can be viewed from various perspectives, depending on our particular interest in it, and that in body psychotherapy we are concerned with the body from an experiential point of view.

Here I would like to go into the two last points more deeply.

The diversity of definitions mentioned above is also due to the fact that in medicine the concept of therapy is used semantically in two different ways: on the one hand in relation to **what** is being treated, on the other to **which means** are being used (Figure 2.1). Thus *cancer therapy* or *AIDS therapy* mean the treatment of the respective illnesses, whereas concepts such as *balneotherapy* or *pharmacotherapy* relate to the means. Similarly we talk of *borderline therapy* or *trauma therapy* when we treat borderline disorders or the effects of trauma, whereas of *EMDR* or *hypnotherapy* when we refer to working with those methods.

PSYCHOTHERAPY

The concept of psychotherapy is often understood in that former sense as a treatment of mental and psychosomatic illnesses and disorders of psychosocial origin (Stumm, 2000, p. 569). This definition, linked to the object of treatment, is however rather vague, since psychotherapists also treat the mental suffering of, for example, cancer patients, whose primary illness is somatic. Also the borders between *organic* and *psychosocial* conditions fluctuate, as do those between *somatic* and *mental*, since it is always the whole person who is suffering.

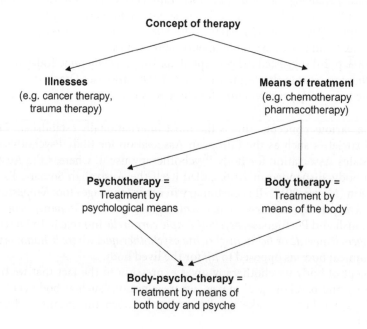

FIGURE 2.1 The concept of body psychotherapy

Mental suffering can also be treated in other ways, for example with psychiatric medication or relaxation training.

Historically, psychotherapy was an attempt to heal or alleviate pathological conditions in human beings through verbal means alone, and it first blossomed under Freud. Initially it was known as the *talking cure*. Freud wrote that the concept of psychological treatment did not mean treating pathological phenomena of the soul:

> Psychical 'treatment' denotes, rather, treatment taking its start in the mind, treatment (whether of mental or physical disorders) by measures which operate in the first instance and immediately upon the human mind.
>
> (Freud, 1890, p. 283)

For him, verbal means were the essential tools (Freud, 1890).

Thus a more precise definition of psychotherapy in the sense of the latter concept would be the treatment of illnesses or disorders **with psychological means** - not only talking about associations, memories, feelings and ideas, but working also with images or guided attention.

Freud spoke of *psychical* treatment; generally the word *psychological* is used nowadays. He spoke also of a treatment of the soul (*Seele* in the German original text). I make no distinction between the terms **psyche** and **soul** or **mind** in this book.

BODY THERAPY

Having considered all this, we see more clearly how to understand the notion of *body therapy*, a term which is unfortunately often used as synonymous with *body psychotherapy* (e.g. McNeely, 1987). In the 19th century, women began to treat tuberculosis using only the patients' bodies and their own, with no technical instruments such as devices to increase breathing, which were often used at the time (von Steinaecker, 2000; Section 3.1.2). The breath and body therapy which then developed were treatments **using bodily means.** According to this understanding, we can include in modern body therapy all methods which aim at healing and relief using only the body. Unlike physiotherapy, however, these approaches seek to improve body awareness and are based on the assumption that healing follows the internal intelligence of the organism (Johnson, 2000). Thus techniques such as craniosacral therapy or many of the methods of classical massage are not included in body therapies, as they are not aiming for 'embodied self-awareness' (Fogel, 2009, pp. 154–5), even if they do have a psychological effect through deep relaxation.

Among the body therapies we find the Alexander Technique, the Rosen Method, the Feldenkrais method, Eutony, Qigong or Rolfing. With their respective approaches, these all aim at a mindful engagement with the bodily functions, tonus, posture, movement or coordination, but they are different from body psychotherapy. For example, yoga also aims to calm the mind and connect people to something beyond themselves, but the path of yoga is above all a physical one (Heller, 2012, pp. 28–30). Rolfing, also known as Structural Integration, works manually on the connective and muscle tissue and aims at reorganising bodily structure; it is, however, not body psychotherapy (Jacobson, 2011). These approaches are not working with psychological methods even when the bodywork has an emotional effect and can influence psychological pain through change in the physical posture.

This is also true of Charlotte Selver's **Sensory Awareness** (Brooks, 1986), which she herself called a psychagogic method in which changes take place involuntarily through focusing attention on the inner perception of the body. However, Selver's attitude and her techniques for body awareness had a great influence on body psychotherapy, especially in the USA. In this respect we can posit a continuum along which bodywork methods approach body psychotherapy (Caldwell, 2015; Chapter 4).

The boundary between body therapy and body psychotherapy is in my view less a methodical than a conceptual one. Unlike body therapy, body psychotherapy is always connected to psychological and psychotherapeutic models and to an understanding of psychological functions, personality and development (Ollars, 2005, pp. 32–3). For this reason I will not be covering functional body therapy approaches in this book. However, body psychotherapy does use their methods and techniques to explore and change psychological processes, attitudes and habits through breathing, posture or movement. In addition, because of the psychological effect body therapy methods can elicit, in practice it is often difficult to draw the line between the two. For whoever touches the body in a helpful way, also touches the soul.

Important
Somatic and mental problems can be treated with various means. Psychotherapy is a treatment with psychological means, body therapy with bodily means.

In body therapy as well as in body psychotherapy, we use **objects** such as cushions, balls, ropes, cords, scarves, puppets, foam hitting cubes, tennis racquets or batakas. However, these are not therapeutic means in the sense that we are trying to achieve change through them as with a drug, an inhaler or an extension bed. They are **auxiliary aids**, which help create experiences (Geuter, 2019, pp. 55–7). This is why I do not include them in the definition of basic therapeutic means.

BODY PSYCHOTHERAPY

The special feature of body psychotherapy is that it systematically combines work by means of the psychological and by means of the physical in one treatment and focuses on mental as well as physical structures and processes. From all these considerations we can develop the following **definition of body psychotherapy**:

Important
Body psychotherapy is a treatment for illnesses or disorders using bodily as well as psychological means. In the same way, one can talk of body-mind therapy as a treatment via the body and the mind.

As far as I know, Buentig was the first to advance this definition. He calls body psychotherapy a form of treatment which organises 'the process of the animation of the body and the embodiment of the soul in an eventful life by means of the body-mind of the patient and that of the therapist in their mutual relationship' (Buentig, 1992, p. 180).

Other basic psychotherapy approaches may share the view of body psychotherapy – that all cognitive and emotional processes are connected to the body and to bodily experience – and some even utilise both psychological and somatic means, for example when inducing a trance in hypnotherapy or working with mindful body awareness in Gestalt therapy.

However, what distinguishes body psychotherapy is the comprehensive use of body experience and bodily treatment methods, which are systematically combined with psychological treatment into a holistic therapeutic process. 'Body psychotherapy treats each human being as essentially a unity, existing simultaneously and entirely in both the realm of embodiment and the realm of mentality' (Totton, 2020, p. 94).

The definition I offer here disentangles some of the snarls that result from mixing up the **what** and the **with what** – the object and the means. When Totton (2003, p. 136) deplores the fact that the term *body psychotherapy* does not really describe the essence of the matter, namely a holistic approach to the human being, then he is trying to describe the object of treatment, which elsewhere he calls *bodymind* (2003, p. 29). Heller (2012) is also attempting to define the object which he sees in the organismic regulation processes. Petzold (2009, p. 40) bases his concept of living body therapy in part on the argument that we are not treating the physiological body as doctors do, but rather a subjective and personal living body. **What** we are treating in psychotherapy can be described as the mind, personal living body or organism. I prefer to say that we are treating human beings who are in pain, even though today it is fashionable to use the language of reification and to call it the treatment of disorders. If we want to describe the **object** of treatment, then, as Petzold (2003) suggests, we should use the concept of **human therapy**, as we do that of human medicine. The broad concept of human therapy could encompass all therapeutic means of treating mental suffering, including art and music therapy, mototherapy, ergotherapy, sociotherapy or bibliotherapy.

Dance therapy

Dance therapy works principally with the medium of dance and is usually numbered together with music and art therapy among the **creative therapies**, which use an artistic medium such as painting, making music or dancing (Trautmann-Voigt, 2006). Since dance therapy is based on movement and bodily expression, we can also classify it as a body-oriented psychotherapy approach. In the English-speaking world, it is usually known as dance movement psychotherapy. By virtue of the fact that it works with the medium of dance and has its own theoretical tradition, dance therapy presents itself methodically and conceptually as a relatively autonomous approach. Despite all they have in common, we can view body psychotherapy and dance therapy as two separate approaches (Tantia, 2019). In this book, I will mention dance therapy only occasionally. It would be quite another task to build a bridge, based on the approach presented here, to the diversity of dance therapeutic theory and practice, a task that is not for me.

We get into a similar snarl when we try to define body psychotherapy in contrast to the verbal therapies and refer to it as involving non-verbal or extra-verbal methods (Fuchs & Koch, 2014, p. 8; Mueller-Braunschweig, 1998, p. 202). 'Verbal' therapies work with the medium of words. However, body psychotherapy is **not a non-verbal therapy approach**, as is often falsely claimed, but one in which both words and body are deployed as therapeutic means.

When doctors assert that body psychotherapy is unnecessary, since psychologists treat the mind and they themselves the body, they display a lack of understanding of these concepts. Doctors themselves rarely work with bodily methods such as chiropractic. Usually they deploy methods foreign to the body, such as drugs or surgical procedures, to heal disorders of the bodily system.

Approaches – methods – techniques

For the theory of psychotherapy, Wampold (2001, pp. 7–10) differentiates four levels of abstraction: meta-theoretical models, theoretical approaches, therapeutic strategies and therapeutic techniques. A meta-theoretical model provides the philosophical background for an approach. The holistic understanding of the human being as a body-mind being in relation to the environment is such a model.

According to Wampold's distinction, next to the psychodynamic, the cognitive-behavioural, the humanistic and the systemic, body psychotherapy is one of the great approaches within psychotherapy. It is not synonymous with the techniques used, which can also be utilised in other approaches.

On the level of therapeutic strategies I speak of principles (Geuter, 2019). Principles provide a superordinate view of process-oriented interventions in therapy, for instance the principle of encouraging awareness, or the principle of deepening inhibited emotions. Consistent strategies implementing these principles can be called methods: in body psychotherapy, for example, working with the breathing, with mindfulness, with stress positions or with re-enactments. Techniques are the practical means by which we can, for instance, stimulate the breathing, enlarge breath volume or evoke expression through breathing.

BODY OR SOMA

In body psychotherapy we find the concepts of *body* and *soma*. In the Reichian tradition, body is the notion more used and is associated with needs, sexuality or 'life energy'. The more perception oriented tradition in contrast uses the idea of soma, introduced by Thomas Hanna and meaning the body as perceived from within (Mullan, 2014, p. 225; Payne et al., 2019a, p. 9); this is from the ancient Greek and was used by Homer for the material body and the corpse, whereas for him life was to be found in the psyche (Sonntag, 2008). The conceptual distinction between body and soma is rooted in the distinction in the German language between the *Koerper* (body) and *Leib* (soma), something not found in other languages such as French or Chinese (Korischek, 2020). The concepts of *somatics* or *somatic psychology* used in the USA contain the legacy of this older German notion.

The distinction between these two concepts in the German language is also a legacy of the philosophical movement of *Leibphaenomenologie* (phenomenology of the body) going back to Husserl and Merleau-Ponty (Zahavi, 1994). Thus the French philosopher Gabriel Marcel (1976) differentiates between the body that I am, *Leib*, and the body that I have. The phenomenology of the body describes *Leib* or the lived body as the subjectively sensed body perceived from within and reserves the concept of body for the objectified body perceived from without. For the phenomenal world of subjective perception is only accessible in its sensing aspect to the subject themselves (Schmitz, 1986). From the outside, nobody can perceive **how** something feels for the subject. This is why some approaches to body psychotherapy prefer the concept of *soma (Leib)* to that of body.

Historically, as the instrumentalisation and objectified research on the body progressed in the 19th century, philosophers began to use the concept of *Leib*. The Swiss educator and school reformer Pestalozzi began to advocate physical exercise to promote fitness for work and earning a living (Jaeger & Staeuble, 1978, p. 138), and psychophysics started to measure the performance of the sense organs. Klein (2005, p. 83) says that it is thus the modern age which has created the sensation of having a body, which produces an instrumental and reflective relationship to one's own body. Therefore the distinction made between the *Leib* and the body in the phenomenology of the body could possibly be describing a sense of alienation. In connection with this feeling of alienation, a new discourse about the body and the philosophy of the *lived body* developed (Boehme, 2003, pp. 30–9).

In the philosophy of the 19th century, it was Schopenhauer and Nietzsche who regarded the body in a non-objectifying manner and called it *Leib*, lived body (Boehme, 2003). It is Schopenhauer who first forwarded the idea which shaped the philosophy of the body in the 20th century: that the body is twofold, being seen from outside and sensed from the inside (Fellmann, 1996, p. 278). Nietzsche later lauded the lived body as the self and the essence of reason: 'body am I through and through, and nothing besides'; and *soul* is just a word for something on the body (2006, p. 23). The following aphorism is often quoted:

> Behind your thoughts and feelings, my brother, stands a powerful commander, an unknown wise man – he is called self. He lives in your body, he is your body. There is more reason in your body than in your best wisdom.
>
> (Nietzsche, 2006, p. 23)

Nietzsche, however, wanted to respect the body because in it there is a bridge to the *Uebermensch* (superhuman), who overcomes the weaknesses and infirmities of human existence. He countered the pessimistic Schopenhauer with a life-affirming will that transcends the self (Nietzsche, 2006, pp. 89, 173). Maybe this is why Reich liked to read him (Section 3.4).

In the 20th century, Husserl, the founder of phenomenological philosophy, described the lived body as something which both senses and is sensed. The lived body as a medium of perception is also the medium of the perception of itself: only through my lived body do I experience what really constitutes my bodiliness (Husserl, 2012, p. 234; cf. Section 5.3: 'Phenomenology'). Merleau-Ponty (2012) subsequently stated that as opposed to other objects, which can be in my field of perception or not, the lived body is always there. In this constancy it is a medium of communication with the world and can be the body that touches and that which is touched and thus subject and object in one. It is the source of experience and the object of experience simultaneously (Jonas, 2001).

Bergson (1911) determined that the surface of the body is the only part of the extended world that can be felt and perceived at the same time. Both Bergson and Plessner (1975) link the concept of the lived body to the philosophy of life, which has been so influential in body psychotherapy (Chapter 3). In his *Philosophical anthropology*, first published in 1928, Plessner described the body as twofold: it owns itself and is owned, being its own means and own purpose; it is life itself, since only life unites these two in itself (Plessner, 1975, pp. 189–90).

The idea in the philosophy of life and in phenomenology of the twofold nature of the lived body, which can only be perceived from a first-person perspective, is among the basic premises of an experiential body psychotherapy. Nevertheless I still think it unnecessary to substitute the term *soma* for that of the *body*. The idea of the lived and experienced body includes this aspect. In general, the notion of *body experience* is used by most authors as the generic term for the subjective relation to the body (Braehler, 1995a; Joraschky et al., 2009; Schreiber-Willnow, 2000; Chapter 6). In experiential psychotherapy, the term *body* is commonly used. When Gendlin (1993) uses the word *Leib* in a text written in German, he means the usual physical body, which however senses something about the situation and communicates meaning (Gendlin, 1996; Section 5.3).

For both the reasons given at the beginning of this chapter, I therefore argue for holding on to the notion of the body; for allowing the idea of soma and lived body to merge into a concept of the experienced body; and for defining the focus on body experience as being the specific perspective on the body of body psychotherapy.

PERSPECTIVITY

There is only one body, not the lived body and the objective body as two distinct objects. Whether as psychotherapists we look at the lived body or as doctors at the objectified body is just a matter of different perspectives (Chapter 7). From both viewpoints, we are looking at the one body. The experienced body is both internal and external, sentient and substantial, mental and material. The psychological and the physical are not radically different from one another, but also not identical (Fuchs, 2017). They are two aspects of the living, two sides or perspectives of the same life process, as the philosopher Max Scheler (1966, p. 78) wrote. The whole that they belong to is a living being in interaction with their world (de Haan, 2020, p. 13). Therefore we can only differentiate various perspectives from which we view the body. The distinction between an objectifying and a subjective perspective of perception is only one of many and can itself be divided up into even more perspectives.

Let us take the simple example of a person who is picking up a glass. We can explore this action as follows:

- Haptologically: what is happening in the skin as the person picks up the glass?
- Biochemically: which metabolic processes are involved in the movement?
- Neurobiologically: which neuronal processes are involved in the movement? How does the sensorimotor coordination take place in the neurons and muscles?
- Phenomenologically: is the movement coordinated or not? What shape does it have? What impression does it make? Are the hand movements flowing or inhibited, precise or erratic?
- Psychologically: what does the person experience as they reach for the glass? What is it they need as they do so? What do they associate with this act? Are they perhaps afraid that they will drop the glass? Are they thinking about the grandmother who gave them this special glass? Are they looking forward to the drink in the glass? Is their mouth watering? Can they feel the smoothness of the glass with their fingertips?

What we are observing is a person's interaction with the world, which only exists as a whole: in the skin, the cells, the brain, the hand, the movement, the thoughts and feelings. The various questions about this same observable event are the result of the viewpoints of the respective scientific disciplines. The psychological point of view regarding experience and behaviour is one of these.

In everyday life we usually take the first-person perspective towards our bodies. We experience the world from the body and through the body. We assume the third-person perspective when the body is not functioning well, when it is not able to do its bit or starts to hurt. Then in our self-perception it morphs from 'me' to 'it'.

I want to illustrate the significance of this perspective view with another example. When a violinist makes a string vibrate through the movement of the bow, then we hear a sound. What is the sound and what is the cause of it? From the point of view of physics, the sound is the air vibrating caused by the vibration of the string and the resonating body of the instrument. But does the sound that I hear exist in this vibration? Or a melody consisting of several sounds? Physically, we can depict a melody as a sequence of vibrations. But from the subjective point of view, the aesthetic experience of the listener transcends the vibrations. In addition, these last are produced by the actions of the violinist, who again is playing a composition and who creates the effect in the ears of the listener. The sound is therefore a complex affair that I can view from various sides. It is identical with the vibration of the air and yet it is not, according to how I look at it. We could also say that only in the complex relationship between composer, musician, instrument and listener does the sound exist, but that it can be described from various perspectives. I can describe it with the concepts of physics but also with those of psychology, without need of a theory of how the one is related to the other.

Thus when Grawe asks whether one has ever been astonished at 'how a monotonous sequence of magnetic potentials can *create* songs as beautiful as Schubert's Symphony in C-major' (2007, p. 29, my emphasis), he is taking a technical point of view: how music can be created through the medium of a data carrier. Grawe's question corresponds exactly to his perception that neuronal activity creates psychological processes (Grawe, 2007; Section 7.2). However, this is a mere metaphorical idea and, moreover, a false one. Psychological processes originate in a complex interplay of body, brain, situation, environment, biography, memories and the whole of life in all its vibrancy and abundance of forms (Emrich, 2007, p. 208).

Now we can apply these examples to the processes we are dealing with in psychotherapy. It is not possible to limit emotional experiences to actual bodily, psychological or even central nervous processes. If we look at these from various scientific perspectives – physiology, brain science or psychology – then the differences lie not so much in the subject matter of their studies as in their questions. If a person is afraid, then we can:

- Physiologically: examine the blood circulation, for instance the fact that the forehead grows cold.
- Neurobiologically: examine the neuronal firing patterns emanating from the amygdala.
- Psychologically: ask the person what the fear means and how it is related to their life and to their biography.

From the point of view of the subject matter, these are all various aspects of a coherent life process in a living body. However, from each perspective, we can both look at and influence what is happening in a person. Scientific subdisciplines distinguish themselves from one another not on the basis of objectively defined areas of study, but on that of their various questions. Researchers compel nature to answer their questions, as Kant (1996, pp. 25, 28) asserted; knowledge is not determined by the objects.

Bergson (1911) illustrates the fact that we have to think about the physically living human being differently than does natural science with Zeno's story of Achilles and the tortoise. The fallacy that Achilles can never catch up with the tortoise, because as he approaches it, the distance between them can again be divided up, is based on the fact that mathematically, the distance can be divided up ad infinitum, but the sequence of the movement of a human being cannot. We can never really capture Achilles' run with nomothetic methods, which are dedicated to setting up universal laws. In psychotherapy, we are interested in how a person cuts their own path, even though researchers attempt to determine distances on this path with the help of quantifiable indicators.

Just like the experienced body, the living, moving body is not a static entity that can be quantified in any given moment, but **a process**. We experience it when we walk as well as in the rhythm of our breathing, when we feel pain or relief from pain, when desire rushes up or dies away.

Referring to Ken Wilber, Wehowsky (2006, pp. 191–2) suggests a model of four perspectives on the body:

1. The individual **objective body**, observed from without; this is the usual vantage point of natural science and medicine.
2. The individual **subjective body**, observed from within.
3. The **interobjective body,** observed in relation to social and ecological systems (e.g. 'I am the father of my children').
4. The **intersubjective body**, observed in experiencing interaction (e.g. 'I feel as if I am failing my children as a father').

With the help of these perspectives we can ask how a patient's body is presented from the outside, how the patient feels it from the inside, what relationship their body has to others and how they feel in this relationship.

The two perspectives of psychotherapy are those of inner experience and behaviour in relation to oneself and to others. These are **first-person perspectives**, those of the I and the we (Choifer, 2018). In body psychotherapy, we are not dealing with the body as an object from a third-person perspective, but with the owned body of the patient, with our own body as the therapist and with both in their relationships and in relation to one another. Experiential and relational body psychotherapeutic practice is not technical work on the body as an objectifiable physis, but work with the personal, experienced body of a living person in a living relationship.

Important
In body psychotherapy we see the body as a personal, experienced body of a living subject in relation to their life world.

Perspectives of body experience

Schatz (2002, pp. 77–8) distinguishes seven kinds of body experience, to which he assigns seven perspectives that he understands in part to be treatment approaches.

1. The **objective body** = the body from a **medical-biological perspective**; the body that I have; this body is seen as healthy or sick, can be palpated or x-rayed and treated functionally.
2. The **subjectively experienced and expressive body** = the body from an '**individual' perspective**; here Schatz means how someone experiences their body and expresses this experience, including the use of symbolisation (I give meaning to my bodily experience).
3. The **body moving in space** = the body from a **spatial perspective**: moving in space and moving around; walking, approaching, retreating.
4. The **body as the bearer of the past, present and future** = **chronological perspective**: bodily memories, bodily experience, sensing the body in the present, organismic projections, bodily intuition.
5. The **body in relationship** = the body from a **relational perspective**: how someone relates to another person with their body and how we can develop relationships through the body.
6. The **body surrendered** = the **autonomic perspective**: here Schatz means phenomena that happen of their own accord, as for example autonomic, uncontrolled

movements of the body, or autonomic processes such as crying or laughing, which can also occur in therapy when strong feelings come up.

7. The **creative body** = the **creative perspective**: bodily creative, artistic processes expressed for instance in music, language, art, dance or mime.

From these different perspectives we can put various questions to the body: how does it communicate meaning, how does it experience pain, how does it move, how has life experience formed it, how does it express itself in interaction when affect motor patterns surface, how does it surrender or control itself, what creative resources does it harbour? In this way, through questioning the body, we can approach the whole living person.

From a psychological perspective, the experienced body is the body that is perceived and experienced as the subject and the medium of human needs, the locus of sensation and the setting for affects. This body is always the body of a human being in their natural and human environment. Since it is also a social body, we have to look at it from a historical and sociological perspective. When we sense the body, we sense not only its 'nature', but also how it exists in historical and social reality: occupied by the dispositives of power, as Foucault has shown; identified with a social habitus learned through the body, as Bourdieu demonstrated; controlled by social constraints embedded in the behavioural apparatus of self-constraint, as Elias describes in his historical studies (Section 1.5); moulded by the adoption or rejection of family models of bodiliness (Young, 2002. p. 26). If we want a comprehensive understanding of human beings in all their bodiliness, then we have to include the perspectives of history and social science.

Clinical application

Bulimia is a prime **example** of this. People suffering from bulimia experience a conflict between the desire to surrender to their greed and the desire to curb their greed. This conflict takes place in and through the body. We can explore the body experience of bulimic people psychologically; we can examine the weight or the effects of frequent vomiting on the teeth; and we can study the socio-historical issues of how far the conflict between societal pressure to consume and the ideal physical body of this society, as well as the contemporary compulsion to present the body publicly, have contributed to these symptoms. The various perspectives give us various insights into bulimia.

If we understand the body as the living body of a living person who lives in and with this body, this attitude covers those aspects of bodiliness represented by the concept of *Leib*, soma. In *Leibphaenomenologie* (phenomenology of the body), the notion of *Leibsubjekt* or somatic subject is often used as synonymous with the human being or the person and the terms **human being** or **person** are used hardly at all. Fuchs (2017) currently spotlights the idea of the person (Chapter 5). He also called the *Leib* or soma all that I become aware of as myself when I close myself off from the outside world (Fuchs, 2000, p. 89). Thus the soma would be that of which I can say 'This is me'. The terms *soma* or *somatic subject* would then be identical with what is called in the terminology of humanistic-experiential psychotherapy *the person*: a sensing, experiencing, feeling, thinking, striving and acting human being, whose living body is part of their being as a human.

As for the question of whom we are dealing with in psychotherapy, it must be human beings, people, living beings. We treat not the body or the soma but the person in distress. However, we look at them from certain perspectives, including various perspectives on the body, which we can define without using the notion of *Leib*, soma. The understanding of the living body encompasses the concept of soma.

Neither do we need the concept of soma for the definition of body psychotherapy as therapy with bodily and psychological means. Bodily means are those of the relevant body with all its needs, demeanours or tensions, its various states or its inner experience; a body that a person has **and** at the same time is.

3

The quest for natural aliveness

On the origins of body psychotherapy

Body psychotherapy developed as the first split from Freudian psychoanalysis, which not only forged new paths theoretically, like Adler or Jung, but also developed new treatment methods. Next to psychoanalysis we also find the origins of body psychotherapy in reform movements in gymnastics and dance of the early 20th century. Initially we can recognise three central ideas about the body (Geuter, 1996):

- According to the **Reichian idea**, the body is the site of blocked energy and the medium for the expression of repressed material and of character armouring. This tradition works with the idea of restoring the flow of blocked energy by, for example, liberating affects from the defence system through bodily expression and thus bringing repressed emotional material up into consciousness.
- The concept of the body as a natural human resource grew out of **reform gymnastics**. Without direct psychotherapeutic intent, body therapy here strives to reappropriate the body through consciously paying attention to sensing it, its breathing and its movements and in so doing to restore the harmony of the bodily functions.
- In the psychoanalytic line stemming from **Ferenczi**, the body is seen as the bearer of meaning in transference. In a dialogical process of sensing and interaction, this meaning is then revealed.

From the late 1960s, the contemporary **growth movement** and **humanistic psychotherapy** became the third source. In connection with *Leibphilosophie*, meaning lived-body philosophy, a phenomenologically oriented body psychotherapy developed, which takes the inner sensing of the body as the starting point for the therapeutic quest for meaning and significance.

From the beginning of body psychotherapy, the Reichian tradition has been prevalent (Chapter 4). In the German-speaking countries, schools developed out of the reform movement in gymnastics, which emphasised perception and exercise. Later in the USA, a more experiential body psychotherapy developed, based on the functional body therapy approaches of Sensory Awareness or Body-Mind Centering, which, according to D. Johnson (2015), is well suited to the pragmatic American philosophical tradition.

These traditions are not only connected through the personal experience of their protagonists. They share far more intellectually than they are generally aware of. Some of their fundamental ideas are rooted in the spirit of philosophy of life and of the life reform movement (Geuter, 2000a; Marlock, 2015b). The two earlier traditions converge in a desire for the

DOI: 10.4324/9781003176893-3

unhampered development of human nature in the face of the burden of modern civilisation, in their longing for aliveness, wholeness, movement, rhythm and experience. Both are clearly children of their times and more inclined to inner inconsistencies than the history written to date, based mainly on the works and the personalities of Reich (Boadella, 1973; Sharaf, 1994) and Gindler (Ludwig, 2002), would have us believe. Of late, even analytical body psychotherapy employs concepts such as 'life movement' (Geissler & Heisterkamp, 2007), without, however, establishing a connection to philosophical sources or linking it to the other traditions.

In this chapter, I first want to show the intellectual basis of body psychotherapy in the history and context in which in Germany the initial ideas were formed. I will aim to depict both the common guiding ideas as well as the conflicting ones of the two larger and older traditions as part of contemporary discourse. Elsewhere I have already described the history of the ideas of the various schools and the teacher–student relationship of the founders (Geuter, 2000, 2000a, 2015). Since in this book I depict body psychotherapy as an experiential therapy approach based on body-mind unity, I will concentrate here on how the origins of body psychotherapy are connected to a mentality that, from its philosophical theories to its everyday practice, was shaped by the quest for new forms of relating to our lives.

FOREBEARS

As Freud and later Reich appeared on the stage of psychotherapy, the question of how emotional and bodily processes are connected was fashionable in physiological research. Emotions were often described in concepts of '*visceral physiology*' (Dror, 2019, p. 76). In the beginnings of psychotherapy, we also find the idea that psychological processes are connected to motor and vegetative processes. Marlock (2015b, p. 85) distinguishes two directions of development: one in which the psychological is emphasised and which leads to Freud, who was the first to grant the 'psychic apparatus' a special status in relation to the life of the organism (Starobinski, 1987, p. 23); and another which focuses on the corporeal in the therapeutic process. Marlock includes in this last the physician Franz Anton Mesmer, who at the end of the 18th century was already treating illness by touching and stroking the body and who explained the effectiveness of his methods with animal magnetism (Peter, 2001), as well as **Pierre Janet**, who since the end of the 19th century had created the foundations for a dynamic psychiatry. Janet studied the breathing patterns of his patients and the contraction of the muscles in neurotic processes and propagated the cathartic method and the significance of massage in a non-verbal dialogue. For this reason Boadella (2002, p. 20) calls Janet 'the first body psychotherapist'. In his theory of strength and tension he connects physiology and psychology (Ellenberger, 1970, pp. 377–9). Like his contemporary, the psychologist Theodule Ribot, he explains personality through the body (Starobinski, 1987).

At that time psychotherapy was not yet a discipline separate from medicine. Some physicians practiced medical treatment and psychological dialogue in one unified approach. We can observe this most clearly with **Georg Groddeck**, who is seen by Downing (1996, p. 346) as the first body psychotherapist and who is also regarded as the founder of psychosomatics. At the end of the 19th century, Groddeck took over from his famous teacher, Ernst Schweninger, the concept of an individualised medicine, massaged his patients daily and, through strong pressure on the diaphragm, mobilised their breathing (Will, 1987). With the help of psychoanalysis, he then attempted to explore the meaning of organic symptoms (Will, 1987, p. 52). All his life, Groddeck (1931) championed the view that massage and psychotherapy belong together. With massage you could treat resistance and transference, as well as alleviating functional disorders and tensions and thus strengthening the healing powers of the organism itself. Groddeck thus practised the model of verbal psychotherapeutic work and body-work in one treatment with one therapist, as Reich also did later on.

Since 1900, Groddeck had run a sanatorium in Baden-Baden, where he treated mainly chronically ill patients. Early on he developed some of the initial guiding principles of body psychotherapy:

- Repression is not least a bodily act and bodily symptoms can therefore be the defence system itself without having need of symbolic conversion as in the Freudian theory of hysteria (Will, 1987, pp. 113–4).
- Not only psychological associations, but also bodily associations disclose information about the patient (Will, 1987, p. 149).
- Psychological energy can be bound up in the breathing (Groddeck, 1931); the id expresses itself in the breathing style (Groddeck, 1992, p. 154).
- Healing takes place not through making repressed material conscious, but by removing the resistance to healing and thus releasing the repressed material hindering recovery; then the id of the patient can come into a healing movement (Groddeck, 1992, pp. 180–1).

This understanding of healing corresponds to the ancient notion of medicine 'medicus curat, natura sanat' ascribed to Hippocrates: the physician can treat, but nature heals. In the light of contemporary system theory, we would say that the therapist gives the impulse, so that the faculty of self-regulation inherent in the human system can unfold (Chapter 17).

Whereas Reich, like the later Chicago school of psychosomatics of Franz Alexander, was searching for a typology of neurotic patterns, Groddeck was pursuing the idea of understanding the sick person and the meaning of their illness individually (Giefer, 2019), an idea which later became a guiding principle in the psychosomatics of Viktor von Weizsaecker.

The concept of the id also comes from Groddeck. Freud took it over from him (Ellenberger, 1970, p. 516). But above all, Groddeck inspired those analysts who were interested in bodily expression in psychoanalysis. Ferenczi visited him often when he was developing his own active techniques (Will, 1987, p. 66). Since 1920, Groddeck had also been a member of the Berlin Psychoanalytical Institute, to which Reich and Fenichel later belonged (Bocian, 2007, p. 187).

3.1 PSYCHOANALYSIS AND REFORM GYMNASTICS – TWO EARLY SOURCES OF BODY PSYCHOTHERAPY

When we look at the two early sources of body psychotherapy (Figure 3.1), then among the psychoanalysts it was above all Sándor Ferenczi and the left-wing Freudians Otto Fenichel and Wilhelm Reich, who were pondering the significance of the body for repression and the suppression of emotions and who were looking for new approaches to treatment. In reform gymnastics, however, the focus was not on psychotherapy but on a new attitude to the body in posture and movement. Experiencing the body was meant to loosen up functional constraints and allow the use of one's body in accordance with its natural functions. This approach was a kind of somatic education and developed at first into new forms of body therapy. Then it was taken up by psychotherapists; body psychotherapy approaches developed from it but not until the second and third generation.

3.1.1 Psychoanalysis – the earliest source

In psychoanalysis there was initially much deliberation as to the significance of the body in psychotherapy, which, as psychoanalysis was reduced to the Freudian mainstream, was later forgotten. It was not only Freud's drive theory that was based on the body. In the beginning, he massaged patients, applied pressure on sensitive parts of the body to provoke reaction or massaged the head to awaken memories (Totton, 2002, p. 9), practices he later abandoned.

Psychoanalysis	**Reform gymnastics, breath therapy, body education, expressive dance**
	Impulses from movement teachers such as
• Georg Groddeck	• Elsa Gindler
• Sándor Ferenczi	• Dorothee Guenther
• Wilhelm Reich	and expressive dancers such as:
	• Mary Wigman
	• Rudolf von Laban
Leading to:	Leading to:
• affect oriented body psychotherapy methods focused more on uncovering conflicts	• more functional body psychotherapy methods focused more on breathing and movement

FIGURE 3.1 The two early sources of body psychotherapy

Freud (1923, p. 26) wrote that the ego is 'first and foremost a body ego'. Freud connected the ego to the bodily sensations which emanate from the surface of the body.

Freud was aware of the fact that a 'man's states of mind are manifested, almost without exception, in the tensions and relaxations of his facial muscles, in the adaptations of his eyes, in the amount of blood in the vessels of his skin, in the modifications in his vocal apparatus and in the movements of his limbs and in particular of his hands' (1890, p. 286). However, he did not use these bodily signals in his therapeutic work. He remained true to the enlightenment idea of the self-knowing spirit. Over time, the body became for him just a representation in the psyche. In not one of his case studies do we find interpretations of non-verbally, non-cognitively represented material (Balint, 1984).

Simmel

Some of Freud's notable contemporaries view this differently. At the 5th International Psychoanalytic Congress in Budapest in 1918 on the theme of war neuroses, Ernst Simmel (1993, p. 22) presented the treatment of a soldier whose sullen rage had led to spasms of the pharynx, and another who as a result of the shock of an injury had lost the muscle tonus in one arm. Apart from Ferenczi, Simmel was the only participant to speak out for psychocatharsis (Schultz-Venrath, 1996). He believed that the enormous affect block from the traumatising situation needed an adequate abreaction, as in the situation itself the soldiers had not been able to carry their actions through to a close. 'I have for a while now been providing the neurotic person with a padded phantom, so that they can fight against it and triumphantly free themselves with all their primordial human instincts' (Simmel, 1993, p. 31). Here in 1918, we already find the model of expressing a feeling in the therapy room by using an object. The idea that after trauma there is a tendency 'to complete the action which was interrupted by the shock' re-appears in Ferenczi (1988, p. 59) and today takes centre stage in the trauma treatment method of Peter Levine's Somatic Experiencing (2010).

Fenichel

Simmel's idea that there is a connection between muscle tone and emotional repression was a common theme of several leading theorists of the psychoanalysis of that time, such as

Fenichel, Ferenczi and Reich. Otto Fenichel followed it up theoretically, and Ferenczi and Reich did so in their treatment practice as well. Fenichel (1927, p. 118) wrote, in a similar vein to Groddeck, that suppression 'consists of holding back certain impulses from motility'. He attributed this to the fact that children are urged to hold back motor impulses connected to drives. Through muscular hypertension, suppression is maintained and free movement is restricted. Thus 'in every neurosis full control of motility is forfeited' (Fenichel, 1927, p. 119). Fenichel was ahead of Reich's theory, but did not draw the conclusion of working with the body in psychotherapy. In a lecture in Berlin in 1927, only published in 2015, he advocated a treatment consisting of body therapy and psychoanalysis consecutively, in which gymnastics would help initially to reduce the tension of repression. For patients who were particularly estranged from their bodies, he recommended harmonic gymnastics in the style of Elsa Gindler (Fenichel, 2015). He had himself got rid of his headaches through taking part in Gindler's courses (Muehlleitner, 2008, pp. 147). On the question of psychoanalytic techniques, he was basically in agreement with his closest friend, Reich (Muehlleitner, 2008, p. 196). However, when Reich started vegetotherapy, he was afraid of him working aggressively on the body armouring and warned him against it (Fenichel, 1935, p. 333).

Fenichel laid a foundation stone for our understanding of somatoform disorders with his theory of 'affect equivalents'. Like Groddeck, he assumed that functional affect reactions – for example, muscular hypertension – will persist as long as there are suppressed emotional images. Bodily symptoms are in this case not symbolic signs of conflict, but rather real consequences of psychological stress (Kuechenhoff, 2008, p. 115; Section 7.1). Alongside the psychoanalytical theory of conflict, we can find this concept in body psychotherapy right from the beginning.

Ferenczi

In the 1920s, Ferenczi was probably the most creative innovator of psychoanalytic technique next to Reich. He was also Groddeck's closest friend (Will, 1987, p. 13). He too lamented neurotics' restricted motility (Ferenczi, 1925, p. 167) and experimented in treatment with patients' bodily activity as well as the conscious holding back of motor impulses (Ferenczi, 1925, pp. 149, 176). With these bodily methods, he wanted to heighten inner tensions and so obtain more material for interpretation (Ferenczi, 1926, p. 188). Sometimes he recommended relaxation exercises in order to overcome 'psychic obstacles and resistance to associations' (Ferenczi, 1926, p. 190). Thus Ferenczi (1930, p. 264) was aware of the increase in tension through denying impulses as well as relaxation through allowing them, and this was an expression of his advocacy of 'elasticity' in psychoanalytic technique (Ferenczi, 1928). He encouraged patients to pay attention to the language of the unconscious in facial expression, gestures, posture and behaviour and he offered to enter into a bodily action dialogue with them so that they could become aware of material that could not be verbalised in their relationship to the analyst. Consequently, some psychoanalysts – such as for example Reich's first wife, Annie – started to pay attention not just to what the patient said, but also to their body language without, however, giving up the couch setting (Jacobs, 2001, p. 6).

In psychoanalysis, Ferenczi (1931, p. 276) was considered a specialist for 'difficult cases'. Unlike Freud, he adhered to the idea that for many severely disturbed patients, it was not oedipal phantasies but real traumata such as sexual abuse that were the origins of their illness (Dupont, 1988). Such patients were more likely to present their childhood traumatisation in their behaviour rather than to verbalise it (Ferenczi, 1931, p. 279). Ferenczi saw in this a therapeutic opportunity: if the patient was allowed to behave like an 'unruly child' and to reproduce the traumatic experience, then they could work through the shock in therapy. Thus, Ferenczi encouraged regression so as to unlock pre-verbal psychic material

and would let the patient hold his hand, or he would stroke their head, to prevent dissociation (Ferenczi, 1931, pp. 280–9). In his clinical diary from 1932, we find several therapy
examples in which he lets the patient's traumatic experience come up into affective motor
arousal (Ferenczi, 1988, e.g. p. 54). Later, however, he complained that these methods did
not have the required effect (Ferenczi, 1933). As Downing (1996) observes, he was lacking
a concept of how to bring people out of this regressive state in a manner in which the reliving of traumatising experiences in relation to the therapist leads to a new and healing
experience.

Because of these experiments, Freud attacked Ferenczi quite fiercely and accused him of
'pampering'. The background to this was certainly the fact that he had appealed to Freud for
help when he fell in love with a patient, the daughter of his lover, and was seriously confused
(Haynal, 2000, pp. 50–1). But what Freud was attacking was perhaps the fact that Ferenczi
represented a more motherly pole of the analytical relationship, one focused on experience
rather than on the strict methods of interpretation of the patriarchal Freud. From his clinical descriptions we can sense his strong emotional presence as a therapist, something that
was only recognised later as a change mechanism of therapeutic treatment. Ferenczi laid
the foundation for this understanding of psychotherapy, which his student, Michael Balint,
later called two-person psychology (Ermann, 1994).

Ferenczi always understood his technical experiments as an extension of psychoanalysis
and not as a new form of therapy. Despite the fact that he ignited a storm of creativity, he
was not the initiator of any great innovation. This was related to the fact that established
psychoanalysis violently rejected him, defamed him as a paranoid schizophrenic and with-
held his letters and writings from public view for decades (Nagler, 2003; von Polenz, 1994,
p. 191). Today, both Integrative Therapy (Petzold, 2003) and analytical body psychotherapy
draw on Ferenczi and his experimental, body-oriented approach. As Ferenczi was searching
for corrective emotional experiences, Schrauth calls him 'the spiritual father of all the more
experiential therapy forms' (2001, p. 73).

Reich

Of all the psychoanalysts mentioned, only Reich developed his own original body psychotherapy (Boadella, 1973; Buentig, 2015). In his vegetotherapy he not only brought together
verbal work and body-work in a single therapeutic process, as did Groddeck, but he connected this way of working with a systematic theory of the relationship between psychological and bodily defence processes.

Three things had brought him to this point (Geuter & Schrauth, 1997):

- Firstly, he was working with numerous patients who had experienced deprivation, abuse
  or neglect and who today we would identify as borderline patients. Reich (1925, pp. 246)
  was the first to describe their pathology and to advocate a therapeutic method which
  focussed on ego analysis and on working with the current transference.
- Secondly, he upheld Freud's theory of actual neurosis. For him, blocked sexual tension
  was the energetic source for all mental illness (Harms, 2017). Therefore, healing was
  only possible when the neurosis was deprived of this energetic source. However, this
  meant that the patient would have to become capable of the ultimate vegetative involuntary surrender in the sexual act (Reich, 1927). Reich called this 'orgastic potency'.
- Thirdly he initiated a technical discussion among analysts about their experience that
  resistance often prevented patients from associating freely. Reich was looking for a way
  of working with the resistance in order to restore the original energy of the suppressed
  drive by loosening the defences.

Reich was interested in patients who had problems regulating their affects or had dissociated them. In connection with this last, he referred to a psychological *contactlessness* (Reich, 1972, p. 310) and an affect block (Reich, 1972, p. 80). He referred to patterns of emotional defence as character resistance. He understood character as the result of the struggle of the ego with the drive and with reality. With Groddeck, Fenichel and Ferenczi, he assumed that psychological suppression is accompanied by muscular tension. He described psychic defences by means of 'character armouring' as 'functionally identical' with muscular hypertonus (Reich, 1973, p. 270), neurotic character and muscular dystonus as a 'functional identity' (Reich, 1972, p. 345). This means that both suppression and tension as defence mechanisms function as protection against a person's painful feelings and thus that both constitute the neurosis. Reich described the respiratory block as the central mechanism of affect suppression and repression (Reich, 1973, p. 308). All neurotically sick people, according to Reich, suffered from a tonic contraction of the diaphragm and breathe out shallowly and in snatches (Reich, 1973, p. 306). From these deliberations, Reich concluded that biographically not only a character attitude but also a physical attitude developed, both of which we can view as expressions of the relevant defence patterns. He spoke of character and muscular armouring (Chapter 13).

In his chief work, *Character analysis*, he described, on the basis of the body language of his patients, how character resistances show themselves in facial expressions, gestures and muscle tone or in the breathing. At first, he would just point this out to the patient. Also, he would suggest that they pay attention to their breathing and encouraged them to take notice of feelings which were held back on the body level and to express them. For example, he asked a masochistic patient to let himself go completely until he was throwing himself about on the couch and screaming out his hate of his father (Reich, 1972, p. 242). Whereas Breuer and Freud (1895) had described in their *Studies on Hysteria* that the path from hysterical, physical symptoms back to the memories would dissolve the emotional tension, Reich went in the opposite direction, going from the emotional tension in the body back to the memories. He utilised the body's affective memory.

> It never ceases to surprise how the loosening of a muscular spasm not only releases the vegetative energy, but over and above this, reproduces a memory of that situation in infancy in which the repression of the instinct occurred. *It can be said that every muscular rigidity contains the history and meaning of its origin.*
>
> (Reich, 1973 p. 300).

From the time of his exile in Oslo, from 1934 onwards, Reich moved on to working directly on the muscle tensions of his patients. For example, he massaged the tense neck muscles of a stiff-necked patient. If a patient's breathing was shallow or forced, then Reich would try to deepen it through touch (Sharaf, 1994, p. 237). With a patient whose defence system froze his face in a permanently friendly smile, he wrote that he could either describe to him his chronic facial expression or by disrupting the muscular position, for instance by pulling the chin down, he could 'eliminate' it (Reich, 1973 p. 271). He called this 'an enormous step forward'. He gave the name **vegetotherapy** to this new therapy method, as working with the body often produced vegetative reactions:

> The loosening of the rigid muscular attitudes produced peculiar body sensations in the patients: involuntary trembling and twitching of the muscles, sensations of cold and hot, itching, the feeling of pins and needles, prickling sensations, the feeling of having the jitters, and somatic perceptions of anxiety, anger and pleasure. I had to break with all the old ideas about the mind–body relationship, if I wanted to grasp these phenomena. They were not 'results',

'causes', 'accompanying manifestations' of 'psychic processes'; they were simply these phenomena themselves in the somatic realm.

(Reich, 1973 p. 271)

At first, Reich's therapeutic style tended to be thorough, slow and not invasive. Only in his
later years did he work in an invasive manner with the idea of loosening blocks in the body
swiftly (Totton, 2002, p. 12). This was related to a linear-causal way of thinking, in which
for each mental disorder there was a cause, which Reich wanted to 'attack' and 'eliminate'.

Character

Historically, it is interesting to see that Reich with his focus on the idea of character was firmly in
the mainstream of contemporary psychology, but still presented his own concept (Section 13.2).
The French philosopher Henri Bergson, whom Reich (1973) regarded as his philosopher of refer-
ence, described character as the 'actual synthesis of all our past states' (Bergson, 1911, p. 146).
In 1910 the philosopher Ludwig Klages (1926) published *The Science of Character: Principles of
Characterology*. Thus, the concept of characterology came into being.

Klages said that the soul, in touch with both the inner and outer worlds, communicates
in 'the semiotics of the body world' (1926, p. 12) and that a person's inner life is revealed
in their movements (Klages, 1926, p. 17). He devised a system of character qualities which
influenced contemporary psychological diagnostics (Geuter, 1992, pp. 94–105). This used
expressive media such as handwriting, facial expression, gestures, physiognomy and voice
(Geuter, 1992, pp. 95–105). In emphasising body expression, this diagnostic was in agreement with the gymnastic movement, with expressive dance and with the search for authentic movement in the performing arts (Moscovici, 1991, p. 13). But its intentions were static:
to infer a person's character from body expression as a congealed form of movement is a
'natural fact' (Klages, 1926, p. 29). The study of expression and character in contemporary
psychology had no dynamic concept of character. This is perhaps the reason why Reich
never referred to them. Reich considered character not as a natural fact in the sense of our
modern idea of temperament, but as the result of dynamic processes of a biographically
specific and phase-related struggle of a human being with the conflicts between their needs
and an environment which denies them.

Political reservations will have played their part. Klages placed his characterology in the
context of a conservative critique of civilisation and followed the ideal of a body ruled by the
will (Geuter, 1992, pp. 105–9). Reich, on the other hand, stood for the ideal of surrendering
to the autonomous, pleasurable bodily arousal processes. Klages also did not understand
the body from its inner, perceptible corporeality (Schmitz, 1992a, p. 17). Thus, his characterology and study of expression were useful for a static diagnostic system, but not for the
dynamic understanding of character in psychotherapy that was already set out in Bergson's
concept. Similarly, we can say the same of the morphological and physiognomic theories on
the relationship between 'physique and character', for example from the psychiatrist Ernst
Kretschmer, presented in his eponymous 1921 book. The psychoanalytic and body psychotherapy theory of character developed completely independently from psychological characterology, which flourished simultaneously.

3.1.2 Reform gymnastics – the second source

Some schools of psychotherapy developed not out of psychoanalysis but out of a trend
towards subjectification, self-awareness and self-experience within the German reform

gymnastics movement. In this tradition, the starting point was not working with loosening the defences but one of aesthetic and educational work with the body.

At the beginning of the 19th century, the Swede Pehr Henrik Ling established a system of gymnastics resting on the following four pillars:

- Medical gymnastics to strengthen the body.
- Military gymnastics to steel it.
- Educational gymnastics to learn discipline.
- Aesthetic gymnastics to learn graceful movement.

In Berlin, Friedrich Ludwig Jahn founded the German gymnastic movement to strengthen young Germans for the fight against the Napoleonic occupation. This was part of military gymnastics. The Swiss educator Johann Heinrich Pestalozzi recommended movement as an instrument of discipline so that children could learn to control their limbs. In the second half of the 19th century, as part of the Nature Cure movement and above all in the struggle against tuberculosis, a form of healing gymnastics was propagated. Sebastian Kneipp especially promoted treading water as a cure for the endemic disease of tuberculosis. Above all, breathing, fresh air and movement became synonymous with a healthy life (von Steinaecker, 2000, p. 40).

Within the German-speaking countries, physicians were trying to strengthen the respiratory function with breathing exercises supported by mechanical devices, whereas teachers of breathing and physical education were warding off tuberculosis using the natural means of the body (von Steinaecker, 2000, pp. 53ff). These women were committed to the principle of helping people discover natural breathing and natural movement. At the end of the 19th century, their reformative efforts came together with reforms in other areas of life, such as the vegetarian settlement movement, healthy clothing reform, reform pedagogy and the body culture movement, to form a greater movement of 'life reform' in the society of the time. It was then that the foundations for modern breath therapy were laid.

During the German empire and the Weimar Republic, Wedemeyer-Kolwe (2004) identifies four developments in the body culture movement, which at the time was very diverse. These are:

- Bodybuilders, who admired physical strength.
- Nudists, who looked for meaning in light and air.
- Followers of Asian body arts.
- 'Harmonic' gymnastics.

Among these last, Wedemeyer-Kolwe counts all those who seek meaning in the rhythm principle. They are often referred to as reform gymnasts and banded together in 1926 as the German Gymnastic Federation. Here, body therapy impulses originated which later developed into various body psychotherapy approaches. These followers of reform gymnastics aimed not at training the body for competition, nor for the external effects of speed and strength, but of attaining a natural sense of the body in rhythmic learning (Nitschke, 1990). Their attitude to the body was focussed on inner sensing and experiencing. According to Ling's four-pillar model, this would count as aesthetic gymnastics.

In contrast to the development of psychoanalysis, the idea of reform gymnastics flourished in an early transatlantic exchange (Mullan, 2016, 2017). At her New York School of Expression, the actor Genevieve Stebbins had been teaching emotional and aesthetic body expression and how to increase life energy through physical exercises such as dynamic breathing since the end of the 19th century (Stebbins, 1893). She built on the idea developed by the French voice coach François Delsarte that emotional experiences involve body movements (Wedemeyer-Kolwe, 2004, p. 29). The German gymnast Hede Kallmeyer, who later taught artistic expressive movement in her school in Berlin, studied with Stebbins (Arps-Aubert, 2012 pp. 119). One of her students was Elsa Gindler. In 1917 in Berlin, she founded the School for Harmonizing Body Formation, which became a great influence on the development of body psychotherapy and somatic psychology (Geuter et al., 2010).

Gindler

Gindler left very little written material: one published article, several lectures and a few notes (Arps-Aubert, 2012; Ludwig, 2002). In her article from 1926, she wrote that her students should not learn any exercises, but rather try to heighten their intelligence through gymnastics (Gindler, 1926, p. 85). She taught them to explore their own body in their own way, in stillness and in movement, and thus to become aware of what was happening in it. Each student could practice in their own way: 'In this manner we can achieve something quite essential. The student begins to sense that they can work with their own body themselves' (Gindler, 1926, p. 86). The means of attaining this sensing awareness were through breathing, exertion and relaxation. The music teacher Heinrich Jacoby, who worked closely with Elsa Gindler, wrote that the heart of her work was entering into an attentive relationship with the regulating and regenerating processes of one's own body through consciously sensing its present state (Ludwig, 2002, p. 54).

Gindler never gave her work a name. Today we would perhaps call it working with inner body mindfulness. Thus, she wrote that the aim of her work was not to learn certain movements, but to reach concentration (Gindler, 1926, p. 83). She summed up what she taught in a pithy sentence: 'investigating what happens while trying something out' (Ludwig, 2002, p. 164). This shows Gindler's attitude: to experience something, not to achieve something. One of her students says that from a philosophical position of acceptance, Gindler made their own body experience into a form of knowledge within an experimental setting (Rothe, 2014, p. 201). The path of her work consisted not of pre-formed exercises, but rather in working with the body she represented an experiential and experimental approach, which later became characteristic of humanistic-experiential psychotherapy.

To sense precisely, to observe attentively and to be mindful of the body, to feel what is happening and to work with what we encounter in life (Arps-Aubert, 2012, p. 154); these principles taught by Gindler had an enormous effect on psychotherapy. Basically, Gindler taught an attitude of mindfulness on a bodily level in which people could relate to their own sense of the body and of movement. Gindler's work as well as other related body-work approaches in the reform gymnastics movement laid the foundations for a sensory, bodily way of exploring oneself. The people she taught carried this attitude into psychotherapy (Figure 3.2). She gave body psychotherapy sensory experiencing as an approach to the body in a psychotherapeutic process of self-exploration and self-reflection (Marlock, 2015a, p. 393). Gindler herself never attempted to combine her body-work with psychotherapy and she never viewed the work as therapy (Ludwig, 2002, p. 159). She understood it as working on the bodily functions. However, she recommended students who wanted to teach her work – all women – to go into psychoanalysis as well (Ehrenfried, 1991, p. 35). In turn in 1931 she recommended her body-work to psychoanalysts:

The curiously affective matter of course with which some analysts reject the necessity of consciously engaging with the body – let alone with their own! –should really arouse their suspicion. It would be interesting to show psychotherapists what they could gain for their understanding of their main task through the conscious exploration of their own body.

(Gindler, 1931, p. 102)

Gindler's was one of the smaller gymnastics schools of the day – in 1929, for example, she had 56 members (Wedemeyer-Kolwe, 2004, pp. 49–50). However, Gindler's significance for psychotherapy is due to the attitude she taught and to the circle of her students. To this circle belonged Lore Perls, the wife of Fritz Perls, the founders of Gestalt therapy, as well as Klara Nathansohn, later Clare Fenichel, who married Otto Fenichel. The psychoanalyst Ernst Simmel took part in courses held by Heinrich Jacoby (Arps-Aubert, 2012, p. 145). Elsa Lindenberg, Reich's partner at the time, was taught by Clare Fenichel and, after the Second World War, by Gindler herself (Ludwig, 2002, pp. 184–5); according to my research there is no evidence for the hypothesis that Reich himself was a 'patient of Gindler' (Petzold, 2009, p. 28).

In addition, one of her students was Charlotte Silber, who later in exile in USA called herself Charlotte Selver. Selver had earlier learnt rhythmic gymnastics at the Rudolf Bode School in Munich and also studied with the expressive dancer Mary Wigman. From 1926 she had her own school of gymnastics in Leipzig. In US American exile, she founded the method of Sensory Awareness and had a great influence on humanistic, experience-oriented psychotherapy; there she taught Gindler's work to Perls and to her friends Erich Fromm and his wife, who practised it for the rest of their lives (Geuter, 2000a, p. 61; Weaver, 2015). Fromm (1976) saw in the work with body perception a possibility to experience oneself being the body instead of having the body. Perls took conscious sensing from Selver and probably also the concept of awareness as a method of Gestalt therapy. With Perls, as with Gindler, we find an experimental approach to therapy, which was also taken up by Greenberg in his Emotion-Focused Therapy (2011). The therapist makes suggestions so that the client can discover new aspects. The client observes how they experience themselves in different ways when they try this out.

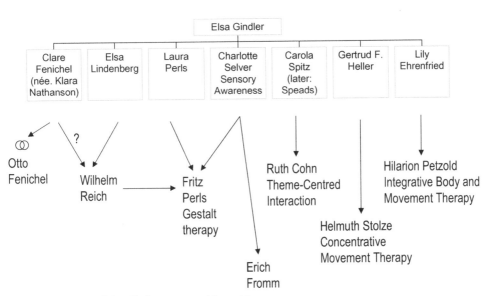

Upper row: students of Elsa Gindler, movement therapists
Lower row: psychotherapists

FIGURE 3.2 Elsa Gindler's influence on psychotherapy and body psychotherapy

Students of Gindler also included Carola Spitz, Lily Ehrenfried and Gertrud Heller. Ruth Cohn, the founder of Theme-Centred Interaction, studied this work with Spitz. Heller trained Helmuth Stolze, the founder of Concentrative Movement Therapy, in the work.

Concentrative Movement Therapy

The emergence of Concentrative Movement Therapy is probably the most important consequence of Gindler's work in body psychotherapy in the German-speaking countries (Geuter, 2015). During the Nazi regime, Heller emigrated, as did all of Gindler's students in the top row of Figure 3.2. In a psychiatric hospital in Scotland, she worked with exercises for experiencing the body, which she linked to becoming aware of the corresponding feelings and thoughts. After the war, Stolze spread the word among psychotherapists in Germany about her work. From her movement therapy, Stolze developed a body psychotherapy method which was linked to theoretical ideas mainly from psychoanalysis. For the name he used a concept from I. H. Schultz, who had originally called his autogenic training 'Concentrative self-relaxation' (Geuter, 2004a, p. 175). In Concentrative Movement Therapy, patient and therapist explore together the unconscious meaning of an action or a movement as symbolic and then work through it verbally (Chapter 4).

Functional Relaxation

Another body psychotherapy approach widespread in German-speaking countries is Functional Relaxation (Bartholomew & Herholz, 2019), which also emerged from the somatic education movement. The founder, Marianne Fuchs, studied first in 1926 at a school for gymnastics, music and dance, which the gymnastics teacher Dorothee Guenther had founded in Munich together with the composer Carl Orff. They taught functional gymnastics with musical and rhythmic elements (von Arnim, 1994, p. 196). In 1928, Fuchs arrived at the Institute of Sports at the university of Marburg and worked at the university together with the psychiatrist Ernst Kretschmer. In 1936, she moved to Heidelberg, where after the war she worked under the psychosomatic physician Viktor von Weizsaecker.

Fuchs treated her son, a 1-year-old, who suffered from spastic bronchitis. With the help of gentle touch to the rib cage and of sounds which adapted to the boy's laboured breathing, she succeeded in calming him down and dissolving or alleviating his asthmatic fits (Fuchs, 1989, p. 23). At first, she called her method 'rhythmical relaxation of breathing'. Later she used the name Functional Relaxation because her aim was to harmonise the breathing rhythm and the vegetative functions and to dissolve tensions in the expiration phase (Chapter 4).

3.2 CONNECTIONS – EXPRESSIONISM, EXPRESSIVE DANCE AND BODY PSYCHOTHERAPY

Through people like Fenichel, Reich, Perls or Selver, numerous connections developed between psychoanalysis and reform gymnastics. In addition, Gindler's gymnastics studio was within a few blocks of the Berlin Psychoanalytical Institute (Geuter, 2004a), which was the centre of the psychoanalytic movement in the 1920s (Mueller, 2004a, p. 61) and of critical left-wing psychoanalysts such as Fenichel, Reich, Simmel or Fromm (Muehlleitner, 2008, pp. 180–3). They were both places from which body psychotherapy originated. At that time, Berlin as a city was a hub of artistic and intellectual experiments which gave this development numerous impulses.

Only recently were the beginnings of body psychotherapy and Gestalt therapy connected to the art form of expressionism (Geuter, 2004). Bocian (2007, p. 18) talks about an **expressionistic generation**, who saw themselves as outsiders of society and, in the face of the rapid modernisation process gripping Berlin after the First World War, were animated by an almost messianic belief in the transformation of the human being (Bocian, 2007, p. 28). In 1922, Hermann Hesse linked transformation to sensuality in his novel *Siddhartha*. The Dadaists were preaching the person's own experience. Expressionist writers depicted a human being who rebelled and strove to find truth in inner experience (Geuter, 1986). Expressionism attempted to transform intensity of feeling into inner knowledge and to escape from alienation by intensifying experience (Fellmann, 1982).

Perls and Reich were inspired by all this. As a young man, Fritz Perls took part in the acting classes given by Max Reinhardt at the Deutsches Theater in Berlin and was drawn to expressionist dancers and writers (Sreckovic, 1999, pp. 20, 28–9). Bocian (2007) shows how deeply this has shaped the expressive style of Gestalt therapy. Wilhelm Reich, who was Perl's training analyst in Berlin, saw in the bodily expression of emotions a healing path, just as in expressionism the merit of the artwork lay in its expressive intensity (Geuter, 2004, p. 100). The same expressionist scream could be heard on Reich's couch as on the theatre stage.

In expressionist literature, the '**new human being**' was heralded, as for example in Georg Kaiser's drama *The Burghers of Calais*. Similarly, Franz Hilker, president of the German Gymnastic Federation, the association of reform gymnastics, described the cultural task of somatic education as shaping a new human being through working with the body (Ludwig, 2002, p. 43). Both Perls and Reich longed for the ideal of a liberated human being.

Berlin was also a centre for modern **expressive dance**. Elsa Lindenberg worked as dancer at the German State Opera house. There, the ballet master Rudolf von Laban (1926), who had arrived in Berlin in 1930, the same year as Reich, represented a kind of dance wherein the outer bodily movement should be the expression of an inner soul movement. In Berlin as early as the beginning of the century, the dancers Isadora Duncan, Mary Wigman and Valeska Gert had promoted expressive dance, which later gave birth to dance therapy (Fiedler, 2004; Geuter, 2000a, p. 66; Trautmann-Voigt, 2015). Duncan attempted to portray sensations in her dance, and in the 1920s Wigman depicted in dances titled 'Dance of Life', 'Witches Dance' or 'In the Sign of Darkness' unconscious, suppressed and frightening material on stage (Hoelter, 2002, p. 180).

In Vienna the psychiatrist Jacob Levy Moreno published an expressionist journal while working as a doctor in a factory (Kriz, 2001, p. 165). He later founded the group therapy method of **psychodrama**, which, despite the fact that Moreno was working at the same time as Freud in Vienna, takes its basic elements from the theatre and not from psychoanalysis. Moreno emphasised spontaneousness and creativity, as does the art of acting. Perls later adopted Moreno's principle of working in scenes (Petzold, 2007), which then crossed over from Gestalt therapy to psychoanalysis and psychodynamic body psychotherapy.

Berlin was also a centre of Western Buddhism. Here the physician Paul Dahlke established 'Das Buddhistische Haus' (The Buddhist House) in 1924. At the beginning of the 1920s, Franz Alexander was studying possible parallels between Buddhist meditation and the psychoanalytic process (Goldstein, 1995, p. 241). The psychoanalyst Johannes Heinrich Schultz discovered **yoga** and with elements of hypnosis developed his **autogenic training** from yogic concentration techniques as well as from autosuggestion as a body-oriented relaxation method (Geuter, 2004a, pp. 175–6; Wedemeyer-Kolwe, 2004, p. 149). According to the understanding of yoga at the time, Schultz did not aspire to experiencing the body through sensing, but rather bringing it by force of will into a certain state. This is the reason that autogenic training and body psychotherapy developed separately as the latter was interested in the experience of the liberated self. Instead, autogenic training became a body method of mainstream psychotherapy. Schultz propagated it during the Nazi era as a performance-enhancing and short-term therapy method at the German Institute for Psychological Research and Psychotherapy in Berlin (Cocks, 1997, pp. 158–9, 227; Cocks, 2019). Yoga too was popular in SS circles (Tietke, 2011).

3.3 YOUTH AND LIFE-REFORM MOVEMENT

The common cultural roots of body psychotherapy reach back to earlier times than the Berlin of the Weimar Republic. In order to understand the early ideas, we have to go back to the life-reform movement, which started to develop at the end of the 19th century. This included diet reform, rural communes, loose reform clothing and nudism. It was also connected to the youth movement of the time. Body psychotherapy owes its creation to the spirit of a time that, in contrast to modern civilisation, was searching for a way of preserving natural vitality and of achieving personal change and whose avant-garde abandoned themselves to subjective experience. There was a widespread thirst for new experiences, so that at the end of the century the German word *Erlebnis* (experience) first came into use (Gadamer, 2010, pp. 66–70).

At a time when railways and trams were replacing physical locomotion such as walking and riding and the telegraph system was making it possible to communicate even when physically separated, the body culture movement began to propagate the natural beauty and the natural rhythm of the body (Geuter, 1996, p. 99). The body was being simultaneously suppressed and enhanced (Section 1.5).

Due to the enormous speed of technical, economic and social change, nothing stayed as it was. Intellectually, the idea of the unity of the world began to break down: in biology the unity of creation, in physics the unity of space, in painting that of form and perspective, in music tonality and linearity of composition. Time and space were at least in art no longer separate categories. According to Freud, the linearity of time was also invalid for the unconscious. The unconscious was thought of as timeless, somewhere where the past and the present were totally mixed up.

Given the vacuum in orientation one question moved to the forefront in the philosophical thinking of Schopenhauer, Nietzsche, Bergson and later Driesch or Klages: what is life or the living? The philosophy of life attempted to answer this question. Reich and also leading representatives of the life-reform movement were rooted in this thinking.

Numerous exponents of psychoanalysis and of reform gymnastics came from the **youth movement**, which started up as the 'Wandervogel' in Steglitz near Berlin in 1901. These young people shared with the life-reform movement the same 'desire for a remodelling of the body in the age of naturalness' (Linse, 1998, p. 435).

According to contemporaries in the 1920s, the youth movement was closely connected to the gymnastic schools (Korn, 1963, p. 102). Hedwig Kallmeyer, in whose school Gindler learnt, was friendly with artists from the youth movement (von Steinaecker, 2000, p. 165). Leaders of the youth movement such as Hans Blueher consulted Gindler (Ludwig, 2002, p. 36). Marianne Fuchs, the founder of Functional Relaxation, also belonged to a youth movement group (Dietrich, 1995, p. 85). The Jungian psychotherapist, Gustav R. Heyer, who was interested in combining psychoanalysis with gymnastics and developed a physical-psychological theory of psychotherapy (Heyer, 1931, 1932), came from a group of Free German Youth (Dietrich, 1995, p. 85). Carola Spitz, a student of Gindler, was a member of the Girls' Wandervogel (Schoenberger, 1992, p. 409). In Vienna too, Siegfried Bernfeld and later Fenichel and Reich became members of the left-wing, bourgeois-intellectual and emphatically sexually-oriented youth movement (Fallend, 1988, p. 22), which however was only on the fringes of the mainstream youth movement in the German-speaking countries (Linse,

1986, p. 400). All three later moved to Berlin to work at the Psychoanalytical Institute there, which in comparison to Vienna was much more progressive.

Many of the exponents of reform gymnastics were also interested in the various **nutritional** ideas and **physical education practices** of the life-reform movement. The most important of these was the Mazdaznan movement founded by Otto Hanisch, who at the beginning of the 20th century propagated specific teachings on nutrition, breathing and bowel cleansing (von Steinaecker, 2000, pp. 94–5). Gindler followed this diet and had a connection to the lodge of the movement in Leipzig (Ludwig, 2002, pp. 24, 27; Wedemeyer-Kolwe, 2004, p. 157). The later well-known breath therapist Ilse Middendorf also followed these teachings (Moscovici, 1991, p. 142), as did the artist Johannes Itten, with whom Gindler studied drawing and who also taught in her classes, and who began his painting classes at the Bauhaus in Weimar with Hanisch's breathing exercises (Haag, 2018; von Steinaecker, 2000, pp. 97–8). Von Steinaecker thinks that almost all the protagonists of breathing and somatic education came into contact with this doctrine.

3.4 A MENTALITY SHIFT: 11 IDEAS

If we look at the fundamental ideas of the somatic educators, the body-oriented psychoanalysts and those physicians who at the time were interested in psychosomatic and holistic concepts of healing, then we can distinguish 11 basic ideas or themes, the roots of which we can trace back to the life-reform movement and to the philosophy of life. These are figures of thought which have crystallised out of my studies of the early texts in their historical context. They reveal a mentality shift in which, in culture, in science and in everyday life, the rigid thinking of the Victorian (in Germany Wilhelmine) era is breaking apart and giving way to a new attitude to life. Together they form a collective mental vessel for the two body psychotherapy traditions, the shared interest of which seems to consist of the wish to experience the living-body with the living spirit. I see these ideas not as a system and the order in which they appear here not as a hierarchy. The way in which they are described and the order is just as associative as the manner in which they appeared to me.

1. Relating to life

'Man has alienated himself from, and has grown hostile toward, life', wrote Reich (1973, p. 7). He wanted to awaken people's aliveness. He was not only searching for new methods of treatment, nor did he just want to substantiate Freud's first drive theory and he was not only the theorist of sexuality, as he is often portrayed. His great interest was a 'science of life' (Reich, 1973, p. 18).

> 'The question "What is life?" prompted each new acquisition of knowledge'.
>
> (Reich, 1973, p. 22)

Following his research on cells, Reich wrote both euphorically and presumptuously in his diary in 1939: 'I have discovered life!' (Reich, 1994, p. 159). Sexuality was so important because for him it was synonymous with life (1994, p. 71). 'Sexual, vegetative energy is active in everything that lives' (1973, p. 116). Orgastic potency was therefore for him much more than uninhibited pleasure in a sexually charged era. It was 'the basic biological function which man has in common with all living organisms' (1973, p. 109).

With the question of the nature of life, Reich positioned himself squarely in the context of contemporary philosophy of life, a philosophical movement which was particularly strong in Germany and which took as its starting point not reason but experiencing life (Fellmann, 1996). At the same time, Reich attempted to answer a question which was at the root of the great scientific controversy between mechanists and vitalists. The mechanists held that living bodies were machines whose energy balance obeyed the laws of physics, whereas the vitalists insisted upon the autonomous principle of the living and called themselves 'organismic', 'integrative' or 'holistic'. The dispute was basically about the essence of life (Sinding, 1998). In the 1920s, it was the focus of a bio-philosophical discourse which was greatly influenced by Ernst Haeckel, proponent of a mechanistic biology and author of the book *The Wonders of Life*, and by the philosopher Hans Driesch, who was also a biologist, and a proponent of vitalism (Ebrecht, 1992. pp. 143, 156–62).

Reich was not alone in establishing his theory in the context of the philosophy of life. For Groddeck, for instance, the id was not a psychological entity but a kind of **life force**, the 'totality of the living being' (Will, 1987 p. 124). The id exists beyond the flesh and the soul as the energy which determines both aspects of life. Human beings are lived by the id, wrote Groddeck (Will, 1987, p. 119). Similarly, the conservative philosopher and characterologist Ludwig Klages, who in 1915 described life as a category beyond consciousness and matter, wrote succinctly: 'The mind perceives, the being exists, but only life lives' (Klages, 1937, p. 43). We can find Klages world view – that mind stands in opposition to the soul and as such to life – echoed by Gindler in her remarks about certain male students: 'They are all becoming more and more aware that the work of the brain alone must always lead away from the aliveness of life' (Ludwig, 2002, p. 37). This sounds like the description of rationalisation later given by Fritz Perls as 'mind fucking'. Interestingly, Charlotte Buehler (1979, p. 7), one of the seminal figures of humanistic psychology, writes in a personal retrospect that in the 1920s, one of her main questions was 'what is human life really all about?'

Since the 1920s there has been a broad endeavour to bring psychology and biology together as a combined science of life (Harrington, 1996). The psychotherapist Gustav Heyer (1932) set out a theory of '**life-circles**' and differentiated between the vegetative life-circle, the animal life-circle of 'blood life', the pneumatic life-circle of breathing and the mental life-circle of ideas. The philosopher Helmut Plessner (1975, pp. 191–2) referred to functional circles, as did Viktor von Weizsaecker and Thure von Uexkuell later on, a concept that Functional Relaxation then inherited (von Arnim et al., 2022). Marianne Fuchs refers to a concept of life when she writes that her interest is 'raising the awareness of the senses for the sake of an aliveness oriented towards the centre' (Moscovici, 1991, p. 137). Fuchs describes the intention of her method as 'experiencing what is still alive in me' (Dietrich, 1995, p. 105). In Heyer, we encounter the idea that there are functional principles of the living or the organic, which encompass mind and body. Today we find this idea in body psychotherapy in Heller (2012).

Since the 19th century, four philosophers have highlighted the concept of life and established ideas which we later see in psychotherapy and psychology: Schopenhauer, Nietzsche, Bergson and Dilthey.

- **Schopenhauer** is considered the founder of the philosophy of life. He saw the definitive impulse of all life in the **will to live**. This will intended nothing less than life itself. In contrast to the primacy of reason that reigns in the idealistic philosophy of Kant, Hegel and Fichte, Schopenhauer set the primacy of life. In so doing he saw human beings as part of nature. An act of will was for him identical to an act of the living-body. The concept of will denoted for him 'the direct experience of the reality of one's own body' and 'the drives connected to corporeality' (Fellmann, 1996, p. 279). Schopenhauer understood consciousness as dependent on the living-body and sexuality as the focal point of the will, and his idea was to overcome passions through contemplation – all thoughts which Freud later followed up (Nitzschke, 1998).

- **Nietzsche,** whose *Thus spoke Zarathustra* was one of Reich's ten favourite books (Laska, 1981, p. 15), developed Schopenhauer's position. In his *Untimely Meditations* he describes the human being as a living being, an animal and not a 'cogital' (Nietzsche, 1980). He paraphrases Descartes' famous sentence as: '**Vivo, ergo cogito**': *I live therefore I think*. In *Zarathustra*, Nietzsche took up those great themes which should also be of interest to body psychotherapists: experience, affects, drives, the living-body. His life-philosophy turned philosophical questions into the subjective and addressed them to humanity (Chapter 2).
- **Bergson** criticised the association psychology of early experimental psychology, which assumed that consciousness consists of elementary sense impressions. He advocated the view that we can only grasp the life of the psyche with the help of **intuition**, through an awakening to experience (Bergson, 1946). Reich made an 'exceedingly careful' study of Bergson's writings. 'My present theory of the *identity and unity of psychophysical functioning* originated in Bergsonian thinking' (Reich, 1973, p. 23). Reich referred to Bergson very early on, since he described pleasure sensations as an attraction inherent in the movement of the body. We can read in Bergson's *Time and Free Will*:

> acute desire, uncontrolled anger, passionate love, violent hatred. Each of these states may be reduced, we believe, to a system of muscular contractions coordinated by an idea … The intensity of these violent emotions is thus likely to be nothing but the muscular tension which accompanies them (Bergson, 1950, pp. 28–9).

The classic biographies of Reich have omitted this connection to Bergson and to the philosophy of life. Sharaf (1994, p. 55) only mentions Bergson once, Boadella (1973) twice, but neither of them says anything about the connection in terms of content. Only Mannhart and Backhaus (1993) have pointed out the forgotten roots of body psychotherapy in the philosophy of life.

- **Dilthey** was the exponent of the philosophy of life, who by dint of his proposal of a hermeneutic psychology as an experiential science is deemed to be the initiator of psychology as one of the humanities. For him experience was the ultimate entity of consciousness and not sensation as the mainstream psychology of the time maintained, and the category of experience was key to the theory of the humanities in general (Habermas, 1987). Dilthey (2002) said in 1910 that the world presents itself to human beings through experience and always in a life-context. However for Reich not Dilthey, who was much discussed in psychology, was important, but Bergson; Bergson connected the philosophy of life with a discussion of natural science questions, as Dilthey did not. Here too, as in the case of the concept of character, we can see what a divide already existed between psychoanalytic and psychological discourse.

Finally, the phenomenologist Edmund Husserl spoke about a **stream of experience** in which the content of experience exists (Hehlmann, 1963, p. 284) and William James (1994), for whom experience was the subject-matter of psychological study, speaks of a **stream of consciousness**. From here it is not far to Perls' principle of the flow of awareness that has been adopted by experiential body psychotherapy, or to the stream of events, reflections, memories and images that in 1922 James Joyce presented to the world in his 'Ulysses'.

2. Critique of civilisation

Freud relocated conflicts which made people neurotic to the inside, the world of fantasies and ultimately that of antagonistic drives. Ferenczi, however, emphasised that not incest fantasies, but real traumatisations, including real sexual abuse, were at the root of most mental disorders (Dahmer, 1982). Reich stayed with Freud's original view that the 'psychic

process reveals itself as the result of conflict between instinctual demand and the external frustration of this demand' (Reich, 1972, p. 287). Thus, the inner conflict is secondary.
It develops as the result of pressure from the outside world where the frustration of the
instinct is generated. This is why a critical examination of society was so important to him.
In Vienna and in Berlin, he was actively involved in the sexual-political movement and in
sexual advice bureaux for the proletariat (Boadella, 1973; Fallend, 1988; Peglau, 2013).

Among left-wing Freudians, it was a given that repressive social conditions were responsible for people having to suppress their experiences, affects and needs. They saw the source
of suppression as being in society, and Reich in particular saw it in the suppression of sexuality in which a 'mechanized and authoritarian civilization' (1973, p. 7) is anchored. So right
from the start of Reichian body psychotherapy, a paradigm of repression developed which
interpreted psychic problems as the result of inner suppression due to external repression. In
this approach, the super-ego was 'a piece of introjected and unassimilated society' (Bocian,
2007, p. 281). Body psychotherapy has always preserved this knowledge of the consequences
of real traumatisation, real emotional injury and real experience of relationships (Marlock,
2015b, pp. 88–90).

At the beginning of the 20th century, the anarchistic psychoanalyst Otto Gross had
already wanted to set up a Utopia of erotic and social revolution against repression (Bocian,
2007, p. 160). Gross, whom Bocian sees as the godfather of left-wing Freudianism in Berlin,
established the crucial idea that inner conflicts are conflicts that have been internalised. He
spoke of the child's need for contact and how, because of social restraints, biological regulation, the child's affects, cannot be followed through; to achieve individual self-regulation,
the results of upbringing would have to be undone (Bocian, 2007 pp. 167–8). Reich and
Perls also later linked social criticism with biology. They saw psychological problems as the
result of the internalisation of demands, prohibitions and damaging repressive experiences
in upbringing. Through Ferenczi's student Michael Balint and Donald Winnicott, this view
later became part of the object relations theory in psychoanalysis.

In his *Character Analysis* from 1933, Reich understood the inner character armour as the
result of interpsychic experience. In this he was conform with the cultural-historical school
of Soviet psychology, which had formulated just this assumption as the cultural-historical
law (Slunecko & Wieser, 2014). Reich had met proponents of this school in Moscow during
his short communist phase (Heller, 2007).

A critical attitude towards civilisation was not confined to left-wing Freudians. It was one
of the great issues among the intelligentsia of the first half of the 20th century. Nietzsche
had provided many keywords for this discussion. Klages criticised the destruction of nature
(Bishop, 2019). That healthy human nature was deformed through the dominant civilisation was also a prevalent subject in reform gymnastics. Von Laban (1926) aimed to preserve
the natural strength of the body, which was damaged by working life, through gymnastics.
Gindler spoke out against 'hostile acts' in body education (Ludwig, 2002, p. 45) and criticised the fact that children's desire to find things out for themselves was broken in their early
years (Ludwig, 2002, p. 197). Her criticism of civilisation was focused on the restriction of
free movement through an education in which the naturalness of the body was neglected.
In 1924, the gymnast Dore Jacobs founded with her husband the Community Association
for Socialist Life. In her school in Essen, in the heart of the wretchedness of industrialisation on the Ruhr, she offered training in body-work and rhythmic education to the workers
(Hoelter, 2002).

Some of the gymnasts, expressive dancers and breath therapists such as von Laban,
Wigman, Schlaffhorst and Andersen brought a distinct nationalist note to social criticism
(Wedemeyer-Kolwe, 2004, pp. 114–5), and Rudolf Bode, who used expressive gymnastics to
treat muscle tension caused by civilisation (Wedemeyer-Kolwe, 2004, p. 99), joined the nazi

party in 1932 and became a leader of national socialist physical education (Seewald, 2002, p. 28). The *Verein fuer Koerperkultur* (Association for Body Culture) founded in 1905, where Duncan and Gindler were both members, aimed to achieve 'racial improvement' through life reforms (Wedemeyer-Kolwe, 2004, p. 33). The teachings of Mazdaznan considered the 'Arian race' to be degenerate because of bad diet and false breathing. According to them, Arians had the task of cleansing the body, eating raw fruit and vegetables and contributing to the development of their own person and of their own race (Wedemeyer-Kolwe, 2004, p. 155). This all shows just how multifaceted and contradictory the protests against modern civilisation were. Gindler was a follower of the teachings of Mazdaznan, but she was no racist. In fact, a memorial stone was erected in Yad Vashem to commemorate her humane actions during the NS era (Ludwig, 2002).

For all the contradictions from nationalist to revolutionary criticism of civilisation, the common ground of the emerging body therapy and body psychotherapy approaches was the view that inner conflicts and deficits are the result of internalised emotional and physical experiences in a society hostile to the body, to human needs and drives. Both Gindler and Reich aimed at the development of a healthy human being, whose true nature has been deformed through society and who recovers it either through natural movement and readiness to react or through uninhibited sexual surrender. These were their responses to the alienation of aliveness through civilisation.

3. Rhythm

The contrast between **rhythm** and **beat** was one of the main issues in the social criticism of the time. The clock cycles set by machines in this era of rapid industrialisation were contrasted with the rhythms of nature. The philosopher Max Scheler (1966, p. 18–9) wrote in 1928 that rhythm is a characteristic of instinctive and not of learnt behaviour. This linked rhythm philosophically to nature and thus we can use it as a way of connecting with our inner nature.

As society, so the individual: we can perceive rhythm, but we have to give ourselves the beat (Nitschke, 1990). Klages gave a lecture in Berlin in 1922 on the nature of rhythm, in which he described the mind and with it beat as the antagonist to the vitality of rhythm. The breath therapists Schlaffhorst and Andersen followed this idea and saw in breathing the link between mind and body (Dietrich, 1995, p. 28). Other breath therapists saw in breathing the human rhythm itself (von Steinaecker, 2000, p. 86). Rhythm also became a guiding principle in Functional Relaxation, which was originally named 'rhythmical relaxation of breathing'; here we see the reform gymnastics idea of looking for the living rhythm in the body.

There was hardly an issue so predominant in breath therapy, expressive dance and reform gymnastics as rhythm. This was also true for the first generation of the various life-reform movements. In 1911 the music educator Émile Jaques-Dalcroze established an institute for music and rhythm near Dresden, which became a place of pilgrimage for European intellectuals during the 3 years of its existence (Guenther, 1990, p. 20). Jaques-Dalcroze is seen as the founder of rhythmic-musical education. Movement would flow out of the music and into the body and stimulate the inner human rhythm (Wobbe, 1992). Whereas Jaques-Dalcroze had the body taking a subordinate role to the rhythm of the music, Rudolf Bode saw rhythm as a 'primal phenomenon of life' (Seewald, 2002, p. 27). Bode, who founded his school for rhythmic gymnastics in 1910 in Munich (Wedemeyer-Kolwe, 2004, p. 48), advocated a rhythmic physical education, in which students would develop their own individual rhythms. The ideological principle of the 'new rhythmic world order' (Wobbe, 1992, p. 29) was that by immersing themselves in their own rhythm, people can experience cosmic rhythm. In the same period, the anthroposophist Rudolf Steiner developed the movement art of eurythmy. Lore Perls, later a Gestalt therapist, studied eurythmy and expressive dance from the age of 8 (Sreckovic, 1999, p. 23). The modern dancer Isadora Duncan said that dance is a primal rhythm and a primal movement of nature (Jeschke, 1990). Its task was to communicate mood and express inner impulses. Mary Wigman spoke of the rhythmic language of the dancer's gestures (Wilke, 1986, p. 468).

This orientation towards inner rhythm and a holistic approach to the body was proclaimed an antidote to the nervousness of modern life. Rhythmic gymnastics would calm the nervous system. This was also part of a response to the question of how in times of emancipation, girls should move. The goal was similar to that of callisthenics, a rhythmic body training taught in the UK and the USA, which Lowen later studied: controlling the body gracefully and promoting health through rhythmic grace (Linse, 1998, pp. 436–9). Accordingly, of the 90,000 members of the German Gymnastic Federation in 1930, 85,000 of them were women (Wedemeyer-Kolwe, 2004, p. 57).

Not just the gymnasts but also the psychotherapists Heyer and Reich were studying the idea of the rhythm of nature. Heyer speaks of the polar phenomenon of rhythm and calls tension and relaxation primal phenomena of life (1932, p. 39). Reich noted in his diary: 'But the truth lies in rhythm, ecstasy, love' (1994, p. 98). He understood the life process as a state of oscillation between 'parasympathetic expansion and sympathetic contraction' (Reich, 1973, p. 295). His concept of the pulsation of life was rhythmic. In his theory of sexual arousal, he established the rhythmic curve of tension-charge-discharge-relaxation, which he later called the actual life-formula (Reich, 1973, p. 272). In the quotation I refer to, however, he called it not a rhythm but a four-stroke cycle and thus used a concept from the technology of the internal combustion engine. Perhaps this shows Reich's ambivalence in wanting on the one hand to follow the ideas of the philosophy of life and on the other to define life processes in terms of physics. I will return to this later. Fuchs taught a different rhythmic curve of life processes in four steps: 'ebbing away-end-new beginning-swelling' (1989, p. 33). In both cases, the idea of rhythm is related to quantitative changes, which then culminate in a qualitatively different state.

4. Movement

Just as rhythm was seen as counter to beat, so in social criticism, movement was counter to rigidity. The dissolution of boundaries in modern times created new spaces of freedom, particularly for those living in the city. The young psychoanalyst Fritz Perls rode through Berlin on a motorbike wearing a leather jacket (Bocian, 2007, p. 135). In town, young people danced the Charleston, while youth movement people chain danced in the parks. In the Weimar Republic things were on the move; people were on the move. In the body culture movement, there was a destandardisation of movement. Rudolf Bode countered the muscular tension of civilisation with natural, pain-free, unconscious and rhythmic movement (Wedemeyer-Kolwe, 2004, pp. 99–100). The youth and body culture movement sought 'the pleasures of free movement in fresh air and sunshine, at the beach and in the forest' (Korn, 1963, p. 118).

Gindler's ideal was the 'wonderful mobility of reacting', the free transition from activity to passivity and back (1926, p. 87). Reich shared with Bergson the ideal of freedom based on total mobility (Mannhart & Backhaus, 1993, p. 166). Stoerig writes about the life-philosophers that 'movement, becoming, developing meant more to them than inflexible being' (1969, p. 232). In contrast to the dominant association psychology of the time, Bergson, the main proponent of the philosophy of life, linked perception with movement: perception has its roots in 'the tendency of the body to movement' (1911, p. 41). This is because from what the world around us offers to the senses, it selects whatever affects the body. In Bergson's view, perception is directed towards action – or, as it was said at the time, towards the deed – as is memory. For him the human being was a being who acts. The fundamental law of life is a 'law of action' (1911, p. 194).

Long before the philosophy of the embodied mind (Section 5.2), we find here the source of a fundamental attitude of body psychotherapy. Human beings are seen not as beings whose psyche represents reality as a cognitive-affective reproduction, but as beings who discover and perceive reality in movement and action. Bergson (1911) was already using the concept of motor schema, which Downing (1996) later developed into the affect-motor schema (Chapter 12). We also later find Bergson's theory of the unity of perception and movement in the theory of the Gestalt cycle of von Weizsaecker (1997), who however does not mention the source. He also neglects the link to Schopenhauer, who wrote even before Bergson, that in the experience of one's own body, perception of movement coincides with sensation (Fellmann, 1996, p. 278).

As Bergson lamented how human beings became rigid through habit and hardened into characters (Mannhart & Backhaus, 1993, p. 162), Ferenczi recognised the restriction of motility, the excessive stiffness in all the limbs as characteristic of many neurotic people (1925, p. 167). Reich spoke, as did Bergson, of character rigidity. The 'Bergsonian' Reich, as he called himself (1973, p. 23), also linked drive to movement. Initially he understood drives as affect-motoric in origin and not as biophysical energy. He took sexuality out of the realm of the imagination and into the experiencing body with its memories, when he described it as the motor memory of lust experienced or as the motoric part of all experienced feelings of pleasure (Reich, 1923, p. 163). He later wanted to measure in the laboratory the polarity of streaming and rigidifying on the skin surface's electric potential (Section 3.6).

5. Breath

'As soon as we let go of the breath, we notice that the rigidity has gone', wrote Gindler in her essay about gymnastics (1926, p. 88). Breathing is seen as an important way of dissolving the rigidity which reduced flexibility. Fuchs (1989) aimed at stimulating the **autonomic breathing rhythm** of her patients.

Working with the breathing in the treatment of tuberculosis was the beginning of modern body therapy (von Steinaecker, 2000). The first to work on the body with only the means of the body were breathing teachers such as Schlaffhorst and Andersen. In the body culture movement, breathing played an important role. Numerous breath schools emerged, such as that of Emil Baeuerle in Baden-Baden, who belonged to the inner circle of the Mazdaznan movement. The breath therapist Ilse Middendorf studied with him (Moscovici, 1991, p. 142). In 1890, the translation from the Sanskrit of *The Science of Breath* by Rama Prasad was published in England and in 1896 in Germany. In the Weimar Republic, the subject of breathing was ubiquitous in sport and even in bodybuilding (Wedemeyer-Kolwe, 2004, pp. 147–8).

In psychotherapy too interest in the breathing was growing. C. G. Jung attempted to capture psychological change through physiological information with the help of a pneumography among other things, and thus to prove the existence of complexes (Peterson & Jung, 1907). Groddeck wrote that the way we breathe is the language of the id, an expression of life (1992, p. 154). He saw breathing, as did Jung, as an indicator of the unconscious, but was not prepared to teach proper breathing because it was not helpful for some patients. For his autogenic training, I. H. Schultz established the famous breathing formula: 'it breathes me'. Gustav Heyer (1932, p. 40) regarded breathing as a rhythmic polarity between tension and relaxation. In psychoanalysis, the disorder of the breathing in asthma became the first great psychosomatic issue (Will, 1987, p. 12).

The physiotherapist Marion Rosen, who was born in Germany, studied breath therapy in 1914 with the gymnastics teacher Lucy Heyer-Grote, who until 1933 was married to G. Heyer. Later in the USA she developed the Rosen method, a gentle experiential form of working with movement and bodily touch (Rosen & Brenner, 1991), which Fogel (2009) utilises for psychotherapy.

Reich (1972, p. 375) supported a psychodynamic understanding of breathing, as did Groddeck, Jung and Heyer, and he described the attitude of inhalation as an instrument in the suppression of emotions. As Sharaf reports, Reich always paid attention to the patient's breathing as an indicator of emotionality: 'When the patient's breathing was shallow or forced, Reich would make use of touch to stimulate an emotional flow' (1994, p. 236). He also tried to trigger the orgasm reflex with the help of breathing techniques (Reich, 1973, p. 333). However, this is not a breathing exercise but an attempt to mobilise the **involuntary breathing**. This is why Reich opposed the breathing techniques of yoga: they led to a stiff bodily expression, reminding him of obsessive-compulsive acts and suppressing affect arousal instead of freeing it up (Reich, 1973, p. 358). Discussing matters of treatment, Heyer also pointed out that working with the breathing often 'elicited and released emotional material from the unconscious' (1932, p. 43). Thus, he criticised the unpsychological breath work practised by some contemporary breath trainers. Heyer, who was initially an opponent of the Nazis and later a staunch National Socialist, also criticised yoga for quite different reasons than Reich: it was pointless and dangerous to take Indian breathing methods, developed in a very different climate, for a very different race, and use them on modern Westerners (Heyer, 1932, p. 44).

Breathing was at the centre of nascent body psychotherapy in many different ways: as the expression of a basic life rhythm, as a central function of the body, as a method of harmonisation and relaxation and as an indicator of emotional processes.

6. Function

Next to the more life-philosophical concept of rhythm, the factual concept of function played a large part in the infancy of body psychotherapy. Tension between the orientation towards rhythm and that towards functionality permeates the first generation of body trainers and also Reich's work. We find this also in art, where the New Objectivity movement succeeded expressionism, which still looked for rhythm in works of art. Beth Mensendieck, a gymnastic trainer born in 1864, who was active in Europe and the USA, taught functional gymnastics for women to improve the health and functioning of the body (Wedemeyer-Kolwe, 2004, pp. 29, 67–8). Students were to know the functions of the body 'as if it were a machine' (Seewald, 2002, p. 29) and should learn how to move in a useful manner (Hoelter, 2002, p. 177). In reform gymnastics, people intentionally focused on the inner functioning of bodily processes and not, as in sport, on external achievement (Arps-Aubert, 2012, p. 92).

Breathing was regarded not only as an expression of rhythm, as Fuchs saw it. 'Breathing is most importantly a *functional* process', wrote Heyer (1932, p. 45). In his theory the various life circles corresponded to physical and mental functions. Gindler described the goal of her work as capturing people's interest in a way of behaving in which their movements and their organism can react and function undisturbed (Ludwig, 2002, p. 120). In Sensory Awareness later on the word was: 'We are not interested in the healthy mind in a healthy body. We are interested in the total functioning person' (Lowe & Laing-Gilliatt, 2007, p. 99). This concept also appears in Rogers' theory of the *fully functioning person* (Rogers, 1959).

We find this connection between economy and functionality in a completely different context in Reich's sexual theory. For him, orgasm was not just the sensation of pleasure. In fact, he studied it, as the title of his book *The Function of the Orgasm* from 1927 demonstrates, in terms of its function within the energy balance of psychological processes. Starting from Freud's metapsychology, he regarded neurosis from the economic point of view as the expression of blocked sexual energy. By allowing the tension to flow out, orgasm regulated the biological energy balance of sexuality. Ultimately, sexuality was meant to fulfil the biological function of homeostasis.

Reich used the concept of function in other respects. Thus, he spoke of the 'functional identity' of character armouring and muscular armouring, meaning that 'muscular attitudes and character attitudes' have the same defensive function (Reich, 1973, p. 270; Chapter 13). He also spoke generally of the functional unity of mind and body 'having at the same time an antithetical relationship' but both functioning 'on the basis of biological laws' (Reich, 1973, p. 379). Here the unity is mediated by an underlying third.

Various theorists regarded breathing, movement and sexuality as bodily functions depending on their background; Heyer (1932) included the circulation. Generally, there was a search for a 'functional' order (Fuchs, 1989, p. 7). The body should be able to fulfil the functions assigned to it, and therapy would create the necessary preconditions.

Bocian, who also depicts Perls as a representative of functional thinking (2007, p. 148), links functionalism to the new leaning towards objectivity, then widespread among the intelligentsia of the 1920s; the life-philosophical complaint of alienation and the critical attitude of the expressionists to technology turned into praise of technology and an appreciation of functionalism (Bocian, 2007, p. 176). In architecture and design, the new Bauhaus style, in which form should follow function, began to take over. For housing development as for furniture, the same principle applied as it did to the body. They should fulfil their intended function optimally.

7. Sensing

The concept of conscious sensing developed from the body-work tradition in body psychotherapy and was accompanied by the idea of abandoning oneself to the body's autonomic processes. They share the notion of awakening sensory perception and paying attention to the sensuality of the body.

Moscovici (1991, p. 20) wrote that Elsa Gindler was the first to recognise the importance of sensing. It is more accurate to say that she applied it to body-work. The concept of sensing had already been used in philosophy by Husserl, who, unlike Kant, wanted to start not from general categories of knowledge but from directly existing phenomena (Section 5.3). Husserl understood sensing as consciousness becoming aware of the lived body (Boehme, 2003, p. 44). Thus, Gindler adopted the idea of sensing rather than having discovered it.

Gindler understood sensing not as emotional, but as appropriating the body for the self through perceptive consciousness, as did Husserl, who used for this the concept of *sensings*. In reform gymnastics, special attention was paid to the inner sensing of the body. Stolze calls it a characteristic of Concentrative Movement Therapy to ask not only what the patient is thinking or feeling, but also: 'What are you sensing just now? What do you notice in yourself? What is the body telling you?' (Stolze, 1959, p. 29). This unlocks a dimension of self-experience different from feelings, that of bodily sensation. Sensing means opening the inner senses. According to Gindler, sensing applies to proprioception (Ludwig, 2002, p. 136). In Concentrative Movement Therapy as in Functional Relaxation, proprioception, the sense of the position of the body and of the various parts of the body in space and in relation to each other, is a central theme. But visceroception is also part of self-perception (Section 6.3). Generally speaking, it is about a bodily awareness of oneself. Today we would call it mindfulness. Therefore, it is no surprise that the 'body scan' of Kabat-Zinn (2017) from Mindfulness Based Stress Reduction (MBSR) is none other than the systematic journey through the sensations of the body which Gindler was already practising in the 1920s (Ludwig, 2002, p. 146). In MBSR this is presented as new, with no mention of where it originated.

'Sensing' the body or 'sensing into' the body (Stolze, 1959) is the modus operandi of those branches of body psychotherapy oriented towards perception. Their source is Gindler's idea of sensing, which we also find in Charlotte Selver's Sensory Awareness. In the USA this *somatic awareness* is well represented. In Body-Mind Centering, an approach to motion and development which Aposhyan (2004) integrated into body psychotherapy, the attentive sensing of one's own body is the basic path to the self (D Johnson, 2015). Perls took up this tradition and declared attentive sensing to be a fundamental mode of exploring the self in Gestalt therapy. In 1947 he wrote to his wife Lore about his sessions with Selver:

> What she does is really interesting. She calls it sensitising the body ... At last, I've found what I've been looking for all these years and what I never found in any school. And it confirms and supports my whole theory ...
> Here is the method which not only achieves what I've always striven for with concentration exercises, but is also so subtle and the opposite of stress (completely different from Reich's current method of releasing the patient's cramped up body by force).
>
> (Sreckovic, 1999, p. 116).

Those approaches which came to body psychotherapy from Gindler's work have brought the idea of sensing with them. We can find this not only in Gestalt therapy but also in Hakomi, which, referring to Buddhist traditions, views mindful sensing as a basic method of therapy (Kurtz, 1983; Chapter 4).

The idea that the patient should surrender to their own corporeality was closely connected to sensing. For example, Gindler wrote about falling asleep, that 'when we try to sense the heaviness all over the body as well as in the head, then we enter into a state where nature does the work for us' (1926, p. 92). If we let gravity work when standing up, then we become lighter. The student should surrender to the inner processes of self-perception.

In the Reichian tradition, surrendering was seen not only at the level of sensations but also at that of emotions. For instance, orgastic potency meant, to Reich, surrendering oneself to the autonomic process of involuntary pleasure (Sharaf, 1994, p. 95). He called this the capacity to surrender. In the Reichian and Gestalt therapy traditions, sensing was extended beyond proprioception to desires and emotions. This attributed to sensing as a mode of self-exploration a far greater significance for psychotherapeutic work (Geuter, 2019, pp. 87–90).

Sensing was about the sensation and experience of one's own affects. Reich wanted to help people who could no longer feel anything because they suffered from *contactlessness* and *affect blocks* (Reich 1972, p. 310) to be able to feel again. Using methods which were at times hefty, confrontative and, as Perls complained, violent, he wanted to break through their unhappy consciousness and to liberate the inner stranglehold of denial, so they could again sense the vitality of their innermost core.

8. Experiencing

Experiencing is a guiding motto of body psychotherapy (Geuter, 2019, pp. 60–4), as seen in the first of the 11 ideas Dilthey wanted to make experiencing the basis of philosophy. Life experience is, according to Dilthey (1910, p. 54), where we generalise our memories of our life-story. This philosophy was well-suited to a time of hunger for experience where reaching back to the subjective helped to understand an ever more complex world (Section 3.3). Reich took the liberty of declaring the inner life, which is after all subjective, as a measure for the accuracy of scientific views, when in 1936 he wrote: 'My organic, vegetative conviction of the correctness of my views is the source of the strength that people admire in me' (1994, pp. 83–4). He used his body as a research instrument by acting on what he saw and sensed (Sharaf, 1994, p. 279). Thus, the subjective gave access to the external world. Reich did not however adhere to a subjectivistic idealism, nor did the philosophy of life, which assumed an independent world accessible to human beings subjectively through experience.

In the technical discussions within psychoanalysis, Reich argued that interpreting repressed instinctual needs, which until then had been the psychoanalytic technique, was not enough: patients had to re-experience the suppressed material. This motivated him to work on resistance and to help patients experience it in the body. He described this in numerous case studies (1972). In his *Character analysis*, the **how**, meaning the form of the behaviour, took precedence over the **what**, the content of what was said. Thus, it was more important for Reich that patients experienced something than that they understood it: 'The patient no longer talked about his hate – he experienced it' (Reich, 1973, p. 171). He saw the sensation, the experience as a more reliable source of self-certitude – 'perceiving what we sense', as Gindler said (Ludwig, 2002).

Philosophically we can recognise the link to Bergson. Bergson placed cognition at the point where the tension of consciousness towards an action is interrupted by becoming aware, a being-as-it-is experience, that Bergson called **intuition** (Bergson, 1946). With this idea he legitimised philosophically a source of knowledge other than thinking, which Freud favoured in therapy. The idea of knowing something by experiencing a certainty in the body emerges later in Gendlin's concept of *felt sense*. In the tradition of Carl Rogers, Gendlin (1961, 1996) places the concept of experiencing at the centre of his body-oriented psychotherapy.

9. The present

Emphasising the *here and now* began in psychotherapy back then. One of the basic shared ideas of body psychotherapy is paying attention to the present – in other words, to realise things as they present themselves to consciousness. This is also linked to the philosophy of life. In it, Stoerig (1969, p. 232) recognises **actualism** as a common characteristic, which emphasises movement and becoming. This is related to the thought of the ancient philosopher Heraclitus that you cannot step into the same river twice. Presence is a necessary precondition of conscious experience (Metzinger, 2010).

Bergson (1911) assumed that life flows. His theory is that the present is what happens and not what is. In relation to the outside world, each present moment is only ever a sensation of what has just been and a movement towards what comes directly after. In this sensorimotor relationship to the world, the present can only exist in the awareness that I have of my body. The present comes into contact with the past through recognition, when what I perceive of things recalls the past into the present through the present image that I have of the body. This is a very modern theory, which corresponds to Damasio's view that subjectivity consists of the unity of external perception of the world and internal perception of somatic processes (Section 6.5).

Here too Reich was a Bergsonian. He placed the emphasis of analysis firmly on the resistance which became visible through actual behaviour in the therapy session. This was the resistance of the ego to experiencing the feelings lurking under the surface. This was compatible with the ego psychology of Fenichel, which advocated that interpretation should proceed step by step from the surface into the depths and not head directly towards unconscious instinctual needs and fantasies.

Gindler also took as her starting point what happens in the moment and what occurs during practice (Section 3.1.2), and her focus in teaching was on the awareness of the perception of the body in the present. If for example somebody had a tensed-up shoulder, then Gindler (1926) would address not the history or the meaning of the tension, but would just help this person to consciously sense how they produced and maintained it. Becoming conscious of the tension was the path to loosening it in the immediate present. From this follows the body psychotherapeutic principle that change in the present moment comes about through being able to abandon the defence (Geuter, 2019, pp. 356). Then we can have a different experience or we can understand directly in the present (Chapter 16).

The psychoanalyst Otto Rank (1929, p. 316) said at the time that the end of the neurosis could be seen in the capacity to surrender to the present. Later on, it was above all Rogers and Perls who, starting with the idea of experience, brought psychotherapy into present time and space, in order to work with what the patient was experiencing here and now in the session. Perls encouraged patients to describe the current manifestation of their symptoms and called his therapy at first concentration therapy during his time in South Africa (Walker, 1996, p. 130). Psychoanalysis took this turn into the present a few decades later.

10. Wholeness

The concept of wholeness first gained significance in humanistic psychology. However, ideas of wholeness were already widespread at the beginning of the 20th century. The call for wholeness, authenticity and a natural life echoed through this age of rapid technological modernisation, which had begun at the end of the 19th century. The fear of modernity generated a downright longing for wholeness and community (Gay, 2001). These ideas of 'wholeness' were directed mainly towards cultivating a whole body-mind self as the basis for a collective wholeness (Harrington, 1996). Harald Schultz-Hencke, later a psychoanalyst, wrote at the age of 24 in his diary that he was convinced that humanity must become an organism (Theilemann, 2018, p. 71). In psychology as in other fields of knowledge, as much sense as nonsense was written about wholeness and organism, as these concepts lent themselves to exploitation from every part of the political spectrum, allowing even psychology to open up to National Socialist ideology (Geuter, 1994).

In the early days of body psychotherapy, we come across the idea of the wholeness of the human being as a psychological and corporeal being. The breath and body therapists followed the motto: 'from individual experience of wholeness to the process of cognition' (von Steinaecker, 2000, p. 86). Gindler wrote that 'in the human being we have a whole, which is itself just a part of a social organism' (Ludwig, 2002, p. 100). In body pedagogy, though, no theory of wholeness was developed. This is also true of Reich. He did speak of the 'identity and unity of psychophysical functioning', which idea originated in Bergsonian thinking (Reich, 1973, p. 23) and later of seeing the 'patient first of all as a biological organism' (1972, p. xii). However, neither Bergson nor Reich formulated a theory of wholeness such as that of Gestalt therapy or holistic psychology.

The neurologist Kurt Goldstein, who was a member of the Gestalt group and whose concepts became part of humanistic psychotherapy, advocated in 1934 the theory of a **holistic organism** (Goldstein, 1995). He saw each normal or pathological phenomenon as the expression of its comprehensive activity. After the First World War, Goldstein worked with patients with brain injuries and had observed that areas of the brain could take over the functions of other areas, which according to the localisation theory of the time, should not have been possible. Thus, deficits could be compensated by other parts of the whole. Through this he arrived at the idea of a self-realising brain (Harrington, 1996). In his biological theory of the organism, Goldstein assumed that the organism had the capacity for self-regulation of defects, and he spoke of its self-actualisation (1995, pp. 300, 303). According to Votsmeier, with the concept of organism he meant not only the physical body, but the idea, the image or the concept of the organism as a whole (1995, p. 5). For him the organism was the unit whose reactions we can observe and whose physical and psychological aspects can only be differentiated from each other through reflection (Goldstein, 1931, p. 6). Mind, feelings and bodily processes were all part of a whole, the living being (Goldstein, 1995, p. 361). As a biological theorist of the organism, Goldstein wanted nothing to do with the philosophy of life. He saw his holistic ideas as in opposition to the drive theory of psychoanalysis, as this latter made the methodological mistake of regarding one phenomenon as the primary 'on which the others are supposed to be depending' (Goldstein, 1995, p. 257).

The concept of **self-regulation** of the organism was closely connected to the idea of wholeness. Ideas about 'self-regulation' or 'organic regulation' of life processes had been around since the 19th century, for example those of the vitalist Hans Driesch, whom Reich had studied. Walter B. Cannon spoke later of an 'organised self-government' which would lead to what he called homeostasis in 1929 (Tanner, 1998; cf. Heller, 2012, pp. 200–2). Reich too spoke in the original German of 'self-steering' and not yet of self-regulation. Self-steering meant for him that actions form themselves according to an internal principle. In its function of establishing an inner harmony, self-steering 'is not only compatible with natural instincts; it is in fact functionally identical with them' (1973, p. 181). The psychoanalyst Otto Gross, however, was already using the concept of 'individual self-regulation' (Bocian, 2007, p. 168). Bocian sees a link from Gross to Reich and then to Perls that emphasises organismic self-regulation, 'because the conflict and relationship theory as an affect theory had as its basis the body' (Bocian, 2007, p. 168). The left-wing Freudian idea of self-steering also stood for the assertion of subjectivity in the face of external control through society.

Neither the idea of wholeness nor self-regulation, however, play an important role in the beginnings of body psychotherapy. We have to imagine them both more as ideas prevalent in the intellectual discourse of the day, and thus they provided a background for other concepts as, for example, Reich's concept of the functional identity of the physical and the psychological. Only later did the concept of self-regulation gain significance, above all in the context of systemic ideas or infant research (Chapter 17).

11. Unity of nature and culture: a shared dream

Faced with the destruction of nature through civilisation, establishing humanity's unity with nature was a common dream of both conservative cultural critics such as Klages and of left-wing Freudian revolutionaries such as Reich. The various wings of the life-reform movement and the youth movement shared this desire for unison with nature. So Gindler went out into nature with her groups (Ludwig, 2002) and Reich with his family (Geuter et.al., 2010, p. 65). Klages, whose theories were well-received in the gymnastics movement, complained in 1913 that human beings have lost all knowledge of the world-creating power of all-uniting love (1937, p. 34). The biologist Jakob von Uexkuell, on whose theories Functional Relaxation is based, was also looking for healing from a destructive, capitalistic system. Whereas he saw this healing in a renunciation of democracy (Harrington, 1996), for a while Reich saw it in revolutionary change. Criticism of 'mammonism' (Klages) and the quest for healing were common to both sides; the responses differed.

Reich's anti-capitalism was saturated with life-reform ideas. He regarded mental disorders as a disruption of the 'natural capacity for love'; healing was for him the regaining of involuntary life functions, the capacity to surrender to orgasm (Reich, 1973, p. 6ff). He sought fulfilment in the sensuality of nature:

'Children who blossom, flowers that bud, breasts that swell, lips that kiss, arms that embrace, life, life'.

(Reich, 1994, p. 98)

His dream was the 'unity and congruity of culture and nature' (1973, p. 8). Just as Schopenhauer assumed that moral values can only be found empirically in the deeds of human beings (Fellmann, 1996, p. 287), so Reich sought morality in the nature of sexuality and the loving person. In his later work he regarded the innermost core of a human being as encompassing goodness, God, life and love, including the genital embrace, and which creates a natural moral sensitivity (1953, pp. 41–2).

The attitude that human beings are naturally good was also a basic tenet of contemporary reform pedagogy. This went against the earlier educational system of drill and discipline, just as reform gymnastics went against the earlier gymnastics of toughening up. They all had in common an image, resonant of Rousseau, of the goodness of human nature, which is then deformed by humans themselves. It is no coincidence that a long friendship united Reich with Alexander Neill, who founded his boarding school, Summerhill, in 1921 and whose ideas on education were widely read in the student movement, as was Reich.

Also, a theme of Rousseau's thinking is that turning away from nature is bad for one's health. In breath training, illness was seen as an impurity of the body (von Steinaecker, 2000, p. 99). Reich too set up his understanding of nature as a norm. He saw orgastic potency as a therapy goal and allowed no exceptions as it is a biological function (1925, p. 222).

Both Gindler and Reich wanted to liberate the beast in human beings, the 'animal' of which Nietzsche spoke. Gindler often referred to the free-flowing movements of animals as a model for movement originating in the body and not in the mind, Reich to the pulsating movement of the amoeba as a model for the free pulsation of a non-armoured human organism (cf. Barlow, 2001).

Gindler was happy when students became livelier and more natural (Ludwig, 2002, p. 38). But not being a theorist, she developed no ideology out of this. Her dream of naturalness was linked to the ideas of naturopathy. Franz Hilker, who was on the board of the German Gymnastic Federation with her, wrote that after an illness in her youth, Gindler asked herself whether it was possible to find in nature herself the conditions for mobilising the body's immune system; later she studied 'whether we can find answers in human nature itself and the need for an orderly and undisturbed functional flow' (Ludwig, 2002, p. 76). Today we could see in this a model for working with resources. Gindler, the reform movement and early body psychotherapy were all anchored in the context of a counter-civilisatoric practice of body-work, which ultimately reconciled with modernism through the emphasis on the personal responsibility of human beings who were becoming increasingly individualised.

3.5 NATURE AND SEXUALITY – DOMINATION OR LIBERATION

In the early days of body psychotherapy, there were great differences in the way the sensuality of the body was seen (Geuter, 2000a, pp. 68–70). Left-wing Freudians were faithful to the drive theory. Reich stood for the concept of the *genital character*, free of neurotic inhibitions. When he was a student in Vienna, he and Fenichel had studied the sexual misery of young people (Fallend, 1988). In Vienna and Berlin, he campaigned for a liberation of sexuality (Peglau, 2013). For Reich, the aim of releasing physical blockages was always to gain more freedom in sexual surrender. Thus, he was beholden to the heroic image of the human being prevalent in early psychoanalysis (Altmeyer & Thomae, 2006), in which the human being, caught in the conflict between lust and anxiety, struggles against sexual frustration.

In the gymnastics movement, the attitude to sexuality was quite different. They followed the separation into 'vulgar carnality' and 'noble sensuality', which the middle-class reform movement had constructed (Linse, 1998, p. 441). Andersen wrote that in the breath school of Schlaffhorst and Andersen, stimulants such as coffee and chocolate were prohibited as were movements of the pelvis, so that Germans could achieve their highest performance (Wedemeyer-Kolwe, 2004, pp. 93–4). Schlaffhorst wanted to tame lust with breathing and singing (von Steinaecker, 2000, p. 77). Body culture methods were aimed at desexing body sensation and eliminating sexual desire (de Ras, 1986, p. 415). The so-called New Spirit Movement of the time cultivated breathing exercises, mantras and meditation to control 'lustful thoughts' and the 'lustful soul' through asceticism and self-discipline (Wedemeyer-Kolwe, 2004, pp. 170–1). The Mazdaznan movement advocated diet to cleanse the intestines and the vagina, as otherwise man and woman would be too passionate and disharmonious (von Steinaecker, 2000, p. 97). Von Laban (1926, p. 111) held that gymnastic movements would deflect sexual desire downwards; when dancers danced naked or almost naked, this cooled sexual curiosity down. Gindler said that people should come into a relationship with their organism (Ludwig, 2002, p. 98); however, the organism stopped short of the pelvis and of lustful sensations.

In this self-sensing, aesthetic pleasure was opposed to sexual pleasure (cf. Linse, 1986, p. 400). Desire is then felt in a living-body, which experiences itself as free for itself alone. Starobinski sees in this a narcissistic component of modern civilisation, as conscious listening to the body has a certain degree of instinctual gratification (1987, p. 28). The body, cleansed of the need for a sexual partner, would be narcissistically gratified. 'There remains the desire to become primeval and thus to live at last', said the philosopher Ernst Bloch (1979, p. 333) in a searing critique of Klages. Klages (1926, p. 61) excluded 'the animalistic drive' from his model of character.

Thus, we find in early body psychotherapy the polarity of

- Sexuality versus asceticism.
- Sexual liberation versus liberation through movement.
- Relinquishing control through surrender versus controlling the body through sensing the self.

The system of callisthenics already mentioned also aimed at controlling the body gracefully (Linse, 1998, p. 439). According to Wedemeyer-Kolwe (2004, p. 85), the movement of rhythmic gymnastics produced not a liberated body but a self-disciplined one. Laban wanted to create a discipline of the spirit through physical self-control (Bender, 2020, p. 63). After his emigration to the USA, the German bodybuilder and yoga student Joseph Pilates, who had collaborated with Laban, called his system of gymnastics 'Contrology' (Pilates & Miller, 1945). The gymnastic movement was concerned with strengthening the individual through physical self-awareness, Reich with the surrender of the ego to the 'we' in shared sexual gratification. For him pleasure was not streaming towards oneself, but streaming towards the world. It was expansion. The polarities described above persisted throughout the development of body psychotherapy; however, it is not possible to follow this up in a short introduction to its history.

These differences were also connected to the differing aims of body pedagogy and of Reich with his vegetotherapy. Gymnastics teaching was not about opening up feelings. The only feeling allowed for was joy in movement and in self-discovery. Anxiety, sadness or pain just did not appear. The goal was the optimal development of the bodily functions. However, when Reich thought of bodily functions, he thought primarily of the sexual function and its inhibition through affects. Reich thought in psychotherapeutic terms. Whereas Gindler interpreted physical symptoms through physical tension and relaxation, Reich interpreted them through the tension between desire and defence. Thus, his vegetotherapy was emotional. Gindler wanted people to become more awake and ready to react (Ludwig, 2002, p. 120), so as to be able to make optimal use of their organism. For Reich, the readiness to react was an emotional problem:

> 'We speak of a "genital" character when the emotional reactions are not governed by rigid automatism, when the person is capable of reacting in a biological way to a particular situation'.
>
> (Reich, 1972, p. 363)

Despite the differences in their attitude to sexuality, both the gymnastic movement and Reich himself stood for hope in an era full of tension. Their counterpoint would be the main work of phenomenology of that era, Heidegger's *Being and Time* from 1927. If the gymnasts paid homage to joy and said nothing about Eros or anxiety, Heidegger speaks neither of joy nor of Eros, but only of worry, fear, anxiety or decay, out of which 'Dasein' is pre-reflexively revealed. The sombre atmosphere of his book is well-suited to the sombre troubles of the time, whereas in its early stages, body psychotherapy was quite dedicated to the joy of living.

3.6 THE MATERIALISATION OF LIFE – REICH'S PATH TO NATURAL SCIENTIFIC ENERGY WORK

With his orgone theory, Reich distanced himself from 1939 onwards from body psychotherapy and began to explore areas that remained unproductive for it. We can only understand this if we look at Reich not as he has been viewed up to now, but in the tradition of the philosophy of life. His later work is permeated with the attempt to identify life-energy scientifically. Even though he had relinquished Marxism, he was still searching for a materialistic solution to the question of what life is. From Bergson's book *Creative evolution* he adopted the idea of a creative power, in the original *élan vital*, which is meant to explain the development of organisms. This was one of the three Bergson works he specifically says he has read (1973, p. 23). In this book, Bergson advances the view that the life-force could be awakened electrically.

We have to take into consideration that at the time Bergson's book first appeared in 1907 as well as in Reich's time, electrotherapy was fashionable in medicine. Reich's orgone accumulator, a special cabinet in which he wanted to collect the life-energy, is constructed in a similar way to the electric 'light bath' of the firm Siemens and Halske from 1911 (Museum fuer Energiegeschichte, n.d.). In the 1920s, the high frequency radiation device 'Energos', a gadget for use at home, was supposed to alleviate pain, rheumatism, influenza or diabetes with high-frequency alternating currents (Museum der Dinge, n.d.). In an advertisement for such devices from 1931 it reads: 'the best natural rejuvenator'. The model 'Anapol' from the firm of Foerster was supposed to cure impotence (Museum fuer Energiegeschichte, n.d.). Lastly, in 1929, Hans Berger of Jena for the first time published the results of measurements with an electroencephalogram, which gave a further impetus to the quest for an electrical explanation of life processes.

In psychoanalysis, Siegfried Bernfeld had attempted since 1929 to measure libido electrically, whereby together with an engineer he had built a 'libido gauge' (Peglau, 2013, p. 275). He believed libido to be a form of energy subject to the laws of physics and published many papers on 'libidometry' (Peglau, 2013). Reich began to measure sexual energy electrically in the 1930s. He measured skin potential at the erogenous zones when test subjects reported pleasurable sensations (Sharaf, 1994, p. 212). He wanted to prove the existence of Bergson's *élan vital* on a material level. And he wanted to find a way of working directly on the 'living organism itself' and not just on conflicts and character armouring (Reich, 1972, p. 358). Orgasm research was the way to penetrate 'deep into the secrets of nature' and to develop psychology into 'biophysics' and a 'genuine experimental natural science' (1973, p. 386).

Reich later claimed that he had discovered orgone energy, a universal energy until then unknown, which determined organic as well as inorganic processes, such as the weather, and which he would collect in his orgone accumulator for healing purposes. He understood it as a universal force of regulation of all natural processes throughout the cosmos (Heller, 2012, p. 117; Young, 2015a). From 1945, Reich equated orgone energy with the id and with *élan vital* (Reich, 1972, p. 297, fn1). He went from a biological to a physical understanding of energy: 'This something called "id" is a physical reality, i.e., it is cosmic orgone energy' (Reich, 1972, p. 297). He now believed he was able to treat psychological problems in a purely energetic manner. At times he spoke of a biological energy that encompassed more than 'bio-electricity' (1948), but ultimately of a 'strictly physical energy' (1973, p. ix).

'Living matter does indeed function on the basis of the same physical laws as non-living matter … At the same time, it is fundamentally different from non-living matter'.

(Reich, 1973, p. 380)

The difference lay in the specific arrangement of the mechanical and electrical functions.

With orgone research, Reich believed he had reached his goal. Philosophically, this was to overcome dualism by tracing both the psychical and the physical back to laws of life valid for both; scientifically, it meant resolving the controversy between mechanists such as Haeckel and vitalists such as Driesch about the nature of life (Section 3.4), which in the Weimar Republic was a contentious issue (Geuter, 1992, p. 111). By defining the immaterial life-force of the vitalists as physical in an explanatory model acceptable to the mechanists, he thought he was doing justice to both sides. He believed through physics he had solved the 'riddle of the universe', a phrase Haeckel used in 1899 in his eponymous book. What the orgone was for Reich was for Haeckel the ether.

As for therapy, Reich now thought he could work 'not through the use of human language' (1972, p. 361), but directly on the living organism, on the biopathy instead of the psychopathology (Reich, 1972). He aimed to penetrate into the 'biological depths' so as to 'restore the motility of the body plasma' (1972, p. 365). Theoretically, he was looking for an explanation of the biological through physics.

Reich's oeuvre is permeated with the life-philosophical question: what is life? The impasse he reached was that he wanted to solve this question through physics and so had to postulate an energy that could be measured. He reduced vitality and soul-experience 'to a positivistic and materialistic construction of the term "energy"' (Marlock, 2015, p. 150), and his scientific explanations tended towards a scientism of natural scientific explanations, which Husserl (2012, first pub. 1936) had roundly criticised (Section 7.3). Here he is still in the grip of the tradition of the organic physicists such as Emil DuBois-Reymond and Freud's tutor Ernst Bruecke, who in the mid-19th century had looked at the activities of the organism from the point of view of physics and claimed that it was subject to the same laws as inorganic matter.

The physiologist DuBois-Reymond proposed the theory that electrical energy was the juice of life and of the soul (Harrington, 1996). Reich never freed himself of this position. At the end of his book *Listen, Little Man*, he wrote in 1946 that 'I have given you an instrument with which to govern your lives with the conscious purpose which thus far you have applied only to the operation of machines. I have been a faithful engineer to your organism' (Reich, 1948, n. p.). This conforms to the spirit of behaviourism, which at the time dominated in psychology, but from which Reich radically differed through his respect for life and for children, as we see in his work with infants (Harms, 2013). With brilliant psychological insight, Reich had developed psychoanalysis into vegetotherapy. However, in his later work, he asserted the primacy of a physics point of view. The medical psychoanalyst longed to be an engineer of the organism.

3.7 EXPERIENCE AND GROWTH – THE HUMANISTIC THERAPY MOVEMENT AS THE THIRD SOURCE OF BODY PSYCHOTHERAPY

From the 1960s onwards, in the wake of the human potential movement and of humanistic psychology and psychotherapy, body psychotherapy blossomed anew (Geuter, 2015, pp. 28–31). These movements became the third source of body psychotherapy and had a greater impact internationally than did Gindler's ideas (Wolf, 2010). The humanistic psychologist Charlotte Buehler wrote at the time that the body-oriented approaches increased in significance through humanistic psychology and the human potential movement (1974, p. 8).

As were the years at the beginning of the century, so those since the late 1960s have been a time of yearning to feel and experience intensively. Through the student and hippie movements, young people were searching for liberation, creativity, overcoming boundaries, ecstasy and a post-religious spirituality. They wanted to liberate passion from the rule of reason, experimented with new lifestyles and were committed to the emancipation of the individual. This included not only a radical attack on the body etiquette and sexual prohibitions of society, but also an anti-psychiatry, which interpreted madness as protest. Dancing ecstatically to loud music, letting one's hair grow and throwing away your bra were all part of a body-oriented liberation scenario. 'Sexuality once again became the great metaphor of happiness and liberation' (Marlock, 2015b, p. 96–7). In the student movement, Reich was seen as the theorist of sexual liberation and 'posthumously, Reich became an honorary member of the growth movement' (Totton, 2002a, p. 220).

At that time, humanistic psychotherapy and body psychotherapy blossomed in the context of countercultural, alternative movements (Hutterer, 1998, p. 401). Theoretically and therapeutically, they formed an alternative to the monolith of established psychoanalysis and to behavioural therapy; humanistic psychology even called itself the 'third force' (Bugental, 1964). Maslow (1968), the theorist of humanistic psychology, set his thinking in the context of cultural criticism and assumed that human beings could be happy if their inner nature was not suppressed but encouraged (see box). In contrast to Freud's metaphor of the psychic apparatus, where psychological energies and entities struggle with one another, or to Reich's battle metaphor of the neurotic person, whose 'resistance' must be broken and 'eliminated', humanistic psychotherapy developed the image of the human being as a blossoming plant in need of cultivation.

'At that time, many people became involved in personal-growth, therapy and encounter groups as a way to expand their inner possibilities and to seek an identity that they believed they had lost' (Geuter, 2015, p. 29). With the aid of therapy, they wanted to awaken potential and overcome barriers. Reichian body therapists urged their clients to grow into the ideal of orgastic potency (Cornell, 2015, pp. 694–5.). Therapy groups offered an intensity of relationships and feelings not available in society as a whole (Wolf, 2010). In Esalen, Poona and elsewhere there were group marathons. In many places a *workshop-cult* developed. The psychiatrist Stanislav Grof experimented with LSD and later with trance induced through forced breathing and loud music, in order to foster *The adventure of self-discovery* (Grof, 1988). In all this, the body was a point of reference in the quest for the self.

Self-actualisation

Maslow (1968) saw humanistic psychology as part of a new philosophy of life, in the centre of which stood the concept of self-actualisation. This was a concept very in vogue in the social movements of the time, related to the idea of *wholeness* (Section 3.4; cf. Corsi, 2012), and was introduced in 1934 by Goldstein (1995). Goldstein regarded a healthy person as a freely active being aiming to fulfil their potential. Pure survival was a motif of sick people (Votsmeier, 1995, p. 9). Maslow differentiated between *deficit needs* and *growth motivations*. In his concept of a hierarchy of needs, self-actualisation was right at the top. In his view, this is not a state but a development of the personality, in which people free themselves from limitations and become capable of seeing things as they are and of acting to change them (Maslow, 1959). This also includes being able to perceive oneself and reality more accurately; accepting oneself and being able to react spontaneously; being decisive and able to deal with conflicts; the ability to be creative, autonomous and productive; and the ability to live values such as courage, kindness, honesty, goodness and love, as well as realising one's own potential and personal, human essence (Maslow, 1968). This far-reaching idea of self-actualisation was an ideal image which Maslow believed that some people he had met fulfilled. Self-actualised people had a feeling of rootedness and belonging, were content, had self-esteem and focused on tasks outside of themselves (Maslow, 1968).

As the protest movement subsided, people turned back to the individual, discovered again this listening to themselves and the search for meaning in the finer sensations of bodily self-perception. In particular, the feminist movement put the question of body identity on the agenda (Staunton, 2002a, p. 1). In the years of the second flowering of body psychotherapy, the two sources from the early days flowed again: first free your own lust for life, then find yourself. Just as at the beginning, body psychotherapy believed in those days that it could make people more liberated, more creative and less conformist (Totton, 2002a, p. 220).

The understanding of freedom that humanistic psychology was propagating at the time was, however, something new. Freedom was to them not freedom from repressive instinct denial or the freedom of inner movement and self-expression, but rather freedom to shape possibilities. Maslow (1968) held the view that the self-actualising person was relatively independent of their environment. Humanistic psychology strove for autonomy and self-determination. This matched the spirit of the times. Buehler (1979) found that in the 1970s there was a process of awakening to new possibilities in Western society.

The gravitational centre of the new psychotherapy was the Esalen Institute on the Californian coast. Also in California was the second innovative centre of psychotherapy, the Mental Research Institute in Palo Alto, with the group around Gregory Bateson, Jay Haley and Paul Watzlawick. The first events in Esalen were titled *Human Potentiality*. Also living and teaching in Esalen were Stanislav Grof, founder of Holotropic Breathwork; Jack Lee Rosenberg and Marjorie Rand (2004) of Integrative Body Psychotherapy; Ida Rolf, founder of Rolfing; Fritz Perls or Moshe Feldenkrais as well as Abraham Maslow; Carl Rogers, founder of client-centred psychotherapy; the family therapist Virginia Satir; the Jungian James Hillman; the dance therapist Mary Starks Whitehouse; and the singers Bob Dylan and Joan Baez as well as George Harrison, lead guitarist of the Beatles (Kripal, 2007). Also, Gregory Bateson, who as an anthropologist was one of the fathers of systemic therapy, stayed for a while in Esalen. The theoretical physicist of the New Age, Fritjof Capra, the Nobel prize-winner for chemistry Linus Pauling and the meditation teacher Deepak Chopra gave courses there. In Esalen in 1963, Selver gave the first ever self-exploration workshop (Weaver, 2015, p. 44). The body psychotherapist George Downing (1973) studied Esalen Massage, and Will Schutz developed encounter groups there (Wolf, 2010). In California, John Lennon and Yoko Ono had Primal Therapy sessions with Arthur Janov. Therapy methods that intensified emotions were very popular in this cultural climate. Heller (2012, p. 635) says that it was in California that body psychotherapy liberated itself from the fanaticism of the American East Coast Reichians, who were strongly orgone therapy oriented, so that it could absorb the ideas of other therapy approaches.

At the centre of therapeutic endeavour was now the 'search for the true self' (Miller, 1980). Children too had a right to an individual self, and authors such as Alice Miller criticised repressive education. Therapies promising to loosen blocks and attain more inner freedom were at a premium, for example Janov's Primal Therapy (1971), which promised fast deliverance from painful childhood experiences, but which tended to push traumatised patients back into old painful wounds (Young, 2015b).

Common to both body psychotherapy and humanistic psychology was the focus on experience. Body psychotherapy then adopted the therapeutic attitude of Carl Rogers, offering a secure, supportive, understanding and authentic relationship. Also, there was a growing interest in Buddhist ideas. This led to the revival of mindfulness, which Gindler had taught without using the concept. In Hakomi therapy, Reichian concepts were explicitly combined with Buddhist teachings of non-violence and mindfulness (Kurtz, 1983). Now therapeutic change was seen as transforming how people organise their experiences.

Humanistic psychology was based on contemporary values: dignity, the right to personal development, authenticity, self-determination, individuality, meaningfulness, responsibility, empathy and kindness (Hartmann-Kottek & Kritz, 2005). From these values were derived a different view of psychotherapy, particularly of the role of the therapist. The therapist was no longer seen, as in psychoanalysis and for Reich and Lowen, as an omniscient physician, but, as with Rogers, as a helpful person who makes themselves available for interaction (Geuter, 2019, pp. 398–9). Bohart et al. (1998) name the following *humanistic principles* which the therapist follows:

- Discovery.
- The clients decide for themselves.
- The therapeutic relationship is democratic with equal rights on both sides.
- The therapist is committed to an empathic understanding of clients within their own frame of reference.
- The therapist is in a respectful manner authentic in relation to the clients.

These and other principles of humanistic psychotherapy influenced the body psychotherapy schools which developed at that time, and later intersubjective psychoanalysis and behavioural therapy, especially Acceptance and Commitment Therapy. We can discern this influence in the following ten characteristics of the body psychotherapy flourishing at the time:

1. Since that time, a new understanding of the role of the therapist in body psychotherapy has prevailed. The distant, omniscient therapist of one-person psychology, formerly represented by psychoanalysis, was superseded by the more empathic, supportive, respectful therapeutic companion, who shows themselves and is available for interaction (e.g. Brown, 1990).
2. Humanistic psychology saw subjective experience as the basis of knowledge (Maslow, 1968). This renaissance of the concept of experiencing facilitated a therapy approach in which, as in Gestalt therapy, the experience of the here and now in the therapeutic situation was the focus of attention. The emphasis of the work shifted from uncovering biography to discovering what was happening in the present moment. The guiding principle became the idea that only what was deeply felt and experienced would result in change.
3. Through humanistic psychology, sensing, which in Gindler's work was centred on the functions of the body, became a fundamental therapeutic principle extending to the whole lived-body experience. Change would originate not through insights stimulated

from outside, but from inner, sensed experience. From client-centred therapy, Gendlin (1996) developed Focusing, a method in which a systematic exploration of bodily sensations is used to gain responses to questions from the body and to generate meaning.

4. The adoption of Eastern meditation and mindfulness exercises in the humanistic therapy movement inspired individual body psychotherapists to propagate a radically non-invasive approach and in particular Ron Kurtz (1983, 1990), to focus on systematically working with mindfulness as the central aspect of therapy – a first in the history of psychotherapy.

5. Humanistic psychotherapy liberated itself from Freudian psychoanalysis and took up some of C.G. Jung's ideas, such as the interpretation of dreams on both a subjective and an objective level or working with active imagination. In Unitive Body Psychotherapy, Stattman (1989) emphasised creative work with inner images. Brown (1990) adopted Jung's archetype theory.

6. In both humanistic psychotherapy and body psychotherapy, the preference was for group over individual therapy (Soth, 2015; Wolf, 2010). The personal is political and the psyche public. Some body psychotherapy methods, as for example Concentrative Movement Therapy in the German-speaking countries, are to this day practised mainly in a group setting (Schreiber-Willnow, 2013). For inpatient therapy, body psychotherapy has hitherto been group therapy (Roehricht, 2000, p. 19).

7. Since humanistic psychology investigates the characteristics of a healthy and satisfying human life (Buehler & Allen, 1972) and is not only concerned with the pathology of unconscious dynamics or learning experiences, it emphasises growth towards a fulfilled life. Body psychotherapy schools, which had developed since the 1960s and 1970s, shared this impetus. This corresponds to the ideas of C. G. Jung, that through therapy patients would grow out of their neuroses. Buehler and Allen (1972) preferred to speak of a tendency towards higher complexity rather than of growth.

8. At that time body psychotherapy rejected diagnoses, as did Rogers and the anti-psychiatry movement. The focus was not on the treatment of symptoms but on transformation and growth (Soth, 2009, p. 71). The idea, shared with humanistic psychotherapy, was to arrive at *process diagnoses* in the course of therapy (Bohart et al., 1998). The humanistic model assumed an individual human being experiencing themselves and not patients as the bearers of disorders. Correspondingly, the aim of therapy was not to eliminate disorder, but to transform patterns of experience.

9. The theory of humanistic psychology focused on the experiencing individual (Buehler & Allen, 1972). This was one of the basic tenets of the Association for Humanistic Psychology at a time when it was not of interest to psychoanalysis or behaviourism. Until today it is a characteristic of humanistic-experiential therapies that 'the person is viewed holistically, neither as a symptom driven case nor as a diagnosis' (Elliott et al., 2013, p. 496).

10. Initially Maslow (1968) called humanistic psychology 'holistic, dynamic psychology', as its aim was to study and understand the individual as a whole (Buehler & Allen, 1972). Modern body psychotherapy shares this view of the human being as a body-mind whole with humanistic psychotherapy (cf. Eberwein, 2012; Schneider & Laengle, 2012).

Despite body psychotherapy having been closely associated with these ten characteristics to humanistic psychotherapy since the 1970s, most schools have retained the understanding of child development and mental disorders from psychodynamic psychotherapy. This is in part due to the weakness of humanistic theories in this regard. To date, many body psychotherapy schools lean more towards the psychodynamic theory than the humanistic, even if implicitly, in my view, many basic humanistic ideas have influenced the thinking of most body psychotherapists.

The humanistic therapy movement not only influenced body psychotherapy, but was in turn influenced by it. In Rogers' client-centred therapy, a body-oriented way of working developed with Focusing and various authors discuss combining verbal and body therapeutic approaches (Kern, 2014; Mueller-Hofer et al., 2003). Gestalt therapy uses paying attention to bodily processes as an essential tool (Kepner, 1993), even if no direct body interventions are used. Psychodrama has the physical portrayal of issues in the group as its main method.

Certain body psychotherapy schools developed in those days are based explicitly on humanistic psychotherapy. Malcolm Brown (1990), founder of Organismic Psychotherapy, was first trained in client-centred therapy and numbered Maslow and Rogers among his most important teachers. Rosenberg et al. (1985) begin their body psychotherapeutic textbook by pointing out that it is about growth and development. Rosenberg at first named his approach Gestalt Body Psychotherapy and later Integrative Body Psychotherapy (Wolf, 2010). Petzold (2003) based his Integrative Body and Movement Therapy on Gestalt Therapy and body therapeutic methods. Stattman's Unitive Body Psychotherapy (1989) and Keleman's Formative Psychology (1985) see themselves as in the tradition of humanistic psychotherapy.

The humanistic therapy movement spawned a wild creativity of therapeutic ideas and methods, which thrived in an environment of alternative self-discovery. At the beginning, creative experimenting counted for more than developing reliable scientific theories. However, in distancing themselves from established psychotherapy, some of the founders of therapy schools became themselves the defendants of dogmatic positions (Soth, 2013), and for years there was a distinct touch of anti-intellectualism in a vibrant therapy scene (Totton, 2002, p. 13).

Since then, however, body psychotherapy has gone through a great transformation and has developed into a clinical method. The diversity of praxis and theory developed by the various schools and the legacy of the three sources have been gradually integrated into a body psychotherapy that is recognisable as such above and beyond those schools. Also communication with other psychotherapy orientations such as the psychodynamic, behavioural, cognitive, systemic and hypnotherapeutic approaches is on the increase (Chapter 18). We can describe our present-day task with a phrase from Perls (1981): There is no end to integration.

4

The legacy of the schools

Since the 1970s, body psychotherapy schools have proliferated. Some were tightly bound to the personality of their founder and offered no ideas or concepts with any enduring influence. Others developed basic theoretical ideas or treatment methods that are still widely used today. These schools of body psychotherapy constitute the legacy from which a comprehensive theory of body psychotherapeutic practice can draw. I would include the following:

- **Bioenergetics**: releasing sympathetic tone by overstretching tense muscles where the affective energy is bound up.
- **Biodynamics**: both mobilising and harmonising psychological processes through massage.
- **Biosynthesis**: working with sensing, grounding and facing in equal measure on the three levels of vegetative life streams, motor fields and contact.
- **Hakomi**: utilising the state of inner mindfulness to experience the body and the mind, so that they reorganise themselves.
- **Integrative Body Psychotherapy**: combining sensing, feeling and thinking in an eclectic way so as to become more aware of all levels of experience and to realise the self.
- **Functional Relaxation**: letting go of tension through the outbreath and so reorganising the body.
- **Concentrative Movement Therapy**: stimulating body awareness in order to find meaning.
- **Focusing**: developing an evaluation of questions or problems through mindful perception of the body – so-called *felt sense*.
- **Integrative Body and Movement Therapy**: utilising the perception of the body for therapy by focusing systematically on it and experimenting with breathing, posture, facial expressions, gestures and movement.
- **Analytical body psychotherapy**: retrieving unconscious relational expectations and patterns from early object relation experiences and working through them in the therapeutic situation through scenes or body language within the transference/countertransference process.
- **Pesso–Boyden System Psychomotor**: reviving the structure of an early experience or an early disturbed relational constellation in therapeutic role-playing and, with the help of ideal relational figures, allowing the client to experience an alternative.

DOI: 10.4324/9781003176893-4

TABLE 4.1
Schools and movements in body psychotherapy

Schools and their founders	Orientation, methods	Body image
Perception oriented: Concentrative Movement Therapy (Stolze), Functional Relaxation (Fuchs), Body-Mind Centering (Bainbridge Cohen), Integrative Movement Therapy (Petzold), Focusing (Gendlin), Rosen–Method (Fogel)	Examples: – CMT: perception, experiencing the inner and outer worlds; sensing relationship to oneself. – BMC: exploring the body and its systems in movement. – IMT: working with perception, posture, breathing, movement.	A moving body exploring itself.
Affect oriented/neo-Reichian: Bioenergetics (Lowen), Biodynamics (Boyesen), Biosynthesis (Boadella), Core-Energetics (Pierrakos), Organismic Psychotherapy (Brown), Orgone Therapy (Baker)	Examples – Bioenergetics: mobilising expressiveness, releasing muscle blocks through stress positions. – Biodynamics: massages, vegetative digestion of rest affects, body rooted talking.	An expressive and energetic body; body as the means and the location of the repression, of expressiveness and of the regulation of affects.
Relationship oriented: Analytical body psychotherapy (Moser, Heisterkamp, Geissler), Pesso-Boyden-System-Psychomotor (Pesso), relational body psychotherapy (Rolef Ben-Shahar, Sletvold, Totton)	Becoming aware of the latent meaning of body expression in transference; working with resonance in an embodied encounter, re-enactment and transformation of relationship patterns of early childhood in embodied dialogue.	A dialogic and moved body in transference.
Movement oriented: Dance and Movement Therapy (Caldwell, Espenak, Chace, Whitehouse, Schoop)	Experience in movement, expression of the unconscious in movement; extending the behavioural repertoire through movement.	A moving, expressive and learning body.

Starting with these schools as our source, we can distinguish basically **four great directions**:

• Perception-oriented.
• Affect-oriented.
• Relationship-oriented.
• Movement-oriented schools (Roehricht, 2000, pp. 15–6).

These are all based on certain body images which are connected to the focal points of their treatment techniques (Geuter, 1996). Whereas schools such as Concentrative Movement Therapy focus on body perception and move from there to meaning, the neo-Reichian methods tend more towards the expression of feelings, mobilising and regulating repressed affects and analytical body psychotherapy more towards revitalising the object representations of early childhood in a body language dialogue in transference. Dance therapy, however, works with movement and bodily expression and is often numbered among the creative therapies (Chapter 2).

Hakomi is not included in the table (Kurtz, 1983, 1990). Connected to the neo-Reichian theory of character structure, it is more oriented towards perception and experience than to affect expression (Weiss et al., 2015). Thus, Hakomi does not fit well into the schema of the table and neither does the Integrative Body Psychotherapy of Rosenberg et al. (1985).

Wolf (2010) classifies Hakomi and various other schools such as Focusing, Unitive Body Psychotherapy, Holotropic Breathwork or Bonding into a **fifth direction**, which she calls the 'self-actualising movement'. She includes here psychodrama, Schutz's Encounter and Gestalt therapy, which Rolef Ben-Shahar (2014, p. 51) sees as a process-oriented body psychotherapy. We can include some of these schools, such as Holotropic Breathwork, in the affect-oriented movement, which works with the expressive body, and others, such as Focusing, in the perception-oriented direction. However, I would describe these last three mentioned by Wolf as more humanistic, experiential approaches, related to the body but not really belonging to body psychotherapy. Self-actualisation is also not a concept to which much attention is paid in body psychotherapeutic schools. Wolf's idea, however, does pay tribute to the fact that in many of the body psychotherapy schools, the understanding of the focus of psychotherapy and of the way it works has been deeply influenced by humanistic psychotherapy (Section 3.7).

The proliferation of the schools is connected to the history of emigration. As a result of National Socialism, Reich, Perls and all the Gindler students from the top row of Figure 3.2 (Section 3.1.2) emigrated. Gindler's work returned to Germany after the Second World War to some extent through these émigrés (Figure 3.2). Helmut Stolze, founder of Concentrative Movement Therapy, was a student of Gertrud Heller, and he invited Miriam Goldberg, who had trained with the Gindler students Vera Jaffé and Lotte Kristeller in Israel, to the Lindau Psychotherapy Weeks, where from 1963 on she gave courses for 20 years (Remus, 2008).

Reich emigrated in 1933 first to Denmark, then via Sweden to Norway, where he stayed until August 1939. In Oslo he met the psychoanalysts Ola Raknes, Nic Waal and Trygve Braatøy, whom he knew from the Berlin Psychoanalytical Institute and who had taken up his ideas (Bassall & Heller, 2015; Heller, 2007; 2012, pp. 523–8). David Boadella (1987), Malcolm Brown (1990) and Gerda Boyesen (1987), all later founders of neo-Reichian schools, were students of Raknes (Figure 4.1). As a psychiatrist in Norway, Braatøy worked closely with the physiotherapist Aadel Buelow-Hansen, who with his support developed a special psychomotor treatment for psychiatric patients, in which symptoms were viewed as an expression of a lack of balance in the whole body (Thornquist & Bunkan, 1991, p. 14).

This tradition lives on in Scandinavia today. In Norway, the cooperation between Buelow-Hansen and Braatøy produced a special form of psychomotor therapy which views the body as the centre of experience and the bearer of biography (Ekerholt, 2010; Thornquist, 2010).

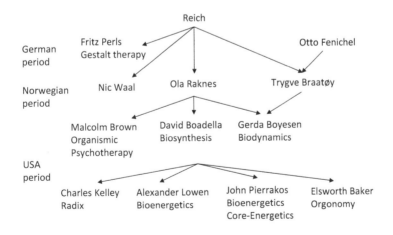

FIGURE 4.1 Wilhelm Reich and neo-reichian body psychotherapy

In Sweden, under the name of psychomotor therapy, massage and vegetotherapeutic techniques are combined in an academised psychosomatic physiotherapy (Eriksson et al., 2007, p. 3207). The Norwegian psychologist and physiotherapist Gerda Boyesen, who worked in the psychiatric clinic with Buelow-Hansen and Braatøy, also propagated this combination. She founded the school of biodynamic psychology, which is widespread in Central Europe and in the UK, and taught massage techniques for the regulation of affect tension. In Belgium and France, psychomotor therapy is regarded as a psychotherapeutic method (Probst et al., 2010; Wolf, 2010).

In the USA, Reich left behind a small group who studied his later orgonomy and viewed body psychotherapy as an energy treatment. Among them were Charles Kelley (2004) and Elsworth Baker (1967). This group had hardly any effect on psychotherapy. However, one student of Reich's, Alexander Lowen, had a great impact on it with his bioenergetics. At the same time, inspired by the Gindler student Charlotte Selver and her work in Esalen, as well as by other body trainers such as Carola Speads, Bonnie Bainbridge Cohen and Marion Rosen, an experiential body psychotherapy was developing, which focuses on the nuances of body perception and from there to awareness (Aposhyan, 2004; Fogel, 2009; D Johnson, 2015). This movement is strongly represented in the curriculum of academic somatic psychology in USA.

The Reichian school in body psychotherapy is the most prevalent internationally. In South America, Spain, Italy, Bulgaria and Greece, it is predominant. In Italy, for example, Jerome Liss taught his approach, Biosystemic Therapy (Liss & Stuppiggia, 1994), Malcolm Brown (1990) Organismic Psychotherapy and Luciano Rispoli (1993, 2006) a body-oriented, functionalist theory of the self. In the UK, various neo-Reichians founded influential therapy schools, such as Gerda Boyesen (1987) with biodynamics or David Boadella (1987) with his biosynthesis.

Because of the strong tradition of object relations theory in the UK, an animated dialogue between psychoanalysis and body psychotherapy has recently developed (Young, 2012). The Chiron Centre in London, once neo-Reichian, was influenced by intersubjective analysis and now advocates **relational body psychotherapy** (Soth, 2009, 2019), as do Rolef Ben-Shahar (2014), Totton (2015, 2019) or Westland (2015, 2019), and also Sletvold (2014) in Norway and Cornell (2015) in the USA. This latest development already belongs to an era beyond the schools, in which an author is concerned with the theoretical basis for body psychotherapy without wishing to create a new school.

In German-speaking countries, the tradition of living-body therapy continues with Concentrative Movement Therapy and Functional Relaxation, and the specific tradition of European, phenomenological philosophy in Integrative Body and Movement Therapy. Also, analytical body psychotherapy has developed, which seeks meaning in the language of body actions (Geissler & Heisterkamp, 2007).

The concepts and treatment techniques of the larger and smaller schools, which together with some body-work methods that Kogan (1980) and later Caldwell (1997) have documented, are based less on scientific explanation as on clinical experience. Their fascination lies in the wealth of practical knowledge on the one hand and, on the other, in their simplicity. Simplifying theories are generally more easily accepted than complex ones; they are succinct, make thinking easier and offer a clearer course of action. This is not only the case in body psychotherapy. In psychology, reductionist behaviourist theories were dominant for decades; today, how people understand neuroscience shows again these reductionist tendencies (Section 7.2). In body psychotherapy, we encounter ideas such as that 'people would be free of suffering if only they would breathe out properly and let go', or 'if only their muscle blocks were released'. Some schools such as Biosynthesis or Integrative Body and Movement Therapy did attempt to develop a more comprehensive approach. All the different schools, however, offer some elements for a general body psychotherapeutic theory, and for this reason I will briefly describe them here.

BIOENERGETICS

Of all the neo-Reichian schools that can be traced back to students of Reich in Oslo and the USA (Figure 4.1), and then to their students, Alexander Lowen's bioenergetic analysis (1975) is the most well-known. Lowen (1958) assumed, as did his teacher Reich, that all life processes are regulated by a fundamental energy that can be measured physically, which manifests psychologically and somatically and which he called bioenergy. In a neurotic person, this energy is bound up in muscular tension. Whereas in the end Reich pursued the idea of a purely energetic treatment, it is to Lowen's credit that he reconnected body psychotherapy to psychoanalysis. Lowen (1958) understood bioenergetic therapy as an analytical approach, which practised analysis on the psychic as well as on the bodily level. The more conflict- and affect-oriented schools of body psychotherapy retained the dynamic thinking of psychoanalytical theory as their framework. The majority shared the view that the life of the soul is guided by dynamic and unconscious processes and that conflicts between desires and defences against them generate psychopathological symptoms.

Lowen went further than Reich in several respects. He further developed the theory of character structures as a dynamic theory of character formation and augmented Reich's model with the oral and narcissistic character types (Section 13.2). Moreover, he expanded Reich's horizontal view of the tension segments of the body (Section 13.1) into the vertical. In terms of the energy theory, he looked at the flow of energy between the top and the bottom and emphasised the therapeutic value of grounding (Anagnostopoulou, 2015). This means that through their way of standing and their connection to the earth which supports them – both literally and figuratively – people can experience the feeling of being connected to this ground (Lowen, 1977). And finally, Lowen was the first to develop therapy work in the standing position, and he created a system of body exercises which could be utilised in psychotherapy (Lowen & Lowen, 2012). With the help of stress exercises, he aimed to discharge the tensions held in the body and to release the affects bound up in them. Bioenergetics is well-known for these body techniques.

BIODYNAMICS

Gerda Boyesen (1987; Boyesen & Boyesen, 1980) refers back to Reich's theory of the vasomotor movement of feelings and advocates a model of layers of defence, according to which affective energy accumulates not only in the muscles, but also in the connective tissue and the internal organs (Southwell, 1988). In biodynamics, she links psychological and physiological concepts and deploys various forms of massage as body psychotherapy, which she calls manual body psychoanalysis (Boyesen, 1987, p. 73). While Lowen's exercises helped to loosen up hypertonic structures through working on the underlying muscular tension, Boyesen shows us the importance of working with hypotonic structures, which need an increase in tension instead of a reduction. Furthermore, bioenergetics and biodynamics complement each other in the sense that bioenergetics has developed a multitude of techniques to dynamically loosen up the muscle blocks in body expression – a relinquishing of emotional arousal – while biodynamics looks for a way to melt such blocks in a gentle manner – an inner metabolising of arousal. This method has its origins in Boyesen's physiotherapeutic experiences in Oslo.

BIOSYNTHESIS

Of all the neo-Reichian schools, it is David Boadella's Biosynthesis (1987) which has accomplished most for integration. Boadella characterises principles and techniques of body psychotherapeutic work on the vegetative or emotional, the muscular or the vital, the psychological, verbal-cognitive or mental levels (Section 6.1). Centring through breathing and sensing, grounding through action and movement and facing through perception and thinking are, according to his theory, the three basic elements of a psychotherapy which works simultaneously with the vital, emotional and mental processes. He links these with the three embryonic germinal layers: entoderm, mesoderm and ectoderm, which then differentiate into the structures belonging to each layer. Keleman (1985) assigned the function of digestion and energy supply to the entoderm, support and movement to the mesoderm and communication to the ectoderm. From Blechschmidt's theory of embryo-dynamic fields, Boadella (2000) adapted a system of motoric fields, whose deficits could be balanced out and strengths developed (Section 14.2).

Boadella introduced the principle of working with polarities into body psychotherapy and saw the task of therapy as being to develop a balance between the antipodal motor fields or between poles which were too strongly or too weakly charged, grounded or focused, or boundaries which were overly strong or too weak. If a cathartic vision of therapy had dominated the encounter groups of the 1970s, now it became accepted that in addition to loosening inhibitions, body psychotherapy had to work on strengthening boundaries.

OTHER NEO-REICHIANS

John Pierrakos, a student of Reich's, first collaborated with Lowen in developing bioenergetics, but then moved towards a more spiritual therapy. In his **Core Energetics**, he aimed to liberate a person's direct, unrefracted, original energy (Pierrakos, 1973), so that they could get beyond the walls of denial and discover their true potential. In every human being there exists an indivisible *core energy*, which Pierrakos regarded as a substance. He diagnosed the psychic and energetic state of a person by means of their aura.

Malcom Brown (1990) studied with Raknes in Oslo, as did Boadella, and was trained in client-centred therapy (Section 3.7). He embedded the Reichian techniques of de-armouring in the theoretical framework of humanistic psychotherapy and understood his **Organismic Psychotherapy** as a means of helping patients attain a greater degree of awareness, individuation and self-fulfilment. Brown talks of a *healing touch* in psychotherapy, which, as nurturing touch, triggers awareness of early deficits; as consciousness-inducing touch, that of bodily sensations; or, as cathartic touch, can provoke feelings (Geuter, 2019, p. 256).

Stanley Keleman, who studied with Lowen, among others, has depicted how emotional experiences are incorporated into the somatic architecture and, by means of physical defence structures, shape an emotional anatomy. His system of emotionally influenced body forms is built on patterns of stress reaction (Keleman, 1985, 2015; Section 13.2). Keleman speaks of a **Formative Psychology** because he wants to understand the wound patterns reflected in a person's body form. Also, early on he described the therapeutic relationship as a somatic bond between two people who relate to each other through muscular-motoric language. The concept of **somatic resonance** for the bodily perception, through which the therapist senses processes in the patient, originated with him (Keleman, 1989; Section 15.2).

Jay Stattman (1993) linked transference to the imitative behaviour of the child in the early somatopsychic attachment. In his **Unitive Body Psychotherapy**, he brought together Reichian character analysis and vegetotherapy, Gestalt therapy, object relations theory and existential approaches (Marlock, 1993).

INTEGRATIVE BODY PSYCHOTHERAPY (IBP)

Jack Lee Rosenberg aimed to develop Gestalt therapy in a body-oriented direction. He described knowledge and esteem of the self in the sense of humanistic psychotherapy as the basis and the goal of psychotherapy work, but drew as well on the Reichian energy concept (Rosenberg et al., 1985). In his model of personality, he differentiates four layers: core self, primary scenario, character style and agency, a concept for protective and coping strategies learnt in childhood (Fischer, 2016). In terms of Gestalt therapy, IBP sees therapy as a process in which unresolved situations in one's own biography are brought to closure (Rosenberg et al., 1985). Akin to Biosynthesis, Integrative Body Psychotherapy is less a specific method and more an integration of various ways of working with breathing, movement, grounding or awareness (Kaul & Fischer, 2016).

HAKOMI

In the Hakomi method, Ron Kurtz (1983, 1990) has elaborated on the character structure theory of Reich and Lowen, but his methods are informed by the meditative principle of inner mindfulness, which he has declared to be the basic principle of treatment. Kurtz places body psychotherapy in the framework of the philosophical vision of constructivism, which was emerging at that time. His goal is that in therapy, clients attentively explore and realise how they shape their experiences themselves, so that a new organisation becomes possible. At a time when confrontative work with resistance was all the rage, Kurtz rejected any way of working which put pressure on the client. He saw the therapist as a companion – similar to a master in the Buddhist tradition – and not as an interaction partner in the transference process.

BREATHING METHODS

Those schools centring on deep breathing such as Stanislav Grof's **Holotropic Breathwork** (1985) or Leonard Orr's **Rebirthing** are closely related to the affect-inducing approaches in body psychotherapy. Both utilise a technique of deep, connected and accelerated inspiration and expiration without a pause between them, so as to induce changed states of experience. In Holotropic Breathwork, breathing is supported by loud, rhythmic music. The aim is a reactivation of perinatal experiences in states of non-ordinary consciousness (Section 11.1). Hyperventilation is induced voluntarily and can lead to strong bodily sensations, intense feelings and a shift in perception in an imaginative-symbolic direction (Teegan, 1986). Re-birthing is seen in body psychotherapy as problematic because of the strong destabilising effect and the problem of not handling hyperventilation well (Boadella, 1987; Levine & Macnaughton, 2004; Young, 2015b). In many cases, the use of invasive breathing techniques has led to re-traumatisation (Heller, 2012, p.306).

In his **Primal Therapy**, Arthur Janov (1971) gave therapeutic permission to scream with a theory, which saw the primal scream as the expression of childhood primal pain or even the pain of birth. Petzold (1984) rightly criticised this as pathologising birth. Janov thought that psychological pain is always a result of suppressed pain from traumatic childhood experiences. The concept of the key or 'primal scene' originated with him. According to this idea, a cluster of traumata gather into one scene, where the child reaches the point of denying their experiences and splits off thinking and feeling from the body. Janov aims to access these experiences through mobilising the body.

CONCENTRATIVE MOVEMENT THERAPY

The more experiential body psychotherapy movement developed in a different way from those schools derived from Reich. Concentrative Movement Therapy developed in Germany and Austria out of inpatient work with people not suited to verbal psychoanalytical therapy. This method can be traced back to Gindler (Section 3.1.2) and works through offering possibilities for self-experience with the aid of objects such as a ball, a rope or a stick, which Gindler had also used (Stolze, 1983, 2002). Movement is then interpreted symbolically in relation to its unconscious meaning. Thus Becker (1989) describes acting as a way to remember and to reawaken the unconscious. Concentrative Movement Therapy sees itself as a psychodynamic body psychotherapy (Schreiber-Willnow & Seidler, 2013) and draws theoretically mainly from the psychoanalytic theory of child development and theories of body image and body schema (Schmidt, 2006; Stolze, 2002). Concentrating on the body-self should lead to an intensification of the body-space image (Becker, 2010, p. 131). Just as in Functional Relaxation, this relates to the theory of the Gestalt cycle of Viktor von Weizsaecker (1997), in which he describes the unity of perception and movement and of speaking and thinking in understanding the world.

FUNCTIONAL RELAXATION

Functional Relaxation was developed by Marianne Fuchs (1989) out of a relaxation method using coordination with the spontaneous rhythm of the breathing (Section 3.1.2) and works with releasing the tension in the expiration (Bartholomew & Herholz, 2019). The patient should be fully awake so as to encourage proprioception. In contrast to the autohypnotic technique of autogenic training, Functional Relaxation is concerned with sensing the body in a state of full awareness. Therapy is seen as a sensory process of learning which works by broadening subjective experience. The approach is experiential and not self-disclosing, which is why in clinics the method was long used in addition to verbal psychotherapy and usually for somatic symptom and functional disorders, and is now used however also for anxiety or depression (Herholz et al., 2009). Von Arnim et al. (2022) link Functional Relaxation theoretically to the neurophysiology of proprioception, the theory of signs and psychoanalytic development theory.

EXPERIENTIAL BODY PSYCHOTHERAPY

Starting from Gindler's work, Charlotte Selver developed **Sensory Awareness** (Section 3.1.2), which Selver herself saw as an education to more awareness and not as a therapy (Lowe & Laing-Gilliatt, 2007) and which we have to number among the body therapies (Chapter 2). In this method, the senses are awakened through exercises and the faculty of perceiving in the 'here and now', for example the physical and emotional quality of the voice, of the posture or of movement (Brooks, 1986). After having met the religious philosopher Alan Watts, Selver linked her method to Eastern teachings of awareness, and as a teacher at the Esalen Institute, she had great influence on the development in the USA of somatic psychology and psychotherapy (Weaver, 2015; Section 3.7). Perls adopted her concept of awareness for his Gestalt therapy (Section 3.4).

Another source of experiential body psychotherapy in the USA was **Body-Mind-Centering** from Bonnie Bainbridge Cohen. Cohen was a dance teacher and ergotherapist and had studied also with the physiotherapist Berta Bobath, who was herself a student of Carola Speads (Hartley, 1995; Figure 3.2), so in a way she is a great-granddaughter of Gindler. Body-Mind-Centering focuses on self-knowledge through directly experiencing the body in its physical systems and aims to educate movement and restructure psychomotor patterns. The method sees itself as somatic learning, but was developed by Aposhyan (2004) into *Body-Mind Psychotherapy*. The same is true of the **Rosen Method** (Rosen & Brenner, 1991; Weaver, 2015, pp. 44–5). Rosen worked with psychiatric patients in England

and the USA and taught relaxation through breathing, massage and body-work as a gateway to awareness. Fogel (2009) integrated her work into psychotherapy. D. Johnson (2015) adds **Authentic Movement** from dance therapy and Gendlin's Focusing to the experiential methods. Authentic Movement teaches how to experience one's physical self directly through free associative movement and attempts to heighten awareness of the inner world through *kinetic meditation* (Payne, 2006). We can allocate this method to the dance therapies.

FOCUSING

Gendlin (1996) developed Focusing out of client-centred therapy. Focusing is a method of exploring the emotional appraisal of cognitive processes and situations on the basis of bodily sensations. The term was originally used in cognitive psychology for a style of perception in which people scan several stimuli at once. Focusing means therefore not focusing on details but directing awareness to the general perception of the body, organising from this a general emotional impression and then symbolising it. In six specified steps, the patient explores the feelings that arise in the belly and the chest in response to a situation or a question. With the help of this feeling, they can then test whether a perception or a thought is appropriate and whether a bodily sensation and a corresponding word fit together. The meaning felt in the body Gendlin calls the *felt sense*.

PESSO-THERAPY

Pesso-Therapy – or Pesso Boyden System Psychomotor, to give it its full name – is a completely independent school. Like dance therapy, it developed out of modern dance; however, it does not work with dance elements (Pesso, 1997). Originally, Pesso taught dancers how to convert emotions in the interaction with other dancers into dance movements. From there he developed a group therapy method whereby clients could explore their inner reality by sensing what the body does through role playing. By experiencing inhibitions in their emotional expression, body freezing, unfeelingness or actions not leading to the desired outcome, they can identify their childhood deficits in need satisfaction. Other members of the group play the role of important attachment figures in their biography, not as in psychodrama as these people themselves, but rather as the internalised object images of the client (Pesso, 1986). In bodily dialogue with these figures, for example with a fantasised mother, transference feelings are mobilised and old experiences presented as if on a stage, so that we see them as belonging to the past. In a next step, the role players offer as ideal parents what the child would have needed and so facilitate a corrective, healing experience (Pesso, 2015). Nowadays, Pesso's approach is also used in individual therapy (Schrenker, 2008).

ANALYTICAL BODY PSYCHOTHERAPY

The German psychoanalyst Tilman Moser adopted Pesso's approach (Moser & Pesso, 1991) as he was searching for a way out when psychoanalytical processes were stagnating because of the insistence on a method of mere verbal interpretation. Through body-work in scenes and through touch, Moser (1992, 2001) aims to discover split-off emotions in the transference relationship as a dialogue between the wounded child and its attachment figure. Similarly, Guenter Heisterkamp (1993) and Hans-Joachim Maaz (2001, 2008) aim to explore the transference in psychoanalysis and thus approach the experiences of early childhood.

From the initiatives of these psychoanalysts and the schisms in bioenergetics in Germany and Austria, analytical body psychotherapy has developed, in which working with the body is closely linked to intersubjective psychoanalysis (Geissler, 2009; Geissler & Heisterkamp, 2007). The body is seen as a medium of re-playing unconscious representations of early object relations experiences in facial expressions, gestures and actions. Psychotherapy is understood as being the situation wherein psychological complexes in the unconscious behaviour of the participants are restaged non-verbally – this is called enactment (Jacobs, 2001). In these scenic interactions, transference and countertransference processes can be worked through by interpreting the body language in the action-dialogue. Because of this broadening of the setting through enactments and action-dialogues, Heisterkamp calls analytical body psychotherapy an 'enhanced form of analytical psychotherapy' (2010, p. 301). From a body psychotherapy perspective, we can regard it as a direction within body psychotherapy.

INTEGRATIVE BODY AND MOVEMENT THERAPY

Integrative Body and Movement Therapy developed in a fusion of Ferenczian psychoanalysis, Gindler body-work, experiential approaches and the sensing mode of Gestalt therapy as a body-oriented therapeutic method within the broader theoretical framework of Hilarion Petzold's **Integrative Therapy** (Petzold, 2003; Petzold & Berger, 1980). The focus is on perceiving one's own living body, accessed through experimenting with posture, facial expressions, gestures, breathing and movement as well as the systematic exploration of the body (Waibel et al., 2009, p. 7). Petzold grounded his integrated approach in existential *Leibphilosophie*, lived-body philosophy, scientifically in psychophysiological and psychological research and on a broad base as a multimodal therapy. We can regard Integrative Body and Movement Therapy as one approach within body psychotherapy, but at the same time as part of Integrative Therapy founded by Petzold, which, in contrast to the other schools described here, is theoretically beholden to modern scientific research.

Petzold (2009, p. 30) describes all the schools as 'methodically grounded praxeologies' in which there is a pool of experience of treatment techniques. Many of them have hesitated to apply themselves to the task of integrating their experiential concepts in the formation of a scientific theory and offering them for discussion (cf. Heller, 2012, p. 105). However in the student generation this is changing. Whereas for example Lowen wanted to go *back to basics* and to working only with the body and its energy (J Miller, 2010), some of his students abandoned his one-person psychology (Schindler, 2002) and developed bioenergetic analysis further to a method which recognises the body, the relationship and the transference as three dimensions of therapy (De Clerck, 2008). A body psychotherapy which transcends the various schools should aspire to integrate the experiential knowledge they have bequeathed us with more recent clinical findings and scientific theories.

5

The living subject

Psychotherapeutic models are based on ideas about human beings (Buehler & Allen, 1972; Parfy & Lenz, 2009; Petzold, 2012). Body psychotherapy is based on a **holistic view of human beings** and sees them as body-mind beings in interaction with the world. We see this entity not from the outside as scientifically objectifiable, but as a unity in experience. In terms of time, this entity is the whole life process of a human being.

In the early stages of psychology, Wilhelm Wundt must have meant something similar when he wrote that the body and the soul are 'included in the direct reality of psychological experience' (Wundt, 1911, p. 393). Mental processes are processes of an embodied individual. Mental experience is founded on body experience, and body experience in turn is a mental process.

Greenberg and Van Balen see all experiential psychotherapy approaches as based on the assumption 'that human beings are aware, experiencing organisms who function holistically to organise their experience into coherent forms' (1998, p. 28). They are agents who purposefully act, create meaning and symbolisation and strive for survival, growth and meaning. Their subjective experience is an essential aspect of being human. Organisms being in uninterrupted self-movement generate a world of meaning (Froese, 2011, p. 211). Jakob von Uexkuell (2010) says too in his ecological theory that for a living being, the world is always a subjective, meaningful environment. The significance that human beings attribute to events is always embedded in communicative and culturally determined intersubjective meaning structures (Kriz, 2017, p. 238).

With this background, experiential body psychotherapy views humans as embodied, experiencing and acting beings in affect motor relationship to the world around them and organising their experiences in affect motor patterns. This is in accordance with the view of the theory of enactivism, whereby humans are beings acting in interactions (Varela et al., 1993). In my opinion, a fundamental theory of body psychotherapy should therefore be based on the idea of a subject in their lifeworld, on the theory of enactivism and a theory of experience and also be in line with a dynamic-systemic view of life (cf. Barlow, 2001; Section 7.3).

The notion of systems theory that in complex dynamic systems their components are working together is probably best able to integrate different scientific approaches to the human being, such as the biological and the psychological (Capra & Luisi, 2014). Also, systems theory is well-suited as a metatheory to integrate various psychotherapy approaches (Kriz, 2010). However here I will not be discussing this metatheoretical classification and will confine myself to developing a theory on a level that we need for therapeutic practice.

DOI: 10.4324/9781003176893-5

5.1 THE SUBJECT AND THEIR RELATIONSHIP TO THE WORLD

In the natural sciences, living beings are called organisms (Toepfer, 2005). From the point of view of systems theory, organisms are the elementary units of the living (Laubichler, 2005). The concept of wholeness applies mostly to organisms. Goldstein (1995), a neurologist and Gestalt psychologist, who was later involved with humanistic psychology, saw all that happens physiologically or psychologically as fundamentally taking place in the general context of the wholeness of an organism (Section 3.4, 10. Wholeness). Similarly, Maturana and Varela (1992) understand holism as being when all psychological functions are those of a single organism acting in relation to the world.

In body psychotherapy, it is not always clear whether as in systems theory **organism** is understood as the human being or whether the physical-chemical body is meant. Heller (2012, p. 3) uses the concept of the organism as a fundamental idea and equates it with 'the individual system' (Section 1.1); however, he also speaks of an 'organismic process' when addressing regulation processes of the immune system or of the cardiovascular system (e.g. Heller, 2012, p. 9)

Body systems

The physical body is a complex system, in which we can differentiate various subsystems: the nervous system, the cardiovascular system, respiration, skin, muscles, skeleton and the gastrointestinal, endocrine, reproductive and immune systems (Kutas & Federmeier, 1998, p. 136). However we can understand **body systems** not only as formations and structures but also **as processes**, since all cells or organs are in constant change and in constant exchange with one another in coregulating the body as process (see Fogel, 2009, pp. 41–2). Mental processes as well as brain activity depend on these body systems (Kutas & Federmeier, 1998) and are connected to them in a complex manner. Physical and psychological processes are, however, always manifestations of the activity of the whole system; it is not a case of one causing the other. For example, tears, which appear when we cry deeply, have a different chemical composition from those that appear through irritation such as dust (Fogel, 2009, p. 111). Moreover, we experience them differently. These connections should not be understood as causal, but as systemic (see Heller, 2012, p. 256).

A theory of the physical body requires one of the body systems, which a theory of body psychotherapy does not. Body psychotherapists should have sufficient knowledge of physiology, for instance of the connections between nutrition, neurotransmitters, metabolism and mood, when they are treating the depression of an overweight patient (Heller, 2012, p. 203), but they should not just connect clinical-psychological models with those of biology (Heller, 2012, p. 195).

In body psychotherapy, we are only dealing with the physiological regulatory systems of the physical body indirectly. Body psychotherapy necessarily influences these systems; for example, when someone cries deeply, then toxic stress hormones are flushed out (Fogel, 2009, p. 111), but it does not work directly with them as such. For instance, we have no means of regulating blood pressure to a specific level as does medicine, even if therapy does lead to a change in blood pressure. Our medium is that of working with the person and their subjectively experienced and acting body (Section 6.1).

Psychological experience is inextricably connected to physical function, but is not identical to it. When in body psychotherapy we describe an increase in pulse rate or a perspiring forehead, then we do so as part of the stress experience, as bodily behaviour. But we do not measure the pulse rate or the psychogalvanic skin reaction. Natural science is concerned with the observer's experience of things, psychotherapy with the way things *experience us* (Laing, 1967), i.e. with how something touches and moves us. As a subject, a human being is identical to their experience (Strawson, 2014).

Thus, psychotherapy cannot base itself on the concepts of the natural sciences (Chapter 7). The natural sciences provide us with concepts for understanding the world as objective nature, for instance, the chemical composition of a cold sweat, but not, however, for what makes a person at this moment in their lives break out in a sweat. The world appears differently to a living subject than it does to natural science. We can therefore understand living subjects with concepts which describe their experience and behaviour and which are accessible to us both introspectively and intersubjectively through our own self-experience (Heilinger & Jung, 2009, p. 26; cf. Gendlin, 1997, p. 227).

Therefore I propose a theory of body psychotherapy which focuses not on the concept of the organism, but on that of the **living subject in relation to their world** (Kriz, 2017). In this theory, the idea of wholeness refers to the **wholeness of experience** (cf. Soth, 2012, p. 63). Body experience is seen as the basis for self-experience. This perspective seems to me the most likely to do justice to the practice of body psychotherapy, where we work with the body on the experience and behaviour of our patients.

Important
The human being as an experiencing and acting subject in their life-world takes centre stage in a theory of experiential body psychotherapy.

The concept of the organism is important on a higher level for the development of a theory of dynamic systems such as Maturana and Varela (1992) advocate, where it can encompass the biological, neuroscientific and psychological view of the human being. Bringing together theories from these and other disciplines in metamodels is a task which goes far beyond the scope of this book. I would only ask that the concept of the organism not be made the focus of a **theory of therapy**, so as to avoid the danger of biologistic thinking and to concentrate on a theory of the human being as an experiencing subject.

Seeing a human being as a subject or as a **person**, a concept that William Stern (1927, 1930) introduced into psychology, is a hallmark of the humanistic approach to psychotherapy (Hartmann-Kottek & Kriz, 2005). A subject encounters the world from a **first-person perspective** and experiences this world in their own particular way. The concept of subject is therefore closely related to that of experience. It is a person who senses and feels. If someone has difficulty breathing or a pain in their hand, then this is a fact, but only a person can say that they are having difficulty breathing or have a pain in their hand. And the 'sufferer' is the one we comfort, not their organism (Wittgenstein, 1967, p. 125). Only a living subject can feel and articulate pain or need and have an interest in their own wellbeing.

From this point of view we can apply the concept of wholeness beyond the organism to the organism-environment system. Gendlin (2016) calls body-environment **one** concept, since both together are one process. He offers the example that when walking, both the ground and the foot participate in a living event. As parts of an interaction process, together they are an event. The body consists of 'body-environment-process events' and so is not just 'what is within the envelope of the skin' (p. 88). According to him, events determine the whole (Gendlin, 2016, p. 89).

Thompson (2010, pp. 427–31) follows such a relational concept of wholeness already on the level of the organism itself, since the properties of the parts have to relate to each other so that a whole is created consisting of these relationships. Thompson therefore speaks of **relational holism**.

With human beings, we have to include something more. Since a person can react reflexively to their organism-environment relationship, this simultaneously becomes a **person-world-relationship** (de Haan, 2020). They can relate to what they experience, describe the 'experiencing experience' and so bear witness to mental processes – for Damasio (2012) the hallmark of consciousness. As a person we are not only an organism, but we also have a conscious relationship to ourselves as an organism and to our biological response to the world; we can distance ourselves from ourselves, which Plessner (1975) has called 'eccentric positionality'. A **phenomenological psychology** therefore looks at a person in their relationship to themselves and to their lifeworld, at a *situated person* (Graumann, 1980; Graumann & Métraux, 1977).

Psychological processes belong to the **life processes**. They are generated by biological organisms and are dependent on a particular arrangement of matter, which, however, they transcend. Systems or wholes possess qualities which do not exist in the parts, but are created by the interaction between them. These are called **emergent properties**. Holistic and Gestalt psychology called this oversummativity. Mental processes belong to these emergent properties of organisms. They are not matter but events (Edelman, 1992, pp. 3ff).

One example of this is colour perception. Through light waves that we can measure but not see, stimuli in the external world induce the experience of a colour. However, this experience is not predetermined by the qualities of the light (Varela et al., 1993, p. 166). In fact, colour perceptions vary from species to species. Human vision is trichromatic, yellow-blue-red, whereas that of other living beings is not. In humans, colour impressions can be created by dreams or imagination. Sacks (1995) reports that a patient who could not see colours after an accident saw the world in 'rat colours' and was sometimes disgusted by it. Someone who does not see the world in colour experiences it differently (Sacks, 1997). Thus, the way we experience colour goes beyond the mere biological.

In philosophy, such phenomena are known as qualia, for instance the quality of the experience of a certain red colour (cf. Damasio, 2012, p. 241). Experience is created as organisms deal with their environment in their own particular way. It is not just a simple reflection of sensory stimulation (Hutto, 2011).

This theory is also well-suited for psychotherapeutic work, since we are always concerned with how people perceive reality in their own way. Because of their life story and current situation, they generate their own inner world in their dealings with the outside world. For example, depressives see the world sometimes as grey and colourless, metaphorically speaking.

Three models in body psychotherapy

Theory construction in body psychotherapy consists up to now of two basic models of how living beings relate to their environment and regulate inner processes:

- The one model is based on the **energy** involved in these processes. Most neo- Reichian schools adhere to this model. Reich thought that a unified force lies behind not only psychological and physical, but also organismic and non-organismic phenomena (Wehowsky, 2015, p. 164). This model sees the body as an **energetic body**.
- In another model, bodily manifestations are read as **signals** for inner processes, which in turn are coordinated by an exchange of signals (von Arnim et al., 2022, p. 39). This model presupposes a **semiotic body** as the conveyer of meaning. Psychodynamic body psychotherapists who do not adhere to the energetic model tend towards this one.

The one model corresponds to an energy paradigm, the other to an information paradigm (Section 7.3). Where the energy model ascribes psychological and physical manifestations to a common life energy, the information model sees the body as a network of signalling processes, accessible through deciphering the codes of the cells, the hormones or the language (T von Uexkuell, 2001).

The theory of enactivism, which I will discuss in more detail in Section 5.2, suggests a third model, according to which living beings relate to their environment through living activity itself (Varela et al., 1993). They constantly establish their identity anew and give the world meaning (Thompson, 2010, p. 153). Similarly, from a phenomenological perspective, Gadamer asserts that it is a fundamental fact of life that beings nurture themselves on something alien to them (2010, p. 257). From this point of view, life is essentially connecting to something, an **event in relationship** to the environment (Jonas, 2001). Human beings create their inner world in this event, in this life process, themselves (Section 5.2). This model is based on a **phenomenal body** in its living presence and relatedness.

Seen from the perspective of this model, mental disorders are not something that exist inside a person or in their 'energetic system', but are disorders of being-in-the world (Fuchs, 2019), in the relationship of a person to themselves, to others and to their lifeworld (Bolis et al., 2017; Spremberg, 2018).

Reich was looking for what was common in physical and psychological processes. Since his thinking was materialistic, he looked for this in the physical world and saw energy as something that forms both the psychological and the physical (Section 7.3). However, if we understand life not as something material but as processes, we reach a different conclusion: mental and bodily processes are aspects of unitary **life processes** (Chapter 2).

The three models influence the understanding of therapeutic treatment:

- In the **energy model**, therapy is focused on the regulation of energetic processes (Tonella, 2000). Thus, body psychotherapy can consist of steering the energy flow of a 'bioelectric field' (Boyesen, 1987, p. 166), or of an electromagnetic field, whereby Pierrakos (1987) does not rule out the use of apparatus. The energy model concurs with the ideas of early psychoanalysis in attributing symptoms to unconscious forces at work in the patient, which the therapist, however, can recognise. Here the therapist is working on the patient's energy flow, energy blocks or energy level with charge and discharge (Pechtl & Trotz, 2019, p. 37).
- In the **information model**, the body is understood as the bearer of meaning. The aim is to translate bodily sensations into language, the so-called semiotic progression (von Arnim, 1998, p. 34). This is seen either as intrapersonal, i.e. deciphering signals in their significance for the patient; or interpersonal, i.e. in their significance for the interaction. We find the interpersonal viewpoint in Geissler (2009, pp. 209ff), who views the body as an organ of communication for unconscious scenes in therapeutic interaction. According to this model, body psychotherapeutic methods aim at an understanding of the body as a communicator of processes to be interpreted symbolically. Here the therapist creates a process in which the patient learns to sense and read the body and its symbols on the intra- and interindividual levels.
- From the philosophy of **enactivism** and **phenomenology**, we can develop an understanding of therapy as working with the experience of meaning in an embodied relationship (Roehricht, 2015, p. 52). Here body psychotherapy means that through feeling all that is happening within themselves in the situational moment of the therapy session, a person experiences themselves psychologically and bodily in the relationship field in their whole being and lifeworld by discovering themselves and learning to regulate their needs, emotions and interactions.

I would like to illustrate this with a more detailed case study.

Clinical example

A patient with severe depression is going through a serious life crisis. Paul is searching for a new orientation both privately and professionally. He has feelings of worthlessness and guilt and is full of shame towards his daughter; he wakes up early full of self-reproach and believes that he is such a failure, he should die. As a Christian from a pious family, he prays a lot and asks God for mercy. He cannot forgive himself his sins.

Since his self-reproach is linked to a concept of God, I ask in the therapy session whether he has some unfinished business with God. He feels ashamed in front of God. God has given him many talents and is disappointed with how he uses them. I suggest that he speaks with God here in the therapy room. He should choose a place for God and one for himself. Spontaneously he lies down on the ground and starts with: 'Please don't hit me so hard'. He was never beaten as a child, but now he is afraid of blows to the back of the neck.

He kneels up, bows his head, puts his hands at the nape of the neck and in this position with a desperate and beseeching voice, he says to God: 'I'm sorry that I'm like this. Please forgive me my trespass, that I'm such a failure. Tell me what I have to do so that I will be okay. I don't know'. Then I ask him to speak to Paul as God. As God he sits down next to Paul, holds his hand over his head and says: 'I love you. Everything is alright. This is a misunderstanding. You don't have to lie on the floor'. Again we change the roles, so that he can experience how he reacts to God's words. He says: 'I don't believe you, you're not God, you're the good Samaritan. If you were God, you'd see what a piece of dirt I am'. Afterwards he feels empty, as if God was no longer there and he is left behind alone.

He does not see God in this figure. God has sent a 'snowflake' and is watching Paul and this Samaritan; he himself is cool, distant and 'hard as bone'. Paul is disappointed. He gets angry with this God and wants to get up and confront him. 'Tell me what you want from me!' In his fantasy, God says: 'I know the answer, but you have to find out for yourself, if you want to be worthy of me'. Standing and facing God, he is outraged. 'I'm sick of your arrogant smartass spiel!' he yells.

He learnt this kind of religion as a child. His successful father always felt like a poor sinner. In the child's eyes, his father was right up there with God. There are two parts of him in conflict: one rebels and refuses to let God destroy him, and the other is afraid of how he confronts God. In the session the rebel wins: 'Now I'm talking!' The 'earthworm' dares to attack God: 'I do my best and all you can do is moan on!' He recognises his father in this hard God and his mother in the Samaritan, who however used to say: 'It makes me so sad when you're like that', which he found poisonous.

In the following sessions, the patient came back to this theme again and again. It became a key experience. He was terrified that he would lose God. Nevertheless he also recognised that he would feel like a 'little turd' if he stayed with this idea of God. In the face of this gigantic, wordless and silent existence, he could only ever be guilty. It became distressingly clear to him that this God would never respond. In this non-response, he could also recognise his girlfriend. In later sessions, he said that he wanted to try 'God-fasting' and to take more responsibility for himself. The idea of not being guided by a higher power, but creating his life himself, was completely new. Concentrating on his own needs was very difficult for him.

The session described here begins with thoughts and feelings. These all have to do with the patient's relationship experiences, with his relationship to God and to his parents. Facing up to his relationship to God in a bodily confrontation evokes new ideas and feelings in him. He does not believe God and in the end gets angry with him. If he felt pathetic while lying down, standing up he felt stronger. The rage he felt in the confrontation changes his image of God. Everything that happens in the session is an integral process, consisting of thoughts, feelings, images, bodily postures, sensations and actions, which changes something in his relationship to God. As a child, he grew into a relationship pattern that is still operative today. The exploration of both himself and this relationship goes deeper and deeper as more parts of his experience come alive in the scenic work.

This description is a simplified sketch. In the one scene, I stood in for the girlfriend, which the patient found very enlightening. However I only sketch examples from therapy so as to illustrate some aspect of it. Here I wanted to show that body psychotherapy means not just extending therapy to bodily interventions, but promoting and deepening a holistic body and mind experience and shedding light on its significance for a person's relationship to themselves and to their lives. For this particular patient, what happened in this session, both bodily and psychologically, was a unified and interdependent experience.

Important
Body psychotherapy is not just about supplementing psychotherapy with bodily methods, but about treating human beings holistically as experiencing and acting subjects in their relationship with their environment and the world of others.

The holistic view of body and mind as a unified experience includes the idea of a unified process that we can observe on various levels: from the metabolic processes involved up to the thought images. Seen from outside, these can be separated, but they work together in the experience. This is always an integral experience of physical and psychological processes (Section 6.1). There is no body nor mind that can experience alone; both are 'abstracted aspects of the flow of organism-environment interactions that constitutes what we call experience' (M Johnson, 2007, p. 12).

In self-observation we can focus our attention more on the psychological or more on the physical processes. Accordingly, Fogel (2009, p. 43) differentiates between a 'conceptual self-awareness', which uses language, and an 'embodied self-awareness' of what one senses. Both exist, however, only in the relationship between brain and body and thus are both mental as well as embodied. In life processes such as affect expression, they appear together.

In psychotherapy, **body expression** is often regarded as a revelation of the soul. Even in the word **ex-pression**, the soul is the main part (Chapter 14). According to this, a person who throws their arms up is **showing** joy. While it is true that they communicate it in this way, it is not so – that first they feel joy and then they express it. Someone feels joy and the gesture itself is the joy. Psyche and physis do not interact in joy; they are one in the joy event. I can differentiate the inner feeling 'I'm happy' from the throwing up of the arms and speak about it independently of the gesture, or about the gesture independently of the accompanying feeling. However in the differentiation, both are still one and the one does not develop out of the other (cf. Geuter, 2000, pp. 1349–50). Goldstein (1995, p. 232) speaks similarly in his discussion of anxiety about the mental and physical phenomena of 'a unitary life process'. C. G. Jung expressed it as follows:

The spirit is the life of the body seen from within, and the body the outward manifestation of the life of the spirit – the two being really one.

(Jung, 1971, § 195)

Circular causality

We often hear of mutual feedback (Aposhyan, 2004, p. 28) or **bi-directionality** between body and mind (Goodill et al., 2013, p. 67; Tschacher & Storch, 2017, p. 118). These ideas are problematic, as they suggest that physical and psychological processes take place separately and then influence each other. However, psychological and bodily experience is not divided in two; it is one whole (Depraz, 2008; Payne et al., 2019a).

We can better describe the connection between mental and physiological processes with a model of **circular causality** (Fuchs, 2020, p. 9). According to this, the living physical body is the organic foundation for the experienced body, whereas the experienced body forges both the processes and the structures of the objective body. In systems theory, circular causality is regarded as an attribute of self-organisation phenomena, in enactivism as a systemic characteristic of life (Thompson, 2010, p. 138; cf. Dumouchel, 2019). Physical processes do not create mental ones, nor do mental processes create physical ones. Both are connected in circular causality as co-emerging processes of a living system (Chapter 7).

The causalities that matter in psychotherapy are life causalities. If we have the flu, we have caught a virus that causes changes on the basic level of bodily regulative processes. We become aware of this in our body experience as heat or weakness. The reason behind this body experience is, however, not the bodily changes, but the virus. If my stomach constricts because someone has offended me or I have diarrhoea because I am afraid, then it is not my feelings that are the reason for the reaction of the body, but whatever has offended me or made me afraid. The idea of bidirectionality misses these lifeworld causes of events.

With somatic symptom disorders, for example, it is of no help to look at whether the body is influencing the psyche or the psyche is influencing the body. These are always the problems of a human being, and clinically we have to base our therapy on the whole process (Heedt, 2020). From a pragmatic point of view, however, we can act on the assumption that psychological processes are influencing the bodily ones and vice versa. For instance, we can improve a depressive mood by encouraging the patient into fitness training, running or jumping (Blumenthal et al., 2007; Koch et al., 2007; Mei et al., 1997). In body psychotherapy, we can evoke a feeling of joy through thoughts, memories or images as well as through expressive movements such as throwing up the arms. Both approaches activate joyful feelings as a whole. We can augment the exploration of experiences by asking about both bodily and psychological aspects and connecting these. Thus, for example, we can ask patients:

- How does your thought affect your body?
- What happens inside when you have this or that memory?
- What thoughts or images come up when you have this or that feeling?
- What occurs to you when you throw your hands up?

The essence of an experiential body psychotherapy consists of helping the patient to learn how to discover themselves in their whole process of experience and action and how to regulate it.

We work not with body–mind interaction, but with the body-mind human being, with their thinking, dreaming, remembering, feeling, reflecting, sensing, moving, perceiving, breathing, playing. And as therapists we are also body-mind beings. Thus psychotherapy is an encounter between two living, embodied subjects.

Phenomenologically we start out from the 'life movements' (Heisterkamp, 2007) of the experiencing subject (cf. Sheets-Johnstone, 1999). As psychotherapists we are concerned with subjects who are suffering and failing to live a satisfactory life. Their suffering is not an objective diagnostic finding, but a subjective state. This state can consist of individual symptoms, physical or psychological, but it is always a state of the whole person.

Fuchs (2005) describes depression as a state in which a person no longer feels connected with their environment through their body, but that the body is more an obstacle in their way, separating the subject from the world. In psychopathology, this is described as a psychomotor inhibition. It is accompanied by feelings of emptiness, shame and guilt or by negative thoughts about oneself. A depression is neither a biological nor a mental disorder, but an illness of the whole person, which can be treated with technical methods (transcranial magnetic stimulation), biochemical methods (psychotropic medication), social methods (moving house, moving to a new job, changes in the relationship), psychological methods (psychotherapy) or somatic and psychological methods (body psychotherapy) (Chapter 2). Whichever method is chosen, they all influence the whole person and have an effect on the physical, the psychological and on the relationship level. We are not treating the disorder; we are treating the suffering person as a bio-psycho-social being with a specific disorder.

Change through body psychotherapy is only one of many possible avenues of change. Human experience and behaviour can also be altered through a brain operation, psychotropic drugs or physical movement. In particular it can change when the larger contexts of life change: friendship, family relationships, work conditions, financial situation or living conditions. At times these can all have more influence than psychotherapy.

5.2 ENACTIVISM AND THE EMBODIED MIND

As one of the major psychotherapeutic approaches, body psychotherapy today could take as its theoretical base that of **enactivism** (Di Paolo & Thompson, 2014; Gallagher, 2020; Hutto, 2013; Kyselo, 2013; Thompson, 2010; Varela et al., 1993). Now it is the leading theory in the field of **embodied mind** (Heiner, 2008) and emphasises in particular action, an active relationship to the environment and social interaction (Gallagher, 2019). The theory contends that living beings create their perception and cognition 'in action', meaning in embodied activity in the world, which is based on sensorimotor skills (Stewart et al., 2010a; Velmans, 2007). Accordingly, consciousness is neither a product of the mind nor a function of the brain, but is created in the living relationship of a being to the world (Fuchs, 2017; Noë, 2010).

According to enactivism, cognition always involves an individual in relation to the world, making sense of it. Thompson (2010, p. 158) equates *enaction* with *sense-making*. Since this view corresponds to the phenomenological theory of intentionality, enactivism is especially connected to phenomenology (Gallagher, 2008; Gallagher & Bower, 2014; Sheets-Johnstone, 2010). The enactivist theory, however, applies the idea of embodied relating not only to cognition but also to affects and social interactions (Colombetti, 2014, 2017; Gallagher, 2021).

Hutto (2013) sees in enactivism a possible new paradigmatic basis for psychology as a whole. However, it is debatable whether the theory is also valid for higher cognitive processes such as conscious, distanced reflection, or whether we have to differentiate embodied strategies of intelligence from abstract ones (cf. Clark, 1999, p. 150; Froese, 2011; Gallagher, 2005, p. 4). At all events, the claim is that the theory conceptualises a general non-dualistic idea of psychological activity (Velmans, 2007).

Embodied mind, however, means not just that there is mind or consciousness only in a body and its relationship to the world, but also that there is only a **subjectively experienced body in a mind that experiences this body as experiencing** and being aware of itself. We can call this last the **mindful body**. When I use the term embodied mind, I mean both.

Important
The basic starting point of body psychotherapy is the notion of mind and body as a unity, which at the same time we can differentiate from one another.

Another concept we encounter in the context of embodied mind is that of **embodiment** (Section 1.3). Several areas of psychotherapy have taken up this concept (Bohne, 2008, 2012; Garcia et al., 2022; Hauke & Kritikos, 2018; Jahn, 2016, 2018; Leuzinger-Bohleber, 2015; Leuzinger-Bohleber et al., 2013); however, it is not used consistently but on three different levels:

1. **Theoretically**, it describes the aforementioned idea that mind is embodied and is always related to the whole body. Mind, brain and body in turn are seen as embedded in the environment. Thompson and Varela (2001, p. 425) express this in the formula '*embodied and embedded*'. Leuzinger-Bohleber and Pfeiffer (2013, p. 16) describe embodiment in this sense as a basic scientific concept (cf. Glenberg, 2010).
2. **Phenomenologically**, embodiment is seen as experiencing oneself through one's body, living in the body and being aware of this self-perception (Giummara et al., 2008, p. 151; Totton, 2015, p. 9; Westland, 2019, pp. 256–7). The inability to do so is referred to as *lack of embodiment* or *disembodiment*. Kozlowska (2005) speaks of a *disembodied mind* when self-perception is separated from the body by anxiety (cf. T Fuchs, 2005).
3. **Clinically**, the concept of embodiment is used for the practice of awareness, in which the patient is somatically alert for all inner processes (Aposhyan, 2004, pp. 52–3; Caldwell, 2018; Cheney, 2019) or integrates the sensory, emotional and intelligence aspects of the self within the limits of its bodily structures (Bloom, 2006, p. 5). Aposhyan also uses the concept for the embodied presence of the therapist.

Around the concept of embodiment, a whole field of research has developed in psychology, the cognitive sciences and phenomenological philosophy and in interdisciplinary, empirical research on body experience, studying empirically the basis of cognitions and emotions in sensorimotor processes (Adams, 2010, p. 619; De Preester & Tsakiris, 2009). In experimental psychology, the relationship between somatic states, above all bodily expression and body posture on the one hand and thinking and affects on the other, have been extensively researched. As embodiment, Barsalou et al. (2003, p. 43) describe posture, arm movements or facial expressions which are generated in social interaction and play a large part in processing social information. I will depict the relevant research in Chapter 8. In this chapter I am concerned with the theoretical concept.

The theory of embodied mind originated in the cognitive sciences. These had for decades followed the theory that the human mind processes symbolic information as does a computer and that emotions are amodally registered pure information (Heiner, 2008, p. 118; Winkielman et al., 2008, p. 264). The mind was seen as the guiding central instance of thinking and the brain as its seat. In this age of huge ecological destruction, however, the enlightment faith in the power of reason and governing centres is shattered. Moreover, the digital revolution of communication forms has resulted in people perceiving the connection between things that they earlier would have seen as separate; empathy with others has matured and with it the recognition of the worlds of feeling (Rifkin, 2009). The new social net, developing from the bottom up, encourages a new way of looking at human nature (Section 6.4). We no longer see it as a system controlled from the top down, but as the interaction of various functions and experiential spheres. This opens our eyes to the connections between thinking, feeling, bodily sensations, attitudes and behaviours.

Artificial intelligence and the living body

In the wake of the failure of research into artificial intelligence, the long dominant computer models of the mind began to flounder. The prognosis of the 1960s, that we would quickly be building **humanoid machines**, did not come to pass (Tschacher, 2006). It soon became clear that this was because machines have no independent relationship to the world, which in living systems is mediated by the body. For example, when we walk, the elastic movement of the knee is so fast that it most probably has to be explained by a two-way system in the muscles, as a neuronal network in the central nervous system cannot react so quickly (Pfeifer & Bongard, 2007). If we want to build robots that perform more than the simplest tasks, then we have not just the problem of the hyper-complexity of human movement (Heller, 2012, p. 186), but also that of how we can make them emulate the skill of living beings in adapting to their environment, reacting creatively to unexpected damage and repairing themselves (Bongard et al., 2006; Froese & Ziemke, 2009; Pfeifer et al., 2007). In order to develop real artificial intelligence, the machines would have to be connected to the world through a body. As yet complex human actions, such as catching a ball, cannot be emulated by digitally reproducing these functions.

Robots can learn to move, but their basic difference from living beings is that the latter have their own energy budget, which they can continually refresh through a metabolic exchange with the environment and thus maintain their balance (Boden, 1999). Also, they can create meaning for themselves from their bodily relationship to the environment. In self-sustaining biological systems, the organism develops consciousness by contextualising on a higher level what it embodies. Jordan and Ghin (2006) call this *embodied aboutness*. Computers are not equipped to do this.

Thus, in the cognitive sciences, the body has returned to cognition (Heiner, 2008). The view that cognition belongs to embodied subjects existing in the world has become the leading paradigm (Adams, 2010, p. 619). This paradigm brings together theoretical biology, phenomenological philosophy and empirical research in psychology and the neurosciences. Body psychotherapy fits into this paradigm.

Inner purposiveness

Unlike functionalism, which sees the body from the perspective of its functions, enactivism sees it as a self-individualising system that generates meaning and has its own intrinsic purpose (Di Paolo & Thompson, 2014). The body determines what a person perceives, how they act and how the world affects them (Gallagher, 2005, p. 17). For example, three-dimensional vision develops only in a moving relationship to the world. Thus Noë (2010) compares consciousness to dance, which is created in movement in the world. Mental content is not viewed as projections of the internal world, as it is in the knowledge theory of idealism, nor as representations or images of the world. Rather it consists of experiences with the world, made possible by the body. Varela et al. (1993) call this the 'middle way between subjectivism and objectivism'.

In an experiment, Reed et al. (2004) studied the evidence that we represent a bear according to its appearance, a bicycle according to its function and the body according to what it can do. Perceived objects were not all stored according to the same set of categories. Probably each object representation depends on how we interact physically with the object (cf. Gallese, 2003, p. 521).

Living systems have an inherent purposiveness and an independent activity which cannot be predicted (Heilinger & Jung, 2009, p. 23). As early as 1962, the Gestalt psychologist Wolfgang Metzger said it was characteristic that they were the source of their own forces and impetus (Kriz, 2001, p. 164). Living systems create a world through cognition, but at the same time recognise the reality of the outside world. In the framework of their constructivism, Maturana and Varela (1992) emphasise that we are without a doubt in the world, but at the same time, only what we experience is a given. The significance of continually experiencing the world only becomes clear when the connection is broken.

That living beings create their own inner world as experiences in the life process in interaction with the outer world has been called **autopoiesis** by Maturana and Varela. From a biological viewpoint, because of their metabolism, autopoietic systems also have the capacity for **self-regulation,** meaning regeneration and self-preservation (Jordan & Ghin, 2006). Psychology can accept this point of view: we view the capacity for psychological self-regulation as being developed through interactive experiences. When there are psychological difficulties, it can break down. Reviving self-regulation is a relevant goal of therapy (cf. Watson et al., 1998, p. 3; Chapter 17).

Living beings as operationally closed systems

According to the theory of autopoiesis, multicellular living beings are operationally closed systems characterised by a network of dynamic processes whose effects do not exceed the net (Maturana & Varela, 1992). Both the nervous system and the cognitive system count as operationally closed, as their processes retroact on themselves and the networks involved are determined by inner mechanisms of self-organisation. The outcomes of processes carried out by elements of the system remain in the system (Colombetti, 2017). However, this does not mean they are independent of the environment; living beings are connected to it. Maturana and Varela (1992) call this **structural coupling**. They assign communication and consciousness to the area 'social coupling', since mind as the phenomenon of being-in-language is not found in the brain but in the interaction.

The concept of the operationally closed system does not therefore contradict the understanding of the human being as an **open system** (Allport, 1960; Bertalanffy, 1950). Openness means here that because of their inner characteristics, the human being is constantly developing new states in their interaction with the environment. These in turn affect the system itself which, being operationally closed, can maintain its identity over time (Thompson & Varela, 2001). From a systems theoretical perspective of living beings, their organisation constitutes their relationship to the world.

Action and experience

Maturana and Varela (1992) talk of the circularity of action and experience, Varela et al. (1993) of the unity of perception and action. In 1940, von Weizsaecker (1997, p. 124) expressed something similar with his principle of the unity of perception and movement in his teaching on the Gestalt cycle, as did Jakob von Uexkuell (2010) in 1956 with his combining of perception in the 'perception world' and action in the 'action world' into a common functional cycle. Today movement scientists accept this interconnection (Wollny, 2012, pp. 67–8).

According to Bergson (1911, pp. 219–20) there is no fundamental separation between the object and perception of it, since perception consists of a relationship with the object. When I hear something, I experience this perception as if it is there where the sound is coming from. When I lift a heavy object, I feel the weight through the tension in my muscles, but this sensation is bound to my action and to the object I am lifting (Reddy, 2008, p. 121).

Perception takes place in a mostly moving, active, bodily interaction with the environment. A person makes their environment accessible by focusing with their eyes on an object, turning towards something, taking something in their hand, listening to a sound, approaching something and examining it or turning away from it. This is particularly true of life experiences and social interactions, the effects of which we are dealing with in psychotherapy.

For therapy, this means that the more a person extends their field of perception, moves around and looks at things, listens, senses or tastes them, the more of the world they perceive. The world does not just present itself to us, but it emerges through the way in which we each relate to it. When patients can perceive themselves more attentively, this can change the way they experience the world. This is why *perceiving* and *awareness* are the basic principles of body psychotherapeutic practice (Geuter, 2019).

Clinical example

A patient with anxiety and depressive symptoms is sent to me by a psychiatrist. He speaks of his enormous restlessness. I notice that he is sitting on the edge of the chair, as if he was just about to leave. I point this out to him. He was in the navy, he says, and always sits as if on a heaving boat with no foothold. He likes to sit where he can see the door, so that he can leave quickly. Here he is talking about a schema: he approaches the world with a feeling of insecurity and vigilance.

I suggest we do a behavioural experiment: he could sit back in the chair and lean on the backrest. When he does this he notices an uneasiness. He presses his lips together.

Leaning back is 'a bit funny'. I ask him what he means by that and whether he can describe in more detail what he senses. His neck and shoulders are loosening up. I ask him how this loosening up feels, and he says he has a feeling of having more time, as if stress and pressure were fading away. A small change has taken place in his schema. I point out that he often presses his lips together. He had not been aware of that. I suggest we do another experiment in which he consciously presses his lips together and then let's go. He does so and says: 'This is somehow better'. His jaw is looser. Then he starts to speak about his anxiety. The fear is like being tied up tightly. He always has to tense up so as not to make a mistake. Now we can speak about his fear as something he has and which he can at the same time observe. As the tension sinks he can face the feeling of fear governing his schema. Experimenting with bodily behaviour and becoming aware of the ideomotor signals have changed his experience of himself and have opened up the possibility of experiencing the world differently.

The theory of enactivism builds a bridge to the theory of experience. De Jaegher and Di Paolo (2007, p. 487) allocate five concepts to enactivism: autonomy, sense-making, embodiment, emergence and experience. Autonomy means here that living systems have their own self-created identity as differentiated entities. Thus the enactive paradigm becomes part of the systemic perspective of autopoiesis (Hutto, 2010). Sense-making means that through actively connecting to living beings and objects, meaning is created, formed by relationships and coloured by affects (cf. De Jaegher & Di Paolo, 2007, p. 488). Embodied perception does not simply reproduce the environment; rather, it enacts meaning (Varela et al., 1993). The body is an inner universe of meaningful experience. As embodied beings, we absorb the world in the form of experiences, which constitute patterns of organism–environment relationship (M Johnson, 2007, p. 117).

At the end of the 19th century, the philosopher Franz Brentano called the fact that the mind focuses on objects **intentionality**. Beings with a mind can refer and relate to others (Edelman, 1992). Enactivism understands this directionality as a phenomenon anchored in perception and action (Newen, 2013, p. 42). Thus, simple directionality is coupled with perspective vision and the seizing of objects (Newen, 2013, p. 47). Images of objects are only a higher level of directionality whereby, for example, the understanding of the intentions of others takes place. Husserl understood experience too as intentional, because it is always something that is being experienced and meant (Gadamer, 2010, p. 72).

What in everyday life people call an object is always something they can relate to actively. Blood cells are not seen as objects since we cannot interact with them. However, cells can become the objects of viruses, when they are attacked by them, or objects of scientific investigation in the lab. Also the Milky Way is not seen as an object as we cannot interact directly with it.

Thus, objects have affordance (Chemero, 2011; Gibson, 1979; M Johnson, 2007, p. 47). When we recognise something, we relate to it. Gallese and Sinigaglia (2011, p. 127) even think that the action-related perception of the affordances of objects is our primary connection to the environment. Objects with affordances activate the motor neurones even if we do not act. Thus, we would perceive the world in terms of possibilities for bodily action. However, in perceiving something as graspable, we perceive ourselves as bodies which can grasp. Therefore the self would be first of all a bodily feeling for the possibility of action (Gallese & Sinigaglia, 2010; Section 6.5).

Rubber hand illusion

If you stroke a finger of a test person's hand, which they cannot see, several times with a small stick and at the same time that of a rubber hand that they *can* see, then after a while they are quite sure that their own finger is being stroked even when only the rubber one is (Botvinik & Cohen, 1998). The body has an illusion of sensation.

Tsakiris et al. (2006) modified the experiment by moving the fingers of the test person's own hand and of the rubber hand. In the case of movement, the illusion spread to other, neighbouring fingers, even though they were not moving nor were their muscles stimulated. In the case of touch, the illusion only developed in the touched finger. The researchers deduced that the active body is more readily perceived as coherent and uniform than the passive one (Tsakiris et al., 2006, p. 431). A sensory input does not have the same effect on a body part as does an action.

In another experiment by Senna et al. (2014), the test person laid a hand on the table and, invisibly to them, the back of it was lightly tapped with a hammer. When at the same time they heard the sound of a hammer hitting marble through earphones, after 5 minutes they had the sensation as if their hand were stiffer, heavier and less sensitive.

Mental processes extend to objects in the world (Clark & Chalmers, 1998). This is especially true when we act practically in the world with our bodies or when we test the resolution of a task, for example, when we determine the point at which we can catch a flying ball (Clark, 1999, p. 346). In cognitive science, this is known as **extended mind**. An example used by Merleau-Ponty (2012) is that of a blind person feeling their way with their stick. The blind person extends their body image into the tip of the stick and can perceive objects with it, even though they know that the stick does not belong to their body (De Preester & Tsakiris, 2009, p. 3, 10–11). The stick is part of their active exploration and recognition of the environment.

The intelligence of the living not only extends to the environment; it is also connected to it. You cannot separate the swimming motion of a tuna from the flow of the water, which it uses to speed up. How children learn to walk depends on what stimulation their feet receive (Thelen & Smith, 1994); how an adult walks depends on whether they are on a staircase, in the forest or carrying a load on their back (Koch & Fischman, 2014, p. 5). Dynamic systems are continually interacting with a changing world. This is called **embedded mind**.

Thus for a new understanding of mind we have the '**four Es**': *embodied, enactive, extended* and *embedded*. Gallagher (2021) adds the 'four As': *affect, agency, affordance* and *autonomy*.

Human consciousness is, according to this view, neither a mental construction (for example by the brain) nor a reflection of reality, but a state in which the whole person is in an active interchange with the world with their body (cf. Fuchs, 2008, p. 369–70). It is 'a kind of active attunement to the world' (Noë, 2010, p. 166).

Clinical application

Merritt (2015) applies enactivism to dance: as Hutto and Myin (2013, p. 8) see mental phenomena as activities, so for her in dance thought and movement melt together. Here movement does not express something, but is itself the meaning.

Dance improvisation is not the translating of thoughts into movement, but allows movement to happen; similarly, affect motor dynamics develop in a body

> psychotherapeutic session when we allow an inner process to happen and we look for what this happening itself reveals. In this way, we allow the patient to discover meaning in the whole of their own experience. As in dance improvisation a story unfolds which the dancer has not previously devised, so in therapy a story unfolds in autonomic bodily processes (Chapter 2, Perspectivity).

The theory of enactivism is in accordance with the emphasis on **experience** in humanistic and body-oriented psychotherapy. Rogers (1959) saw in experience the fundamental facts of existence and made conscious experience the main focus of treatment (cf. Greenberg, 2011; Weiss, 2015). Since the humanistic turn, body psychotherapy has embraced this (Section 3.7). Koch and Fischman (2014, p. 4) also see an accordance of enactivism with basic principles of dance and movement therapy.

> For enaction, experience is central both methodologically and thematically. Far from being an epiphenomenon or a puzzle … experience in the enactive approach is intertwined with being alive and enacting a meaningful world.
>
> (De Jaegher & Di Paolo, 2007, p. 488)

For Myin and Hutto, 'subjective experiences are identified with environmentally embedded, temporally and spatially extended and worldly interactions of organisms' (2009, p. 28). They are what sensitive beings make of their perceptions (Hutto, 2011). Early experiences live on in the way in which we experience the world today and how we approach it:

> The secret to explaining what structures an organism's current mental activity lies entirely in its history of previous engagements and not in some set of internally stored mental rules and representations.
>
> (Hutto & Myin, 2013, p. 9)

From the perspective of body psychotherapy, early experiences are not only stored as cognitive schemas but constitute **life and experience patterns**, which with Downing (1996), we call affect motor schemas. These patterns, acquired in early life, organise experience and predetermine the individual structure of experience (Chapter 12). They exist in a person's psychological organisation and their corporeality and at the same time in interaction.

A statement of Leuzinger-Bohleber and Pfeifer, a psychoanalyst and a robotics researcher, reads like body psychotherapeutic theory:

> Early experiences of interaction determine as 'embodied memories' further development and the spontaneous (non-cognitive) expectations and unconscious interpretation of new interaction situations.
>
> (Leuzinger-Bohleber & Pfeifer, 2013, p. 23)

In a different conceptual language, this means that it is not pure cognition but the affect that motor schemas acquired biographically that shapes present experience of interpersonal relationships. The past lives on in the patterns in which we experience the world, out of which results how we think and speak about it and how we are active in it.

Clinical application

Body psychotherapy pays particular attention to embodied action in the present moment in the therapy session. The therapist takes notice not just of what the patient says, but also how they behave (Heller, 2012, pp. 13ff). This corresponds to the phenomenological method of focusing on the how instead of on the what: how does the patient speak about themselves, how do they present themselves physically, how do they experience their symptoms and how does what they say feel in the body?

In body psychotherapy, we regard the human being as someone who creates their own inner world on the basis of their life-story and of the relevant present situation. Meaningful experience is created from their own subjective way of approaching reality, which developed out of and is inscribed in living experience. We do not see the inner world as determined. Experiences create patterns, but these patterns are actualised in every moment by the living human being, who experiences in them the world and acts accordingly. In this way they can be writ anew. As a rule, however, we tend to follow well-worn paths. Therapy means to deviate here and now from these, to follow new ones and thus to have more satisfying experiences.

Therapy – changing dispositions

In therapy we are trying to change **patterns** of experience and behaviour, as these are the **dispositions** which create symptoms and are therefore what psychotherapy essentially treats. Due to a disposition, for example when there is concealed anger that someone else might notice, we could feel arousal only as anxiety.

Dispositions are characteristics that appear when something happens. For instance, if it is the manifest quality of a pane of glass to be transparent, then one of its dispositional qualities is that it will shatter when a stone is thrown at it (Newen, 2013, pp. 22–3). Thus we need, in addition to the symptom of the shattering, a disposition and an event. In psychodiagnostics we therefore differentiate between structural dispositions and triggering events (cf. Arbeitskreis OPD, 2009, p. 114).

Psychological dispositions are assumptions about characteristics. For instance, intelligence is not a manifest quality because it is only what we define as intelligence and which we ascribe to something we can measure, such as the ability to solve certain problems (Velden, 2013). A manifest characteristic would be someone having red hair, a dispositional one someone being inclined because of a vulnerability to be anxious in intimate situations, or because of a fear of loss developing a depression when they have lost a loved one. Only in interaction with the world do dispositions appear as structuring causes (cf. Newen, 2013, p. 25). From the point of view of systems theory, they are ordering forces or so-called operators which create order (Kriz, 2004a, p. 39).

5.3 EXPERIENCE AND MEANING

A person's interaction with the external world creates a phenomenal world of experience. As early as 1962, Gendlin (1997, p. XIV) emphasised that experiencing is never only an inner reaction, but always a meaningful interaction. Through our subjective experience, we realise the world in its meaningfulness for us and our recognition of our place in the world is 'immediate, embodied, holistic, and contextual' (Bohart, 1993, p. 52). In experience, a subjectivity that cannot be verified objectively expresses itself (cf. Gadamer, 2010, p. 359). Therefore in therapy there are no 'right' experiences which, from the point of view of the therapist, a patient should have, but only familiar ones or new ones, which prove to be of value or not. And the valuable experiences are often those we would never have expected.

In their seminal paper on the function of experience, Heilinger and Jung (2009) see phenomenal experience as a feature of the natural world. It belongs to human nature. In the interaction with the environment, experience fulfils many functional roles, for example the integration of cognitive and sensorimotor processes (Heilinger & Jung, 2009, p. 3). Experience shows us how something is for a subject, how the subject produces and processes information in interaction with the environment and how this affects their well-being (Heilinger & Jung, 2009, p. 2). Qualitative experience guides human action in many ways: the sense of self stabilises our feeling for action, 'intentional feelings motivate us to act, perceptive qualities secure our orientation in space' (Heilinger & Jung, 2009, p. 8).

For body psychotherapy, Weiss writes: 'Here, I will use the term "experience" in reference to the *qualities of subjectively perceptible events within*, such as emotional nuances and their depth, variations of complex body sensations, or the related networked mental processes' (Weiss, 2015, p. 419). Rogers (1959) understands experience as everything that happens in an organism and is accessible to consciousness. 'To experience means to receive the impact of sensory or physiological events happening in the moment' (Greenberg & Van Balen, 1998, p. 30). Gendlin writes: 'I use the word "experiencing" to denote *concrete* experience...' and later: 'we can direct our attention inward, and when we do that, there it is' (1997, p. 11). He considers experience to be so complex that we can only ever capture it approximately.

Qualitative experience contains a wealth of associations which attach themselves to a psychological process such as a perception or an intention and lend each one a certain colouring. The basic determinants of this colouring are the emotional states (cf. Greenberg, 2011), ranging from a fundamental state of mind through moods to violent affects (Chapter 10). Emotional states also determine people's cognitive access to the world (Bermpohl, 2009). Since emotional dysfunction is at the core of mental disorders, we try to influence disturbed experience through the modification of emotions according to body psychotherapeutic principles (Geuter, 2019).

Important
In experience, perceptions gain personal significance through their emotional colouring and relevance for a person's needs.

Living beings relate internal and external inputs to themselves according to the principle of self-relevance (Bermpohl, 2009, p. 223). Through emotional experience, they evaluate relevance for their needs and well-being (Chapter 10). Subjects process inputs not through rules like a computer, but according to their significance, which is not dependent only on the present situation, since various experiences merge into one composite. What we experience is a Gestalt formed through our biography. How someone experiences the colours of the setting sun or the sting of pain is all part of a flow of experience formed throughout their life (cf. Heilinger & Jung, 2009, p. 10). Meanings are always part of how current life events combine with past ones and what this implies for present or future experiences and behaviours (M. Johnson, 2007, p. 265).

In experience, therefore, a temporal entity is created, among other things. Human beings carry their past within them as embodied memories, but also as fantasies, bodily impulses and needs, as well as outlines of their potential (Gendlin, 1997, p. 25). We feel all this primarily in the body. Body experience is thus the most important access to experiencing as well as to deciding and acting (Chapter 6). The body is our 'store' and our 'compass'; it tells us where we come from and where we want to go (Koeth, 2013, 2014).

However, we only experience what we sense in the body as congruent when we can name it. Thus, differentiated language is a central agent of differentiated experience (Heilinger & Jung, 2009, p. 12). If the therapist uses language richly and exactly, this helps the patient to become aware of what they have felt and experienced (Geuter, 2019, pp. 371–86).

Our task in therapy is to help the patient become conscious of and understand their experiences. This presupposes that they are not avoiding experiencing something of importance. Therefore, therapy focuses particularly on the undefined, implicit feelings and on what is not yet known (Hendricks, 1986).

> Body psychotherapy works basically with **change in awareness**. Whereas in everyday life we pay most attention to the environment or to the intentional objects of what we are planning to do (Gallagher, 2005, p. 27), for example the dishes that I am setting the table with, in therapy we direct our attention to the inside, to what we are experiencing. We change gears from our everyday connection with the world more or less on 'autopilot' (Crook, 1987) to conscious perception. The body, which interacts with the world in everyday activity, now becomes the explicit object of our conscious perception and thus appears as clearly distinct from the world (Gallagher, 2005, p. 29). The body now becomes explicitly **my** body, which mediates my subjective relationship to the world. When my attention is directed inwards to the body as object, I can then perceive it as subject. Gindler spoke of 'listening inwardly' (Ludwig, 2002, p. 111). An awareness of the body as an object seen from outside, for example as anatomy or physiology, is not a determining factor for self-awareness (Cassam, 2014).
>
> Paying conscious attention to the experience of the body brings a person into the present in which the experience exists (Metzinger, 2005). We tend to quickly forget what we are not observing consciously. However, we cannot call something an experience unless we are paying attention to it (Lamme, 2003).

Feeling

We can only experience something when we sense something. Having sensations is a characteristic of living beings (Wittgenstein, 1967, p. 124). Feeling is when we become sensually aware of our bodily sensations (Gendlin, 1997). Feeling means here mindfully and consciously perceiving what we are sensing in the body. People only experience something when something happens inside them and they can feel it, meaning when bodily signals or states surface in consciousness (Chapter 6). For me, feeling is one of the basic principles of body psychotherapeutic practice: *perceiving and feeling* (Geuter, 2019, pp. 83–108).

We can only experience something that cannot become conscious, such as biochemical processes in the body cells, in its effects. For instance, we cannot directly sense the activity of the immune cells when the organism is reacting to a pathogen, but we feel the effects through a rise in temperature or feeling cold. My subjective experience is of fever or infirmity. I can observe and describe their possible function, but I can only perceive it through these qualities of experience (cf. Heilinger & Jung, 2009, p. 5). Homeostatic regulation processes become conscious when we have a sense of well-being, of illness or of pain (Damasio,

2012). This perception of wellness or illness is a fundamental emotional dimension of feeling (Section 10.1).

Experiencing something means that subjective meaning is created from bodily sensations. In therapy, therefore, we try to feel what is activated right now (Weiss & Daye, 2019). Qualities of experience are communicated in emotionally meaningful sensations which are significant and not just the pure feeling of something pinching, tingling or hurting. Feeling means tracking my experience by paying attention to bodily sensations, trying to perceive exactly what is happening in the body and then reflecting on it. For example, I can **sense** in my body whether or not am I satisfied with the sentence I have just written (cf. Gendlin, 1993; Chapter 8). In order to find out, I test whether or not I feel good with it. Only in the case of facts do I **know** whether according to my explicit memory they are right or not (Chapter 9).

Thus feeling also points to the future, for instance when a feeling of dissatisfaction makes a rethink necessary. Working with feeling in the body not only opens us up for experiences, but also clarifies our intentions. Liss (2001, p. 182) speaks of the link between working with exploration and working on resolution. In the following therapy session, the patient discovered the solution when she could feel all she was experiencing in that moment:

Clinical example

A patient comes to therapy because of depression with suicidal tendencies, a fear of loss which sometimes overwhelms her, problems concentrating and feelings of inferiority. In the session, she tells me about a conflict with her boss. He shouts at her and she cannot manage to ask him to use another tone of voice. Sometimes when she comes home from work she has to cry; once she even cried in front of him. He makes her feel very small and she cannot understand why this feeling is so strong.

In an assertiveness training, she would work on how she could face him with more confidence. In the experiential approach, I explore with her how it feels to be so small.

I ask her to fantasise an interaction with her boss. She chooses a large, devilish figure as a symbol for him, which she then puts on a bookshelf about 1.6 metres high. When I ask about her position relative to him, she sits on a low stool in front of him. For a second she slumps over, but then she sits up straight and becomes rigid. I point this little change out to her. She says that she noticed it too. I ask her to explore what this change means and to move back and forth between the two positions again.

Hardly has she tried this than she begins to cry deeply. With the rigid posture she is protecting herself from her tears. All she wants to do is turn away. I suggest she follow this impulse. First she turns to the side, then she slides down from the stool. She wants to crawl into the corner. I suggest that she do this. She crawls across the room into the corner, kneels down with her face to the floor and cries bitterly. She doesn't want to be seen, she wants to hide. I put a blanket over her. That is good. Suddenly she is calmer. Now she can come back out of the corner. She slides across to the stool. I ask her to look how she wants to position herself relative to the boss. At first she sits, then she wants to stand up. She is amazed to find that the eyes of the devil on the bookshelf are at just the same height as she is. That is good. Now she can look at him with only a small feeling of trepidation in her chest.

We talk about this sequence of experiences. Until now she had to use her strength not only for the conflict itself, but also to suppress the child part of herself, which felt so small. When she allows this part to live here, she no longer has to do that. Even though no biographical material related to the child-feeling has surfaced in the session, this experience alone is transformative. Having recognised the weakness, she can now use her whole power to stand up to the boss. As she realises this, she formulates her wish that he should keep a suitable distance between them. The last time she tried to speak to him about it, he came too close to her in a very unpleasant way.

In the next session, she reports that she went to the boss, closed the door and said to him in a calm voice that she wants him to speak to her in a more friendly manner. He was quite upset and she was the stronger. She did this without a rehearsal. The change she went through in the experiential confrontation had made her feel more confident. A few sessions later, she says that since this important experience, the situation has improved.

We also experience the world of objects by feeling them, for example, when we experience how a surface feels by touching it. Then the self-perception of the skin becomes the perception of the external object. We approach other people in a similar feeling way and resonate with them bodily (Husserl, 2012, p. 235; Chapter 15).

When we talk about feeling, we mean an exact, fine and differentiated perception. To feel or sense also means to enrich and deepen our experience through bodily perception. The more we feel the more it becomes clear how something is for us. We can only understand what we experience precisely. In therapy, therefore, experience goes before understanding. 'Understanding follows on from experiential knowledge' (Staunton, 2002a, p. 3). Here experience and reflection are combined. If we want to become conscious of what we experience, we have to use language. In reflection, feeling the present is linked to feeling the past and to notions of the future. In this way, conscious feeling leads us to understanding. Marlock (2015a) therefore calls body psychotherapy a process of **sensory self-reflexivity**.

Clinical example

A patient tells me angrily about how an acquaintance has treated her. She talks in strong terms about this woman, but in me there is no resonance, so that I begin to think there must be some other emotion at the root of this. I therefore ask her to feel her chest area while she is talking about her acquaintance. Her mood changes quickly. Now she begins to notice that there is a tightness in the chest and a feeling of sadness, which I too can sense. Basically she is disappointed and sad that other people do not like her as much as she would wish. This reminds her of how she felt neglected by her dominant mother.

The combination of felt experience and understanding is not just a characteristic of body psychotherapy, but of all experiential-humanistic therapy approaches. Watson et al. write as follows: 'The main objective of experiential therapy is working with the client's awareness both by focusing on subjective experience and by promoting reflexivity and a sense of agency' (1998, p. 3).

In psychoanalysis too we find increasing support for experiential thinking (Section 1.1). Stern (2004) advocates focusing more on implicit than on explicit experience in therapy. With his theory of vitality, he ventures theoretically almost into body psychotherapeutic territory (Stern, 2010), without, however, engaging with concepts inspired by the philosophy of life or the humanistic tradition, from which he derives his ideas (Geuter, 2012).

According to Greenberg and Van Balen (1998, p. 45), experiential therapies have remained silent on the subject of how the body-feeling basis for experience is created. Body psychotherapy fills this vacancy by assuming that body experience is the basis for experience and gives rise to all psychological functions such as thinking, feeling and remembering (Chapter 6). Characteristic of treatment practice in body psychotherapy is 'a therapeutic mode of working grounded in sense perception and awareness' (Marlock, 2015a, p. 393).

Conscious experience

In psychotherapy, some problems can be treated without them becoming conscious or being understood. The patient can heal through an implicit relationship experience with the therapist without them having to talk about the stable, supportive relationship being the primary healing factor. Trauma patients, who suffer from over-arousal, can find relief when their implicit ability to regulate stress increases (Geuter, 2019, pp. 208–13). To achieve this, becoming conscious of the traumatising situation is not necessary. Thus we can speak of an implicit, non-conscious experience. As a rule, however, experiential psychotherapy aims to use inner, implicit experience as a gateway to conscious experience (Elliott et al., 2013, p. 495). It is the sensorimotor interaction with the environment in movement, gestures or facial expressions that is preconscious. Experience is only possible when these become conscious (cf. Velmans, 2007). In conscious experience, the implicit is brought up into the explicit sphere.

Experiencing something is not the same as having something happen to me. During an operation, we experience nothing, even though what is happening will have long-lasting effects in the body and in experience. During narcosis, pain is not felt as pain, as the sensation is disabled; nor do we feel the pain afterwards. Conscious experience presupposes that I can say that I was aware of what was happening.

Experiential psychotherapy works primarily with conscious perception. Based on what we feel, in verbal reflection the perception itself becomes the object of perception. Thus consciousness is relating to itself. However, consciousness is not confined by human language. Studies have shown how on the basis of memories, animals can change their behaviour in new situations, plan for the future and communicate with each other about their intentions (Brensing, 2013). This too is a form of experience and consciousness.

Clinical example

A depressive patient with low self-esteem, who cannot stand up for himself at work, describes how his mother had worked hard all her life as a waitress up until her retirement. She had always been 'rank and file'. 'And I'm just like her, the hard-working, subservient lowly employee'. This sentence, spoken offhand, seems to me a key expression. I repeat it slowly and solemnly, so that he can experience its significance. Repeating something meaningful can often have a deepening effect. The patient is breathing more deeply, as if the words were affecting him on a vegetative level.

So I go a step further and ask him to say the sentence slowly and clearly himself and to pay attention to any sensations, feelings, images and thoughts he may have. He says it again and then: 'My legs are stiff. When I say that I become like a pillar of salt, as if I couldn't move anything except my eyes'. A new body sensation has emerged.

I try to expand the associative space and ask him what crosses his mind in connection to this bodily feeling. He says it is like feeling not alive: 'That was always my survival strategy'. In his school report in the second form, it says his behaviour is not satisfactory; in the fourth form it is 'satisfactory'. 'I gave up drawing attention to myself'.

When he became a timid schoolboy, he got good grades for behaviour. 'This attitude of resignation was my basic life feeling for years'.

In the rest of the session, we talk about the other little boy, who in second form had a bad grade for behaviour. Memories pour out of him of naughty things he did and he becomes quite lively. Once with his stepfather's loaded pistol he shot at the kitchen cupboard. His stepfather refused to admit that he had left the loaded pistol lying around the kitchen. So to avoid a beating he had to 'confess' that he had stolen it from the gun cupboard. This story is like a metaphor for his experience at work: he does as he is told, shows no will of his own and gives in at the least sign of conflict.

In an explorative process during the session, one of the patient's affect motor schemas, a way of living and experiencing his life, becomes more conscious, as he feels the significance of a verbal expression; then out of this bodily feeling, new meaning develops. This goes on to produce further associations, which allow him to see how he approaches conflicts with other people and the unlived potential in his life more clearly. This experience is driven by the conscious feeling of bodily states.

Grawe (2004) has proposed a model of four common factors of psychotherapy: motivational clarification, problem solving, activation of resources and actualisation of the problem. According to this model, we can work towards both clarification and problem solving by activating resources and by actualising the problem (Geuter, 2019, pp. 429–30). A patient's problems cannot all be treated from the same perspective. An experiential approach is better for clarifying, a more action-centred method for resolving problems. Body psychotherapy has both approaches at its disposal, an understanding of treatment in which both **experience-centred** as well as **action-centred** methods are inherent.

Meaning

Meaning becomes conscious as qualities of experience. Only when a person is aware of the significance of the environment for their well-being can they act intentionally (Heilinger & Jung, 2009, p. 3). Meaning enables patients to draw conclusions for their lives from their experiences. Meaning gives value to experience. In the last case study, the patient could draw conclusions about how he could behave in order to feel better in his work situation. In a therapy session, we can act this out in a fantasy and at the same time see how the patient feels when they fantasise about and perhaps try out a different way of behaving. If they feel better, then the new possibility is anchored in the body. Hence we experience meaning by accessing our bodily feeling towards something and simultaneously using our imaginative skills (cf. M Johnson, 2007, p. 12).

Clinical example

In another session, the patient is concerned with the fact that he always ducks his head in front of others. I suggest that he imagine himself growing. He has the image of a tree with roots deep in the earth. We try anchoring this image in the body in that he stands up like the tree and tries to feel the strength of it in his body.

Meaning develops in the interaction between bodily experience and **symbols**. The tree in the example is such a symbol. 'Feeling without symbolization is blind; symbolization without feeling is empty' (Gendlin, 1997, p. 5). Meaning cannot just be thought. Just the idea of a tree does not create in a patient the feeling of meaningfulness. Meaning can only be experienced while we are talking about something or thinking about it and at the same time feeling something towards it (Gendlin, 1997, p. 45). We can only know meaning when we have a feeling for it. Felt meaning develops in an inner bodily feeling (Gendlin, 1997, p. 11–12).

> ... meaning is grounded in bodily experience; it arises from our feelings of qualities, sensory patterns, movements, changes, and emotional contours. Meaning is not limited only to those bodily engagements, but it always starts with and leads back to them.
>
> (M Johnson, 2007, p. 70)

Felt meaning is always part of an interaction in which we are involved either in reality or in imagination. It is not just there in the body, but lives in the **situation** and is felt in relation to something in the body. M. Johnson (2007, p. 83) speaks of *embodied situations*, in which a connection between the organism and the environment develops. We give meaning to the world in which we find ourselves (Noë, 2010).

Emotions lie at the heart of generating meaning (Johnson, 2007, p. 61). If someone feels no emotion, then the world no longer has meaning for them. This is the case in a state of depressive emptiness. People with alexithymia are not able to experience meaningfulness; those with severe obsessive-compulsive disorder (OCD) tend to subordinate themselves to an inner system of assigned meaning. The body communicates in emotional reactions what a stimulus or an event means to us (Chapter 10). Emotions are internal, usually at first unconscious, responses to situations. However, which emotions someone feels is shaped by their whole experience and behaviour. This is why working with emotions and with affect motor patterns is the focus of therapy.

Phenomenology

If we assume that felt meaning is grounded in bodily sensations, this opens the door to phenomenology. Phenomenal concepts are those in which we describe experience and subjective qualities, as opposed to categorial concepts for facts determined by the natural sciences. Phenomenology is based on the first-person perspective. The understanding of cognition is bound up with the cognising subject, which Husserl (2012), the founder of phenomenological philosophy, saw as a lived-body-subject in the world. For Husserl, a person's 'lifeworld' is always a subjectively given world. This is the necessary perspective for any therapy. For psychotherapy, Greenberg and Van Balen (1998, p. 29) therefore equate an experiential approach with that of phenomenology.

Phenomenal concepts describe how something is for a person, for example how it is to see or taste a red tomato. This is something we cannot express in concepts such as the wavelength of red light. The phenomenal qualities of tomatoes are experiential qualities (cf. Newen, 2013, pp. 78–80), which cannot be included in physical descriptions without being at odds with them (Heilinger & Jung, 2009, p. 5). The wavelength of their colour can be determined but not experienced (Husserl, 2012, pp. 137–40). In therapy, we talk about love, hate, disappointment, despair, insecurity, hesitancy, trepidation, hope, confidence, strength – qualities of experience which need to be described in phenomenal terms. We can only do justice to experience processes in the language of experience and not in the language of science (Geuter, 2004). To reach a diagnosis, psychopathology is dependent on what the patient says about their subjective world of experience. Diagnostics therefore are also based on phenomenal experience (Bermpohl, 2009).

> In phenomenology, Husserl (2012, p. 290) was concerned with recognising subjectivity through self-elucidation and not with how we can learn empirically about subjective states. He wanted to analyse life phenomena purely introspectively through 'inner or self-perception' (Husserl, 2012, p. 231), without referring to the experienced empirical world. Varela et al. (1993, pp. 16–21) hold that he neglected the pragmatic dimension and the embodied aspect of experience. This is perhaps the reason for the fact that phenomenology has not been important in the history of body psychotherapy as has the philosophy of life. Phenomenological philosophy reflects on experience without really capturing how people make lived experiences. This distinguishes Husserl's phenomenology from the Buddhist approach of cognising cognition by observing the activity of the mind in embodied everyday experience (Varela et al., 1993, p. 22).

For Heidegger (1962), phenomenology is a method of treating philosophical questions according to Husserl's maxim of turning to the 'things themselves', the phenomena. Heidegger identifies as phenomena 'that which shows itself, the manifest ... "phenomena" are the totality of what lies in the light of day or can be brought to the light' (Heidegger, 1962, p. 51). This is the basis of experiential psychotherapy. Hartmann-Kottek (2008, p. 161) emphasises this also for Gestalt therapy. However, this does not mean that we linger on the surface of phenomena. What Heidegger wants to bring to light with phenomenology we can also apply to psychotherapy:

> Manifestly, it is something that proximally and for the most part does *not* show itself at all: it is something that lies *hidden*, in contrast to that which proximally and for the most part does show itself; but at the same time it is something that belongs to what thus shows itself, and it belongs to it so essentially as to constitute its meaning and its ground.
>
> (Heidegger, 1962, p. 59)

We do this too in psychotherapy. We look at the phenomena and at the same time at the grounds beneath them – grounds not in the sense of cause but of depth. In treatment, we are looking not for reasons but for deepening. Often we look at what presents itself initially and understand that it is an aspect of what is hidden, for example an aloof manner as the expression of an affect motor schema of avoiding intimacy. A phenomenological approach does not mean that we simply accept things as they appear to be, but that we understand how something can reveal itself as it is (Zahavi, 2007, p. 13). A person's world is what presents itself in their experience and behaviour, but this presentation can be fleeting, distorted or perhaps unaffected and profound. It can also be an illusion as, for instance, in the experiment with the rubber hand that I described in Section 5.2.

Thus, phenomenology is not just about describing phenomena, but unlocking them: 'The phenomenology of Dasein is a *hermeneutic* in the primordial signification of this word, where it designates this business of interpreting' (Heidegger, 1962, p. 62). We describe so as to understand. Marlock (2010, p. 49) classifies body psychotherapy, therefore, as one of the hermeneutic humanities.

Understanding often becomes accessible through bodily self-awareness in the immediate present, so that the patient notices: 'Yes, this is how it is, I can feel it' (Chapter 16). The patient I mentioned before, whose legs rigidified, understands this rigidity as the way he conformed by sacrificing his aliveness. The therapist too can reach a greater understanding through their own bodily experience in somatic resonance (Chapter 15). De Jaegher and Di Paolo (2007) speak of 'participatory sense-making', whereby meaning develops directly out of affect motor interaction. Dilthey (1924) had already contrasted the psychology of causal explanation with that of an understanding one, which accesses the psyche by means of original experienced context. For Dilthey, understanding as a method of the humanities is based on being able to comprehend someone else's life manifestations through one's own experience (Habermas, 1969, pp. 185–99). In therapy, understanding is a shared process:

> The relationship with oneself and with others cannot be measured or stripped down to its component parts or to cause and effect, but only illuminated in the hermeneutic circle of shared interaction.
>
> (Fuchs, 2008, p. 314)

6

Body experience

The basis of self-experience

Body psychotherapy acts on the assumption that self-experience is based on body experience and the self on that of a bodily self (von Arnim et al., 2022, p. 141). Inherently, human beings possess a body feeling, which is the basis for the feeling of themselves (Gallese & Sinigaglia, 2010). Living in one's own body is the essential element of the feeling of 'being somebody' (Metzinger, 2010). This is why psychotics, who have lost their sense of the body, lose a part of themselves. Unless we are suffering from a severe disorder of body experience, the body is a constant point of reference for perception separate from the unceasingly changing stream of perception of the environment (Bergson, 1911, p. 44). The bodily sense of self is the foundation of our personhood (Schmitz, 2014, p. 45).

> The simple fact that we are capable of action with, and sensation in, our bodies is sufficient to set out our relations with our bodies from our relations with other objects.
>
> (Eilan et al., 1998, p. 12)

We are always in the world as bodies; in them we experience the world and ourselves. The subjectivity of our relationship with the world is established in embodied experience. Working with body awareness, therefore, is working with the awareness of self and thus with self-reflection, self-confidence, self-control and self-regulation. Since mental illness takes place in embodied self-experience, this is both the starting point and the goal of all psychotherapeutic experience (Fuchs, 2020a, p. 58).

The **concept of body experience** is a generic term for various aspects of the relationship to the body, including body image and body schema, body perception, body awareness and body cathexis (Roehricht, 2009a, p. 39). Body experience encompasses all that we perceive or are able to perceive in the body and with the body, how we do this and what it means for us. I deal with the concepts of body schema and body image in Section 6.7.

According to Donald (2001), from the perspective of evolutionary biology, the body self is the first rung on the ladder of the development of specifically human consciousness. He calls this the 'mimetic' phase of evolution, in which human beings began at first through

DOI: 10.4324/9781003176893-6

bodily expression to communicate and developed the ability to associate their own actions with their perceptions of events. Thus evolution created a bodily self-awareness and developed accordingly neuro-anatomic structures, the connections of which are regulated by the prefrontal cortex.

The sense of self as a bodily subject presupposes an explicit recognition of the mineness of the body and the ownership of my actions (Gallese & Sinigaglia, 2011, p. 135; Section 6.5). In the 14th week of pregnancy, twin embryos show different movement profiles when they are touching themselves and when they are touching their twin (Gallese & Sinigaglia, 2011, p. 136). According to Stern's (1985) developmental psychology model, the initial organisation of self-awareness is created by the bodily exchange between the baby and the mother (Section 11.2). Thus, right from the beginning, the body self is formed through interaction with other bodily beings. In such encounters, babies practise sensorimotor skills, share motoric intentions and experience bodily interactions as coherent and predictable (Gallese & Sinigaglia, 2010, p. 752; Wehowsky, 2015a, p. 324). Thus the early self is an intersubjective bodily self (White, 2004a, p. XXIV).

In therapy, we want to find access to this self and help patients gain insight into themselves and how they feel about their lives, so as to improve their self-regulation capacity (cf. Levine & Macnaughton, 2004, p. 376). To get on better in the world, they need an awareness of how they perceive themselves and the environment subjectively. This awareness is connected to a sense of self. In my view, the therapeutic goal is an authenticity in the sense of Heidegger (1962), which includes being conscious of one's own being co-existing with the phenomena of life. The basis for this is the bodily sense of self.

Important
Making the self accessible by tapping into body experience through many methods is the main specific contribution of body psychotherapy to the psychotherapeutic spectrum.

In a therapy session, bodily sensations can indicate inner and relational processes: whether something touches the patient or not, whether they are suppressing something, are depressed, irritated, relieved, engaged or soothed. If someone is relieved and can relax in connection to some psychological issue, this shows that they have made a move towards healing (Zanotta, 2018, p. 31).

Clinical example

With one patient, I have been talking about the inner tension that she feels in the body. We have often looked at the tension in the chest and the feeling of not being able to breathe properly through the throat and at the connection this has to her problems with exams and with concentration. She reports that her jaw is often so tense that the muscles hurt. This was especially strong when she suffered from anorexia that threatened her life. After being treated in a clinic for this, she then came to me. In her youth she had been treated over several years by an orthodontist and had worn a craniomandibular appliance around the jaw and the head to change the position of the teeth. She still sometimes wears a brace at night.

At the beginning of the session I notice that in a brief moment of silence she draws back her jaw into a tense position, in which her mouth is formed into a forced smile. I point this out and ask her what is going on inside her just now. She starts to tell me about a feeling of insecurity; other people had said to her that she was rather unapproachable. It seems as if with this jaw movement the body is showing a need to withdraw, while at the same time with the forced smile she communicates a need for connection. The small movement of the jaw is revealed as a way of regulating her feelings and needs in contact with other people: there is a fear of asking for something that she has had since childhood and a need to be alone without being rejected for it.

The body psychotherapeutic approach here is to point out the bodily symptom and to ask how she experiences it. This leads to a discussion of the way she relates to other people. We pay attention to the fact that the jaw movement is determined by several factors and that she has a history of forcible orthodontic corrections. I ask her about this. We work primarily on the function of this movement in contact with others by looking at its function in our interaction: how she experiences the movement and the tension with me now, how this changes when we are both silent, when I ask her something, when she tells me something, when I loosen my jaw in a way that she can see and react to, or how the tension changes when she loosens it, in this particular session by humming quietly. In this way, through bodily expression, she experiences something about herself and her relationship to the world and at the same time finds a way to change and regulate it herself.

A sense of self develops essentially through inner perception: 'consciousness of the "self" most likely depends to a substantial extent on awareness … of the body per se, including its visceral organs and functions' (Cameron, 2001, p. 708). Body awareness is the foundation of self-knowledge (Butterworth, 1998) as well as of awareness of others and of the world around us (Gallese & Sinigaglia, 2011, pp. 118, 136); body experience is the foundation for experiencing our own emotions and those of other people. We feel ourselves while we are feeling something or someone else (Waldenfels, 2008, p. 133). We perceive the world not only through our outer senses. Inner senses communicate to us the meaning of what we perceive. '*What* is meaningful to us, and *how* it is meaningful, depends fundamentally on our ongoing monitoring of our bodily states as we experience and act within the world' (M Johnson, 2007, pp. 56–7).

Our self experience extends out into the world and can transcend us, when for example we feel at one with a beautiful landscape we see, with a piece of music we hear or with a person whose skin we feel with our own. It is not just *embedded* but also *extended* (Section 5.2).

Example

If we react to meeting a specific person with tension in the stomach, then this can signal that experience is telling us to be careful. We perceive the other person and our relationship to them bodily, not only through the external sense organs but through inner senses too.

Damasio's neurobiological theory supports this perspective. In contrast to LeDoux (2002), who views the self as a constellation of brain systems and thus as an aggregation of information, Damasio (1999) sees the basis of the self in body experience. The question of how the subject develops meaning for themselves would only be answered when we start from the body as the point of reference for experience.

Neuro-anatomically, there is evidence for consciousness being connected to bodily self-perception. In a coma, only damage above a certain divide within the reticular formation, where body signals enter the central nervous system, leads to a loss of the proto-self (Section 6.5), meaning the perception of inner states, which are constantly monitored in the brain (Ansermet & Magistretti, 2007). Then a person has lost the substrate of cognition, namely the current inner bodily state and the perception of changes in it. From this point on, according to Damasio (1999), consciousness no longer exists.

For Damasio, the sensory experience of the self – the self sense – is the **fundament of subjectivity**. De Preester (2007) thinks that bodily self-awareness of the 'in-depth-body' creates a person's subjective perspective. Accordingly the interoceptive **is** the subjective (De Preester, 2007, p. 617). If we only looked at it as material **for** a cognisant subject, then the split between subject and object persists, as inner perception is seen as an object. In a clinical sense, for body psychotherapy this theory means the following:

Important
Becoming aware of inner bodily perception means to become aware of oneself. Sensing constitutes subjectivity.

We can go further: inner sensing communicates what events in the outer world mean for us and how we want to relate to them. Sensing, according to Merleau-Ponty (2012), is a living communication with the world.

> If inner perception is physically blocked, distorted cognition and emotions are the result. An interesting older study on sensory and perceptual deprivation shows this. For 24 hours, academics were given a headcollar which locked their necks into a certain position. As a result their cognitive capacity was reduced: exaggerated emotional reactions and unusual bodily sensations increased (Zubek et al., 1963). For therapy this indicates that a **purely functional physical intervention, which loosens bodily rigidity, can change thinking and feeling**, since the body becomes accessible to inner perception.

Inner sensing, however, is not necessarily true knowledge, as is often thought in body psychotherapy, when it is said that the body never lies (Section 14.1). This idea, which is also prevalent in kinesiology (Diamond, 1979), is itself an illusion (Section 5.2: Box 'Rubber hand illusion'). Because knowledge of inner states has a quality of immediate certitude, we tend not to question it. Thus it has a kind of immunity from error (Eilan et al., 1998, pp. 22–3). A patient with coenaesthetic schizophrenia insists that the sensation of a thousand ants running over their skin is a reality. It would be absurd to say to them: 'The body does not lie'. Also, because of damaging experiences. the body can mislead us just as can our thoughts, for example if the daughter of a violent alcoholic is repeatedly attracted to alcoholics, or when people who experienced violent abuse are aroused by violence. Neither bodily sensations nor thoughts are essentially right or wrong. As therapists, therefore, our task is to question inner certainties by comparing the patient's perceptions with our own and directing their attention to what they are not yet aware of.

6.1 THREE LEVELS OF EXPERIENCE

In experience, we differentiate phenomenally whether we are feeling something or sensing it, thinking or moving and willing to act, or imagining something. These aspects of experience (Geuter, 2019, p. 74) are not independent of one another. Emotions, needs and intentions, which are what we are primarily dealing with in psychotherapy, are experienced

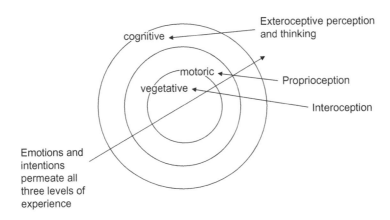

FIGURE 6.1 The three levels of experience

as a whole, but at the same time we can discern images, thoughts, inner sensations, movements and impulses as those components, which communicate them to us (Chapter 10).
The model of the three levels of vegetative, muscular-motor and cognitive processes that we
encounter in various schools of body psychotherapy does this justice (Geuter & Schrauth,
2001; Southwell, 1988; Figure 6.1).

Von Arnim et al. (2002, p. 156) talk about the vegetative, the animal and the human
levels or even layers (p. 184), which they link to ontogenetic development. With reference to the Gestalt cycle of Viktor von Weizsaecker, they describe them as levels of
the 'regulation circle', the 'functional circle' and the 'situational circle' (von Arnim
et al., 2022, pp. 212–3), which are similar to the life circles of Heyer (1932; Section 3.4).
Similarly, in enactivism, Thompson and Varela (2001) distinguish three operative life
circles, which they call organismic regulation, sensorimotor coupling and intersubjective interaction.

Boadella (1987) organises the three levels into a layered model of developmental biology
corresponding to the three germ layers of the foetus, the endoderm, ectoderm and mesoderm; the respiration and digestion systems develop out of the endoderm; the skeleton, tissue, muscles and blood vessels out of the mesoderm; and the skin, the nervous system and
external sense organs out of the ectoderm. Boadella connects them to the three therapeutic
modes: centring, grounding and facing.

In his later work, Reich advocated an understanding of psychotherapy in which he saw
the vegetative as the basis of all psychological processes (Section 3.6). He no longer wanted
to work 'merely on individual conflicts and special armouring, but on the living organism
itself' (1972, p. 358). He saw this in biology. For him the biological was 'at a depth' (p. 361),
and hence the psychological was on the surface.

Layers models

We can trace the model of the three layers of the soul back to platonic philosophy.
Plato differentiated the upper layer of the *logos*, as the ruling and immortal part, from
the two lower, more bodily layers of the *thymos*, to which he assigned the heart and
the will, and the *eros* with all its vital needs: the charioteer of the reason, the noble
white horse of courage and the black horse of greed (Werner, 1966, pp. 87–8). In the

psychology of the 20th century we find Plato's classification in the characterology of the life philosopher and psychologist Philipp Lersch, in which will and intellect as the upper levels are superimposed upon the feelings (Geuter, 1992, pp. 100–1). Reich stood this on its head and declared the vegetative fundament to be the seat of a desirable vitality.

In Germany at the end of the 19th century, parallel to the development of a centralistic state under Bismarck, hierarchical models of the localisation of cerebral functions emerged (Pauly, 2005). In the 1920s, Friedrich Kraus, to whose physiological theories Reich (1973) referred, deduced on the basis of brain research the two levels of a 'deep person' and a 'cortical person' (Gilbert, 1951, pp. 5–6). Later, in comparative psychology, the three layers of the soul were linked to the architecture of the brain: the brain stem as a 'primitive' core, responsible for physiological equilibrium; the 'midbrain' for affects and instincts; and the cortex for cognitive and volitional processes (Gilbert, 1973, p. 104). Similarly, the theory of the triune brain in evolutionary biology differentiates between a reptilian brain and an old and new mammalian brain (MacLean, 1974; Panksepp, 1998, pp. 70–2).

In his movement therapy, Feldenkrais (2005) assigns vegetative, reflexive and conscious activities of the nervous system to the vegetative system, the 'old' and the 'new' brain.

Models such as the triune brain are often cited in somewhat simplistic theories. Reflexes then belong to the reptile brain, emotions to the limbic system and thinking to the neocortex. Then catchphrases such as 'think limbic' come up. However these ideas are only metaphors for mental processes. Neurophysiological connections between the various brain centres and their possible assignment to psychological functions are far more complex than these simple models suggest (Heller, 2012, p. 237).

I understand the three levels model not as a biological layering of the human organism, but as a model of **levels of experience**, which can be differentiated one from the other but are always connected. In body psychotherapy we are dealing with what a person experiences **vegetatively** in the inner perception of body sensations; **muscle motor** in their perception of their posture, movements and action impulses; and **cognitively** in their thoughts, fantasies or images. We always pay attention to the perception of bodily sensations and spontaneous movements and impulses of the body. Since the therapist is aware of the patient on all three levels of their own self-experience, von Arnim et al. (2022, pp. 211–3) extend the model to include therapeutic communication (Chapter 14).

Emotions, intentions and needs are communicated cognitively through language; by muscles through gestures, facial expressions or posture; and vegetatively through signs such as stomach rumbling, blushing or sweating (Chapter 10). Affect motor schemas too reveal themselves on all three levels. However, the three levels do not each communicate separately. In humanistic psychology they are understood as levels of conscious experience, existing simultaneously and interconnectedly (Hutterer, 1998, p. 316).

This model offers an alternative to the notion that in body psychotherapy we are working on 'body-brain-communication' (Aposhyan, 2004, p. 27; Section 5.1). We should not view the links between the levels of experience as causally determined, as the impact of one level on the other, but as systemic. Experience is a holistic process taking place on all levels.

A case in point: yawning

Self-regulatory processes often encompass all three levels. When we yawn, the muscles of the entire respiratory tract are stretched in a unique manner, and the throat quadruples its diameter (Walusinski, 2006). Yawning thus connects breathing and movement. It activates both the trapezius and the masseter, which is involved in chewing (muscle level). These muscles are in turn involved in waking up. Thus yawning leads to enhanced bodily alertness (vegetative level). Interoception is stimulated and this enhances body awareness (cognitive level). Thus through bodily activity, yawning connects conscious and unconscious inner perception and the higher mental functions. It is experienced on all three levels.

From a **systemic perspective**, I assume that a change on one level, such as the motor level of yawning, can trigger changes on all three levels. This is also true of psychotherapeutic interventions. The bioenergetic exercise known as 'the bow', which increases the tension in the muscles of the front of the body, results in a measurable reduction in the concentration of CO_2 in the blood, probably because of increased respiration. Subsequently muscular activity or the vocal expression of feelings brings the concentration back to its original level (Koemeda-Lutz, 2012). A person experiences such a change through bodily processes, such as needing more or less air. If they feel vitalised through increased respiration or through yawning, then in a bottom-up process, their self-experience changes correspondingly.

However, top-down processes also operate on all levels. Talking about something can calm down vegetative agitation or trigger affect motor impulses. Just imagining the contraction of a certain muscle brings about an increase in muscle strength, albeit not to the same degree as physical training (Ranganathan et al., 2004). The interruption of the vocal and facial interaction of a mother with her baby in the still-face experiments (Section 11.3) leads to a decrease in vagal tone in the child (Weinberg & Tronick, 1996).

Processes of perceiving and regulating emotions, intentions and needs can be inhibited or blocked on any of the three levels. An inner coolness or obtuseness, tension in the muscles and fascia or prohibitive thoughts can interrupt or prevent experience as an integrated whole.

Body psychotherapy addresses all three levels of experience through words, expressivity, movement, breathing or body awareness. We can work with vegetative regulation through relaxation, with the exploration of action impulses or by discussing with the patient what they have reported verbally. We are always working with the whole person. In the case of anxiety, for instance,

- Modulating the vegetative arousal level through relaxation or breathing exercises or meditation.
- Helping the patient to use the motor action potential, to face their fears and cope with anxiety-inducing situations.
- Clarifying the context in which anxiety arises and helping the patient to develop alternative feelings in triggering situations.

We can contact patients in their thoughts and feelings, gestures and expressive movements or in their shivering and trembling, their heaviness or lightness (Geuter, 2000, p. 1350). We communicate with them on all three levels and connect these to one another. Van der Kolk (2011) speaks of communication in therapy encompassing mind, brain and viscera, which he sees as the royal road to affect regulation. I would prefer not to refer to this communication as physiological, as does van der Kolk, but as communication over various levels of self-experience.

However, the levels of experience can be classified physiologically as belonging to the sensory systems on which in a physical sense experience depends:

- The vegetative level of visceral sensory interoception.
- The muscle motor level of sensorimotor proprioception.
- The cognitive level of the external senses.

I will deal with this in more depth in Section 6.3.

From a psychological point of view, self-experience consists of all three levels. I see no hierarchy here but rather an interaction. Human beings experience and process their experiences on the vegetative, muscle motor and cognitive levels. Their bodily sensations, movement impulses or thoughts are part of an integral experience of self and are in this sense mental processes.

In body psychotherapy, we ask how something feels or what someone is sensing when they direct their attention inwardly, become aware of their inner state and of their breathing, when they move or try out a new way of doing something, when they express an emotion or observe what is happening in interaction with the therapist. The focus is not on the functionality of bodily systems. When we work with the mobility of the shoulder, for example, our focus is not on the degree of outer rotation at which the muscles are blocked and then releasing this, so as to increase the radius of the rotation, as physiotherapists do. We are primarily interested in whether a movement, such as reaching for something in the world, is blocked in the shoulder, or how a conflict between approaching someone or withdrawing from them is recognisable in the same expressive movement of the shoulder. Nor do we study vegetative processes from a physiological perspective, but seek to learn how someone experiences cold or heat and what this means to them, whether they feel frozen up or sense how something stirs their the blood, or whether rising heat is a sign of general unrest or perhaps of anger or shame. We explore the sensorimotor or vegetative experience as aspects of self-experience.

Clinical application

Patients with chronic pain have often lost their self-perception and defend themselves with pain against feelings they cannot regulate. They are often fixated on the pain and on the perception of the outside world. It has been shown that it helps them more to feel the pain by becoming conscious of the body than to distract themselves from it (Mehling et al., 2009). Turning their attention towards the pain is concomitant with a reduction in the sensation of pain. Brain studies indicate that in this process, sensory perception increases and cognitive control decreases (Gard et al., 2012). Mindful experience seems to lower the fixation on controlling the pain.

Roehricht (2011c) describes the case of a patient who felt constricted by pressure in the body. He asked him how strongly constricted he felt and asked him to act out and experience the constriction with his body. In this way, the patient could give new meaning to his pain.

When patients with chronic pain gain a better sensorimotor and vegetative perception of themselves, this induces self-regulatory healing processes. Self-perception often results in what before felt very painful becoming somewhat lighter (Fogel, 2009, p. 69).

Only recently has psychotherapy taken the **vegetative** level more into account. The impulse for this came mainly from trauma research, as dissociated affects often emerge in vegetative reactions such as sensations of being cold or being hot or of pressure. However, all emotional states are linked to signals of a visceral, tangible or nociceptive nature (Porges, 2009). Vegetative body processes are often a component of the regulation of emotions (Levenson, 2003; Section 7.1). Conflicts can be sweated out and tensions exhaled. In groups I have often experienced that after a piece of especially strenuous emotional work, participants were sweating, had the runs or even got spots.

When we are angry or afraid, the pulse rate increases; in grief, psychogalvanic skin resistance decreases more than with anxiety or anger; with anger, the temperature of the fingers increases more than with anxiety (Ekman et al., 1983). People also react emotionally with their digestive tract. Thus, for example, fear can be accompanied by diarrhoea or the desire to urinate. Both the fear we notice cognitively and our vegetative processes are then part of an anxiety process.

Since psychological and biological states are connected in a circle (Section 5.1), different vegetative states stimulate different kinds of experience and behaviour and thus co-determine our emotional condition (Critchley et al., 2001). We can be soothed via vegetative regulation mechanisms; we feel better without knowing why (Koole & Rothermund, 2011). Implicit emotional regulation, beyond conscious control and explicit intention, is probably often the result of vegetative processes, which modulate core affective experience in particular and help to induce desired emotional states (cf. Koole & Rothermund, 2011, pp. 390–1; Geuter, 2019, pp. 194–9; Section 10.2). By working with the breathing or with body awareness, vegetative regulation processes can return to a certain equilibrium without significant psychological material becoming conscious. A well-balanced rhythm of physical processes such as respiration, heartbeat or digestion is associated with a coherent experience of the body (Porges, 2011).

If the vegetative level is an indication of inner movement, experience is conveyed **motorically** in outer movement such as ideomotor signals. People express also the intention of their actions mainly motorically (cf. Gallese & Sinigaglia, 2010, p. 749). Interpersonal intentionality is expressed on the motor level through approach and withdrawal. We often regulate closeness and distance motorically and thus our boundaries and our connection with the environment.

When we applaud together we create a common action and a common experience. The motor action of clapping is communicated aurally, and out of a variety of clapping rhythms, a common rhythm develops in a self-organising process (Kriz, 2004a, pp. 25–6). The process that appears on the motor level is experienced as a collective feeling of enthusiasm. I had a similar experience in a group with the dance therapist Anna Halprin. All participants were asked to feel their pulse and to stamp in the rhythm of their heartbeat. Within a few minutes 70–80 people were all stamping to the same beat. We had all synchronised our steps and perhaps too our pulses.

With its various methods, body psychotherapy can access a diversity of experiential processes on all levels. Often it is a matter of achieving integration, particularly when the processes of experience are kept apart on the various levels and a person feels in their bodily impulses something different from what their beliefs dictate.

Clinical example

A patient begins the therapy session by saying that since Tuesday there has been a black cloud hanging over him, just like in the dark days of his depression. We talk about what happened just before this. He had a successful preliminary exam and spoke with the tutor about taking the final in two months, so that he could then move to K, where he wants to work. He has hoped for this for a while. But he is also afraid of moving away. It feels like fear of dying. He is ashamed of this fear. He often chickens out and is full of doubts about what to do with his life.

I know that he is not only interested in the job in K but also in one in W and at the same time he would like to stay in B, so I suggest that we sound out this difficult decision situation. He could choose a place each in the room for K, W and B, then mark their positions with objects and explore how he feels in each place. He chooses a thick blue cord for K and puts it about a metre from the chair where he usually sits. For W he arranges a thin green cord in a circle form at his side. For B he chooses the chair. First he wants to try out the position for K. He stands in that place and feels quite heavy-hearted. His breathing falters. There it feels like an exam. At the position for W he sits down in the cord circle. Here it is nice, familiar, but not interesting, as if he is pensioned off. It makes him drowsy. The feeling is so strong that I start to feel drowsy too. Then he sits down in the chair for B. He likes sitting here and he feels calm, but he is looking around for something outside, that cannot be found here.

In all three places in the room he has reacted on the vegetative level (change in respiration, tiredness), the sensorimotor level (standing, sitting, eyes wandering) and the cognitive-imaginative (exam, pension), and he has had a different emotional experience in each (heavy-hearted, boring, searching). Now the question is what these reactions on the various levels of experience signify for his decision. So I ask him to sound this out as a whole: he should look for a place outside these three, from where he can look at them all and then see how he feels about them from there, or whether there is perhaps even a fourth place that would be right for him at the moment. Spontaneously he goes to the chair, perches half on the backrest and leans forwards towards K, as if curious. His posture is dynamic and feels good. This is right. As we talk about it the meaning becomes clear: really he would like to stay living in B, but mentally he is directed to what he would find in K, so that the solution would not be moving to K, but to somehow actualise the spirit of what he would be working on in K so that he could then stay in B. He had not been able to gain this insight in a purely cognitive manner, but in feeling on all levels of self-experience the options acted out in scenic work, it becomes directly manifest.

6.2 BREATHING AS A GATEWAY TO SELF-EXPERIENCE

Self-experience can be induced through focused concentration on what we perceive of ourselves in the body: our inner sensations, our movements, our movement and action impulses and our breathing. Whereas in dance and movement therapy it is primarily movement which is used to access experience, first Reich and after him various schools of body psychotherapy have concentrated especially on the respiration (Macnaughton, 2015).

Breathing is present on all three levels of experience in a unique way. It is a characteristic of the living, connected to all life processes and involved in the regulation of emotional and physical states (Ekerholt & Bergland, 2008). The process of breathing allows us to experience the existence of the living body (Boehme, 2020, p. 36). It lends itself like no other bodily function to being utilised as a gateway to experience.

This is because of its special features. Respiration is a function controlled by the vegetative nervous system, which we can however change voluntarily through muscle motor intervention. It is located on the interface of inner sensation and outer expression. Unlike other unconsciously regulated bodily functions, we can become aware of it relatively easily (Depraz, 2008, p. 246). Through breathing, we can become conscious of our vegetative state, our myofascial tensions and our emotional life; these states are also communicated through breathing in therapy (Chapter 14). In this respect, awareness of the breathing is in a sense awareness of the living body altogether (Boehme, 2003, p. 69).

Breathing is also connected to the environment and to other people. Each inhalation and exhalation of air is an interaction with the world around us. Just as the respiration is a movement of opening and closing, so we can open ourselves to or close ourselves off from the world around us by the way we breathe. Deeper breathing is a preparation for approaching the world.

In Hebrew, the word *rûach* means breath, wind and spirit. In the Koran the Arabic word *ruh* stands for spirit. In classical Greek, the word for breath is *pneuma*, also meaning whiff, airflow, life, soul, spirit, courage. In the Greek text of the New Testament, the Holy Ghost is referred to as *pneuma to hagion*, the holy pneuma, which we could also translate as 'holy breath'. In the second creation story, God breathed the breath of life into the body of Adam, whom he had formed from clay. In the occidental tradition as in other cultures, breath represents the etheric spirit–soul or life itself.

In all body psychotherapy traditions, the breathing plays a significant role:

- Gindler (1926, p. 87) states that in emotionally strained situations, breathing is reduced and this includes a voluntary bodily tensing up inaugurated by the diaphragm. She saw holding the breath as the main respiratory disorder, accompanied by rigidity. In a notebook from 1912, she wrote that through body education the breathing should become strong, smooth and regular (Arps-Aubert, 2012, p. 323). Conscious breathing was for her the way to become aware of oneself, to feel fresh and to relieve tension.
- Reich saw in the breathing an important instrument of body defence. In shock we would breath in involuntarily and not fully out again. The holding of the breath and the chronic contraction of the diaphragm were in his view the bodily means of preventing sensations of lust in the belly and of stifling anxiety (Reich, 1973, p. 306). Thus he called the respiratory block the 'physiological mechanism for the suppression and repression of affects' (Reich, 1973, p. 308; Section 13.1). Neurotic people would all inhibit a deep exhalation. Reich worked with his patients on inducing a deep natural exhalation through an attitude of surrender. As Sharaf (1994, p. 313) reports Reich paid careful attention to 'subtle manifestations of blocked respiration'.
- In the humanistic therapy movement, hyperventilation techniques, such as those practised in Kundalini or in other forms of yoga to induce transformative experiences, were introduced into body psychotherapy (Chapter 4). This is a second approach borrowed from the eastern tradition of breathwork after that of concentrating on the breathing (Heller, 2012, pp. 41–3; Levine & Macnaughton, 2004, p. 369). In the experimental work of Gestalt therapy, the therapist observes the breathing process of the patient so as to gauge their level of arousal (Kepner, 1993).

The breathing function is regulated by the vegetative nervous system (Section 7.1). The vagus nerve is involved in the respiratory reflexes. Due to the parasympathetic innervation, breathing out stimulates psycho-physical relaxation. Conversely muscular relaxation stimulates breathing out; proprioceptive afferent neurons then stimulate the reticular formation to a stronger innervation of the parasympathetic nervous system (von Arnim et al., 2022, p. 219). In turn, by means of the breathing, we can influence the autonomic nervous system. Calm breathing and interventions which communicate the presence of the therapist activate the tone of the ventral vagal nerve. Increasing breathing with its intensive muscle activity, on the other hand, stimulates the sympathetic tone, facial expressions, gestures and contact to emotions (Macnaughton, 2015).

With each breath, the largest and most important respiratory muscle, the diaphragm, oscillates up to eight centimetres in the direction of the inner organs; the organs are massaged and their function stimulated. Thus we can promote vegetative changes in physical functions through working with the bodily means of breathing.

By breathing more deeply, we activate the intestinal peristalsis or ease a stitch we may have after physical exertion (Bunkan, 1991). A deeper release in the breathing influences the heart rhythm, heart rate, skin temperature and the function of the bladder (Johnen, 2010, p. 70). In relaxed exhalation, the mouth and the pelvis move in a little arc towards each other, a movement of surrender. Faster and more intensive breathing releases endorphins and thus helps to suppress pain (Pert, 1999). Perhaps this explains why people have relief from pain when they laugh.

Clinical example

Von Steinaecker (2010, pp. 181–2) reports on the treatment of a woman patient who, after the death of her father and a serious car accident, was suffering from bronchial asthma. The therapist stimulated her respiratory function and her body awareness through stroking and some light stretching. The patient could feel an easing in the sternum, which positively affected her mood. Symptoms such as wheezing and rhonchus, a pathological sound during exhalation, decreased. In the course of treatment the patient became increasingly sure that she would have no further severe attacks. This feeling of more freedom helped her to change her behaviour in distressing situations and in interaction with other people. The change in the psycho-vegetative tone was accompanied by a decrease in anxiety.

Just as the vegetative state and muscle tone both change when feelings change, so too a change in vegetative tone and the release of muscle tension modulates the feelings. It is difficult to maintain a bad mood when we breathe deeply and change our body posture (Hendricks, 1995).

This is not only intrasubjectively valid but also intersubjectively. If, as the therapist, I inhale more deeply, so as to open up my chest, after having reacted to a patient by developing a constriction in that area, that is not just self-regulation. This is an embodied interaction which influences the patient consciously or unconsciously, since in body dialogue I am also demonstrating my willingness to open up a space for their feelings whose holding back has reached me via the body.

Many muscles are involved in respiration, and they are all active even when the body is at rest (Fogel, 2009, p. 228). Next to the diaphragm, the most important are the intercostal muscles that are active in each inhalation. In order to change breathing we can employ many other accessory respiratory muscles in the abdomen, neck, shoulder and chest area, such as the scalenes or the sternocleidomastoid. This is why for instance a stiff neck affects the breathing.

We can contract the respiratory muscles both **voluntarily** and, in emotional events such as a shock reaction, also **involuntarily**; this means mental experience is closely connected to the respiratory function. Through muscle activity we can halt the breathing, release it, compress it, deepen it or make it shallow and also alter its rhythm. Emotional reactions are thus inscribed into breathing patterns. In the same way we cannot change other bodily functions controlled by the vegetative system. Therefore restricting breathing by tensing up the muscles is a crucial means of conscious and unconscious emotional regulation and of the bodily defence system (Section 13.1).

Mental disorders and breathing

If emotional reaction patterns of breathing are repeated often enough unconsciously, they can become entrenched and create **chronic breathing patterns**. Depressive people often display a shallow, restricted, thoracic breathing (Maurer, 2001, p. 27; Section 6.7). Schizoid people, who often have a stiff posture, breathe at times as if their breath were trapped in horror and childhood fears (Schrauth, 2001, p. 53). In people with somatic symptom disorder, we can often observe a restriction in the movement of the diaphragm: sometimes it only oscillates 2–3 centimetres at most instead of 8 centimetres. Krizan (1992) links this to cardiac and circulatory insufficiency, general weakness and listlessness and spinal problems. Tonic stuttering is aggravated when the breathing is blocked by tension in the larynx as a result of anxiety.

Breathing patterns are connected to **postural patterns**. Someone constantly showcasing themselves develops in the long run an inflated chest held in a posture of chronic inhalation, which can lead to a frozen ribcage and hyperlordosis. Other people have a chest which is chronically almost collapsed and tend more towards hyperkyphosis. Breathing patterns are therefore a body component of defence structures (Section 13.2). They can indicate core issues in development, as for instance when someone always holds the breathing back, or another person breathes as if they are desperate for more air and yet another always forces the breathing (Fischer & Kemman-Huber, 1999, pp. 66–83). 'Breathing is always as the person is' (Lowe & Laing-Gilliatt, 2007, p. 73).

Autonomic respiration is innervated by the spinal cord, and voluntary respiration by the motor cortex (Butler, 2007). Autonomic breathing is unconscious, but it can however become conscious much more easily than other autonomic functions. Voluntarily altering the breathing is necessarily a process very close to consciousness. Thus breathing forms an **interface between conscious and unconscious processes** and so is an ideal place to become aware of discrepancies between them (Hendricks & Hendricks, 1993). Any attempt to control oneself shows up in the breathing. Consequently, many schools of meditation focus on respiration (Totton, 2002, p. 23). In autogenic training, the formula 'It breathes me' is a consciously suggestive evocation of autonomic respiration. Consciously letting autonomic unconscious respiration happen and being aware of it is what Middendorf (1995) calls the **breath experience**. Experiencing myself in breathing helps the breathing to win back and strengthen my bodily sense of identity (Maurer, 2001, pp. 14, 46).

In meditation we can see how difficult it is to experience breathing. I once took part in a week in a meditation centre, where we were to spend 1 hour five times a day following and counting the breathing and thinking of nothing else for ten breaths – and we were to start again from the beginning if our thoughts had wandered off. I completely failed at this task. 'Meditators discover that mind and body are not coordinated. … Even when they attempt to return to their object of mindfulness, the breath, they may discover that they are only thinking about the breath rather than being mindful of the breath' (Varela et al., 2017, p. 25). In meditation we can thus realise how far away we are from experience. In Buddhism this dissociation of the mind from the body is seen as a bad habit, which we can transform into mindfulness through practicing concentrating on our breathing.

The body psychotherapy approach differs from that of breath therapy. Traditional breathing therapy aims at a eutonic state in which a person is both psychologically alert and physically open, has good muscle tone and has optimal joint mobility (Fischer & Kemmann-Huber, 1999, p. 12). Breath therapy attempts to restore natural breathing as a bodily function, often using the movement rhythms of the body to this end. In addition to the functional goal of finding the person's own breathing rhythm, which is central to Functional Relaxation (Bartholomew & Herholz, 2019), body psychotherapy has the following aims:

- Letting the unconscious speak through the breathing.
- Encouraging conscious experience.
- Regulating affect tension.

We use the breathing to influence tone, stimulate self-perception, modulate emotional arousal or open up access to emotions. This last distinguishes it from the approach of biofeedback, which uses respiration to gain information about and regulate stress states (Dixhoorn, 2008, p. 55), without exploring or deepening emotional experience through the breathing.

Being aware of the breathing promotes self-awareness. Consciously sensing it encourages the move from exteroception to interoception and, in a non-judgemental mode, the ability to feel the core affective difference between pleasant and unpleasant (Mehling, 2010, pp. 164–5; Section 10.1). For the mindfulness-based therapy of depression, Williams et al. (2007) recommend concentrating on body experience as soon as we notice an unpleasant feeling and linking the awareness of the breathing to it. In body psychotherapy we ask the patient to breathe into a certain part of the body, a body sensation or a feeling localised in the body, so as to heighten awareness of it and create consciousness.

Clinical example

A patient feels guilty at work when female colleagues criticise him and he cannot live up to their expectations. He wakes up in the night and agonises about not having been able to do the right thing, puts himself down as a failure and generally beats himself up. I ask him which Jan, as I will call him, is involved in this. He sees a little person who feels guilty and has a bad conscience. This is a feeling connected to his mother, who was severely depressed and for whose salvation he was responsible, a task he never managed to fulfil.

I suggest that he could embody this little boy at some place in the room. At first he stands up, then he crouches down, turns his face away from me and lets his head hang down. As I ask him what is happening, he says he has a sad feeling, something shameful: 'You're not worth anything!' This was the mother's voice. He feels very lonely, he says, his breathing is becoming shallow: 'What should I do? I'm always doing something wrong'.

At this point I could make various suggestions to help him find a way out of the familiar affect motor pattern and discover something new. I decide to go with the breathing and propose that he could breathe deeply five times and see what happens. He does so and straightens up a bit whilst still crouching. He notices a feeling of resistance. His arm comes forward with the open hand towards him as if he could make a powerful fist with it. The sentence occurs to him: 'No we won't be doing that'. He notices a desire to bite and is astonished how much can change in five breaths.

Now he stands up properly and says: 'I'm standing up'. He feels powerful and proud, as if he is winning back his dignity. I suddenly think of Bob Marley's song: 'Get up, stand up, stand up for your right' and I tell him this. He improvises on Marley's ' Don't give up the fight' to 'Give up the fight'. He wants to liberate himself from always having to fight to do the right thing for his mother/women, to save her/them. He turns around, comes 'out of penitents' corner' and towards the world where he wants to live and 'go my own way'.

In another session he says it was good that I interrupted him in his old pattern by suggesting he breathe more deeply and so inviting him to experience something new.

This example is not about breathing heavily in order to soften up the defence system, as Reich understood breathwork (Macnaughton, 2015), but about observing carefully what changes when someone takes a few deep breaths.

Breathing and feelings

The breathing not only reveals who somebody is but also their momentary mood (Lowe & Laing-Gilliat, 2007, p. 73). 'The way we breathe is almost identical with the way we feel' (Thornquist & Bunkan, 1991, p. 34). The breathing changes involuntarily when we are in shock, receive a message that moves us or when we are thinking intensely. Then we tend to hold the breath in the inhalation. People 'cannot breathe' when they feel under pressure or their breath catches when they are startled. In panic we breathe agitatedly in the upper chest and possibly end up in hyperventilation (cf. Levine & Macnaughton, 2004, p. 374). When we are afraid we take rapid short breaths, when we are excited rapid, deep ones; when we are lying in the sun completely relaxed, we breathe deeply and slowly; when we are overjoyed we emphasise the exhalation.

In therapy we can take advantage of this connection between categorical emotions and respiratory patterns so as to trigger emotions via the breathing (Geuter, 2019, pp. 177–8). A corresponding method, Alba Emoting (Kalawski, 2020), is based on the experimental evidence of Bloch et al. (1991) that voluntary changes in breathing parameters can induce emotions.

The emotional tone of language is also connected to respiration, as speaking consists of an outflow of air. When we ask a question out of curiosity then we have a slight tension in the chest. If a question has an element of hidden annoyance, then we ask it on the exhalation. A compassionate 'What have you done now?' is accompanied by a relaxed, indulgent exhalation; if this same sentence is spoken critically, then we hold the breathing back as we go into a mode of action readiness. Answering a question is usually begun on the exhalation, since then we are more aware of our feelings and thus of our own point of view.

By means of the breathing, we can regulate anxiety and thus resistance. Shallow breathing lessens the depth of feeling and therefore we feel the anxiety less. In order to feel less anxiety, we can restrain the breathing. Thornquist and Bunkan (1991, pp. 25–6) differentiate between this '**breathing to prevent fear**' from a '**breathing in fear**', in which there can be a slight acceleration in the breathing rate, an uneven breathing rhythm and more breathing into the chest. In this way of breathing we can feel the anxiety. With increased abdominal breathing, we can regulate the level of anxious arousal (Acolin, 2019, p. 41), which we can also do by consciously pausing between breaths (Macnaughton, 2015, p. 641).

If a patient blocks their feelings by inhibiting respiration, we can help them to feel the tension hindering their breathing, to relax it and then to release the feelings connected with it (Lowen, 1967, p. 172). By breathing into the feelings they can become more aware of them, since just as breathing against feelings serves as a defence, so breathing into the feelings softens it up. When a patient has little connection to their feelings, we can increase core affective arousal through breathing techniques. This intensifies emotional experience (Geuter, 2019, pp. 166–70). This can lead both to a deepening of experience as well as to a resolution of feelings; then the intervention has a paradoxical effect.

Important
In therapy we take particular care that people breathe into their feelings and not against them or calm down heightened emotional arousal with the breath.

If a patient is overwhelmed by feelings, then the arousal can be alleviated through the breathing – for instance, not breathing out too deeply when they have revealed something that moves them. Since the voluntary respiratory change affects the reticular formation, the soothing effect of a consciously calm breathing spreads to other vegetative functions such as circulation; this in turn stimulates self-healing. Consequently we can modulate breathing in various ways according to whether we want to induce emotions or calm them down (Boadella, 1987, p. 82):

• Concentrating on the exhalation helps to relinquish tension and control, to let feelings flow and to digest them.
• Concentrating on the inhalation helps to induce feelings, to hold them and to increase control. However, inhalation that is too strong can lead to loss of control.

In body psychotherapy, working with the breathing encourages conscious experience of affects and not liberation from them as yoga breathing aspires to (Section 3.4: '5. Breath'). In body psychotherapy we are not interested in teaching the patient to breathe 'correctly', but in gaining more latitude for breathing and thus for affect regulation and a differentiated experience of self (cf. Thornquist & Bunkan, 1991, pp. 30–1). If someone with limited respiration gains more 'breathing space', then their whole way of perceiving and reacting to the world will change. Breathing exercises and activities which promote breathing can be of help here (Heller, 2012, p. 205).

Clinical example

A patient, who is in a difficult exam situation, often speaks in a low voice; the breathing does not reach the abdomen, but is shallow and confined to the chest area. Her feeling is that it stops at the solar plexus. Her momentary attitude to life is full of anxiety, tension and exhaustion. We talk a lot about how she can still function in this situation and cope with all she has to do. To increase her strength and vitality I suggest she try an exercise from bioenergetics, the so-called 'bow', in which you extend the breathing volume by pressing the fists into the small of the back and bending the spine backwards (Lowen, 1967, p. 239–41; Geuter, 2019, p. 240). In addition I show her how by tapping the sternum she can activate a sensation of self and how by making the sound 'huh' as well as stretching the arms out behind and upwards she can gain more breathing space.

In the following weeks she did the bow exercise at home every morning. This helped her discover her strength, soothe her anxiety and pass her exams.

Breathing as a gauge of inner states

Respiration acts like a seismograph to thoughts, feelings, movements or touch (cf. von Steinaecker, 2010, p. 177), so that in the therapeutic process, the patient's breathing constantly gives the therapist an indication of their inner state. Thus from observing the breathing we can follow their emotional processes in therapy: 'The more liberated respiration becomes, the deeper the treatment's effect' (Thornquist & Bunkan, 1991, p. 30). Fluttering breathing can indicate increased arousal or a strengthening of the defences. By paying attention to the breathing, the therapist opens up another level of perception where the patient communicates often without knowing it.

Clinical application

From a slight faltering of the breathing, a therapist can tell that the client has encountered a sensation, a thought, an image or a memory that is unpleasant for them, even if they do not notice it themselves. Then it can be helpful to steer their awareness towards this change in the breathing and to ask them what is happening in connection with it. Thus, in the therapeutic process, the breathing can be used diagnostically as an indicator of resistance and also as a guide to gaining awareness.

When the breathing becomes freer and the client exhales more deeply, this can be a sign of a release of feeling or of a liberating insight or that an image has opened up a new perspective. Sometimes a deep sigh accompanies such liberating moments in therapy.

We can also gauge the effect of an intervention by the respiratory reaction of the patient. We can see whether a patient accepts the intervention and resonates with it through for instance that the breathing deepens or becomes more harmonious. If it becomes shallow when being touched this is a negative signal from the patient (Wehowsky, 1994, p. 108), or at least a cautious one. Breathing is, however, not only a signal from patient to therapist but also a transformation process in respiratory dialogue with the therapist, which is often unconscious (Chapter 14). With their own way of breathing, the therapist influences the breathing of the client. If the therapist continues to breathe when the client is holding their breath in connection with a critical issue, this can help to open up a communication space within the client. Beebe gives us a nice example of this, showing how she helps a patient to talk by synchronising her breathing with theirs: She describes a session in which the patient begins to open up to traumatic aspects of her early childhood:

> … at the point at which she might begin to discuss any of the details, she would become agitated, her body would tighten, and eventually she would hold her breath, as if in an effort to hold everything in. She would hold her breath for long periods, unable to stop, until she would begin to panic. Eventually I began to try to get her to synchronize with my breathing. I made soft, rhythmic sounds as I breathed in and out. Dolores called it the 'breathing song'. Together we began to be able to anticipate when an episode of breath-holding was about to begin, and we would do the breathing song together before she became extremely agitated. Over the course of the next couple of years, the breathing symptom gradually became less frequent.
>
> (Beebe, 2004, pp. 22–3)

6.3 SELF SENSES

In the model of the three layers of experience (Section 6.1), I made a distinction between the sensorimotor and the vegetative levels of self-experience. Now I want to look more closely at these two bodily levels. They are both based on the inner senses:

1. **Proprioception**, the sense of the position and movement of the body in space (deep sensibility), also known as the sixth sense.
2. **Interoception**, the sense for the perception of the inner environment of the body and the activity of the organs and the various vessels.

In addition, Damasio (1999) refers to a third system of bodily signals providing information about the inner world:

3. The system of **fine touch** that operates through sensors in the skin.

I will only mention briefly the anatomical and physiological basis for these sensory systems, since for psychotherapy it is primarily the phenomenology of self-perception that is important: a '**subjective anatomy**' and a '**subjective physiology**', which look at the experiences communicated proprioceptively and interoceptively from a first-person perspective (Section 7.1). For the theory of body psychotherapy, it is good to know the function of theses senses, but not necessarily exactly how they work on a physiological level.

Human senses can be divided up into inner and outer senses. The inner senses help us perceive our inner state, whereas through **exteroception**, with the five senses of seeing, hearing, smelling, tasting and touching, we perceive the outside world. However, from a phenomenological point of view, this classification is not distinct. On the one hand, with the inner senses I can perceive things outside myself, for example when my gut feeling tells me about a particular situation or a movement impulse lets me know about my relationship to a person who has just come through the door. On the other, I can perceive my inner state through the outer senses, when for instance I smell a change in my perspiration or see how my skin blushes in a certain social situation. When touching, I feel the contact between inside and out at the border of the skin anyway and also how this border disappears when I cuddle up to someone and we lose the sense of who is touching whom.

In body psychotherapy we work mainly with inner perception. However it is also important to hone outer perception too, so that the patient can apprehend the world more exactly: by looking or listening more closely, by touching something more attentively or by noticing when we smell danger (Geuter, 2019, pp. 85–6). Meditation methods often promote mindfulness by paying attention to the outer senses. For patients who have difficulty being aware of what is happening in the outside world (Section 10.5) it can be helpful to develop the outer senses, for example by asking them to notice the room they are sitting in. If a patient is insecure about my relationship to them, it can help if I ask them what they see when they look at me.

Often it is **somatic markers** which tell us what we feel or want. Damasio identifies somatic markers as bodily signals, conscious or unconscious, which support cognitive processes (Bechara et al., 2005; Damasio, 1994). They can also be seen as those bodily signals the significance of which, according to the semiotic theory of T. von Uexkuell, is deciphered by feelings (von Arnim et al., 2022).

People who are unable to notice their inner sensations because of neurological damage are incapable of making decisions. According to Damasio, we reach a decision through testing the various options available in as-if body loops and assessing the possible consequences through our respective somatic reactions. When a patient has to make a decision, as in the long clinical example in Section 6.2, we can utilise the direct bodily signals of intuitive knowledge that appear in connection with the various alternatives, when we locate them in symbolic positions around the room. Sensing somatic feedback in a differentiated way promotes self-congruence, because through the patient's awareness, explicit intentions align themselves with signals from the implicit mode of bodily reactions (Storch, 2002). Body experience is therefore essential for **intentionality**. The same is true of **emotional processes**. We become aware of them cognitively, proprioceptively and interoceptively (Section 6.1). And it is interoception which governs our perception of feelings (Damasio, 2012).

Damasio understands the interoceptive sense as those inner perceptions that result from signals from the muscles, vessels and organs: pain, body temperature, heat, tingling, shivering, visceral or genital sensations, the state of the smooth muscles of the blood vessels, local pH or blood sugar levels (Damasio, 2004). Awareness of our emotions and needs depends on our awareness of these inner perceptions (Craig, 2008). This is also linked to our ability to experience the world through our emotions (Damasio, 1999). Damasio surmises that this is why patients with locked-in syndrome do not feel scared or desperate about their condition. However patients who are paralysed from the neck down are capable of feeling emotions since they have feedback from their facial expressions through the trigeminus nerve.

> An experiment with couples, in which physiological measurements were made during emotionally fraught discussions, shows how emotional experience is directly related to actual bodily processes. The more blood flowed under heightened pressure into the periphery and the warmer the hands were, the more the participants spoke of being hot or under pressure. Thus the visceral and the somatic were one with subjective experience (Levenson, 2003, p. 354).

Interoception

At the beginning of the 20th century, Sherrington saw interoception as being just **visceroception**, the perception of organ activity (gastrointestinal and cardiovascular sensibility) (Craig, 2008, p. 273). Craig (2002) defines interoception more generally as the sense of the physiological condition of the body. This covers a whole array of afferent information from all areas of the body, whether neuromuscular, gastrointestinal, cardiovascular, tactile, respiratory, endocrine, chemical or osmotic in nature (Cameron, 2001, p. 697). The receptors of this system, such as the thermoreceptors in the skin and mucous membranes, pain receptors, muscle metaboreceptors or baroreceptors in the blood vessels, react to temperature, pressure, pain, itching, tension or sensations in the intestines (cf. Fogel, 2009, pp. 45–51). Some afferent nerves are sensitive only to light sensual touch (Craig, 2003, p. 501).

The interoceptive system carries information about the condition of the smooth muscles in the viscera, for instance in the gut, or about the deeper layers of the skin, in which changes in the blood vessels are registered, for example when something gets 'under my skin'. Afferent information from the organs is gathered in the nucleus of the solitary tract in the brain stem and projected from there into other areas of the brain such as the amygdala and the frontal brain. Consequently it influences cognition and emotions (Berntson et al., 2003). The interoceptive system functions not only neuronally but also hormonally – it uses both nerve pathways and chemical signals.

The aggregate of interoceptive perceptions communicates the subjective tone of experience. It forms the basis for moods and emotional states (Craig, 2003), which appear in less specific body perceptions, and indicates whether something feels good or bad. The primary core affective evaluation of events as pleasant or unpleasant in the theory of emotions (Section 10.1) has here its basis in the body. Visceral afferents also signal the perception of discrete emotions such as anger or fear, when something turns my stomach or makes my heart stop. Greenberg (2011) therefore wants to concentrate in Emotion-Focused Therapy on emotions as 'visceral experience'. Someone who cannot perceive these inner signals will find it difficult to orientate themselves emotionally and to recognise their own needs. Interoceptive perceptions give us the incentive to change things (Fosha, 2001, pp. 228–9).

Brain or heart

Depraz (2008) suggests that we can overcome mind/body dualism by using a model centred on the heart, as the subjective view of the world is formed through the physiological dynamics of the heart and the breathing. She says it is in and with the heart that we feel; it exists physically and we experience it as vital. The brain in contrast can never be experienced from the first-person perspective as there are no sensors for the interoception of the organ itself. We experience all the other parts of the body interoceptively from the first-person perspective. A brain model of the human being would be thus of no help in overcoming dualism.

The heart combines the physical and the phenomenal dimension and so communicates the affectively anchored, intersubjective structure of experience (Depraz, 2008, p. 248). When we say that we feel with the heart or we have understood something with the heart, then this is as Wittgenstein (1967, p. 213) observed, not an 'image of our choice' but a 'pictorial expression' of something that we feel to be true. Depraz (2008, p. 243) concludes from this that we feel ourselves as embodied, existing subjects most strongly in the heart. In body psychotherapy, Young (2015, p. 645) sees the heart as 'the centre, source and receptacle of very powerful emotions and a sense of life and well-being'. I assume that the feeling we have towards ourselves is formed through the whole of the body, but that the heart sensations have a special place in relation to the affects.

In body psychotherapy, we access interoceptive perception when we ask a patient to focus their attention on the inside, on what they are feeling. When we turn our attention to the body, then an 'inwardness' develops. To support this inwardness, we need to **slow down** various processes:

Letting … embodied sensations and emotions emerge spontaneously and in their 'I'll-take-my-own-time-thank-you' way. You'll find out that you can't command yourself to feel something but you can ask yourself to wait, pay attention, and keep coming back.

(Fogel, 2009, p. 49)

A technical aid for interoception is biofeedback, in which we practice perceiving inner processes by observing outer parameters.

Interoceptive awareness

In psychological research, sensitivity to inner bodily signals counts as an indicator for how well people grasp emotional situations (Pollatos et al., 2007, p. 939). This is known as interoceptive awareness. Someone who is aware of the inner state of their body is also more emotionally expressive (Critchley et al., 2004).

Sensitivity is usually determined on the basis of the awareness of one's own heartbeat. The more precisely someone perceives their own heartbeat, the more agitated they are when looking at unpleasant images (Pollatos et al., 2007). Awareness of the heartbeat does not, however, indicate any specific emotion, but only the core affective state of arousal (cf. Wiens, 2005, pp. 444–5; Section 10.1). Bechara and Naqvi (2004) also point out this difference: being aware of visceral sensations is not the same as feeling a categorical emotion. Feelings only develop in a process of realisation, in which bodily sensations are linked experientially to the meaning of a situation (Section 10.6).

Someone who is aware of their own heartbeat is more easily aware of the magnitude of an emotional activation. Since core affective reactivity, the potential amplitude of emotional arousal, is a component of temperament (Section 11.5), it is not surprising that cardio-sensitivity is deemed to be a fixed character trait (Herbert & Pollatos, 2008, p. 128). However we can increase our capacity to perceive our own heart beat through meditative practices (Bornemann & Singer, 2017).

Also there seem to be cultural differences in interoceptive sensibility. Asian Americans are less aware of their heartbeat than are Americans of European ancestry (Ma-Kellams et al., 2012).

Pollatos et al. (2007) describe heightened attentiveness for visceroceptive signals in **patients with an anxiety disorder**. This makes sense in that such patients are often in an activated-unpleasant core affective state (Section 10.2). However we have to look more closely at these findings. Critchley et al. (2004, p. 189) are keen to differentiate between general attentiveness to signals and the accuracy of the perception. Anxious people tend to pay more attention to the signals from their body; their awareness of bodily states is generally higher (Critchley et al., 2004, p. 193), but their perceptions are not exact. For psychotherapy it is above all a question of learning to perceive and decipher somatic messages more precisely and not one of turning anxiously to them.

Proprioception

Proprioception is the ability to sense movement, action and location of the body, meaning the awareness of changes of position of the musculoskeletal system via information from the neuromuscular spindles, Golgi tendon organs and joint receptors as well as skin receptors, hair follicles and the vestibular receptor systems. Approximately ten million tactile sensors register cold, warmth, pressure or drafts on the skin as well as skin stretching, joint movement or the stretching and position changes of the muscles. They provide information about the spatial relationship of the body to the environment.

If we lose proprioception, then we also lose the automatisms of body schema; then we have no feeling for our own bodies (Fuchs, 2000, pp. 138–9). Someone who has lost their proprioceptive sense cannot even just sit down, because the implicit process of the movement has also gone (Chesler et al., 2016). However such cases are rare. Cole (2016) describes the case of a man whose proprioception was destroyed by a virus infection. He could no longer move, was very anxious and disembodied and had to slowly learn to guide every movement with his thoughts and visual sense.

Sacks (1993) had an accident in which his quadriceps was torn from the kneecap, so that afterwards he was unable to recognise his leg, because a tear in the nerve lead to the loss of self-perception: 'One has oneself, one *is* oneself, because the body knows itself, confirms itself, at all times, by this sixth sense' (Sacks, 1993, p. 50). One of Sacks's patients who, because of polyneuropathy, had lost her whole self-perception, lost with it the organic anchor of her identity (Sacks, 1985). Patients with back pain show measurable deficits in proprioceptive awareness (Mehling et al., 2009). They are also part of a cultural loss of proprioception in a society lacking in spontaneous movement (Mehling, 2010, p. 172).

However proprioception not only refers to body schema (Section 6.7), but has also to do with our relationship to a situation. We notice proprioceptively whether we want to move towards something, or go through, into, or out of it, and we feel an impulse to approach an object or another person or to distance ourselves from them or them from us. In this way we feel one of the components of an emotional reaction (Section 10.4). Motor impulses convey something of our intentions towards the environment. Proprioceptive signals inform us about the environment itself. For instance, when we are aware of the position of our joints when we are throwing a ball, then we know without looking where the ball will land. We orientate ourselves in the outside world through inner perception.

Proprioception, in contrast to interoception, has long been an aspect in the formation of a theory of body psychotherapy, particularly in Functional Relaxation. Here proprioception is seen as the foundation of the body self (von Arnim et al., 2022, p. 116). Stimulating the development of the body self and of vitality through proprioception is seen by Johnen (2010) as the guiding principle of treatment. Dance and movement therapy too emphasises the awareness of the body in movement. Koch (2011, p. 38) writes that it is because of their inherent, kinaesthetic spontaneity that human beings are subjects and social beings and recognise themselves in their own movements. Self-perception, however, always includes proprioception, interoception and the perception of touch.

Important
Proprioception, interoception and touch perception all contribute to bodily self-perception and thus to the constitution of the body self. Interoception plays an especially important role in the perception of emotions.

Just as with interoception, in body psychotherapy we help patients become aware of proprioception by slowing down (Geuter, 2019, p. 41; Sollmann, 2009). This has its match in the principle of the work of Elsa Gindler, whereby people learn to feel themselves in their bodies by moving slowly. O'Shaughnessy (1998, p. 177) writes of an 'introspective proprioception', when we focus our attention on specific parts of the body. If on the other hand we are using the body for an intentional act, such as catching a ball, then the focus is not on inner perception but on the perception of the outside world by means of the body.

The sense of touch

The tactile sense serves both outer and inner perception, but is more for outside objects. We sense in our hand for example through touch whether an object is rough or smooth. This in turn generates a feeling relationship to the object (Chapter 8). The sense of touch is different from the exteroceptive senses in that I can direct my attention both to the hand and to the object. Then either I feel more my fingertips or more the surface texture of the object. We feel the object on ourselves, on the border between inside and outside.

The other senses do not have this double quality that sensing touch has. When we see something with our eyes, it is difficult to alternate between perceiving what we see and perceiving the eyes. The reason for this is that we sense the eyes and the ears as organs, but we see and hear with them, whereas with touch, we sense both the touching organ and the touched object with the same sensual quality.

From an evolutionary and ontogenetic perspective, the tactile sense is the oldest sense (Montagu, 1971; Section 11.1). The biological basis for it are:

- About 50 receptors on each of the approximately 5 million body hairs, that is 250 million receptors.
- Between 300 and 600 million different receptors in the skin, especially in the denser areas of greater sensitivity such as the tongue, the lips and the fingers.
- 2×10^{12} free nerve endings in the skin (Grunwald, 2012).

These figures alone illustrate that the touch experience is always going to be holistic and will include an abundance of information. We cannot equate it to the scientific knowledge of the receptors (Section 6.5).

Human beings cannot live without the sense of touch (Grunwald, 2012, pp. 45–6). If we lose the skin, the organ of touch, we die. The sense of touch enables us to experience ourselves as physical entities in a spatial relationship to the world around us. Patients who have lost their tactile sense, can no longer control their limbs, since they have no feedback from the body. They are not able to feel that they are lying down and they cannot sit up. When they try to do it by using their visual sense to guide them, they are exhausted after a few minutes (Robles-De-La-Torre, 2006).

Unlike the senses of sight or hearing, the kinaesthetic feedback from the skin in relation to the environment is practically indispensable. Without this body sense, no consciousness can develop, but people born deaf and blind are capable of it (Grunwald, 2012). A sense of self develops in the first weeks of life via the skin, primarily by the child internalising the direct experience of being held (Anzieu, 2016).

In body psychotherapy, touch can help to focus self-perception, for example when a patient lays a hand on their chest and tries to feel in the hand what is happening in the chest. The hand of the therapist can also help the patient to notice a tension, an inner state or a feeling and thus to become aware of themselves. In therapy, touch is a powerful part of healing contact (Geuter, 2019, pp. 248–70).

Self-perception and the brain

The findings of brain research show the connection between the inner perception of the body and that of the feelings. Of all the regions of the brain it is the insula, a small part of the cerebral cortex on the border between the frontal, the parietal and the temporal lobes, which is most involved in interoception (Cameron, 2001, p. 703). In one part of the insula, unmyelinated visceral sensory neurons terminate (Critchley, 2009, p. 91). The more precisely someone recognises their heartbeat, the more activity there is in that region (Critchley et al., 2004). Afferent fibres, existing only in primates, lead to the insula and bring information about the condition of the body (Craig, 2008). Pain, temperature and feelings all activate the respective part of the insula; the anterior is active in all emotions.

Direct stimulation of the digestive organs also leads to activity in those regions of the brain which receive interoceptive signals (Critchley, 2009). This is possibly one of the ways in which biodynamic massage, which influences the internal organs, works (Schaible, 2009; Southwell, 1988), namely by heightening interoceptive awareness (Geuter, 2019, pp. 270–3; Carroll, 2002). In studies, severely traumatised patients with dissociative symptoms, who no longer feel their bodies, show a reduction in the activity of the insula and of the cingulate cortex when the trauma is reactivated (Levine, 2010).

Next to the insula, the anterior cingulate cortex is important for both visceroceptive perception and for the regulation of feelings (Herbert & Pollatos, 2008, p. 130). Here the functional condition of the body is monitored and linked to affective and motivationally important information (Dalgleish, 2004, p. 586). Interoceptive neuronal signals initially engender thalamocortical representations, which lead by projection to further representations in the anterior cingulate cortex of the right hemisphere. Since these are not direct representations of signals from the periphery, Craig calls them secondary representations. For him, they are the neurophysiological basis for the emergence of interoceptive physiological signals as emotional consciousness – Craig (2003, p. 503) speaks of 'homeostatic emotions' and thinks that this is arguably how the subjective consciousness of a feeling self develops:

> These findings signify the cortical representation of feelings from the body as the likely basis for human awareness of the physical self as a feeling entity.
>
> (Craig, 2002, p. 663)

These secondary representations of interoceptive signals are only part of the neuroanatomy of primates. This phylogenetically new system makes it possible for people to perceive the self as a separate and bodily entity on the basis of these signals. The human organism is thus built up on an awareness of the body.

Clinical application

Craig (2002, p. 664) makes a point of clinical interest: pain symptoms or somatisation in the case of stress are connected to a dysfunction of homeostatic body systems. Consequently, in an integrative approach we can treat such patients by helping them become more strongly aware of the corresponding bodily signals. This supports the approach of body psychotherapy of encouraging bodily awareness in such cases. Especially patients with pain symptoms and fibromyalgia profit from learning a more intensive perception of the body (von Arnim & Joraschky, 2009, p. 192; Kuechenhoff, 2009, p. 180).

6.4 THE SELF AS THE LIVED ENTITY OF EXPERIENCE

When in psychotherapy we speak of patients becoming aware of themselves, then we mean not an awareness of self as an object, but of a subject making sure of the world and of their own personal states (cf. Eilan et al., 1998). Hitherto I have demonstrated that to do so, a person has to sense and experience themselves. However, to see ourselves as 'I myself', we also need a cognitive idea of 'me myself' as a person who experiences something (Zahavi, 2016). This idea arises in a non-conscious manner as a feeling for who I am (Nijenhuis, 2016, p. 95). It is based on the continuity of the feeling of being a consistent organism and on the perception of an I that is different from a not-I. Roehricht (2009a, p. 34) defines the bodily experience of unity that lies behind this as the body self.

I and self

Freud had no concept of the self. He saw the I or ego as an instance of control between the id and the superego. In contrast, for Jung, the concept of self was essential; with it he meant the unity of the personality and an inner wholeness, which was the goal of the process of individuation. William James differentiated between the *I* as the subject which has consciousness and observes and the *me* as the self that becomes conscious.

In Kuhl's (2019; Kuhl et al., 2015; Chapter 17) Personality Systems Interactions theory (PSI), the self serves to integrate a multitude of personally relevant experiences and also contains the felt knowledge that comes from experience, whereas the I stores explicit experiences and knowledge of rules. The self learns implicitly through inner dialogue and interaction. Thus the concept of self emphasises more the relatedness of the human being than does that of the I (Fuchs & Vogeley, 2016, p. 121).

The experience of a bodily unity gives people the feeling that there is something permanent in the transience of existence. This lets us think of ourselves as 'I myself'. However we have no self as something material, but just ourselves. The self is an experience of being that person who experiences (Zahavi, 2016). We cannot capture it as an object but can only understand it phenomenologically as a model or a pattern, with the aid of which we negotiate our way through everyday life and organise our vital functions (Ghin, 2005; Metzinger, 2013; Rispoli, 2006, p. 638). As such it is as real as our experiences are:

> What I call my 'self' is simply myself as a fully-fledged embodied entity. What I experience as my self is a select subset of everything the body, which includes the brain, does.
>
> (Gallagher, 2005a, p. 8)

According to enactivism, an autopoietic system 'produces and realizes an individual or self in the form of a living body' (Thompson, 2010, p. 158). My pre-reflective experience of myself is created by my bodily reality. When I experience myself as 'I myself', then I conflate certain current and past experiences, accessible in the actual window of awareness, into a model of 'my self'. Metzinger (2005, p. 248) speaks of a **phenomenal self** as that model of the self currently activated. The self does not exist in perpetuity, but rather reconstructs itself as a relatively stable idea in any given moment (Metzinger, 2010) in that environment in which we currently experience ourselves (Parfy & Lenz, 2009, p. 75). The foundation of the experience of continuity is the pre-reflective feeling of the continuity of the lived body (Fuchs, 2017; Snowdon, 1998).

The concept of the self is, however, not just an idea with which subjects express the feeling of physical unity and continuity. We need such a concept in science too. We cannot speak of self-organisation or self-regulation without positing a self that organises and regulates (cf. Tschacher, 2004).

In psychology, the notion of self has long been rationalised away (Kuhl, 2007, p. 63). In humanistic psychology, however, it has played a central role from the beginning. Rogers equates the self with **experience**, which changes from moment to moment (Rogers & Wood, 1974). Already for Rogers the self was not something immutable, but a moment of activated experience, a flowing Gestalt, a process (Rogers, 1959, 1975).

Experiential psychotherapy understands the self in this way (Greenberg & Van Balen, 1998, pp. 42–5). Emotion-Focused Therapy sees the self as an experience of who we are, mediated by the body at each moment in time (Auszra et al., 2017, p. 31). In Gestalt therapy, it is seen as a process, a system of perpetually changing contacts (Wegschneider, 2020, p. 120).

Whereas in his analytical self psychology Kohut regarded the self as a psychological structure established in relationships and ascribed to it needs such as mirroring, idealisation, melting, bordering and efficacy (Kohut, 1971; Wolf, 1998), today intersubjective psychoanalysis understands the self as a process and at the same time as a co-construction in relationships (Ermann, 2017).

Rogers defines as **self-concept** an idea accessible to consciousness, which consists of a person's perceptions of themselves and their relationships to others and to the outside world (Rogers, 1951, 1975). Rogers wanted to help people to be the self that they really are and to be more aware of their real self (Kriz, 2001, pp. 169ff). The actualisation of the self was at the top of the pyramid of needs developed by Maslow (1968; Section 10.3).

In humanistic understanding, **therapy** is a **reappropriation of the self** in the face of experiences that had to be suppressed, dissociated or disowned as not belonging to oneself (Chapter 18). Therapy should help to re-own what has been shut out of experience and thus is not conscious: therapy 'is the owning and reprocessing of experience to assimilate it into existing meaning structures' (Greenberg & Van Balen, 1998, p. 35). However this is a process deeply connected to the body. Owning means to experience oneself as the person who was sad about something, angry about something or self-destructive. Reappropriation means being able to integrate various aspects of experience (Greenberg & Van Balen, 1998, p. 43).

In Kuhl's PSI theory of personality, the self is a **system** which offers a simultaneous overview of numerous life experiences and operates cross-linked and parallel to emotions in a holistic process (Kuhl, 2007, p. 52). According to Kuhl et al. (2015), an **integrated self** is characterised by a unity of thinking, feeling and acting and establishes a coherence, based on the integration of autobiographical experiences, that is stable over time. We have to add an intersubjective perspective to this intrasubjective one, since an integrated self grows over the course of a lifetime through relational experiences, in which a person learns to see themselves through the eyes of others and shares experiences with them (Kyselo, 2014; Section 11.2). It will encompass a coherence between a person's concept of self and how they experience themselves in relation to other people. It reveals itself in our embodied social interactions and is always a work in progress (Menary, 2014; Bolis & Schilbach, 2018a).

We could therefore describe the self as a dynamic system, the health of which depends on integrating as many parts as possible into consciousness. The unity of experience may be based on bodily experience, but the body alone does not produce it. Otherwise a condition such as dissociative identity disorder, in which various models of the self exist in the same body, would not be possible (cf. Schramme, 2005). However since body experience is an essential constituent, the sense of an integrated self breaks down when the body is traumatised.

For Rispoli, the self is a system that encompasses memory, symbols, fantasies, ideas, the ability to plan and rationality, as well as movement, posture, the form and sense of the body, muscle tension and the respiratory, neurological, neurovegetative and immune systems (Rispoli, 2006, p. 638). However it is not the body systems as objects but the living experience of these systems that belongs to the self.

From the point of view of body psychotherapy, the self is thus not only an idea or a cognitive model, but the embodied experience of being the same person throughout one's life, who despite all the changes goes through experiences and gains a subjective feeling of 'I myself'. The self is what a person continually lives, the particular way that they experience themselves and the environment, especially other people, and the way they treat themselves and the world at large. Human beings constantly create their 'self in action' (Perls et al., 1980). As bodily beings with a life story, we are the embodied self. I understand the self as this lived entity of experience.

Important
The self as the lived entity of experience is activated in the cognitive, affective and motor patterns of the confrontation with oneself, with others and with the world. It is a self based on experience and lived in the present.

This understanding differs from the notion we sometimes find in body psychotherapy of the self as an essence or an inner core of being, which we have to liberate from the experiences superimposed upon it (Rosenberg et al., 1985; Pierrakos, 1987). The self is not a kind of substance existing independently of experience. Bateson (2002) asks who I know when I try to live up to the challenge: 'Know thyself'. We cannot find the answer to this by producing something that lives in the depths independently of our lives, but only in life itself.

The self is a fundamental subjective reality created through experience, which we reveal through our way of living and which we feel. Connecting the idea of the self to the experience of self saves us from the dangers of reification.

Furthermore, the self is never something finished. We do not carry it about to show it to others, because depending on the interaction and the situation, it can change its hue. As a lived entity of experience, it develops primarily out of human relationships as a co-construct. Therefore the theory of a self based on experience does not contradict the theory in social science that the self is a social construct (Zahavi, 2016). The self is connected to the cultural environment and thus can change with it (Hermans, 2001, 2014). We are subjects whose identity is formed by the environment and depends on background, gender, ethnicity or religion (Code, 2014).

The **theory of the self** is also a **social construct** of modern Western civilisation. Gergen (2014) speaks of a cultural and social practice of seeing oneself as a self. In our society, we learn to talk about our actions as if they were all governed by a sole protagonist.

In the times before Homer, however, it was usual to assume the soul was a bicameral system, whereby through the one chamber voices of the gods or of the kings spoke to people, who were guided by them (Jaynes, 1976). Today such thinking would be classified as paranoid. In addition it is a construct of occidental thinking that we can find the 'self' by descending in oneself from the surface into the depths (P Fuchs, 2010).

Ho (2019) also sees the theory of the *self-with-others*, according to which the self relates to others, as being a **Western view** of human beings. In the **Eastern view,** there is more a *self-in-others*, meaning that two people in one room are seen as connected through Qi. Markus and Kitayama (1991) point out that in Eastern societies, the self is regarded as interdependent and not as independent.

Rogers links the theory of self to the **theory of consistency**, which says that needs are satisfied through behaviour connected with the self-concept. Incongruency between experience and self-concept leads to dysfunctions. Grawe (2004, 2007) based his consistency theory of the psyche on Rogers' theory. Brown (1990, p. 292) sees 'continuity, unity, solidity' – whereby solidity equals consistency – as the qualities of a basic feeling of self that he calls 'core self'. They can be seen as qualities of psychological integration deeply rooted in bodily experience.

Clinical example

A patient, in treatment for anxiety and depression, is crying because her boyfriend has hurt her badly. Everything makes her sad. Saying this she slides her chin almost unnoticeably to the front and frowns slightly, both signs of anger. Her voice sounds more compressed than yielding. So I ask her to pay attention to her body while she speaks, to the feeling in her chest, the sound of her voice and the movement of her chin. At first she has to defend against the anger, which is probably too dangerous for her. It is pressing down on her, she feels compressed, she says. I ask her to stay with this feeling and to feel what this compression is saying to her and how she is aware of it in the body. Now she says: 'Something wants to explode'. I ask what this could be and she answers: 'There is anger too'. Now we can go on to work with what this anger wants and whether the anger contains a wish for her relationship with her boyfriend.

In this way we can transform one emotion into another, the sadness into anger and then the anger into a need, which Greenberg (2021) sees as one of the essential principles of Emotion-Focused Therapy (Section 10.6). This transformation takes place in an inner process in which, on the basis of body experience, the patient becomes aware of her unconscious feelings without the therapist having to interpret them. The route to this realisation is through pointing out incongruencies between what she is saying and her bodily expression, which communicates something different, until a feeling of congruency is reached. In body psychotherapy, such incongruencies are a possible starting point for body-oriented exploration (Geuter, 2019, pp. 132–9).

Coherence

In body psychotherapy, we often work with the feeling of coherence. Something feels coherent when verbal and bodily representations are congruent. According to the above-mentioned distinction made by Kuhl, coherence belongs to the self, since only I can feel whether something is coherent for me. I can check something and then consider with others whether it is right. However, only truths that I fully possess myself are therapeutically effective (Cavell, 2006, p. 186). When I describe my inner state or my feeling, then the words can be suitable or not, but they cannot be right or wrong (Geuter, 2019, pp. 375–80).

Coherence is a category grounded in the experiential tradition of body psychotherapy. Jacoby (Section 3.1) spoke of a sense of coherence by which a person could orientate themselves (Arps-Aubert, 2012, p. 129). Recently Plassmann (2021, p. 47) also uses the term in psychodynamic therapy. The feeling of coherence offers an orientation in the therapeutic situation as to whether we have discovered the appropriate emotional meaning, and also whether a person can accept their life as they are living it is revealed through the feeling of coherence it summons up.

In body psychotherapy we find the idea that we can discover our **true self**, when we feel deeply enough. However there is no true self like a trove that we can recover, but only a feeling that something is coherent for us, or, going with Rogers, that my self-concept is coherent for me. The true self is thus a metaphor for this feeling (Boeckh, 2019, p. 7).

The notion of a true self induces a romantic idealisation of an all-round positive primitive state, because, for example, it dates from the merging of the egg and the sperm cells, as Rowan (1987) writes. Reich had a similar view of a simple, loving human nature as the primary personality behind all the blocks. Here we can easily be tempted into accepting as real something for the existence of which there is no evidence.

However, as long as the concept of the true self is used in the sense of an integration of inner and outer experience (Cozolino, 2002, p. 197), it corresponds to that of an **integrated self**. Winnicott (1965) understood 'true self' as being a spontaneous aliveness, which is really felt and can be concealed by a **false self**. This idea of a false self for a psychological state where, in the face of intimidating expectations, a child develops a demeanour not really their own, is clinically helpful; it can be seen as an alienation from the original life expression (Dornes, 2000, p. 197) or as a disintegration, in which it is not possible to incorporate experiences into a coherent self because they conflict too strongly with the person's needs. Grawe (2007) uses Rogers' notion of incongruence.

Some practitioners of body psychotherapy use the spiritual idea of the **higher self**. Here the Christian idea that a spiritual aspect exists in a higher sphere beyond the physical lives on. We cannot know whether this is true. Near-death experiences do support it. However in a science-based body psychotherapy, we cannot work with this concept. In addition, the idea that a higher self transcends the lower self of the body is a dualistic notion (M Johnson, 2007, p. 2). However the principle of body-mind continuity developed by John Dewey asserts that all higher states are based on lower ones and so cannot be separated (Johnson, 2007, p. 122).

6.5 CORE SELF AND NARRATIVE SELF – A STAGES MODEL

In theories, the self is sometimes seen as a dimension of experience and sometimes as a narrative construction (Zahavi, 2008). What appears to be a contradiction can be resolved through a stages model, in which the one perspective leads us to ideas of a core or minimal self, the other to those of a narrative self. This also makes sense from a developmental point of view, since in childhood the self develops in stages (Section 11.2).

In his theory based on neurobiology, Damasio (1999) posits three **stages of the self**, which he assigns to **stages of consciousness** connected to the functions of certain brain structures (Table 6.1). The elementary basis of the self, according to Damasio, is a representation of bodily states in the brain, which he calls the **protoself**. He understands this as being a collection of those neuronal patterns which represent the body's condition. Damasio

TABLE 6.1
Levels of the self according to Damasio and Gallagher

Levels of the self	Cognitive function	Level of consciousness
Protoself	Representation of bodily states in the brain – representations of the first order	Completely unconscious
Core self (= minimal self)	Provides the organism with a sense of self – creates representations of the second order	Core consciousness – momentary awareness in the here and now
Autobiographical (= narrative) self	Provides the organism with a biographical identity on the basis of memory – positions the self in time and space – coordinates the activation and presentation of personal memories	Extended consciousness – enduring awareness of identity over time

calls them representations of the first order. On this level, for example, processes such as the production of thyroid hormones or the degree of perspiration are regulated. Most of these regulatory processes are not capable of consciousness.

From the point of view of enactivism, the construct 'representation' is questionable (Section 9.1). However we can also see the protoself phenomenologically as a stage of unconscious processes of perception and regulation of the self.

Damasio puts the **core self** on a second level above the protoself. On this level a **core consciousness** emerges via the body. The beginning of this consciousness is 'feeling what is happening' (Damasio, 1999).

Damasio sees consciousness in general as a feeling of cognition. Consciousness creates two things: the representation of a perceived object as well as subjective meaning in the act of knowing. When I experience something and simultaneously notice how I am experiencing it, then I give the experience meaning and create the possibility of storing it explicitly. We encourage this in therapy by directing the patient's awareness towards present experience.

On the level of the core self, a person is aware of what they are experiencing at that moment. According to Damasio, the core self creates itself from moment to moment in a pulsating movement that reacts to the continuous changes in the inner state of the organism and to its interactions with the environment. Damasio calls the neuronal patterns of core consciousness, arising in the relationship between the organism and an object in the moment of cognition, second-order representations. From a phenomenological viewpoint, the consciousness of the core self is the self-awareness of subjective experience. This is something we often work with in psychotherapy.

Core consciousness corresponds to what is often defined in laboratory experiments as consciousness: a window of attentiveness opened for about 15 seconds in which we can memorise around seven pieces of information simultaneously, for instance a telephone number.

However, human consciousness functions usually on a medium time level in which, for minutes and hours at a time, it continuously manages behaviour, makes long-term plans, monitors various processes and creates a cognitive self (Donald, 2001). We experience this time level as the present (Geuter, 2019, pp. 66–7). Damasio calls this level of human awareness **extended consciousness**. It positions the self in time and space, creates an inner unity of experience over time (Fuchs & Vogeley, 2016), links current representations to personal long-term memories and thus establishes the **autobiographical self** as the third stage of the development of the self. Only on the level of the autobiographical self does a **narrative identity** develop.

> Rogers' theory of the self as experience (Section 6.4) corresponds to what Damasio calls the core self. His notion of the self-concept corresponds to the narrative self as a coherent idea of who I am.

Huether (2006, p. 86) brings the protoself and the core self together in the concept of the **body self**. The rudiments of this exist from birth onwards (Rochat, 2014). The anatomical brain structures which form the basis for it mature first in newborns (Damasio, 1999). These are the brainstem, the hypothalamus, the somatosensory and cingulate cortex, which belong to the phylogenetically older parts of the brain and are involved in body regulation and representation.

When in therapy we work with processes on the level of the core self, then we are working with what emerges in present experience (cf. Zahavi, 2010). This work connects body psychotherapy with the patient's reflections on their life story, the level of the narrative self. Through affect motor patterns of experience and behaviour, this life story surfaces in the present (Chapter 12). They are components of the autobiographical self, which comes to light in the experience of the core self.

Important
Body psychotherapy methods connect working with core consciousness in experiencing the moment with working on expanded consciousness through biographical reflection.

> For therapy, Damasio's thesis that consciousness is a feeling mediated via the body is of great interest. In body psychotherapy, we work on core consciousness when we help people with derealisation or dissociative symptoms to become aware that they are the person feeling something, or when we help people in denial to realise what is actually happening inside them at that moment. The more aware people are of their momentary feelings, the clearer their subjective perspective on their experience becomes. Basically we could say that **the central principle of working with the body in psychotherapy consists of fostering an awareness of now by helping patients feel in their bodies what is happening** (cf. Marlock, 2015a). This corresponds to the principle of the stream of consciousness in Gestalt therapy. In verbal reflection, what has becoming conscious in the present is connected with the patient's life story, with their experiences as well as with their desires and projects for the future, so that it is woven into the extended consciousness of the autobiographical self.

What Damasio differentiates between the core self and the autobiographical self, Gallagher (2000) and Zahavi (2010) call **minimal self** and **narrative self**. Gallagher is interested in the question of what is the minimal basis for a sense of self. He sees this in the two feelings of being oneself, a *sense of ownership*, and of being the one who acts, a *sense of agency*. Zahavi speaks of a *personal ownership*, when I see myself as the owner of my experiences. The one is a feeling of the 'intrinsic ownness or mineness of experience' and the other the 'pre-reflective experience that I am the one who is causing or generating a movement or action' (Gallagher, 2014a, p. 14).

In the case of a severe mental disorder, both of these can go missing: the mineness when, for example, someone cannot experience their arm as belonging to them, and the sense of agency when a part of the body does not move as the person means it to (Geuter, 2019, pp. 318–9). Schizophrenia can be seen as a loss of the sense of the core self and thus as a disembodiment (Fuchs & Roehricht, 2017; Parnas & Sass, 2010, 2014). The patient no longer knows who they are in relation to the world of objects and to themselves. They lose their embodied points of reference for cognition. When in a multiple personality disorder the feeling of being the one who experiences is lost, then the self falls apart.

Clinical application

The *sense of ownership* arises as a differentiation between 'what is felt to be mine' and 'what is felt to be not-mine' (Henry & Thompson, 2014, p. 233). In body psychotherapy, we can explore this through working with the borders between the body and the environment. As for the *sense of agency*, we can differentiate between an intentional and a motor aspect: the impulse and the movement (Geuter, 2019, pp. 74–6). Sometimes it is important therapeutically to follow an impulse into the movement, sometimes to control the impulse and not express it.

Feeling the body as mine is a form of self-certainty which cannot be assigned to specific perceptions. Rather it is a global feeling or certitude (Bermúdez, 2014). Mineness is based on an integration of different signals from the inner senses and perceptions through the distant senses through which a person takes in the environment in relation to their own body (Tsakiris, 2014; Section 6.3)

I have a sense of agency when I feel that I am the one who reaches for something (cf. David et al., 2008) and one of mineness when I experience the reaching arm as being mine. If someone else guides my arm, the mineness feeling is still there, but not that of agency (Synofzik et al., 2008). An awareness of self on this level is pre-reflective and directly accessible: I know both without thinking about them. This is where I speak of myself as 'I', who is simply there, thinking, feeling or acting. This sense of one's own body was called in early psychoanalysis the body ego (Roehricht, 2000, p. 48).

The **minimal self** is the **perspective of the first person in the moment of the experienced present** (cf. Blanke & Metzinger, 2009). However unless a person loses their memory it never exists for itself alone (Zahavi, 2010). All self-experience takes place within the context of time and space.

The **narrative self** does not arise from the awareness of the present moment; rather we acquire it through living our lives and we can call it up from episodic memories (Chapter 9). It is the **narrator of a life story** with a past and a future. Unlike the minimal self, it is spread out in time (Gallagher, 2000). It is a fiction, in the sense of a story that we tell ourselves, the story with which we create a feeling of continuity and which we call our biography: 'We use words to tell stories, and in these stories we create what we call our selves' (Gallagher, 2000, p. 19). These stories are continually evolving constructs with which we engender a sense of identity. Having created them, we are caught in their net. Often we are unable to control them, and they control us.

The narrative self offers my life story as the answer to the question of who I am. The core self offers my feelings or impressions as the answer to the question of how I see the world in the present moment and how I feel about it. When I see an old photo, I can ask whether that is really me, but not when I have toothache (Gallagher, 2014a, p. 5). On the level of the core self, I am not the psychotherapist who is writing a book, but someone who is pleased about the words he has just written and, when he pays attention to it, notices how tense his shoulders are.

On the level of the narrative self, dysfunction shows up as disorders of the mental integration of experiences. Traumatised patients however also show dysfunction on the level of sensory integration, when their sensory perceptions in the present fall to pieces. Consequently it is essential to include work with the body so as to help them regain a coherent experience of the self.

> The models of Damasio and Gallagher only deal with intrapersonal levels of the self. Beyond that we can identify further levels of a **social self**. People always see and experience themselves in relation to others, for example when they are ashamed (Zahavi, 2010). Patients often see themselves negatively by taking over other people's view of them.

6.6 BODY SELF AND IDENTITY

Despite the fact that both experience and the experiencer as well as the physical body are constantly changing, we still feel ourselves to be the same person. The basis for this is the bodily experience of unity (Roehricht, 2009a). Identity in flux is a characteristic of living systems (Thompson, 2010, p. 150).

Nowadays identity is often created through the body as an object via body styling, body building or cosmetic surgery (Section 1.4). For our purposes, however, it is not a question of outward appearances, but of the sum of lived experiences and personal history, which constitute the subjective sense of identity. Furthermore, these external identity creations often indicate that the person has become alienated from the lived body.

We can see identity from various points of view: as the identity of the evolving organism, as a role identity from the aspect of a person's social function, or as a narrative, personal identity from the aspect of the personal story I can tell about myself. By identity we usually mean this **narrative identity**. It belongs to the narrative self.

Just like the narrative self, the feeling of identity develops in the course of time (Campbell, 2014). That human beings can build it up over time is a result of autobiographical memory and episodic memories (Welzer & Markowitsch, 2005, p. 63; Welzer, 2002, p. 30; Section 9.1). In autobiographical memory, events that were significant emotionally and motivationally are woven together into a narratable individual story. The sense of identity connected to it contains all the changes, which every person goes through in their lives (Parfit, 2014).

The sense of identity, however, does not come from a series of pictures of biographical events. Rather, memories create identity when they are linked to sensory, bodily memories which are also stored with every event in episodic memory (Section 9.3). The autobiographical memory is always both a bodily and an emotional memory; it is related to our body self

(Welzer, 2002, pp. 130, 136). In body memory, our life story is also contained in the form of emotional procedural memories, which we live in the present (Section 9.3).

Life story

For life philosopher Wilhelm Dilthey (Section 3.4), the life story is the elementary entity of the life process. It is a context we can experience and which connects the various parts of our biography – namely by meaning (Habermas, 1969, p. 191). It is not in relation to a concept but in relation to my own life that my identity is established over time. Identity is a meaningful review of all I have experienced over my lifespan. According to Habermas, life experience integrates all the life interactions converging in the course of a life into the unity of a personal life story. This unity is anchored in the identity of the I and in the articulation of meaning or significance (Habermas, 1969, p. 193).

However life experience, as Dilthey said, develops in communication with others, and meaning can only be constituted through this communication (Habermas, 1969, p. 196). Identity is therefore an **experience in relationship**.

Without body experience, a person would have no conception of a personal story. The life story as the encompassing unit of human life processes consists of life experiences which we store both on a sensory, bodily level and symbolically. Damasio (1999) writes that identity is born in the sensory areas of the cortex, from where a complex of coherent identity memories can be brought forward at any time. These memories contain experiences of the person's relationship to the world mediated by the body and of the physical states connected to various events. As this relationship is created in motion, the feeling for movement is central for the sense of oneself. **Identity** is thus not a theoretical construct. It is **rooted deeply in body experience**.

When someone tells their life story, this only creates identity when it is felt to be convincing (Gugutzer, 2002, pp. 129–32). A comprehensive sense of identity connects self-narration with bodily sensation. Conversely, it is necessary to find the right words for what we feel, so that we can be sure of it and can talk about it. Personal identity thus develops through an interplay of bodily sensation and verbal reflection, which together create a secure feeling of who we are. A healthy identity is based on a feeling of self-coherence, in which body experience and verbally reflected ideas are congruent.

In an empirical study, Gugutzer (2002, pp. 171–91) found that ballet dancers see their bodies more from the outside as a little-loved object, a 'dance-body', whereas members of religious orders view their bodies as a gift of God, with which they can feel and experience life. The latter saw themselves as identical with themselves in contrast to the dancers. 'Being identical with oneself means to a great extent *feeling* identical with oneself' (Gugutzer, 2002, p. 130).

This is also important for psychotherapy. If a patient lacks a feeling of identity, then they also lack an elementary relationship to their body. The path to a sense of identity therefore always leads through the bodily experience of oneself.

6.7 DISORDERS OF BODY EXPERIENCE AND PSYCHOPATHOLOGY

In body psychotherapy we also look at body experience from a **clinical** perspective. Disorders of body experience are a crucial indicator of the type of psychological disturbance. To this end, we observe how a person experiences themselves in their body, how they sense it, how they feel in the body, how they use and move it, what kind of image they have of it, what messages they receive through the body and what kind they send out. This analysis of disorders of body experience is the **specific contribution of body psychotherapy to psychopathology**.

Also originating from body psychotherapy is the idea of collating body experience in a patient's case history or with the help of specific diagnostic instruments such as the body image sculpture test (cf. Assmann et al., 2010; Roehricht, 2015b, 2009b; Schubert, 2009). As therapists, we experience it also through our embodied perception in interaction with the patient (Krueger, 2019), since mental disorders always manifest themselves in a person's relationships to others, to themselves and to the world around them (Gallagher, 2020; Krueger & Colombetti, 2018). Whereas diagnostic systems often monitor patients from a third-person perspective, in relational body psychotherapy we approach them as someone attempting to understand their problems from their own, first-person perspective (Galbusera & Fellin, 2014).

Mental disorders are not objective illnesses but experienced ones, a linguistic distinction connected to the differentiation in English between *illness* and *disease* (Aho & Aho, 2008). They are not things but **processes** (cf. Hayes & Lillis, 2013). The roots are in a patient's experience of life, but the suffering is in their experience of themselves (Fuchs & Vogeley, 2016). As in any disease, the body moves from the background of experience to the fore (Fuchs, 2020a). It can be experienced as one's own or as alien, as being part of oneself or as an object, as whole or in pieces (Kuechenhoff, 2003).

Striking changes in body experience, not caused by physical damage to the nervous system, all point to an often severe mental disorder (Joraschky & Poehlmann, 2014). For example, adolescents with a sense of alienation from their bodies, who are unsure of being able to control them and are dissatisfied with their physical appearance, are psychopathologically more stressed than others (Roth, 2000).

Disorders of body experience and of the body self are formative for mental disorders (Joraschky et al., 2009). Their diagnosis therefore gives indications as to which body-oriented approaches may be indicated (Roehricht, 2000, p. 47):

- **Anorectics** have a negative and distorted image of their bodies (Joraschky & Poehlmann, 2008). They suffer from an unbearable tension between the subjective and the physical dimension of their body awareness, as they see the body as merely physical (Legrand, 2010). They make it into an object by looking at themselves as if other people are seeing them as objects (Zatti & Zarbo, 2015). Adolescent anorectics fight against the uncontrollable changes in their bodies by subjecting it to their control. Anorexia is not, as many describe it, a body image disorder, but a fundamental alienation of the self from the body (Fuchs, 2022), which can even affect the body schema and with it their unconscious relationship to the environment through movement (Beckmann et al., 2020).
- **Bulimics** also make their bodies into objects by turning them into the battlefield of their conflict between the need to give in to their greed and give up control and the need to control their food intake and their weight.
- Patients with **somatic symptom disorders** exhibit the presence of pain in the absence of the experienced body and all pleasant forms of aliveness in the body (L Young, 1992, p. 97). **Pain patients** are often not able to express their body experience in words (Luyten

et al., 2012). Their bodies send messages in a language of distress, which often plagues them as engrams of traumatic experiences (Chapter 14). Chronic pain can be experienced as meaningless when the pain is detached from its signal character in the traumatising situation (Sauer & Emmerich, 2017).

- Patients with **fibromyalgia** lack the feeling of taking possession of their own body (v. Arnim & Joraschky, 2009).
- Patients with **factitious disorders** can experience their whole body or parts of it as alien and subject it to various forms of self-manipulation (Plassmann, 2016); in the case of someone wanting an amputation, they see the limb as a foreign body.
- In **traumatised patients**, the body holds on to what has happened (van der Kolk, 2014). They can feel dead zones in the body and experience it as fragmented, without borders, divided or as if governed by an earlier psychophysical state; they can also debase or injure it, experience body sensations as frightening or lose their bodily sense of identity (Joraschky, 1997; Stupiggia, 2019). Also as a result of the trauma, they can experience the body as separated from the I, so that it is no longer felt to be 'my body' (L Young, 1992). Sexual traumatisation can lead to sexual disembodiment, whereby to avoid distress, sexual experiences have to be split off from awareness (Malkemus & Smith, 2021).
- In **borderline patients**, the self has split into various parts (Fuchs, 2020a). They lack the sense of a stable identity (Schmidt, 2020, p. 167). They can experience affects and impulses with such a sense of urgency that they are incapable of distancing themselves from them and regulating their emotions and actions (Fuchs, 2007). In this case they identify themselves with whatever has gripped them and lack a sense of body experience that could provide them with a stable orientation. Often they discharge the tension on and with the body. As a result of traumatic experiences, they often feel their bodily boundaries are threatened. With **self-harming behaviour** they demonstrate that the body is unprotected and lacking boundaries (Tameling & Sachsse, 1996). Self-harming can be an attempt to feel oneself again, but it can also be an expression of distress which cannot be shown in any other way.
- **Autism** is not only the inability to understand the mental state of other people. In fact, the person's connection to bodily self-experience is so disrupted that they are also unable to perceive other people (Bizzari, 2018; Bolis & Schilbach, 2018; De Jaegher, 2013). They have both a restricted awareness of their own body and of the bodies of others.
- **Schizophrenics** can have abnormal bodily feelings, so-called coenaesthetic sensations, so that they have a distorted perception of the body, for instance that they underestimate the size of their lower limbs or they cut the body off from awareness completely (Roehricht et al., 2002). Schizophrenics disembody themselves when their sense perceptions are dissociated from the world of objects and people, when they are unable to map their own body sensations or have lost their sense of the body's boundaries or of the natural flow of actions (Fuchs & Roehricht, 2017; Martin et al., 2022; Section 14.2).
- In contrast, in **depression**, the body is not cut off from experience, but rather the suffering is experienced in the body as heaviness, emptiness, blockages or alienation (Lyons et al., 2021). Physical rigidity or constriction is a basic phenomenon of depression and conditions the loss of emotional resonance, which is dependent on subtle resonances in the body (Fuchs, 2020a, p. 52); it also forms resistance to more expansive impulses (Fuchs & Vogeley, 2016). Depressives take shorter steps when walking, they go more slowly with less arm movement, rest longer when they stop and have reduced interoceptive perception (Michalak et al., 2019; Section 14.2). Their negative thoughts seem to be linked to a slumped posture (Michalak et al., 2014; Chapter 8).
- In patients with **anxiety disorders**, suffering is also experienced in the body (Fuchs, 2005), even when experiences in interaction with others lie at the root of the anxiety

(Glas, 2020). In anxiety, the bodily impulses that protect us from threats through fight or flight are inhibited. Anxiety is thus experienced bodily as being trapped within oneself, and even if it is diffuse, the feeling often condenses into a constriction in the chest or a pressure in the abdomen or heaviness in the legs. The arousal bound up within anxiety can express itself not only in chronic hypervigilance but also in chronic tensions, shivering, shuddering breaths, heart palpitations or perspiring (Fuchs & Koch, 2014; Micali, 2019).

- In **panic**, people get into a bodily state with tachycardia, vertigo and shortness of breath which they experience as not belonging to them. The experience of the self is disengaged from body experience.

- With an **obsessive-compulsive disorder**, the patient is lacking a sensual perception of reality which provides a sense of security (Herzog, 2017). They can no longer rely on their embodied experience. The orientating feedback of body sensation as to whether something is 'good like this' or is sufficient and can be left as it is, is missing (Buergy, 2019; Ecker et al., 2014). Through obsessive thoughts or actions, the patient tries to control strong impulses or feelings from a third-person perspective (cf. Auszra et al., 2017, p. 47). Unlike patients with obsessive-compulsive personality disorder (OCPD), patients with OCD experience this as ego-dystonic: they are the victims of it and cannot control their own thoughts and feelings.

Psychopathological symptoms can also involve an **overemphasis on certain senses**: too much looking in the case of paranoia, too much interoception in the case of hypochondria, too much listening in the case of panic. Being overwhelmed by sense impressions is a symptom of ADHD and autism, whereas a lack of sensory perception can be a result of neglect in early childhood.

Body experience can be a basis for exploration not only on the symptomatic level, but also on the structural level, the capacity for integrating psychological functions (Rudolf, 2006):

- In severe mental disorders on a **disintegrated level**, the relationship to the body self is lost. The body is no longer experienced as 'my body', or the border between 'myself' and the outside has dissolved.

- On the level of **severe structural disorders**, the experience of controlling one's own actions or feelings is lost. On this level, people can feel driven or threatened by their affects and psychological states; they can feel not identical to their body, fragmented or can experience the body as a foreign object. Someone who self harms may have lost their sense of the borders of the I and of the body (Tameling & Sachsse, 1996).

- On a **middle structural level** with **moderate integration**, patients are alienated from the body in certain situations or describe their body experience in an ego-dystonic fashion, in which 'I' and 'my body' are separated (Henningsen, 2002).

- On a **higher structural level** with **good integration**, patients can avoid perceptions, deny experiences or inhibit actions on a bodily level, but they experience themselves as being in the body which is sensing or doing something.

With a healthy body experience, according to Galuska and Galuska (2006, p. 593) we can speak of a **personal structure** in which the whole body is open for an experience at any particular moment, and its sensual qualities are a source of vitality and enjoyment of life. Unfortunately in the daily clinical routine too little attention is paid to this pleasure, both in one's own bodiliness and in one's bodiliness in interaction with other people (Joraschky & Poehlmann, 2014, p. 28).

Important
The experience of the body self provides us with information about the pathology, structural level and identity experience of the patient. Thus it offers us a tool to determine the choice of treatment.

Roehricht (2011a) uses body experience as the basis for a classification of psychological suffering, which he sees as the consequence of a disorder in the regulation of the relationship of the living body to the world. He distinguishes three categories:

- The **fleeting body** of psychotics, where the ego is only partially embodied.
- The **instrumentalised body** in people with personality disorders, which is used as a means of self-portrayal or as the site of affect discharge; this corresponds to the median and lower structural level in Kernberg's (1976) character pathology.
- The **weighed down body**, in which the patient experiences suffering as a burden in the body, for example in the heaviness of depression, the breathing difficulties of anxiety, or the pain of somatic symptom disorder; this corresponds to the higher structural level.

In personality disorders, not only can the body be instrumentalised, but patients can act like slaves of their bodily impulses. In both cases, the congruent relationship to the body has been lost.

Body schema and body image

Often, mental disorders are accompanied by a disorder of the body image or body schema, for example in the case of anorexia or psychological deficits of cerebro-organic origin. The concepts of body schema and body image are central to both theoretical as well as to clinical ideas of body experience; however, they are not used consistently (Gallagher, 2003, 2005, p. 19; Roehricht et al., 2005) and are sometimes replaced by other classifications (e.g. Vignemont, 2010).

The notion of body schema first appeared in neurology at the beginning of the 20th century and was used for patterns of sensory and kinaesthetic representations of the actual body (Joraschky, 1995). The more psychological notion of body image was introduced by Paul Schilder for the subjective experience of the actual body. For him, body image is the result of ideas and not of kinaesthetic and somatosensory perceptions (Starobinski, 1987, p. 26).

Body schema is understood as a three-dimensional and dynamic representation of the spatial and bio-mechanical characteristics of the body, the sources of which are information from the various senses and which is anchored in the central nervous system. Medina and Coslett (2010) distinguish between the following three components:

1. A primary somatosensory representation of the body through the surface of the skin.
2. A representation of body form and size.
3. A representation of body posture, in which the body, the position of the limbs in space and the localisation of stimuli in the relationship of the subject to space is mapped out. The sense of the position of the body is informed by tactile, proprioceptive, visual, vestibular, auditory and interoceptive perception.

Body schema functions automatically and performatively (Gallese & Sinigaglia, 2010, p. 747; Giummarra et al., 2008). Its function is to ensure posture and movement in space below the level of intentional control of the body. The processes involved do not need to be conscious (De Preester, 2007, p. 605; Gallagher, 2003; Roehricht et al., 2005, p. 187).

Body schema contains both long-term information, such as the length of the limbs, as well as short-term information about the current position of the body in space. Therefore it tells us something about the habitual and the present body in the sense of Merleau-Ponty's theory. In times of great bodily change, such as puberty, we can see that people need time to adjust their body schema; in their movements they do not yet 'know' how tall they are. Movement is an essential medium of the differentiation of body schema (Lausberg, 2009, p. 128).

Body image, on the other hand, is subjective, personal and usually conscious (De Preester, 2007; Roehricht 2009a, p. 25). Gallagher (2003, p. 5) defines body image as a system of body-related perceptions, ideas and beliefs with three elements:

1. How someone perceives the body – *body perception*.
2. How they understand it – *body concept*.
3. How they experience it emotionally – *body affect*.

In their consensus paper, a German research group narrowed down the definition of body image to that defined by Gallagher's *body concept*, to designate the multidimensional experiential and evaluation aspects connected to the body (Roehricht et al., 2005, p. 187).

In the clinical literature, the notion of body image is often used in the sense of the broader definition of the three aspects listed by Gallagher and not just for the cognitive aspect. In this sense, both body image and body schema are the result of learning experiences, but in contrast to this last, body image is informed by concepts, ideas and fantasies about the body. It is the **image** that a person creates of their body and not a schema which organises its posture and movements. **Body image is concerned with an attitude, body schema with a faculty.** We could also say that the body image is fed by a top-down process, whereas with the body schema we are dealing with bottom-up processes (Giummarra et al., 2008, p. 146; Table 6.2).

TABLE 6.2
Body schema and body image

Concept	Content/Function	Disorders
Body schema	Sensorimotor representation of the body Function: control of actions Components: • Somatosensory representation • Representation of body form and body size • Representation of posture and the position of the body in space	Autotopagnosia (disorder of the localisation of parts of the body in relation to the whole body) Asomatognosia (loss of awareness of parts of the body) Apraxia (disorder of voluntary expressive movements) Ataxia (disorder of movement control) Anosognosia (not recognising loss of bodily functions)
Body image in the broadest sense	Body image in the narrower sense: Inner image of the body, metaphors, fantasies, concepts, knowledge of the body	Body Dysmorphic Disorder Body Integrity Identity Disorder distorted image e.g. in anorexia
	Body sensation/body perception: sensorimotor-visual – description of the relationship of one part of the body to another, assessment of bodily proportions	Inability to describe correctly the relationships of one part of the body to another; neglect-syndrome; distorted perception of body girth and body dimensions in anorexia
	Body affect/ body cathexis: Inner experience of the body, cathexis of the body with psychological energy, affective evaluation of the body	Rejection of one's own body, narcissistic upvaluation of the body; hypochondriac obsession with the body, hysterical disorders of body experience; deficits in the experience of the borders of the body in self-harming behaviour

A body schema can form psychological experience, as the following example of a session in which a patient grapples with a schema shaped by a physical disability shows:

Clinical example

Because of a foot disability from early childhood, the patient habitually stands so that she takes the load off the left hip and the weaker left leg and shifts her weight onto her right leg. As a consequence she has discomfort and pain in the thoracic spinal area. In her body schema, this malposition is anchored as normal posture. Thus she has a sense of this imbalance as the middle position and the shift to the side as the main axis.

We can correct this either by having her look into a mirror or using the therapist as a mirror and learning to move into the vertical axis and to correct the position of the hips, the torso and the head accordingly. When she has found the median axis optically, however, this does not at first correspond to her body sensation. She has to practise this realignment to the middle by, for example, regularly looking for the median axis in front of the mirror at home. In this way she can correct the proprioceptive feedback, which registers a pathological body schema as a normal state.

After I had tried that out with the patient for the first time, she came to the next session saying the work had put her in a good mood. This was mainly because she had discovered something which she could actively do herself to improve her disability, which she had unconsciously given into until now. Also during the week she had often noticed how she leaned to one side, away from the middle. Every realignment had relieved the burden on the right sacroiliac joint and had relaxed the area of the thoracic spine.

When someone who is not in the middle starts to come into the middle and can feel this, they usually feel clearer, straighter or stronger. With the appropriate exercises, patients become more aware of their bodily reality. Coming into the middle and straightening up can be meaningful both on the level of body schema as well as on a symbolic one (Geuter, 2019, 234–9).

There are various disorders of the body schema or of the body image (Table 6.2). In the case of a neuropathy, when the functions of the body schema break down, movements can only be controlled consciously, no longer automatically. With neglect syndrome, on the other hand, half of the body image disappears as a result of damage to one side of the brain. Neuropsychological disorders, however, usually affect both body schema and body image (Vignemont, 2010, p. 678).

Whereas body schema is significant particularly from a neurological and neuropsychological point of view, in body psychotherapy we are more interested in body image. Body image is always connected to psychological processes, fantasies or ideas. Disorders of body image alone are therefore more psychological. In cases of anorexia or bulimia, the body image disorder is of great significance for the genesis and progression of the disease. Hence including body-oriented therapy forms in treatment seems especially relevant (Konzag et al., 2006, p. 35). It also seems sensible to use body-oriented methods to help patients work through traumatic life experiences held in the body, which surface not only in post-traumatic stress disorder (PTSD), but also frequently in somatic symptom disorders.

Disorders of body experience and body image are generally a particularly strong indication for body psychotherapy. In contrast, an intact and positive body image and a sound body experience are signs of psychological health.

7

The experienced body and the body of natural science

Phenomenology often blends out the material nature of the body (Boehme, 2020). However, we do not just own this material body that we sense and experience; we are it too (Chapter 2). In the previous chapter, I have explained how self-experience is physically rooted in the self-senses (Section 6.3). Only a living, corporeal being can experience something in interaction with the world. However, within body psychotherapy, the question of how we are to understand the unity of the experienced and the material body is viewed in various ways.

The abundance of insights from recent physiological and neuroscientific research has enticed some therapists to seek here a foundation for our profession. These insights have deepened above all our understanding of trauma sequelae and psychosomatic illness (Egle et al., 2020; van der Kolk, 2014). Also researchers are examining more closely the connections between processes of experience and behaviour, mental disorders and measurable neuronal, endocrinal or immunological parameters (Knop & Heim, 2020; Schubert, 2020; Walther et al., 2022). The findings of natural science can show us aspects where body psychotherapy should take into account processes in the material body and affect them, but they cannot show us the means of doing so. This is because we work with intersubjective communication in an embodied encounter. From the findings of natural science we can only derive individual forms of medical treatment. There can be no naturalistic justification of any form of psychotherapy (Richter, 2019).

Nevertheless, it is helpful for psychotherapists to have a basic knowledge of the physical body as an object. This is not only true of understanding mental disorders in which bodily symptoms play a large part. The body we are dealing with in therapy is always also a material body, whose physical condition is a factor in possible development, for instance in such a simple fact that it is subject to gravity (Trautmann-Voigt & Voigt, 2009, p. 153). Body therapy such as the Feldenkrais Method is a training in the way we deal with gravity and views the body as a holistic, biomechanical entity (Heller, 1997). Gindler's work explores how the body creates a relationship to the ground that supports it or how, as an inner framework, the skeleton holds it up. In this work we can experience the body in its physical functions and relationship to the world of objects in a mindful way. This is important with grounding techniques (Geuter, 2019, pp. 230–45).

If in body psychotherapy we aim at releasing contractions on the level of the muscles and connective tissue, with which people are also holding in feelings or chronically fixating

DOI: 10.4324/9781003176893-7

affect motor patterns, then it is helpful to understand muscular structure and function (Marcher & Fich, 2010; Roehricht, 2000, pp. 191–204ff; Chapter 13). Also we should be able to evaluate the effect of our interventions on the level of the physical body, for instance when cathartic techniques, or exposure therapy, produce strong vegetative reactions (Schrauth, 2006).

However, knowledge of the experienced body and knowledge of the objective body are two different things. If I ask someone whether they are in pain, only they as a subject can know the answer. But if I ask whether their toe is broken, this can be answered objectively by an x-ray. If someone says: 'I think my toe is broken', they can be mistaken. But if they say that it hurts, they cannot be wrong about that. This last is the statement **of a person**. Scientific statements in contrast are **about a person**. Acknowledging subjective states reported by someone needs no scientific verification (cf. Frank, 1994, p. 31). It is impossible to talk someone out of it by pointing to an x-ray or a scan. We cannot explain the subjective perspective of experience by means of the material body (Chapter 2). We experience whether we feel groggy, fresh, elated or sad not as a physical or biological description of phenomena, but in our sensations (Schmitz, 2014, p. 71).

Natural scientific methods look at the body as an object, not as the subject's embodied experience. But since subjectivity is in many ways connected to the body in circular causality (Section 5.1), the findings of natural science can help us to better understand various psychological processes and disorders, for example when knowledge of trauma physiology helps us understand posttraumatic stress disorder. This is especially true when changes in the body as object are so serious – for example when the function of one of the senses fails or in the case of severe illness or bodily traumatisation – that they dominate experience and behaviour (Fuchs, 2017). In the sense of Fuchs's model of circular causality, we are then dealing with an upwardly directed causality of a lower level.

However, neither a theory of mental illness nor a description of the objective anatomy or physiology of the body is the subject of this book. In this chapter, therefore, I will limit myself to the question of how far certain models of natural science are compatible with certain models of body psychotherapy practice.

Mental processes are necessarily linked to biological processes. All a person's experiences are engraved in their biology; for instance when in women who have experienced sexual violence as children, the brain cortex is thinner where the genitals are represented (Heim et al., 2013), or when in people who were mistreated as children, there is less grey substance in areas of the brain which process emotions (Edmiston et al., 2011). Also therapeutic changes in experience are accompanied by organismic changes. Studies show commensurable changes in the brain and the immune system (O'Toole et al., 2018; Schakel et al., 2019). These connections are not, however, causally determined. Rather it is a matter of correlations, covariations and structural linkage between various systemic levels as part of life processes (Fuchs, 2017). The reasons for life processes cannot be found in material processes.

For example, the polyvagal theory of Stephen Porges (Section 7.1) does not explain the harmfulness of traumatic experience, but offers a model allowing us to describe the effects on a physiological level, which we can then plausibly connect to psychological descriptions. Post-traumatic stress disorder (PTSD) is not the result of physiology, but of what has happened to a person during their life.

Important
The body is not the cause of psychological processes, nor is the psyche the cause of bodily ones; rather both are part of life processes.

Biological levels and experience

On the level of the material body, processes take place on diverse biological levels, which are not identical with the levels of experience (Section 6.1). Thus there is the level of the molecules and cells, which also interact with the environment, store experiences and develop categories; for example, immune cells differentiate between what belongs to the body and what does not. Such processes, however, are not accessible to consciousness. We experience bodily processes on the cellular level at best indirectly in the form of proprioceptive or interoceptive signals, for instance when as a result of immune cell activity in defence against pathogens, we become feverish. Also in the form of cognitive changes, when for example we hallucinate as a result of oxygen deficiency. Biologically, it seems impossible to me to evoke a 'cell consciousness' and to come into contact with the cellular level of the body, as Hartley (1995) asserts. In addition, the effects of medication on the cellular level, such as those of the SSRI type of antidepressants on the re-uptake of serotonin in the synaptic cleft, are only experienced indirectly. Cellular processes are inaccessible to conscious perception.

In therapy, we are concerned with what someone experiences and has experienced and how they feel, not with what is happening in their cells – with the experienced body from a first-person perspective and not with the material body from the third-person perspective (Chapter 2).

We can derive therapeutic tasks from trauma physiology such as to calm down emotional arousal. However we cannot derive the body psychotherapy methods that we use to do this from the insights of natural science. These methods are not to be found on the level of the biological, chemical or physical regulation of organismic processes, but on that of experience, understanding and agency.

Helpful changes on these subjective levels, however, always bring change in physical states. For the patient to feel better, processes of vegetative and sensorimotor regulation, inaccessible to consciousness, must balance out in an improved state of equilibrium. We cannot react calmly when our heart rate is too fast. Healthier self-regulation requires healthier stress regulation. Successful therapy also works down into the physiological level. This is why Liss (2001, p. 176) describes body psychotherapy as therapy rooted in the organic. However, even though we affect the physiological level, in body psychotherapy we do not work with physical or biological means. The heart rate or the activity of the digestive tract may change through our interventions, but we do not use a pacemaker or probiotic substances to achieve this.

Body psychotherapy practice is working with subjectively experienced distress in relationship with an embodied subject. For a general theory of this practice, therefore, we need theories about subjective processes. Theories about the material body, however, come into play when we need to understand illness more comprehensively and orientate our therapeutic approach to specific disorders. Disease can only be described in all its multidimensionality in a **biopsychosocial model of illness** (von Uexkuell & Wesiack, 1996).

Through the findings of psychoimmunology, psychoendocrinology, psychophysiology and brain research, this model has deepened our understanding of illness to such an extent that Egle et al. (2020a) talk of a paradigm shift in psychosomatic medicine. However, in their text book of psychosomatics, which they describe as neurobiologically sound, they only discuss this aspect insofar as it relates to factors in the genesis of illness which are important for treatment. As regards psychotherapy, they only mention that it can affect other functional levels besides the psychological, but without substantiating a psychotherapeutic treatment theory neurobiologically. From a therapeutic point of view, the findings of neurobiology augment at best the spectrum of medical-technical treatment methods, for instance a more exact treatment with psychotropic medication.

Important
Neurobiological or physiological insights can help us to better understand disease. However they cannot be a basis for psychotherapy methods, since psychotherapy is a communicative and not a technical process.

The biopsychosocial model was first formulated by the cardiologist Engel (1977) for the genesis of heart diseases. According to this model, in illness, biological, psychological, social and ecological factors are linked and mutually determined. Illnesses are an event within the framework of these factors. PTSD, for example, is a somatopsychic disorder which manifests in the formation of relationships and in stress physiology (Reddemann & Sachsse, 2000, p. 560), in intrusive thoughts and in endocrinological or immunological reactions (Barratt, 2010, p. 122). Life events always affect the whole of a person's system, never the interpersonal, psychological, physiological, neuronal or cellular level alone.

   The same is true of therapeutic measures (Koemeda-Lutz, 2012). The biopsychosocial model demonstrates that we can influence disorders on the biological, psychological, social and ecological levels, for instance by treating PTSD through psychotropic medication or through changing the patient's social environment. An intervention on one level can potentially affect all the others. In the helping professions, we must always ask ourselves on which level a problem can best be treated (cf. Ollars, 2005). We can also influence all levels of experience with non-psychotherapeutic means (Section 5.1). Treatment with a virostatic drug can completely change the self-experience of a patient with HIV, the granting of an invalidity pension that of a depressive patient. If we understand the biopsychosocial model not just as one of pathology, but as a **recovery model**, then it becomes clear that health can be fostered on all levels that are involved in the genesis of illness. Body psychotherapy works with bodily and psychological means on the level of the person and their body based self-experience, even when through this work changes are achieved on other levels, such as on the organic level or in partnerships or family situations.

> A **pathology** of mental disorders should do justice to the biopsychosocial model. However it cannot be derived from a **theory of treatment**, but only from an understanding of the illnesses. At best, a treatment theory raises our awareness of certain factors in the genesis of a disease, as does behavioural therapy for personal learning history, psychoanalysis for unconscious conflicts or body psychotherapy for disorders of body image, pathological affect motor schemas or bodily defence structures (Section 6.7; Chapter 12; Chapter 13). Psychotherapy approaches cannot form the basis for understanding pathology. An understanding of cancer does not depend on whether a tumour is treated with surgery, radiology or chemotherapy. Conversely, however, an understanding of the illness will influence the choice of treatment.

In the following discussion, I will deal with several aspects of the psychophysiology of psychosomatic illness and trauma sequelae and I will go into various theories of the vegetative nervous system, which in this context are often debated within body psychotherapy. Later on, I will go more deeply into my reasons for not basing a general theory of body psycho-therapy on the scientific models of neurobiology, nor on a theory of energy.

7.1 THE VEGETATIVE NERVOUS SYSTEM AND HUMAN EXPERIENCE AND BEHAVIOUR

Since the beginning of body psychotherapy, the combination of psychological models with models of the vegetative nervous system have played a special role (Bhat & Carleton, 2015). Reich saw in neurosis 'a chronic disturbance of the vegetative equilibrium and of natural mobility' (1973, p. 300). Boyesen (1987, p. 36) argued, in line with the psychoanalytic conflict model, that repressed, conflicted feelings can persist in vegetative symptoms and thus psycho-logical problems can only come to a conclusion when emotional-vegetative cycles have run their course (Section 10.5). M. Fuchs (1989) worked on the assumption that therapy must access the 'vegetative unconscious' and bring about self-regulation through unconscious breathing and the re-establishing of the patient's inherent vegetative rhythm (von Arnim, 1994, 2009; Section 3.4: 3. Rhythm). Carroll (2005, pp. 17, 29) considers that self-regulation of the auto-nomic nervous system (ANS) is still today at the heart of body psychotherapy (Chapter 17).

Vegetative life runs through a multitude of biological rhythms such as the heartbeat, the respiratory rhythm, the rhythm of the cerebrospinal fluid or the rhythmic contraction of the brain ventricles (Maier et al., 1994). Regulated by pacemaker cells, the stomach contracts about three times a minute, the duodenum about 12 times and the ileum, the last section of the small intestine, about eight times (Schaible, 2006).

Healthy rhythms are not necessarily regular ones. In healthy people the duration of the intervals between breaths or heartbeats varies. People with a higher so-called heart rate variability can suppress memories more easily and so can protect themselves from intru-sive thoughts (Gillie et al., 2014). A lower heart rate variability counts as a stress indicator.

Theories of the vegetative nervous system connect certain subjectively experienced states of tension, relaxation and immobilisation, generated by confrontation with environmental stimuli, to certain physiological states mediated by the ANS. Therefore it is interesting, also for an experiential body psychotherapy, to compare psychological models and concepts with these theories. The starting point for clinical theories is, however, the observation of experi-ence and behaviour, which we then relate to physiological processes and not vice versa.

In therapeutic practice we always start with **subjective physiology**, meaning how a per-son experiences vegetative processes. We can then connect this to the body as object and thus to a scientifically comprehensible **objective physiology** (cf. Geuter, 2019, p. 72). This is what I will do in the following passages.

Intersubjective physiology

Experience and physiology are not only connected on the subject level. Interactive pro-cesses also take place, usually completely unconsciously, on the physiological level. In relationships, people synchronise their physiological rhythms (Field, 2012; Section 11.3: on the mother/child relationship). Women who live in groups tend to menstruate at the same time of the month (Weller et al., 1999). When people sing together, their heart rates speed up and slow down collectively (Vickhoff et al., 2013), and when building with Legos, heart rate is synchronised (Fusaroli et al., 2016).

Tschacher and Meier (2020) recorded the synchronisation of the breathing, heartbeat and heart rate variability between patient and therapist during the session. In couples therapy, the amplitude of the skin conductance response increases when the issue of violence in the relationship comes up (Paananen et al., 2018). When two therapists are working with a couple, then it is the co-therapists who react with a high synchronisation of their electrodermal activity (Tourunen et al., 2016). This is also true of synchronisation between patients and therapists (Wiltshire et al., 2020). Kleinbub (2017) and Palumbo et al. (2016) talk about an interpersonal physiology, as did Di Mascio et al. (1957), and Dana (2018) sees the ANS as a relational system.

The vegetative nervous system is responsible for the regulation of all processes connected to the inner organs and the glands. Since its activity, unlike that of the somatic nervous system, can be only voluntarily influenced to a minor degree, it is also known as the **autonomic nervous system**. It looks after activation and deactivation and controls reactive survival programmes, basic bodily states and metabolism; it is also involved in the regulation of functions such as heart rhythm, respiration, digestion and the flow of saliva or of tears (Fogel, 2009, p. 148).

Anatomically and functionally, we can divide the ANS into the:

- Sympathetic.
- Parasympathetic.
- Enteric nervous system (Schaechinger & Finke, 2020).

In the periphery of the body, the ANS is separate from the somatic nervous system (Figure 7.1). This is why often only the peripheral part is referred to when the ANS is meant. However, vegetative functions are also controlled on the level of the central nervous system (CNS), above all from the hypothalamus and the limbic structures. There are bi-directional connections between the peripheral and the central structures (Porges, 2011).

Since the ANS is connected to the somatic nervous system in the CNS, we can influence autonomic processes deliberately through breathing exercises, meditation or yoga (cf. Heller, 2012. p. 208). The ANS is **not** really **autonomic, but interconnected**. It is also not autonomic in the sense of acting independently of the outside world. In fact, it has a regulatory effect on the interchange with the environment, whereby it is regulated itself by interpersonal relationships (Carroll, 2005, p. 14). It is only autonomic in the sense that it functions beyond conscious control.

The vegetative nervous system plays a special part in the genesis of trauma sequelae and psychosomatic illness. Vegetative dysregulation, accompanied by dysfunctional patterns of emotional stress reaction, is characteristic of these disorders. Patients with post-traumatic stress disorder are often trapped more in specific states than in specific experiences. Their memories can be encoded mainly vegetatively. The psychophysiological reaction to an extreme threat persists despite the fact that the threat is over. Thus in treatment it is helpful, and sometimes essential, to reach these patients on a vegetative level and to help them shift to a physiological state associated with safety and social engagement (Porges, 2011).

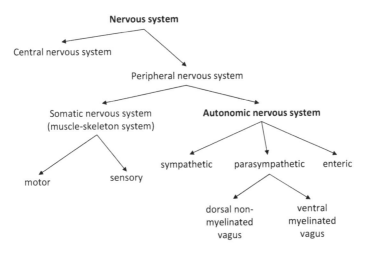

FIGURE 7.1 The nervous system

Von Uexkuell differentiates between:

- Diseases that utilise the somatic nervous system and
- Diseases that use the activity of the vegetative nervous system (Johnen, 2010, p. 71).

In the former case, emotions are held back through tensing the muscles and find their expression in this tension. With diseases mediated by the ANS, however, we are dealing not with a symbolic body language, but with the processing of stress. This corresponds to Ermann's (2004, p. 235) differentiation between conversion and somatisation.

Vegetative symptoms, such as breaking out in a sweat, tachycardia, sleep disorders or diarrhoea, often appear as affective body reactions with a dissociation of the perception of feelings (Schrauth, 2006, p. 659). When people are unable to process and regulate stressful emotions, then the body absorbs the agitation in the form of vegetative stress reactions such as somatisation or PTSD (Plassmann, 2021, p. 103).

Psychosomatics was for many years determined by the psychoanalytical conversion model. Alexander (1950) regarded stomach ulcers, asthma, rheumatoid arthritis, neurodermatitis, hypertonia, hyperthyroidism and inflammatory bowel disease as the consequence of defensive processes. According to this model, conflicts are expressed symbolically in particular symptoms as the suppressed psychological arousal transforms into body language. However, the model was often used to describe symptoms with a hysterical background, for example the so-called *globus hystericus*, a lump in the throat, which can lead to difficulties swallowing (Stern, 1952, p. 149). It became speculative when, for instance, constipation was seen as the expression of repressed sexuality and infantile regression (E Stern, 1952, p. 163). This was taken to extremes by Dethlefsen and Dahlke (2016) with the assertion that each illness has its own symbolic meaning and who began their book, published first in 1983, with the statement that this would take away people's alibi for unsolved problems, hence defining illness as the fault of the individual patient.

> Speaking today for psychoanalysis, Plassmann (2021, p. 103) states that the whole spectrum of psychosomatic illness does not develop through conversion and so the conflict model is not applicable. Schaechinger and Finke (2020, p. 103) regard only fragments of the old theory as being scientifically tenable.

In neo-Reichian body psychotherapy, we again find the conversion model of psychosomatics. Ehrensperger (2010, pp. 114ff), for instance, describes cardiovascular disease and asthma solely on the level of possible muscle blocks connected to these disorders, which he views as an expressive language to be understood psycho-dynamically – for example, asthma as the expression of separation anxiety and a disturbed relationship with the mother. Headaches are interpreted as an expression of hostility (Hortelano, 2015, p. 749). These and other ideas, such as ear disorders having something to do with listening or digestive disorders with swallowing one's anger, sound plausible, but cannot be substantiated scientifically.

Looking at the vegetative level, it becomes clear that an asthma attack is not communicating something in a symbolic body language, but showing an inability to process emotional agitation in any way other than through the body. For these patients, therefore, experience is de-emotionalised for self-protection (Kuechenhoff, 2008, p. 120). The most common psychosomatic disorders, such as high blood pressure and bronchial spasms, always involve the malfunction of the ANS (Velden, 2007). In an asthma attack, a parasympathetic overinnervation of the bronchia occurs. If the functions of the ANS are severely and persistently dysregulated, bodily functions can alter to such an extent that pathological changes in the tissue develop, leading to physically diagnosable symptoms. These are then the result of an **unspecific** reaction of the ANS, which cannot differentiate between a real and a symbolic threat and so in its reaction cannot symbolise conflicts (Velden, 2007).

Studies show that stress results in unspecific inflammatory activity which can manifest as organ damage (Schubert, 2020). However, stress physiology is also dependent on how someone deals with emotions, which is why Schubert (2019, p. 187) considers it reasonable to connect autoimmune disorders with suppressed aggression. Calming down, on the other hand, stimulates parasympathetic innervation and helps to prevent chronic inflammatory processes.

The outdated idea that psychosomatic illnesses are caused by a conversion of psychological conflicts into bodily symptoms corresponds to the dualistic concept of the reciprocal effects of the mind on the body and vice versa (Section 5.1). If on the other hand we see them in the framework of the stress model, then we can understand them as the bodily components of a holistic reaction in the life process. They communicate the experience that a person cannot cope with the burden of stress. Psychosomatic illness protects them from being overwhelmed by even more stress. Their significance is not to be found in innerpsychic processes, as the defence theory supposes, but in what has happened, or been done, to the patient.

Clinical example

A patient with fibromyalgia spent almost the whole of her second year of life as a healthy child in a children's hospital, often tied to her cot, because her mother was in a sanatorium and her father was studying in another city. As a child she felt very lonely inside and was full of aggression towards her parents, which she turned against herself in the form of suicidal thoughts. The pain symptoms flared up as one of her sons broke off contact with her temporarily and another went to Australia for two years. She was unable to cope emotionally with these separations.

Since psychosomatic illnesses are almost always associated with an altered perception of autonomically regulated bodily processes, the expression of emotion is not the silver bullet of treatment, as would follow from the conversion model, but rather the fostering of body awareness and self-regulation. Here the task of therapy is to help the patient become aware of vegetative signals and deepen the perception of their body and its functions controlled by the ANS (Geuter, 2019, pp. 224–8). Just doing this can instigate change (Joraschky et al., 2002, p. 91). Beyond that we have to track the signs of emotional stress and change the dysfunctional patterns with which the patient attempts to regulate them (Plassmann, 2021).

Sympathetic and parasympathetic nervous systems

For a long time, body psychotherapy followed a model of the ANS based on the antagonistic activity of the sympathetic and parasympathetic nervous systems. According to this model they act as adversaries and essentially regulate the basic functions of **activation and vitalisation** on the one hand and **soothing and relaxation** on the other (Table 7.1).

TABLE 7.1
Sympathetic and parasympathetic nervous systems

	Sympathetic nervous system	Parasympathetic nervous system
Basic functions	Preparing for a fight or flight reaction, mobilisation of energy, build-up of arousal	Preparing for withdrawal, build-up of energy reserves, rest and relaxation
Respiration	Dilates the bronchia, accelerates the breathing rhythm and expands the exhalation	Contracts the bronchia, slows down the breathing rhythm and calms the breathing
Heart and circulation	Accelerates the heart rate, increases blood pressure, contracts the blood vessels	Decelerates the heart rate, decreases blood pressure, dilates the blood vessels
Digestion	Decreases salivation, inhibits production of digestive enzymes and intestinal peristalsis, constricts the bladder and the sphincter	Increases salivation, activates intestinal peristaltic and digestion, relaxes the bladder and the sphincter
Eyes	Dilates the pupils	Constricts the pupils, stimulates lacrimation
Skin	Increases perspiration, heightens skin conductivity, contracts the arrector pili muscles ('goosebumps')	
Resources	Acting, coping, keeping something at bay, fleeing	Self-soothing, taking something in, withdrawing
Body psychotherapy equivalent	Activation of emotional arousal, upsurge of feelings.	Deactivation, fading away of feelings, relaxation, recovery

Sources: Carroll 2005, p. 16; Fogel 2009, p. 149; Jaenig 1980; Ruegg 2006, p. 56.

The sympathetic nervous system (SNS) provides energy, the parasympathetic nervous system (PSNS) builds up reserves of energy. This is known as the ergotropic and trophotropic response. Both branches can be differentiated neuroanatomically. The nerves of the SNS exit the spinal cord at the thoracic and lumbar vertebrae, the nerves of the PSNS at the medulla oblongata and the sacrum; from there they go to their respective target organs (Ruegg, 2006, pp. 58–9).

In the fight or flight response stimulated by the **sympathetic nervous system**, the skeletal muscles, the heart muscles and the brain are given priority in blood supply and, through vasoconstriction, the volume of blood flow is increased. Blood pressure goes up and the heart beats faster. Simultaneously the secretory and motor functions of the gastrointestinal system are suppressed. The metabolism also reacts and nutrient depots are mobilised; liver and muscles release glucose, and fatty acids and glycerine flow out of the tissue into the bloodstream. On the level of the brain, the release of neurohormones and neuropeptides stimulates a state of increased awareness and activates the readiness to react with fear, flight and aggression (Uvnaes-Moberg, 1998, pp. 821–2).

In positive social interactions, in contrast, there is a change of direction from the sympathetic to an increased parasympathetic tonus. Also in psychomotor relaxation such as autogenic training, the nervous activity of the PSNS dominates and there is synchronisation between breathing phases and blood circulation in the skin (Perlitz et al., 2004).

The **parasympathetic nervous system** is controlled primarily by the nervus vagus, the tenth cranial nerve, which innervates the throat and the roof of the mouth in the head and, lower down in the body, regulates parasympathetic functions. It forms the connection between nerve cells in the head and in the abdomen. The parasympathetic system is therefore also called the **vagal system**. Since the vagus also innervates the immune system, the ANS can also prevent an inflammatory overreaction of the immune cells (Ruegg, 2006, pp. 154, 193). This explains how a realignment from a sympathetic tonus to a vagal tonus can strengthen the immune system. This realignment can be seen as one of the traditional goals of body psychotherapy.

Sympathicotonia

Reich (1973, pp. 288–98) saw in the activity of the vagus an expansion of the organism towards the world, which represents 'pleasure and joy', in the activity of the SNS in contrast a contraction or movement away from the world representing 'sadness and unpleasure'. A chronic sympathicotonia, a heightened activity of the sympathetic nervous system, was for him the physiological equivalent of anxiety. Boyesen (1987) considers the surplus of energy in a sympathetic tonus to be a physiological component of neurosis (Section 13.1: on the startle reflex). On a physiological level, the goal of therapy consisted of reducing sympathetic tension and facilitating a free and healthy interaction of sympathetic and parasympathetic activity (Schrauth, 2006, p. 659).

Today, on the basis of the stress theory, we see that severe or traumatising stress can lead to long-term stimulation of sympathetic excitation, because the stress processing system is unable to cope; self-referential emotional arousal states develop, disconnected from the reflective and regulating influences of the cortical centres (Rudolf, 2006, p. 20). Such a person is then in a state of **chronic hypervigilance**. Guendel et al. (2002) found that test persons with a high level of alexithymia also showed a heightened basic sympathetic tonus. This suggests that alexithymia should be seen as sustained stress reactivity in which the inability to adequately perceive and express individual feelings results in a permanent increase in sympathetic activity (Guendel et al., 2002, p. 462).

When the organism is focused on fight or flight, this leads to an allostatic reaction. It produces changes instead of stability as in homeostasis (Chapter 17). This is helpful in the short term. When, however, needs are constantly frustrated because, for example, a person's ability to act is inhibited, the organism is destabilised in the long run (Huether et al., 1999). As a cumulative negative consequence of stress reactions which happen too frequently, are too strong or persist for too long, a so-called **allostatic load** develops (McEwen, 2007; Section 11.4). This concept from stress research is similar to that of sympathicotonia. An allostatic load entails changes in the endocrine system which stimulate the sympathoad-renal system. This increases the risk that people get into a state of chronic stress, which through psycho-biological feedback mechanisms can be very detrimental to the organism and can even lead to depression (Gilbert et al., 2004, p. 150).

Traditionally body psychotherapy has two strategies for vegetative realignment:

- Releasing the original affective arousal via the muscles, as Lowen does in bioenergetics with expressive exercises.
- Stimulating parasympathetic activity and thus engendering relaxation in the body, as does Boyesen with massage and M. Fuchs with Functional Relaxation.

Often the affective arousal is first increased in small doses so that what is then released can be processed and digested (Section 10.5: affective cycle).

Lowen's model of tension release stands in the tradition of the ideas of Fechner and Freud, that the 'psychic apparatus' and the nervous system are pushing towards a release of excess energy. This is why initially in therapy, Freud aimed to release affective arousal deriving from the original situation, the content of which had been suppressed, in an emotional catharsis.

Freud saw pleasure as a state in which the level of arousal has sunk. Reich, on the other hand, depicted sexual arousal as a curve running through the stages of tension-charge-discharge-relaxation (Section 3.4: item 3). The model of the ANS was connected to a cyclical model of activation and deactivation.

The polyvagal theory

The theory of a consistently antagonistic innervation of the two branches of the ANS is no longer advocated in neurophysiology today. Rather it is assumed that there are three kinds of autonomic control (Hopper et al., 2006, p. 84; Schaechinger & Finke, 2020, p. 96).

- Reciprocal: this is the old model.
- Joint: the activity of the SNS and that of the PSNS are aligned with each other.
- Uncoupled: changes in the tonus of one branch do not lead to change in the tonus of the other.

A joint aligned activity occurs, for instance, during sex. During a **shock reaction**, in the midst of a sympathetic stimulation of alertness, a parasympathetic inhibition of muscle activity, heart rate and respiratory volume occurs that triggers a **freeze reaction**. Then the increase in blood pressure is accompanied by a decrease in heart rate and, at least temporarily, with a reduction in the blood supply to the muscles and digestive system. At the same time, muscle tonus is increased so that the body posture freezes (Uvnaes-Moberg, 1998, p. 820). This freeze reaction is biologically determined and can be studied in prey animals.

We can differentiate between a freeze reaction in a more sympathetic tonus and one in a more parasympathetic tonus. The latter is a state of capitulation with no self-defence (Aposhyan, 2004, pp. 41–4; Sachsse & Roth, 2008, p. 71) and will be referred to in the following text as **immobilisation**. Patients with a major depression have increased levels of cortisol, a sign of SNS activation, as well as a PSNS hyperarousal, possibly as a result of fear blocking the activated fight or flight response (Gilbert et al., 2004). The combination of muscular torpor and heightened vegetative arousal corresponds to what people experience in a panic attack (Huether & Sachsse, 2007, p. 168). In 1973, Schmitz had already described immobilisation from a phenomenological perspective as a technique of avoiding anxiety and pain by shutting down all expansive impulses (Schmitz, 1992, p. 143).

> After having been raped, 70% of women report on a tonic immobilisation during the attack (Moeller et al., 2017). Such a reaction occurs when we cannot actively eliminate the danger. In women who have been abused as children, the regulation of vagal tonus is proven to be reduced (Porges, 2011).

Porges (2011) has called it a **vagal paradox** that when vagal tonus in babies is **too** high this leads to a potentially lethal bradycardia, whereas a high vagal tonus is generally seen as an index for resilience and health. In his polyvagal theory, Porges resolves this paradox by showing that neuroanatomically there are **two branches of the vagus**, each with different functions: a dorsal, unmyelinated and a ventral, myelinated branch (Figure 7.1). Each branch has its own source nucleus and they can be active independently of one another. As the vagus is not just a single nerve but a whole family of nerve pathways with the main branches as mentioned, Porges calls his theory polyvagal. Next to the aforementioned efferent vagus branches, 80% of its fibres are afferent and keep the brain informed of the condition of the body.

- The **dorsal branch** of the vagus regulates physiologically mainly the activity of the organs situated below the diaphragm and thus the metabolic and digestive processes. It is responsible for gastric and intestinal motility. Here an overly strong tonus can lead to the development of stomach ulcers and colitis (Heitkemper et al., 1998).
- The **ventral branch** exists, according to Porges, only in the neuroanatomy of mammals. However this is contentious as myelinated nerve fibres connecting the brain and the heart have been found in lungfish (Monteiro et al., 2018). It came into existence in evolution, so Porges contends, as the muscles of the face and the head developed into a system for breast-feeding and social connection. This branch innervates the larynx, the throat, the oesophagus, the bronchia and the heart and already functions in babies when they turn towards a trusted person. The cranial motor nerves also belong to the ventral vagus, so that it is also involved in facial expressions. In addition, it innervates muscles connected to sucking, swallowing, breathing and vocal expression. The ventral vagus calms the breathing and the heart rate, inhibits defensive strategies and promotes behavioural states in which growth and recuperation are possible. As this branch is covered by a sheath of myelin, it can react more quickly than can the dorsal branch. Physiologically, it facilitates the ability of mammals to react to danger voluntarily by sustaining their level of attention and communicating with emotional facial expressions. Reptiles cannot do this. They are not able to alter their facial expression. The young of mammals in contrast have a whole repertoire of distress calls (Schrauth, 2006, p. 662), so-called distress vocalisations (Panksepp, 1998, pp. 266–7). Through emotional communication, human beings can receive affection with minimal effort (Porges, 2011).

Porges connects the two branches to **three subsystems of the response to danger.**

On the lowest level, the organism reacts with **immobilisation**, which is regulated by the dorsal branch of the vagus and accompanied by its typical over-reactivity. Such a response occurs in the face of life-threatening events, when a person has lost the possibility of reacting to the threat and has given up trying to do anything. On a second level, in the case of a dangerous event, there is a **mobilisation** regulated by the sympathetic nervous system. On a third and higher level, the organism responds to challenges within the framework of a basically safe situation by activating the myelinated, ventral branch of the vagus, which promotes a calmer behavioural state and inhibits the influence of the SNS on the heart and the HPA axis. Porges calls this reaction the **social engagement system**.

All three responses are experienced on all system levels (Section 6.1):

- Immobilisation in the form of shallow breathing, coldness, paralysis and mental blackout.
- Mobilisation in the form of increased breathing, quick-temperedness, readiness to act and mental alert.
- Need for social engagement in the form of calm or slightly increased breathing, adaptive movements and intentional thoughts.

We can relate these three forms of reaction in the theory of psychobiological emotional systems of Panksepp (1998; Section 10.3) to the **fear and anxiety system**, which responds to threats to physical integrity. They regulate anxiety in their different ways (cf. Heller, 2012, pp. 199–200). People can also be overwhelmed by attractive stimuli, when for instance they perceive the experience of desire or of falling in love as threatening and go into dissociation and immobilisation (Fischer, 2008). The panic system, which Panksepp (1998, pp. 261–8, 274–5) differentiates from the fear and anxiety system, on the other hand, reacts to the fear of losing the attachment object. For this reason Sachsse and Roth (2008, p. 71) call it the attachment system. If the attachment object itself is the source of the threat, as is the case with physical and sexual violence in the family, then both systems are activated and the capacity to react is paralysed (Carroll, 2006).

Under favourable conditions, people use the third level reaction system. Porges (2011) speaks here of an immobilisation without fear, neurochemically mediated by oxytocin (Section 11.4). Depending on the degree of stress, people fall back onto the next lower level. Bentzen (2015) illustrates this with the example of a baby expressing their wishes.

- In stress, the child starts to cry, and the startle and grasp reflexes become stronger. With this behaviour they are trying to establish safety in the attachment (**level 3**).
- If this is unsuccessful, then they fall back on **level 2**, the fight or flight system. Crying becomes an angry screaming.
- If this is also unsuccessful, then **level 1**, the lowest, dissociative, parasympathetic coping strategy comes to the fore: the child withdraws completely from contact with the world.

We can observe such a sequence in the still-face experiments (Section 11.3). While on level 3 and level 2 the child still looks for contact, on level 1 they avoid it. If the immobilisation of level 1 remains chronic, then action patterns are frozen permanently (Jarlnaes & van Luytelaar, 2004, p. 250). According to a long-term study done by Seiffge-Krenke (2000), this avoidant coping style is connected to depression later in life.

The hyper- and hyporeactivity of the muscles can be related to the two coping styles of approach and avoidance. In child development, muscles take up their functions in specific stadiums (Marcher & Fich, 2010). According to Marcher's theory, in a muscle test, the child's muscles react hyper-responsively, meaning excessively, when a trauma or conflict occurred after an action associated with the corresponding muscles had already developed. In contrast, the muscles react hypo-responsively when in the corresponding developmental phase there was a very early or a very intensive traumatic experience (Bernhardt, 2004a, p. 115). In therapy, we work with hypertonic muscles in such a way as to release the tension, and with hypotonic muscles, on the other hand, with gentle touch to revitalise impulses deactivated through resignation (Bernhardt, 2004, p. 102).

Two types of traumatic response

Analogous to level 1, immobilisation, and level 2, mobilisation, Levine (2010) differentiates between two types of traumatic reaction corresponding to the above-mentioned two kinds of freeze reaction of parasympathetic tonus and of sympathetic tonus:

- In people who have been chronically neglected or abused, usually the dominant system is immobilisation, which leaves them stranded in a no man's land of non-existence; following Kohut, Schore (2003, p. 128) speaks here of a **depleted self** in a state of **parasympathetic overarousal**, which is experienced as implosion and is characterised by dissociation and withdrawal of energy to the inside.
- In contrast, when in traumatised patients the fight or flight system continues to be active, symptoms consist of flashbacks or palpitations. Schore speaks here of a **fragmented self** which in the wake of traumatic experiences is in a state of **sympathetic overarousal**, experienced as panic.

We can infer from Porges' theory how we can allow for the basic problems of the physiological regulation of stress in our work with disturbed emotionality. We can correspondingly allocate **three therapeutic tasks** of arousal modulation:

1. When working with the dissociation and depletion resulting from the immobilisation reaction after, for example, severe trauma, it is necessary to calm people down; to acknowledge an existing immobilisation as a sensible reaction; to differentiate it from intense, negative emotions; to release the paralysis; and to offer the security of a relationship, which helps the patient make the transition to a behavioural programme of coping with stress on the higher evolutionary levels. A parasympathetic immobilisation also necessitates the regaining of the sympathetic innervated ability to fight or flee as a resource.
2. When working with sympathetic overarousal as a result of persistent or blocked anxiety or anger, then we have to release tension and compensate the stress on a physiological level by facilitating a parasympathetic state; with trauma patients however, we need to use the appropriate dosage (Levine, 1997, 2010).
3. When the ventral vagal parasympathetic activity is restricted, then people lack the ability to approach challenges in the knowledge that they will be supported by a secure attachment. In this case, our therapeutic task is above all to mediate a feeling of secure attachment. This will stimulate the resources of the vegetative nervous system.

When we work with trauma patients, we thus need to utilise the body psychotherapy treatment principles *regulating and modulating* and *centring and grounding* as well as providing security in the therapeutic relationship (Geuter, 2019).

TABLE 7.2
Bio-behavioural response to safety and danger according to Fogel (2009, p. 148)

	Threat situations	*Safety situations*
Primarily parasympathetic activity	**Immobilisation**; disorganised attachment	**Restoration**
Homeostasis of parasympathetic and sympathetic activity	Normal absorption of the **challenge** in a state of flow	Emotional **presence**, embodied self-awareness, engagement; secure attachment
Primarily sympathetic activity	**Mobilisation** of fight or flight reaction; insecure-avoidant attachment	**Vigilance**, alerting, attention, arousal; insecure-ambivalent attachment

The deliberations on the ANS can explain how bodywork such as breath therapy, yoga, Tai Chi or certain massages can have a harmonising effect on the psyche without striving for psychotherapeutic insights or changes in behaviour. These and other methods can bring about a parasympathetic calming effect, leading to an emotional calming. This in turn can change thinking. Then an autonomic regulation takes place via the ANS, which retroactively influences psychological processes. Massage releases oxytocin (Uvnaes-Moberg, 1998, p. 831), lowers blood pressure and releases gastrointestinal hormones, the production of which is regulated by the vagus nerve. This shows that these methods can retune the ANS from a sympathetic dominance to a parasympathetic one (Uvnaes-Moberg, 1998, p. 829; Geuter, 2019, p. 237). Most probably, the effects of meditation, often experienced cognitively as a more serene attitude, have to do with the calming down of autonomic nerve activity and the emotional regulation implicit in it.

Deep relaxation and calm can also have a paradoxical effect and trigger a high level of affective arousal, such as intense grief. Then we speak of a dynamic relaxation (Section 10.2).

Fogel (2009, pp. 148, 175) connects the bio-behavioural response to situations of threat and safety to the vegetative nervous system and links this to attachment styles (Table 7.2). In his model, the second reaction to danger, which he classifies as an equilibrium between the SNS and the PSNS, corresponds in Porges' theory to the dominance of ventral vagal activity.

According to this, protective mechanisms and vulnerability are determined psycho-biologically by attachment experiences (Blunk, 2006, p. 45; Section 11.6). In therapy, we promote states favourable to the organism such as recuperation, presence and engaging with a challenge in a state of flow, wherein the patient is completely absorbed in the activity in the here and now (Csikszentmihalyi, 1998).

Clinical application

In body psychotherapy, we invite patients for instance to consciously give themselves over to autonomic processes in the here and now ('just let it happen', 'let it come up'), in which the body takes the lead and deliberate control is reduced. This is similar to other autonomic processes such as falling asleep. We cannot deliberately fall asleep, but can only let sleep take over. Reich pointed out that this is also the case with sexual desire and orgasm.

He called this surrendering to the flow of vegetative energy (cf. the autonomic perspective of Schatz in Chapter 2). In some forms of Reichian therapy, therapists try to release the orgasm reflex, which probably leads to a streaming feeling in the body.

The gut brain

The fact that the gut reacts to the vegetative retuning of the organism led Boyesen (1987, pp. 73–9; Boyesen & Boyesen, 1980) to speak of an intestinal emotional digestion. Similarly, shortly after the First World War, the psychoanalyst Ernst Simmel spoke of an 'intestinal libido' (Schultz-Venrath & Hermanns, 2019; Section 3.1.1). In biodynamics, the sounds the intestines make are regarded as indicators of psychological processes, especially as signs of a transition to a parasympathetic state, which supports auto-regulation (Heller, 2012, p. 209). Fogel (2009, p. 111) too describes involuntary relaxation noises from the belly as psycho-peristalsis. Boyesen goes beyond this and sees in **psycho-peristalsis** a 'channel of the instinctive emotional energy' of the id (1987, p. 78).

Through Gershon's (1998) research into the enteric nervous system, some people in body psychotherapy view this theory as proven. Gershon showed that only in the intestines are reflexes communicated without impulses from the brain or the spinal cord, and he therefore speaks of a 'second brain' in the gut, which is independent of the functional hierarchy between the central and peripheral nervous systems, autonomously controls the wavelike movements of peristalsis and could have its own 'psychoneuroses'. The enteric nerve plexus of the small intestine consists of more than 100 million neurons. However we have to see this number in relation to others: it corresponds approximately to the number of neurons in the spinal cord (Schaechinger & Finke, 2020). The number of neurons in the brain is estimated to be over 100 billion and thus exceeds those in the small intestine by a factor of 1000.

The enteric nervous system can function independently of the brain, but it is connected to it by various neurotransmitters and by the immune system and is subject to the control of the CNS (Jaenig, 2006; Schmidtner & Neumann, 2020). The innervation of the intestines is complex. The whole of the digestive system is innervated by the vagus nerve, and the gut has in addition parasympathetic sacral nerves. Here parasympathetic fibres have the function of stimulating digestion (Schaible, 2006). The smooth muscles of the gut, which promote peristalsis, are controlled by the inner intestinal nerve circuits, but receive information via the parasympathetic nervous system from the CNS (Schaechinger & Finke, 2020). An electrical stimulation of the cingulate gyrus in the limbic system stimulates the gut and accelerates the passage of intestinal content. In contrast, if the tonus of the smooth muscles is too high, so that the flow of movement is reduced, then we can speak of a visceral armour.

There is no doubt among scientists that disturbed intestinal motility is connected to negative emotions and acute or long-term stress (Musial et al., 2008). Hence **irritable bowel syndrome** appears to be associated with imbalances in autonomic nerve activity (Aggarwal et al., 1994). A study shows that women suffering from this also have low parasympathetic tonus (Heitkemper et al., 1998). This perhaps explains why a tonus-raising massage of connective tissue can significantly reduce the symptoms of IBS (Uhlemann, 2006). However we cannot ascribe IBS to one single cause, since the causality is circular and connected to ecological, social, psychological, diet-related and genetic factors (cf. Wahida et al., 2021).

The gut is also connected to the emotions by other systems. Next to the various neuronal connections, there are many hormones in the gut and all the neurotransmitters of the brain. For example, 90% of the body's serotonin is produced here, which is one reason that antidepressants also affect the intestines.

We often speak of our **gut feeling** or of visceral perception whereby people can perceive moods or intuitively grasp the meaning of something. These perceptions indicate for instance whether someone feels socially secure or not. Information from the viscera which reaches the CNS via nerves, hormones and immune messengers is an important somatic marker (Gottwald, 2005, p. 120). Moods are experienced in the belly, and the gut communicates a person's overall condition. However, gut feelings are based less on the gut's own nervous system, which is important for intestinal functioning, and more on the fact that numerous signals from the gut influence neuro-behavioural processes on a higher level (Berntson et al., 2003). More than 80% of the nerve cells of the gut are efferent. Only about 20% of the vagus fibres connected to the gut send information to it (Schaible, 2006). The rest send information from the gut to the brain, where inner states are processed.

Da Silva (1990) interprets the **sounds of the gut** symbolically when he reads them as messages about transference. Boyesen (1987, p. 152) interprets specific sounds as the expression of specific emotional processes, which we can read literally. Both points of view contradict the findings of neurobiology on the innervation of the intestines (cf. Heller, 2012, p. 211). The enteric nervous system has no mapping representative of other bodily states. In addition, intestinal peristalsis is not connected to the expressive behaviour of the somatic nervous system. Thus belly noises provide information about the overall vegetative state, for instance the level of relaxation, but they contain neither symbolic information nor are they a direct expression of categorical emotions such as anger or fear.

The **intestinal wall** has also another significant function. Often the skin is described as the largest area of contact with the outside world. However, the intestinal wall with 300–400m^2 is a much larger area and regulates contact with substances that we ingest, not all of which are meant to really penetrate into us. Thus the wall of the gut is, like the skin, the **site of barrier regulation**. Not for nothing do more than 70% of defence cells live in the gut so as to protect the body from harmful micro-organisms. Research on mice intestines show that the immune cells in the tissue surrounding the gut have multiple connections to nerve fibres (Ma et al., 2007). Since both cortisol as well as the vagus nerve can inhibit the immune response of the intestinal mucosa, Ruegg thinks it conceivable that inflammatory conditions of the gut such as colitis ulcerosa are influenced by the brain and the psyche via the vegetative nervous system (Ruegg, 2006, p. 25).

Experiments with mice indicate that information about the microbiome of the gut is transmitted via the vagus nerve to the brain (Bravo et al., 2011). Bercik et al. (2011) were able to show that mice become more reckless when certain gut bacteria are destroyed by antibiotics. It is now under discussion whether there are similarities between the effects of antibiotics and antidepressants (Hiergeist et al., 2020). In any case, emotionally regulated behaviour seems to be directly related to the condition of the microbiome in the gut. When mice were fed a particular probiotic bacterium, they developed a higher resistance to stress (Bravo et al., 2011).

7.2 LIMITS OF A NEUROSCIENTIFIC FOUNDATION
FOR BODY PSYCHOTHERAPY

After physics, biology and computer science, since the end of the 20th century neuroscience has become the leading science of the day for other disciplines. Its reception has also raised hopes of establishing a scientific basis for body psychotherapy. The findings and models of neurobiology are proving to be compatible with psychotherapeutic thinking. In all therapy approaches, this has led to the hope of increased legitimation in a scientific culture dominated by the prestige of natural science. Even the models offered to patients to explain the effects of therapy are often adapted to a neuroscientific *zeitgeist*. In an experiment, Fernandez Duque et al. (2017) showed that people tend to accept explanations of psychological phenomena as plausible when these include neuroscientific information, even if it is totally irrelevant.

Many body psychotherapists feel validated in their theories and their concept of human beings through neuroscience (Aposhyan, 2004; Carroll, 2006; Fogel, 2009; Gottwald, 2015, 2007; Koemeda-Lutz & Steinmann, 2004; Kuenzler, 2010; Maurer-Groeli, 2004; Stauffer, 2009; Westland, 2015). From the perspective of brain research, Huether (2010, p. 119) writes that body-oriented approaches do justice to neuroscientific ideas of the unity of thinking, feeling and acting, and Roth (2004, p. 68) that access to the unconscious can never be exclusively verbal as the limbic centres do not understand language. Gottwald (2005, p. 127) seizes the idea by pointing out that body and emotion-oriented approaches would be more likely to access subcortical structures. He says explicitly that the body–mind unity, which has always been emphasised by body psychotherapists, now has a solid basis in neurobiology (Gottwald, 2005, pp. 121–2). Klopstech recognises a biological foundation, an empirical verification or a parallel scientific objective for the essential hypotheses of our theory and our clinical approach (2005, p. 72). Some authors are even hopeful of finding in neuroscience a unifying scientific basis for body psychotherapy, indeed for all therapy methods:

- Sulz (2005, pp. 21–2) says that, astonishingly, modern neurobiological research has become the exact scientific basis for body psychotherapy.
- Storch (2002, p. 281) says that neuroscientific research has the potential to serve as an integrating basis for the estranged psychotherapeutic schools.

The attraction of neuroscience seems to lie in the fact that its theories support the basic idea of the unity of physical and mental processes (Section 5.2). In this respect, body psychotherapy is probably more compatible with neuroscience than other therapy approaches. However this should not induce us to describe mental and relational processes in metaphors of brain mechanisms (Rolef Ben-Shahar, 2014, p. 106) or to believe that knowledge of the brain can show us how to treat a human being in psychotherapy (Totton, 2015, p. XXII).

Notwithstanding the trend, I am not convinced that neuroscientific research can form the basis for a theory of body psychotherapeutic practice. The subject matter of this research is how the nervous system is constructed and how it functions. Body psychotherapy could only be based on neuroscience when we assume that the experience and behaviour of a human subject can be explained by neuronal processes. However, naturalistic descriptions cannot achieve this (Stauffer, 2009, p. 143; cf. Heilinger & Jung, 2009, p. 34). Even if neuroscience could show that experiences are transformed into biology and change gene expression, we could never understand experience from biology. While there are attempts to connect experience, the first-person perspective, with objective neurobiological data from a third-person perspective, we cannot, however, reconstruct experience from this (Northoff et al., 2006). Neurobiology is only able to demonstrate the biological conditions of experience; it cannot show the substance of the experience itself.

Nevertheless, body psychotherapy should correlate its theories with those of neuroscience, so as to test their mutual compatibility and to seek an exchange of ideas (Leuzinger-Bohleber, 2001, p. 101), which can be just as fruitful here as with the ANS (Section 7.1). The exciting thing about the encounter between psychotherapy and neurobiology is namely not the attempt to justify the former by the theories of the latter, but the connections we can establish between their respective conceptual models, theories and ideas (Huether, 2005, p. 22).

This relationship has stimulated theoretical discussion in psychotherapy since the 1990s:

- In the face of academic psychology, which for decades has negated the existence of feelings, neuroscience has rehabilitated the essential significance of the realm of affects (Panksepp, 2006). The effects of emotions and of stress have been demonstrated down to the cellular level (Carroll, 2006; Oliveira et al., 2016; Schubert, 2020).
- Proven neurobiological sequelae of traumatisation, for instance the reduction in volume of the hippocampus as a result of severe neglect or war traumata (Smith, 2005), have stimulated the psychotherapeutic trauma debate. We now have a greater understanding of what brain processes are involved in retaining often the shock of a situation, but not the context, and that key emotional stimulants from the traumatising situation can be unconsciously reactivated by triggers (van der Kolk, 2014). Thereby the idea of a dissociation in the body put forward by Janet has been rehabilitated (Nijenhuis, 2004).
- The findings of brain research now support the psychoanalytical dream theory, which was attacked for many years by this same research (Kaplan-Solms & Solms, 2000).
- Studies show that psychotherapy alters certain patterns of brain activity and that symptom improvement reported psychologically correlates with a reduction in specific neuronal activation (Barsaglini et al., 2014; Buchheim et al., 2012; Cao et al., 2021; Freyer et al., 2011; Karch et al., 2012; Linden, 2006).

The parallelism of these findings does not, however, imply that neuronal changes explain changes induced by psychotherapy, nor does it justify psychotherapeutic methods. We cannot translate the findings of brain research into psychotherapeutic methods (Gottwald, 2015, p. 127; Huether, 2005, p. 25). The direct application of these findings must remain speculative (Gottwald, 2005, p. 106).

Moreover, up to now, neuroscientific research has confined itself almost exclusively to processes within the organism. Only recently have there been attempts to include interactional processes, such as take place in every psychotherapy, in a second-person neuroscience (Redcay & Schildbach, 2019).

Overestimating the results of research in neuroscience can lead us to adopt biological models too hastily. Our ability to link psychological processes to neuronal ones is still rudimentary, despite the fact that we increasingly understand their interplay and their connection to endocrinal and immunological processes. Beckermann's (1996, p. 7) statement that nobody can link even one mental state exactly to a neurophysiological one still holds true. The solution to the qualia problem, which is the essential question in any psychotherapy of how a sensation feels, is not even on the horizon.

As Nagel (1974) determined in his legendary essay, we can only attribute something to scientifically explainable mechanisms when we have understood it. The hermeneutic understanding of experience and behaviour precedes the scientific findings and not the other way around. Neuro-determinists claim that the brain creates our experience. However in reality, human beings experience something and this is accompanied by brain processes. Neuroscientists observe on the level of the physical body, from a third-person perspective, processes the meaning of which they can only know from what their subjects communicate to them from the first-person perspective. The study of activated brain areas makes no sense without a phenomenological elucidation of the processes studied (Gallagher, 2014b).

No neuroscientific research can see experience. No study of a state of the brain shows the lived experienced of fear (Frazetto, 2013) or the intentionality of experience (Richter, 2019, pp. 42–3). When I feel love for my wife and my children, the state of my brain can be monitored, but a scan will never show this love **for them**.

In psychotherapy, in contrast, mental and physical phenomena are often seen as one and the same, for instance when we read that a memory is a series of electrical impulses generated by a specific sequence of nerve cells (Pollani, 2016, p. 158). However, if we examine these impulses scientifically, we will never find a memory. Statements such as 'ego states are brain patterns' (Pollani, 2016, p. 166) or 'neuronal networks are the neurophysiological substrate of schemata' (Stauss & Fritsche, 2006, p. 214) are based on a category error and cannot be proven empirically. The mistake lies in viewing neurobiological and psychological data as one and the same. The idea behind this is that the brain is the substrate of the mind.

According to the theory of enactivism, however, mind is an expression of the living that transcends the temporary dynamic patterns of brain activity (Thompson & Varela, 2001; Noë, 2010; Section 5.2). Mind is not in the brain, but is connected 'to the whole environment, the whole of life' and the whole organism (Emrich, 2007, p. 208). For example, we **feel** feverish, while the immune system triggers a myriad of reactions to deal with a virus. Experience and behaviour do not originate in the brain, but in a complex interaction of the embodied subject with their environment (Chiel et al., 2009). The brain is part of this interaction. Chiel and Beer (1997, p. 555) offer the following metaphor: the nervous system is not the conductor of an orchestra, but one of the players in a group of improvising musicians.

No-one can point to part of the brain and say that there is where what I am now experiencing takes place. There are no brain structures for our consciousness of ourselves (Vogeley & Gallagher, 2014). Our experiences are embodied where they are; for instance we experience a pain in the foot in the foot. Velmans (2007) thinks experiences are therefore there where we experience them. Processes in the brain notify us that the pain is in the foot. However, this does not mean it is in the brain. In phantom pain, the brain can project a perception, but this does not mean that the pain experienced in the foot is not in the foot. From the first-person perspective, the pain is there where it hurts. It is experienced there and can be monitored there. From a third-person perspective, we can examine which neuronal processes are involved in this experience, but how a person experiences themselves in the body cannot be observed in the brain (Velmans, 2007, p. 561).

The brain and the person

The insight that interactive experiences programme neuronal connections has led some authors to formulate the goals of psychotherapy neurobiologically: to weaken dysfunctional neuronal connections or arousal patterns and to develop and consolidate new ones (Grawe, 2007; Kuenzler, 2010). However such statements are purely metaphorical, since nobody can describe the patterns of experience and behaviour on a neuronal level. Attempts by Cozolino (2002) and Grawe (2007) to establish a 'neuropsychotherapy' are characterised by the translation of psychological concepts metaphorically into a neuroscientific language. The authors fail to engage with the epistemic problems this entails.

Cozolino (2002, p. 25) asserts that psychological symptoms have a 'brain based explanation' and are 'a reflection of suboptimal integration and coordination of neuronal networks'. Yet to date, not one single mental disorder can be diagnosed by neuroscientific means (Tschuschke, 2020, p. 135). He does not consider whether neuroscientific findings can explain mental disorders generally in a reasonable way. Thus he reinterprets parallel findings on the laterality of brain processes and on the dysregulation of affects into cause and effect relationships by making the established dysregulation between processes of the left and right hemispheres of the brain the cause of dysregulated affects (Cozolino, 2002, p. 118). In this way, a materialistic concept of the genesis of mental disorders creeps in, which sees them as ultimately caused by hypostatised brain processes.

The problem with this concept is that first it divides up mind and body into separate entities and then it attempts to connect them (Fuchs, 2008). As a starting point, however, this construction creates in itself the question of how one causes the other. Only when we philosophically separate the brain from the person to whom it belongs can we claim that the causes of experience and behaviour lie in the brain (cf. Pauen, 2007). Yet if our starting point is the actual person, then psychological processes and brain processes are only parts of their essential living being, two aspects of an embodied subject (Fuchs, 2008, p. 357). When musicians are playing a duet and their brain waves synchronise, this synchronisation develops through their interactive coordination process and not the other way around (Gugnowska et al., 2022). Attributing psychological and interactional phenomena to neuronal phenomena is as if we tried to explain the duet through the brain waves.

Some psychotherapists claim, for instance, that ADHD is the **result** of a delay in the thickening of the cortex (Shaw et al., 2007). This is no different from saying that a thinner muscle is the cause of muscular weakness. In patients whose hippocampus volume has shrunk due to developmental or war trauma, it is not the shrunken hippocampus causing their problems but the state of neglect or of war. Heim et al. (2020) however describe the sequelae of early stress in such a way that brain development – not that of a human being – is disturbed, and the risk of mental disorders is due to disturbed brain development. But this last is just as much a result of the stress as the mental disorder itself.

The neural explanation of psychological symptoms follows the natural scientific concept of causality. As Rank (1929, pp. 312–3) said in early criticism of Freud, psychic causality is different from scientific causality. The **causalities of human suffering**, which we are treating in psychotherapy, **are of life** and not 'causalities of a material, scientific nature' (Marlock, 2015, p. 151).

The same is true of our understanding of psychotherapeutic change mechanisms. A reorganisation of cortical areas is not a central mechanism of body-oriented mind-body therapies and thus a cause of the relief of suffering, as Mehling (2010, p. 170) claims; at most, it describes hypothetically the effects of therapy on the level of brain physiology. Echoing a remark made by T. Fuchs (2008a, p. 126), I would formulate it as follows:

Important
Between neurophysiological, subjective and social processes there exists only a circular causality, no foundation of one process in any of the others.

As the starting point for psychotherapy as a clinical neuroscience, Cozolino (2002, pp. 3, 157) focuses on a question which we have not even begun to resolve and is at the same time wrong, namely how the brain generates the mind or constructs the self; he completely omits any consideration of the philosophical dimensions. He substantiates the idea of neural networks, which is only a model, and calls it the 'neural substrate for what Freud called the *ego*' (p. 29). Here Cozolino is following an implied idea of the brain as the subject: the brain, not the person, learns (p. 16), 'psychotherapy teaches a method to help us better understand and use our brains' (p. 291) and 'to foster neural growth and integration' (Cozolino, 2002, p. 27).

Grawe (2007) is also trapped in this 'property physicalism' (Beckermann, 1996) when he says that psychotherapy can only be effective by changing the brain. The idea of an autopoiesis of brains and not of living beings surfaces in his phrase that 'concepts such as mind and soul are ultimately – in their existence as well as their particular characteristics – a product of neural networks' (200, p. 3). Since Grawe's understanding of the human being manages without the body (Section, 1.2), he also ignores even the close relationship between the brain and other body systems. In reducing psychological processes to those of the brain, we are in danger of overlooking the fact that they are in many ways linked to hormonal, metabolic, immunological and vascular processes and not just to neural ones (Fogel, 2009, p. 41).

Recently the findings of brain research have so impressed science that the old question of the relationship between body and mind has only been formulated in terms of the relationship between the **brain** and the **mind** (Tretter & Gruenhut, 2010, p. 231). This has led to an update of the old **dualism** in the sense that the *res extensa* of Descartes, the material substance of the body, is now the brain. In psychotherapy, we can find statements such as 'the physical brain, the body's experiencing organ, and mind, the psyche, are one unity' (Slavin & Rahmani, 2016, p. 154), that 'emotion is created in the brain' (Fogel, 2009, p. 56) or develops there (Sulz, 2021) or that the brain regulates feelings and the amygdala has something 'to say' (Berking, 2017, p. 49). If the brain has become the 'cerebral subject' (Vidal & Ortega, 2017), then we can ascribe human properties to it as in 'finding happiness in the brain' (Amen, 1998), or an 'anxious and fearful brain' (Cozolino, 2002, p. 235). However, emotions do not originate in the brain, but in life, in the living interaction between a subject and the outside world (Chapter 10).

In contrast to this brain-centredness, my view, in accordance with enactivism, is that the brain is an organ of a living being in interaction with their environment (Chemero, 2011, p. 178). As part of such a being, it does not make its own decisions (Gallagher, 2018; Gallagher et al., 2013; McGann et al., 2013). A person, not an orbitofrontal cortex, as Sulz (2021, p. 25) asserts, reviews their decisions. As a relational organ it belongs to a dynamic system that includes the body and its surroundings (Di Paolo & De Jaegher, 2012; Fuchs, 2017; Noë, 2010). People do not **have** a 'social brain' (Cozolino, 2002); they **are** social beings. Whoever looks only at the brain and its interaction with psychological processes will never find the human being we encounter in psychotherapy.

Neuro-body-psychotherapy?

Following Grawe (2007), Kuenzler (2010) has coined the term neuro-body-psychotherapy, to which he added a question mark. The question, however, should not become a statement, since Grawe's own concept of **neuro-psychotherapy** makes no scientific sense. If we adhere to a definition of psychotherapy based on **what** we treat (Chapter 2), this would mean we treat both the neurons and the psyche, but no psychotherapist treats nerve cells. And if we want to express **how** we treat, this would mean we treat by means of the nerve cells or the brain, which is just as absurd. This may apply to methods which use electrodes attached to the brain to activate the reward system (Heller, 2012, pp. 239–40) or transcranial magnetic stimulation, but not psychotherapy. Nevertheless unconsidered ideas, such as a 'brain-based psychotherapy' (Cappas et al., 2005), are still being used.

Informing patients that they can change their brain, as Cappas et al. (2005) do, is basically a hypnotherapy technique, which uses their belief in an desired objectivity (cf. Fuchs, 2008, p. 310). Hypnotherapists who successfully treat herpes simplex by having their patients imagine that healing dolphins are swimming through their blood vessels (Gruzelier, 2002), are not claiming that dolphins are really doing that. Badenoch (2008), on the other hand, acts as if she really is changing synapses when she has her patients visualise those synapses changing that contain, for example, memories of a menacing father. Her 'brain-wise therapy' is just a cognitive, suggestive technique. Stauffer (2009) understands the use of neuroscientific information for patients who are not suffering from organic brain damage rightly as the introduction of an interpretative model, which helps to reduce stress and to develop ego strength. For patients who like to be up to date on the latest scientific trends, this suggestion might be useful.

> Knowing about neurophysiological processes in the brain is relevant for the neuropsychological treatment of disorders of the brain function, but not necessarily for psychotherapeutic change processes. As interesting as it may be to know what happens neurophysiologically when someone is thinking, feeling or moving about, therapeutic change takes place in thinking, feeling or moving. We cannot sense how thoughts are thought, feelings are felt or the movements of the muscles produced; we can only experience the thoughts, feelings and movements themselves. It is on this level of sensing and feeling and moving that body psychotherapy works.

There is no sound reason for formulating a new paradigm for body psychotherapy on the basis of neurobiology. Natural scientific research can only form the basis for a technical practice in which a human being is treated as an organism in relation to their physical functions. Therefore there is only a neuroscientific basis for a body psychotherapy which makes the patient into an object of therapy technology. Grawe (2007) comes close to this notion with his focus on the therapy goals set by the neuropsychotherapist and not the patient.

Important
Natural science can penetrate deeply into the secrets of biological, chemical and physical life processes. However it cannot teach us what it means to feel alive or not, happy or not, healthy or not. Science has no answer to the question of what makes a fulfilling life.

As psychotherapists we encounter patients as subjects; we see them above all as a person with their own unique lives and their own suffering, and less as subjected to laws valid for the physical human organism in general. Here we see the difference between a hermeneutic and a natural scientific approach (Section 5.3).

Neuroscientific knowledge and conceptual models can nevertheless stimulate the formation of a theory of body psychotherapy (Carroll, 2005, pp. 13–4) and can be included as perspectives when we consider questions of body experience, memory, emotions or child development. This is why in the chapters on these themes I also refer to neuroscientific findings and theories. In the practice of body psychotherapy, however, we are not working with brain processes, nor with physical or biological energies, but with the life, experience and behaviour of subjects. We can understand these with the aid of theories on the level of subjective processes, not with those of natural science.

7.3 THE WEAKNESSES OF THE ENERGY MODEL

The Reichian energy model is an explicit attempt to ground body psychotherapy in natural science. This model assumes that behind psychological and physical processes lies a universal energy as a unifying element (Ferri & Cimini, 2012, p. 19; Section 5.1). This energy is often understood as being physical and/or biological (Koemeda-Lutz & Gutzat, 2022). The energy model bases body psychotherapy on a theory of the material body of natural science and not on one of the experienced body and the communication between embodied subjects.

Rolef Ben-Shahar (2014, p. 164) holds that the assumption 'that bodymind energy could be felt and interacted with' is one of the foundations of body psychotherapy. For him, energy is a kind of monitoring of bodily rhythms such as vibrations or pulsations. The idea of energy is often used in such a vague manner in body psychotherapy, without a definition of what is actually meant by the concept of energy (Totton, 2002a, p. 205). Throughout his entire work, Lowen advocates the concept of bio-energy, without once formulating a theory of this energy (Carle, 2002, p. 161). Trotz (2019, p. 138) talks vaguely of the 'energetic functions' of the self and counts among them bodily functions such as breathing and heartbeat, passivity and activity or an undefined 'pulsation'.

In body psychotherapy, the idea of energy has often been used to describe **intense experiences**, which are difficult to express in words. As Marlock says, it helped to record the 'intensity of emotions, feelings and passions; vital and powerful self-expressions; flowing pleasurable sensations; and even ego-transcending orgasmic experiences, sometimes referred to as cosmic or oceanic' (Marlock, 2015, p. 150). Thus since the 1970s, the energy concept has been popular in approaches which attempt to reach inner freedom through increasing the energy level (cf. Caldwell, 2018, p. 82). For Barratt (2010, p. 77) the notions of *élan vital* or libido stand for a living, embodied being in the world and an 'erogeneity of our entire body'. This is a congenial, emancipatory aspect of the life-energy concept, which points to sensual vitality and sexuality. However, we should not use a scientific construct for something that we cannot really specifically identify. Nevertheless, the energy concept has been overloaded in an effort to explain 'the quantitative aspects of affective processes, their vegetative basis' (Marlock, 2015, p. 149) and life as a whole.

The neo-Reichian energy model is a legacy of both drive theory and of vitalism in body psychotherapy (Sections 3.4 and 3.6). It is an attempt to derive all life processes from one final force circulating in the physical body. This distinguishes the Reichian concept from the psychic energy of C.G. Jung, which Jung explicitly did not equate with a physical energy as life force (Jung, 1928).

- Lowen (1958, p. 18) works on the assumption of energy as a 'physical phenomenon, that is capable of being measured' and which he sees as the source of psyche and soma. He defines bioenergetics as 'the study of the human personality in terms of the energetic processes of the body' (Lowen, 1977, p. 45). Helfaer (2011, p. 79) describes the energetic perspective as key to the theory and practice of bioenergetic analysis.

- Keleman (1985) uses the metaphor of a pump spreading energy throughout the body, and so builds on the hydraulic imagery of drive theory.
- Boadella (1987) understands character not only as patterns of preferred behaviour but also as an organisation of energetic charge.
- Pierrakos (1987) speaks of energy as a basic substance of the personality and considers illness to be the blockage of energy and health the flow of life energy. For Rosenberg et al. (1985), a healthy person is an aggregation of free-flowing energy.
- Boyesen et al. (1995, p. 83) consider that in his orgone theory, Reich has provided bio-physical evidence of libido energy. Boyesen speaks of a 'discovery' and sees this energy as an indubitable fact of nature and not as a hypothesis. She also assumes that energetic illness is a given (Boyesen et al., 1995, p. 96).
- Fuckert (2002, pp. 93–5) writes that arousal and emotion are the result of bio-physical energy, a primal bio-energy without mass or life energy. How energy with no mass is to move around the body and why on the one hand it is a bio-energy and on the other a bio-physical energy, she does not say. We can already find this coexistence of a biological and a physical concept of energy in Reich's work (Section 3.6).

The fundamental problem of the energy model is the claim, as formulated by Pechtl and Trotz, to try to describe 'human processes as part of nature with the laws of physics' (Pechtl & Trotz, 2019, p. 37). From there we arrive at a therapeutic practice in which working with muscle tension is seen as 'energy work' in a physically defined sense. Greene (2013) even goes so far as to say that all psychotherapy is energy work, since energy is omnipresent.

We cannot discuss these statements rationally when the authors neither name the physical laws they rely on nor define what they mean by energy. The same is true of the idea that life is the expression of a life energy. This idea is circular, because we can also speak of life itself if one does not determine the energy which creates it. While it is true that we can describe life processes in terms of the dynamics of energy, we cannot however derive these from physical laws. Energy is not the cause of life. In fact it is living beings who invest energy, that they themselves have produced, into achieving their goals. The causes lie within these beings themselves and in their learning experiences (Fuchs, 2017). The difference between the enactivist approach I advocate here and the energy model is thus related to whether we see life as an interaction in the sense of systemic theory (Capra & Luisi, 2014; Chapter 5) or as the expression of a 'primal, creative force in the universe' (Davis, 2020, p. 47), as do the spiritual schools within body psychotherapy (Heller, 2012, p. 277).

In addition, there is the problem that the concept of energy in body psychotherapy is mainly used diffusely on an abstract level for which there exists no generally accepted scientific theory. On this level of abstraction, energy is thought of as a substance the effects of which can be recognised without anyone being able to prove its existence (Downing, 1996, pp. 366–77; Heller, 2012, pp. 638–9). On a general level of abstraction, we can at best use the notion of energy as does Capra (1982) as a systemic concept to describe dynamic structures of self-organisation.

The idea of a physical energy is a legacy of the scientific world view of the 19th century. The physicist and physiologist Hermann von Helmholtz formulated the law of the conservation of energy in 1847. According to this law, a system can only transform energy – for instance, a motor can transform chemicals into kinetic energy, but the energy itself remains constant (Osietzki, 1998, p. 322–3). The ideas of the Helmholtz school shaped Freud's psycho-energetic thinking (Nitzschke, 1989). Freud and Reich created a metaphorical world of congestion, pressure, charge and discharge fitting for an age fascinated first by the steam engine (Osietzki, 1998; Russelman, 1988, p. 28) and later by electricity and radioactivity

(Section 3.6). Also at the beginning of the 20th century the fascination with sexuality led to Freud and Reich seeing the central energy of the body in the sexual drive (Section 3.5). Neither of them ever abandoned the correlation of mentalist concepts such as drives, arousal, pleasure and displeasure with the model of the circulation of energy and with 'physical processes'. Habermas (1969, pp. 300ff) sees in this the scientistic self-misunderstanding of psychoanalytical metapsychology, to which the energy model in body psychotherapy has succumbed.

Right from the beginning the idea that, if we only knew enough, we could heal mental illness with physical, biological or chemical means, has been linked to the energy model. Freud (1940) thought we could work with psychological methods as long as we have no others with which to directly influence the distribution of energy in the psychic apparatus. Both Boyesen and Pierrakos imagine working directly with energy quanta (Section 5.1).

Schore (2003) appeals to psychoanalysis to update the energy concept to neuroscientific standards. It is his view 'that affectively charged psychobiological states are known to be a product of the balance between energy-expanding and energy-conserving components of the autonomic nervous system' (Schore, 2003, p. 267). The problem with this formulation is the description of these states as products of ANS processes. In fact they are a product of the life movements of an organism, to which experience and the biological processes in the ANS both belong. The observation of parallel processes does not mean that processes of experience are identical to or are produced by organic processes. Schore also writes that 'energy shifts are the most basic and fundamental features of emotion' (Schore, 2003, p. 267), but he does not define this energy. The observance of arousal states in emotional processes is, however, not proof that we are dealing with a life energy supplying both psychological and organic processes; it just describes an expression of life, not identical with experience, on another level of scientific exploration.

In Asian schools of thought, the concept of Qi stands for an energy and a material reality (Carle, 2002, p. 157). What we feel at the pressure points of acupuncture is seen as the manifestation of this energy. Fred Gallo's **Energy Psychology** is based on this. Gallo (2000) assumes the existence of a subtle bio-energy, the streaming and disruption of which he diagnoses with the muscle tests of kinesiology. In his system, subtle energies serve in the body as a control system for feelings (Wehowsky, 2015). Negative affects are resolved by tapping points on the meridians. On the basis of a theory of unknown energies in the physical body, the therapist determines what treatment the patient needs. This acupressure tapping is thus following a medical model. Today some therapists forgo the energetic explanation of the tapping techniques and base their work on the empirical values of therapeutic transformation and other possible factors (Bohne, 2019; Geuter, 2019, p. 211; Pfeiffer, 2022).

Phenomenal level

Heller (2012, p. 277) points out the importance of the **differentiation** between the **concept of energy** and the **experience of energy in the body**. This corresponds to the differentiation between causal-explanatory and phenomenal concepts. On a phenomenal level, body psychotherapists sometimes describe various different sensations, such as tingling, tension, pressure, vibrating, arousal, flowing, streaming, seizing up or a languorous feeling of vigour, as the expression of energy. Patients, too, describe body-centred therapy experiences as energising. On a phenomenal level, we can therefore speak of the energy in processes of arousal. Therapists can talk with their patients about an energy moving somewhere, or being blocked, without having to define what is meant. It immediately makes sense when a patient says she can feel how 'the energy' is moving from her chest up into her head, but not down to the pelvis. Patients also understand what is meant when they feel the arousal in other parts of the body but not in the extremities, and when we say they should let their anger move into their arms. On this level, the idea of energy is an abstraction for various ways of experiencing. If we relate it to vigour, vitality or the ability to act, then we can demystify the energy concept.

Important
On a phenomenal level, the concept of energy can describe certain experiences sensed in the body. However, as a concept for an alleged physically determinable life force, it has no explanatory power for a theory of the practice of body psychotherapy.

On the level of body experience, the concept of energy describes **phenomena of arousal and vitality**. Aposhyan (2004) uses the concept of energy consistently when she talks of emotional arousal felt in the body. Caldwell speaks of the flow of energy when we are under stress and have the feeling of shrinking or inflating oneself; 'My stomach feels fluttery and I label this energetic event embarrassment' (Caldwell, 1997, p. 8). Harms expands the energy concept into the interpersonal field when he views attunement and coordination processes between parents and child as the expression of a deeper energy process and considers the energetic factor as determining the quality of the contact (Harms, 2008, pp. 64–5).

Such observations seem to be classified as energy above all when we are unable to explain them with current scientific knowledge (Heller, 2012, p. 638). Clinically, however, we should avoid labelling the various phenomena of body experience, emotional life or affective interaction with the single concept of energy since this restricts our perception (cf. Downing, 1996, p. 375). From a clinical point of view, we need a differentiating, phenomena-oriented language (Section 5.3; Geuter, 2019, pp. 371–86).

We have to **distinguish observable facts from scientific constructs**. For example, objectively, we can detect a hardness in the muscles. This is a fact. If we then talk about a muscular armour, this is a metaphorical idea with the help of which we are describing a phenomenon. The muscular armour is a construct of observation. In body psychotherapy, however, constructs such as muscular armour are often treated as if they were objects that we could nail down. Having formed a construct from our observations, we tend to believe we could actually see this construct itself. The same is true of psychological concepts such as that of intelligence. This too is a construct, in which we conflate various observations. Then, when looking for the biological basis of intelligence, we look for the substance of the construct (Velden, 2013). When we reduce metaphorical ideas to the material level, they become reified. The concept of energy, too, is a construct for describing observable processes. We tend to confuse the signifier with the signified when we think the concept exists in reality, for instance in the reified idea that a substance is flowing through the body (Heller, 2012, pp. 278, 639).

The physical body

On the level of the physical body too we can describe our observations in terms of the energy concept: phenomena such as electrical and chemical processes between neurons, the state of arousal in the nervous system connected to this, body heat radiation, light radiation, magnetism, metabolic or bioelectrical processes in the muscles. Organisms connect to their environment through electromagnetic, mechanical or chemical energies (Johnson, 2007, p. 158). Living beings have energy budgets, which they can refill through metabolic exchanges with the environment and through which they attain and retain their equilibrium (Boden, 1999). When describing such processes, we should always name the **specific** energy meant (Wehowsky, 2015, p. 172), e.g. the change in temperature or in skin conductance, bodily processes which also occur in therapy. Eberwein (2009, p. 92) calls the energy created metabolically, which can be mobilised by motivation and dysregulated by defensive processes, body energy. The concept of body energy can link subjective experiences of psychosomatic arousal to biological processes. However we should avoid understanding it as a kind of general life energy (Wehowsky, 2006, p. 197).

> From internal medicine, we already know that pathological processes produce changes in local body heat radiation. For instance, we can accurately diagnose renal insufficiency in 75% of cases by means of a spectroscopy (Folberth et al., 1987). The most likely reason for this is the segmental innervation of the skin, which creates a connection between inner organs and certain areas of the skin, as in the theory of Head's zones (Duus, 1983, p. 301). Infrared thermography produces images of moods, which are translated into posture (Cantieni, 2006). In these cases we can reasonably speak of thermal energy, but not of a general bioenergy.

Energy and information

Decades ago in psychoanalysis there was a discussion about replacing the energy model with an **information model**. W. Koenig (1981, p. 90) criticised the fact that the metaphorical concept of psychic energy was being confused with the scientific concept of energy in physics, and this was a source of conflict in metapsychology. Generally there was a tendency to draw on the energy concept as an explanation for events not understood (W Koenig, 1981, p. 97). In body psychotherapy, Kurtz (1983) advocated the same change of model. At that time in his school of Hakomi, there was a change of focus from working with the body and releasing blocks to a mindful self-observation. Both these introductions of a new model marked a movement towards cognitive theories in which, according to Fodor (1975, p. 198), physical change was seen as a change in information.

Petzold (2006, p. 102) also suggests replacing the energy concept with that of information. However I see no solution in this, since the concept of information relates to signals which are interchanged without containing any of the related living processes themselves (Section 5.1). Petzold does bring both aspects together in his idea of the 'informed living body'. Wehowsky (2015) wants to complement the concept of energy with that of information. However, this co-existence of both concepts leaves body psychotherapy oscillating between drive theory or vitalist life theory on the one hand and a cognitive theory on the other, instead of giving it its own foundation in an interactional theory of life processes (Section 5.1).

Time-bound metaphors

Scientific theories use the ideas of their times, which stem from daily life. The **energy model** is a legacy of steam engines, pumping stations and electrical grids and is well suited to the **second industrial revolution** of electrotechnical industrialisation; the **information model** is well suited to the **third industrial revolution** of automation, control engineering and communication technology and is a legacy of cybernetics (Wiener, 1961). The energy model follows the excitation of electricity, the information model the possibility of dealing with reality in the form of symbols, through television, audiotapes, and computers. The energy model mirrors the endeavour to monitor and control forces, the information model the endeavour to decipher and use character codes. Von Uexkuell (2001) expressly links the paradigmatic change in medicine from a machine model to a semiotic understanding of symptoms to the transition from an industrial to an information society.

Today, notions of the organism as a **network**, in which a multitude of interconnected control entities exist and in which we can intervene from any one point, are based on the technological paradigm of **internet communication**. Varela et al. (2001) referred explicitly to the World Wide Web (WWW) as they launched the idea of a brainweb. Just as in the WWW, information is not stored in one single computer, but is created in a networked interexchange, so it is also in the brain. According to this metaphor, phase synchronisation, analogous to the simultaneous electrical activity in the net, connects brain processes to one another. The net metaphor can also be found in biochemical information models such as Pert's (1999), based on neurotransmitters and receptor–ligand communication and sees information as the bridge between mind and body (Pert, 1999). Perhaps the systemic model of the embodied mind with its idea of an integrated interconnectivity of all living processes and of the constant interexchange in movement is a metaphorical expression of our current technology (Section 5.2). Later generations will be able to evaluate this when they outstrip this model.

A living system

As a counterpart to both the energy and the information models, I prefer the idea of a **systemic theory of the living** (Capra & Luisi, 2014). This does more justice to an experiential and subject-centred as well as a relational understanding of body psychotherapy than does the energy model, which tends towards a body technology view; or the information model, which tends towards a cognitivist view. If Reich was looking for the foundation of life in a new form of energy inherent in matter, the systemic theory sees this in its inner organisation (Maturana & Varela, 1992). According to this theory, the living is characterised by the fact that because of its structure it constantly creates, namely maintains and renews, itself and determines its own borders in interaction with its environment. Living beings have an **autopoietic organisation**, and as **autonomous entities** they develop borders to the environment surrounding them (Section 5.2) to which they adapt and with which they interact. They are self-sustaining metabolic systems (Ghin, 2005).

Since living beings create themselves, in them, being and doing are a unity. Cells divide and proliferate without the need for an external cause. Their being consists of the self-movement of their doing. However their existence, as that of all living beings, is bound to a milieu in recursive interaction, which forms their subjective life world (von Uexkuell, 2010). Thus, in addition to their organisation, the second characteristic of living beings is the regulation of their relationship with the environment and finally the third, that they develop from simple to more complex forms and reproduce themselves (Toepfer, 2005).

From this concept of living systems there follows a different concept of healing than from the energy model. In his later phase, Reich wanted to steer life like an engineer steers a machine (Section 3.6). This is why he put patients in the orgone accumulator. With Lowen, we see a similar idea of the therapist as an expert who, from outside, recognises the blocks and the bottlenecks of the flow of energy in the patient's body and then releases them. Here the therapist looks at the energy flow of the patient from outside and knows how to heal them. Healing consists of bringing the energy back into circulation, which, according to Downing (1996, p. 372), is a mechanistic understanding of the therapeutic healing process.

From the autopoietic theory of life, it follows that **the living organism heals itself**. Hence the therapist can only help to remove obstacles to self-healing (cf. Kuhl, 1998, p. 71); Groddeck had already advocated this (Chapter 3). Therapists can provide a healing environment and give impulses to help healing take place, but patients can only heal themselves. Basically it is no different for doctors. Even a surgeon can only set a broken bone; it has to grow back together itself. The understanding of healing in an experiential relational body psychotherapy thus integrates well into a systemic theory of the living. From a systemic perspective, therapy is also seen as an impulse for self-regulation, in which at all times the results of the process in turn affect the process itself (Chapter 17). According to this understanding, a patient's biopsychosocial system changes in ways we cannot predict (cf. Schiepek, 2004, p. 258; von Schlippe & Kriz, 2004a, p. 10). In body psychotherapy, too, somato-psychic processes such as emotional arousal, the expression of feelings or changes in the breathing are self-regulative learning and developmental processes of the subjects 'rather than a mechanical process of rearranging the distribution of energy, or the conversion of energy, within the body' (Marlock, 2015, p. 151).

From the dynamic-systemic view of life there follows a different understanding of the concept of **blockage**. The energy model sees this as the blockade of a flow of energy. Sometimes a water metaphor is used as an illustration, wherein the therapist removes the rocks hindering the flow of water from the riverbed. According to the model of living systems, it is the self-regulation of dynamic processes which is blocked, hindering the system in its effort to maintain and renew itself and to interact. In this metaphor, the therapist prompts the patient to remove the stones themselves, or to let them be borne away by the flow of the river or to find some other way of getting around or over them, so as to restore the freedom of self-regulative processes.

8

Embodiment research

The sensorimotor basis of thinking and feeling

In both psychology and psychotherapy, the theory that the psychological expresses itself in the body, gestures, posture and facial expression has a long tradition (Section 3.1.1). The body is viewed as animated, as **mindful body**. This is the perspective of the old expression psychology. More recent empirical embodiment research addresses the effects of bodily processes on mental ones: **embodied mind** (Payne et al., 2019a). As mentioned at the beginning of Section 5.2, this research is concerned with how body posture and behaviour influence thoughts and affects and what impact sensorimotor processes have on them.

As I introduce some of the results of this research, you will recognise various aspects from your clinical experience or from everyday life. The astonishing thing about this research is not so much the results, but that such familiar processes can now be confirmed experimentally (cf. Huether, 2006, p. 75). Body psychotherapy has always assumed that human beings experience 'through the body' and that the quality and intensity of experience is dependent on the vitality of the body (Lowen, 1967, p. 45). Embodiment research now bridges the gap between this way of thinking and experimental psychology (Michalak et al., 2019).

Lakoff and Johnson (1999) showed in their book *Philosophy in the flesh* that thinking depends on the input communicated to the brain via the body. Abstract thinking is derived metaphorically from practical, sensuous bodily experiences. For example, we structure our mental activity metaphorically around our bodily presence in space. We say that something is in front of us or behind us, that we will put it aside, that it weighs heavily on us or that we unburden ourselves. The experience that something enters and then leaves our body forms the metaphorical space for expressions such as 'withdrawing into oneself' or 'coming out of one's shell'. The idea of being absorbed in a task or snug in a relationship corresponds to the experience of being a body in a room – Lakoff and Johnson call this a container schema. The nature of the body and its relationship with the world shape the possibilities of cognitive concept formation.

Near and far, sudden and prolonged, straight and curved, intense and weak: all such concepts are basically non-linguistic concepts deriving from our experiences of movement. They are the bedrock of our foundational capacity to think in movement, a thinking that is grounded in non-linguistic corporeal concepts.

(Sheets-Johnstone, 2010, p. 115).

DOI: 10.4324/9781003176893-8

Cognitive processes are closely linked to body movements. For example, the ability to visu-ally rotate an object in imagination is connected to the ability to anticipate motor processes (Gibbs, 2006, p. 7). How long it takes to recognise a hand rotating on its own axis corre-sponds to the time needed for the movement (Parsons et al., 1998). Humans perceive the world and themselves first and foremost through the senses (Section 6.3). The structure of our consciousness is determined by our subjective and embodied experience of the world (Legrand, 2007). Embodiment research shows that not only the structure, but also the **phe-nomenal field of consciousness** and thus the respective experience in the moment is formed by a person's overall **current bodily condition** (Gallagher, 2005; Gibbs, 2006).

Actions structure our field of consciousness. Therefore acquiring knowledge is deeply connected to sensorimotor processes (Coello & Fischer, 2016). If we encourage children to make gestures, this stimulates their learning of language (Goldin-Meadow, 2015). The body is also involved in thinking. When we count silently we tend to make movements, and when we think about a certain situation we sometimes use sensorimotor simulation to make it clearer (Wilson, 2002). If we literally take a step back, we feel more cognitive control (Koch et al., 2009).

In a phenomenological analysis of thinking and language, Gendlin (1993) pointed out that the body communicates whether we consider a thought to be correct or whether we need to think some more. This inner decision is reached through a process of verification and reassessment on the basis of bodily sensations (Section 5.3). I feel in my gut whether I consider an idea to be right or not. If these sensations signal a 'yes', then I can let the thought stand; with a 'no' I need to go through it all again, or to formulate it differently, until my feel-ing says 'yes, that's right'. We feel a persistent doubt in the body. Thus meaning is generated in a visceral process (Johnson, 2007, p. 53). The body promotes thinking.

Visceral feedback is however unspecific and non-symbolic (Section 6.3). It lets us know whether a thought is acceptable or not. This feedback runs along the perception axis of pleasant–unpleasant, but gives us no clue as to the content of the idea.

Proponents of enactivism (Section 5.2) refer more often to the kinaesthetic met-aphorics of thinking and speaking (e.g. Merritt, 2015) than to those concerned with the vegetative and affective. However the metaphorical language of thinking is motoric, vegetative and affective. Thoughts move forwards or get stuck, they hit the mark or miss it, they arouse our curiosity, agitate us, leave us cold or fascinate us; they weigh heavily on us or wake us up; we float ideas or take them on board and accept them.

THINKING

Many experiments have shown how body postures, movements and body schemas influence cognitive processes. Reed and Farah (1995, p. 337) had subjects compare human figures in photos to one another. If they moved their own arm they were more easily able to recognise differences in the position of the arm in the photos; the same result was found for move-ments and positions of the legs. In an experiment of Tucker and Ellis (1998), subjects could answer questions about a cup in a picture faster when the handle of the cup was pictured on the side of the hand with which they were giving their answers. When reading a text, subjects could better remember humorous passages when they smiled, annoying ones when they frowned (Barsalou et al., 2003, pp. 57–8).

> **Clinical application**
>
> These experiments support the approach of body psychotherapy of activating cognitive processes through body postures and movements. Memories too are more easily triggered when we evoke the dominant affects of the earlier situation through the body. For instance, one such technique would be to voluntarily assume a posture or to execute a movement connected to the relevant life situation or the supposed affect.

If we imitate the expression we have seen on a face, we are more likely to recognise the face later on (Barsalou et al., 2003, p. 58); someone who cannot move their face does not recognise the other face so readily (Section 14.4). This accords with the finding that injuries to the somatosensory cortex and not to the visual cortex make it more difficult to evaluate facial expressions. This is also true of body posture: when we imitate someone else's posture, we notice their feelings and intentions more clearly (Reed & McIntosh, 2008, p. 94).

> **Clinical application**
>
> For patients, this means that they can sometimes empathise more with the feelings of others by, for example, acting out a scene, which evokes their presence in the therapy room; for therapists, it means they can understand their patients better if they also empathise with them in their facial expressions and gestures (Chapter 15).

However we can also use the body to shield ourselves from stimuli. Test persons who look at faces while chewing gum are not good at recognising these later on, probably because they are less able to empathise with the facial expressions on account of the gum-chewing.

> **Clinical application**
>
> In therapeutic work when memories of situations experienced as threatening come up, stereotypical actions can help the patient feel less. This can be used in treatment for example to facilitate a controlled confrontation with traumatic experiences. Possibly this is an effect of bilateral stimulation (Geuter, 2019, p. 211).

In these experiments the thoughts and feelings of the subjects are often modulated by a cover story. Riskind and Gotay (1982) let subjects take part in an experiment allegedly about the relationship between electrical skin resistance and muscle reaction, in the course of which they had either to assume a bent posture or sit up straight. Subsequently they took part in a 'separate' experiment, in which their stamina in puzzle solving was tested. Those who sat up straight in the first experiment persevered longer in the second. If you cross your arms over your chest and solve problems in this position, you will be able to work longer and more persistently than someone whose arms are at their side (Friedman & Elliot, 2008).

People sitting up straight during an experiment have more confident thoughts than people sitting slumped down (Brinol et al., 2009). A stooped posture is more likely to result in negative thoughts and negative moods and also lets people recover more slowly from them (Veenstra et al., 2017). If in an experiment depressive patients are asked to sit up straighter, then they tend to speak less in the first person singular, but use more words related to sadness (Wilkes et al., 2017). They seem to have less thoughts revolving around themselves, to feel less empty and more emotional.

Schubert and Koole (2009) found that using a story to camouflage the gesture of making a fist increased self-esteem in men but not, however, in women. The authors conclude that self-concept is based not only on the symbolic idea of who one is, but also on the sensorimotor state of the body and its interaction with the environment. They relate this to the change mechanisms of psychotherapy:

> It is possible that successful interventions that are traditionally considered 'cognitive' are partly effective in changing people's self-conceptions because they change embodied components … altering people's postures and movements can be a potent way of changing their self-views.
>
> (Schubert und Koole, 2009, p. 833)

Bodily processes not only induce thoughts; they can also hinder them. Body movements which contradict a verbal statement interfere with people's ability to understand it. They create an incongruity in the experience. Subjects who are told to press a button while listening to the sentence 'You told Liz the story' understand it more slowly if they have to move the hand towards themselves than if they have to move it away from themselves – almost as if the hand then moves towards Liz (Glenberg & Kaschak, 2002). If the direction of the movement and the direction of the communication are congruent, this facilitates understanding. If you hear 'Liz told you the story', then the opposite movement to the above accelerates or slows down understanding. **Cognitive processes** flow **optimally when** they are **aligned to bodily states** (Barsalou et al., 2003a, p. 87). I described this in Section 6.4 as the concept of coherence. When consciousness is at one with the action of the body and if a person is at one with what they are doing, then that person is in a state of what Csikszentmihalyi (1998) calls flow experience.

Clinical application

Establishing a balance between cognition and body states is a principle of body psychotherapeutic work. In biodynamics there is a style of therapeutic dialogue known as rooted talking, whereby verbal expression is related to somatic experience (Geuter, 2019, p. 379). As therapists, we can monitor by means of the congruence, or lack of it, between verbal and bodily expression, whether a patient is at one with what they are saying.

With Focusing, Gendlin developed a technique connected to the body, so that people could find the felt sense – a sense of meaningfulness perceived in the body, in which a body sensation and a word come together to create an overall impression of what I feel in relation to a question or a problem (Chapter 4). When in a therapy session language and bodily sensation coalesce, then a therapeutic flow develops and the patient can have an experience of congruence.

Felt sense is not something that we have; rather it is something that happens in a flowing process and that we can notice and name. Working with the felt sense is a practice of engaging with inner perception, which can generate meaning and significance. In the following example, we can see an incongruence between words and gestures:

Clinical example

A woman says that she really wishes her husband would be more affectionate. At the same time she makes an involuntary gesture of pushing away with her right hand. When I point this out we can get into an exploration of the ambivalence that she was not aware of until now.

FEELING

It is not only thinking that we describe in a metaphorical language related to bodily experience, but also feelings. When we are happy, we are high or on top of the world, when unhappy we are down, dejected, hangdog. When angry we are in high dudgeon, when miserable downcast, in disgust repulsed. We connect pride with uprightness, shame with stooping, hate with coldness and affection with warmth. The feeling of being excluded from a group is directly connected to a need for physical warmth (Bargh & Shalev, 2012).

How closely **posture** and **bodily expression** are related to moods and feelings has been documented in a great number of experiments. For quite a while now, psychological research has been concerned with what is one of the main issues in clinical body psychotherapy.

In a much-quoted experiment, Strack et al. (1988) showed that the activation or inhibition of the muscles involved in smiling by holding a pencil in the mouth in a certain way – either horizontally with the lips or at the front with the teeth – influences how funny the participants found the cartoons they were being shown at the same time. This did not hold up in several repeats of the experiment (Wagenmakers et al., 2016). However in contrast to the first study, in the replication studies the test persons were monitored. Other studies show that the feeling of being watched reduces trust in the perception of one's own inner signals and judgement (Noah et al., 2018). Martin et al. (1992) demonstrated that, in addition to the feedback from facial expressions, the overall level of arousal co-determines how we evaluate ambiguous situations. They let subjects put on either a happy or an angry facial expression while reading a text; also they had some of them do two minutes of dynamic physical exercises before the experiment. The emotional reaction to the stories read was dependant on both these preconditions. Activated subjects were more likely to report angry content than the non-activated.

Stepper and Strack (1993) manipulated the body posture of test persons on the pretext of testing office furniture ergonomically. People who were praised while standing up straight were prouder when they had good results in a later test than were people who were praised in the same way, but in a crooked posture. In a similar experiment people told different stories about an ambiguous picture according to their body posture (Doering-Seipel, 1996). If someone taking part in an experiment where the goal is hidden assumes an anxious posture, they are more likely to feel anxious afterwards (Barsalou et al., 2003, p. 53).

Thus body postures can demonstrably induce and reinforce feelings; however, they are not identical to the feelings. Posture represents the action impulse inherent in the feeling (Sheets-Johnstone, 1999, pp. 264–5), for example the erect posture corresponding to the impulse to show oneself or face up to something, but it does not constitute the whole of the feeling (Chapter 10). Also physical activity cannot induce specific ideas (Adams, 2010, p. 626). Action is not identical to thinking; however, it can lead thinking in a certain direction.

These experiments support body psychotherapy's approach of influencing patients' emotional states and their self-esteem through changing body posture and embodied expression.

For example we can work on straightening up the vertical axis along the spine so as to induce more dignity, pride and presence (Geuter, 2019, pp. 234–9).

Clinical example

In role play, a patient is talking to her father about how he humiliated her. In doing so she starts to stoop. I suggest that she pursues the dialogue while slightly rotating her shoulders towards the back and stretching the spine, i.e. taking up an erect posture, and noticing the difference in her experience in contrast to the original position.

Depressive moods are also connected to physical posture. Kraepelin described depressive patients as follows: 'The head is lowered, the back bent and the whole body sunk into itself by gravity'(Bader et al., 1999, p. 613). Recent studies confirm that in the vertical plane, the attention of depressive people tends to be downwards (Meier & Robinson, 2006).

Sugamura et al. (2007, 2008) make use of this insight in an experiment. Subjects who, on a pretext, have to adopt a slumped posture for a while were more likely to end up in a depressive mood than those who, in the same experiment, were told to keep an erect posture. In another experiment, people got into a more depressive mood just by looking downwards without changing their posture (Sugamura et al., 2009). An erect posture was concomitant with an increase in feelings of pride and strength.

In a *Peanuts* comic, Charlie Brown explains how you should let your head hang down if we want to get the most out of your depression; the worst thing you can do is to straighten up and hold your head high, because then you will immediately feel better. The cartoonist, Charles Schulz, seems to have known that body psychotherapeutic means to vitalise or straighten up the body can influence moods through body feedback.

The explanation of the effects of such experiments is that proprioceptive feedback generates feelings with no need for cognitive understanding (Stepper & Strack, 1993). With this thesis, experimental psychology rehabilitates Dilthey's view (Section 3.4), that lived experience is in itself a way of processing reality (Section 5.3), supports the view that body experience becomes significant for the forming of lived experience. However, until now, embodiment research has mainly concentrated on proprioceptive feedback from the sensorimotor system and has paid little attention to interoceptive information from the vegetative system (Section 6.3).

It is not just posture, expression and activation, but also the **sensations** we feel when touched, or **movements** which affect our emotional evaluation. Someone holding a rough object in their hands evaluates social interaction as more difficult than does a person touching a smooth object (Ackerman et al., 2010). In one experiment, subjects were asked to look at neutral Chinese characters, not known to them, while moving their arm to press against a tabletop either from below upwards, corresponding to a gesture of approach, or from above downwards, corresponding to a gesture of pushing away. In the first case, the supposed content of the characters was evaluated more positively (Barsalou et al., 2003, p. 53). In another experiment, subjects whose arm was active in the approach gesture were more likely to reach for biscuits casually placed near them (Foerster, 2003). Similar effects emerged when subjects moved their heads in an affirmative or negative manner (Wells & Petty, 1980).

Additional findings from embodiment research support the following clinical conclusions:

- Participants who are in a good mood recognise earlier than others in a film when a happy facial expression morphs into a sad one; in a sad mood, people are more likely to recognise a change from sadness to joy (Niedenthal et al., 2001). Clinically, we can utilise this by helping patients through somatically induced moods to experience how their perception is dependent on their inner state.
- Empirical research shows that the vocal expression of feelings reinforces the relevant feeling (Niedenthal et al., 2005, p. 29). Clinically this means that we can intensify a patient's feeling by giving vocal expression to it – a technique often used in body psychotherapy (Section 14.5).
- When subjects are asked to speak about an issue that makes them angry, slowly and with a soft voice, then they feel less angry and their heart rate slows down. When someone speaks fast and loudly, they become angry and aroused (Niedenthal et al., 2005, p. 30). In psychotherapy, when a patient is over-excited or the feeling sensation is too weak, then we can use vocal expression – and also other expressive channels – to regulate the intensity of emotional arousal.

Winkielman et al. (2008, pp. 265–6) propose that to induce anger we activate the muscles with which we make a fist, or that we make a scowling face. They call this 'embodied simulation' of feelings. What may seem new to experimental psychology is in reality a classic method of affect induction in body psychotherapy, which I include in the principle of *activating and expressing* (Geuter, 2019).

Experiment: the scientific vs. the therapeutic approach

In applying the experimental findings of embodiment research directly to clinical practice, we are in danger of understanding psychotherapy in a purely technical way: clenching your fist to better feel your anger, or jumping around to get into a more joyful mood. This is the logic of 'when you do this, this happens', the logic of experimental research, which examines the effects of certain conditions on certain variables.

In clinical work, this kind of logic – assuming a certain posture in order to create a certain effect – is of little help, since there is no clear-cut, linear relationship between bodily posture or activity and experience. Scientific experiments manipulate conditions so as to test effects. However the understanding of experiments with posture, movement and behaviour in body psychotherapy is that each is an **offer for the individual patient**, to experience something in their own unique way. What we are really interested in is **what the actual patient experiences subjectively in each experiment**. In a process-oriented body psychotherapy, our intention in an experiment is to affect the process, but not to achieve an effect the therapist has previously decided upon (Geuter, 2019, pp. 42–3).

SENSORY MODALITIES

We can also draw certain clinical conclusions from the findings of embodiment research on the modality-specific processing of perception. Stimuli are processed faster when they are confined to one sensory modality, e.g. hearing or seeing, than when they change modalities

(Barsalou et al., 2003a, p. 87). Stimuli from the same modality, in which an object has formerly been recognised, activate the idea of the object more easily later. This is how traumatic experiences are triggered. If something is stored in a certain modality, then, when we encounter a similar stimulus again, the characteristics of this modality are more readily accessible (Pecher et al., 2004).

Clinical application

It is sensible to follow an event in the same modality in which the patient experienced it. If they remember a smell, then we should first try to substantiate it. If they talk about the tone in which someone said something to them, then we first ask how they felt about this tone; was it for instance shrill, bitter, sharp, contemptuous?

When reactivating early experiences, it is useful to approach the patient in the modality in which they experienced the event. When the issue is for instance how their parents used to scold them, then we can use hearing: when you remember the voice, how did it sound, where did it come from? Later in the process we can include other modalities. However if the memory is blocked, then it can be useful to offer several different modalities in the attempt to open it up.

Body psychotherapy works in principle **multimodally**, meaning that we utilise all the various modalities of sensory experience (Section 9.1). This approach is much more likely to evoke experiences, memories and resources than a purely cognitive procedure and is in line with the theory of the research group led by Barsalou and Niedenthal. Since self-confidence disintegrates when there are conflicts between the various sensory modalities (Metzinger, 2010), we are thus simultaneously working to restore the unity of experience.

SIMULATION

In body psychotherapy we often sound out emotions by exploring bodily states associated with them. This approach is in accord with the theories of embodiment research. Niedenthal et al. (2005, p. 22) explain their findings on the relationship between body and affects as follows: acquiring emotional knowledge involves the embodiment of emotional states, so that emotional knowledge is linked to those bodily states in which we found ourselves during this learning experience. We can utilise this by invoking these states. For example in experiments it was shown that even when people speak about abstract emotional concepts, they exhibit very subtly the corresponding facial expressions (Winkielman et al., 2008, p. 279). This means that we involuntarily generate somatic feelings when we just **think** about them.

Therapeutically, we use this when we voluntarily activate emotional experience through expressive movements or when we explore intentions through action impulses. Actions too seem to be internally simulated when we think about them. If subjects hear the sentence 'He hammered a nail into the wall', they can then draw an object lying in a horizontal plane more quickly than can those who heard the sentence 'He hammered a nail into the floor'. In these last, the perception of a vertical object has been invoked (Zwaan et al., 2002). Brain studies show that the motor cortex becomes active when someone only hears the word hammer (Just et al., 2010). The Broca area of the brain, which is responsible for language, contains representations of the hand and mouth (Gallese, 2007, p. 663). This argues for the close link between gestures, facial expressions and language. According to Gallese (2003a,

p. 174), we simulate an action internally when we perceive it. He comes to this conclusion through research into mirror neurons. Gallese (2003, p. 521) considers bodily simulation to be a basic functional mechanism of the brain. Whether, as Gallese thinks, this mechanism is also the basis for empathy with others is, however, disputed (Chapter 15).

When a person has an experience and stores it in memory, sensoric, motoric and intro-spective states from that situation will always be stored with it (Barsalou et al., 2003, p. 44). According to Barsalou, cognitions are generally anchored multimodally and located situationally. Memories are therefore never purely cognitive, since in every idea that comes up, we bodily recall the sensory, motor and introspective states associated with the situation, which gave rise to the memory (Chapter 9). Thus evoking these states is the central mechanism for recalling stored knowledge (p. 63). Barsalou et al. use for this the concept of re-enactments. By recognising in themselves emotional states connected to specific states of the senses and of the body, people simultaneously interpret social situations (Niedenthal et al., 2005, p. 40).

Therapeutic relevance

This theory supports the concept of enactment in clinical practice, according to which early experiences communicate themselves through acting out (McLaughlin, 1991), as well as enactments in body psychotherapy, in which we actively evoke experiences by restaging them with all their emotional implications (Geuter, 2019, pp. 286–8). Furthermore, the theory also supports the idea that a multisensory storing of experience in a therapy session anchors the experience far more than just speaking about it. If an insight leads to an embodied experience then it will be 'incorporated' and impresses itself much more deeply on the patient's consciousness.

Embodiment research offers no new principles of action for body psychotherapy, but it validates the principles we already follow. It provides us with experimental evidence for the notion that cognitions, emotions, bodily sensations, postures, movements and motor impulses are all inextricably connected. This supports the holistic idea of the importance of looking at the human being as a unified entity in all areas of experience, of life and of vital expression (Section 5.1).

9

Memory

Embodied remembering

Like thinking and feeling, memory is connected to the body. According to the theory of embodied mind, experiences are embodied and determine as embodied memories later experiences and behaviour (Section 5.2). Hence memory is not a function of the mind or the brain. It is a **function and** a **faculty of living systems**, which already quite simple organisms possess (Kramar & Alim, 2021). Memories arise in a person's life and are incorporated into the living system itself as a kind of sediment of the interaction of the system with the environment. They are based on sensorimotor affect experiences and manifest in behaviour (Leuzinger-Bohleber, 2001, p. 119). In the here and now of interaction, analogies to earlier situations are recognised not only cognitively but also bodily (Leuzinger-Bohleber & Pfeiffer, 2013a). The brain is the central organ in this process, but as a part of the whole living being (Section 7.2). Earlier experiences express themselves as embodied memories in spontaneous (not cognitive) expectations and unconscious interpretations of new interaction situations (Leuzinger-Bohleber & Pfeiffer, 2013, p. 23). In therapy, memories therefore appear not only in thoughts, but in bodily sensations, reactions, gestures, movements and interactions with the therapist.

Clinical example

A patient tells me that the house where the practice is smells like her grandmother's place. Every time she comes here, she feels safe because of the smell.

Here a sense impression induces a positive memory accompanied by transference, not explicable by a sheer cognitive-emotional, unembodied concept of memory.

Not only what we experience in interpersonal relationships, but also what we have learned and what skills we have acquired constitute human self-experience and human identity. When someone says 'I'm a heap of misery and all my life I've just kept my head down', they define themselves via autobiographical experiences in a body language metaphor. But when another person says: 'I'm a racing driver with all my heart', they define themselves via their performance. In both cases, the body and the memory are part of the self-image. In the first case, through inner time-travel, the memory can be retrieved from how a person has lived their life; in the second, the memory rests as if timeless in what a person does.

DOI: 10.4324/9781003176893-9

Here we are dealing with two different kinds of memory systems (Roediger, 1990). In memory research the one is called **declarative** or **explicit** memory and the other **non-declarative** or **implicit** memory. Bergson (1911) already differentiated two systems, memory images and habits, and the last he designated the memory of the body.

Both aspects belong to **autobiographical memory**, not only what we can symbolically 'declare' but also the way we breathe, speak, walk or give someone our hand.

Memory is often seen metaphorically as like the hard drive of a computer. However, in memory theory, the computer metaphor is unhelpful (Leuzinger-Bohleber & Pfeiffer, 2013a, pp. 45–8; Section 5.2). For example, it cannot explain that in everyday life we are constantly acting from experience without having to access explicit knowledge. The necessary contents of memory are at our disposal as inner procedural knowledge. The metaphor also does not explain how we are able to continually adapt to a changing situation. Thus Edelman (1992) distinguishes a replicative memory for coded information – semantic memory belongs here – and a dynamic memory, which on the basis of similar input in an earlier situation, generates a similar output. This memory is a characteristic of a whole living system.

Remembering, retaining, forgetting are **faculties** like moving, thinking or feeling. When we speak of 'the memory' with a noun, it tempts us to want to find a special hardware for a faculty of the whole living system.

No generally accepted selective classification of memory systems exists (Welzer & Markowitsch, 2005), as we are dealing with an extremely complex subject. Table 9.1 shows a classification based on Markowitsch (2005, p. 89). Welzer (2002, p. 130) proposes that we

TABLE 9.1
Memory

Declarative/explicit memory		*Non-declarative/implicit memory*		
Semantic memory	Episodic memory	Priming	Conditioning	Procedural memory
Facts, knowledge, more from the left hemisphere. Example: Rome was founded in 753.	Events, tellable memories, more from the right hemisphere. Example: it was wonderful in Rome with Grandma.	Processing repeated stimuli without consciously storing them. Example: bicycles come nearer faster than pedestrians.	Connection of stimuli with reactions through repetition. Example: I am startled when a cyclist rings their bell	Acquiring motor skills and behaviour. Example: I can ride a bike.
Acquired through cognitive learning.	Acquired through significant experiences.	Acquired through repeated perception.	Acquired through the connection between stimulus and reaction.	Acquired through doing and practising.
Almost no significance for psychotherapy.	Contains the dynamic unconscious of psychoanalysis.	Learned unconscious of behavioural therapy.		

regard the various memory systems as functional systems, interdependent and organised by autobiographical memory. For all that we remember, regardless in what way, originates in biographical experience. Concerning therapy, Cozolino states that 'just about everything we do … depends on the patient's memory' (2002, p. 84). The memory relevant for psychotherapy is, on the one hand, what shows itself in the implicit patterns of experience and behaviour and, on the other, what we are or are not capable of.

Explicit memory is subdivided into

1. **Semantic cognitive memory**, in which we store our learned cognitive knowledge and which is not very important for psychotherapy. However, it is not independent of the body. Sometimes we use body movements to evoke a memory.
2. **Episodic memory**, which contains memories of those life events we have filtered out of innumerable experiences and retained; this is central for psychotherapeutic work.

Implicit memory is subdivided into

1. **Priming**, a non-semantic memory for perceived objects, whose contents we store when they are repeated.
2. **Conditioning**, in which we combine one stimulus with another out of our experience.
3. **Procedural memory**, which contains skills, competences and behaviours that we have learnt through practice.

Welzer and Markowitsch (2005) also speak of a **perceptual memory**, which enables us to recognise something we have previously encountered. All the functional subdivisions mentioned describe different abilities of retaining and remembering.

Initially psychoanalysis and behavioural therapy had focused respectively on certain aspects of memory – psychoanalysis on the suppressed content of experience and behavioural therapy on learnt behavioural readiness. Accordingly they have **two different concepts of the unconscious** (Sonntag, 1988).

• Freud assumed an unconscious that contains suppressed material. From the perspective of the psychology of memory, this is the unconscious of episodic memory, consisting of the content of experience, for example desires, which through dynamic processes were shifted into the unconscious. The **dynamic unconscious** is thus not a memory system (Ansermet & Magistretti, 2007), but an **unconscious part of the content of experience**. When I refer psychodynamically to the unconscious, this is what I mean and not Freud's (1915) theory that the core of the unconscious consists of drive representations.
• In contrast, behavioural therapy based on learning theory assumed an unconscious of learnt actions, conditioned habits and behaviour acquired through reinforcement. From the perspective of the psychology of memory, this is the **unconscious of implicit memory,** only that it is not referred to as such in behavioural therapy. This unconscious functions even when through brain damage the explicit processing of information fails (Kandel, 1998).

Cognitive behavioural therapy on the other hand assumes that dysfunctional behaviour is an expression of dysfunctional perceptions, which in turn are an expression of dysfunctional beliefs. We could say that, as automatic thoughts or schemas, these form a pre-reflective, cognitive unconscious.

The dynamic unconscious reveals itself through its manifestations (dreams, associations, fantasies), the learnt unconscious through behaviour.

Body psychotherapy utilises both memory systems and so draws on both concepts of the unconscious. Reich was concerned with the unconscious of psychoanalysis and with liberating repressed sexuality. His paradigm of liberated movement were the orgastic movements, the vibrating and shuddering. Perception-oriented body psychotherapy, like behaviourism, turned to the conditioned and procedural unconscious, movements the body had learnt and could learn anew. Their paradigm of liberated movement was the involuntary, 'non-deliberate movement', which would open up new experiences (D Johnson, 2015, p. 121; Section 3.5). Hypnosis in turn uses priming when it links new content precognitively to situations and experiences. C.G. Jung and Milton Erickson extended the concept of the unconscious to include creative space in which an internal world of images and potentialities could be produced and utilised. This unconscious points not towards the past but to the future, similarly to the concept of 'not-yet-conscious' of the philosopher Ernst Bloch (Blohm, 2015).

The dynamic unconscious and the procedural unconscious can both express themselves in the body in different ways. The body psychotherapeutic theories of affect motor schemas, and character structures accommodate both concepts of the unconscious (Chapters 12 and 13). In body psychotherapy, we assume that an unconscious attitude and disposition for experiences and behaviour originates in relationship experiences being largely unconsciously internalised. Reich's idea that muscle tension contains the history and meaning of how it originated is basically a theory of body memory, whereby life experiences are transformed into emotional-procedural dispositions for experience and behaviour. Thus I would propose that we speak of an **emotional-procedural memory**, which contains emotionally significant, implicit experiences from childhood and with which body psychotherapy characteristically works (cf. Erskine, 2014; Figure 9.1).

In memory theory there is no reference to such a memory; however, there are ideas such as that of emotional reactivities, which are stored in the implicit, emotional memory (Grawe, 2004). Such an idea illustrates how we need an extended concept of memory for psychotherapy. We can for example assign the experiences stored in sub-symbolic and nonverbal-symbolic mode – below the symbolic, verbal mode, according to the Multiple Code Theory of Bucci (2001) – to an unconscious that is part of an emotional-procedural memory. Before exploring the emotional-procedural memory more deeply, I will elucidate the concept of body memory and the differences between episodic and procedural memory.

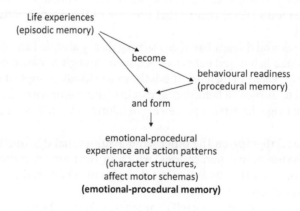

FIGURE 9.1 Memory in body psychotherapy

BODY MEMORY

In recent years there has been an increasingly lively debate about body memory (Koch et al., 2012). Firstly we know that the body possesses a genetic, an immunological and a hormonal memory, whereas here we are essentially concerned with those stored in the central nervous system. In the genes we have the memory of evolution, so to speak, where depending on how they are activated, epigenetic programming translates psycho-social, biographical experiences into biology (Binder, 2020; Section 11.4). Experiments on mice show that traumatic experiences can be passed on genetically via epigenetic programming of insulin and blood sugar levels (Gapp et al., 2014).

The **immunological** memory can be conditioned (Ruegg, 2006, pp. 94–6) and is thus autobiographical, as it contains life experiences of resistance to pathogens. This resistance is an interaction of the organism with the environment through which the organism changes, mediated by psycho-social experiences. Adolescents and children who are physically abused and still live in the family, or who have spent their childhood in an orphanage and were then adopted, show in comparison to a control group a sustained increase in levels of antibodies against herpes simplex. Early experiences determine this level to a greater extent than do their present health or stress situations. Hence the immune systems of early traumatised patients have in the long run more difficulty with resistance to pathogens (Shirtcliff et al., 2009). Its functioning does, however, improve through psychotherapy (Schubert, 2015).

People who as children were subject to abuse have increased levels of the stress hormone cortisol (Schubert, 2020). This is the result of a sustained epigenetic alteration in the activity of the gene regulating the production of stress hormones (McGowan et al., 2009). If trauma causes a genetic alteration, then there is an increased risk of developing post-traumatic stress disorder (PTSD) (Klengel et al., 2013). Women who as children were subject to sexual or other violence show a level of adrenocorticotropic hormone six times that of normal (Blunk, 2006, p. 48). Children of depressive mothers develop a higher baseline of noradrenaline, which enables stronger or less modulated shock reactions (Cozolino, 2002, p. 261). Life experiences are therefore not only activated on the level of the episodic memory, but also on that of the immunological and **hormonal** memory, since they continue to have an effect on all levels. This is an important issue in trauma research. People with PTSD suffer not only from psychological phenomena such as intrusions, but also from weaknesses in the immune system and/or permanently increased levels of stress hormones. With Pert (1999) we can assume that emotional experiences are stored even in the peripheral body cells, so that we also have a **cellular memory**. Biological research shows that what we have learned can be stored not only in the central nervous system, but also in the cell nucleus as epigenetic changes (Bédécarrats et al., 2018). However this is only true of very basic learning – associative learning requires a neural network.

For body psychotherapy, it is not these physiological aspects of body memory that are crucial, but rather those in the explicit, implicit and particularly in the emotional-procedural memories, which are retrievable through the body. The contents of implicit memory is also often referred to as the 'body memory' since it is accessed via the body and not in verbalised remembering (Section 9.2).

T. Fuchs (2009, 2016, 2019) uses the concept of body memory for all body mediated forms of implicit memory in everyday behaviour, of which he names five: procedural or sensomotoric, situative, intercorporeal, incorporative and traumatic memory. He describes situative memory as how we find our way bodily in space through experience;

intercorporeal as the attitudes and behavioural dispositions we have developed in contact with other people, which generate implicit relating styles; incorporative as the attitudes and roles we have learnt through our culture; and traumatic as the implicit memories of traumatic situations.

In any case, the list of various forms of memory is not exhaustive. We could for example include **pain memory** as a body memory not necessarily connected to episodic memory, which can function precognitively. Babies who have had their heels pricked frequently so as to get blood samples react later with stress symptoms when their heels are touched (Gaensbauer, 2002, p. 262). Possibly these body memories are not just neuronal but also molecular memory (Ruegg, 2006, p. 43).

The living memory of the subject

In psychotherapy we are dealing with those aspects of memory connected to the living subject. Swathes of memory can be delegated to other storage systems. Thus we speak of a cultural memory of humanity which is stored in our creations, such as books, artworks, buildings, musical scores or electronic data storage.

However, there are two kinds of memory which cannot be delegated to other media. Firstly everything we have **learnt procedurally**. I cannot look up on the internet how I learned to guide a spoon to my mouth, to climb a tree or to develop a fear of heights and how all this lives on in me. The other is **how something feels** that **I have experienced**. I can describe how my father beat me and how humiliated I felt, just as I can describe my vertigo. But my living experience exists only in me. And the feeling of humiliation or the vertigo can in certain situations be activated in the form of vegetative sensations, motor impulses, thoughts or fantasies, so that I then feel humiliated or scared in the here and now.

In psychotherapy we are dealing with these aspects of memory. Mainly they are experienced and lived in the body, but not exclusively. Therefore here I will not call it body memory. It is much more a question of procedural memory and of a living human being's memory of their experiences. Thus in psychotherapy we work with the **memory of a person's lived experience**.

9.1 EPISODIC MEMORY

Episodic memory is the memory of life experiences. It also contains those events which, because of defence mechanisms, are not accessible to consciousness. These are not unconscious in the sense that they cannot be made conscious, but rather in the sense that they are fallen into oblivion. In psychoanalysis they are activated through verbal free association to thoughts, feelings, images, dreams or other memories. Episodic memory is however not disembodied, as its content is embedded in sensuous experience and moved interactions. If it was wonderful in Rome with grandma, then memory will be linked to the taste of the food, the walk through the Forum Romanum or the atmosphere in one of the churches. For in memory we store not only the physical aspects of an object but also the sensual context, our emotional reaction, our motoric involvement and our general bodily and mental condition at the time we were concerned with the object (Damasio, 1999). Long-term memory contains the experience of our body with the world (Wilson, 2002, p. 633).

Sometimes memory content can only be read from a bodily reaction. Patients who have prosopagnosia or face blindness, for example, fail to recognise the faces of people they know from photos, but do react to the photos with a distinct vegetative arousal: 'their implicit body memory recognises the familiar without it becoming explicitly conscious … Body memory is therefore more enduring than explicit memory' (T. Fuchs, 2000, p. 317). In research little attention has been paid to this remembering of the body on the vegetative level.

> Memory retention is better when the content is connected to the body. In an experiment, people who dramatised the monologue of a play could remember the essence of the story better than those who just reproduced it in words or wrote it down (Scott et al., 2001).

Ansermet and Magistretti (2007) assume that the state of the organism in which something is perceived is passed on together with all the associations which later attach themselves to the memory content. In so doing, this state can connect itself to later fantasies and associative perceptions. With this thesis we can explain one of the mechanisms of how early childhood experiences, even those of the prelingual stage, irrupt into the present. This can happen because a somatic state from an earlier experience connects to someone's present experience and, out of their compulsion to discharge the tension they are now feeling, they do something which does not help to resolve the present situation, but to end the old unbearable state. Then present behaviour is guided by the old affect tension, and unconscious memories are re-enacted in the present.

> Many studies substantiate that memory does not store experience reliably. An experiment of Oeberst et al. (2021) showed that in interviews where the questions were asked repeatedly, subjects generated false memories of autobiographical events, for which their parents had previously provided information on their plausibility. Their conviction that they remembered a specific event decreased, however, when, as a follow up, they were asked to reconsider whether they really remembered the event after another interviewer had informed them about 'false memories'.

Remembering is not like reading off the hard drive of a computer or Plato's wax tablets. As they are recalled, memories can become instable and modified under the special conditions of the moment (Beutel, 2009, p. 386). Then they are stored anew and frequently rewritten (Roediger & Abel, 2022), often in such a way that they correspond to present needs and ideas (Schacter, 2001). This is why episodic memory never contains exactly what 'really happened'. Current ideas and perceptions as well as a person's general condition at the moment of remembering all flow into the reframing of memory.

At the same time, this is a way in which psychotherapy can work: memories can be coupled to a new state or a new experience if they are recalled in a different physical and emotional condition, then reviewed and re-experienced (Maurer-Groeli, 2004, p. 102). Thus in therapy, regression is never a simple route back to the past. In fact, in regressive processes, the past is redrafted from the perspective of the present needs and motives of the subject, so as to find new possibilities for self-regulation. Therefore it is more helpful therapeutically to achieve a reframing in the present than to overcome repression and search for the causes of problems in the past.

Clinical application

The perception of the state of the body is a central focus of body psychotherapy as a way of evoking and transforming autobiographical memories. This is why body psychotherapy uses not only cognitive associations but the **associations of the body**: sensations, bodily impulses, the quality of sense experiences which appear in a therapy situation and lead to the experienced past, or which as a momentary quality express something about a certain event. If therapy is limited to thoughts and feelings, then these memories are neglected.

Clinical example

A patient reports being very restless at night. He regularly wakes up with a start in the early hours, his mind races and he thinks about where he has not lived up to people's expectations. He calls it his 'horror programme'. To understand what lies behind this, I ask him to imagine that he is just at the point where the 'horror programme' begins and to observe what happens. He notices a roaring in his head, his breathing stops and there is a hardness in his chest. He says it is as if he freezes and the muscles become hard right down to his thighs. He feels as if he is dead. This description of the body freezing while the mind races points to a trauma physiology, in which the parasympathetic and the sympathetic nerve systems are both powered up and the freezing is accompanied by heightened arousal (Section 7.1).

I ask him what image he has of the feeling. He is lying frozen on his back on the bed and is afraid: 'What's happening?' He starts to cry: 'I don't want to die', 'I'm afraid', 'I'm so afraid because I don't know what I've done wrong'. He is choking. He is all alone and does not understand what is happening. Through concentrating on his bodily state and the images connected to it an early childhood memory comes up. He is having a pseudocroup attack and is being pushed hectically through a hospital corridor, further and further away from his parents. He is asking himself, as that child, why they are leaving him alone and what he has done wrong.

Events are more easily stored and later more easily remembered when various sense channels are involved. In body psychotherapy, therefore, all channels are used as a multimodal access to memory. Maurer (1999, p. 93) has used the acronym VAKO: visual, acoustic, kinaesthetic-tactile and olfactory perception. The cognitive psychologists Engelkamp and Zimmer (2006, p. 290) describe 'motor processes of action execution' as relevant for remembering verbal stimuli. From research in memory psychology, we know too that people remember images better than names (Engelkamp & Zimmer, 2006, p. 295) – this underscores the value of working with images in psychotherapy. We remember actions we have executed ourselves, whereby proprioception accompanies visual perception, better than actions we have only

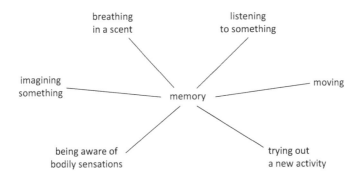

FIGURE 9.2 Multimodal activation of memory

seen (Engelkamp & Zimmer, 2006, p. 309) – this underscores the value of working with sensomotor experiences. Transmodal retention facilitates remembering. Mnemonists file dry information spatially and pictorially (Foer, 2011). The memory artist Shereshevsky linked numbers to images or things heard to odours or taste sensations (Mecacci, 2013). Through a multimodal approach which includes body experience, we can extend the associative space to access content of the episodic memory not yet remembered (Figure 9.2)

Representation

The memory theory ideas considered here result in a different concept of representation for body psychotherapy. In psychotherapy, representations are depicted only as linguistically coded ideas of significant others, events or interaction experiences. However people store not only cognitive ideas of interaction experiences, but memories in all modalities of experience with all the accompanying body states. Thus there are no purely cognitive representations that can be accessed only through the zone of language. We access interaction experiences just as well through feelings, sensations, attitudes or actions. These shape 'a whole tissue of beliefs about other people' coded in motoric or vegetative form (Downing, 1996, p. 118).

Representation is a concept from computer models of the mind and refers to symbolic representation of non-symbolic input (Thompson, 2010, p. 5). This is criticised or seen as unnecessary in the theory of embodied mind (Chemero, 2011; Hutto & Myin, 2013). Varela et al. (1993, pp. 193–4) argue that this concept assumes that we can reproduce the world as it is. This presupposes a world with specific characteristics which a mind, separate from it, represents internally. In regarding representations as mental entities, cognitivist theory sets up an 'inner theatre of the mind' (M Johnson, 2007, p. 131). Embodied mind theory, however, views these as **patterns** in which a living being experiences a world. Experiences persist in the integral, lived relationship of a person to the world and not in mere mental ideas in the head (Johnson, 2007, pp. 114–34). When I use the concept of representation, then I mean these lived experiences which can appear in cognitive and somatic form.

From the cognitivist concept of representation follows **clinically** that therapeutic changes take place cognitively. According to this understanding, the aim of treatment is to replace inadequate representations with adequate ones: for example an inappropriate image of the mother with one more appropriate, or an inadequate belief with a more adequate one. Psychotherapy is then mental work on the optimisation of ideas of reality, whereby the adequacy of those ideas can only be measured against other ideas.

The purely cognitive concept of representations only makes sense when we differentiate between a correct representation and a false one (Newen, 2013, p. 48). In the practice of psychotherapy, it ensnares us in debates with patients on whether one point of view is right or not. In therapy, however, it should never be about right or wrong, but always about whether an idea is subjectively significant and helpful or not.

Body psychotherapy is not about fabricating the 'right' ideas, but about helping patients to discover and to experiment with possible ways of relating to reality, so that they can live less in painful and more in what are for them coherent and satisfying patterns of experience and behaviour. For this purpose, the concept of schema is more suited than that of representations. In Chapter 12 I will go into this in more detail.

9.2 PROCEDURAL MEMORY

Procedural memory is an embodied form of knowledge. First of all it is the memory of motor skills. This memory is forgetful in a completely different way than is episodic memory (Table 9.2). In episodic memory we can forget content. We can remember it again by asking ourselves: what was that again? Through association we can recall what we have forgotten; however we cannot intentionally realise what we have forgotten. Procedural memory, on the other hand, knows no time. Some skills we might lose, but generally speaking we retain the content of procedural memory timelessly in our actions, for example when, after a break of several years, we sit down at the piano and play something. Here memory is what we do (Caldwell, 2012). What we forget is how hard it was to learn the skill (Welzer, 2002, p. 50). Since the procedural unconscious is learnt and lives on in everyday actions, it is not suppressed in the depths, but located rather on the visible surface of our behaviour. This memory is not revealed through questioning or through associative remembering. It is simply there. We experience its existence in the immediate present. The whole of implicit memory 'does not make the past present, but contains it in itself as active in the present' (Fuchs, 2000, p. 316). Fuchs therefore calls it the memory of the lived-body.

Forgetting is, in these two memory systems, as different as acquiring. The content of episodic memory is not learned. We retain it simply because it is significant to us. We forget most of what we experience. What we learn is the way in which we tell what we remember, the narrative form. Implicit memory is quite different. All content of priming, conditioning or procedural knowledge is acquired by learning and is based on repetition (Table 9.1). Neurobiologists assume that recurrence of action potential sequences stabilises neural connectivity patterns. Since they are learnt and stable interconnections, body memories, which present as habits and behaviour patterns, are less prone to disruption than the content of the verbally determined explicit memory.

TABLE 9.2
Memory – forgetting and recollecting

Episodic memory	*Procedural memory*
Forgetting content	Forgetting how we learnt it
What happened? What comes to mind?	What is going on? How do I experience it now?

9.3 THE EMOTIONAL-PROCEDURAL MEMORY
IN BODY PSYCHOTHERAPY

Constant repetition can, however, transform the content of declarative memory into procedural memory (Kandel, 1999, p. 508), for example when we learn to drive a car by having it explained to us in detail. This is also true of the emotional-procedural memory, where learning processes from interpersonal relationships are stored. These learning processes create 'a knowledge of interaction free of language or fantasy' (Dornes, 1997, p. 313). Its content consists of experiences that could, in principle, be dealt with by episodic memory, but the effect of which is procedural; we learn a certain behaviour in relationships and later we continue with it. We learn unconscious 'procedures' (Beutel, 2009, p. 386) and with them a social habitus (Bourdieu, 1984).

Important
In the emotional-procedural memory significant experiences become implicit, unconscious reaction readiness.

Much of the content of implicit memory dates back to a time when episodic memory was not yet functioning. Episodic memories are only then possible when a child can verbally classify memories as 'mine', i.e. when they are capable of speech and of ego-consciousness (Draaisma, 2004). This is related to a leap in the maturing of the prefrontal cortex (Roth, 2001, p. 336) and is usually possible around the third year. Thus earlier life experiences are necessarily stored not verbally but as action potential. The content of these experiences, inaccessible to consciousness, influences, however, consciously accessible content and forms core beliefs for which there is no explanation on a cognitive level (cf. Roediger, 1990).

Not only early experiences but also 'all later affect, sensory and motor impressions are stored in the brain initially without connections to the language centre or to cognitive structures' (Huether, 2006, p. 89). Accordingly, Fogel (2003) suggests that we speak of a 'participatory memory', which contains **implicit relational knowledge**. Since this knowledge regulates the way in which we shape relationships, he also talks of a *'regulatory*, automatized, and unconscious' implicit memory (Fogel, 2003, p. 207). Schore (2001, p. 43) says the same:

> Such nonconscious regulatory mechanisms are embedded in implicit-procedural memory in unconscious internal working models of the attachment relationship that encode strategies of affect regulation.

Children of depressed mothers, for example, learn in their first years of life to smile at their mother more or less, according to the situation and what they need from her (Chapter 11, Box 'Depressive mothers').

Fogel's thoughts on participatory memory go in the same direction as those of Gaensbauer (2002) and of the concept suggested here of an emotional-procedural memory. Gaensbauer argues that early childhood experiences do not easily lend themselves to being divided into explicit and implicit memories, since the memories of small children operate as a whole and there is no hard border between the two systems. Moreover, he questions the notion that procedural memory precedes explicit memory in child development:

> To the extent that habits, learned skills, and unconscious scripts are the product of individually registered events which are aggregated over time into more automatically operating neural circuits, one could argue that in many cases explicit, episodic memory precedes implicit, procedural memory, i.e. that memories start out as declarative and become procedural.
>
> (Gaensbauer, 2002, p. 271)

However, this formulation implies that explicit remembering, as with adults, is already possible. With implicit relational knowing (Lyons-Ruth, 1998), we are dealing with experiences that could generate episodic memories by their very nature, but not with young children, since they still lack episodic memory. Here bodily patterns of experience and behaviour in interaction are coded (Section 11.3). This uses structures in the brain which function from birth onwards: the amygdala and other limbic regions for emotions, the perceptual cortices for perception, the basal ganglia and motor cortex for behaviour (Siegel, 1999).

According to Fogel (2003, p. 210), participatory memories appear as enactments of significant personal experiences which are not yet integrated into a narrative; they are behavioural and emotional, and can be conscious in the sense that a person can become aware of them without knowing their origins. Here we are not remembering the past but are living it here and now. Thus we experience it as a life in and with old experiences. They emerge when the present reminds us of the past and they manifest in relationships, in therapeutic regression and in transference. Similarly, Stern et al. (1998, p. 302) refer to patients in psychotherapy revealing an implicit, procedural knowledge of what to think, do and feel. Human beings act, feel and have ideas about things without recognising the influence previous experiences have on present reality (Siegel, 1999). This is characteristic of emotional-procedural memories on which affect motor schemas are based (Chapter 12).

When emotional-procedural memories become active in therapy, then we can relate what the patient is experiencing today to what they had for certain reasons previously learnt. Such an awakening helps them to recognise that a familiar pattern of relating to people engages automatically, even if it is not at all helpful and functional in their present life.

Clinical example

A patient, in therapy because of severe depressive states, and who is always doubting herself and putting herself down, comes to the session with the following wish: she wants to throw herself into someone's arms and cry. But she thinks that people only like her when she does what they expect. Last time she saw my face as we said hello, and she had the impression I was laughing at her. Today she saw me looking more benevolent. But she often thinks that it is of no importance to me whether she is there or not. This is her feeling about the world in general.

I try to imagine hugging her, something I have never done before, and I notice that it does not work. As I ask myself why not, it strikes me that her way of shaking my hand in greeting always seems to me like a gesture of distance. After speaking about her image of me when we greet each other, I suggest that we look together at what message she is conveying in that moment and whether she can communicate her need to be hugged.

When we say hello, she always raises the right shoulder a little and bends the elbow up and at a right angle, then from this position she stretches her hand forwards so that from the bent elbow it forms an angle of about 45 degrees to the body in front of the chest. Then she throws her head back slightly. In our experiment in the session she is not able to spontaneously reproduce this gesture. I tell her what I notice physically in this greeting and ask her to do it slowly and consciously once just as she usually does. This movement and posture are immediately familiar to her, yes, 'that is what I do', and straight away she has an association: 'It's just as if I were holding a shield in front of me'. Indeed her movement is exactly that of someone who is holding a shield in front of them and just a little to the side with their forearm. Immediately she sees in this movement the message 'Don't come too close'. Until now she had never seen this physically familiar gesture in all its significance. In our exploration we include the slight turning of the head sideways and back and we see it as a defensive position, away from the open position face to face with another person, so that she withdraws and at the same time holds her shield in front.

In her greeting schema, the patient shows how she herself avoids the closeness that at the same time she longs for, and how she signals to others not to give her what she desires. I had noticed this ambivalence at the beginning of the session in my response to her wish. Her schema was an embodiment of what she had learnt in relation to her mother. She described her as a 'highly polished column of marble', always perfect and always dismissive and critical of her daughter. She had projected this experience of rejection onto me, was ashamed that she was not worthy of me as of her mother and thought that I must find her boring, annoying, tiring and inadequate. With her affect motor schema, she protected herself from repeating a rejection she had experienced.

Dornes' considerations correspond to the idea of the affect motor expression of an emotional-procedural unconscious. Dornes writes that even babies have unconscious beliefs, which exist as 'procedural rules' and form a 'procedural unconscious' (1997, pp. 306, 311). We learn how to behave in emotionally meaningful situations from these rules. They constitute **habits of feeling**, which are 'the precipitation of such experiences without them ever reaching explicit status' (Dornes, 1997, p. 309). Thus **unconscious emotional rules** emerge right from the beginning, which later on, when they are in part verbalised, can also become conscious. In the chapter on developmental psychology (Chapter 11), you will find more clinical examples that demonstrate the repercussions of early emotional–procedural memories.

Dornes illustrates the formation of habits of feeling with the example of a child, 'which in the course of her first year learns in numerous interaction episodes that she has to suppress her anger when the mother goes away, because when she expresses anger then she will be rejected even more' (1997, p. 312). This child learns the implicit emotional rule that she will be told off if she does not suppress her anger. Such a rule can later determine behaviour and experience in the sense of an emotional-procedural memory, but is also capable of becoming conscious. According to Dornes, this cannot be changed through insight, but only through 'repeated experience of the opposite' (Dornes, 1997, p. 323).

Traumatic experiences in adulthood are also frequently stored implicitly, above all when in an overwhelming traumatic situation, a victim of trauma dissociates the explicit from the implicit processing of what has happened. This is also a predictor for a later post-traumatic stress disorder (Siegel, 1999). Memories then have a continuing effect on behaviour and experience as if timeless, without having become part of the life narrative. The present is experienced as if it were the past (Fogel, 2003). Hochauf (2008) speaks of an '**impression memory**', in which non-verbalisable experiences that, because of the dissociation, after the moment of switching off in the traumatising situation, cannot be held in the event memory and so are stored in the body. What has happened then breaks out into present experience and behaviour in the form of images, sensations or feelings. Intrusion takes the place of explicit memory. The kinaesthetic or sensory memory store opens of its own accord in traumatic flashbacks. Here an experience, inaccessible for conscious memory because of traumatic dissociation, can trigger a flood of re-experiencing.

The crucial memory for psychotherapy is neither that with which we call up coded information, nor that of conditioned responses. In psychotherapy, we are dealing primarily with a memory that leads people to an embodied response to similar inputs with similar outputs, all related to their formative early experiences. We cannot capture this memory with a representation model or with a conditioning model. It is in fact a dynamic memory that is a property of the whole system and not separable from interaction with the environment (Leuzinger-Bohleber & Pfeiffer, 2013a, p. 48). The response dispositions gathered in the emotional-procedural memory, which, because of early experiences, are stored affectively, cognitively, sensorially motorically and vegetatively, determine perception and behaviour in the present and are **embodied memories**. In its model of memory, body psychotherapy is thus in accord with the theory of embodied mind.

The emotional-procedural memory is just as present and forgetful as the other content of procedural memory. We often do not know its origins or have forgotten them. It surfaces in a person's experiences and behaviour, physically sometimes in small gestures, facial expressions or breathing patterns. We can unlock someone's emotional-procedural unconscious by paying attention to what they reveal in their experiences and behaviour, not just to what they say. There we can look for old imprinting and explore possibilities for new pathways. In therapy we address this memory verbally, not with questions about where and when life experiences took place, but with questions in the present (cf. Fuchs, 2000, p. 322; Geuter, 2019, pp. 380ff):

- What is happening inside?
- What is coming up just now?
- What is it like? What are you feeling?
- What do you feel like doing right now?

With these and similar questions, we are looking for unconscious patterns in the present. The emotional-procedural unconscious is not dynamic, but consists of acquired patterns of experiencing and behaving; thus it is not a question of uncovering defence or repressed material, but of a process of 'exploring and discovering' habitual affect motor schemas or, as transactional analysis would have it, life scripts (Geuter, 2019, pp. 131–56).

Important
The emotional-procedural memory of affect motor schemas, character patterns or traumatic experiences contains the past in the present. We can address it with the question of what is now and not with what comes into mind. This is a central concept of body-related exploration.

Grawe (2004) holds that the content of implicit memory can only be dealt with by activating it through a bottom-up process. This would mean creating a situation with similar stimuli to that in which the content was acquired. Talking alone does not help. However, the situation does not have to be reproduced from the outside as in exposure therapy. It can be activated through sensations, feelings or images, or through the dynamics of transference. Since the emotional-procedural memory can only be accessed in the present, it comes alive through 'sensorimotor and affect states and experiences' (Beutel, 2002, p. 8).

In therapy, a body movement, for example, can activate an experience which is no longer conscious, just as musicians can sometimes reactivate a forgotten piece of music by moving their fingers. In this way the body creates a gateway to biographical experiences. And the body often remembers more accurately than does thinking (Caysa, 2008, p. 79).

Emotional-procedural memory is the determining early basis of the self (Section 6.4). Basic self-experience depends on it, whereas the autobiographical self reproduces what we tell ourselves about ourselves. Thus, we could speak of a timeless self on the one hand and of a self that we construct in a kind of mental time travel on the other.

In language, we can only communicate those memories that we tell ourselves as our life-story. Emotional-procedural memories, however, are communicated through body language, tension, movement, moods, impressions, diffuse sensations or images and show themselves too in beliefs which cannot be justified from experience. A body-oriented style of working is the royal road to access and work with this form of memory.

> Therapy that acknowledges and works with body memories may give therapists and their clients their best chance at facilitating change that lasts.
>
> (Caldwell, 2012, p. 261).

10

Emotions

Models of emotionality and the practice of body psychotherapy

Emotions are a central theme of psychotherapy. Mental disorders are always connected to the intra- and intersubjective regulation of emotions (Lincoln et al., 2022; Panksepp, 2006). Each mental and behavioural disorders of the ICD 11 involve emotional disturbance. Plassmann (2019, p. 135) describes the main task of psychotherapy as being rendering uncontrollable, negative, emotional material controllable and making transformative processes possible when they are blocked. All body psychotherapy is concerned 'with the perception, clarification, differentiation, fine-tuning, regulation, interpretation, verbalisation and transformation of feelings' (Petzold, 2003, p. 609). Emotionality is the core of our vitality (Boadella, 1996, p. 8). Emotions are the most important generators of meaning in what we experience (M Johnson, 2007, p. 61). When patients are no longer afraid of emotions – no longer suppress, deny or split them off – then emotions connect them to themselves, to other people and to the world. This is one of the foundations of mental health (Barnow, 2012, p. 117).

A cognitive approach is not enough to regulate emotions in psychotherapy (Fuchs, 2020b). If feelings cannot be allowed and negative emotional states not regulated, then patients are hardly able to clarify and reflect on them. Then we need other ways of working. The Reichian branch of body psychotherapy and Gestalt therapy have right from the beginning concentrated on working through affective experiences (cf. Revenstorf, 2000). Meanwhile this is happening in other psychotherapy approaches, especially Emotion-Focused Therapy (Greenberg, 2011). One of their goals is that patients become capable of perceiving deeper, sometimes painful feelings, accepting them, symbolising, regulating, expressing and, if necessary, transforming them (Auszra et al., 2017, p. 20).

In the early stages of psychotherapy, the suppression of emotionally significant experiences or the inhibition of emotional expression was a central theme. At the same time, at the beginning of the 20th century, neurological theories of nerve activity were dominated by the model of the conflict between arousal and inhibition (Traue, 1998, pp. 19–22). Also Breuer and Freud (1895) assessed hysterical symptoms as being an expression of affective arousal which could not be discharged and thus broke through into symptoms. Later Reich saw the economic core of neurosis in the inhibition of orgastic experience, and Schultz-Hencke (1940) focused on impulse inhibition in his neo-analytical theory. In 1925, Reich had already pointed out that because of their fragile ego structure, some patients, later known as borderline personalities, would bring their aggression or other problems directly into the analytical situation. These patients were not suffering from an inhibition; they were rather uninhibited impulsive characters with a lack of defences (Reich, 1974).

DOI: 10.4324/9781003176893-10

Emotionality can be disturbed in many ways. Some people are not even aware of their feelings; others have difficulty expressing them. Some people inhibit emotionally significant experiences, others their behaviour; some are trapped in the ambivalence of whether to express or suppress a feeling (Greenberg & Bischkopf, 2007). Some patients identify their feelings falsely or they substitute or disguise their primary emotion with another, secondary one, for example by crying when they are angry or becoming angry when they are ashamed, or masking their shame with pride, or their grief with a smile (Greenberg & Safran, 1989). Others have the tendency to sustain an emotion without the object – then we are dealing with a personality disorder, for instance, the pathological expression of rage and grief, which can lead to further health problems (Greenberg & Bischkopf, 2007, p. 167). Often patients lack the basic capacity to regulate their emotions themselves (Siegel, 1999). In severe mental disorders this is always the case because repair mechanisms have no respite to recover (Schore, 2003).

Traumatised people display an inordinate emotional reaction ranging from numbing to overexcitation. With borderline patients, the affective arousal and the related object are disconnected. Thus the emotional arousal can be high without there having been an event which caused it. At times they are in the grip of an emotional storm. Also they can sometimes wrongly attribute emotions, when for example danger is experienced as exciting or neutral situations as a threat (Russell, 2003, p. 151). Some people cope with the tension of arousal pathologically by self-harming to discharge it, or by displacing the tension into the body and thus silencing it. Reich (1972) sees this as an affect block. In these patients, defence is archaic and prevents any access to meaning (Kuechenhoff, 2008).

The treatment of emotions therefore has to be oriented towards what problems patients have and what kind of help they need. There is not **one** cause of mental disorders which can then be explained by one model; rather there are many (Greenberg & Van Balen, 1998, p. 50). Therefore there cannot be just **one** correct way of treating emotional problems. Some body psychotherapists have concentrated on encouraging emotional arousal. This can help patients whose access to their emotions is blocked off. But sometimes feelings can be overwhelming, especially for people who are in an emotional tumult because of their experiences and not in need of being brought into contact with their feelings in therapy. Often it is necessary just to accept and tolerate the arousal.

Important
Therapists have to decide clinically when to encourage emotional arousal, when to calm it down and when to just respect and accept it.

The clinical decision is based on whether an emotion is beneficial for the needs of the patient and of their significant others or not (see Section 10.3). As defined by EFT, it is primarily a question of transforming maladaptive emotions so that adaptive emotions can take their place.

Depending on their therapeutic approach, therapists assess emotional processes in different ways. According to studies, interpersonal therapists evaluate a session as helpful when the emotional experience of the patient becomes more intense, cognitive therapists when it becomes less intense. Presumably the former see it as important for the patient to experience their feelings, the latter for them to control them (Bischkopf, 2009). In body psychotherapy, Lowen (1977, pp. 43–4) wants to release blockages so that the person is free for the 'flow of feeling', whereas M. Fuchs (1989, pp. 46–7) wants not to reactivate feelings but to achieve behavioural control, support or change through sensation and relaxation. Both positions have their merits.

EMBODIED APPRAISAL

Researchers have come to no uniform definition of emotions and to **no uniform concepts**. We can find notions such as affects, vitality affects, core affects, interrupt affects, basic emotions, primary emotions, pre-emotions or self-referential emotions. In addition, emotions are classified very differently, for example according to their valence (whether the emotion is more positive or more negative), activation (whether it is calmer or more excited) and dominance (whether it is stronger or weaker). Other systems classify emotions according to the pattern of their expression.

Damasio (2004, p. 6) differentiates between emotions and feelings. Emotions are for him what appears on the stage of the body, feelings what is happening in the mind. Rogers (1959) saw this similarly when he spoke of feeling as including both the emotion and its cognitive content. Emotions come and go. Their meaning is preserved in feelings.

In the following, I use the term **emotions** for all holistic, embodied responses of a subject to a significant internal or external event, appearing in the form of an emotional reaction, for example arousal, freezing, grief, anxiety or anger. I generally use the concepts of emotion and affect synonymously. I use the term **affect**, however, in the sense of a distinction made by Russell (2003), more in connection with the arousal dynamics of an emotion, activated when something affects us. In Section 10.1 I will go into this further. I use the term **feeling** in contrast for the conscious integration of how, in an act of perception and processing of our body sensations and thoughts, we succeed in emotionally grasping a situation or an event.

Scherer (2009) understands emotions generally as a **system for appraising the relevance of events and for preparing reactions**. Emotions do not simply exist in a person; they take place in relation to others, to the world or to oneself, this last for instance in reaction to one's own actions, which is then the object of the emotion, as is often the case with guilt or shame. From the point of view of the theory of embodied mind, they are the **embodied responses** of a living being to internal or external events or situations, interrupting the orderly flow of relations with itself and the world (Thompson, 2010, p. 365), which lend meaning to an event for said being. This view is also called **embodied appraisal theory** (Prinz, 2004). In contrast to cognitive appraisal theories, which lead to a therapeutic strategy aimed at changing emotions through cognition only, this theory works on the assumption that emotional evaluation occurs mentally and bodily at the same time and that the perception of somatic changes is a vital characteristic of emotional perceptions and reactions. In interaction with an event, emotions dynamically alter experience on the cognitive, sensomotoric and vegetative levels (Section 6.1). From this perspective they are **processes** and not representations; 'Saying that my sadness is *about* the death does not mean that my sadness represents the death; rather it means that the death is what has caused me to become sad' (Prinz, 2004, p. 62; Section 9.1).

According to Ekman (2003), there are universal affect programmes for emotional response, which are triggered by certain events. Levenson (1999) calls emotional response patterns involuntarily generated by prototypical situations, such as grief at the loss of someone, the core system of emotionality (not to be confused with the concept of core affects, which we will come to later). This system of affective response patterns allows us to react quickly and comprehensively in situations of great significance (Levenson, 2003). This is true at least for intense feelings of grief, anxiety, disgust, anger, curiosity or joy, whereas other feelings such as awe, humility or sorrow are experienced more quietly (Johnstone, 2012; Section 10.4). Furthermore it has the advantage of communicating to others how someone appraises the situation. Affects reach out to others and influence them. This is their communicative aspect.

We experience, for instance, **anxiety** in the body and it shows itself bodily to the outside world. This can include cold hands, rapid heart rate, sweating, dilated pupils, chest constriction and possibly laboured breathing or the feeling of losing one's balance. If someone is very afraid, then the lips are tense and narrowed, the mouth open, the eyes rigidly towards the front, eyebrows and upper eyelids are raised and the lower lids are tensed up. This is the pattern of fear that another person can recognise.

This pattern expresses a core theme in a person's relationship to the environment, as do all emotions (Prinz, 2004). However, anxiety can be related to various specific themes such as fear of abandonment, of ghosts, of school; existential anxiety; fear of getting ill; or fear of dying. These themes are not visible in the anxiety reaction; we have to explore them in psychotherapy.

Presumably throughout evolution, emotional systems have developed not only in humans on a biological level, which in certain situations trigger certain reactions such as approach, withdrawal, flight, fight or connect. Panksepp (1998, pp. 52–4) distinguishes the following:

- The seeking system.
- The fear system.
- The rage system.
- The panic system.

To these 'primitive systems' he adds the more 'sophisticated' systems of lust, care and play. In his view, these are based on the brain systems involved in each case. However, Dalgleish's (2004) assessment that we have no hard facts to show how exactly which regions of the brain are involved in emotional processes is still valid.

How a person responds to a situation is not determined, only the affect programmes with which they can do so. Thus I could react to a frightening situation with fear, but neither do all people react in the same way to the same situation, nor does my response to it always have to be fearful. An emotion is therefore a **subjective process in interaction**. If the fear is disconnected from the situation, then it is generally an unhealthy process, which, if it becomes chronic, can result in an anxious personality. In this case the pattern is imprinted in the person as a chronic embodied appraisal: in fantasies, convictions, postures, movements or sensations.

According to constructivist theories, categories of emotion are not evolutionary but determined by convention and language. Thus Russell (2003) regards specific emotions as a specific kind of bodily feeling, to which we allocate concepts such as anger, sorrow or disgust. Cultures and subcultures determine the classification of these concepts and of feeling rules (Hochschild, 1996). Different languages have different inventories of emotional concepts (Russell, 1994). The Ifaluk of Micronesia have only one word for grief, love and compassion. Also for them, concepts of emotion describe not a person's inner state, but their relationship to events, above all to those they share with other people (Lutz, 1982).

However, the theories mentioned here do not have to contradict each other. Emotional reactions can be pre-determined through evolution and yet understood in culturally developed categories. Intercultural studies show differences in how unambiguously facial expressions are assigned to emotional states (Russell, 1994). The facial expression of basic emotions can be universal, as Ekman (2003) says, but the degree and the interpretation are regulated culturally.

Today science generally recognises that the whole person is engaged in emotions and that 'somatovisceral and motor systems' are involved (Scherer, 2009, p. 3459). Emotions flow through the whole organism (Johnstone, 2012). Bodily reactions are not just a by-product of emotions; they are part of them (Fuchs, 2020b).

After many decades, research is finally catching up with the early insights of William James (1894–1994) and with the clinical experience of body-oriented and experiential psychotherapies (Geuter, 2006, p. 258; 2019a). Fenichel and Reich had already described the connection between motor function and emotions (Section 3.1.1). This is why encouraging emotional expressivity was, for Reich, the royal road of vegetotherapy (Traue, 1998, p. 339). Lowen describes emotions as 'the perceptions of internal movements within the relatively fluid body' (1977, p. 52). Perls accepted the idea that muscular contraction interrupts the cycle of experience (Kepner, 1993).

There is no emotion without bodily sensation (Downing, 2000, 2004). Emotions are experienced in interaction with the environment or with inner experiences in the body (Garvey & Fogel, 2008, p. 64). Thus Welzer (2002, p. 75) rightly describes emotions as 'body-based appraisals, which attribute positive or negative value to representations of experience and are therefore the actual creators of meaning and significance, ultimately of consciousness' (Welzer, 2002, p. 83).

Kernberg (1992) defines affects as psychophysiological behaviour patterns characterised by cognitive evaluation, a pattern of facial expressions, pleasant or unpleasant subjective experience and a muscular and neurovegetative pattern of discharge. As with the first theory of Breuer and Freud, corporality is allowed here only as a pattern of discharge and not as the basis of experience.

COMPONENTS

As experiential entities, emotions encompass not only the somatic perception of emotional reactions. Krause (1997, p. 67) names six different components, three of which designate the visible parts which appear in the body and three those experienced more inwardly (Table 10.1).

When an emotion arises, all these components become active. We react to an emotion-provoking event with bodily expression, with proprio- and interoceptive signals and an increase or decrease in action readiness. We become conscious of these emotions through these somatic signals and our perception of them, as well as through our fantasies and thoughts. This is true of everything in the following discussion. In psychotherapy, therefore, we can influence the whole affective process through each single component. We can pick up our patients at any point, through gestures and facial expressions (1), vegetative signals (2), movement and spontaneous gestures (3) and awareness of body sensations (4), as well as through language and inner images (5 and 6).

TABLE 10.1
Components of the affect system according to Krause

Occurring emotion	Experienced emotion
1. Motor-expressive components	4. Perception of bodily correlates
2. Physiological components	5. Naming and explaining the perception
3. Motivational components (action readiness in the voluntary motor functions)	6. Perception of the situational meaning

The various components are like aspects or elements of a homogeneous process. There is no hierarchy or system of mutual contingency. For example, the appraisal of a situation and the reaction to it are not connected one after the other. In the reaction an appraisal occurs and through the appraisal a reaction. The overall emotional response usually takes place unconsciously and as a whole is made up of the various components. It always includes cognitive, muscular and vegetative processes (Section 6.1).

10.1 THREE STEPS OF APPRAISAL IN AN EMOTIONAL PROCESS

In the following, I introduce a model of the origins and development of emotional processes, on the basis of which we can study various tasks of body psychotherapeutic work. According to this model emotions arise in a process consisting of several stages of perception and evaluation. We can distinguish them as consecutive steps in the model, but not in reality as they take place within milliseconds.

1. At the beginning of an emotional process, there is a trigger (Figure 10.1), an event in the outside world or in the internal psychological or bodily world, for example a hefty emotional reaction to a dream or to a somatic illness – in behaviouristic terminology, a stimulus. According to the component process model of Brosch and Scherer (2009; cf. Sander et al., 2005), an event is appraised initially with regard to its **relevance**. The first question is whether it is new, remarkable or significant for us. This question is then

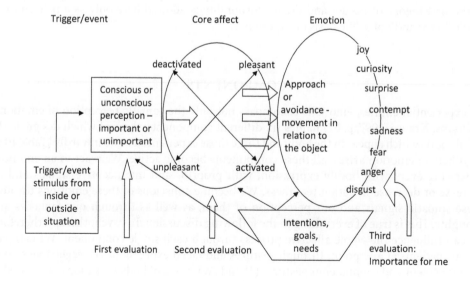

FIGURE 10.1 The structure of emotional processes - an embodied appraisal model

answered with the help of our memory of emotional experience. Our perception does not just reproduce reality; it compares it to previous experience.

If the importance of the event has been established, our attentiveness increases. Neurobiologically this means that in certain cortical regions, information processing is intensified (Roth, 2004, p. 63). This corresponds in part to what Siegel (1999) calls the phase of **orientation reaction**, which I will explain later (Table 10.2). This is the first prerequisite for emotional perception. Without perception there can be no experience.

When we experience a discrepancy between our expectations or attitudes and actual events, our attention is more alert and is directed towards what is different from what we expected (Ritz-Schulte et al., 2008, p. 37). This is why we pay more attention when something unusual or even threatening happens.

This process is not necessarily conscious. An event can pass over the threshold of perception, be appraised as relevant and still not lead to an emotional reaction because the trigger is dissociated. Whether someone can focus their attention depends on their overall emotional and physical condition. This condition is a more deciding factor than reason (Greenberg & Van Balen, 1998, p. 49). I will come back to this in the discussion of the affective cycle (Section 10.5). In any case, most perceptions are rejected as not relevant, so that only a few are processed emotionally. This is because a person's needs and intentions determine what they pick out from the flood of information.

2. The second question of the appraisal according to Brosch and Scherer (2009) is whether an event is **pleasurable or unpleasurable**. This evaluation occurs unconsciously within 200 milliseconds. Panksepp (2006, p. 45) calls this faculty an 'inborn, fully embodied, neuronally energised capacity to feel good and bad about the world'. Roth (2001, pp. 319–20) thinks that on a median level of the limbic system, everything the body does is evaluated as to its positive or negative consequences. An activation of the limbic system, however, is accompanied by complex somatic reactions (Huether, 2005). We sense whether or not something is pleasant for us, and the corresponding evaluation of how pleasant or unpleasant an event is is known in emotion research as **valence**. Pleasant means in accordance with one's needs, unpleasant the opposite.

3. In a third appraisal, we experience the **quality of an emotional reaction**, which lends **meaning** to an event with regard to our relationship to it. This meaning determines whether and in what way we position ourselves in relation to the event, for example if we are anxious about it and prefer to withdraw, or curious and drawn to it, or sad and in need of support, or jealous and wanting to do harm, or angry and looking for a fight. Now we experience a discrete or categorical quality in our reaction, which determines our relationship to the object of the emotion. This is why we speak of discrete or categorical emotions.

In contrast to the first, we experience the second and third appraisal as emotional. In the next part, I will discuss the second and in Section 10.4 the third.

Core affect

Feldmann Barrett and Russell (1998, 1999) put forward a theory which differentiates the stages of the second evaluation: when an event has been appraised as significant in the first step and processed further, it then encounters an **already existing core affective state**, which can be reproduced in two independent polar dimensions (Figure 10.2). Along the dimension of **activated-deactivated**, a person feels a degree of energy mobilisation: from sleeping to relaxed to awake to hyperactive or frenzied arousal. Along the dimension of **pleasant-unpleasant**, there are various ways in which someone can feel good or bad. In combination, these two dimensions give us **four basic affective states**, each with four different shades:

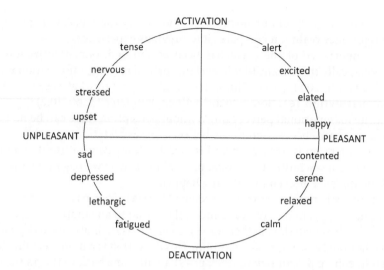

FIGURE 10.2 The two-dimensional structure of core affect according to Feldman Barrett and Russell

- Passive-pleasant.
- Active-pleasant.
- Passive-unpleasant.
- Active-unpleasant (Feldman Barrett & Russell, 1999, p. 11).

In Kuhl's PSI-theory, there is a similar distinction made between facilitated or inhibited positive affects and activated or down-regulated negative affects (Ritz-Schulte et al., 2008, p. 32).

A person is always activated or deactivated in some way, and they feel well or not. This **connection between activation state and valence** is identified by Feldman Barrett and Russell as **core affect**. This notion of core affect, however, does not mean the *actual* affect or core. Fosha (2001, p. 228) uses it in the latter sense to denote emotions which surface in therapy when resistance is abandoned. The term core affect also does not mean a central theme of existence, as Kolbe (2019) uses it in existential analysis. Here I follow the concept of Feldman Barrett and Russell.

Wilhelm Wundt (1911, pp. 36, 94–5), founder of experimental psychology, assumed that each feeling is characterised by a particular quality and intensity. He differentiated three *main dimensions* of polarities:

- Pleasure and displeasure.
- Arousing and subduing.
- Tension and relaxation (Wundt, 1911, pp. 99–100).

Here we already have the model of core affects connected to the dimension of an activation contour in time, which is important for psychotherapy.

The **basic core affective state** is not linked to any trigger. It represents the **continual flow of feeling** which categorical emotions then interrupt. For example, we can be in a pleasant activated state, where we are attentive, interested, elated or even happy; or in an unpleasant deactivated state where we are sad, depressed, lethargic or exhausted, according to how far away the state is from one of the poles. We have to see the adjectival concept of 'sad' for instance as a **mood**, whereas sadness as a feeling belongs to the categorical emotions. Similarly, on the core affective level, we could be in a basic state of apprehensiveness, which would make us receptive to acute anxiety.

The core affective baseline colours the manner in which we experience an emotion and sometimes even determines which categorical emotion we can experience. When we are under a great deal of highly unpleasant tension, we can hardly experience joy, or when feeling upbeat we tend not to become angry. A person's whole momentary mental, emotional and bodily condition feeds into this underlying state, which manifests among others in the physiological state of the autonomic nerve system (Porges, 2009). Damasio (2004, p. 43) calls this baseline background emotions, which are a crucial factor in our general feeling of wellbeing. Unlike categorical emotions, core affective moods are not specifically directed towards anything, but characterise how we generally relate to our environment. However, we can pay attention to them and feel and evaluate our own state. Then we sense how we are at the moment. Plassmann (2021) uses here the idea of self-emotions. We do this also in therapy when we ask patients about their momentary condition.

> In Lewis's (2000) model, emotions can also be differentiated according to their **time duration**: emotional **episodes** last from seconds to minutes, a median **mood** development hours or days and an **emotional attitude** closely associated with the personality months or years. When we speak of emotions in everyday life, we usually mean short episodes.

On the level of core affects, we have to include what Craig (2008) called **homeostatic emotions**, meaning emotions which respond to the need of the body for warmth, air or rest, for example when we feel unwell because we are cold. This unwellness motivates us to change the situation. It is possible that only primates feel this disruption of homeostatic needs such as freezing or needing air subjectively as emotions because they have the necessary afferent nerve pathways (Craig, 2008; Section 7.1). Humans then feel unwell and can communicate this emotionally. Frequently people with mental problems only notice their inner states on this core affective level of wellbeing or lack of it, without being able to feel categorical emotions (Chapter 14: Body talk).

According to the theory of Feldman Barrett and Russell, an event which touches off emotions and is appraised in the first step as relevant does not create a hedonic tone or activation, but **changes the existing core affective state**. This change therefore constitutes the second step of emotional appraisal. Then, for example, we are interested in something or irritated by it, without knowing which categorical emotion we are feeling (Figure 10.2). We evaluate it core affectively. The trigger makes someone increasingly activated or deactivated, increasingly feeling pleasant or unpleasant. We can view this as two simultaneous appraisals, which take in both the intentions and needs of that person, for example, whether they are hungry, need the presence of another person or are totally concentrated on what they are doing.

Three phases

We can assign core affective reactions to the first two phases of Siegel's (1999) three-phase model of emotional processes (Table 10.2). Unlike Brosch and Scherer (2009), in the concept of the orientation reaction Siegel brings together the appraisal of the relevance of an event and a preliminary core affective evaluation. He ascribes our ability to perceive this change in core affectivity to the second phase.

TABLE 10.2

The three phases of the emotion process according to Siegel and their clinical significance for body psychotherapy (modified by Geuter, 2009, p. 82)

Phase	Significance	Therapeutic task
1. Orientation reaction	– State of increased alertness: attention: something important is happening! – Initial appraisal as good or bad – Arousal	– Becoming aware of something – Engendering awareness – Working on modulating arousal – Allowing the arousal, weakening or reinforcing it
2. Elaborating appraisal (Feeling of an increase in energy and alertness)	– Sensing a change in alertness and energy – Sense of the valence – Approaching or avoiding the stimulus = primal emotion	– Clarifying whether something feels pleasant or unpleasant – Clarifying whether we want to turn towards it or turn away from it
3. Differentiating categorical emotions	– What does this mean for me? – What do my somatic markers indicate? = categorical emotion	– Becoming aware of the discrete emotions and their significance through bodily sensations, thoughts and images – Clarifying the relationship between the subject and the object or event

In the **orientation reaction**, the organism shifts into a heightened state of attentiveness or arousal and makes an initial appraisal of an event as good or bad: the person feels energised or alert. If the event is evaluated as irrelevant, then deactivation can increase and the person can feel bored or tired (Feldmann Barrett et al., 2004, p. 684). This corresponds to the psychophysiological concept of arousal. Neurobiologically there is an unspecific activation of the cortical and limbic brain structures, which stimulate the central and peripheral noradrenergic system (Huether, 2009, p. 98). Arousal means not only an increase in sympathetic tone; vagal tone can also be increased as with attachment related triggers (Section 7.1). The autonomic arousal reacts to different emotional triggers in a similar way and does not represent the categorical emotional experience, so that it also does not explain goal-oriented action. For example, the heart rate increases when subjects look at sad or angry faces; looking at happy faces or someone expressing disgust reduces it (Critchley, 2009). The polarity of the reaction is here: activated or not activated, aroused or calm.

If there is a change in the valence dimension of core affect, meaning pleasant or unpleasant, and the person senses this hedonic tone, then in Siegel's model we are dealing with the second phase of a reaction to an emotionally triggering event. The organism **senses** something as pleasant or unpleasant and **reacts** on first impulse with approach or withdrawal. Since it is on this level that an event is first experienced as emotional, Siegel speaks of a *primary emotion*. Zinck and Newen (2008) call this a stage of unspecific emotional reaction, a so-called *pre-emotion*. In developmental biology, this would correspond to the reaction of the reptilian brain, which contains systems of activation/deactivation and pleasure/unpleasure. When a change occurs solely in the core affects without any further emotional participation, then we experience this as a change of **mood**.

Mental problems can interfere with our orientation reaction. A study by Kaletsch et al. (2014) shows that borderline patients have less confidence in their perception of emotions expressed bodily in interaction.

In a third step, according to Siegel, the **categorical emotions** are differentiated. In this step the affect programmes of the limbic systems of mammals, developed through evolution, are at work, eliciting rapid reactions as prototypical response patterns – those emotions that we know as fear, anger or disgust, in which somatic markers (Section 6.3) signal what the events mean for the subject. Now specific emotional reactions are assigned – not always consciously – to an event or an object, so that Russell (2003) speaks here of an *attributed affect*.

The quality of these reactions is only experienced as emotional when it coincides with a change in the dimension of core affect. Then, for example, something that inspires fear will only be felt as scary when it is linked with an arousal and a valence. **In order to be felt, categorical emotions need core affective experience.** This matches Stern's (1985) assessment that each discrete affect, such as anger, fear or joy, is experienced at least in the two dimensions of 'activation' and 'hedonic tone'. In the model presented here, this means that behind each emotional experience there is an experience of change in those two core affective dimensions.

Important
Each emotional experience involves changes in the two dimensions of core affect: the activation state and the hedonic tone.

Therapeutic relevance

Without core affective change we are not able in therapy to clarify the meaning of emotions. If a patient talks about sadness, she can only experience the sadness and those needs connected to it (for example for comfort) when the grief really takes hold of her (= activation) and distresses her (= hedonic tone). These core affective changes are experienced bodily.

When in the dispute over the primacy of cognition or emotion, Lazarus (1982) argues that an appraisal precedes every emotional event; this belongs to the perception of categorical affective quality. When on the contrary Zajonc (1984) asserts the primacy of emotional arousal, this belongs to core affects. Perceiving an appraisal only cognitively lets a person remain cool or calm. They will only experience it emotionally if there is a change on the core affective level.

However, even though a categorical emotion needs the perception of core affective changes, these last alone do not convey which emotion we are feeling. For example, a high level of arousal connected to a negative valence could mean anxiety, anger or disgust. We can only recognise the significance of a change in core affect in relation to an object by the specific emotional reaction: we become angry, are afraid or are disgusted. On the other hand, perception of the specific emotional significance depends on the core affective state; experimentally, for example, it could be shown that anger is experienced in various ways depending on whether we express it loudly and rapidly or quietly and slowly (Siegman et al., 1990). Thus both perceptions of the meaning of an event and changes in the core affective state flow into categorical emotions.

The pleasure-arousal theory represents emotions in a coordinate system with the orthogonal axes pleasure and arousal (Larsen & Diener, 1992). Feelings of anger or anxiety, for example, are assigned to the quadrant unpleasant/activated with negative pleasure and positive arousal (Lang, 1995, p. 374). Since the theory does not differentiate between core affect and categorical emotion, the classification of emotions is not clear-cut. Jealousy, anxiety, guilt, disgust, hate, pain, humiliation and general bad mood are all listed in one corresponding quadrant (Reisenzein, 1994). With this model we can only describe the valence and intensity of emotional experience quantitatively, not the specific emotion. For example, arousal alone does not reveal what patients experience in therapy: 'emotional arousal at one point in therapy maybe a sign of distress and at another point a sign that the client is actively working through distress' (Elliott et al., 2013, p. 517).

If a person's core affective experience is blocked, then an emotion-triggering event does not lead to a change in arousal and valence. Clinically this is what we call an affect block. When arousal is inhibited, a person has difficulty feeling anything. Here we speak of alexithymia, which can also mean that a person does not feel the existing arousal. When arousal is lacking because of dissociation, then the person feels emotionally numb. If in contrast the tension of the arousal is too high, this hinders a conscious, reflexive emotional experience. Borderline patients in particular have problems coping with core affective tension (Garcia & Arandia, 2022, p. 12). If, as a result of trauma, a person is triggered into a state of hyperarousal, then they will often dissociate so as to reduce the unbearable level of excitation. In this way they protect themselves from reliving the old pain. Mental problems are often problems of the dysregulation of emotional arousal.

If the arousal is too low, there is no emotional experience. If it is too high, the emotion takes over the person. As therapists, we have to work differently with each of these conditions. It is only possible to process an event emotionally within the so-called **window of tolerance** of median emotional arousal (Geuter, 2019, p. 159).

If a person has no sense of what is pleasant or unpleasant for them, then they are not able to pursue any goals. They suffer from volitional inhibition. If the sense of valence and thus of pleasure is arrested, this deadens the vital sensing of all emotions. Then a person seems lifeless. Often they will displace the arousal or the hedonic tone into the body.

10.2 THREE THERAPEUTIC TASKS

Before discussing categorical emotions, I want to show what the distinction between event perception, core affects and emotions means for body psychotherapy. From the model in Figure 10.1, we can derive three different therapeutic tasks concerned with clarifying and regulating emotional processes:

1. We can work on a person's **attentiveness for perception** of what is happening to them or what they encounter, for example by encouraging mindfulness and directing awareness

towards what they perceive and what it means for them. This is working on the first appraisal in the emotional process. Body psychotherapy methods which prioritise working with mindfulness or self-awareness are most suitable for this task.

2. We can work on the **perception of core affective changes** and on a **modification of the core affective state**. This is working on the second appraisal. Both the affect-oriented as well as the trauma-adapted methods of body psychotherapy are suitable for this.

3. We can work on the **perception, clarification and transformation of emotions**. This is working on the third appraisal, which is concerned with the significance of an event or a situation for the person in relation to an object. For this task we can use enactments and methods taken from Gestalt therapy.

These three tasks correspond to Greenberg's (2004) three principles of emotional change, which were distilled out of empirical research: *emotion awareness*, *emotion regulation* and *emotion transformation*.

The second of Greenberg's tasks includes, along with regulation, also the perception of core affective changes. In the following, I consider the difference between the second and third tasks. I will discuss briefly some of the principles of body psychotherapeutic treatment, which I have described in full in my book about the practice of body psychotherapy (Geuter, 2019).

Specific schools have their specific focus

Several of the body psychotherapy schools have developed their work with a focus on certain aspects of the emotional process:

- On mindfulness in Hakomi.
- On awareness of the body as the basis of attentiveness and wellness in Body-Mind-Centering.
- On the perception of feelings through the language of the body in Concentrative Movement Therapy.
- On the regulation of the breathing, which supports core affective wellbeing, in Functional Relaxation.
- On the blocked expression of emotions in bioenergetics.
- On the melting of defences and the digestion of affects in biodynamics.
- On the clarification of the relational aspect of emotions in analytical body psychotherapy.

The emotion theory model presented here facilitates an integrative perspective, which helps to collate these various focuses into a comprehensive body psychotherapeutic practice.

Russell (2003) differentiates between a regulation to sustain or change the core affect and one to change the kind of emotion related to an object. He calls them affect and emotion regulation. We influence our core affects and our emotions in different ways:

- We cannot change core affect, arousal and hedonic tone in the same way we can categorical emotions, but we can influence them so that our basic state improves. Psychotropic medication works on this level. If the arousal is muted with drugs, then events are interpreted as less important (Siegel, 1999). Through a change in the breathing, we can heighten or mute our general emotional state (Keleman, 1985). We can also manage our core affective state through our behaviour. In everyday life we distract ourselves when we want to lower the level of arousal, or we go out and run when we want to feel more vital. In therapy, I can do energising exercises with a patient to make them feel more alive, grounding or body awareness to centre, ground or calm them down. Core affect can be modified without reference to the source of an emotion (Russell, 2003, p. 149).

- In order to change a categorical emotion, we have to relate it to the object of the emotion and alter the appraisal. Object relations patterns cannot be altered through psychotropic drugs (Fuchs, 2008a). Emotions can only be changed through other emotions (Greenberg, 2011). I will go into this more deeply in Section 10.6.

It is of vital importance in body psychotherapy to differentiate between these two regulative tasks. Activating **work on core affective arousal** is often called charge and discharge work (Totton, 2003, p. 67); these two concepts originated in drive theory (Geuter, 2019, pp. 161–2). This work can be done with any affective quality just as we can contain and soothe any emotional arousal. In contrast, other **experiential ways of working** relate the emotional quality to another person or a situation. We can explore the emotional evaluation in a back and forth between the thoughts that occur and the sensing. It is a characteristic of body psychotherapy that it works with both modulating arousal levels and methods of clarifying or enacting to resolve and regulate emotions and combines both these in one therapeutic process.

Important
Body psychotherapy brings working on the modification of core affect and working on the exploration, regulation, clarification and transformation of object-related emotions together in one therapeutic process.

Clinical example

One patient always shakes my hand very forcefully and usually speaks that way too. He is of medium height, an extremely slim but muscular man. Shortly before our session, he was in a therapy group and had charged several times headfirst into a man-sized block of foam, which had done him a lot of good. This was all about his childhood anger at his mother, who clung to her son after the death of his father. The question was whether behind this forcefulness was a strong feeling of suppressed anger. Looking at it in this way would mean locating the forcefulness as suppressed anger on the level of categorical emotions. However, we could also see it as a core affective quality of an already heightened level of arousal, which colours his whole experience. The one view does not preclude the other. If I work with the anger arising from his relationship to his mother, then I focus on the emotion. But I could also work with him experimenting with being gentle instead of forceful, rounder instead of angular and, instead of shaking hands so robustly, doing so sensitively and connectedly. Then I would be working with the general intensity of his reaction. As we worked, he realised that he never felt seen in his sensitivity and so as a teenager he tried to play the hard man. For him, the work with both the emotion and with core affectivity was important; both were relevant in their different ways.

Verbal psychotherapy has traditionally focused on all those evaluative processes which express themselves in categorical emotions. Emotion-Focused Therapy works with this too. Carryer and Greenberg (2010) have said, after years of experience with this approach, that too little attention was paid to the emotional arousal. On the other hand, in-patient treatment often centres on methods such as running for depressive people to raise their activation level, since core affective flattening does not allow them to experience distinct emotions; or on methods to lessen the arousal of traumatised or borderline patients (Geuter, 2019, pp. 208–13). Exposure therapy works with increasing arousal when the anxiety is heightened through a situation deliberately contrived to do so. The patient is then asked to become aware of the ensuing rise and fall of arousal. This method regulates core affectivity. Methods such as relaxation exercises, mindful body awareness, meditation or, as in body psychotherapy bodily containment are all useful in tempering arousal.

Important
We can change core affectivity more easily through bodily methods than with words.

When core affect is changed, all emotional experience changes. Buddhism basically teaches us how to stay alert and mindful on all levels of being from the spiritual to the vegetative in a pleasant-deactivated core affective state and thus to assuage the reactions of discrete emotions connected to the ego. In the schema of Feldman Barrett and Russell (Figure 10.2), this is the quadrant in which a person is perfectly happy. We call this serenity. Boyesen (1982, p. 10) speaks of **independent wellbeing**. In such a state, things do not affect us so much emotionally. We can use the mind to achieve this in the body, or the body to reach it in the mind. This is what meditation, mindfulness training or yoga seeks to do. I assume that the psychological effect of body therapy methods and of most meditation forms on people's emotional balance is realised through the modification of core affect (Geuter, 2019, pp. 205–8). However, they transcend this level when practitioners reflect on the meaning of their observations.

Since a differentiated emotion can only be changed in its internal or external relationship to an object, working on the emotions themselves is not possible without psychological means. Here we have to clarify, for example, what is making a patient angry, what the anger is aimed at and what they want their anger to change (Section 10.6).

At this point we can see how useful it is to be able to utilise both psychological as well as bodily methods in the therapeutic process; this allows a more targeted influence on the different aspects of emotional experience in the treatment of emotional dysregulation.

Regulation of arousal

Through the body we can change emotional processes, especially in their intensity, while at the same time – and this is how therapy differs from, for instance, running as sport – we can explore, experience, express or contain object-related emotions and arrive at a new emotional appraisal. Dialectic behaviour therapy tackles these two aspects in separate treatment modules. However, if we want to work with the full intensity and quality of emotional processes, it makes more sense to combine both in one therapeutic process.

Working with heightened arousal is productive also from a systemic point of view of therapeutic change, according to which change is a shift in the organisational structure of the dynamic system in which the patient is trapped. Therapy then means destabilising the old system by first creating a high-energy, volatile situation, which then allows a new and stable state to replace the old.

Clinical examples

The therapist asks the patient to stand with the feet shoulder-width apart and to move up and down in the knees. This exercise leads to an activation, the legs begin to tremble and he starts to clench his fists. This activation (= core affect) also brings up a feeling, a categorical emotion (= anger). Phrases leap into his mind : 'Leave me alone!' or 'I don't want to!' This flow of energy lets him really experience the rage he felt towards his brother and some of his schoolmates and to sense its innate power (for more detail cf. Geuter, 2009, pp. 85–7).

In another case, a patient is chronically exhausted and listless (= core affect: deactivated and highly unpleasant) and at the same time completely hopeless (= emotion), so that she cannot even speak. She feels like a helpless toddler. Only when she lies in the arms of the therapist does the inner tension relax enough for her to find some peace of mind and to speak about herself.

In body psychotherapy, we work on the one hand with **raising the tension of the arousal** so as to increase *emotion awareness* – the first principle of emotional processing in Greenberg's (2004) Emotion-Focused Therapy. In this way we encourage a processual activation of problematic schemas without which corrective emotional experiences are not possible (Grawe, 2004). And on the other hand, when they get into disproportionate or unpleasant states of arousal, we help our patients to **down-regulate the arousal tension,** independently of the meaning that the corresponding emotions have. We help them to become aware of and to guide their somatic reaction to internal or external stimuli and thus to modify it. To do this we have techniques to modulate breathing and to regulate motor tension, basic body exercises for calming down and supportive touch, as well as the soothing and stabilising effect of the therapeutic contact (Geuter, 2019, pp. 199–203). Sometimes we can even mitigate the tension by first increasing it. This is because of the cyclic dynamics of affects over time (Section 10.5): the arousal curve tends to flatten out when it has passed its zenith.

Here we have to differentiate between a permanent and a situational activation and deactivation:

- In the long run, the arousal level should be neither too high nor too low, since both are inconducive to a healthy emotional experience.
- In certain situations, it can be helpful to work with very high tension or to induce an extremely deep state of relaxation, loosening defences beyond the limits of their normal functioning, so that unconscious, repressed material can emerge (Boyesen & Boyesen, 1987, p. 7). In contrast to everyday relaxation, we can call this last a dynamic relaxation (Schrauth, 2001, p. 43). In the same way, we can distinguish an everyday activation from a dynamic one, which entails the mobilisation of affects and of material from the dynamic unconscious (Geuter & Schrauth, 2015). In both cases, the arousal must remain within the window of tolerance, as otherwise no helpful change is possible.

Thus, before we start to work with the activation or deactivation of affective experience, we have to ask ourselves whether we are dealing with an **over-regulation** of affects, which allows the patient to avoid painful emotional experiences; with an **under-regulation** of intensive negative affects (Greenberg & Paivio, 1997); or with an over- or under-regulation of pleasant, joyful affects, which Greenberg and Paivio do not mention and with which psychotherapy in general is reluctant to engage (Heisterkamp, 1999).

On the level of cultural emotional feeling rules, Scheff (1983) speaks in a similar way of over-distanced and under-distanced feelings. This can apply both to the current situation as well as to a person's personality, since many people border their affects too strongly or not strongly enough (Boadella, 1987; Keleman, 1985; Section 13.1). Following a processual indication, we can then work either with the principle of *activating and expressing* or with that of *regulating and modulating* (Geuter, 2019). The long-term goal of psychotherapeutic work is neither to heighten nor to lower arousal tension, but to enable the patient to develop the ability to pulsate freely between these two poles according to the needs of the situation and thus to integrate their affective states and to achieve self-regulation (Monsen & Monsen, 1999).

Valence perception

The body can also serve as a source of orientation for whether something is perceived as pleasant or unpleasant or neutral, i.e. for working with valence. When a patient is uncertain in this dimension of core affect, then the first question is what they sense in their body. The Focusing method is concerned with this level of inner perception. Gendlin and Hendricks-Gendlin (2015, p. 249) talk about an inner sensing 'less intense than emotions' but also different from a sheer bodily sensation. The *felt sense*, a holistic inner sensing, is in Focusing a signal as to whether a person feels good or not good with a situation. The sensing of valence appears often as an interoceptive signal in the chest, the abdomen and the genitals. Johnstone (2012) speaks accordingly of the chest and abdomen as a hedonic centre. It manifests more in the middle of the body but also in vegetative processes at the periphery, as, for example, in a sensation in the skin. It expresses itself differently from categorical emotions, which are connected to action impulses and thus are noticeable in the muscles in the periphery of the body.

We can find numerous examples of how to differentiate through bodily sensations between pleasant, unpleasant and neutral in the work of Williams et al. (2007) on the mindfulness-based cognitive therapy of depression. The authors aim to help patients become aware of different sensation qualities, so that they need not automatically shy away from experiences just because they are unpleasant. To this end they use many techniques of somatic awareness which are also prevalent in body psychotherapy.

Mindfulness trains the ability to tolerate arousal tension and unpleasant feelings and to modulate them. A mindful attitude towards bodily sensations associated with problematic feelings helps the patient to distance themselves from them. It also helps them stop defending themselves against emotional experience and creates awareness for the unpleasant feeling and its meaning.

10.3 EMOTIONS AND NEEDS

As I described in Section 10.1, a person's intentions and desires are involved in their perception and processing of emotion triggering events (Figure 10.1). This is true as well for the emotions themselves, since these also reveal needs (Bischkopf, 2009): the need for security, encouragement and soothing when we are anxious; for comfort and support when we are grieving; for security, inviolacy and sometimes also attachment when we are angry; or for sharing when we are happy. Desires and needs can also be experienced affectively themselves. They can impel us to act, change our core affective state and trigger emotions. Colombetti (2017) sees them as part of affective life. Especially the experience of incongruence between needs and their fulfilment leads to psychological activity (Grawe, 2004, 2007).

Emotions regulate a person's balance of needs (Damasio et al., 2000). When someone is mentally ill, usually emotions are hindering the fulfilment of their needs, and they have no skills to deal with them. They perceive themselves and the world in a way that obstructs their need-fulfilment (Troesken & Grawe, 2004). According to Grawe's (2004) consistency theory, not being able to fulfil one's needs is a cause of illness.

Mental problems develop when vital needs remain unfulfilled or are violated and people react with maladaptive emotions or are not able to react adequately. In psychotherapy, we therefore work with such difficult emotions so that people can learn to live more according to their needs. Working with emotions helps us to sense what we need to live (Plassmann, 2019, p. 79). When patients bring their needs 'back into consciousness' (Auszra et al., 2017, p. 55), then we can work how they can fulfil them in harmony with the needs of others. Thus we go from emotions to needs and from there to action. In psychotherapy, therefore, we need not only a theory of emotional processes but also an idea of the needs that are important for a satisfying life.

Important
In mental disorders obstructive, dysfunctional emotions or a lack of skills stand in the way of the fulfilment of needs.

In the theory of psychotherapy, needs have been often neglected. Initially psychoanalysis regarded needs as instincts. Humanistic psychology was the first to emphasise that human motivation consists of more than just instinct or the avoidance of pain and the search for pleasure as advocated by learning theory. Maslow (1968) devised a model of a hierarchy of needs, at the top of which came the need for growth and self-actualisation. The impulses of humanistic psychotherapy were taken up by body psychotherapy at a time when many people were searching for an enhancement of their inner potential through experiential and encounter groups and believed they would discover the wellspring for this in bodily experienced needs (Section 3.7).

Lowen (1958) grafted a concept of needs onto Reich's theory of character structures when he described these last as reaction patterns formed in childhood as responses to typical conflicts between needs and their frustration (Section 13.2). In body psychotherapy today, many authors draw on Lichtenberg's theory of motivational systems. Lichtenberg differentiates five motivational systems based on **five needs** and the response patterns associated with them (Lichtenberg et al., 2001):

1. The need to fulfil physiological requirements, such as food, sleep, tactile stimulation and warmth.
2. The need for attachment and affiliation.
3. The need for assertion and exploration.
4. The need to react aversively through antagonism and/or withdrawal.
5. The need for sensual and sexual pleasure.

However there is no uniform concept of need systems. In his theory of the four basic needs, Grawe (2004) recognises the need for attachment and the striving for pleasure and avoidance of pain, but not the other three named by Lichtenberg. Instead he adds the need for control and that for the enhancement of self-esteem, which Maslow puts at the top of his five-level pyramid. In the context of their theory of self-determination, Ryan and Deci (2000) see competence, autonomy and relatedness as three basic human needs. Pesso (1997) names five basic needs for place, nurturance, support, protection and limits. In schema therapy, we find a model of five core emotional needs: for secure attachment; for autonomy, competence and a sense of identity; for freedom to express important needs, opinions and emotions; for spontaneity and play; for boundaries and self-control (Young et al., 2006). For existential analysis, Kolbe (2019) names the need to be recognised as an individual and for one's achievements, as well as the need to lead a life that has meaning for that person.

All these models emanate from a phenomenological description of needs as the authors perceive them. This is also true of psychobiological theories such as Panksepp's (1998) motivational and emotional systems. Here it is the needs which activate the corresponding systems:

- Bodily needs for food and warmth, Lichtenberg's first system, activate for example the **seeking system**, with the main emotion being interest.
- The need for attachment can activate the **care system**, and in the case of separation anxiety also the **panic system** with feelings of panic and sadness.
- The need for exploration can activate the **system of play and joy**.
- The need to avoid danger, the **fear system**.
- The need for expectations to be fulfilled, the **rage system**.
- The need for sensual and sexual pleasure, the **system of love and lust**.

The classification shows that it is not always easy to distinguish needs from emotions. I would identify lust not as an emotion but as a need, which can be connected to a feeling of joy. Needs like the sensation of lust can be directly and deliberately satisfied. Feelings of joy or love, however, cannot be deliberately conjured up. We can be open to them, but then they just happen to us.

> **Sexuality** is not an affect but a need. However, it is regulated emotionally and at best is experienced core affectively as pleasant and with joy as the basic emotion, at worst as unpleasant and connected to fear, disgust, anger or post-coital tristesse. As a need, sexuality activates emotions and can also be activated through emotions. Because of its tradition of drive theory, Reichian body psychotherapy is not always able to clearly recognise the difference. In the first Freudian drive theory, which Reich inherited, affects were seen as the progeny of the drive. Even today, Kernberg (1992) views libido and aggression as drives, which integrate positive, pleasant and negative, unpleasant affects. This means there is no clear differentiation between needs and emotions. Sexuality belongs to the needs, but aggressive rage to the affects.

To satisfy our needs, we have to take action. Thus Trautmann-Voigt and Voigt (2009, p. 123) assign to Lichtenberg's five motivational schemas specific movement themes such as carrying or holding as themes of the attachment system; grasping, touching or crawling as themes of the exploration system; pushing oneself up, screaming or turning away as themes of the aversive system; or sensual stimulating touching as a theme of the sensual/sexual system.

Each need/motivational system leads to certain affective experiences of satisfaction or of stress. Psychotherapy is also an attempt to help people satisfy their legitimate needs and to avoid frustration and stress. Psychotherapeutic work with emotions must therefore always be linked to the question of needs. Auszra et al. (2017, p. 115) call it the royal road to facilitating new and helpful feelings when a patient can experience a painful feeling and at the same time sense what they need. In the case of anger, we can ask them what they want or what action they want to take; of sadness, what they need or what is missing; of disgust, what is so repulsive or what they want to get rid of; of anxiety, what they need to protect or save themselves from. We can also reinforce this approach in the therapeutic relationship by asking 'What do you need from me?' or 'What could I give you that would help?' (cf. Auszra et al., 2017, p. 103). By paying careful attention to somatic signals, body psychotherapy can be particularly conducive to exploring the patient's needs when their own perception is blocked.

10.4 CATEGORICAL EMOTIONS

Now I want to go into the third appraisal of my emotion model, in which we notice the emotional significance of an event through a categorical emotion (Figure 10.1). As a spontaneous emotional reaction in a certain situation, we usually first experience one of the basic emotions of joy, curiosity, surprise, anger, sadness, fear, disgust or contempt. However other emotions such as pride, shame, guilt, embarrassment or jealousy can also convey the meaning of an event for us.

These emotions establish a specific relationship to something that is expressed in fantasies and motor impulses. Often action readiness is inherent in emotions (Frijda, 1986) as long as they are not just experienced inwardly. This is shown in the model as **approach** or **avoidance**. Elsewhere I have classified the approach and avoidance system as part of the core affective system of pleasant/unpleasant (Geuter, 2009). I now see this differently. On the core affective level, we have attraction and aversion as fore-contact emotions, as they are called in Gestalt therapy (Dreitzel, 2021, p. 48, 136). Approach and avoidance, though, belong more to the emotions since their form is determined by the concrete emotion.

However the movement between subject and object cannot be allocated unequivocally to either the valence of core affect or to the categorical emotions, since it also includes the polarity of pleasant and unpleasant, which helps determine approach and avoidance. But it is only when the subject experiences categorical emotions that a concrete **locomotor tendency**, to approach an object, to distance themselves from it or to distance the object from themselves, develops. This is why in the model shown in Figure 10.1, the movement of approach and avoidance appears in the transition to emotions but already belonging to them.

Karen Horney speaks of three emotional vectors:

• Going towards someone.
• Going away from someone.
• Going up against someone (Boadella, 1996).

Gustav Kafka describes four primal affects:

• 'You come to me'. 'I come to you'.
• 'You get away from me'. 'I get away from you'.

These all describe movements between subject and object (Koch, 2011, p. 65). Reich advocated a similar bipolar model of affective flow towards the world = lust and away from it = fear (Boadella, 1973).

Grawe (2007) writes that approach serves the goal of satisfaction and avoidance that of protection, and that because of these two different aims, we should not assume them to be two poles of the same dimension. Approach and avoidance can lead to psychological suffering when a person turns towards something not conducive to their needs and avoids what would be good for them. Psychological processes are more fulfilling when the appraisal of good/bad is compatible with the tendency to approach or to avoid.

Emotions always mean something for the desired interaction between subject and object and thus also involve a locomotion impulse. This does not have to mean that the person wants to do something with an object; it can also mean that they withdraw from the world of objects when these are perceived as dangerous, as happens with the freeze response (Section 7.1). Curiosity, for example, paves the way for someone to approach an object. If in addition they want the object to come closer, this indicates joy; if they want to push it away, then anger. In the case of disgust, the object should be removed from the vicinity or should be excreted from the body; in that of anxiety, the distance between subject and object should be increased by one or the other moving away.

Clinical application

In body psychotherapy, we can explore this tendency through locomotion, for example through a patient's movement impulse: is this an impulse to approach or to turn away or to go against something? In this way we can discover the vector of the relationship with the object. For example, I can ask a patient who is working on issues with their father to imagine he were here in the therapy room and to symbolise him with some object. Then I ask them to find out at what distance and what angle they need to stand in relation to him and whether they have a movement impulse linked to him. Such pointers are essential elements in enactment work (Geuter, 2019, p. 296).

Basic emotions

What I have said here is true above all for a certain class of emotions, the basic emotions, which Krause (1996, p. 252) calls **interrupt affects**. These emotions interrupt the psychological process. They tend to be situational, highly intensive and short-term, the most important for clinical purposes being fear, disgust, anger and grief. As mentioned at the beginning of this chapter, basic emotions are affect programmes developed in the course of evolution, with which we react to events. Sadness is usually a reaction to separation or loss, fear to threats and danger, anger when others hurt someone emotionally or physically, when a person's potential is denied or expectations frustrated. Experiences of self-efficacy, attachment, social acceptance and pleasure create joy. Experiencing something as harmful or extremely unpleasant engenders disgust and in so doing creates distance. Experiencing something as useful, stimulating or pleasant leads to curiosity.

From a phenomenological viewpoint, basic emotions are higher-level categories of emotional reactions which we can then differentiate further. Their fundamental themes are determined by evolution, but how we experience them depends on our individual lives (Feldman Barrett, 2017). Thus in sorrow we can be shocked, aggrieved, despondent or broken up; or in anger upset, furious, enraged or helplessly pent up. Psychotherapy can be about discovering emotions in their specific tonality as well as identifying and experiencing the basic emotion.

We call other emotions such as envy, jealousy, stoicism or humility **self-referential emotions** (Table 10.3). Zinck (2008) offers pride, shame, embarrassment, humiliation, hubris and guilt as typical examples. Damasio (2012) calls them social emotions; Krause calls them me-emotions, because they are directed towards the person producing them and develop out of a process of confrontation with our inner values and with the ideas others have about us. For example, pride can be authentic or presumptuous (Wubben et al., 2012). In the first

TABLE 10.3
Classification of emotions

Basic emotions (Ekman & Friesen)	Self-referential emotions (Zinck)
Interrupt affects (Krause)	Me-emotions (Krause)
Attributed affects (Russell)	Social emotions (Damasio)
Affects (Kernberg)	Emotions/feelings (Kernberg)
Bodily perceived emotions (Lowen)	Feeling states (Lowen)
• Joy/happiness	• Pride
• Interest/curiosity	• Shame
• Surprise/shock	• Guilt
• Grief/pain	• Humiliation
• Fear/anxiety	• Arrogance
• Rage/anger	• Envy
• Disgust	• Jealousy
• Contempt (debatable)	
Complete list	Open list

case, someone sees themselves through the eyes of the others as good; in the second, they see the others in their own eyes as bad. Self-referential emotions involve an **inner comparison** with a standard of feeling and behaviour. They are not necessarily tied to a certain trigger, but can be reinforced by one. Usually they build up slowly and tend to persist or even to become the basic mood of someone's personality. In child development they come up later, even though there are precursors such as when a baby apprehensively withdraws; however this tends to be more a question of fear (Reddy, 2008, p. 129). Shame develops in the second year of life, when the child can see themselves through the eyes of an observer (Dornes, 1997, p. 267). The same is true of pride. However we can observe facial expressions corresponding to basic emotions in the very first months (Dornes, 1993, pp. 116–20).

Lowen (2013) differentiates between feelings such as humiliation or pride as 'generalized feeling states' and emotions which are usually linked to more intensive vegetative body sensations (Table 10.3). The latter often literally burst into our consciousness, but equally they can remain hidden from our awareness by our psychological defences and so lead a subterranean, haunted existence.

It is the class of basic emotions for which Ekman (2003) in his transcultural studies found universal patterns of **facial expressions**, which Darwin had already studied in both humans and animals. Despite cultural differences in the presentation of emotions (Section 10.5), we can still recognise them in the patterns of the facial muscles. Ekman distinguishes those basic emotions named in the Table 10.3.

Sometimes contempt is assigned to disgust, and shame or pride are listed under basic emotions (e.g. Tracey & Robins, 2004) although shame is not easily recognisable in the facial expression and requires an examination of one's inner values. However compared to the other emotions, shame is the one most easily identified in bodily expression (Walbott, 1998, p. 889). With pride, people often smile slightly, raise their heads and expand a little; sometimes they put their hands on their hips or over their heads (Tracy & Robins, 2004; Section 14.1).

The facial expressions of basic emotions can be identified with the *Facial Action Coding System* (FACS), in which observable movements of the facial muscles are recorded and assigned to the emotions. Clinically, we find that borderline patients for example show a lot of disgust, contempt, and rage in their facial expressions and little anxiety, sadness or surprise; however as a group they are very heterogeneous (Benecke & Dammann, 2004). But the reverse conclusion, that people who display the facial expression of a basic emotion are actually feeling it, is not possible (Krause, 2006, p. 24). If we ask subjects about their subjective feelings when watching a film and then compare this with a video of their facial expressions, we find less matches between these last and their reported feelings than the expression theory would suggest (Fernandez-Dols et al., 1997). However, when subjects are asked to voluntarily mimic an emotional face, then they start to feel it too; the autonomic nervous system reacts exactly as it would if a person was remembering a life situation linked to this emotion (Levenson, 2003, p. 353).

Clinical application

In therapy, we can use this to advantage by letting the patient consciously assume a facial expression which can then activate a feeling, for example when they knit their brows to activate anger, or let the eyelids and the corners of the mouth hang down so as to intensify the feeling of sadness. Basic emotions can also be experienced strongly through voluntary bodily movements (Geuter, 2019, pp. 170–9).

Research to determine the emotional significance of facial expressions is usually done by means of static impressions using photos. However, it is difficult to identify a more subtle emotional expression that way. According to experimental studies, a subtle expression is more discernible in a brief, dynamic movement of the face (Ambadar et al., 2005). This corresponds more closely to everyday experience, where we tend to observe processes of emotional expression and not momentary snapshots.

Posture and movement are also a means of recognising emotions (Bachmann et al., 2020). Reportedly we recognise grief and joy more easily through the body than through the face (Walbott, 1998). But assigning specific body movements to the basic emotions is difficult. We raise our shoulders when we are enraged, but also when we are in a state of euphoria; we bring them forward when we are disgusted, afraid or in despair and pull them back in antipathy (Walbott, 1998). In addition, feelings can be expressed in very different ways (Dael et al., 2012).

Bodily signals tend to display more the positive or negative meaning of an experience than do facial expressions when emotions are strong. If we show subjects photos of tennis players after a match, they can tell from body cues whether the player has won their game or not; the same is not true of facial expressions (Aviezer et al., 2012). In body psychotherapy, this correlates with the fact that we can evoke strong emotions much more readily through bodily than through facial expression.

Wallin describes the **body expression** of five basic emotions and of shame as follows:

Happiness: deep breathing, sighs, smiles, laughter, bright eyes.
Sadness: choked up feeling, lump in the throat, mouth turned down, moist, reddened eyes, slowed down body movements, crying.
Fear: racing heart, mouth dry, rapid shallow breathing, eyes wide with raised eyebrows, impulse to flee.

Anger: muscular tension particularly in jaw and shoulders, pursed lips, clamped jaw, often thrust forward, lowered eyebrows drawn together, glaring eyes, upper eyelids raised, reddened neck, yelling, impulse to fight.
Disgust: nausea, nose wrinkled, raised upper lip, turning away.
Shame: rising heat in the face, blushing, averted gaze, impulse to hide.

(Wallin, 2007, p. 295)

Wallbott (1998) has examined to what extent we can recognise emotions through posture and movement. In a discriminant analysis, he isolated two general factors: most importantly the factor activity/passivity, and secondly the factor approach/avoidance. The first of these is a dimension of core affect, the second of general locomotor object relations, which cannot be assigned to a certain emotion. Evidently both can be identified by means of body language in particular. Atkinson et al. (2004) had actors portray anger, disgust, fear, joy and grief on several levels of intensity. Subjects recognised the feelings even when the face of the actor was hidden and they could only see their expressive movements in the form of points of light. However, recent studies indicate that subjects assign emotions to people filmed carrying out certain movements, even when the people had been instructed just to perform movement associated with an emotion and not to express an emotion itself (Melzer et al., 2019).

Clinical application

Patients can often only communicate emotions with the qualities activation/deactivation, pleasant/unpleasant and approach/avoidance when they prevent themselves from experiencing them for psychodynamic reasons. In body psychotherapy, we can address these qualities on the somatic level and so work with affects even when they cannot be communicated symbolically (Chapter 14: Body talk).

It is not only the facial muscles and those of the locomotor system that react to emotionally triggering situations – the heart muscles, the smooth muscles of the intestinal walls or the tiny erector muscles of the ca. five million body hairs do so too (Grunwald, 2012). They help express self-referential emotions such as guilt or shame. Emotions are also expressed through the skin: we get goose bumps when we are scared or excited. The skin reacts vegetatively too (Section 6.3): we blush, sweat or feel cold. Skin temperature sinks when we are afraid or sad (Ekman et al., 1983), so that we can also recognise emotions through touch (Hertenstein et al., 2006). Basic emotions are accompanied by specific breathing patterns (Bloch et al., 1991) and with particular voice qualities. They also have a certain rhythm, which is why we can experience music as sad, joyful or sometimes even fierce.

However, it is not possible to deduce a person's emotional state with any accuracy from the quality of the voice (Section 14.5). An observer can attribute the wrong emotion to someone, whereby it is mostly those emotions adjacent to one another which are confused, for example hot anger with cold anger, or contempt with pride, or interest with happiness (Banse & Scherer, 1996, p. 632). However in psychotherapy, we must not be daunted by such studies. For one, we gain insight into the emotionality of a patient through various channels. Secondly, we explore a patient's emotional expression together with them in therapeutic communication so that we come closer to a person's subjectivity in a dialectical process of forming and verifying hypotheses.

When exploring emotions in body psychotherapy, we pay attention not only to facial expressions, posture and movement, but also to **body spaces**. Emotions capture us by taking up space in the body. We tend to experience them more in those body spaces in which we express them, since they are connected to the muscles and their function of expressive movement (Jarlnaes & van Luytelaar, 2004, p. 263; Roehricht, 2000, pp. 194–204). Also that is where we inhibit them, for example sobbing or screaming in the throat (Boadella, 1987). Attachment related emotions such as love, longing, desire, grief, fear and in part anger are felt more in the front of the body, boundary-setting anger more in the back, the nape of the neck and the shoulders. We feel excitement more in the lower abdomen, anxiety in the stomach area and panic in the head as agonising thoughts. In the case of anxiety, it is as if the arousal wanders upwards with the increase in intensity, so that in the end the connection between the head and the rest of the body is lost.

However, emotions cannot with any certainty be assigned to specific parts of the body. We experience them in various areas; for example, excitement, fear and panic can also be felt in the legs when they go weak and shaky. Likewise we cannot deduce an emotion from a sensation in one part of the body, since sorrow or joyful expectation can also make the legs go weak or heavy, and anger or joy can tense them up. In the abdomen, we can feel both the melting sensation of pleasure as well as the falling sensation of fear, when the heart sinks (Keleman, 1985; Lowen, 1977, p. 52). Surprise as well as shock shoots through the body as does the startle reflex (Section 13.1). Artists often hit the mark in this respect, for example Feuchtwanger, when he writes about a woman: 'She felt that oppressive feeling of annihilation creeping up from her heart into her throat and grabbing her by the shoulders' (1998, p. 721). Therapeutically we can encourage patients to become aware of their feelings by letting them sense exactly where the emotion is located in the body – sadness or anger that they feel in the throat, the arms, the pelvis and so on (Downing, 1996, p. 92).

On the basis of questionnaires, Nummenma et al. (2014) drew up **bodily maps of emotions**. The subjects were asked to assign various emotions to different areas of the body. The results were the same for people in Finland and in Taiwan. Emotion-specific maps of activated body sensations proved to be statistically independent of one another. Changes are often felt in the chest and seem to be connected to the breathing and the heart; in addition people feel them in the expressions of the face (Nummenma et al., 2014, p. 648). Anger or joy are felt more in the arms and are also recognised more in the arm movements (Bachmann et al., 2020), since they express a need for more closeness or more distance in relation to others, whereas sadness leads to a sense of deactivation in the arms. Disgust leads above all to sensations in the throat and digestive system. Happiness is the only emotion which evokes sensations in the body as a whole.

Children too can differentiate patterns of bodily arousal associated with happiness, fear and surprise (Hietanen et al., 2016).

10.5 REGULATION OF EMOTIONS AND THE AFFECTIVE CYCLE

In this section, I present a model of working on regulating emotions as they process and, in the following, some thoughts on reorganisation. The model in Figure 10.1 referred to three aspects of appraisal in an emotional process, whereas this one refers to the basic emotions, which interrupt the flow of experience and communicate an evaluation of an event. In this model we look at the core affective dimension of arousal of a categorical emotion not only in terms of its intensity, but also in its temporal dynamics, focusing on the therapeutically relevant blocks.

In contrast to other emotions, basic emotions usually have a short-lived dynamic activation contour (Geuter & Schrauth, 2001, 2015). They swell up, reach a peak and then ebb away. This sequence can be faster or slower, shorter or more prolonged according to the nature of the trigger and how rapidly the situation changes for the relevant person. A surprise can be sudden and fade away immediately; aggravation can build up slowly and last longer; sobbing in the therapy session can flow through the patient like a wave (Meyer, 2009). We always experience affects in a temporal dimension (Stern, 1995). Basic emotions can be like a drizzle or a downpour, but they always have a beginning and an end.

This temporal-cyclic structure holds true for basic emotions which appear as primary emotions, but not for secondary ones, such as anger superimposed on sadness, or fear covering up shame.

> Impulses and actions can follow a similar dynamic process to emotions. Gallagher and Hutto (2019) describe four phases: from the affordance, to what the acting person considers themselves capable of, to the actual deed and finally to the resolution or affirmation which consists of an appraisal of the events. They see this as an arousal curve with its high point in the deed.

Parents intuitively deal with basic emotions differently than with other emotions. If a child is sad or angry, they calm her down bodily or let her express her rage until she quietens down. To regulate a basic emotion, they influence her on a core affective level and subsequently find out what it was all about. In contrast they try to modulate self-referential emotions such as envy, jealousy or shame right from the start by talking the child through them. Body psychotherapy is similar. Working with emotional arousal is usually work with basic emotions (Geuter, 2019, p. 171). 'Working with more complex emotions needs to be done in enactments or by clarifying them on a cognitive-emotional level. We cannot resolve guilt or jealousy by crying or punching the bag' (Geuter & Schrauth, 2001, p. 10). However we can utilise expressive techniques with these feelings too, as long as we have exposed the basic emotions hidden in them, for example anger in jealousy or fear in arrogance.

The following **model of the temporal cycle of affective processes** by Geuter and Schrauth (2001, 2015) is based on the concept of the vasomotor cycle as submitted by Southwell (1988). It depicts in abstract the process of the arousal of an emotion as a curve. In this it resembles Reich's (1973) sexual excitation curve and the arousal curve in the contact cycle of Gestalt therapy (Gremmler-Fuhr, 1999, p. 362).

The model (Figure 10.3) assumes that starting from a state of rest, an increase in arousal occurs due to a trigger, leading to an expression of feeling or to a discharge of affective energy, resulting in a decline in arousal, followed by a phase of recuperation and the integration of the experience. The corresponding processes take place on the following levels: vegetative, autonomic body processes, voluntary and involuntary muscular activity and cognitively experienced conscious feelings (Section 6.1). During the increase in arousal, there is usually a movement in relation to the object, whereas during the decline in arousal, there is usually an inward movement towards the auto-regulation of the emotional event. This model is based on the notion of homoeostasis, whereby after having been challenged by a stimulus, living systems always attempt to return to a state of equilibrium. However this does not mean that the system strives towards the lowest set point, but rather that it is always in dynamic motion between reaction and equilibrium (Chapter 17).

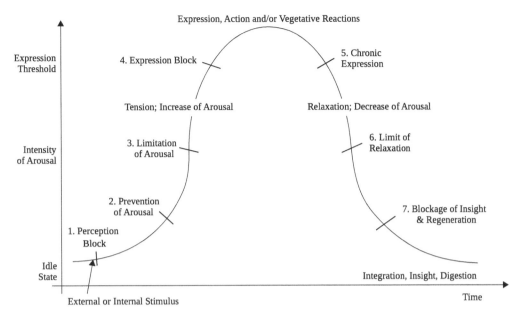

FIGURE 10.3 The affective cycle and its blocks

In this model, we can distinguish various points where the cycle of an emotional event can typically be blocked and which necessitate different approaches in therapy:

1. The first possible block is that a person is **not aware** of an emotion-triggering event or of the first signs of emotion associated with it. This is a **dissociation of the event**. An important situation is perceived as unimportant. Dealing with this limitation is essential for progress in therapy (Storch, 2003, p. 17).

The therapeutic task in this case is to help the patient become aware of the situation and its personal relevance. Here we need to sharpen awareness. Developing their bodily self-perception helps the patient to become aware of signals that an event is significant.

2. A second block could be that a patient perceives an event or an object consciously or unconsciously, but the emotional **arousal is inhibited**. A **dissociation of experience** can prevent it completely: the emotional relevance of what they have experienced is kept out of consciousness. In the body this is achieved for example by a sudden rigidity accompanied by holding one's breath. It is possible that only the vegetative signs of an affect are in evidence, for instance a reddening of the skin or pressure in the chest, or that the affect expresses itself in the clenching of fists without the patient being aware of it. Then they communicate their emotional state without perceiving it (Griffith & Griffith, 1994, p. 46).

Therapeutically, it is helpful to point out these affect signals or to invite the patient to tolerate the arousal that they inhibit through freezing. This last can be done in various ways: for example trauma patients can relate their experience again, all the while mobilising resources and letting the body shake out the tension (Levine, 1997), or well-integrated patients can be provoked through therapeutic interventions to increase their arousal level.

3. The third block is when the patient perceives the emotional arousal but inhibits it. For example, a child becomes sad and their throat starts to open for crying. They promptly tighten the throat and so prevent the crying; Downing (1996, p. 193) views this as countermobilisation (Section 13.1). A man feels his longing, but then his voice fails or he skips over it and makes perhaps an untimely joke. This is a **dissociation of the impulse**, not of the experience, the **suppression of a lived reaction**, not of the emotional experience; he is conscious of the feeling (Greenberg & Bischkopf, 2007, p. 171). Trauma patients can experience hyperarousal, but because of the hopelessness they lived through during the trauma, they have to suppress their action impulses. The intensity of the emotional experience can also be chronically dampened, for example in children of depressive mothers, who control their enjoyment (Chapter 11).

Therapeutically, the task here is to help the patient to stay with their feeling and its intensity and to tolerate it while noticing its dynamics; for example the therapist directs the patient's attention towards sensing the arousal and to becoming aware of the signs of the feeling in the body. Trauma patients have to learn to perceive the arousal, to maintain it and to control it, so that they can make contact with strong sensations (Levine, 2010). Here the patient must be able to regulate core affect so that they can then cope with the categorical emotion.

4. Some people can feel the magnitude of the emotion they are experiencing, but they cannot express it because of shame or fear of the consequences. For example, a patient is sad, but resists admitting this to his wife because he is afraid that she will reject him as a man. Another patient is angry but afraid that the anger will destroy their relationship and so keeps it hidden. People caught in this block **suppress their emotional expression and action impulses**.

Here the task of therapy is to encourage emotional expressivity in general and towards the relevant object in particular, in words or deeds. This could be, for instance, expressing despair by clinging to someone or anger by hitting or kicking something.

5. Then there are people whose experience of emotional arousal is so overwhelming that they express their feelings with an intensity others find inappropriate. It is also difficult for them to stop. They **maintain the arousal** without it abating. This overly strong expression is usually accompanied by an 'over-identification with the emotional state' (Reddemann, 2004, p. 83). These people often do not see their emotionality as an issue; however they do have problems with the consequences of their actions. This is often the case with borderline patients.

When the arousal does not die down, then each new stimulus hits this high level of excitement and adds to the drama. Some patients are permanently in a pseudo-cathartic state. When emotions go on for a longer period of time without abating, then we are dealing with a personality disorder: chronic sadness, chronic anger or chronic anxiety. In therapy, the task is to limit the arousal, to recognise the defensive function of the dysfunctional expressivity or to find the affects buried beneath the excessive affectivity.

6. The next block is when someone can let go of a fierce outbreak or expression of emotion, but **cannot** completely **calm down**. This is not only the case with problematic emotions such as fear or anger. Sometimes we are so happy that we cannot quieten down and feel that we are too excited or even in a hypomanic state. In this case we need a way of helping the excitement to abate, letting us become calm. To do this we employ basically the same methods as those used to influence core affect (Geuter, 2019, pp. 208–13).

7. The last block in an emotional episode is when, despite the reduction in the level of arousal the patient, cannot integrate the experience cognitively and emotionally and thus cannot find their way to an inner equilibrium. Here we could speak of an **insight block**. Here it is important that the patient can process, understand and integrate their experience and reach their own conclusions about it. If they can also feel in the body what they have understood, if there is congruence between the words and body sensations, then the understanding is more profound.

However, emotional processes can begin in a different way than described in this model, for instance with a parasympathetic freeze, which needs to be balanced out by a recovery and activation phase (Section 7.1). Patients can also suffer from hypervigilant perception or an overly rapid build-up of tension (Kern, 2014, p. 62). Then the arousal curve was too high from the outset. These patients need stronger borders in relation to stimuli or an easing of their tensions. The above model does not do justice to these aspects.

Affect integration

Solbakken et al. (2012) refer to the capacity to access and utilise the adaptive properties of affects for personal adjustment as affect integration. Their definition of affect integration includes the ability to consciously perceive and tolerate an affect, to reflect on it and to express the experience related to it, i.e. accessing and dealing with affects. In this broad understanding of the concept, we could regard the affective cycle as one of affect integration.

The evaluation of the data of a Norwegian multicentre study on outcome in psychotherapy shows that patients who have difficulties with affect integration benefit from unlimited, open, long-term therapy.

Geuter and Schrauth's model is similar to Mergenthaler's (1996) model of cyclical processes in therapy. According to this model, the sequence of relaxation – arousal – experience and reflection – pure reflection – relaxation is favourable for the course of a therapy session. Geuter and Schrauth's model too can be applied to an individual session when it includes working with a strong emotional process in body psychotherapy and the patient goes through an emotional cycle (see the last case study in this chapter). There are also similarities to Rudolf's (2006, pp. 38ff) model of the affect cascade. However, Rudolf does not link his process model of affective experience to core affects, so that he only differentiates two levels: the experienced affect and its expression and communication.

In any case, emotions do not surge up and then ebb away, going through schematically determined phases in the process, as it would seem from this model. Rather they are then processed further (Figure 10.4). Emotions communicate something not only to the subject but also to the environment. They are a **communication** tool. Moreover, we rarely express our emotions in the raw prototypical form of the biologically determined affect programmes. A person's actual emotional response to a situation is generated through a complex inner process that subjects the primary reaction to **feeling rules** (e.g. 'Do not wear your heart on your sleeve!') and personal rules on the presentation of emotions, so-called **display rules** (e.g. 'Let no one see how upset you are!') (Levenson (1999, p. 499). People also follow **cultural rules**, which partly determine whether and to what extent we reveal an emotion, e.g. in one context being especially cool, in another acting out emotions histrionically, in a third not showing our tears (Kitayama et al., 2006). It is also defined culturally when an

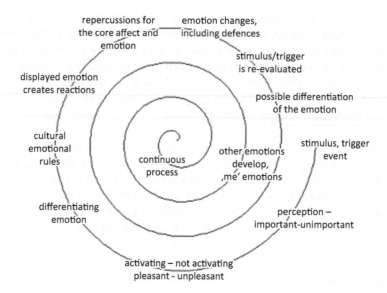

repercussions for   emotion changes,
the core affect and   including defences
emotion
                                   stimulus/trigger
                                   is re-evaluated
displayed emotion
creates reactions
                                   possible differentiation
                                   of the emotion
cultural
emotional   other emotions   stimulus, trigger
rules   develop,   event
            continuous ,me' emotions
            process
differentiating   perception –
emotion   important-unimportant

activating – not activating
pleasant - unpleasant

FIGURE 10.4 Progression of an emotional process

emotion should be over, e.g. the rules about the year of grief to get over the loss of a loved one. When today the DSM defines a period of grief longer than two weeks as pathological, this is less a case of cultural emotional rules and more one of disease mongering for the benefit of the manufacturers of anti-depressants (Kleinman, 2012).

Emotions often call on other people to behave towards me in a certain way, for example to be careful in the case of anger, or to offer comfort for sadness. They create resonance. This in turn reflects back on the emotion, which perhaps becomes milder or more intense, is repressed or held back, maybe even goes through a change in mood. Basic emotions can change into self-referential emotions – from anger perhaps to envy or jealousy, from joy to pride, from surprise to shame. Thus emotions change in the course of dealing with a situation or another person. The process of appraisal of a situation begins with the interruption through a basic emotion, but it does not end there, especially when the question is what implications, both cognitive and behavioural, this emotional experience has for someone and how this affects the world around them (Brosch & Scherer, 2009). As part of an intersubjective world, feelings are atmospheres in which people are collectively immersed and which they also create collectively (Schmitz, 1992, pp. 135–52; Wildt, 2001). Feelings connect people to the world. In this being-together they develop a range and power which often accounts for the fascination of body-oriented and experiential therapy groups.

Vitality affects

Stern (1985) has described the temporal changes in the flow pattern of affects as vitality affects. With this he means that affects can, for example, explode, rush in or fade away. A person's behaviour can exhibit the corresponding qualities without them experiencing a particular categorical emotion. In this, Stern's concept is similar to that of core affects; however the difference is that he is looking at the dynamics of the process. Vitality affects are **activation- and process-contours**, such as adults express in dancing or in music. According to Stern, they appear in the affective interchange between people as dynamic, kinetic feeling qualities, which are an essential part of affective attunement. Working with emotional regulation in psychotherapy, we can directly influence these process-contours (Geuter, 2019, pp. 203–5).

> When listening to the lullabies or dance music of other cultures, in half the cases people can identify the content (Mehr et al., 2019). It appears that characteristics similar to process-contours are important here: tempo, rhythm, accentuations, the length of the intervals or of the notes.

Stern names three properties of vitality affects as intensity, time pattern and Gestalt. They correspond to the three notions of weight, time and space, which von Laban used to describe movement (Section 14.2). So, the intensity of an affect can be high or low and change over time. In terms of the Gestalt of a movement process, an affect can surface abruptly or develop slowly; it can have a more expansive or contractive tendency. It is in the activation-contour of an affect that we often recognise its specific quality. For example, we can be brought to tears through various feelings such as helplessness, loneliness, burn-out and sympathy (Barthelmaes et al., 2022), and the process of crying also varies. Depending on its form we can differentiate between helpful crying, protest crying, dramatic crying or persistent crying that has uncoupled from its original cause (Fogel, 2009, pp. 110–1).

Clinical application

A mother harmonises with her child by attuning herself to their affective experience in intensity, time pattern and Gestalt (Nicely et al., 1999). Similarly a psychotherapist must engage with the vitality contours of the patient if they want to help them explore and change their emotional experience (Geuter & Schrauth, 2015). In so doing, they can take up the respective contour and change it, letting the intensity increase or decrease, speeding up or slowing down the time or reinforcing the Gestalt, for example if it is expansive, exaggerating this or mirroring it through a contraction, or changing it or transposing it into another modality (Trautmann-Voigt & Voigt, 2009, p. 119).

According to Stern (1985), the affect interchange between people follows not only these three features, but also a beat, a rhythm and an intensity contour. Emotions too can be described in terms of their movement contour in time and space, which also express affect-motor schemas in the relationship (Chapter 12).

10.6 THE RESTRUCTURING OF EMOTIONS

Downing (1996, pp. 92–3) has designated three procedural steps for working with affects in psychotherapy:

1. Becoming clearly aware of the affect and letting it act on the body.
2. Naming the affect.
3. Establishing a relationship to the intentional object of the affect.

Downing is concerned here not with the regulation of the arousal, but with clarifying and restructuring the emotions. Clarification is always a subjective matter, since emotional experience and its relation to the intentional object are highly subjective, even if emotional reactions follow certain patterns (Frijda, 1996). One aspect of clarification is understanding the motivational and intentional significance of an affect, for instance, why I am afraid of someone or of a situation and what would have to happen so that I would no longer need to be afraid. Fear of, fear itself and fear for are, according to Heidegger (1962), three questions regarding fear. An emotion only has personal significance when the client knows what they feel towards whom, regarding which need and which issue (Boritz et al., 2011, p. 17). Affect consciousness only develops when activation, perception, expression and reflection are all present (Monsen & Monsen, 1999). Clarification and restructuring need to be done on the basis of reflection.

Clinical application

In therapy we have to clarify the following: what feeling is it exactly? In what situation does it appear? What is the relationship between me and my opposite number in that situation? What do I need and what skills do I have to fulfil these needs? And what do I conclude from all this (cf. Rudolf, 2006, p. 41)? The connection to the needs and intention in an emotion is essential (Section 10.3). Examples: Am I sad? What makes me sad? What would I wish for in this sadness? Who do I expect this from? What could I do myself? And what does all this tell me? We can facilitate this verbal psychotherapeutic work with body psychotherapeutic techniques such as exploring these questions with the help of somatic sensations and motor impulses.

For Downing (1996, p. 98), restructuring means that the patient finds a new affect-motor schema that helps them to express the affect in a different way and that they become familiar with this new schema (Chapter 12). We can go through this with the patient, for example by letting them try out what they can achieve with an imagined partner through their affect. Affects are connected to patterns and schemas, scenes and scripts and are organised around them (Monsen & Monsen, 1999). We can access and change them through affect awareness. Restructuring means also that the function of an affect has been understood and if necessary an adaptive affect substituted for a maladaptive one, for example a constructive anger that can change a relationship, instead of a nagging, destructive jealousy.

This corresponds to one of Greenberg's (2011) basic principles as mentioned above, that emotions can only be changed through emotions. If someone can feel the anger hidden in their grief at having been abandoned by someone, then they can deal more easily with the sadness. I have presented an example of this elsewhere (Geuter, 2019, p. 287). And if someone can feel the sadness concealed behind their anger, then they can learn to let go of the anger. If someone can follow their curiosity despite their fear, then they will learn to overcome it. And if someone experiences the comfort of attachment while grieving, this can soothe their grief.

According to a model of Emotion-Focused Therapy, patients move 'from a state of global distress through fear, shame, and aggressive anger to the articulation of needs and negative self-evaluations; then they would move on to assertive anger, self-soothing, hurt, and grief as states indicating more advanced processing' of unfinished emotions (Elliot et al., 2013, p. 517).

In Emotion-Focused Therapy, Auszra et al. (2017, p. 87) name seven criteria by means of which we can determine whether a patient is experiencing an emotion in a helpful way:

- Does the patient turn towards the feeling?
- Do they symbolise it?
- Are the emotional expression and the verbal symbolisation congruent?
- Does the patient accept themselves and the emotion?
- Do they accept responsibility for the feeling and are they prepared to work on it?
- Is the emotion sufficiently regulated?
- Is it sufficiently differentiated or becoming more differentiated over time?

Living through affective processes eventually changes memory, particularly when avoided emotions become conscious. This is because affective processes are represented as episodes with the subject experiencing them, an object related to them and a specific interaction between the two (Krause, 2006, p. 23). These episodes form the building blocks of the episodic memory, which can be modified when the contents are invoked with an intense emotional involvement and then stored anew (Chapter 9).

Case study

A depressive patient, who feels a lack of orientation both in his work and in his private life, talks about a man in his men's group. He experiences it as if this man is saying to him that he is not a real man. He connects this to his overpowering father, who always demanded that he perform well, but never gave him any support as a child. We set up a fictional scene in the therapy room, whereby he encounters both the man from the group and his father. He says to both things like 'You shouldn't dictate to me! You are not the boss. I want you to respect me!' Initially he stands there slumped over, his head lowered, chest caved in and pelvis too. I suggest that he change his posture somewhat and try to straighten up. The change in posture is meant to help improve his self-esteem.

This little change releases a flood of anger. He wants to hit a foam block I have there. I tell him I will stand opposite him on the other side of the block as his father. The reason for this is that then, in enacted transference, he can direct the massive rage he feels in his body towards an intentional object. He growls at me: 'Leave me alone! Go to your new wife! I want nothing more to do with you!' Then this makes him sad; the reason for the anger is that his father never really saw him, never appreciated him. He only acknowledged him when he learnt to recite the Greek alphabet very early on. Using one of Pesso's techniques, I offer to be his ideal father and say to him that I see him and am glad he is there. He cries deeply. I stretch my hands towards him as an offer of contact and he grasps them over the block. Then he wants to embrace me.

In this example, the feeling of impotence towards the man in the group is transformed first into rage, which is greatly intensified by the change in posture and by directing it at the father. By becoming aware of this rage and letting it flow through the body, naming it, and expressing it in relation to the intentional object, the father, as Downing describes the three steps of working with affects, the patient can feel the disappointment and sorrow he felt in the face of his father's attitude towards him. Experiencing his rage in this intensity creates an autonomous overturn from one emotion into another. As he goes through this in the enactment with me, he can articulate his need to be seen and can accept a corrective experience. This leads to affective restructuring, and in his memory he can see his father slightly differently. In the embrace, he experiences affection and a safe attachment. When after the arousal of a negative emotion a positive feeling emerges, as is the case here, then there is a period of calm in which autonomous self-regulation can take place (Fredrickson, 1998, pp. 313–4).

For an emotion to be restructured, it has to be consciously connected to the object and its significance in relation to the subject. What I defined as a feeling at the beginning of this chapter is basically the relatively conscious perception of these aspects in the course of an emotional process with all the other aspects listed in Figure 10.4. Information of various kinds comes together in a feeling. According to Damasio (1999), a feeling develops when a change in the state of the organism is represented. In a feeling, specific bodily sensations connect to conscious information (Stepper & Strack, 1993, p. 219). In a feeling, we consciously perceive the situational significance of an emotion and we symbolise the emotional experience. In a feeling, the affect sensed in the body comes together with the mental image, which as Freud asserted, is separated from it in the repression of the affect. 'Feelings on the other hand are always hidden, like all mental images necessarily are, unseen to anyone other than their rightful owner' (Damasio, 2004, p. 28).

In an emotional process, the consciously perceived feeling comes later than the somatic reaction, because the cognitive processing of information, a function of the cortex, takes longer than the emotional reactions controlled by the limbic system. In this respect, James (1994) was right in saying in 1894 that an emotion follows the bodily reaction, but not that it is a result of the perception of a physical act of expression – meaning that we feel afraid as a result of running away from the bear. An emotion is a coherent process in which the external and internal somatic emotional reactions happen faster than the cognitive components of the emotional experience, but then come together with them in the conscious feeling. In this coherent process, the feeling does not originate in the bodily sensations, nor does the emotional sensation originate in the cognitive evaluation; rather both arise from the interaction with the triggering event. In feeling, however, we can reflect in language on the emotional reaction. Thus feelings encourage our human capacity for flexible and complex action.

Le Doux (1996) confirms neurobiologically that in the case of fear, the bodily reaction is faster than the cognitive. In the brain, fear is processed in two ways: a fast one, independent of the neocortex, and a slower one via the neocortex. Because of the faster path, I flinch first and only later do I see through the slower path what rustled. The observation that the body reacts faster than the mind is explained here in a different way than in the theory of William James and Karl Lange at the end of the 19th century, in which emotions are seen as conscious perceptions of body reactions.

Working with restructuring emotionality requires a dialectical process between implicit experience and conscious reflection (Bischkopff, 2009). Only then can patients become aware of and influence their feelings. This work fulfils the third of the three principles of emotional processing that Greenberg (2004) has identified as promoting change: transforming and reflecting on the emotion. The first two of Greenberg's principles, increasing awareness of emotion and enhancing emotional regulation, both belong to the classic tasks of body psychotherapy and its corresponding techniques. Therapeutic work on emotionality encompasses all of these principles.

11

Child development

The shaping of experience in early affect motor dialogue

Children acquire basic patterns of experiencing the body and the self, of emotional experience, affect regulation and an interactional repertoire of expression through their early lives, which in their first few years are deeply rooted in the body (Frank & La Barre, 2011; Marmeleira & Duarte Santos, 2019). In order to understand patients and their suffering and also to correlate some of the phenomena that appear in therapy, we need to tap into those life experiences which shape their present-day lives and behaviour. Knowledge of developmental psychology can help us here. We need it too when in a session we invite a patient to explore and express early experiences through pre-verbal sensorimotor movement patterns such as clinging, sobbing or throwing a tantrum (Heisterkamp, 1993, p. 50).

It is impossible to describe here everything one needs to know about child development. The aim of this chapter must be to elucidate various aspects which seem to me important specifically for the theory and practice of body psychotherapy. Among these I include how, through both pre- and perinatal as well as early pre-verbal experiences, through affective bodily dialogues an early self develops and lifelong patterns of need, stress and affect regulation and attachment are formed, all of which we are concerned with in treatment.

Until now, body psychotherapy has concentrated on the developmental theory of the early years. Bentzen (2015) criticises that there is no research on the significance of pre-puberty and puberty for character development. I too will concentrate on the early years, since it is then that the basic patterns of regulative and affect motor interactive strategies are formed. They are stored in the emotional-procedural memory, the only repository available to the small child as a store of affective experiences (Kandel, 1999, p. 513; Section 11.3). Episodic memories can only begin in the middle or at the end of the second year (Knopf et al., 2011). Furthermore, earliest childhood is crucial in the genesis of mental disorders; according to Grawe (2007), empirical research leaves no doubt about this.

Psychoanalysis and behaviourism both initially regarded the baby as passive and unrelated, governed by instinctual drives or formed through conditioning. Humanistic psychology, on the other hand, understood babies as active and interested beings (Buehler, 1979, p. 12). Modern developmental psychology confirms this view: the child is from birth onwards relational and competent (Dornes, 1993, p. 16).

- Newborns recognise the voice of their mother, prefer her scent and in their first months can combine stimuli from various sense areas.
- Three-day old infants love to control the singing of a female voice through sucking movements on a pacifier (Dornes, 1993, p. 237).

DOI: 10.4324/9781003176893-11

- When newborns hear the recorded crying of another baby, they cry more than if they hear their own recorded crying. They seem to live in relationship (Reddy, 2008, p. 124).
- When they are shown a film of one of their own movements, they coordinate their movements with what they are seeing. According to Reddy (2008, p. 125), this shows an awareness of their own body.
- Newborns prefer the drawing of a human face to one where the face is turned upside down.
- Six weeks after birth, they copy behaviour seen 24 hours before, namely sticking the tongue out or opening the mouth (Meltzoff & Moore, 1994). This shows that they already have motor memory, since they can convert something seen into movement. Linking visual perception to motor function is a sign that infants have a body schema, which was probably acquired in the womb (Gallagher, 2003, p. 19; Reed & McIntosh, 2008, p. 86).

Babies show their intentions and needs through body language and call for a response (Trevarthen & Aitken, 2001). Therefore relational psychoanalysis now sees infants as relational beings. However, they underestimate the significance of the body in experiencing the outer world and the moulding of the inner (White, 2004a). Babies take possession of the world through grasping, biting or crawling. Sensorimotor experiences shape their development of the body self. Their cognitive learning processes are initially organised in a sensorimotor fashion (Piaget & Inhelder, 2000). When parents rock their babies, push against their kicking legs, lift them up or put them down, they not only interact on a personal level but are also showing their children space, pressure and gravity (Cheney, 2019).

> The early stages of development are frequently described as pre-verbal. This designates language as a reference point of development. However, we could say instead that language is post-kinetic (Sheets-Johnstone, 2017), as communication takes place first of all through movement and bodily expression. Primary intersubjectivity is established through bodily communication.

According to Adolf Portmann's idea (1951), human beings are physiologically premature births. Having arrived in the world, we depend for quite some time on someone else for survival. The child therefore expresses its needs so that others take care of them. They learn what their needs are, and the strategies required to get them met, in interaction with others. In this way they grow into the culture.

Infants show the tension between needs and their fulfilment and whether or not they have reached their goal through affect expression (Tronick, 1989). The way infants communicate their needs and how the environment responds mould their psychic structure. If need regulation goes awry, this leaves bodily memory traces and experience patterns that can lead to disorders (Dornes, 2000, p. 29).

Psychopathological symptoms often develop through a long chain of difficult experiences faced by children struggling to satisfy their desires (Tronick, 1989, p. 117). Such early experiences can effectively shape a person's vulnerability (von Arnim et al., 2022, pp. 64–8). According to the diathesis stress model, they predispose to psychopathology. Grawe (2004) maintains therefore that interpersonal relationships and their traces in memory are the most important breeding ground for mental disorders. In the beginning of psychoanalysis, Ferenczi, Rank and Reich all held the view that neuroses were based above all on real childhood experiences and not so much on fantasies as Freud and Klein assumed. Thinking in body psychotherapy follows this tradition (Marlock, 2015b).

Depressive mothers

Studies on the interaction between children and depressive mothers show how early affect motor strategies develop. More than half of small babies of depressive mothers did not smile to attract the attention of their mother (Moore et al., 2001). When a mother is manifestly depressive over a longer time, then the infant tends to adopt her 'slowed-down affect motor style of interaction', so that the depression is introjected 'on the behavioural and physical level' (Dornes, 1997, p. 68). As adults they can then transfer this style of interaction onto non-depressive people and thus induce despondency in them. Communication of emotional states takes place here 'in the medium of non-verbal affect signals (body posture, vocalisation, speed of movement, facial expression)' (Dornes, 1997, p. 69). In this way, the child unconsciously acquires an affect motor schema (Chapter 12).

As shown in still-face experiments, in which the reactions of babies to a sudden voluntary rigidity of the mother's facial expression and gestures are studied (Section 11.3), it is more difficult for babies of depressive mothers to find their way back to a self-regulation of the tension that still-face caused in them than for the children of healthy mothers. They do show self-soothing but also more agitated behaviour, and only with difficulty can they move their attention to other things (Manian & Bornstein, 2009). Also, they try less to attract their mother's attention vocally. When however they are reunited with the mother, they are more active than other children (Field et al., 2007, p. 321).

We could interpret this as being a schema that babies have who are worried about their mother: their attention stays with the mother rather than moving to something else, and when she returns to them, they reward her with intense displays of affection. This can lead to them controlling their own needs and to an oral character structure (Section 13.2), characterised by unrequited desires and a resigned attitude in interactive behaviour. Such a schema of experiencing and behaviour can originate long before the development of language.

11.1 PRE- AND PERINATAL IMPRINTING

Children's very first experiences are those with their own bodies in the womb. During pregnancy, the foetus develops all the senses early on (Graven & Browne, 2008):

- First the sense of touch develops. The earliest sensitivity reaction of the foetus is for pressure stimuli on the lips (Grunwald, 2012, p. 42). In the fourth week the innervation of the skin of the extremities begins: now they can sense their hand on the wall of the womb or on the placenta (von Arnim et al., 2022, p. 183). From the eighth week, touch triggers motor reactions. From the tenth week on, the hand moves recognisably to the face (Piontelli, 1992). From week 12–13 of pregnancy, the foetus purposefully grasps the umbilical cord.
- From week 16 on, they hear the heartbeat and the voice of the mother and notice light (Chamberlain, 1997).
- Proprioceptively, the foetus notices that they are swimming in the amniotic fluid. From the seventh week, they move spontaneously without stimulus from outside. At this stage the limbic system matures (Roth 2001, pp. 335, 456).

The foetus learns by using and practising bodily functions. They begin to construct a sensorimotor body schema when, for example, they put a thumb in their mouth and can sense themselves both in the thumb and in the mouth. Also they learn to differentiate between their own body and that of others. With twins between weeks 14 and 18, movements directed towards the partner increase in comparison to self-related movements (Castiello et al., 2010). After birth, children can differentiate between whether they are touching themselves or someone else is touching them (Rochat, 2003, pp. 262–3). They learnt the implicit knowledge they need for this in the womb.

However, people who were born without a limb can still have phantom sensations. Gallagher (2003, p. 22) sees this as an indication that we have an innate body schema. But these phantom sensations could also be a co-sensing of the limbs of others and as such the result of learning processes at a later stage.

The significance of pre- and perinatal experience for the life of the psyche has hardly been broached in psychology textbooks. In body psychotherapy, however, it is an important issue as experiences which are difficult to articulate verbally are often the subject of treatment (Boadella, 1998), relying on clinical observation. Apart from some research on the aftereffects of pressure and stress (Section 11.4), empirical research has paid little attention to the relationship between pre- and perinatal experiences and the psyche of adults. Also, by its very nature, such research is extremely difficult, so that statements about it tend to be hypothetical. However, behavioural observation and neurobiological research support the basic assumption that psychological and social life begin before birth and that experiences from that stage are stored in the body (Glenn, 2015). Our knowledge of the long-term effects of these experiences is growing (Hartmann & Belsky, 2018). We know that in the womb the initial imprinting of the ability to manage stress takes place. In addition, attachment problems and traumatisation can occur during pregnancy, for example if the mother experiences violence (Hochauf, 2006). This is particularly important in body psychotherapy with children and adolescents (Schmitter-Boeckelmann, 2013; Unfried, 2006).

In theories of the development of the self (Section 11.2), a joint focus of attention is viewed as a prerequisite of intersubjectivity. **Joint attention** however already starts **in the womb**. The foetus participates directly in the intentions, emotions and behaviour of another person, whether it is the mother or a twin, and this shared experience precedes any cognitive involvement (Ciaunica, 2019). The encounter through the skin precedes that through the eyes. Piontelli (1992) observed single babies and twins in the womb via ultrasonic scans and after birth. They showed similar affect motor patterns:

- A girl who in the womb had sucked on her hands and on the placenta, sucked as a newborn intensively on the hand and skin of the mother.
- One-year-old twins loved to play a game where, separated by a cloth, they rubbed their heads together. In the womb these two had done the same thing with the membrane that separated them.
- Piontelli noticed that with another pair of twins, in the 18th week of pregnancy, the girl, who was very active, would move towards her more passive brother and touch him. He in turn would move away from her. This pattern of approach and withdrawal typified their later relationship.

Piontelli inferred from this that the womb is not a dark, quiet place, but rather an individual physical environment and an interaction space. In this space the mother and child interact. The mother's lifestyle and feelings affect the unborn child. Children of mothers who are afraid of pregnancy and of giving birth are slower in their mental and motoric development than children of less anxious mothers. The same is true for children of mothers exposed to pressure and stress in their daily lives (Huizink, 2000). Children of extremely anxious mothers move more in the womb and tend later to have attention deficit problems (Van den Bergh, 1990).

Newborns of depressive mothers have lower motor tone and are less expressive. During pregnancy, depressive mothers pass on their altered hormone levels to their babies (Lundy et al., 1999). The children later have increased levels of cortisol and noradrenaline and lower levels of dopamine; they enter the world with a sympathetic arousal level that is too high. On a biologically programmed level of stress regulation, they are basically disturbed in their capacity to regulate affects. This is important in psychotherapy. Often, disturbed affect regulation can only be treated in tandem with this stress regulation disorder (Section 11.4).

Predisposition to illness on a physiological level can already develop in the womb. Nathanielsz (1999) did an epidemiological evaluation of the long-term effects of the winter of starvation in Holland in 1944–1945. People whose mothers were starving in the first trimester of pregnancy were later more likely to be obese than those whose mothers starved in the last trimester. This was because at the beginning of pregnancy, the deficit leads to an increase in growth of the placenta. A deficit at the end of pregnancy, in contrast, leads to a lower quantity of fat cells in the foetus. These pre-dispositions are passed on through the generations. Women who weighed less at their own birth were more likely to give birth to smaller babies in their turn.

Thus, prenatal experiences can show themselves in symptoms. A baby who was almost miscarried withdrew into the womb and became immobile; later the child suffered from claustrophobia (Piontelli, 1992). According to an epidemiological study in Finland, children whose fathers died before they were born were more likely to be schizophrenic (Huttunen & Niskanen, 1978).

Prenatal traumatisation

Traumatic experiences during pregnancy can disrupt the perception and regulation of bodily needs and of cold or warmth, hunger or fullness, or of pain. Later on this comes up more in sensorimotor impressions than in images (Hochauf, 2006, p. 129). These often form matrices for further traumatic experiences. Hochauf illustrates this with a patient who coped with her near-death experience by floating, losing her body awareness and longing for death (Hochauf, 2006, pp. 131–2). During pregnancy, her mother had had serious medical complications.

If the child is rejected during pregnancy, this can show up later in the form of dreams, fantasies, anxiety or illnesses. In transference an abortion attempt can come back as a persistent, inexplicable feeling that the therapist wants to be rid of the patient (Sonne, 1996).

Clinical example

Huber (2000) writes of a patient who believed that she had no place on this earth, who numbed her feelings and suffered from abdominal cramps, diarrhoea and migraines. In her dreams she was always in danger. In a therapy session, as she breathes deeply into the belly, she sees herself in there, is scared to death and thinks she can see something pale and pointy coming towards her. She knows from her mother that after her she aborted several babies. The image and the sensations convince her that the mother had tried to do it to her too and that this is linked to her condition.

Studies with ultrasound show that some foetuses recoil from the needle during amniocentesis and freeze up or reduce their breathing (Chamberlain, 1997, p. 29). We can observe the foetus withdrawing from touch from the 5th week of pregnancy onwards. The Moro reflex is an early form of startle response in which the embryo suddenly breathes in, the arms move quickly upwards, the legs open and then close again (Trautmann-Voigt & Voigt, 2009, p. 60). After birth, the reflex is triggered when the baby's head is not held and he loses support (Frank, 2001, pp. 83–4). At the age of 2–4 months, it is cortically inhibited as are other primitive reflexes (Cozolino, 2002, p. 76). When adults go through severe traumatisation, this inhibition can be released and the reflex reappears. Then the body regresses to this most primitive form of the startle response (Section 13.1).

Clinical application

In emotionally very difficult therapeutic situations, patients find that when the therapist holds their head, this calms them down and can contain the shock of the regression.

Lost twins

Piontelli (1992) reports on a boy of 18 months who was suffering from restlessness. When the therapist offered the interpretation that it seemed as if he was always looking for something he had lost and could not find, the parents said that there had been a twin brother who died two weeks before the birth and with whom he spent this time still together in the womb.

Almost 30% or more of conceptions are said to be twins or multiples (Noble, 1996). A number of embryos miscarry with bleeding, and foetuses are absorbed by the placenta.

Clinical example

The symptoms of one patient pointed to her having had a twin who died in the womb. For weeks she is painfully absorbed in the fact that she cannot let go of the twin, who had lived on in her fantasies all her childhood. In addition she cannot distinguish herself from the other or accept that she lives on while the other has died. She cannot think of herself as one of two, as she has no experience of a real twin and of differentiating herself from them. In her case, there is no paranoid belief, as she is mentally completely clear. For a long time, she had carried a little heart around with her in a pouch as a symbol of the lost twin, but now she has discarded it. However she cannot separate herself from them, since she cannot know which is her heart and which is theirs. In an active imagination she sees a little being, which is both outside her and also half of her head. When I ask her what this little being wants, she says: it wants to play.

In body psychotherapy, we can work with this fantasy on the level of pre-verbal childhood experience. I invite her to play twins, to which she happily acquiesces. We lie down on the floor next to each other and roll around separately. She nudges me tentatively with her fingers. I respond by nudging her. We play this game for a while. She touches herself and me as if it is difficult for her to perceive who is who. So I touch her in a way that she can feel: we are two. I respond to her touch with some pressure as a sign that here another body is at work. I gradually guide the contact so that our fingers touch and hers press against mine and vice versa.

From outside our play probably looks just like an amusing game; however there is a therapeutic purpose behind it: to let her experience on a sensorimotor level the sensation that her body is separate from the other. To tell her that in words is useless. She knows it already but she cannot feel it. Because of her erstwhile experience, her body works against this knowledge. She says: 'I know I'm a single person, but it's not true.' Because it does not feel like that; the knowledge does not **live** in her. The body supports a belief which overrides rational insight. This can only be changed through a corrective bodily and ultimately deeply emotional experience either in life or in therapy.

Birth experiences

Otto Rank, who wrote *The Trauma of Birth* in 1924, was convinced that human beings were shaped by the birth experience and would re-experience birth sensations in psychoanalysis. Rank believed that fear experienced at birth would repeat itself in separation anxiety. Together with Ferenczi, he thought that psychological symptoms emerge in the form of compulsory repetition of unconscious content. However now that gentle birth is generally advocated, unless we accept Rank's assumption of a paradise lost, we cannot presuppose that birth is unavoidably traumatic. But clinical experience suggests that traumatic birth experiences do exist. Pre- and perinatal traumatisation can be an early, extreme and often near fatal experience that can shape the child's relationship to the world (Hochauf, 1999, p. 514). Elsewhere I have written about my own experience, that under emotional stress, sensations of constriction in the chest would appear. In a body psychotherapy group, as I relived my own birth, this developed into a prolonged choking fit – a repeat of a birth experience of almost suffocating (Geuter, 2002). A patient who got stuck in the birth canal had as her greatest fear that she would be tortured and often felt that she was helpless and not able to get through something, as well as having repeated nightmares in which she was strangled – possibly a result of a nuchal cord.

When traumatic experiences are reactivated, they tend to reproduce themselves 'with a similar psychosomatic and affective response as in the original event' (Hochauf, 2001, p. 49). The early trauma is 'fixated in a precise action schema of the situation' (Hochauf, 2001, p. 50). And being stored without context, it is also timeless (Section 9.3). In the first two years of life, the connection between the hippocampus and the cortex is not sufficiently developed for a sense of space and time to be stored in long-term memory. The body grows and the traumatised body lives on timelessly in it. When a traumatic memory is reactivated in therapy, it has no reference to space and time or relationship and is experienced in its original dissociated state.

Clinical example

A patient nearly died at birth. After her twin sister was born, the doctors were not expecting a second child. They had not palpated the child and ultrasound was not yet available. As she then came out, she was squashed by the mother's vaginal spasm. The mother was anaesthetised and the baby delivered with the help of a vacuum pump. She and her sister were premature and put into an incubator. At that time, this meant that in their first weeks they had no body contact with the parents. As an adult she suffered from intense feelings of paralysis. In therapy sessions she would suddenly freeze up physically. She often had swollen eyes, periostitis around the nose, frequent headaches, constant anxiety that something terrible was going to happen and feelings of disgust and foulness about herself. She presented herself not in feelings but in states; in my presence she felt empty, as if lacking oxygen, cold, sensations of hammering in her head, a sore throat, a feeling as if her head was being torn from her shoulders. One curious symptom was the physical sensation that she was being pulled up diagonally towards the left when she sat opposite me. She was afraid I would break off therapy because she was not worth the trouble. In these symptoms, the experience in the incubator with the noise of the machines and also a kind of birth transference appeared. Often the therapy room became foggy and it was remarkably difficult for me to think clearly. She felt the need to be held like a baby. She longed for death as if she had not yet arrived in her body even now. Only through bodywork in contact with me in our sessions did she find a way out of her dissociative stupor and dissociative trance (cf. Geuter, 2019, pp. 124, 264–5).

Neurotic inhibitions can also have their source in a birth trauma, for example if someone almost suffocated or went through the shock of narcosis. To release the tensions held in the body through such experiences, body psychotherapy has a number of techniques to reactivate birth traumas. This work is often psychologically very helpful.

Grof's theory of the birth matrix

Grof (1985) differentiates four *perinatal matrices* in the birth process:

- The matrix of the original *amniotic universe* stands for the experience of the ideal, undisturbed state in the womb before birth begins. Here belong feelings of unity with the cosmos, *oceanic ecstasy*; or, when this level is under threat, feelings of being engulfed by the cosmos; or, as an introject of rejection, often feeling cold.
- The second matrix of the birth beginning is linked to the pressure on the child before they enter the birth canal. Here belong images of danger for life and limb, or feelings of hopelessness.
- The third matrix of expulsion, as Grof calls it, is the experience of the foetus of being moved through the birth canal. Here belong a simultaneous sensation of pleasure and pain or feelings of pressure pain and imminent suffocation or a struggle for survival.
- The fourth matrix stands for the experience of coming out of the birth canal, so that the build-up of pain and tension resolves itself in relief and relaxation.

Experiences of these phases of birth can appear in the images or sensations which emerge when people in experimental LSD sessions or after guided breathwork (intensifying and accelerating the breathing – Holotropic Breathwork) enter into altered states of consciousness and re-experience their birth. Grof associates these experiences with pathologies such as paranoia, schizophrenia, severe depression, sadomasochism or mania. There is no evidence to support this and it remains speculation.

11.2 THE ORIGIN OF THE SELF

We can substantiate the argument that the self has its basis in body experience (Chapter 6) through developmental psychology. At birth, the child already has a bodily experience of the self, since they know the difference between when they touch themselves and when someone else touches them (Section 11.1). The experience of it being me who moves and touches myself shows the first differentiation between self and non-self (Gallagher, 2003, pp. 27–8; cf. Butterworth, 1998). Motor activity and interaction are the starting point for the development of the body self (Gallese, 2003). Trevarthen (2003) reports on an experiment with a 20-minute-old child, who was already following the movements of a ball with its body. This newborn moves their body coherently in time and space, which for Trevarthen is reason enough to speak of a child self.

For body psychotherapy, Stern's (1985) theory of the development of the self is very valuable (Geuter, 2018). Stern shows that the self is based on body experiences and forms itself in a cognitive-affective-motoric exchange between subject and object. This is in accordance with the view of body psychotherapy that early relational experiences are dynamically inscribed in the body structures and the psychosomatic patterns of experience and behaviour, and also with that of Gestalt therapy, that the self is created in interactive sequences of creative adjustment between the individual and the environment (Frank, 2005, p. 117). In contrast to many researchers in developmental psychology, Stern was looking for scientific evidence of the infant's **inner experience**. His work comes close to clinical practice. Kern (2014) linked Stern's theory of the layers of the sense of self with clinically significant breaches in self-development and the relevant body therapeutic tasks.

Stern (1985) differentiates **four senses of self**, which develop in stages and then remain as forms of self-experience. In therapy we can explore earlier stages. However this is not regression as understood by Freud, who used the concept in the sense of one stage supplanting the previous one. Rather, all the stages of the sense of self remain active during one's whole life. Each corresponds to a certain orientation:

1. Stern calls the first stage the **emergent self**. This is the sense of self of the first two months of life. At this stage the infant learns to recognise the **relationships between sensory experiences**. Their sense of self is directed entirely towards the coherence, the actions and the emotional states of the body. Stern thinks that at this time, a supramodal form of perception exists, in which information from various sense channels can be perceived as a whole.
2. Somewhere between the second and the seventh month, there develops from the emergent sense of self a **core self** as a separate, coherent and **distinct bodily entity**. According to Stern, the organisation of this sense of self is based in the body and contains experiences of
   - Self-agency.
   - Self-coherence, i.e. an ordering of places, movements and time sequences.
   - Self-affectivity, i.e. a cohesive affective experiencing in the form of motoric patterns, inner sensations and certain feeling qualities.
   - Self-historicity, i.e. a motor memory.

The core self develops out of these four experiences. Stern regards the sense of core self as the foundation for all later more differentiated senses of self.

> This sense of a core self is thus an experiential sense of events. It is normally taken completely for granted and operates outside of awareness. A crucial term here is 'sense of', as distinct from 'concept of' or 'knowledge of' or 'awareness of' a self or other.
>
> (Stern, 1985, p. 71)

In psychoses, we see deficits in this sense of self, when people have no feeling for their own agency and no affective sense, and when their feeling of coherence is lost in a state of depersonalisation or that of historicity in a state of dissociation.

3. Between the seventh and the ninth month, the **sense of a subjective self** develops. The infant learns that they can **share subjective experiences with others**. Now they can read other people's inner states and can share a joint focus with someone else; for example, they can follow a hand that is pointing to something. And they can show through gestures what they want. A new form of intentional communication is beginning. The child learns to orientate themselves on the facial expression of the mother. Stern speaks of a quantum jump in intersubjective relations.

> In an experiment, Kanagoki et al. (2022) were able to show that already at the age of 8 months, when shown aggressive interactions on a screen, children turn their gaze against the aggressor. They interpret this as the expression of an early 'punishing' of anti-social behaviour.

4. In the second year, the **sense of a verbal self** begins with language. The child is increasingly able to **construct their own life narrative** and to relate to others through speaking. Communication can now extend to things and people who are not present, and children start to objectify themselves by talking about themselves.

   Stern saw **language** as a *double-edged sword*, since it allows a separation between what we experience interpersonally and what we say about what we experience. With the development of language, part of the child's experience starts to lead a double life: a non-verbal experience and a verbalised version of the experience. Stern emphasises that the force and wholeness of early experience goes missing and children become alienated from their own personal experience. However, language can also help to differentiate experience. According to Schramme, full self-awareness consists of a human being creating their self themselves by shaping their own story in which they create themselves as a figure (2005, p. 401).

Stern's thinking is interesting in that here, in developmental psychology, bodily sensation is ordered ahead of cognitive functioning. In my view, this holds true not only for child development but also for self-experience in general in the present (Section 6.3). Therefore we can understand the stages of self-experience that unfold in childhood development as living on in the form of layers within personality. Thus Stern's model comes close to what body psychotherapy strives for: to unlock areas of experience which are less accessible through language, but which have a highly real existence; to establish congruence between bodily experience and linguistic reflection, between world knowledge and word knowledge; and to counteract the alienation of experience which makes language possible.

The autobiographical self, which mentally spans different eras and, with the help of autobiographical memory, brings together various life experiences in one life story, can only develop on the basis of language (Section 6.5; Chapter 9). Children can only do this from about 4 or 5 years of age, when they succeed in integrating their own experiences into a coherent, temporal-causal organisation, the core of which forms a self-concept extended over time (Fonagy et al., 2002).

Bodily touch, both self touching and touching in interaction, is vital for the development of the sense of self and for self-regulation. This is also true beyond the first years of life. S. Weiss (1990) could show that the specific nature of parental touch affected the body image of their children. In children of 8–10 years, body concept and body feeling were more exact the more the parents had touched the various parts of their bodies. According to this study, it was above all dynamic touch that encouraged an exact body concept. Time was also a factor: if the mother touched them too long, it had the opposite effect.

Joint attention

The theory of Fonagy et al. (2002) on mentalisation corresponds basically to Stern's ideas. However, these authors describe child development without depicting the affect motor elements of interaction. Here, **mentalisation** means that the child forms cognitive assumptions about the intentions of others. They see this ability as significant for psychotherapy. Fonagy et al. ascertain a revolution in the 9-month-old infant corresponding to Stern's third stage. At this age, children begin to remove obstacles so that they can get to where they want to go. At the same time, they start to understand other peoples' actions as having a goal. This makes joint attention possible, which psychologically enables collaboration as in human culture (Tomasello et al., 2005). The child looks in the direction someone is pointing and points to things themselves. From the end of the first year, they look in the direction someone else is looking.

Joint attention is however not only a cognitive occurrence, but rather a **behavioural procedure** (Messer, 2003) and develops as a physical faculty in early childhood (Gallagher, 2014a, p. 16). It presupposes that the child is starting to act intentionally and can differentiate between the aim and the means of an action. In joint attention, this *being-with-the-other* is built up on the sensorimotor, cognitive and affective levels. Children now try to initiate joint attention. By beginning to recognise the difference between their own state and that of others, they are gaining a subjective view of the world. In the gaze of the other, they look for information on whether something is dangerous or not. Hence at this age, separation anxiety develops (Rochat, 2003). Children now need to share their emotional states (Dornes, 1997, p. 143).

At 15 months, they can successfully locate a goal object. This is a watershed in development. The eye movements show that the child understands another persons' intentions. In the next developmental step, from about 2 years of age, they can ascribe to themselves and to others intentions, which precede actions (Fonagy et al., 2002). Now the child also recognises the emotional states of other people. At the age of 4, children can abstract joy, sadness, anger and anxiety from their own experience to the extent that they can represent these feelings through moving a teddy bear around (Boone & Cunningham, 2001).

Theory of mind

The cognitive ability to attribute mental states to oneself and to others is known as the theory of mind (Povinelli & Preuss, 1995). An assumption about an inner state is called a theory, since the state itself is not directly accessible. The concept of the theory of mind presumes that an interpersonal self develops when the child is able to see things from the perspective of someone else.

Intersubjectivity, however, does not develop by inductively penetrating the other person's mental sphere (Fuchs, 2016). The interpersonal self is not just the result of reflective interactions. The child **lives** the interpersonal relationship, even if they are unaware that they and the other person can have different perspectives on the world. We can be relational without being aware of the fact that we are relational (de Haan, 2010, p. 13). Children could thus have direct access to the experiences of others. In cognitive psychology, they are currently discussing also the thesis that children are born with the innate ability to grasp the mental states of other people (Vincini & Gallagher, 2021).

In contrast to the theory of mind, a phenomenological and enactive theory would emphasise the processes of a vital and embodied interaction. We can only perceive others from a third-person perspective when we step outside of this interaction (Gallagher, 2018).

Brain development

The stages according to Stern have interesting parallels in the process of the maturation of the brain (Schore, 2001, pp. 30–2). In newborns, the function of the amygdala and the sensorimotor cortex are on the level of the emerging self. This is why newborns know from the smell whether a nightdress belongs to their mother or to another woman. The faculty of face-to-face interaction from the age of 2–3 months is concomitant with an increased myelinisation of the visual area of the occipital cortex; the beginning of joint attention with the establishment of the relevant functions in the orbitofrontal cortex at 10–12 months. Approximately at this age, the subjective self comes to maturity, according to Stern. Now visual and auditory information can be linked to emotionally expressive gestures and voices. At this time, when the child also learns to walk, the orbitofrontal cortex is connected more closely to the sympathetic nervous system (Carroll, 2005, p. 20). Lastly, the verbal self develops during the maturation of the orbitofrontal cortex in the middle of the second year. At this time, the child possesses less than 70 words, however. Therefore Schore (2001, p. 42) writes that the core self is acquired unconsciously and non-verbally and is founded in the patterns of affect regulation. The whole of the prefrontal cortex, of which the orbitofrontal cortex is only a small internal part, being sometimes allocated to the limbic system, is the last part of the brain to mature. This is why more complex regulation of behaviour is only possible after puberty. With the ability to foresee the long-term consequences of actions, autonomy develops (van der Kolk, 2006, p. 279).

Levels of consciousness

As Stern distinguished the stages of the development of the self, so Dornes (2000, p. 183) distinguishes various levels of the child's emerging consciousness (Table 11.1), which have parallels to the consciousness levels of Damasio (Section 6.5; Table 6.1):

- On the first level, children live in the immediacy of their sensations and perceptions, to which belong a vague sense of being hungry or sad or happy, but also of looking different from another baby. This consciousness is according to Dornes one of **self-perception**. In Damasio's theory, this corresponds to the protoself and extends into core consciousness (arrow in Table 11.1).

- On the second level, according to Dornes, children become aware of their own person as a self. When they look in the mirror with a dot glued to their forehead they know 'That's me!' This is approximately at the end of the second year of life, when they become capable of self-objectification through the verbal self. Now children have **self-awareness**. This is however not necessarily linked to language. Chimpanzees too recognise themselves in the mirror (Gallup et al., 2014). And gorillas touch a dot that has been glued to their forehead, where macaques in contrast do not. So probably a gorilla can develop an elementary area of self (Maturana & Varela, 1992).
- On a third level of **self-reflection**, children can think about their own thought and feeling processes. Now they are capable of inner dialogues in which they create their own story. We can assign this level of consciousness to Damasio's stage of the autobiographical self.

11.3 THE BODY IN THE INTERACTION OF THE EARLY YEARS

The most important interactive experience of the infant is generally the experience of the mother, since in a psychophysical dialogue she regulates nourishment, sleep and bodily needs such as relaxation of tension, as well as proximity, safety and attachment. In this dialogue, they practise patterns of regulation of attention, needs, tension and stress, which become models for later experience and behaviour. This is often identified as early affect regulation.

I speak here usually of the **mother**, because she is the one who carried the child and brought them into the world, who nurses them and who is for the earliest bodily interaction the most important person. Infant and attachment research have also usually concentrated on the mother–child interaction. For further development, however, the **father** or other **attachment figures**, as well as the **siblings**, can be just as important. Also children relate to different attachment figures in different patterns and forms of interaction and bonding.

Early childhood is especially significant for the development of affect regulation for two reasons. Firstly, infants experience intersubjectivity as a commonality of states which

TABLE 11.1
Levels of consciousness according to Dornes and Damasio

Level of consciousness development according to Dornes	Level of consciousness according to Damasio	Level of self according to Damasio
Immediate self-awareness – vague noticing (until about 18 months)	Completely unconscious	Proto self
Self-awareness – 'This is me' (from about 18 months)	Core consciousness – momentary awareness in the here and now	Core self
Self-reflection – awareness of one's own mental world – beginning of inner dialogue (from 4–5 years onwards)	Extended consciousness – enduring awareness across time	Autobiographical self

are regulated in a dyad (Tronick, 1998). They experience the actions of others in direct participation via bodily resonance (Dornes, 2002). Thus they absorb into their affective texture much of what other people feel and sense and how these persons treat them. Secondly, from late pregnancy until the second year of life, the brain goes through a phase of accelerated growth such as never occurs again in life; during this time it develops more rapidly than any other system of the organism (Schore, 2001, p. 27). Since in early childhood experiences are processed far more in subcortical realms than in cortical ones, early emotional experiences have lifelong consequences for a person's affective structure (Panksepp, 2001, pp. 138–9). Only when the cortical structures mature and participate can more complex behavioural strategies develop through inhibition (Cozolino, 2002, pp. 75–8).

What babies take in from others is at first stored affect motorically, because in the first three years, the right brain hemisphere matures more than the left, where linguistically coded memories are processed (Cozolino, 2002, p. 80). Also the corpus callosum reaches full maturity after the tenth year (Cozolino, 2002, p. 107) so that only then can the two hemispheres fully communicate with each other and integrate experiences through language. Babies learn completely unconsciously, for example, whether the world is safe or not, or how they can connect with other people. Since the prefrontal cortex only matures later, a cognitive regulation of emotional processes based on experience is not yet possible in early childhood (Schore, 2003).

Important
Early experience is stored in the body independently of reflective processes and forms an unconscious framework for personality.

Clinical application

Asking a patient to look for an inner image of how they were held and carried as a child can trigger an immediate reaction, even if they cannot answer the question through their linguistically coded knowledge.

The infant has only bodily expression as a medium of communication. By communicating with others through touch, voice and expressive movements, their inner life develops in dialogue. Following a concept of Braten (1988), Trevarthen (2004, p. 8) speaks of **protoconversations**, when adult and child synchronise rhythmic patterns of movement with each other and also vary these. The dialogue is two-way. When mothers calm their infants, their heart rate and respiration synchronise and they become calmer themselves (Ham & Tronick, 2009). Hence, we could speak of **affect motor and vegetative communication**. Eight-week-old babies already notice whether the reactions of their mother seen on a screen are in attunement with their own actions or not (Trevarthen, 2003). After only a few weeks, they are able to imitate particular facial expressions. The older they get, the more they make contact through imitating facial expressions and bodily gestures. Playful affect motor dialogues develop in an interactive regulation from moment to moment (Beebe, 2000, p. 422). Infant research assumes that persistent mismatching in this dialogue can form the basis for mental disorders (Dornes, 2000, pp. 25–31). Koehler describes the following example:

Example of interaction

A child turns their head away from the mother as soon as she overstimulates them. She however reacts to this by chasing after eye contact with them. She tickles the child and lifts them up. The child evades contact, turns away, keeps their head down and pulls their hand away from hers. However 'the mother fails to see this defence as a sign to wait, but thinks it is a stimulus to make contact in other ways. In the end the child just looks straight through her, becomes limp, shows no interest and stops reacting at all ... as long as the mother is after them' (Koehler, 1990, p. 44). Only when the mother's face relaxes and she turns her head away does the child lift his.

Koehler says that an aversive reaction normally makes the mother slow down, but here it only makes her double her efforts. By turning away, this child is obviously trying to regulate the level of arousal. Such a pullback is not aggression (Beebe, 2000), but is about modulating attention and core affectivity (Section 10.1). In the example, the child experiences that they are not being soothed, and rather the mother increases her activities; therefore they have to do even more in order to be soothed (Koehler, 1990, p. 44). If this continues, the child could learn a strategy of calming down a state of strong arousal by becoming limp. In body psychotherapy, we would speak of an affect motor schema of responding to a strong state of affect arousal by withdrawing or becoming apathetic. This pattern of core-affective regulation would be the result of many mismatched interactions, which leave traces on the unconscious level of the emotional-procedural memory.

According to Kiersky and Beebe (1994, p. 393), timing, relatedness to space and the degree of affective stimulation and of proprioceptive arousal are the significant parameters of early interaction. These correspond approximately to the three categories of space, time and weight of the Laban movement analysis (Section 14.2). According to Stern (1985), every infant has an optimal level of arousal which needs the response of an optimal level of stimulation and the infant regulates this themselves. Through this experience of mutual regulation, they learn the mechanisms through which arousal levels can be managed.

Important
For an infant, affect regulation means first regulating the core affects of the level of arousal and feelings of pleasure and unpleasure; only then do categorical emotions have their turn. Body psychotherapy sees here a fundamental level of personality development that is key to the regulation of need and affect tension and thus for therapeutic work.

Interactive regulation of core affective states

In early interaction, infants can learn to maintain an optimal level of arousal, to deal with unpleasure and to enjoy pleasure. Soothing and stimulating are the essential tasks of parents in the affect regulation of the infant in the first year of life (von Salisch & Kunzmann, 2005). This is mainly the regulation of a state. Infants acquire the ability to recover from an unpleasant state either on their own or with the help of others. Huether (2009, p. 100) identifies being able to control a threat or a loss of equilibrium through one's own efforts and to find safety and protection as the two most important experiences a human being can have during early childhood.

Through successful interactions tolerance for emotional arousal grows (Miller et al., 2002, pp. 405–6). Parents encourage this with tickling games when they gradually increase the child's arousal level and stop at the right moment. Deficits in this area call for therapeutic interventions with the help of which patients can learn to tolerate a higher level of arousal or to curb it as needed and to notice appetitive and aversive tendencies (Section 10.2; Geuter, 2019, pp. 158–70).

Since regulation difficulties are formed early on, they are not sufficiently symbolically encoded, so that body-oriented methods are well suited for their treatment. However, mere therapy **techniques** are not sufficient. A mother successfully helps a child to regulate core affectivity not only by adapting to the child's behaviour, but also by attuning herself on a deeper level to the rhythms of his inner state (Schore, 2001, p. 20), which Stern (1985) calls vitality affects (Section 10.5).

Clinical application

In terms of psychotherapy, this means that there is a connective and healing level in the relationship to the patient, which we cannot describe as therapeutic behaviour, but is rather a quality of being with the other person and which involves attuning oneself to their inner state. This quality is in itself soothing and as a relational experience it regulates core affective processes (Geuter, 2019, pp. 199–203).

Still-face experiments

The still-face experiments of Tronick and his colleagues in 1975 demonstrated for the first time how children react when they get no response from the mother (Adamson & Frick, 2003). In these experiments, mothers were asked to first behave normally with their child and then suddenly to freeze their movements and facial expressions for two minutes. The child's usual reaction is at first to turn away, then to smile, to stretch towards the mother and make sounds in order to regain her attention. If no reaction comes, they cry, turn away and try to soothe themselves by for example sucking their thumb, or else they become apathetic. The first signs of these reactions can already be observed at two months (Moore et al., 2001). The type of reaction depends on whether the mothers are normally well-attuned to their children in their reactions. Children whose mothers are not aware of their signals or who disregard them are less active in trying to evoke a reaction from the mother (Downing, 1996, p. 140).

Through the unsuccessful efforts of the children in the experiment, the mothers themselves become stressed. We see this through measuring electrodermal activity. When they are reunited and the mothers can soothe their children and synchronise their behaviour with that of the child, then their parasympathetic reactivity increases. Therefore Ham and Tronick (2009) speak of a **relational psychophysiology** and, with respect to therapy, they consider it possible that, just as in the mother–child relationship, a high level of empathy on the part of the therapist can help the patient develop something new and therapeutically effective.

The still-face experiments are basically **still-body** experiments. The mothers freeze all their bodily movements, not just their faces. Stack and Muir (1992) examined to what extent it was the gaze or the touch which led to the reported reactions. If the mother keeps her face still but moves her hands without touching the baby, this attracts the child's attention, but they do not smile. If she touches them while her face remains frozen, then the baby looks and smiles, even if the hands are invisible underneath a blanket. Interesting too is that in a normal still-face experiment, the child looks 50% at the face and 30% at the hands of the mother (Muir, 2002). The significance of the hands for affective communication is often overlooked. Early communication, however, is face-to-face and skin-to-skin. In therapy too, hands can be very important.

RIGs

Frequent repetition of interactive experiences gives rise to pre-symbolic schemas of the self, the others and the interaction (Kiersky & Beebe, 1994). Stern (1985) calls them generalised representations, so-called RIGs (representations of interactions that have been generalised), which integrate various attributes of action, perception and affect. RIGs are based on episodes of experience and reveal the expectations of what will happen next that have developed out of them. According to Stern, they should not be regarded as memories. Later he called them *schemas-of-being-with*, consisting of sensorimotor sensations, visual perception, conceptual schemas, schemas of chronology, feeling forms and the so-called *proto-narrative envelope* (Stern, 1995). The last concept refers to episodes into which an infant divides up an event before they can narrate it. For example, mother comes in; I lift my arms and she picks me up; we smile at each other. RIGs already start with breastfeeding, since this is always embedded in a specific affective dialogue between mother and child. The concept of RIGs is similar to that of emotional-procedural memory (Section 9.3), as this memory shows itself in present day expectations of what will happen, but is not accessible in explicit memory.

Example of interaction

Stern (1985) tells the story of a girl whose mother had divorced and could not share her child's enthusiasm, so that she would never take on the upwards regulation of the arousal. The child became inhibited in a phase in which the core self develops and could only experience a narrow spectrum of pleasurable excitement. If the child persisted, however, the mother started to react.

This experience leads to the creation of an RIG: exerting oneself, struggling to interest the mother leads to an experience of togetherness. The girl has learnt early on to be 'a "Miss Sparkle Plenty" and precociously charming' (Stern, 1985, p. 198). All this developed non-verbally through bodily communication, and later it appears in her adult body language.

In a good mother–child relationship, there will have been about 30,000 circles of happy interaction by the time the child is 6 months old (Krause, 2006, p. 38). This impressive number of interactions establishes a basic feeling of being lovable and anchored both affect motorically and cognitively. Malatesta describes this as an *emotional life-script* (Krause, 2006, p. 39).

Body micro-practices

Stern's concept of the RIGs relates to the inner world of the infant. To emphasise the action character of the implicit knowledge the child has learnt in interactions, Downing speaks of body micro-practices. With these he means strategies of deploying the body in interaction (Downing, 2007, p. 563). As embodied affective faculties, micro-practices are based on implicit knowledge and are modes of action in which in a 'two-body-field' – from the third month on also in a triad – closeness and distance are regulated.

Body micro-practices are learnt very early on through the smallest characteristics of repeated interaction during the first 2 years of life (Downing, 2000). Tronick (1998) talks of the micro-regulation of social and emotional processes. For example, the infant learns to dampen down their arousal when the intensity of the emotional response of the caregiver is often too high (Downing, 2015). They thus develop a bodily strategy to regulate core affects. Such a strategy can be auto- or co-regulative (Chapter 17). In early childhood interaction, micro-practices occur in an interconnection of *body with body*, since adult and child communicate with their whole bodies. Adults move when they are in contact with the child and talking to her (Downing, 1996, p. 142). Micro-practices are recognisable as procedural techniques in motor interactive behaviour. What was termed 'defence' in the interaction example from Koehler is actually the regulation of a state with the help of motor micro-practices in relation to the mother. Downing (2000) also counts as a body micro-practice the ability to feel emotions in the body, to tolerate and observe them and to follow the bodily changes they effect.

Clinical application

Thielen (2013b) describes an exercise with which he explores childish micro-practices in a transference dialogue in body psychotherapy. The patient lies down and is brought into a regressive state through an emotionalising breathing technique. In this state, Thielen then asks her to imagine that his hand represents the hand of her mother or her father. He then says that the hand is very slowly coming near her forearm lying next to her body. According to him this usually leads to spontaneous movements of the patient's forearm and hand. 'These can then become approaching, aversive or neutral movements. Sometimes however the body freezes' (Thielen, 2013b, p. 314). Thielen sees this body language as a repeat of the micro-practices of early interaction. We could also call them a depiction of interactive affect motor patterns, which give us a diagnostic clue to early relational experience.

In **micro-coordination**, mother and child adapt their behaviour to one another in intervals of 3–5 seconds (Tronick, 1989). This runs along the lines of opening a dialogue, withdrawing from it and then beginning it again in a constant rhythm (Schore, 2003, pp. 8–10). Schore sees the essential channel of these micro-regulations in the mutual transference of affects in a rhythmic mirroring of expressive movements (cf. Trevarthen, 2001). An attunement between mother and child in rhythmic affective dialogue is fundamental for the child's wellbeing. Here infants learn basic regulatory strategies, which, as emotional-procedural knowledge, shape the way they later deal with both stressful as well as joyful situations. However there is also a regulation, upstream from the emotions, in which the infant organises their physical relationship to themselves in interaction. This is shaped by how the mother holds herself in the body, how she holds her child, how she breathes and in what kind of rhythm she moves (Downing, 2015).

Clinical application

In a teaching film, Moser (1994) shows how in therapeutic dialogue he picks up fine signals of body language communication, in which some of the child's feelings are visible in the adult patient, who cannot easily verbalise them. For example, the patient feels an impulse in their finger, as if it wanted contact. In the sense of a micro-regulation, Moser explores on the level of the finger how this approach could proceed. What is happening on the body level is simultaneously verbalised, so that the adult ego of the patient can be conscious of it.

In another scene, Moser shows how the patient inhibits pleasure. In a mutual affect transference in which the patient approaches the pleasure and the therapist encourages them by being pleased himself, the patient can finally access a childish pleasure by bouncing.

Moser writes about this process as follows:

> This access through the body, through acting scenes, through touch and active regression is an attempt to make contact with the real child in the patient, with the child who keeps most of their formative experiences outside language and so can only rediscover them outside language.
>
> (Moser, 1993, p. 134).

The experiences and patterns which developed back then can only be understood and changed in the present (Frank, 2005). This is why we have to seek out the arousal stress resulting from the past (Geuter, 2006, p. 121).

Traumatisation

Not only accumulated interactive experiences but also traumata can be psychopathologically significant. Traumas from the first 2 years of life are stored in the emotional-procedural memory, just like those from the pre- and perinatal stages. Since small children are less able to protect themselves, they are much more vulnerable to traumatisation.

An infant reacts psychobiologically to a traumatic situation in two ways: with hyperarousal and with dissociation (Schore, 2003, p. 67). Hyperarousal is a result of the alarm reaction of the sympathetic nervous system; dissociation is part of the subsequent parasympathetic reaction of the autonomic nervous system, whereby the child disengages themselves from the outside world and turns inwards to safety (Section 7.1). Schore sees this as a primary regulatory process of conservation-withdrawal. The infant withdraws to an autoregulatory strategy, so as 'to modulate overwhelming levels of distress' (Schore, 2003, p. 68).

When a child of this age is abused, sexually or otherwise, they are not able to communicate their experiences verbally, but they show up in their behaviour. A child who has been abused as a baby exhibits, when playing with dolls, for example, sexualised behaviour which they have experienced; corresponding memories are possible from the second half of the first year onwards (Gaensbauer, 2002; Section 9.3). The memories are stored multisensorially and are preserved in the form of images, sensations, feeling states and sensorimotor processes even if they cannot be consciously reproduced. However, an adult can express sensory memories in words even though they are not able to assign any meaning to them from episodic memory (Gaensbauer, 2002). To work with early-traumatised people, we must be able to access and understand the significance of pre-verbal expression.

Motor activity

The child relates with their body not only to other people, but also to themselves and to the world of things. Primarily they comprehend the world through the muscle sense: their exploration is basically haptic. By experiencing through action how the world resists our intentions, they realise the difference between self and world. In active encounters with the material environment, they develop faculties and become aware of their self-efficacy. Their cognitive appropriation of the material world is a result of these sensory motor activities. In the first 18 months of life, the infant's thinking is mainly sensorimotor (Dornes, 1997). This is why the psychomotor theory views the physicalness of the child as the lynchpin of their existence (Fischer, 2000, p. 25).

Mental activity is based on the fact that we perceive and act in the world (Section 5.2). A child learns what a hammer is by knocking little plugs into a plank with holes in it with a wooden hammer; they learn what a room is by crawling around it; they learn to want something by moving towards it. Language and concepts, ideas and desires are all learned in connection with bodily movement. The goal of child development is, according to Thelen (2000), not to grow beyond sensorimotor operations with cognition, as Piaget's research indicates, but to be at home in the body with one's cognition. This corresponds to the goal of body psychotherapy, which unites verbal reflection and bodily sensation in a holistic approach.

Clinical application

In body psychotherapy, we can explore assumptions about relationships with other people motorically in movement. With a patient who cannot let anyone get close, I can explore what they feel when we stand opposite each other and I take one step towards them. For example, one patient noticed in this experiment that with an intake of breath they pumped themselves up and at the same time closed themselves off inside so that they could avoid the feeling of being threatened. In such an action dialogue, patients can discover how they experience closeness.

The development of a child shows itself in **movements** (Trautmann-Voigt & Voigt, 2009, p. 16). Dance therapy therefore works with movement themes of early childhood, such as raising and lowering, upwards and downwards, moving with or against gravity (Trautmann-Voigt & Voigt, 2009, pp. 80–3). According to Haeckel's biogenetic law, a child replays in their development all the movement patterns of evolution. The basic movement of the simplest life-forms is the **pulsation** of single-celled organisms. Simple multicellular life-forms with a radial structure move from the centre towards the periphery and back. Following the stages of evolution, we find in life-forms with a bilateral structure **serpentine movements** along an axis just like fish or snakes; **homologous movements**, in which the upper or the lower limbs are moved together, like a jumping frog; **homolateral movements** like lizards, which move upper and lower limbs on one side of the body simultaneously; and lastly **contralateral movements** as in mammals.

At first infants move along the spine; then they raise themselves up with homologous movements, belly crawl with homolateral and crawl with contralateral movements until they learn to walk (Aposhyan, 2004, pp. 205–10). In body psychotherapy, we can look at the body from a functional perspective as to whether the respective form of movement has developed, or whether, because of developmental difficulties or illness, there are deficits specific to certain stages, which could be treated with the corresponding physical activities. As an infant, I missed out the belly crawl stage because of a serious illness. This showed up motorically as an adult in restricted movement in shoulders and arms. My body therapist noticed this and gave me the exercise of belly crawling with babies.

Relational disorders can lead to restrictions in mobility. For example, if the parents push the child to walk too early because they expect them to be a high achiever, this can overtax the child physically as they try to please them. This can result in stiffness in the knees and the hip joints to balance out the lack of stability, which can then lead to hypertension in the leg and pelvic musculature.

> We acquire our motor skills in auto- and co-regulation. When an adult helps a child who cannot yet sit up themselves, then it is best when they adapt to their tonus and movements (Fogel, 2009, p. 16). They can feel in their hands whether the infant is pulling themselves up on them and wants to use their own strength, or whether they are not yet able to do so, or what the relationship between the pulling of the adult and the movement of the child is. The child too is aware of the adult pulling them and their own pulling, and they regulate their actions accordingly. This helping up is thus an interactive regulation of tension in tiny increments. 'The total force exerted is a smooth function over time but it can only be achieved by a mutual sensing of when to pull more or less in relation to the partner' (Fogel, 2009, p. 16).

Treating developmental delays in children is a classic field of psychomotor therapy. In body psychotherapy, however, we are more concerned with the meaning of movements, since psychological problems are always connected to how people relate emotionally to the world and to themselves. Therefore what interests us in childhood development is above all motor activity in interpersonal space, i.e. how patterns of affective interaction are communicated through the body between adult and child. Developmental patterns of movement emerge in relational space and reflect the needs that are significant at that time. The child experiences the growth of their psychological functions and expresses them through movement (Frank, 2005, p. 118).

Bentzen et al. (2004, p. 62) therefore suggest that we divide psychomotor development into stages grouped around the child's specific needs or rights:

1. To exist – this is connected to the stretching and avoidance response in the foetus.
2. To have needs met – this is experienced through sucking, grasping or biting.
3. To be autonomous – this manifests in crawling, walking and acting.
4. To act intentionally and purposefully of one's own volition – this is experienced in strong controlled motoric movement.
5. To express feelings of love and sexual desire – here children discover gender-specific behaviour.
6. To have one's own opinion while learning control and motor activity.
7. To be accepted and respected as a member of a peer group – here children learn to better coordinate their motor skills as individuals as well as in the group.

According to the theory of Marcher, which lies behind this model, each developmental stage requires the child to master new movements that are connected to specific muscle groups (Marcher & Fich, 2010; Section 7.1). When they have movement patterns consciously under control, they can then actively utilise them, for example, crawling in order to explore (Bernhardt et al., 2004b, p. 135). To act intentionally, for instance turning one's attention towards an object, presupposes not only cognitive faculties, but also the ability to guide the muscles controlling the movement of the head (Bernhardt et al., 2004b, p. 145).

Here psychomotor development is connected to the relevant psychodynamic developmental themes, so that we can link this to the theory of character structures (Bernhardt et al., 2004a). The psychomotor theme of stretching is related to the schizoid structure with its conflict focused on existence and the threats to it; that of sucking and grasping to the oral structure, with its conflict focused on needs and their not being adequately met; the movements of autonomy to the oral, but also the narcissistic structure; the acts of will to the masochistic structure, with its conflict focused on independence and submission; the movements of love and desire to the rigid character with its typical conflict (Section 13. 2).

11.4 THE SHAPING OF STRESS REACTIVITY THROUGH ADVERSE EXPERIENCES

In the following I will go into two aspects of early development that are important for body psychotherapy: the shaping of stress reactivity and the way in which the regulation of categorical emotions is trained in early relational experiences (Section 11.5). How an adult deals with pressure is basically learnt in the first years of life. This level of early imprinting is not paid enough attention in psychodynamic theories and therapies, which concentrate on the consequences of interactive experiences for psychological development. In contrast, working with stress regulation is a traditional field of treatment in some of the body psychotherapy schools such as Functional Relaxation, biodynamics or the breathing therapies.

Research on animals shows that lifelong stress reactivity is biologically imprinted through early experiences and is passed on epigenetically (Gapp et al., 2014). When mother rats lick and groom their young, this changes the epigenetic mechanisms of gene expression at the hippocampal receptors for glucocorticoids, one of which is the stress hormone cortisol. If the mothers neglect to do this, the gene expression is later missing. The effects of this appear in the first week of life and persist into adulthood (Weaver et al., 2004). It has been proven that this is due to the behaviour of the mother and not to genetic factors: in cross-fostering experiments in which researchers swapped the embryos in the womb immediately after conception, the offspring's behaviour is determined by that of the mother who bore and raised them and not that of the mother who conceived them (Francis et al., 1999). The behaviour of mother rats affects their young in their anxiety reactions, attentiveness, learning and memory reactions under stress (Zhang et al., 2006, p. 83). Chicks of barn fowl who after birth were denied contact to a mother hen or a substitute did not carry out synaptic pruning in the limbic region, which results in learning difficulties. In rodents who have been separated from their parents and siblings, we can observe a reduction in metabolic brain activity (Bock et al., 2003). Because of the similarities in the physiology of stress management in mammals, these experiments are relevant for human beings (Huether et al., 1999, p. 90). However, the cultural and social transmission of such traumatic experiences would be much more significant than the epigenetic (Horsthemke, 2018).

Nurture

The crucial factor for the long-term effects of stress events is the behaviour of the mother. When young rats are separated from the mother daily for 3–6 hours in the first 2 weeks of life, their stress reactivity increases in the long run because the mothers then ignore them (Kandel, 1999). If the separation is only for 3–15 minutes, however, then the young animals later deal better with stress than those who had no separation. This is obviously because these were then licked and groomed intensively by their mothers when they were reunited (Panksepp, 2001, pp. 151–2). Experiments with primates have also shown that the behaviour of the mother can counteract emotional problems (Panksepp, 2001, pp. 135–6).

The vulnerability, traditionally viewed as genetic, is according to this research the expression of interaction between the genotype and early experiences with the environment. Thus neurobiological studies support findings from observations, such as those Harlow carried out on baby monkeys or Spitz on the emotional deprivation of orphanage children. When for example in developmental studies the factor of parental care is statistically controlled, there is no demonstrable effect of poverty on children (Zhang et al., 2006). The quality of parental care seems to be the determining factor, so that the more difficult a child's attachment style is, the worse the effect of traumatising relational experiences (Spinazzola et al., 2018).

McEwen (2007) has applied the results of animal research to human psychology. The accumulation of stress factors often leads to an allostatic reaction: adaptation without equilibrium (Section 7.1 on 'allostatic load'). This takes place at the cost to the body of the dysregulation of neurotransmitters such as serotonin and CRF (corticotropin releasing factor). Thus abuse and neglect in childhood determine the lifelong regulation of the activity of the HPA (hypothalamus-pituitary-adrenal) axis governing stress reactions. In the long term, base levels are higher and circadian rhythms modulated (McEwen, 2003, p. 152; Chapter 9, Body memory). Also a lack of maternal nurture in childhood leads to an increase in the release of cortisol in the adult and thus to a higher stress reactivity (Fries, 2008, p. 476). Women who were maltreated or subjected to sexual violence in childhood also show changes in the energy metabolism of the immune cells, which, however, is not passed on to their offspring (Gumpp et al., 2020). On a biological level, these findings support what numerous long-term studies on the psychological consequences of maltreatment, abuse and neglect have shown (Egle et al., 2016). I point them out here because they illustrate how a psychotherapeutic treatment of the resulting adverse psychological effects has to include regulation of stress reactivity. Body-oriented methods are especially suitable for this (Geuter, 2019, pp. 224–8).

According to the findings of the Felitti study (Felitti et al., 1998), more than six adverse childhood experiences shorten life expectancy by 20 years. Today we know about biological mechanisms by which such experiences determine coronary heart disease or autoimmune disorders. Someone who experiences the distress of neglect or abuse in early childhood will have increased levels of inflammation parameters in adolescence (Ehrlich et al., 2016). A sustained level of stress in childhood leads to hypercortisolism, which makes one susceptible to inflammations (Schubert, 2020). Chronic depression can also be a result of emotional abuse and neglect (Nelson et al., 2017).

Traumatic experiences of the attachment figure also affect the stress reactivity of the child. Mothers with PTSD can experience stress with the child as a trigger for posttraumatic stress; for example, they see the child's separation anxiety or helplessness as a threat. If the child triggers the symptoms of the mother, then she cannot regulate the child's affects. She misinterprets signals and thus exposes the child to her own traumatic stress (Schechter & Serpa, 2013). In this way she communicates her traumatic past to the child and shapes their style of regulating basic affects.

Stress is, however, not only noxious, but can also promote development. If an individual masters new and challenging situations, then successful behaviour patterns will be reinforced. But uncontrollable stress results in sustained arousal. However this can also lead to a fundamental reorganisation. Whether it results in a reorganisation or in damage to the organism is dependent on the quality, intensity and context of the stress and at the age at which it occurs (Huether et al., 1999).

On the level of the autonomic nervous system (ANS), we can see the consequences of stress regulation in early interaction (Section 7.1). When children are breastfeeding in a secure, supportive relationship, then their sympathetic tone decreases and the vagal tone increases. The ANS is retuned, a sign of successful stress reduction (Uvnaes-Moberg, 1998, p. 821). This happens not only with the children but with the mothers too. Breastfeeding mothers react to stress with a lower increase of cortisol release than do mothers who feed their infants with a bottle. The activities of the HPA axis and of the sympathoadrenal system also decrease in the long run.

An important means of preventing stress is **touch**. Stroking and touching modulates the activity of the HPA axis; rats who were touched and stroked as young animals recover more easily from an electric shock than control animals (Montagu, 1971). This process is mediated through the production of the hormone oxytocin, which is released in young mammals when they are touched (Insel & Young, 2001). This anti-stress effect grows the more often the subject experiences the situation in which release occurs (Uvnaes-Moberg, 1998). Since the effects of oxytocin last only for a few minutes, it is possible that the long-term effect is produced by increasing the body's own opioids. Thus, in humans, 'positive social experiences are stored as memories which may, in turn, reactivate physiological processes that parallel those induced by the original sensory experience' (Uvnaes-Moberg, 1998, p. 830). In this way, according to Uvnaes-Moberg, mental representations of positive experiences can permanently alter physiology.

Not only mental representations do this, however. In fact it is the experiences lodged in implicit memory which themselves crosslink emotional, hormonal and immunological processes in a network of bodily communication. In the long run, internalised regulators connect biological systems with object relations (Paar et al., 1999, p. 303). When we influence the stress reactivity and equilibrium of our patients by means of psychotherapy, then we affect this level of regulation too.

11.5 PARENTAL BEHAVIOUR AND CHILDREN'S EMOTIONAL REGULATION

In section 11.3, I have described how the regulation of the child's core affects is a crucial parental task in the first year of life. Later on, children learn in innumerable interactions how to **regulate categorical emotions** (Section 10.4). The task of the parents is to notice the child's signals, to read their inner state and to name it. In this way the child learns to perceive and identify their emotions themselves. For example the parents say: 'Now you're sad'. By having their feeling named, the child also learns that we can share emotional states. Children who internalised a form of emotional regulation helpful in childhood probably have effective regulatory abilities later on (Miller et al., 2002, pp. 428–9). If a patient lacks this ability, it is the therapist's task to name their emotions and thus bring them up into consciousness.

Affect mirroring

Small children get to know emotions by seeing their inner states mirrored by other people. Because of the maturation of the visual cortex, infants start face-to-face interaction at the age of 2 months. Now they recognise emotions in the faces of others (Schore, 2001, pp. 17–8). At this age they also start to smile (Rochat, 2003). At 3 months, they start to play with their gaze (Schore, 2001, p. 33). Now children and their caregivers repeatedly synchronise their affective experiences.

According to the theory of Fonagy et al. (2004), the child learns what their feeling state is through maternal affect mirroring. Through mirroring, the child registers how they are feeling themselves, also what they perceive of the body and at the same time what the mother is showing them. The child compares whether what the mother is mirroring fits with what the child is feeling. In order for the affect mirroring to be successful, the mother's reaction has to be congruent. This means the mother should not react too strongly or too weakly or with another feeling than that of the child and thus reinterpret the child's expression. In therapy we see that patients interpret their emotions wrongly because they have adopted a reinterpretation, for example of anger as sadness. Then the task is to access the concealed affect.

Through social feedback, feelings are anchored referentially by being marked. This takes place, for example, through exaggerating slightly as in 'motherese', which uses an over-done intonation to make clear that now it is the **child's feeling** that is meant and not that of the adult. Parents emphasise the child's experience. They say: 'Now you're happy!' and extend the feeling a little. Or they say: 'Oh that hurts!' while they cuddle and rock the child. Through little exaggerations and gestures, they set **emotional markings**. When a small child imitates the slightly exaggerated emotional expression, then they get into the affect state more clearly in their body. The mirrored affect passes over to the child and they become more familiar with it. In good affect mirroring, the attachment figure is attuned to the child but at the same time separated from their feeling – a good model for the relationship of therapist to patient.

Clinical application

We can utilise this in body psychotherapy, for example when we say in a genuinely tragic voice to a patient: 'But that's very, very sad' (Section 14.5; Geuter, 2019, p. 392). The corresponding feeling is anchored referentially. The pitch of the voice communicates that the therapist connects to the patient's feeling on a deep level without it being their own feeling. And it helps the patient to feel the feeling if they possibly could not feel it before.

An emotional marking can also occur playfully as with small children, for example when the therapist through singing, dancing or hopping around helps to arouse childish feelings of joy. In mirroring, the therapist draws at the same time on the experiences of the small child, who could regulate states of feeling through another person.

Another way of marking consists of answering in a different mode, for example by responding to the physically expressed joy of the child by making suitable noises. The transmodal response communicates the feeling state behind the child's behaviour; this encourages development (Milch & Berliner, 2005, pp. 146–7).

Clinical application

Body psychotherapy utilises this when, for example, the therapist responds to a verbal communication with a breathing reaction, or by modulating their voice or with a gesture or a movement or to a bodily expression with a reaction in another mode. This accentuates the vitality contour of an emotional experience.

The child's experience in mirroring is not like that of an ordinary mirror; even though they are shown something about themselves, there is a difference (Dornes, 2000, p. 207). The mother or father say for example to the child pulling the sled up the hill, who has just fallen into the snow: 'You're strong enough, you can pull the sled up the hill'. In this way they nurture an existing feeling of self while at the same time transforming the beginnings of frustration. In mirroring, the child is not just given information about what is happening, but is inspired to develop something new out of the situation (Dornes, 2000, p. 208).

Clinical application

If we speak to a patient who is sad as described above, there is an underlying message: you can feel this feeling, you can bear it, I am with you and if you let it go deeper nothing bad will happen. Through this they have the experience that they can cope with the feeling without having to do anything, and this reinforces their self-efficacy.

Affect mirroring thus has several functions:

- To notice the affect.
- To regulate it.
- To shape psychological structure.

The method of slightly exaggerating helps the child to learn that other people also react emotionally. When the father says: 'Daddy's sad now', combined with a sad face, but without really being sad, he suggests to the child that they can make someone sad, but that they do not need to worry about it. And when the father shows the affect in body language and names it in words, the child learns the congruence of feeling and naming.

Case study

A patient remembers being abused as a child. She talks agitatedly about it and, without consciously noticing, pulls her mouth down in an expression of disgust. Now the therapist could just assert: 'That's disgusting'. They would name the affect that she had not been aware of. However they could also mark the feeling of disgust without words, through a sound, which expresses in a slight exaggeration her latent feeling. In this way, the affect would be marked and mirrored as her own.

The aim of such a sequence would not be to relive the disgust she felt at the time, but rather in returning to the original arousal, to explore a possible new reaction schema, which could grow out of the destabilisation of the existing system – in this case, for example, to be able to express disgust without dissociating.

Internalisation

Through interacting with others, the child learns to identify sensations as emotions and to connect them to certain situations. From the seventh month, on it is possible to do this with anger. In the months before that, infants express stress, disgust, startle, interest, joy or pleasure more in the form of diffuse inner states so that another person will help them to regulate them. As they grow older, they are able to internalise this co-regulation towards auto-regulation (Holodynski, 2004, 2009). The child becomes increasingly able to deal with their feelings in an internal dialogue and through their own actions.

According to Holodynski's theory, children shift the expression of their emotions to the inside. Observations show that for a long time when they are dealing with their emotions alone, they still express them visibly through facial expressions and gestures. From the age of 6, they uncouple themselves from the expression of emotions through body language. They begin to experience and regulate them internally, without expressing them openly. Holodynski uses a notion of Wygotski's for the transition from speaking to speaking internally and calls it internalisation.

However the uncoupling of expression from feeling is in part a cultural imperative of our civilisation. Children learn what society has embraced (Elias, 2000). Today, another desired ideal is added to this: to express a pretend emotion even if this contradicts our inner feelings (Winterhoff-Spurk, 2005). Thus children learn to be happy without showing it, but also to smile without feeling it.

The acquired uncoupling of expression from feelings can become a problem when emotion regulation malfunctions. Other people can only help us to deal with difficult emotions when we show them, and they can only be regulated when the expression is congruent with the inner feeling. This is also one of the reasons behind the body psychotherapy approach to open up emotional experience through expressive body language (Geuter, 2019, pp. 170–9).

Temperament

Based on the responsiveness of the mother, we are able to predict the degree of emotional expression of which the child is capable. According to the studies of Nicely et al. (1999), the crucial factor is how intensely the mother engages with the infant. The authors think, however, that there is a certain degree of expressivity in the child regardless of the mother's behaviour, but that she does modulate the form this expressivity takes.

Goldsmith and Campos (1982) have called the manner in which children express categorical emotions *temperament*. Rothbart and Hwang (2005) characterise the basic elements of temperament as follows:

- The intensity with which a person reacts to events.
- The threshold beyond which a child reacts.
- The degree of their inner psychophysiological arousal.
- The extent to which they can regulate this level of arousal.

According to this understanding, the characteristics of temperament are related to the arousal dimension of core affects (Sections 10.5 and 10.1), so that this aspect of emotionality remains comparatively stable. Fox (1998) also aligns temperament parallel to the various levels of activity with which a child reacts to everyday events and which makes them unique. Newborns already show individual differences in temperament in their irritability to stimuli (von Salisch & Kunzmann, 2005) and in the intensity of their movements (Frank & La Barre, 2011).

Core affectivity can therefore only be changed to a certain extent, mostly through dramatic events in someone's life or experiences that really shake them up. In the treatment of borderline patients, who usually show a great intensity of every emotional experience – a high core affectivity – we therefore work with accepting the basic individuality of the person and helping them to regulate arousal levels (Linehan, 1993). Psychotherapy work with emotion regulation has to distinguish between working on the core affectivity determined by temperament or on particular emotions, since the latter are easier to change and should be treated differently from regulatory disorders on the core affective level (Section 10.1).

Clinical significance

We should consider not the aggressivity of borderline patients as inherent, but rather the impulsivity. Aggression as a behaviour resulting from anger is more likely a reaction to painful or frustrating life experiences (Geuter, 2019, pp. 184–6).

11.6 ATTACHMENT

Attachment research also supports the notion that interactional schemas are anchored deeply in the affect motor coded patterns of experience and behaviour. Bowlby's theory of attachment was always very physical (Orbach, 2004, p. 22). However, according to White (2004a), for reasons of respectability, attachment theory has not asserted that the child desires the body of the mother. In body psychotherapy, however, we regard attachment styles as affect motor patterns.

Attachment theory presupposes a primary need for proximity. Patterns of attachment to the earliest caregivers develop in the interactive regulation of this need (Karen, 1998). Mammals form attachment to their offspring first and foremost through touch. In human development, touch is the basis of experience (Barnard & Brazelton, 1990). It is thus not surprising that Beebe's research shows that negative qualities of maternal touch at 4 months correlate with an insecure attachment at 12 months (Downing, 2004, p. 446). For small children, closeness is physical. Nevertheless, the reception of attachment theory pays little attention to the physicalness of attachment. Grawe (2007) describes attachment schemas as motivational schemas without even mentioning the bodily communication inherent in them. This is also because attachment research has worked out the patterns of attachment, but neglected to show how they are developed through body language dialogue (Downing, 1996, p. 404, fn 11). In any case, there are very few studies on the role of body contact in early development (Downing, 2015).

Fonagy and Target (2007, p. 432) at least assert that attachment research has underestimated body experience, which is the basis for the internal working models of attachment. Without giving their reasons, they write that this is not an argument for body-oriented psychotherapy. Clinically they only utilise gestures, prosody and the emotional use of syntax as mediators of metaphorical meaning.

Dornes (1997, p. 308) speaks of attachment styles as feeling habits with which he wants to make clear that a securely attached child, for example, does not evoke the absent mother in a cognitive image, but instead carries her within themselves because of their experiences with situations entailing separation, soothing and comfort (Chapter 12: 'Basic concept'). These experiences are acquired in an emotional–bodily dialogue and are therefore part of the emotional–procedural memory.

The early development of attachment is connected to the regulation of core affectivity:

> in forming an attachment bond of somatically expressed emotional communications, the
> mother is synchronizing and resonating with the rhythms of infant's dynamic internal states
> and then regulating the arousal level of these negative and positive states.
>
> (Schore, 2003, p. 39)

Schore bases attachment theory on a theory of regulation, since attachment develops by the mother regulating the changing states of arousal and emotion of the infant. Therefore he describes this psychobiological attunement as the 'essential mechanism that mediates attachment bond formation' (Schore, 2003, p. 11). Attachments are 'synchronised dyadic bioenergetic transmissions' (p. 117); the caregiver modulates changes on the level of the arousal. The observation that infants with only a low ability to orient themselves and at the same time a high excitability have greater difficulties in developing a secure attachment (Spangler & Grossmann, 1995, p. 57) is compatible with Schore's view. Here we could speak of the infant's core affective trait factor as part of the shaping of attachment style.

Schore comes close to a body-oriented view of attachment, which takes early, physical togetherness as the origin of the shaping of psychological structure and the development of attachment styles. However in his therapeutic conclusions, he remains strangely pallid and confines himself to a verbal psychotherapy. Orbach (2004) calls attention to another possible conclusion from attachment research. She presumes that patients use the body of the therapist as children do that of their caregiver, when they generate physical sensations in the therapist while seeking help with their own problematic body experiences.

Important
Attachment styles are affect motor patterns for the regulation of needs and feelings in relation to others.

All the findings of attachment research with small children in the so-called 'strange situation' are based on evaluating the affect motor interaction between infant and mother in which the form of physical touch or its absence plays a central role. The four empirically determined attachment styles which children display when they are separated and then reunited with the mother (Ainsworth et al., 1978) are patterns of affect motor regulating of connection and separation, and of the core affects of pleasure and displeasure and the arousal level connected to them:

- **Children with a secure attachment** turn towards the mother when she enters the room again. They greet her, let themselves be soothed and held if the separation has distressed them, and when they are calm, they return to their play. The mother is attentive and responsive to the child.
- **Children with an anxious-avoidant attachment** evade the mother. They avoid bodily contact so as to escape rejection and suppress the expression of negative affects. The mothers refuse to comfort their children and turn away from them or force themselves on them by interrupting their play.
- **Children with an anxious-ambivalent attachment** display a high level of tension and strong affects such as anxiety or anger; they run to the mother, cling to her and then run away again. Some of them hang on to their mothers, but cannot calm down. The mothers sometimes draw the child towards them, sometimes push them away without any clear structure recognisable to the child.

- **Children with a disorganised attachment** behave unexpectedly and in a bizarre way. It is not possible to describe either their behaviour or that of their mothers coherently. They cry when the mother returns after the separation, or they run away from her when they are afraid. They say: 'I want you' and at the same time move away. Sometimes they freeze in a movement, lie down rigidly on the floor or cling unexpectedly. Their movements can be fragmented or suddenly frozen. Such children lack all ability to manage and regulate emotions (Chaffin et al., 2006). This attachment style plays a major role in connection with the after-effects of traumatisation.

Longitudinal studies show that attachment styles are relatively stable into adulthood (Grossmann et al., 2002). With adult attachment interviews, we can explore them as representations of experience:

- Young people with a **secure attachment** regard a reliable relationship as a source of wellbeing and have cognitive and emotional access to their partner.
- Young people with a **dismissive attachment** speak positively about their partner but what they say is not filled with lively feelings and memories; it seems incoherent.
- Young people with **unresolved attachment** talk a lot about emotional issues, but they are not able to evaluate their partnerships.

This is how adult attachment styles are represented cognitively; however, they are expressed in experience and behaviour as psychophysiological patterns in relation to other people.

> Securely attached people are better able to understand the signals of body language than those who are insecurely attached. People with an avoidant attachment style tend to overlook signals of need or stress, whereas those with an anxious style tend to respond too strongly (Wallin, 2007, pp. 262–3).

Which attachment style a child develops depends primarily on maternal sensitivity in the early years. In addition, whether the father is empathic and encouraging towards the child when they play is also a predictor of attachment style. However children can develop different attachment styles towards each parent. Mothers rated by observers as competent in their body contact with the child tend to have securely attached children. The quality of the relationship consists in the parent's ability to respond and attune themselves to the child (Downing, 1996, p. 153). According to an evaluation of videotaped mother–child interactions carried out by Trautmann-Voigt and Zander (2007), this quality is shown in the mothers' movements. Mothers of securely attached children react to them with middling intensity and well-balanced bodily movements; mothers of children with an anxious-avoidant attachment style tend to be passive; mothers of children with an anxious-ambivalent style escalate the interaction or withdraw completely from the reciprocal relationship by behaving just like the child in their movements. Children with disorganised attachment were not represented in this study. However the behaviour of these mothers is often unpredictable and punctuated by extreme mood swings. Often these mothers have not been able to deal with their own traumatic experiences and are ten times more likely than other mothers to have lost an attachment figure before the age of 7 (Grossmann, 2000).

When a sensitive attachment figure explores the wellbeing of the child, they help them to gain an image of themselves, to identify their own feelings and intentions and to get an idea of the feelings and intentions of others. Thus a secure attachment facilitates mentalisation. At this point too we see that the mutuality between mother and child on an affect motor basis precedes the cognitive perception of mental states.

11.7 LIFELONG DEVELOPMENT

The foundations for the basic schemas of experience and behaviour are laid in the first years of life. They are inscribed deeply into the emotional-procedural memory and surface in the physical strategies with which someone approaches their environment and their contemporaries. This does not mean, however, that a person is pre-determined from childhood on or that their development is finished when they are grown up. People change, above all through dramatic experiences, throughout their lifetimes, and so does the emotional structure of their bodies. The body also is transformed during its life cycle and various somatic-emotional transitions have to be gone through. Adolescence especially is a time of fierce transformations whereby huge changes in cognitive and emotional faculties linked to a boost in brain development take place (Fogel, 2009, p. 177). Through the experiences of sexuality and partnership, body image is formed anew, and attachment styles can change. This is why at this age mental disorders related to the body, such as anorexia or body dysmorphic disorder, can develop. Also adolescents are more starkly confronted with society's expectations of the ideal body than are children, which is why illnesses such as hysteria or bulimia develop especially in young people.

In psychotherapy, we always work with a person's whole life story. Being able to access the person through the body helps to open up those layers formed in early life, which are often difficult to reach through words.

12

Affect motor schemas as body narratives

Agatha Israel reports the following observation:

Clinical example

A premature baby is lying in the neonatal intensive care unit. The single mother, who also has two school-age children, is rarely there, and the nurses leave the child alone. The little girl screams rigidly without any tears. The child therapist thinks she is seeking contact and screaming for a good ear that hears her suffering. She has the impression that the child is already splitting off her feelings and is 'just screaming out the unbearable'. Israel infers from this: 'When nobody and nothing is there, then the child armours herself against the emptiness with her rigidity' (Israel & Reissmann, 2008, p. 110).

Thus we could describe early armouring and early affect motor pattern as the way in which the baby deals with experience. Since nobody comes to help her, she has to cope with these unbearable feelings alone, by making herself stiff and creating an inner support through muscle rigidity. She learns affect motorically to behave like this, because all her attempts to find help and support in an attachment relationship have failed.

We can describe such an experience as follows:

- On the level of a **one-person psychology**, as a rigid armouring out of which a character attitude can later develop, an 'emotional anatomy' (Keleman, 1985).
- On the **relational** level as an affect motor schema resulting from interactive experience – or in this case the lack of it – and which can determine the form of later relationships; for example, when she feels a need, the child will make herself rigid, as she expects that it will not be met.

With the theory of character structure, we can name and classify prototypical defensive attitudes (Section 13.2). With the notion of affect motor schemas, however, we can describe **individual patterns of interaction**, which appear in experience and behaviour. Totton (2019, p. 286) speaks of 'embodied engrams of relating, organising our bodymind behaviour and activating accompanying habitual thoughts and attitudes.'

DOI: 10.4324/9781003176893-12

Various schemas can be activated. according to the context. Some of them, such as the search for human contact through the eyes, through sounds and movements, are available from birth on (Section 7.1: distress vocalisations). However most of them are acquired through childhood experiences. Like character structures, they bear witness to stories living in the body, which we retell through our interactions.

Important
In character structures, as in affect motor patterns, a person tells the story of their relational and life experiences in the form of a body narrative. In their posture and movements, people express how they feel towards other people and situations.

Whereas the character structure theory explains this 'body narrative' (Aalberse, 2001; Petzold, 2000) mainly on the basis of drive theory (Section 13.2), Downing has made use of **object relations theory** and empirical infant research for body psychotherapy. His focus is on the quality of the relationship that the child experiences interactively. Downing (1996, p. 130) coined the term 'affect motor schemas', which I have frequently used here as synonymous with 'affect motor patterns'. He understands these as constellations of motoric behavioural patterns, cognitive evaluations and affective tone, also including breathing patterns. These constellations are generalised **patterns of the organisation of experience**, through which we experience the world and which we developed through experience (Johnson, 2007, pp. 131–2). Thus they are the past, the present and the future of an individual. We could call them in terms of transactional analysis **embodied scripts**, which determine the nature of interpersonal *transactions* (cf. Berne, 1964; Monsen & Monsen, 1999, p. 292), or in terms of existential analysis as a person's characteristic way of *being-in-the-world*.

The schema concept

The concept of schema was advanced in Gestalt psychology in 1932 by Bartlett and was first adopted by humanistic psychotherapy (Laengle & Kriz, 2012, p. 433). Today it is used in psychology and psychotherapy for the 'orders in the processes of perception, cognition, action and interaction' (Kriz, 2017, p. 83), although not consistently. Lammers (2007, p. 74) defines a schema generally as 'a preformed emotional-cognitive-behavioural mode of reaction to certain stimuli, which through significant learning experiences in childhood and adolescence have become important'. A schema thus acts as a **complexity reduction**, so that 'through their own experience a person can immediately classify a situation relevant to their needs according to its significance for their lives' (Lammers, 2007, p. 74).

In the language of scientific theory, we can see schemas as **hypothetical constructs**. A cognitive-emotional schema, for example, is posited as an inner structure controlling behaviour, which can itself only be recognised from outside through the verbal and non-verbal expressions of the person in question. Schemas are deduced from observable tendencies in perception, emotional evaluation, felt sensation and exhibited motor behaviour. Wehowsky therefore describes them, in contrast to verbal representations of knowledge, as 'nonverbal patterns' constituting an 'embodied organisation of knowledge' (Wehowsky, 2015a, p. 323).

The theory of affect motor schemas inherits from sociology Bourdieu's theory (1984) that in the **habitus**, the necessities of practical action are transformed into motor schemas and automatic body reactions. Thus, affect motor schemas are also determined by socio-cultural rules of behaviour and the external imperatives people are subject to. A clinical theory of body psychotherapy should not forget that alienation and repression always manifest in the body. Schemas are often a result of desired or enforced conformity to adverse conditions.

From psychology, the theory inherits the notion of Piaget's **sensorimotor schemas**. These contain patterns of sensory information about an object and the motor action associated with it and are related to aspects of cognition and intelligence linked to actions (Wehowsky, 2015a). According to Piaget, new experiences are integrated into existing schemas through a process of **assimilation,** and in turn, through **accommodation**, schemas are adapted to new experiences (Piaget & Inhelder, 2000). In contrast to sensorimotor schemas, affect motor schemas include emotions. They regulate not only the relationship between the individual and the world of objects, but first and foremost between self and other in interpersonal relationships (Downing, 1996, p. 131).

The concept is similar to the idea of **relational schemas** from Grawe (2004). He understands relational or motivational schemas as directing psychological activity towards goals and thus regulating needs. In addition, he mentions conflict and intentional schemas. In the consistency theory of Grosse Holtforth and Grawe (2004, p. 10), **motivational schemas** are seen as a person's potential to satisfy basic needs. They are classified into two groups: **approach schemas** to create experiences where needs are met; and **avoidance schemas** to protect against hurtful experiences of rejection. However, since Grawe's thinking does not include the lived body (Section 1.2), it overlooks motor strategies and motor knowledge that express interactional experiences and implement motivational schemas.

Also similar is Greenberg's (2011) concept of **emotion schemes**, whereby he means cognitive-affective units important for a person's integrated functioning. Despite the fact that Greenberg maintains that the preconceptual, experiential elements which generate action are central here, he does not include bodily aspects in his theory. Bucci (2011, p. 49) sees emotional schemas as forms of memory structure and also leaves out the motoric aspect.

Stern (1995), on the other hand, presumes that **schemas-of-being-with** are made up of perceptual schemas, conceptual schemas, sensor-motor schemas and representations of event sequences. What he describes as RIGs, however, are rather representations of single interaction sequences (Section 11.3). The concept of schema refers to a higher level of generalisation.

Schema therapy

At present, the notion of schemas is often linked to schema therapy (Young et al., 2006). Schema therapy developed out of cognitive therapy and has integrated ideas from other therapy approaches, including the model of ego states from transactional analysis (child ego-, parent ego- and adult ego-state), as well as the psychodynamic notion that the way someone deals with situations and with other people has its roots in the frustration of their basic needs; this is also the basis of character structure theory (Section 13.2). With his schema categories, Young, however, follows no developmental theory.

In schema therapy, the schema concept refers primarily to dysfunctional schemata (Berbalk & Young, 2009). These are formed through harmful experiences in relation to basic needs; schemas of dependency, vulnerability or failure, for example, are linked to the need for autonomy (Section 10.3). Eighteen dysfunctional schemas are grouped into five so-called schema domains. According to this approach, schemas appear in a state called a schema mode. These are classified into the categories of child modes (vulnerable, angry, impulsive), maladaptive parent modes (demanding, punitive), maladaptive coping modes (e.g. detached self-soothing and avoiding, narcissistic overcompensating, surrendering, overcontrolling) and a functional healthy adult mode.

Unlike this categorical model, the theory of affect motor schemas describes individual patterns of thinking, feeling and acting that can be helpful or obstructive. It also differs from schema therapy in prioritising motor patterns. In schema therapy, bodily sensations are included in descriptions of patterns but not systematically in the concept of therapeutic work.

BODY KNOWLEDGE

Bergson already had the idea that something like **motor schemas** exists:

> Consider memory, the body retains motor habits capable of acting the past over again; it can resume attitudes in which the past will insert itself.
>
> (Bergson, 1911, p. 299)

This is already true even at the level of learning bodily skills. This kind of learning leads to a physically encoded knowledge, which the owner can often not describe in words. For example, a football player runs to the exact place where the ball, flying in a great arc, will land. The players know this intuitively. It can be determined roughly by keeping the angle of their view of the ball constant while they are running (Gigerenzer, 2007, pp. 17–8). Probably the players are not conscious of doing this, but they follow the rule in the actions of the body. They know it motorically.

According to the psychologist Karl Buehler (1934), such motor knowledge is **empractical**, meaning that it is connected to physical action and so remains implicit. It does not become explicit and can hardly be made so, because it was learnt and carried out pre-reflectively. From motoric experience, people know what they have to do. They follow a motor schema that links perception to movement. This **sensorimotor intelligence** is for Piaget (2001) the basis for intelligence in general. Bodily intelligence is hypercomplex and to date cannot be reproduced in machines (Section 5.2: Artificial intelligence).

Body knowledge is created by repetition or practice (Section 9.2). This is also true of affect motor patterns. They are not created in moments of heightened emotion, but through repeated experience (Beebe & Lachmann, 1994). Once we have learnt them, they become part of our personality. 'In implicit, empractical knowledge what has become second nature through repetition appears like first nature' (Caysa, 2008, p. 74). It seems not like acquired knowledge but like something that just belongs to us. Since empractical memory is tied to the body, we do not have it, it has us. In sport philosophy, Caysa comes close to the notion of affect motor schemas when he writes that, as empractical knowledge, memory is an affective-mental body knowledge that runs through all stages of life and can be passed on from one generation to another (Caysa, 2008, p. 80; Section 9.3).

Clinical example

Barratt (2010, p. 43) describes a patient who, while speaking, tenses up her shoulders and lifts them, letting her head hang down with the chin close to the chest. All this has no recognisable connection to what she is saying. In the course of a longer process, images and nightmares came back to her showing that her mother would frequently cuff her about the head, often for no discernible reason.

MOTORIC BELIEFS

In dealing with the world of objects, we develop what Downing (1996, p. 115) called motoric beliefs, a combination of motor and cognitive processes. We see them when, for example, a child makes herself ready to hold something with the appropriate tension, when somebody gives her something that she knows. Her bodily strategy contains a motoric belief, which is not necessarily explainable. Downing illustrates this with an experiment from Bower, in which children watch how an experimenter forms a lump of clay first into a long, thin cylinder and then into a ball. The children hold each object in turn. When they are asked which of the objects is heavier, the majority think it is the ball. However, if they are given the two differently formed objects one after the other to hold, then their arms move in the same way to take each of them. Arms, hands and shoulders seem therefore to expect the same weight. The belief shown in their empractical actions is more geared to reality than what they say.

In their motor actions, patients sometimes communicate their symptoms. An example is the little boy in a case of Piontelli's (Section 11.1: Lost twins), who acts as if he is looking for something. According to Downing (1996, p. 125), particularly patients with severe disorders express developmental deficits in motoric convictions. Their life experiences often elude their self-perception (Rudolf, 2018, p. 70). However we can see the affect motor patterns that have been shaped by these.

Clinical application

In the therapy room, we can observe how a patient structures the space. How much room do they take up? Do they retreat into a small space and stay there? Or do they just perch on the edge of the chair? Does this maybe indicate that this is all they deserve? Or do they take up more than their share of the space? Maybe they cannot find a place to settle; could this indicate that they are convinced there is no place for them in life?

Through early experiences, patterns of motor relationships to objects and to people develop. When an infant repeatedly has their nappy changed or is picked up, at some point they will stretch out their arms or lift up their legs, because they know what will happen next. Thus a sensomotor schema develops from experience. The infant learns a habit in which there is as yet no distinction between the means and the end, since the end can only be reached through a necessary sequence of movements (Piaget & Inhelder, 2000). A habit is formed through constant repetition of sensomotor actions until it becomes second nature (Fuchs, 2008, p. 38). The child now knows the tension, rhythm and flow of an action. They learn how it begins, how it continues and when it is over. Downing calls such a sequence a body micro-practice (2000; Section 11.3).

AFFECTIVE EXPERIENCE

In interpersonal interaction, in addition to motor and cognitive patterns, we have affective tone. The child's actions take place in a relationship and thus are tied to emotional meanings. This is how schemas, which are sensory, motor, cognitive **and** emotional, develop.

Example of interaction

When an infant pushes the mother with their hands, she might put them down because she interprets the movement as the child wanting more room. Another mother might start to play with the child, pushing and shoving each other. A third might interpret the movement as aggressive and spurn them with the words: 'You're a bad child!' Each style of interaction leaves the infant with an experience which is stored affect motorically and records what effect the gesture of pushing someone with their hands produces.

Affect motor schemas are the result of frequent interactive experiences, especially of early relationships experienced mainly in bodily contact, and they form an implicit actional and relational knowledge which is inscribed in the body (Lyons-Ruth, 1998; Streeck, 2013). Similarly Totton and Priestman (2012, p. 39) speak of embodied-relational or procedural memory engrams. This knowledge surfaces in the way in which the body regulates social interactions (Streeck, 2018, pp. 29–30).

When behaviour such as that described in the above examples is constantly repeated, the first infant learns that their actions – regardless of why they are doing them – lead to physical separation; the second child expects a happy game; the third expects rejection. Thus for future emotional and relational experiences, it is not so much the contents of the experience stored cognitively (I remember my mother treated me in such and such a way) that are crucial but rather these repetitive 'procedures of past mutual regulations' (Tronick, 1998, p. 299). Affect motor schemas thus create 'future potentialities of experience and action' (Wehowsky, 2015a, p. 326) which appear in body posture, movement, voice expression and the use of the senses, but also in cognitive belief systems. In affect motor schemas, movements are connected to cognition and affects.

Example of interaction

I remind you here of the example described in Section 11.3, in which a mother overstimulates her child to such an extent that they have to shut her off. This makes the mother uneasy, so that as soon as the infant is present again, she is relieved and immediately starts a new cycle of stimulation. She follows a strategy of 'more of the same' to solve a problem in the interaction, that she herself causes again and again through her behaviour. For the child this could be the beginning of an affect motor schema of retreating into a state of emotional numbness when the stimulus is too strong. This pattern then serves to regulate affect tensions and can continue on into adult life without its origins becoming conscious.

In repetitive interactions, children acquire movement patterns with the help of which they regulate tensions. In movement dialogues, they learn whole motor sequences (Gebauer,

2008, p. 50). These patterns are inscribed into body memory (Downing, 1996, p. 129). Caldwell (2012) speaks of motor maps. In their movements and accompanying body sensations, we can later perceive how a person organises their experiences (Frank, 2005, p. 120). Both aspects reveal in the present their embodied life story (Frank & La Barre, 2011, p. 79).

ATTUNEMENT

The affect motor interchange between parents and child is good when the adult can adjust themselves to the rhythm, intensity and form of the child's expression. This attunement takes place on the level of the processual contour of an action determined by an affect, or what Stern calls vitality affects (Section 10.5). There seems to be a basic rhythm of vocal and gestural expression that can be transcribed musically and which we find in children's rhymes and songs (Trevarthen, 2003). For example, if the rhythm is too fast then 12-month-old infants display anxious behaviour (Downing, 2015). If a child expresses anger, sadness or joy, some parents tend to slow the rhythm and thus lead the child to restrict their expressivity. Others increase their movements and stimulate the child to a more intensive expressivity.

> Others join in; and then, neither undermatching nor overmatching, permit the infant to feel
> out and explore her own evolving rhythm (the best outcome, needless to say).
>
> (Downing, 2000, p. 261)

Attunement occurs for the most part unconsciously and over short periods of time. Papousek's studies (1994) show that infants expect contingent reactions without a time lapse. When child and adult often mismatch, this is not worrying. What is important is that that they find each other over and over again.

CONNECTION AND SEPARATION

According to Downing, the first basic issues of affect motor schemas are connection and separation. In psychoanalysis, Mahler described the differentiation between self and object from the age of 4–5 months and emphasised the concomitant autonomy as the primary goal of development. Downing considers the ability to form attachments to be of equal importance. While separation schemas show how we pull away from others, connection schemas show how we reach out to them (Downing, 1996, p. 138). He argues convincingly that both schema types develop from birth onwards and not in phases one after the other, as Mahler assumed. Similarly, Trautmann-Voigt and Voigt (2009, pp. 155–7) distinguish two *affect motor prototypes* of body movement: one they call the type of round, nestling, introverted movement of a baby, with which they entrust themselves to parental care; the other is the type of expansive movement corresponding to the use of autonomous energy as they move out into the world. Here we recognise the attachment and exploration behaviour from Bowlby's attachment theory (Section 11.6).

Children learn a connection schema, for example, in the way in which they are able to make contact with the mother through the eyes and elicit a certain reaction (Downing, 1996, pp. 172–3). This schema develops in interaction with the mother's reactions. Mutual gazing deepens the connection. The pupils of adults dilate when they see a baby, and this in turn lets the child's pupils also dilate (Schore, 2003, pp. 7–8). Children protest when the mother withdraws from contact with them and they turn away when she is too pushy (Tronick, 1989, p. 116). A schema acquired in early life determines the desire for closeness or avoidance of the same later in life. The attachment styles described in attachment research can be seen as prototypical patterns extracted from the array of possible affect motor schemas of connection.

When a baby surrenders or lets themselves go, this allows them to connect with the other, and when they push, to disengage (Frank & La Barre, 2011. p. 27). In body psychotherapy, we can directly address these affect motor schemas of connection and separation.

Clinical application

In the exercise called *reaching out*, in either a standing or lying position, we stretch our arms out to the front with palms inwards and say: 'Come here', 'Mummy' or 'Daddy' or 'Mummy, Daddy, please come'. This activates the desire for connection. A desire for separation or bordering can be activated by the client pushing against the hands of the therapist while standing, trying to push them away. They can also say 'Go away' or 'Leave me alone' or something similar. This is not only about bordering but also about having one's own strength validated or responded to.

BASIC CONCEPT

As a basic body psychotherapeutic concept, the theory of affect motor schemas is connected to the theory of emotional-procedural memory and that of affect and emotion regulation (Section 9.3; Chapter 10). Through interactive experiences, an implicit action knowledge about how to model interpersonal relationships develops in the form of schemas, which usually remain unconscious, but can be made conscious. The affect motor patterns that people exhibit in relationships are not the manifestation of a suppressed unconscious, but of experiences which were acquired implicitly, stored in the emotional-procedural memory and restaged as unconscious, affective-cognitive-motor habits (Figure 9.1; Chapter 9).

Affect motor patterns contain strategies with which a person regulates their core affects and their emotions in relation to other people. They are not summoned from the top down, but activated from the bottom up. They are not 'belief systems', as rules for behaving are often called in cognitive therapy, since they are not purely cognitive and any symbolisation only occurs retroactively. They are also not the unconscious fantasies that psychoanalysis regards as determining action. People trapped in affect motor patterns may act **as if** they have a fantasy, as Dornes (1997, p. 320) writes – for example, that they are afraid of being forgotten if they do not angrily make themselves heard; however, they are living the fear which is inscribed in their memory as an emotional procedure. However, the lived fear can manifest simultaneously as a fantasy or a belief system. Thus affect motor patterns are also not representations acquired through cognitive learning, as internalisations are seen in object relations theory (Kernberg, 2006, pp. 5–6). Rather they are a procedural reflection of co-created regulative patterns (cf. Lyons-Ruth, 1998, p. 285). Also they are not just 'interactional images' (von Arnim et al., 2022, p. 66), since they are deeply rooted in early bodily experiences of interaction. As Dornes (1997, p. 48) writes, a mother is not an image that the infant classifies in their mind and then brings up again as needed, but the sum of sensations triggered by her presence. Experiences with her are not merely 'internalised relational experiences' as attachment theory will have it (Strauss & Schwark, 2007, p. 405). They are present in that they are lived. Affect motor schemas appear in interpersonal behaviour or body strategies, but also in sensations, feelings and thoughts. Often we can only speak of the knowledge inherent in affect motor patterns when it surfaces actively, reveals itself and is experienced (Wehowsky, 2015a). Herein lies the significance of experiential therapy.

Important
Affect motor schemas are lived experiences, stored in emotional-procedural memory, that appear in a person's relationship with themselves, with others and with the environment as affect-cognitive-motor habits or lifestyles.

Without using the notion of affect motor schemas themselves, Fuchs and De Jaegher (2010) take the example of a child with a borderline mother to make the point that schemas are not representations, nor are they cognitive working models. They criticise the view of mentalisation theory (Section 11.2) that the child has to inhibit their ability to understand the state of a borderline mother because the representation of her aggressive affects is unbearable.

> The alternative view is that the mother's hate is expressed through the quality and dynamics of the embodied interaction, e.g. repeatedly rejecting the infant's approach or overriding his initiative. As a result, these interaction sequences are taken up in his implicit memory in their *process* form, not their *content* form, e.g. as a bodily tension and resistance which the infant builds up against his own impulses to approach the mother.
>
> (Fuchs & De Jaegher, 2010, p. 211)

In order to do that, the child does not have to form a representation of the inner state of the mother; instead they show their implicit knowledge in the form of an avoidant coping style.

PATHOGENIC SCHEMAS

In therapy, we aim at changing those schemas that cause suffering and reinforcing those that facilitate a satisfying life. Maladaptive development of affect motor schemas can form the basis for mental disorders (Downing, 1996, p. 149). Neurotic schemas lead people to stick to familiar patterns (Huether et al., 1999, p. 91) even though the old experiences which guided behaviour in the past are inadequate for the demands of the present. Freud called this *repetition compulsion*. When people cling to affect motor schemas because of early imprinting, then they will often experience the same thing again and again. They always approach the objects of their experience in the same manner and organise them within the established pattern (cf. Greenberg & Van Balen, 1998, p. 50).

We could describe the deficits that Rudolf (2006) enumerates in his theory of the so-called structural disorders, and which he views as forming the basis for regulation dysfunction, as pathogenic schemas. According to his theory, the contact between self and others – the connection schemas – is disturbed in patients with structural disorders, as is the ability to differentiate oneself from others – the separation schemas.

Pathogenic beliefs, which, according to cognitive theories such as Weiss's control mastery theory, are at the root of mental disorders (Albani et al., 1999), are incorporated so to speak in affect motor patterns. Examples of such beliefs are:

- If I let someone get close I will be abused.
- If I get attached I will lose myself.
- If I approach a woman/a man I'm so anxious I can't feel anything.
- If I say what I want in life, I will be put down.
- If I make myself independent I'll lose my footing.

Patients do not just articulate these beliefs, they live them in their patterns. They become a problem when a person can only behave and experience the world in accordance with them. Disorders are repetitive patterns. The problem is not that a person has a pattern, but that the pattern has the person.

Clinical example

Meyer (2001) describes a patient who always withdrew when women approached him sexually; however he also felt compelled to seduce any woman who attracted him. This game of wooing and rejecting was rooted in a childish affect motor pattern. He had learnt to perceive closeness initiated by someone else as unpleasant. His mother was always fiddling with him and he always felt pressurised when someone approached him; at the same time he wanted intimacy. This pattern also appeared in his relationship to the therapist.

Therapeutic work is working with such patterns. It can be more profound when we not only address cognitive beliefs but also the narrative of the body.

> Self-narratives seem to be able to dominate a person only when the body is set in a specific state of being ... a binding self-narrative is destructive for the body only so long as it can draw strength from the specific emotional posture embodied in a specific physiological body state ... The important stories of our lives are those that are enacted by our bodies.
>
> (Griffith & Griffith, 1994, pp. 132, 135)

In body psychotherapy, we aim to explore the debilitating schemas so that the patient can attain a new emotional demeanour, a new embodied self-narrative and a satisfying inner state (Griffith & Griffith, 1994, p. 198). Schmidt-Zimmermann and Marlock (2011a) describe how with a depressive patient they explore affect motor schemas of collapse and helplessness on the cognitive level as well as on the level of somatically identifiable patterns, how they understand the coming-into-being of these patterns and, through a regaining of vital feeling movement, develop new, self-supporting and supportive structural components (Schmidt-Zimmermann & Marlock, 2011a, pp. 103–5).

Dysfunctional affect motor schemas are akin to what other theories refer to as maladaptive interpersonal patterns. These are seen as introjects of early relationships to loved ones, which surface in therapy as salient interactive patterns (Horowitz, 1991). They appear in enactments which evolve out of emotional-procedural memory as 'a reproducing action' (Wehowsky, 2015a, p. 327).

Among psychotherapists, enactments are at times seen as resistance. This can be true in the case of hysterical patients, such as Freud treated at the beginning of psychoanalysis. However an enactment is not necessarily preventing something. Often something is 'on the stage' simply because it is there. It is notably those patients with personality disorders or somatic symptom disorders who are driven by their unresolved, sensory affects to show their suffering in this way. Above all, pre-verbal experiences 'pressure for action repetition since they cannot be remembered in any other way' (Dornes, 1993, p. 192). The notion of resistance is completely inapplicable here, since 'implicit regulatory memories and representations, play a constant role ... in making up a large part of our lived past and symptomatic present' (Stern, 2004, p. 143).

In body psychotherapy, we explore maladaptive affect motor schemas not only in what patients tell us about their significant relationships, but also in what we see during interaction with them. We can reflect on both aspects verbally, but in bodily action dialogues, we can make the patterns conscious and slowly change them (Geuter, 2019, pp. 286–312). Since these schemas are based on affect motor learning experiences, they can only change through new affect motor experiences.

Clinical example

Schmidt-Zimmermann (2010) describes a patient who had feelings of helplessness with regard to her boss. She remembered her brother who was two years older and used to attack her as a child, verbally and also physically. In the session, she displays a defensive affect motor schema: she stands with her head down and waves her arms about blindly and impotently so as to keep the brother away from her. Linked to this posture is the conviction that she is small and inferior and not able to defend herself. Schmidt-Zimmermann lets the patient narrate her relationship to her brother with her body. The patient shows how she makes contact, takes up a posture of vigilance and then turns away. Finally she arrives at a posture of 'Don't hurt me' and 'I just want to get away', which are connected to a loss of energy. Schmidt-Zimmermann now lets her stand for a while in this posture so that she can feel what is happening. After a while, an impulse develops out of the body to defend herself against her brother; this is linked to the phrases 'Leave me alone' and 'Go away'. A spontaneous reorganisation is going on in which, out of affect motor intelligence, the old schema is transformed into a new possibility to face her brother.

This sequence fulfils what Worm (2007, p. 218) formulates as the aim of therapy: 'understanding the fixed patterns in connection with their history and their current function of regulating relationships'. The memory of how the patient experienced her relationship to her brother surfaces from her emotional-procedural memory. Sensomotorically, an early scene from the past unfolds, an affect motor condensed experience that shapes her experience and behaviour in relationships today. By experiencing and narrating the affect motor schema intensively with the body, the patient's awareness of herself is heightened. However to the understanding referred to by Worm, we have to add the fact that the body finds a change from the inside and a new locomotive impulse comes up in relation to her brother, which is linked to the feeling of anger. This example shows how in working with a schema, we can implement the body psychotherapeutic principle of *reorganising and transforming* (Geuter, 2019, pp. 342–59).

When someone becomes aware of an affect motor schema and can sense alternatives, then they expand their conscious and unconscious options. This is a principle of body psychotherapeutic work: to trace back the array of possible experiences and behaviour to basic patterns and to help patients become aware of and change them, so that they can discover a much broader, vital set of choices.

Clinical example

Frank (2005, pp. 121ff) describes a session with a patient who came to her after the death of her adult daughter. Since the patient is very structured, the therapist can offer suggestions on changing a pattern, which the patient can accept and act on. In the session, she sits there motionless and breathing shallowly and tells of a dream with a red suitcase. The therapist asks her to open the suitcase and to look at what is inside. She sees a red lining, but she says she cannot touch it and rubs her fingertips with her thumb. The therapist invites her to pay attention to this spontaneous movement. While she does this her head starts to turn slightly in a circle and she purses her lips and relaxes them again and again. The therapist points out these spontaneous signals of the body. Subsequently the patient contracts and expands her feet in a rhythmic movement, then a similar pulsating movement starts up in the torso and the pelvis. During all this the patient says again, increasingly tense, that she cannot touch the lining of the suitcase. As she starts to gasp for air, the therapist has the impulse to support her physically, and after clearing this with the patient, she sits down so that she can take her feet between her own. This touch leads to a cry of 'Please don't leave me!' The patient is crying but calms down as the therapist shows her that she is there and not going away. Thereupon the patient lies down in the therapist's arms and tells her that all her life she has struggled for air even when she was a little girl with panic attacks.

At that time her mother was in hospital for several months. She was afraid of being abandoned. Through the dream image of not being able to touch the lining, which moved her very much without her knowing what it meant, affect motor memories were coming up in the body of this early feeling of loneliness. This had been activated through the death of her daughter. By following the movements of the body and the intuition of giving her support, the therapist helped her to develop something new out of the pattern of separation anxiety and playing dead. In contact, the patient could have a new experience and then say that **she herself** would never leave her.

Staunton's remarks (2002a, p. 4) are appropriate for this case: our core beliefs are embodied and – even if we are aware of them – they determine our lives until we begin to experience directly in our bodies the pain they contain. We cannot, and need not, always fathom the life experiences that lie behind such affect motor schemas and thus understand how they developed, as in this case. But when we enact a schema in the present moment of experience and behaviour, we can become aware of it, and through a new experience we can give the impulse for a new schema to complement it or to take its place.

13

Defence and coping

Bodily forms of processing experience

The defence theory is at the core of psychodynamic theory. Defence mechanisms serve to avoid experiencing conflictual thoughts, wishes, feelings or impulses and to cope with the tension associated with them. In psychoanalysis, where defence was originally understood as being directed against libidinous wishes and fantasies, repression, denial, identification, rationalisation, splitting or projection are viewed as mainly cognitive operations against ideas and affects, whereas other defence mechanisms such as reaction formation take place on the action level (Geuter & Schrauth, 2001, p. 7). The body was long considered only as a symptom bearer of defence processes. Thus, according to the hysteria theory of Breuer and Freud (1895), undischarged affects became stuck in the motor function.

In the tradition of Reichian theory, however, the idea that the body is involved in the defence processes is of vital importance. If emotional reactions are suppressed, we can often observe this in motor functions. Moreover the defence process is maintained by the body; it persists in bodily tensions and strategies. It helps the patient to live their life as they do and prevents them from living it as they would like. Often it is communicated in unconscious bodily expression. For example, we cannot explain projective identification, a defence mechanism by which the patient unconsciously transfers into others parts of the self that are unacceptable to them and then encounters them in their reactions (Chapter 15), without resorting to a theory of affect communication through body language.

Also in Rogers' client-centred psychotherapy, the notion of defence is vitally important. According to Rogers, the defence system serves to prevent the patient becoming aware of threatening stimuli. With the help of a defensive attitude, essential parts of the organism are excluded from the self-concept (Pfeiffer, 1987). But Rogers (1959) describes defence as a purely cognitive process of selective awareness, distortion of reality or denial of experience. Mindfulness-based behavioural therapy has the concept of **experiential avoidance** similar to the defence theory, by which is meant a verbally communicated tendency to avoid psychological experiences so as to reduce unpleasant feelings (Boulanger et al., 2010, p. 107). What a person is conscious of is mapped out through self-reports. Even in cognitive psychology, the notion of defence mechanisms is an issue and suppression is seen as an unconscious mental process, though measured only on the basis of conscious reports (Cramer, 2000). The psychodynamic defence theory, however, assumes that a dynamic unconscious creates defence processes (Chapter 9).

As diverse as these ideas are, a general theory of defence is not bound to a certain psychotherapeutic paradigm. In line with a theory of experience, we can understand defence mechanisms as strategies to avoid ideas, feelings or action impulses. They protect the person from suffering in the face of experiences of incongruity.

DOI: 10.4324/9781003176893-13

The historical source of a body-oriented theory of defence is Reich's analysis of resistance. In an early debate about psychoanalytical technique, Reich's position was to release suppressed content by analysing the defence and not by interpreting drives (1972, pp. 296, 304; Section 3.1.1). Primarily, he wanted to analyse not the suppressed desires themselves but the function of the means by which a patient held them back. In psychoanalysis, this later became a basic principle of resistance analysis. Since each resistance has a specific form and gets its specific character from the personality as a whole, Reich replaced symptom analysis with the analysis of 'character formation' from 1925 onwards (Reich, 1974, p. 6).

Sometimes the concepts of **resistance** and **defence** are not clearly differentiated. By resistance, we mean that the patient obstructs or hinders the therapeutic process and resists something coming up, and by defence unconscious processes which generally regulate unpleasant, unwanted or unbearable affects, impulses or ideas (Chapter 13).

Reich understood character as a structure formed of patterns of defence. In solidified structures, which we could call patterns of affect regulation in relationships, significant basic conflicts between desire and reality become manifest. Reich (1973, p. 353) differentiated between the origin of these patterns in the life story and their current function in thinking, feeling and in the body, between the historical and its current dynamic explanation. He looked for a mechanism with the help of which a traumatic or conflict-ridden experience was being retained in a pathological reaction (Reich, 1973, p. 356). He believed he had found this mechanism in the incorporation of the defence system. This hypothesis has much to commend it.

DEFENSIVE BEHAVIOUR

Defence develops from what are initially protective mechanisms of the body, which through learning are then changed, reinforced or become chronic. Small children are not yet capable of cognitive defence. As the example of the premature baby in Chapter 12 shows, infants' defence systems are purely sensomotoric (Dornes, 1997, p. 49). Infants react to the breaking off of relationship with a contraction of the whole organism, a freezing up (Harms, 2008, p. 56), as for example those in the still-face experiments (Section 11.3). Schore (2003) hypothesises that, because of the early development of the right hemisphere, dissociation as a defence against traumatic affects precedes repression, which is probably more a function of the left hemisphere. Utilising their motor abilities, children can involuntarily suppress affective arousal and impulses (cf. Dornes, 1997, pp. 296–9). This suppression is a defence using the body. We can speak here of protective, defensive **behaviour** as a reaction to fear, intrusiveness or rejection (Miller et al., 2002, pp. 428–9). Such behaviour is a means of actively adapting to adverse conditions. Successful defence is therefore an achievement that we must acknowledge in psychotherapy (Rosenberg et al., 1985).

The defensive parts of any of us are very much like frightened little children. They need lots of love, attention, and reassurance. They need to tell what they are afraid of and have those fears dealt with in an adult way.

(S Johnson, 1985, p. 109)

Reich wanted to eliminate the defences like an illness. I see them more in the sense of Fenichel (Section 3.1), as an attempt to protect oneself from damage, analogous to the immune system (Heller, 2012, p. 489). In this tradition, Gestalt therapy also views the muscle tension accompanying defence mechanisms as a function of the ego (Kepner, 1993). For humanistic psychology, Maslow asserts that 'defensiveness can be as wise as daring' (1968, p. 54). It is a self-protective mechanism.

By differentiating between genesis and current dynamics, Reich drew attention to **how** and not what children suppress (Totton, 2002, p. 11). Children avoid bodily core affective arousal and pleasure by making themselves stiff. When they have traumatic experiences, they transfer the fear and the pain to the body. Through tensing up the muscles and breathing shallowly, they can repress emotional arousal or urgent impulses: gritting one's teeth so as not to scream, a ramrod posture so as not to rage, holding one's breath and pressing one's lips together so as not to cry or laugh.

Also substituting one affect for another (Greenberg & Safran, 1989), for example, anger for shame, pride or grief, is 'physical work and chronic tension is the consequence' (Krause, 1998, p. 246). In the case of the *affect block* (Reich, 1972, p. 199), ideas are split off from the affects and the patient appears tense in the body, unapproachable and untouched by everything. Some defence mechanisms such as projection, negation or denial are more of a cognitive nature. Yet even intellectualisation is often linked with a body block against feeling. In what is known in Gestalt therapy as retroflection (Perls et al., 1980, p. 171), affect motor impulses against other people are rerouted towards the self. In splitting, in which the self or objects are perceived as 'all good' or 'all bad', we can find that the good or the evil parts of the self are assigned to certain parts of the body or to certain bodily activities.

Affects can also be displaced so far into the body that they only appear as bodily sensations or reactions. To use an expression coined by Hanna (2004), *sensory motor amnesia* occurs when even the tension is no longer felt. In the strange situation in attachment research, children with an anxious-avoidant style (Section 11.6), who seem apathetic, have the highest levels of the stress hormone cortisol (Spangler et al., 2002). Presumably they have learnt to suppress emotional reactions.

Important
Defence against experiences and affects is a holistic process which includes the body. Defence is perpetuated through muscular and vegetative changes.

Defence processes encompass cognitions and affects as well as motor and vegetative changes. For example in the case of repression, the perception of the emotional significance of a bodily state is inhibited. Thus anxiety is not experienced, even though the body shows all the signs of it. We could call this a repressive coping strategy (Weinberger & Davidson, 1994). Someone who barricades themselves against perceiving their emotions in such a way is also more likely than others to deny that an increase in their pulse rate has anything to do with feelings (Weinberger & Davidson, 1994). Inhibition or repression of negative feelings can provide temporary relief, but results in a long-term increase in the sympathetic activation of the cardiovascular system (Salovey et al., 2000), so that they express themselves vegetatively. It has also been shown experimentally that even in the short term, the repression of emotions leads to strong cardiovascular reactions (Levenson, 2003, p. 362).

However, we have to be wary of jumping to the reverse conclusion here. When defence mechanisms are linked to muscular tension or the activation of the sympathetic nervous system, this does not mean that all tension or every increase in sympathetic activity is a sign of defence. Both can be adequate reactions to a life event. If for instance some shocking news upsets your stomach, then according to the principle of the Head zones, the stomach-ache could be projected onto a skin area on the level of the sixth to ninth thoracic vertebrae, since this is where the afferent nerves of the organs and the skin converge (Duus, 1983, pp. 299–300). Also the fascia of the organs are connected to the fascia in the thorax and in the shoulder/neck area (Fischer, 2011). This is why something that upsets your stomach can trigger pain in the skin or tension in the shoulder. Therefore we have to explore the tension in order to know what it is revealing.

Clinical example

At the beginning of Chapter 6, I described a therapy session with a patient in which we explored the significance of a certain movement of her jaw. She often pulls her jaw back. After saying something, she is not able to let her lips relax together and to loosen the lower jaw. The tension in the jaw increases when she is in stress. As background: since she was a child, an orthodontist had repeatedly tried to bring her lower jaw first back and then forward. To do this he used dental braces, a cranio-mandibular appliance and a device of his own invention to insert, artificial long teeth in a brace. This all reinforced a jaw position acceptable to the doctor.

In this session she is at first not able to sense the tension. However, after paying attention to and exploring it, she has a eureka moment in which she feels that in a relaxed position, the lower jaw can just slide forward without her having to push it. She gets to this point by carefully observing how she holds and moves the jaw; she focuses on it and experiments with tiny movements. When she finds a relaxed position, the tension in her upper chest, which restricts her breathing and which we explored in previous sessions, releases too. I showed in Chapter 6 that her tenseness is a symptom of anxiety regulation; however, it is also an expression of a physical experience.

13.1 BODY DEFENCE

Downing (1996, p. 191) suggests the notion of body defences for defence processes in which the physical body itself, or the perception of it, is deployed to protect against something that the person wants not to perceive, feel or do. Body defence is used above all to inhibit not ideas, but unwanted affects: 'painful memories, forbidden desires, threatening forms of contact with other people and unwanted forms of bodily arousal and activation', that are perhaps at the same time 'wanted and desired', generating conflict (Downing, 1996, pp. 207–8). Body defence is connected to defence mechanisms such as repression, inhibition, reaction formation, undoing, affect isolation or turning against one's own self, but here it is primarily the body which takes care of controlling the unwanted aspects and thereby adapting to reality.

Important
We speak of body defence when the body and not cognition is at the centre of perceptible defensive behaviour.

Downing describes ten mechanisms of body defence, some of which are related to current defensive behaviour, some to chronic defensive behaviour and some to both. I will add an eleventh mechanism.

1. **Breath reduction**: Downing (1996, p. 197) calls this perhaps the most effective form of body defence. Since we breathe more deeply when in the grip of strong emotions, we can suppress feelings through breathing (Boadella, 1994). By restricting the breathing, we can limit affective arousal. Reich (1973, p. 300) writes that, without exception, all his patients reported having practised as children certain ways of breathing such as tensing the stomach muscles so as to suppress feelings of hate, anxiety and love. The depth and permeability of our psychological experience is reduced when the breathing is kept shallow and its volume restricted. Physiologically reduced breathing restricts the flow of oxygen and thus the metabolism. If shallow breathing is coupled with swallowing air, a rigid chest musculature or a stiffness in the throat, neck and pelvis, this can suffocate vitality (Heisterkamp, 2002, pp. 120–1).

Breathing is such a convenient means of regulating feelings through the body because it is innervated by both the autonomous as well as the somatic, voluntary nervous systems (Mehling, 2010, p. 162; Section 6.2). Whereas it basically comes and goes automatically, at the same time we can influence it consciously and deliberately, hold it, deepen it or make it shallower. In body defence, however, breathing is usually altered **unconsciously with the help of voluntary muscles**, so as to regulate emotions and thoughts.

This can be done in various ways. Holding the inspiration is perhaps 'the most important instrument in the suppression of *any* kind of emotion' (Reich, 1972, p. 375). In shock, the breathing freezes on the inhalation, so that breathing out becomes difficult. However, there is also a parasympathetic freezing after the exhalation that hinders breathing in (Section 6.2). Also the flexibility and flow of the breathing can be disturbed as can the relationship between chest and abdominal breathing and the transition from exhalation to inhalation (Downing, 1996, p. 197). In paradoxic breathing, through muscular exertion the diaphragm moves upwards during inhalation (Fischer & Kemmann-Huber, 1999, p. 47).

Paying attention to these various aspects of breathing is central to body psychotherapeutic treatment technique. Little moments in a session in which the patient interrupts their breathing pattern can be seen as defensive body micro-practices or as a sign of thoughts and feelings trying to push through and can be utilised in the therapeutic process.

2. Downing calls a form of body defence in which a movement is used against another preceding one, thus suppressing it, **countermobilisation.** For example, a child stretches their arms out towards the mother and then immediately pulls them back, because they know that she will not embrace them. In a child this is a visible affect motor process, but in an adult it can be much more subtle. In a facial electromyography, changes in the innervation of the facial musculature can be monitored which correspond to certain feelings even though there are no contractions, for instance in the case of poker-face (Tassinary & Cacioppo, 1992). Countermobilisation appears in an extreme form when a patient becomes catatonic during a psychotic episode (Downing, 1996, p. 194). Countermobilisation is an actual form of bodily defence that we can also observe during the therapeutic process.

In countermobilisation, the original impulse is held back from what Fenichel (2015) calls *motility* and thus repressed. It is not, however, an idea which is being repressed as it forms, as in the classic concept of repression. It is the holding back of an action impulse. This is also known as **impulse repression**. If a thought is already on its way into action and this is then interrupted, the activating thought is repressed as well. With the help of countermobilisation, the emotional arousal accompanying an impulse to act is also inhibited (Section 10.5). A typical example is the suppression of anger which has just welled up. In retroflection, there is also a tensing of the muscles against the swelling impulse (Perls et al., 1980, pp. 190–1).

3. Whereas in countermobilisation, muscles are activated, in **deactivation** they are shifted into hypotension. This leads to a feeling of reduced vitality and thus avoidance of action. This parasympathetic deactivating can also spread to other systems besides the musculature. For example, anxiety and grief lead to a reduction in measurable girth due to changes in connective tissue (Krause, 1996). Bodily deactivation is an avoidance mechanism of both core affective arousal as well as emotions. In this way, people can diminish the amplitude of their feelings. They lapse into a neutral flow of movement in which there is no variation in the tension (Bender, 2007, p. 27).

4. **Muscular stiffness**, described by Downing (1996, p. 195) as chronic holding, is at first an acute defence mechanism, which serves to prevent unpleasant thoughts and feelings from becoming conscious. To this end, muscles are contracted. Reich (1973, p. 300) said that this bodily tension is the 'most essential part in the process of repression'. For example, the thorax is hardened so as to defend against being moved emotionally, or the shoulders and neck are stiffened to control anger. If such a form of body defence becomes chronic, then chronic muscle tension ensues.

The startle reflex

A startle reflex is an involuntary contraction of the skeletal muscles, above all the flexors, accompanied by an abrupt holding of the breath, which occurs as a reaction to a sudden, strong stimulus. The torso and the knees move towards each other, the shoulders move forward, the upper arms are turned outward, the lower arms are pulled in and the head is pulled down between the shoulders towards the sternum (Sheets-Johnstone, 2019, p. 93). A shock is expressed swiftly and clearly in the lid-reflex (Lang, 1995, p. 379). The closing of the eyelids makes it clear that a protective mechanism is being activated (Boyesen, 1987, p. 27). The organism makes itself less vulnerable by protecting soft parts such as the eyes and inner organs. Here we are not dealing with a defence mechanism; the startle response is a brain-stem reflex that is then modulated through the amygdala (Barnow, 2012, p. 115). The trigger can be, for example, a loud bang or the sudden movement of another person towards someone else.

In the Moro reflex, small children contract their arms and legs towards the torso (Section 11.1). In the Feldenkrais method, this movement pattern is seen as the neuromuscular reaction of the stop reflex, in which the upper part of the thorax is pulled forward and down and the pubis forwards and up (Czetczok, 2010, p. 150). According to an experimental study by Hillman et al. (2005), the startle reflex appears motorically only in this sagittal plane. The startle reflex also involves vegetative reactions such as a rise in blood pressure. It corresponds to the alarm reaction in animals in which they are immobilised in the readiness potential (Section 7.1).

It has been proven experimentally that the extent of the reaction is dependent on whether a person hears a frightening noise in a pleasant or an unpleasant situation (Bradley et al., 1993), which means on their core affective state. Also context determines the reaction, for example, whether I hear a shot at the shooting range or in the night in a dark street. Frequently repeated shock experiences, even minor ones, can lead to chronic **startle reflex patterns** (Schrauth, 2001, p. 29). In this case, the shortening of the flexors caused by fear impacts the whole musculoskeletal system, resulting in changes in body posture and tension in the antagonists, which have to compensate (Czetczok, 2010, p. 149).

Next to shallow breathing, the **chronic hypertension** in stiff muscles is probably the form of bodily defence most often described. It appears in the form of chronic patterns of muscular contraction that Reich called muscular armour, which make up characteristic body postures as the physical aspects of character. Muscular armour is a kind of frozen 'holding back' (Reich, 1972, p. 363; Section 13.2). If, for example, the expression of longing through stretching out the arms is chronically held back, this can lead to a stiffness in the shoulder and neck muscles. However they could also be stiff from holding back aggressive impulses. Tension in the pelvic muscles could be due to holding back aggressive or sexual impulses. There is no clear-cut relation between chronic muscle tension and corresponding affective states. But the psychomotor function of the respective muscles indicates the possible significance of the tension (cf. the chart on musculature, expression and psychomotor function by Roehricht, 2000, pp. 194–204).

However, long-term muscle contraction not only indicates a defensive process. This can in itself become a major symptom when chronic pain is the result (Pohl, 2010). Then the dysfunction has settled into the muscles or connective tissue and has to be treated from there. Depressive patients, for example, have more tension in the shoulder and neck areas, which can be loosened up by massaging on the level of the fascia (Michalak et al., 2022a).

5. Just as the mobilisation of the muscles can lead to chronic stiffness, deactivation can lead to a **chronic hypotension** (Downing, 1996, pp. 196–7), which Lillemor Johnson has called a resignation reaction on the level of the musculature (Bernhardt, 2004, p. 102). Chronic hypotension can be a sign of weak defences, which make a person prone to being overwhelmed by affects or to not being able to regulate intense negative affects. If however hypotension is as strong as what is known in trauma physiology as the point of shutdown, then there is a deadening towards all potentially arousing thoughts, feelings and impulses. In this case there is immobilisation without readiness potential (Section 7.1). We find this also in the defence against any motor activity with which infants react to a comprehensive frustration of their needs.

Over-regulation and under-regulation

Stiffness and rigidity on the one hand and deactivation on the other are two possible forms of body defence when a person is psychologically wounded. When the former becomes a habitual pattern, an **over-bordered structure** develops, corresponding physically to chronic hypertension (Boadella, 1987; Keleman, 1985). If however a person yields to chronic trauma, then a puffiness or collapse takes place, and an **under-bordered structure** with chronic hypotension develops. In this case, the sufferer will most likely present an affect motor pattern of seeking out other people for support when they are troubled, whereas the previous patient will keep their distance. With Greenberg and Paivio (1997), we could call an overly strong defence an **over-regulation** of affects, which helps to avoid painful experiences, and a weak defence as **under-regulation** of intensive, negative affects, leading to emotional flooding. In personality psychology, Asendorpf (2004) differentiates between over-controlled and under-controlled people, to which as a third type he adds the resilient personality. This third type corresponds to the body psychotherapeutic goal of attaining free flow and free choice, which I will come back to at the end of this chapter.

Whether the patient is over-regulated or under-regulated determines which principle we follow in treatment: with overregulation resulting from inhibited feelings, it is more likely the principle of *activating and expressing,* but if it results from a traumatic experience, then *perceiving and feeling,* while with under-regulation, *regulating and modulating* (Geuter, 2019).

6. Referring to the theory of affect motor schemas, Downing (1996, pp. 191–3) construes **underdeveloped motor schemas** as signs of a deficit or of a developmental standstill. This standstill serves as a defence insofar as it helps to avoid the tensions associated with the developing and testing of another schema. As an example, Downing mentions a person who when she is angry has no idea what to do with this impulse. He traces this back to the child having been under pressure to leave a schema in its undeveloped state or to inhibit it. The defensive activity consists of someone unconsciously remaining in this state of inhibition. Examples would be assuming a timid self-effacing stance so as to save oneself from rejection and hurt, or an aggressively inhibited servility so as to avoid confronting one's own desires and longings.
7. **Over-developed schemas** – Downing (1996, p. 193) calls them defensively distorted schemas – are a form of body defence in which events generally elicit an excessive reaction. According to the model of the affective cycle, these people, trapped in the fifth blockade of a persistent affect expression described in Section 10.5, would react to each new challenging stimulus with, for example, a dogged, pugnacious aggression, so as to defend against feelings of humiliation or even closeness and intimacy.
8. Downing calls another body defence mechanism **kinaesthetic avoidance**. Here he means that a person turns their attention away from kinaesthesia and attempts to ignore all perception of movement. They 'forget' how muscles feel and move (Pohl, 2010, p. 19). Kinaesthetic processes are rarely treated in body psychotherapy and are more of an issue in dance therapy or functional body therapies such as Feldenkrais work. Von Laban (1926), for instance, described the kinaesphere as the personal movement space. In the framework of his theory, kinaesthetic avoidance can mean that a person confines the kinaesphere to the restricted area of their own skin or to the median area of a space up to the width of their elbows, but avoids reaching out into the broader kinaesphere of the space they would be able to reach with outstretched limbs (Chapter 14: Proxemics). People who have experienced the violation of their personal space, as for example with sexual abuse, or try to make themselves invisible out of fear, often have a disproportionately narrow kinaesphere. A disproportionately large kinaesphere could indicate a person with narcissistic problems who takes up a lot of space in order to avoid intimacy (Bender, 2007, pp. 124–5).
9. Downing (1996, p. 198) calls a body defence in which someone pays a lot of kinaesthetic attention to a particular aspect or area of the body, while avoiding the rest, as **kinaesthetic hyper-concentration**. As an example, he describes dancers who are totally concentrated on the function of the movement of the body in space, but avoid bodily sensations not connected to this function. Worm (1998) describes a patient who used expressive bodily exercises in a defensive actionism to avoid feelings in the relationship.
10. Lastly, Downing names a mechanism in which a person replaces their living relationship to their body with a **visual body image construction** and thus avoids the experience of the lived body; a fetishist would be an example of this.

11. To the ten body defence mechanisms mentioned by Downing, I would like to add **body splitting**. This means that a splitting off of the experience of individual body parts from the rest is used as a defence mechanism (Bender, 2007, pp. 230–4). For example, expansive behaviour can be split off by inhibiting the sensation of action in the arms. Fear of acknowledging reality can be managed by a lack of physical presence in the legs, so that they remain underdeveloped. Frequently we can find a split between the head and the torso, perhaps to keep body sensations out of conscious perception, or between upper and lower body in the waist area. Bender (2007, p. 223) connects the split in some women between a slender upper body and an accumulation of fat in the lower body to an avoidance of strength and assertiveness. A split between the heart and the pelvis could detach feelings of love from sexual desire or vice versa.

Boadella (1987) assumes that there are systematic blockades between individual regions of bodily experience: the neck separates the head and the locomotor system, the throat separates the head and the internal organs and the diaphragm separates the spine – and thus the largest muscles in the body – from the intestines.

Functional identity

A theory of bodily defence and one of cognitive defence do not exclude each other. In fact they describe defence processes from different perspectives. Reich described psychological repression and muscular hypertension as functionally identical in relation to defence; both have the same function and could replace and be influenced by one another (1973, p. 270). Character attitudes could develop out of the defence system and muscular postures from the bodily defences. In the unity and dichotomy of the psychological and the physical, both fulfil the function of regulating tension, emotions and conflicts.

Heisterkamp (1993, p. 24) criticises the theory of functional identity for not defining **of what**, meaning of which superordinate whole, the psychological and somatic aspects of defence are functions, whereas I see their identity in the **what for**. However we cannot derive the somatic from the psychological in the sense of cause and effect, nor vice versa. In fact both are different expressions of the common processes of the living (Chapter 2).

Segments

Reich (1972, p. 368) advanced a model of a **horizontal layering of body defences** into seven segments, which he linked to certain expressive movements but not to anatomical structures. In neo-Reichian therapy schools, these segments are sometimes viewed as being like anatomical structures, despite the fact that the anatomical assignment is only vague and does not provide the model with a scientific basis. Since the segments form so to speak seven rings of armouring, Heller (2012, pp. 474) sees the model as an expression of the metaphorical idea of the human being as a worm. Sometimes they are also linked to the chakras. However there is no evidence that Reich was aware of the concept of the chakras (Fuckert, 1999, p. 136), although it is not impossible, since yoga was widespread at that time (Section 3.2).

Orthodox Reichian schools propagate working systematically on the blocks in these segments, from the eyes down towards the pelvis, and mobilising the respective expressive movements (Baker, 1967). I hold such an approach for overly mechanical. The segment model offers however reference points for distinguishing prominent areas of tension and inhibition in a phenomenological diagnosis of body defences, for discovering their meaning and for working on the expressive movements associated with them (Rosenberg et al., 1985; Rosenberg & Morse, 2015).

1. The **ocular segment**, which includes the cranium, forehead and eyebrows, is connected to the expression of shock and grief, but also of vitality. In this segment, early traumatisation can manifest as a frozen expression (Fuckert, 1999 p. 141). A glassy or blank stare can reveal a shutdown of the organism in the face of transmarginal stress, a frozen look aloofness. We can recognise anger in wide-open eyes with knitted brows, a contraction of the musculus corrugator supercilii (Section 14.4). Kelley (1976) developed special techniques for releasing the tension in the eyes. Baker (1967) describes a technique in which strong feeling reactions are generated by letting the patient follow a moving object or light source with their eyes from a distance of about 20 cm over a longer period of time. Eye movement desensitization and reprocessing (EMDR) utilises similar movements. Shapiro (1995) writes that she discovered this by chance, without mentioning earlier descriptions of similar techniques. Holistic ophthalmology uses relaxing exercises such as following swinging movements with the eyes, for example a figure eight (Schultz-Zehden, 1995, p. 137). We find these today in the Energy Psychology of Gallo (2000).

2. The **oral segment** with mouth, jaw, chin, and upper nape of the neck is the location of expressions of crying, sucking, retching, biting or screaming. The mouth is involved in the expression of all emotions as well as desires and appetites of all kinds. The mouth and the jaw often hold repressed anger (Rosenberg et al., 1985). Tension in the jaw can also bind insecurity, diffidence or grief. Gritting one's teeth is a common mechanism to suppress feelings. This can lead to chronic tension in the jaw muscles. Bruxism can be a sign of a processing of tension during the night. For some children, biting is their way of releasing affective tension.

3. The **cervical segment**, including the throat and neck, is connected to swallowing, speaking, choking, crying or screaming. Rising feelings are sometimes choked down in the throat, or fear is held in the neck with a closed-up throat and raised shoulders. Tonic stuttering involves a laryngeal block, in which the voice box closes up and the breathing stops. In embryological development, the endoderm, mesoderm and ectoderm are connected to the throat and neck; the bridge between the ectoderm and the mesoderm is at the base of the skull (Geissler, 1996, p. 19). Also vital blood vessels and nerves, connecting the brain with the rest of the body, pass through the neck. Thus the throat and neck represent a vulnerable area also prone to tension. Tension in the muscle insertions at the base of the skull is often accompanied by restricted breathing and reduced proprioception.

4. The **thoracic segment**, with the pectoral muscles, shoulder muscles, the muscles between the shoulder blades and the intercostal muscles, give chest resonance and a soundscape for the voice and the feelings. The thorax is the seat of interpersonal, passionate, soft, abandoned, trusting, joyful, compassionate, hearty and loving feelings; it can also harbour sadness, longing, regret, pain and suffering (Rosenberg et al., 1985). Tensions in this area show general self-control, restraint, anxiety, severity or aloofness (Reich, 1972, p. 375). We find hunched shoulders, a sunken chest, an inflated thorax or a barrel-like chest; this last is often the expression of power or of arrested power. The thoracic segment includes the arms and hands, which emotionally are the locomotor connection between the ego and other people; the wish to pull someone closer, to push them away or to hit them (Section 10.4). The arms can be cramped up or pulled back in the shoulder joints.

5. The **diaphragmatic segment** includes next to the diaphragm itself, the upper abdominal organs and the lower back musculature. Since it is anchored to the lumbar vertebrae,

tension in the diaphragm affects the spine and impacts the unity of breathing and movement (Boadella, 1987, p. 66). The diaphragm is the main inspiratory muscle for breathing at rest. Tensions in the diaphragm are involved in restricted breathing and are thus an important factor in body defence. An accumulation of startle responses can result in chronic tension in the diaphragm. Just as the cervical segment separates the head from the torso, the diaphragmatic segment separates the upper body from the lower. Thus tension in the diaphragm limits the exchange of aggressive and sexual impulses in the lower abdomen and the pelvis with the feelings in the chest and throat areas (Rosenberg et al., 1985).

6. The **abdominal segment** encompasses the muscles of the lower abdomen and the lower spine. These include not only the large abdominal muscle and the latissimus dorsi, but also the iliopsoas. Berceli (2005) sees this as the main trauma muscle, since it contracts in shock, pulls up the thighs in the startle reflex towards the torso and also activates running movements. If the tension is not released, then it remains contracted. Even when remembering traumatic experiences, the psoas often contracts. In Jin Shin Do, a method of deep acupressure massage based on the meridians, the alarm point of the large intestine, which when tense is seen as an indication of undigested traumas, lies on the origin of the psoas. In Traditional Chinese Medicine, the lower abdomen – or lower dantien – is regarded as the energy centre of the body. Chronic contraction in this area can numb strong emotions (Eiden, 2009, p. 21). 'The "gut feeling" depends essentially on a relaxed musculature in the lower torso; … relaxed abdominal breathing often has a liberating effect' (Trautmann-Voigt & Voigt, 2009, p. 12).

7. The **pelvic segment** includes the pelvic floor, genitals, uterus and ovaries, the anus, the pelvic musculature as well as the legs. Tensions in this area can manifest in problems with excretion and with sexuality. Reich (1972, p. 389) spoke of a specific *pelvic anxiety* and *pelvic rage*; if the pelvis is not free for pleasure then it can be transformed into these feelings. This segment is also often regarded as the basis for a person's 'rootedness', both in themselves as in reality: in themselves by dint of the body resting in the pelvis as its centre of gravity; in reality by sensing that they are standing with both feet firmly on the ground. Lowen (1977) calls this grounding. Tensions in this segment alienate people from the feeling of being grounded. To centre oneself in the middle of the body and in the ground is one of my ten principles of body psychotherapy (Geuter, 2019).

When we work on tensions in these various areas of the body, our goal is not to eliminate them mechanically. Rather it is to help the patient to understand what function they have performed in the regulation of deficient, hurtful or traumatic experiences (Rosenberg et al., 1985) or else just to change them.

Important
In the long run, it is helpful to release tensions in the body, because flexibility in the relevant bodily areas protects against reacting unconsciously to similar experiences in the present with the same body defences as before.

So far I have looked at body defences mainly on the level of the musculature. Tension, however, always involves the joints (Geissler, 1996, p. 33). Unresolved conflicts are held in the **joints,** for example, in the hip joints, the ban on the impulse to move erotically (Graeff, 2000, pp. 33–4). Tension in the joints can stabilise reaction and behaviour patterns. This is where manual medicine uses techniques to release joint tension. Some of these have been adopted by certain schools of body psychotherapy. Geissler (1996) points out that next to joint tension there is also a condition in which the joints are hypermobile and where we need body work which strengthens, tones and supports them.

Boyesen (1987) assumes that defence processes in the body can also take place at the level of the fascia surrounding the muscles or even underneath them in the periosteum. Physically it is often the fascia that maintain the tension. Chronic contraction is often manifested in the **connective tissue** (cf. Grassmann, 2019). If we regard defence processes as protective measures appearing on all experiential and material levels of the organism, then Boyesen's notion that they also surface in vegetative processes, such as the regulation of interstitial fluid, makes sense (Section 7.1). Downing's third body defence mechanism, deactivation, is a vegetative process resulting from the avoidance of action.

However, it is theoretically more difficult to classify vegetative processes within the concept of body defences. This is because the theory of defences developed out of psychoanalytic ego psychology. Therefore defence is often seen as an unconscious ego decision reacting to thoughts or impulses. However, we should not understand the notion of body defences as if the psyche was doing something which then functioned through the body. Then we are stuck in dualistic thinking (Chapter 2). In fact defence processes are **regulation processes** that we can observe on the psychological, motor and vegetative level and which are connected to physical processes on these levels. Since the regulation of experiences connected to the autonomic nervous system cannot be read symbolically (Section 7.1), it is not easy to account for vegetative processes managing experience in the framework of a theory of defence. In my view, this problem could be a good reason for thinking about whether other concepts for the somatic processing and regulation of experience would be a better way of describing those processes now under the heading of defence, for example the notion of experiential avoidance, which would include the body.

13.2 PATTERNS OF DEFENCE AND COPING – THE CONCEPT OF CHARACTER STRUCTURES

As a result of basic attempts to defend against ideas, feelings or impulses and to regulate those emotions connected to the denial of needs, specific patterns of dealing with deficient or traumatic experiences and conflicts often develop. In body psychotherapy, they are seen as ego syntonic compromises and interpreted as affect motor structures formed in childhood development (Bentzen, 2015). These patterns embody a compromise between needs and their suppression. Usually they are regarded as a consequence of a coagulated defence, but they can also be the result of a lack of defensive capacity (Bernhardt et al., 2004, p. 140). These are just two different attempts to adjust to an environment which denies the child fulfilment of their needs.

Since Reich (1974), the relevant patterns have been called character structures in psychodynamic theory. These appear most notably in interaction with other people. Lowen writes that such a character structure 'bridges psyche and soma' (1958, p. 18); however, it is primarily a hallmark of how someone builds their bridges to others and to the world.

The theory of character structures posits them as the basis of symptom formation, similar to pathogenic schemas in schema therapy. Lowen (1958, p. 123) sees in character the 'basic disturbance'. Hence character does not mean all that constitutes a human personality, but rather a structure which can generate pathologies and is created as a result of certain developmental conflicts that a child cannot deal with in accordance with their needs and thus resolves in a particular manner. For Reich, only a person who corresponded to the romantic ideal of the 'genital character' was free of such pathogenic structures (Section 3.5).

In body psychotherapy, the theory of character structure is a view held exclusively by neo-Reichian schools, especially by bioenergetic analysis (Lowen, 1958), biosynthesis (Boadella, 1996a) and Hakomi (Kurtz, 1983). For the perception-oriented schools, it was never important. Downing (1996) left it out of his theory. Heller (2012, pp. 560–1) rejects it because it does not do justice to clinical phenomena and makes questionable generalisations.

In my view, this model is not an essential component of an experiential body psychotherapy. However I will discuss it here since it does throw light on some typical psychological problems. It shows structural prototypes, which can result from desire-defence conflicts; a rich clinical body psychotherapeutic knowledge has gone into their descriptions. If we separate the model from its old drive theory background, its energy theory metaphors and its pathologising and link it to a theory of developmental needs, then it can take its place in an experiential theory of body psychotherapy. Totton (2015, p. 90) has a similar view.

> With **operationalised psychodynamic diagnosis**, contemporary psychodynamic theory favours a model different from that of character structures (Arbeitskreis OPD, 2009). The structure concept is here related to the psychological functions a person has at their disposal in regulating themselves and their relations to others (Section 6.7). According to this model, there are certain basic conflicts which can be resolved in various ways. Here character is not understood as the result of these resolutions, but as the personal way in which a conflict is dealt with (Rudolf, 2000, p. 149). Thus a basic depressive conflict with typical problems of self-esteem, for example, can be managed in an altruistic, compulsive, narcissistic or schizoid manner. This model is therefore more differentiated than the model of character structures, which only recognises one or two resolutions respectively for a certain conflict.

In psychoanalysis, Freud first understood character as an extension of drives, as their sublimation or as a reaction formation against them (Hoffmann, 1996, p. 51). Abraham saw character structures as forms of coping with drive conflicts, and in 1921 he distinguished between oral, anal and genital characters. In contrast, Fromm (2020, p. 26) defined character in 1929 more generally as a structure of those impulses, anxieties and attitudes which for the most part unconsciously determine typical behaviour. The character models of drive theory contributed to neo-Reichian theory (e.g. Baker, 1967) and to the work with the *Kestenberg Movement Profile* in dance therapy (Kestenberg Amighi et al., 1999). In neo-analytic models, Schultz-Hencke (1940) and Riemann (1972) differentiated between schizoid, depressive, compulsive and hysterical characters. Schulz-Hencke linked these characters to an inhibition of the four forms of impulse experience: intentional, oral-captive, anal-retentive and loving-sexual. König (2004) added the narcissistic, phobic and borderline characters to this classification (Table 13.1).

Reich's most significant contribution to character theory was to understand character as a reaction mode of the ego based on the defence theory (Hoffmann, 1996, p. 54). Hence there is no anal character in Reich's system, only the defensive structures of the compulsive and the masochistic characters. Lowen (1958, p. 142) rejects the idea of an anal phase too. He defines character structures as 'types of defences' (Lowen, 1977, p. 137). He derives the 'oral' character not from a partial drive, but from the processing of privation and loss and thus comes close to the depressive structure. At the same time, however, Lowen (1958, p. 180) connects the oral structure with the searching of the mouth for the breast and describes it as 'pregenital'. Thus, like Reich before him, Lowen commingles an ego-psychological defence

TABLE 13.1

Psychoanalytic and body psychotherapeutic character structure models

Schultz-Hencke/ Riemann	König	Reich	Lowen	Eisman	Rolef Ben-Shahar	Totton
schizoid depressive	schizoid depressive	schizoid	schizoid – oral – oral compensated	sensitive/withdrawn – dependent/ endearing – self-reliant	fragmented oral	boundary oral
compulsive	compulsive	compulsive				
		masochistic	masochistic	burdened/enduring	dense	holding
hysterical	hysterical	hysterical	rigid: – hysterical – phallic-narcissistic – passive feminine	industrious/ overfocused/ expressive/clinging	rigid	– thrusty – crisis
	phobic					
	narcissistic	phallic-narcissistic	psychopathic/ narcissistic	tough/generous/ charming/seductive	inflated	control
	borderline	impulsive				

theory with that of drive psychology. On the one hand he defines character as a type of defence and as a form of compromise, on the other as 'the typical way an individual handles his striving for pleasure' (Lowen, 1977, p. 137). The drive-theoretical connection to a scientifically obsolete theory of psychosexual phases seems not very helpful to me.

Reich (1972) called the defensive patterns of the character **armouring**: the character armour corresponds to a muscular armour, since repression takes place in the body through tension. Since then, the notion of muscular armour has been prevalent as a metaphor describing the somatic aspect of character structures. It brings together individual observations in a pattern (cf. Henningsen, 2002), but sometimes it is used in such a reified manner, as if muscular armour was something a person has and which we can palpate and remove. However what is being palpated are cramped up muscles and not a suit of armour. Armour is a metaphor and not an actual object (Section 7.3).

Connected to the concept of armouring is a metaphorical world of **congestion** and its release, which goes back to Freud and Breuer's early theory of hysteria. Reich proposed an economic model of neurosis in accordance with Freud's first theory of anxiety. This model follows the psychoanalytic metatheoretical differentiation between dynamics, topography and economics and asserts that blocked libido is the economic origin of neurosis (Geuter & Schrauth, 1997). From this perspective, Lowen (1958) describes character as the structure of a person's energy balance. According to his thinking, because of developmental conflicts, energy is held back, and this leads to characteristic energy blockages (Section 7.3). On the basis of this idea, Lowen one-sidedly emphasises therapeutic work with the expression and activation of the body, which I would see as only one of ten principles of body psychotherapy (Geuter, 2019). However Lowen prefers to restrict the concept of armouring to rigid character structures (Lowen, 1958, p. 257) where he holds bioenergetic therapy for particularly suitable (Lowen, 1958, p. 310).

More recently, body psychotherapeutic character theory has mainly followed the notion of the internalisation of real experiences similar to that of object relations theory (Marlock, 2015b). In the reception of this theory in the 1980s S. Johnson (1985) defined character structures as **core themes** resulting from relational experiences. This theoretical change corresponds to the transition from thinking in phases to thinking in phase-typical accentuated themes in Stern's developmental theory (1985; Section 11.2). Here, people with schizoid, oral or masochistic issues struggle with the aftermath of a past, where they have learnt to compensate deficits and conflicts in meeting their needs with defence strategies and compromises (S Johnson, 1985). Johnson sketches a process in five stages in which:

- The child expresses a need.
- The environment reacts unsatisfactorily or not at all.
- The child feels anger, shock or pain.
- The child denies these and withdraws their impulses.
- Through this adaptation a compromise between desire and defence develops. (Johnson, 1985)

The fourth step of withdrawal is not only a mental process but also somatic:

> The need is held back through contraction. This is a serious unconscious step. The conflict between subject and object is internalised. Now the childish organism is in conflict with itself. Only those needs which trigger a positive echo in the outside world will be expressed … Defensive patterns are developing … which aim to prevent the rebuff or the trauma from happening again.
>
> (Koemeda-Lutz & Steinmann, 2004, p. 92).

According to this understanding, character structures are **coping patterns** revealing a deficit and a potential at the same time. Bentzen (2015) shows that embodied in them are not only tensions and deficiencies, but also the abilities and resources that a child develops in the relevant phase when a structure emerges. Accordingly Koemeda-Lutz (2002a, p. 134) describes character structures as **response patterns**, in themselves not pathologic, but representing a tendency towards a protective reaction, which if consolidated leads to restrictions in experience and behaviour. Chronic patterns protect at the cost of 'expansive life movements' or even of expressing needs at all (Koemeda-Lutz, 2002a, p. 133). This understanding is widespread in contemporary bioenergetics (Pechtl & Nagele, 2019).

Hence the theory of character structure largely follows the psychoanalytic model, that mental disorders arise out of desire-defence-conflicts rooted in the relationship between the child and their early caregivers. Basic approaches to experience and behaviour can however also originate in painful or traumatic experiences, which subsequently lead to defences against the real or perceived threat (Nijenhuis, 2016, p. 85). They can also originate in the failed attempt to conform to some social or cultural norm or image.

In modern body psychotherapy, therefore, we speak more broadly of **forms of embodied relating** (Totton, 2015) or **patterns of habit formation** (Eisman, 2015). Totton, Eisman and Rolef Ben-Shahar (2014) put forward new, phenomenal, non-pathologic concepts, oriented to a healthy development. In the case of Rolef Ben-Shahar, a pathologic perspective is nevertheless apparent, when he speaks of fragmented or inflated character structures (Table 13.1). In addition in each character structure, Totton differentiates three forms:

- The *creative* version where the position simply affords a theme.
- The *yearning* version, where people continually search for something crucial which they feel is missing from their world.
- The *denying* version, where they compensate for and deny the underlying yearning. (Totton, 2015, p. 92)

Character structures are similar in their dynamics to the attachment styles, which also develop out of relational experiences. Downing (2015) therefore wants to consider relating both models to each other. Just as the attachment styles can with increasing severity become attachment pathologies, so a mental problem can consist of being too strongly stuck in a character pattern rather than in a symptom created by this pattern, for example in a compulsive personality rather than a compulsive disorder. Then character is itself the disorder, and we are dealing with **character pathology**, formerly known as character neurosis. This concept corresponds to a large extent to personality disorder in the ICD 11, in which the over-development of one normal personality trait becomes pathological.

In **schema therapy** too we find the idea that frustration or denial of core needs creates structures which restrict a person in their cognitive, emotional and physical response to the environment and to other people (Young et al., 2006). Here the assumption is that maladaptive schemas develop when the child's basic needs are not fulfilled. However the concept of needs is here different from that of the character structure theory. It does not follow a developmental theory but defines five basic needs of a child on the basis of clinical experience:

- Secure attachment.
- Autonomy, competence and a sense of identity.
- Freedom to experience and to express one's own needs and emotions.
- Spontaneity and play.
- Realistic limits and self-control (Section 10.3).

If the needs for security and acceptance are not fulfilled, then schemata are created in the schema domain 'disconnection and rejection', and in case of the other needs in 'impaired autonomy and performance', 'other directedness', 'over-vigilance or inhibition' or 'impaired limits' (Jacob & Arntz, 2014, p. 6; Chapter 12: Box 'Schema therapy').

The schema domains are similar to the conflict axis of **operationalised psychodynamic diagnosis**, which includes seven developmental conflicts:

- Individuation versus dependence.
- Submission versus control.
- Desire for care versus autarchy.
- Conflicts of self-esteem.
- Guilt conflicts.
- Oedipal conflicts.
- Identity conflicts. (Arbeitskreis OPD, 2009)

Each character structure designates a style of dealing with experience and relating to the world. This shows itself in behaviour, gestures, handshake, facial expressions, gaze and speech (Reich, 1972, p. 31). Character is a person's habitus and as such cannot be separated from the body. On the bodily level, character structures are habitual holding patterns. Character manifests in the patterns of tension in the body as a person's frozen history (Boadella, 1987), with visible hypertrophies and posture anomalies (Revenstorf, 2000, p. 195). In this respect, character is also subjective anatomy, which, according to the French philosopher Gabriel Marcel, tells the past story of the lived body in the present. Since character structures stem from relational experiences, they are also always active and recognisable as patterns of relationship formation. They pave the way for how a patient experiences themselves and others and vice versa, surfacing in therapy as typical transference dispositions.

Every human being has an idiosyncratic pattern of preferred defence mechanisms. Character structures are therefore only **prototypes** and not objectifiable realities of individual people. Prototype means that unlike in the case of affect motor schemas, they are a standardisation of types emphasising particular attributes, which a patient we have classified with this character structure does not necessarily have. We can regard them as constructs that help to describe people and how they became what they are (Marlock, 2015, p. 154). They are organising points of view which capture a person's experience, behaviour and corporeality. As such they provide a framework that offers diagnostic indications for therapeutic strategies (Eiden, 2002, p. 46). In body psychotherapy, we always look for these indications also in the body of the patient.

Ambiguousness

It is not possible to reliably infer character structures from the physical body (Section 14.1). Since Reichian body psychotherapy all too easily correlates the two, I would like to give a personal example warning against speedy interpretation.

During my training, I frequently experienced the symptom of hiccupping so severely as if I would choke. This was interpreted as a sign of my 'oral character structure'. A psychoanalytically trained instructor went so far as to see in this the 'disgusting mother's milk'. However, when this symptom turned up as I was with my physiotherapist, she said that it sounded like I was gasping for air, but swallowing water. She asked me whether I had almost drowned as a child. It suddenly dawned on me that my earliest childhood memory was of floating peacefully on my back and looking at something green from below. That same evening I demonstrated this symptom on the phone to my mother and asked her if she recognised it. She said she would never forget how I had done that all night after having fallen backwards into a pond. My cousin had managed to pull me out.

The life-story that the body tells is ambiguous. The symptom could have been about character or breastfeeding, but it told of a quite different early trauma.

The classification of the character types has changed over time. Reich worked out his model at a time in which denying needs was considered an ideal in child-rearing, and the compulsive personality disorder, which resembled the later model of the 'authoritarian character', was very common. In the last few decades there has been a predominance of narcissistic and hysterical character structures, these last linked above all to self-dramatisation in the media

(Section 1.5). Reich (1974) described the borderline structure as the 'impulsive character' in 1925; it was not included in the character structure model until many decades later, but is now often discussed. This is because guiding principles change over time, as does the level of impulse control required by society; all of this is incorporated into the character structures. Reich's healthy ideal of the 'genital character' based on drive theory was also a child of its time. Character is not only individual but also **social**.

In the following, I describe seven character structures with regard to their development and their prototypical attributes (Table 13.2). These descriptions are based on Bentzen (2015), Eiden (2002), S. Johnson (1985), Koemeda-Lutz (2002a), Kurtz (1983), Lowen (1958), Reich (1972), Revenstorf (2001) and Sartory (2015). However I refer primarily to Lowen's character structure model as the most prevalent in body psychotherapy. But it is not the only one. Johnson (1985) brings in a symbiotic character between the oral and the masochistic structures, which he links to conflicts of separation and self-esteem.

In contrast to Lowen, Keleman (1985) constructs his typology on the basis of the startle reflex. He identifies four stages of a persistent startle reflex: stiffening, becoming compact, swelling up and collapsing. To these he assigns four structures: rigid, dense, swollen and collapsed. Keleman's structures are prototypes of stress reactivity and are not based on a developmental genesis. They show at what point in a stress reaction a person has got stuck. The foundation of Keleman's emotional-anatomical structures, which I will not go into further here, is the way someone deals with anxiety, whereas Lowen's model is based on the assumption of fundamental conflicts in childhood development, to which he assigns developmental phases. I would prefer to see these as conflicts specific to and accentuated by such a phase.

- With the **schizoid structure**, the right to **exist** has been injured – the need to be welcome in this world and to find a secure place within it. According to the theory of character structures, as a child such an adult experienced elementary loneliness, animosity, coldness or hate, felt the fear of being annihilated, rejected or totally abandoned and withdrew into themselves (Bentzen, 2015; cf. Bernhardt et al., 2004a, pp. 167–73). In order to survive, the schizoid cuts themselves off from the world and retracts their own vitality: 'the organism freezes, stiffens, tenses up and twists itself away' (Koemeda-Lutz, 2002a, p. 119). The schizoid tries to avoid the pain by numbing their feelings. Their deeper desire is to be accepted. The patient described in Section 11.1, who almost died at birth and was then in an incubator, is an example of such a structure.

This seems a good place to elucidate the difference from the new psychodynamic understanding mentioned at the beginning of Section 13.2. According to Rudolf (2000, pp. 147, 165–9) the 'schizoid mode' is not a reaction to the injury of a particular need, but rather it can act as a way of dealing with various basic conflicts, for example the basic conflict of intimacy through a formal, business-like, technical or artificial interpersonal contact; or the depressive basic conflict of attachment security, through emotional withdrawal, protection against frightening or hurtful relational experiences and shutting down towards the environment. Developmentally, the schizoid mode is seen as a lack of competence resulting from relational disorder (Rudolf, 2000, p. 167). The character structure model, in contrast, connects a structure as a habitual mode of dealing with the world with just one basic conflict.

TABLE 13.2
Character structures

Character structure	Basic experience	Conflict or deficit	Basic feeling, fear	Decisions, choices	Strategy, attachment style	Body posture
Schizoid	Rejection, not wanted, early loneliness, early contact cold	Trust versus distrust	Being destroyed, not belonging, not being in the body, fear of intimacy	For existence, against feelings and needs, isolation instead of intimacy	Suppress impulses, withdrawn inwards, over-controlling, freezing	Held together, stiff, frozen, splitting in the body, rigid countenance
Oral-dependant	Deficiency, unmet needs	Caring for versus being cared for, dependency versus autonomy	Not getting enough, having no-one, fear of separation and independence	For needs and dependence, against independence	Seeking help, pleading, becoming dependent	Holding tight, clinging, collapsing, bent over, feeble, searching
Oral compensated	As oral	As oral	Need no-one, do everything alone	Seemingly independent but with unmet needs	Reject help but want it	More highly toned than oral type
Narcissistic	Suppression of identity, being inferior, unimportant, not taken seriously, manipulated	Having to be instead of wanting to be, lack of respect as an independent being	Letting nobody close, showing no vulnerability, fear of closeness and manipulation	For independence, against security, going into the stronger position	Asserting oneself, winning or seductive. being close through controlling, belittling the other person	Holding up, inflated, strong, upper body disproportionally stronger than lower, head up
Masochistic	Suppression of strength and aggression, love connected to pressure and submission	Autonomy versus submission	Guilt for being independent, being bad, repressed rage with danger of explosion, humiliation	For security against freedom, submission instead of independence	Stifle negative feelings, wait, hesitate, obey, submit to get intimacy	Holding on to oneself, stocky, compact, muscled, buttocks pulled in
Compulsive	Discipline and repression of pleasure	Control versus giving up control	Needing security, wanting but not being able, fear of change and risk, aggression	For independence through external rules instead of flow	Rigidity, perfection, reality before feelings, control of feelings	Holding tight, rigid, tense, tight jaw
Hysterical	Lack of attention, suppression of love, feeling oneself as sexual	Independence versus attachment	Need for validation, fear of constraint, commitment, love	For freedom instead of abandonment, not paying attention to realities	Attracting attention, acting out feelings but not engaging with the heart	Well-proportioned, muscular hypertonia, accentuated pelvis

Physically the schizoid structure often displays tension in the muscles of the whole body, an empty gaze and severe tension in the neck and shoulder region linked to the attempt to survive by living in the cognitive faculty and cutting off bodily sensation. Because of a lack of gratification of their basic need for a secure existence, they can have the feeling that the body is alien. Also apparent is sometimes a fragmentation, a splitting of the left/right or upper/lower aspects of the body, as well as a lack of coordination in the body as a whole. According to Lowen, the schizoid is trying to **hold themselves together** in the face of imminent fragmentation.

- The **oral character** was wounded in their right to have **needs** at all. This could be based on the child's experience that fundamental needs for nourishment, support, contact or closeness were not adequately met, for example when a child has been welcomed, but subsequently abandoned. In order to survive, they will revoke their own needs. This can lead to the conviction that they need nothing, while at the same time unconsciously they are very demanding. The oral character therefore collapses in on themselves and characteristically has a lack of vitality, a sunken chest and a slumped posture. Their initiative and the strength to take something for themselves from the world are inhibited. Such a person hopes that their desires will be fulfilled without them having to bring them into the world themselves. Their feeling of emptiness makes it difficult to satisfy their neediness, so that they search wistfully for something without knowing what it is they want. They try to give to others so that they will get something back. They are afraid of their own helplessness and try to motivate others to look after them. The oral character tries to **hold on to someone for support**.
- Lowen differentiates a **compensated oral structure** as a subclass, in which superficial strength and activity is a defence against neediness, whereby the emptiness persists. This type often appears strong without actually being so. Afraid of being needy, they exaggerate their independence. The body is described as having a layer of rigidity over the usual oral lassitude (Kurtz, 1983).

This is the only passage where Lowen distinguishes between a **passive** and an **active coping strategy** for the same basic conflict. However, we could apply this notion to the other structures. Thus the conflict of the right to exist could be tackled actively through an intellectual productivity cut off from feeling or passively by devitalisation. This again would match the two schizoid modes described by Rudolf: the active mode would deal with the intimacy conflict, the passive with the depressive conflict. Also the following narcissistic and masochistic structures each display both a more active and a more passive mode.

- Lowen's old concept of a **psychopathic character**, which is not identical to the antisocial psychopathic personality disorder, is hardly used any more. Today it corresponds most closely to the **narcissistic structure**. The fundamental wound here is to **autonomy** and **self-esteem**. A child injured in this respect is already aware of their needs, but it is made difficult for them to be their own person. This can be through humiliation, exploitation, manipulation or parentification; or by the child being driven to be more than they are, which encourages the grandiose self. The narcissistic character copes with the fear of being treated like that again by denying weakness and vulnerability and emphasising their own independence and brilliance as compensation. Physically such a person seems inflated. Lowen describes the dominating man with a pumped up chest, narrow hips and a belligerent or arrogant look. The expression is often one of injured pride or aloofness. Another way of resolving the conflict about independence would be to internalise the early relational pattern of manipulation and apply it to relationships today. The narcissistic character tries **to hold themselves above and beyond other people**.

- With the **masochistic structure**, not to be confused with sexual masochism, the right to **self-assertion** and **independence** has been violated. The child now knows what they want and tries to assert their needs, but their will is denied or broken. Interactions which make them feel ashamed curb their expansive and pleasurable initiatives. Since they have to do what the other person wants, they internalise a relational structure in which they are dependent and full of suppressed defiance. Their compromise consists of fulfilling the wishes of others and relinquishing their own assertiveness. I encountered a prototype of this structure in a man whose disabled mother could only move around the apartment by crawling on the floor and who always wanted to have her only child close by. The masochistic type submits to the other person, restricts their own movements into the world, swallows their anger and suppresses their contempt. The aggressive power is turned inwards.

Since the character structure model is built on a theory of conflict, it lacks the trauma theory perspective. Depending on the background, there are various possible levels of masochistic reaction. Ermann (2004, pp. 185–6) depicts masochistic submission as a reaction on a median structural level (Section 6.7). The man in this last example coped in this way with the fear of losing his mother. On a lesser structural level, masochism can be a result of the internalisation of real suffering inflicted on that person. Then the traumatic experience in the early relationship is repeated again and again by seeking out situations where the person will suffer. Such a person can for instance get other people to treat them sadistically, so as to cope with guilt feelings resulting from repressed aggressive fantasies against those who maltreated them in their childhood.

Physically, the masochist gives the impression of being under great inner stress. They can appear as if caught in a vice, hunched up like the oral character and at the same time muscle-bound but not supple. According to Lowen, the muscles are more likely to be overdeveloped in order to hold back negative impulses and dominate natural ones. The voice is inhibited and has a complaining tone as the throat is tight and the head ducked down. It is as if the stifling of all expansive impulses is the price for intimacy. This character resists expressiveness and agency and deals with life as a duty. They are trying **to hold on to themselves**.

- Reich described the **compulsive structure**, which Lowen leaves out. This is because of Reich's view of this structure from the perspective of drive psychology (1972). A compulsive personality structure, however, is a common defence against impulses and emotions and can be linked to various conflicts (cf. Rudolf, 2000, p. 233). In early psychoanalysis, the compulsive structure was linked with toilet training. However since the time of Freud and Reich, this has changed a great deal. According to early psychoanalysis, the compulsive develops extreme self-control as a reaction against the **pleasure** of excretion, but also against that of other vital needs and appetites. They suppress the desire to relinquish control by controlling their affects and actions. They deal with the inner tension by striving for perfection. Physically they seem completely self-contained and self-confined. The compulsive tries **to hold themselves back**.
- The **hysterical structure** is concerned with the need for sexual self-determination and finding a **sexual identity**. The injury consists of having been rejected or seduced or ignored, usually by the parent of the opposite sex. We cannot interpret the crises created by the child just as oedipal conflicts, but as attempts to gain **attention** (Kurtz, 1983).

The avoidance strategy, which the child can learn in this phase, consists of not opening up any more so as not to be hurt. The hysterical character chooses independence over love and surrender in order not to feel the anxiety of being vulnerable. The desire for intimacy is acted out in order to gain validation and sexual approval from others.

The main tension in the body is the high charge in the pelvis and a caution in the chest and heart region (Bentzen, 2015). Bentzen also describes a 'romantic' variant displaying the opposite polarisation. In this respect, the hysterical also holds themselves back to some extent. Physically, hysterical structures are well-proportioned and show habitual muscular hypertonia (Koemeda-Lutz, 2002a, p. 130), through which they can resist the anxieties of letting go and of feeling profound love. The hysterical tries **to keep everything open**.

As I indicated in my description of the masochistic structure, with these character structures we cannot describe the personalities of people with severe mental disorders and a restricted structural level. We can, however, understand some of the personality disorders as extreme forms of some of these characters. Generally speaking, most people have the traits of various prototypes. Diagnostically, it is interesting to see which prototype most determines personality and behaviour (Lowen, 1958, p. 311).

Body oriented work on a certain structure is directed at loosening the patient's bodily affect motor inhibitions, so that they can let go of the defensive posture. This then frees up repressed affects as intended (Revenstorf, 2001). This can in turn evoke anxiety, which has to be overcome in order for change to come about. The goal is a relative freedom of the greatest possible vitality, or a midpoint between poles, for example self-confidence midway between being completely unsure of oneself and exaggeratedly self-assured. We can only achieve this when we both understand the pattern and also release the somatic tension which sustains it. This means that only when the body and the psyche are relatively permeable and mobile can present functioning be freed from the influence of the past (Lowen, 1958, p. 363). According to Rogers' idea, a person is healthy when 'experience loses its structure-bound quality and becomes freely flowing' (Greenberg & Van Balen, 1998, p. 36). In therapy, we are concerned with this freedom and not with breaking up character structures, as they are also an expression of a person's ability to protect themselves.

> The aim of therapy is to give a person voluntary choice over when, where and how he defends himself, so that he is not crippled by defences in situations which do not threaten him, nor is he over-vulnerable and hyper-sensitive in situations that do.
>
> (Boadella, 1977, p. 43)

Important
In this sense, healing is the development of the capacity to flow, whereas holding on to a character structure is to limit experience. A flow experience can begin when the person is less constrained by the limits of predetermined structures.

14

Communication with the body

Body behaviour and therapeutic interaction

In the preceding chapters, I have often spoken of interaction, but the emphasis was always on inner experience and those patterns of acquired experience with which a person encounters the world. In this chapter, I discuss how people behave bodily and how they interact from body to body in the here and now. This is not about habitual schemas and structures recognisable in the body, but about the flow of information in the actual process of therapeutic communication, the body as a medium of communication (Roehricht, 2000, p. 23). This also raises the question of how therapists perceive what is happening in the patient when they themselves are unaware of it and thus unable to express it verbally (Bucci, 2001). As a rule, therapists constantly observe the fine changes in the bodily state of their clients (Davis & Hadiks, 1990). However they generally do this intuitively. We have hardly begun to develop a theoretical understanding of bodily communication in psychotherapy. The following remarks are meant to offer some categories for such an understanding.

Up to now in the psychotherapeutic tradition, more attention was paid to what life experiences (schemas, structures) and what symbolisations the body was communicating, for instance how someone expresses emotions in relations to others or reveals their biographical development in their posture. For mental disorders manifest themselves mostly in the realm of interpersonal relationships. Body psychotherapy is traditionally interested in emotions, defence structures, relationship patterns, intentions or meanings communicated by the body and for the relationships between this bodily communication and the verbal one. This is because the emotional content of a verbal communication is conveyed more through the **how** than the **what**. A person's relationship to the world of objects can also be impaired, as is the case in severe mental disorders such as psychoses, and has to be treated. Body psychotherapy therefore is concerned with the body in relation to the world of objects, to the world of interpersonal relationships and to the patient themselves.

With the intersubjective turn (Section 1.4), the focus became more on how the body communicates in therapeutic interaction. In this context, research has turned towards dynamic bodily interaction in the dyad (Ramseyer, 2011, 2022; Wiltshire et al., 2020). Now the body is no longer only examined as to what it reveals of the patient's patterns or what it symbolises, but also how the patient and the therapist communicate bodily. From the point of view of traditional body psychotherapy, when two people embrace, they are expressing their feelings. However, an embrace is an event which unfolds out of a togetherness and not only from the feelings of the partners. Interaction means not just that each person receives something from the other, but also that something is created in a shared space (Froese & Fuchs, 2012). According to the ideas of enactivism, I and the other are a common entity in the

DOI: 10.4324/9781003176893-14

interaction (Colombetti, 2014, p. 87). Interactive processes, for example two people dancing together, have their own embodied dynamics of mutual incorporation (van Alphen,
2014). This develops in a space where the one body is here, the other there, and in the space
between them something happens.

Clinical example

In a session with a patient, I notice that without conscious intention, my left hand has
gone to my heart and my fingers are touching my sternum. This happens in a situation
in which the patient is speaking associatively about something and I am asking myself
what all this really means to him. My initially unconscious gesture is the bodily expression of my question as to what touches his heart. As I mention this and point to the
movement of my hand, he immediately has a feeling of loneliness that he usually covers up, and he sees himself as a little boy in the large and emotionally cool house of his
childhood, all alone with his anxiety. This image gives me an inner impulse to hug him
to me like a father would, to comfort and support him.

When we communicate, the body immediately becomes more visible. One study showed
that people eating a sandwich with far too much salt made faces expressing disgust; however, if they thought they were not being watched, they did not make these faces (Hermer,
2004, p. 27). The living body relates. Orbach says: 'There is no such thing as a body' (2004, p.
28), a reference to a well-known quote from Winnicott (1965) that 'there is no such thing as
an infant', but only ever a body in relation to other bodies. This is valid both for the person
showing themselves and the person seeing them. Body behaviour – posture, movement, gestures, facial expressions, the sound of the voice – is the fundamental source of information
about the feelings and intentions of other people; experiments in the psychology of perception show that we always perceive another body as a coherent configuration, just as we do
the face (Reed & McIntosh, 2008).

Even plants communicate. Tomato plants whose neighbouring plants are infested by
a certain caterpillar develop chemical substances against this caterpillar, as they have
molecular information from these neighbours, carried through the air (Sugimoto et al.,
2014). We are far from understanding all the ways in which living bodies exchange
information.

In body psychotherapy, the body was long viewed from the perspective of a one-person
psychology. Bodily expression was largely understood as an unconscious communication
about the self. In emotion research, this corresponded to the model in which a person
shows their inner self through this expression and others decipher this information. But
there has been a radical rethink. Emotions are also shown so as to influence the receiver in
a way that benefits the sender (Russell et al., 2003). It is not only expression that matters,
but also the impression it makes. When a cat hisses, it is not only angry; it also aims to
intimidate. A person's body language is, however, subject to social rules that have become
second nature.

Important
A patient's bodily expressions are a manifestation of intrapsychic *and* relational processes. In psychotherapy, they are part of a reciprocal event.

This rethink correlates with a relational view that has been around for a while in psychotherapy, that what takes place in therapy is a relationship process (Rogers, 1959). In their body expression, the patient speaks both about themselves **and** simultaneously to the therapist (Davis & Hadiks, 1994, p. 403). Frey (1999) has described this in an information model. According to this, the therapist as the receiver understands from their own experience and with their own special nature, what they assume is going on in the patient as the sender. Furthermore, bodily expressions impress the receiver and provoke emotional reactions in them. This contagion can in turn affect the sender and change their emotionality (cf. Figure 10.4). In communication processes, the roles of sender and receiver switch constantly. Behaviour is meant to make an impression; the receiver can decide which signs they take as indicating something (Frey, 1999, pp. 74–5). For therapy, this means that as therapists, the more open we are to receive these signs, the greater the range available from which we can develop our impressions. However communication does not only function according to the sender/receiver model, since in an interactive loop, everything that happens can be cause and effect simultaneously.

Important
Like emotions bodily expression has an adaptive and regulative (intrapersonal) function as well as a social and communicative (interpersonal) function.

Emotional communication signs can indicate

- An affect related to an object ('I don't like him').
- The state of the sender ('I'm afraid').
- An affect in relation to the receiver ('I despise you', 'I want you to comfort me') (cf. Krause, 1992).

The patient's bodily signals can thus express something about others, about themselves and about the relation to the therapist. Therefore the viewpoint of one-person psychology is just as valid as that of two-person psychology (Geuter, 2019, p. 401). According to the model of the communication square of Schulz von Thun (1981), we can say that the body provides self-revelation, factual information and an appeal and indicates the relationship between sender and receiver.

The concept of **body expression** only refers to part of the interactive process and contains a fundamental problem. Inherent in the word 'expression' is a differentiation between an invisible mental act and a visible sign, in which the mental 'ex-presses' itself. In the analysis of the expression, they are treated as if the one were the cause of the other. The concept of body expression thus finds itself in the tradition of dualistic thinking, which sees the body as the expression of the soul (cf. Box in Section 5.1). However what is visible in the body is only one aspect of a comprehensive somato-psychological process that can express itself both verbally and physically and can only be divided into its component parts in reflecting on it. Lowen put it this way: 'It is not the mind which becomes angry nor the body which strikes. It is the individual who expresses himself' (Lowen, 1958, pp. xi–xii).

In the tradition of expressive psychology the concept of **body language** is often used. This idea is based on an analogy with the spoken language, despite the fact that the latter is usually voluntary, the former more involuntary. In body psychotherapy, the concept of body language usually refers to expressions of affect and movements we can **see** in the patient. Like body reading (Section 14.1), it is bound to the one-person psychology of expression and movement diagnostics, in which the patient speaks with their body and the therapist as an expert reads the message and interprets it. This reflects the fact that in research, the most important medium is the camera (Heller, 2012, p. 583). But there are some things the camera can hardly see: the flash of the eyes, the sensation of a handshake or the shimmer of the skin, and some things such as a tiny gesture or a smell are as good as invisible even if one reacts upon it. In therapy, when our own bodies as resonators are open for the facial expressions, gestures, olfactory or prosodic signals of the patient, we perceive such signals and through them we can access their unverbalised experience and unspoken interactional processes.

Since bodily gestures cannot be read like symbols with specific meanings, in research the notion of body language has been abandoned (Heller, 2012, p. 578). For this reason, Heller makes no use of it. In his model of the four dimensions of the organism, he rather describes the perceptible actions of the body in general as behaviour and reserves the concept of body for the relationship of the organism to the natural world of objects (Heller, 2011).

The concept of body language is also not comprehensive, because not all that the body presents is an expression of or a reference to something. If anything, the behavioural expressions of the body are determined by many factors and are hypercomplex. This makes it extremely difficult to reflect on them in clear-cut terms. They could be the result of a pathological process in the central nervous system (CNS); they could be intentional, when a person is trying to achieve something with a movement; they could be consciously or unconsciously guiding a communication; they could be signs of an inner attitude or an affect motor pattern, an inner condition or a communicative purpose; they could be conventional and controlled by the environment or individual and controlled from inside or completely uncontrolled. In any case, they are not necessarily an expression or a language or a sign of conscious or unconscious inner processes. Thus the concept of body behaviour, analogous to that of body experience, is more suited as the generic term for all a person does with their body and shows in interaction. Whereas under **body experience** I understand all forms of **inner** reference to the body (Chapter 6), all forms of reference to the body towards the **outside** I term **body behaviour.**

Some behaviour is a signal, some an expression. I will therefore use the customary notions of body signals or body language, for example when a patient communicates an important signal through the body, but I will try to make sure not to convey with these notions a dualistic idea nor one which depicts the body as a speaker to whom we are listening and whom we are understanding as if we were looking something up in a lexicon.

In an interaction, body behaviour performs various **functions** (Heilmann, 2009):

- **Syntactic**: it structures what is said, for instance by indicating a classification with the hand.
- **Semantic**: it supports or modifies what is said, for example by emphasising something or toning it down with a gesture.
- **Dialogic**: it structures the conversation, for instance by regulating the change of speaker by lowering the voice at the end of a sentence or by taking a deeper breath indicating one wants to speak, or giving one's partner feedback with movements of the head (Paggio & Navarretta, 2013).

This dialogic function can be disturbed when a patient leaves no room for the therapist to speak (Streeck, 2004, p. 242), or vice versa, as I experienced in one clinic as the
therapist explained the therapy plan and hardly let the patient speak at all.
- **Pragmatic**: it expresses psychological and physical sensations and feelings, communicating them to others.
- **Adaptive**: it helps a person to adjust to their impulses, feelings and interpersonal needs
while speaking (Wallbott, 1998a), for instance pulling at an ear or rubbing fingers on a
jumper.

In psychotherapy, we are interested in the last two functions because we can deduce meaning from them.

Human beings also use body movements per se to perceive something, to bring something to mind or to gather their thoughts (Goldin-Meadow, 1999). This is why we gesture
or scratch our heads when we are talking on the phone. Through the body we regulate our
relationship to the world and to ourselves.

BODY COMMUNICATION

For all body behaviour that people exhibit in interaction with one another and which
changes during this interaction, I want to suggest the concept of body communication (cf.
Waldenfels, 2008, p. 137). This includes for psychotherapy both the one-person and the
two-person viewpoint and focuses on the **communicative process from body to body**.
This communicative process unfolds not only through the therapist seeing something in
the bodily expression of the patient. Another medium of perception are the sensations and
impulses the therapist feels in reaction to the patient, which in turn affect the latter (Appel-
Opper, 2008). Communication takes place when one person discloses something and the
other understands it and gives something in return. For this, the therapist needs their own
body with which they receive and transmit and thus become involved in a circular, interactive process (Chapter 15).

In psychotherapy, the concepts of non-verbal behaviour, non-verbal interaction or non-
verbal communication are often used for body behaviour and body communication (Heller,
2012; Ramseyer, 2022; Westland, 2015). The concept of **non-verbal behaviour** as well as
that of bodily expression usually refer only to the patient and do not embed bodily information in communication as a whole. The concept of **non-verbal communication** in turn
does not clearly indicate that it refers to the body. We can also characterise paranormal or
inexplicable phenomena of communication or one made just with sounds and not words
as non-verbal. Moreover with the word non-verbal, body communication is defined as
something which it is **not**. The body is not included in the concept, and language becomes
a defining line which determines the non-verbal as an entity. This is not only imprecise, it
also implies a subtle devaluation (Heisterkamp, 2002, p. 117), since the verbal interaction
looks like the authentic one. However we have to be careful not to do the same in the other
direction and declare bodily gestures and motor expressivity to be the authentic mirror of
feelings and needs (Keleman, 1989), as sometimes happens in body psychotherapy. I hold
the view that in therapy we should give all the patient's forms of expression the same priority. This is why we should not be working with 'non'-concepts, but should define what we
mean. With the concept of body communication, we mean communication by means of
the body.

In communication science too, body communication is usually defined as distinct from verbal communication. Heilmann (2009, p. 10) differentiates the following:

- **Verbal** communication with the content of language.
- **Paraverbal** communication, the expressiveness of speaking.
- **Extraverbal** communication, so-called body language.

All three are seen as communication. In the first two channels, we receive the communication via the ear, the favoured sense organ in psychotherapy, and the extraverbal communication mainly, but not exclusively, via the eye.

Observing paraverbal and extraverbal communications often opens the door to the patient's unconscious intentions or dissociative states and is frequently the reason for further exploration in the therapeutic process (Cornell, 2016; Geuter, 2019, pp. 132–150). In turn, patients also observe the therapist on this level. When in psychotherapy we discuss whether therapists should communicate anything personal about themselves or not, we often neglect to consider that we reveal ourselves anyway in our therapy room, our clothing, posture, movements or gaze, even if we do not mention it (Rolef Ben-Shahar, 2019). We can directly perceive things such as hierarchies, attitudes towards people of another skin colour (Hamel et al., 2018) or gender typical behaviour (R Johnson, 2019) which are unconsciously acted in an embodied interaction (Krueger, 2019).

Patient and therapist not only speak to each other in the therapy room, they are also constantly behaving bodily towards each other. Thus an **implicit communication** goes on, from which people exchange about 90% of the information in relationships (Stern, et al., 1998). We know implicitly, for instance, how to hug or kiss someone. Cultural rules are also implicit, for example in Japanese culture, there is more emphasis on subtle movements of the body (Kaji, 2019). We learn these things through experience, not by having them explained, and we practise them by utilising our experiential, affect motor knowledge. Implicit knowledge is procedural (Fuchs, 2008b). In psychotherapy, too the bulk of our communications takes place in this space of implicit relational knowing (Lyons-Ruth, 1998; Streeck, 2005, 2013).

All present moments involving intersubjective contact involve actions, be it a mutual gaze, a postural shift, a gesture, a facial expression, a respiratory change, or a change in vocal tone or strength.

(Stern, 2004, p. 145)

Implicit relational knowledge is communicated largely via bodily signals. Such signals are important for the therapeutic relationship and primarily determine the assessment the patient makes of the therapist's competence (Merten, 2001, pp. 80–1). The signals of body communication also provide the only explanation for how phenomena such as transference, projection or projective identification take effect (Chapter 15). Fuchs (2008b) estimates that in a single therapy session, more than a million body signals are inter-exchanged. The interplay of communication occurs in a fraction of a second.

Emotions are often regulated implicitly in body communication, for instance when the therapist breathes more calmly while the patient enters an arousal state of danger, shows their sympathy through a synchronised movement or cries together with the patient; surveys show that 72% of therapists have already done this without this having a place in theory (Donovan et al., 2017, p. 109). Emotional attunement takes place in therapy as it does in the mother–child interaction, through rhythm, coordination or affective tone (Trevarthen, 2012).

BODY TALK

J. Wiener (1994) has drawn an interesting distinction between *body language* and *body talk*. By body language he means a language of gestures accompanying speaking. He describes body talk as a primitive mode of communication which is a precursor to actual talking and in which a body that has been split off from the inner life early on communicates in a 'psychosomatic' language, often in a quite dramatic manner. Here the concept of body talk denotes a special form of expression of incomprehensible suffering via physical discomfort. Whereas body language is symbolic, produced by the voluntary muscles, body talk speaks a more vegetative language which the sufferers themselves do not understand. Patients complain for example of a general unwellness, undifferentiated pains or anaesthesia and emptiness. In therapy they feel nauseous, they are too cold or they have to go to the toilet, they get dizzy, freeze or have the urge to harm themselves; however they cannot see any meaning behind all this. Since these bodily expressions are not symbolic, we miss the real message when we try to interpret it as such (Section 7.1).

Breuer and Freud (1895) developed the model of a symbolic body language on the basis of hysteria. They saw what showed itself in the body as a symptom, which was a substitute for the experience of the soul. Symptoms indicated the original, repressed ideas or impulses. For instance, the *arc de cercle* with its sometimes violent movements revealed a repressed sexuality. Body talk however is not about a somatic language, but about a **language of somatisation**. Here the body presents the patients' **distress**, because they have no other way of drawing attention to themselves. These patients have separated their bodily selves from their emotional selves; they use the body to protect themselves from ominous inner experiences (Wiener, 1994, pp. 339, 343). In such cases, there was often an early disintegration between body and psyche, such as we see with children with a disorganised attachment style (Section 11.6), or the differentiation of experience is missing. Consequently the body is presented as if it were not part of the self. Wiener assumes that with body talk, the disorder is rooted in pre-verbal communication (Wiener, 1994, p. 348). He describes body talk therefore as speaking with a proto-language. Traumatised people also frequently communicate in body talk that is difficult to decipher (Heinl, 2001). Often it is the suffering of the body that brings them to therapy.

Important
Body talk does not symbolise psychological material by means of the body. Rather, it expresses an inner suffering in the form of physical discomfort.

Moser (1987) called these people 'psychosomatic' patients, as did Wiener, since somatic expression is their only form of expression. Today we talk of somatic symptom disorder, in psychodynamic diagnostics also of a structural disorder, when mental experiences can hardly be specified and bodily ones scarcely expressed in words (Rudolf, 2006, pp. 65–6). When people have lost their bodily self-certitude, they fall back on elementary body talk. This tells of 'unrecognisable or non-memorable basic psycho-physical needs, which were never met and now urgently demand fulfilment' (Moser, 1989, p. 126). In the present they could be: 'Hold me tight; I feel I'm going to break into little pieces' or 'Stay with me, I'm not able to live'.

If a patient has a higher structural level (Section 6.7), body talk can communicate the tension held from a chronically repressed affect reaction (cf. Kuechenhoff, 2008, p. 115). However body talk often conveys the archaic brunt of early states of shock, despair, desolation, loneliness, greed, rage, impotence, panic or fear. This is an 'unspoken voice' (Levine, 2010), in which the sequelae of undigested traumatic experiences, paralysis or overarousal, can make themselves heard. Interpreting it symbolically and not letting it affect us can be a form of resistance on the part of the therapist (Moser, 1989, p. 212).

Since body talk speaks a **pre-verbal** language, we should not read it as a commentary on or a substitute for verbal communication. However despite the fact that the patient has no access to them on a verbal level, the experiences expressed in body talk 'continue underground, nonverbalized, to lead an unnamed … but nonetheless very real existence' (Stern, 1985, p. 175). It is precisely those analogue aspects of experiences which the body stores from the pre-verbal stage or from experiences overwhelming the capacity for reflection: how intense something was, how strongly it affected the person or how far away it felt. In therapy we have to explore these dimensions of experience, adequately verbalise them and help the patient to regulate the core affective experience without moving too quickly to the symbolic level.

CHANNELS OF BODY COMMUNICATION

Communication with the body takes place through various channels, in which the body expresses itself perceptibly for others. Most mentioned are:

- Movement.
- Posture.
- Gestures.
- Facial expressions.
- Prosody.
- Proxemics.

The rarely used concept of **proxemics** means the behaviour with which we regulate the amount of space we need between ourselves and others, so that no one crowds us, or we keep someone at arm's length or someone sticks to us (Heilmann, 2009, p. 88). We can differentiate:

- **Close space** of intimacy.
- **Personal space**, between half a meter and 1.2 metres – this is roughly arm's length.
- **Social distance space**, which starts at 1.2 metres (Haas, 1993).

Rizzolatti et al. (1997) talk about personal, peri-personal and extra-personal space.

The behaviour of patients in space can express something about their feelings and needs (Haas, 1993). People with relationship traumas often have a stronger need for a safer personal space (R Johnson, 2019). We can let such a patient mark out the space they need in the therapy room (Ho, 2019). U. Schmitz (2006) encourages a feeling of wellbeing in space by asking the patient which areas of the room seem to them comfortable or less comfortable.

In an experiment on the spatial configuration of relationships, men had oxytocin sprayed into their nose before they were encouraged to approach attractive women. Men in relationships tended to maintain more distance between themselves and the women, presumably because the hormone had activated their attachment system (Scheele et al., 2012).

A great deal of research is being done into movement, gestures, facial expressions and prosody, some of it with regard to therapeutic communication. I will discuss this and the expressiveness of body posture in the next parts of this chapter. However there are other channels which are not alluded to or researched so extensively:

- The importance of smell or of **olfactory communication** in therapy is seldom mentioned. One of my key experiences was years ago as a patient entered the room, said 'It smells of fear in here' and opened the window. In the previous session, a patient had been full of anxiety and I had not opened the window afterwards. According to experimental studies, test persons have difficulty recognising the smell of fear; however fMRI studies show that the smell of sweat triggered by anxiety activates areas of the brain which process social and emotional stimuli (Prehn-Kristensen et al., 2009). Also it can happen that I have to refuse to work with a patient because I cannot bear their smell. This touches on areas of body communication which tend to be ridden strongly with shame and are especially important in groups (Damhorst, 2006, p. 95).
- In communication research generally, tactile or **haptic communication** is not often a theme, despite the fact that communication begins first in the womb via the skin (Muir, 2002; Section 11.1). It is more likely to appear in research under the heading of boundary violation (Schmidt & Schetsche, 2012a). For a long time it was no different in psychotherapy because of the touch taboo. However studies show the value of touch (Smith et al., 1998). With the hands-on techniques of body psychotherapy, such as massage, there is always haptic communication, which can trigger transference feelings (Chapter 15). In body psychotherapy, touch is a significant channel of communication and an important tool of practice (Geuter, 2019, pp. 248–83).
- The body communicates through **signs of change controlled by the autonomous nervous system,** such as blushing, changes in the size of the pupils or goosebumps (Section 7.1; Section 14.4: on eye contact). Such signs can be emotionally contagious, but little research has been done on this.
- One channel that has more often been the subject of clinical observations is **respiratory interaction**. Since breathing is a basic medium 'of self-expression and self-regulation' (Heisterkamp, 2010, p. 97; Section 6.2), people influence each other via respiration. Patients can thus communicate psychic states through their breathing which are then transferred to the therapist. Dornes gives an example:

Clinical application

The patient is lying silently on the couch, and after a while the psychoanalyst becomes anxious. Dornes discusses various fantasies that they could be having. But then, he writes, 'he pays attention to his bodily processes. He notices that he is breathing in a peculiar way – not quietly and deeply as usual, but with short, compressed and tense breaths. Then he notices his unusually sweaty hands and his attention wanders back to the patient who is still lying there, still silent. He sees beads of sweat on their forehead and notices a strange breathing rhythm. Slowly he realises that from the start the patient has been lying there like that and that he, the therapist, has slowly taken on the breathing rhythm of the patient. The analyst's anxiety was a result of this breathing. The patient was not trying to get rid of the anxiety nor did they have any fantasies about it, rather their anxiety transpired quite literally into the analytical situation and in/to the analyst' (Dornes, 1997, p. 71).

Here the therapist has absorbed the patient's message with his eyes and with the help of his inner sensations and, through the vegetative resonance (Chapter 15) of his breathing, has understood the patient's condition.

> In his endeavour to resonate with and thus understand the patient, the therapist in a sense breathes himself into the patient's specific constricted condition and – insofar as he is not trapped in a countertransference resistance – breathes himself out again.
>
> (Heisterkamp, 2010, p. 97).

In the way they breathe, the patient can convey something about themselves and via the breathing they can also communicate with the therapist. We can therefore use a patient's respiratory reactions as an indicator of the effect of an intervention (Section 6.2). When the therapist makes an intervention and has the impression that it should affect the patient, but their breathing has not changed, this can indicate resistance or a rift in the contact (Wehowsky, 1994, p. 108).

The therapist can also consciously deploy their breathing in a **respiratory dialogue of affect regulation**, in which they react to the breathing of the patient, who in turn reacts to the breathing of the therapist. For example, the therapist senses the constricted breathing of the patient in their own chest and gives back a calm and regulated breathing. In this way, subtle respiratory dialogues with a diversity of meanings can develop. Such meanings could be: I will help you to breathe deeply because you can hardly breathe; I feel your anxiety so strongly, that my own chest is constricted; I can feel how happy you are and it makes me breath more deeply too. In this case the breathing is intentionally used as a tool by the therapist.

14.1 THE EXPRESSION OF BODY POSTURE

In body psychotherapy, the subject of posture has traditionally been treated in two different ways. Perception-oriented body psychotherapy sees posture more with regard to gravity. It looks for instance at how a person stands, where they rest their weight and how straight their back is. Graeff (2000) sees here a direct symbolism of experience: to stand up physically or to let oneself go physically means to stand up or let oneself go inwardly. Reich (1972), on the other hand, emphasised that the way someone speaks, makes associations, reports dreams, greets someone or lies down reveals the defence, and therefore he read the language of posture more as the language of defence systems. In this tradition, posture was studied as a chronic and thus characteristic posture of a particular structure (Section 13.2).

Body posture is also studied in other psychological contexts. William James (1932) depicted approach and retreat as well as expansion and contraction as fundamental dimensions of the language of posture. Expansion means a postural pattern of the 'shoulders back, chest up, back straight and head held high' type, which is associated with feelings of self-assurance, pride or triumph. A contracted posture is associated with feelings of dejection or anxiety. In psychotherapy, however, there is little consideration of the fact that posture is always also determined by culture and social status, to the expectations of behaviour of which people conform (Bourdieu, 1984; Heller, 1997).

The attempt to use expression to interpret character goes as far back as the 18th century when Lavater tried to discover the inner human being through their physiognomy. At the time, natural scientist and enlightener Lichtenberg criticised him because people project meaning into what they see (Heller, 2012, p. 269). German expression psychology (Geuter, 1992, pp. 105–9) as well as body reading in body psychotherapy (Eiden, 2002, p. 47; see Box) follow the tradition of Lavater. Both want to determine character by means of the body, even though they have different aims and different images of the human being (Section 3.1.1); in a book published in 1921, German psychiatrist Ernst Kretschmer even relates body stature to character.

Since the 1970s, when the medialisation of the world began, more attention has been paid to body language, and there has been a boom in literature on this subject, which has also exposed the cultural and gender related bias of body language ideas (e.g. Henley, 1977). In their book, Kurtz and Prestera (1976) wanted to show what a person's stature, posture and physiognomy reveal. The keynote is:

> The body never lies. Its tone, color, posture, proportions, movements, tensions, and vitality express the person within. These signs are a clear language to those who have learned to read them. The body says things about one's emotional history and deepest feelings, one's character and personality.
>
> (Kurtz & Prestera, 1976, p. 1)

This is not wrong, but exaggerated in its absoluteness. In body psychotherapy, this 'body reading' was pursued as an objective analysis of the body, with which people thought they could diagnose characteristics from interpretive categories. We have to liberate ourselves from this kind of analysis. This is why I want to go into it here and temporarily leave the focus of this chapter. Even today postures are often interpreted analogously, as if they could be literally translated into a way of life. Crooked is crooked, upright is upright and puffed up is puffed up. While it is true that a solidified body language which has become second nature expresses something about the person's biography, all that Kurtz and Prestera have itemised in their lists could just be the language of the moment and thus part of the particular situation and the particular process. Furthermore, this body reading implies a definition of the therapeutic relationship in which the therapist is the knowledgeable expert and the patient the object of this knowledge: the patient's body speaks, and the therapist interprets it. What they neglect to consider is that what the therapist 'reads' is an impression formation (cf. Frey, 1999) the categories of which are set by the therapist, and that their body behaviour also influences the patient's demeanour.

In neo-Reichian body psychotherapy, **body reading** of character structures is taught up to this day (Heinrich-Clauer, 2008a, p. 162; Section 13.2). Lowen was of the opinion that personality could be captured 'through the interpretation of bodily expression' (1967, p. 76). To do this the therapist has to find the relationship between a person's physical characteristics and their behaviour (Lowen, 1967). This means that Lowen assumes the role of the knowledgeable doctor who knows the meaning of the signs. However he overlooks the fact that body expression always has a communicative function with the aim of creating resonance in the receiver, and that its meaning is dependent on the field in which it takes place (Asendorpf & Wallbott, 1982). When we look at some of the videos of treatment sessions with Lowen, we see him explaining diagnoses and interventions without connecting the patient's body expression to their relationship to him or to the situation. In the interaction, Lowen himself creates the model of the expert relationship through his own body behaviour.

What is also left out of this kind of body reading is the fact that it can be very humiliating. D.H. Johnson (2018) reports on how in a body reading he was accused of stiffness and rigidity, both of which were the result of a congenital disease of the spine.

It was Reich who said: 'Words can lie. The expression never lies' (1973, p. 171), from which Kurtz and Prestera as well as Lowen made the slogan that the body never lies. This sentence is seductive because it lures people to believe they have the power of interpretation because they see the truth. Davis (2020, p. 17) calls this a fallacy; Worm says it is an idealisation of the body since it insinuates that via the body we can get 'directly to the true core of the self' (Worm, 2007a, p. 259). Body language is **not the language of truth**. Just like verbal language, it can try to deceive, whether deliberately or not, for instance when a client produces 'good breathing' because they want to please the therapist. Above all it is ambiguous. Sensations can deceive even the person who has them, for example when the body stays quiet despite the fact that tension would be an adequate reaction, or when it desires something that damages the person. Caldwell (2018, p. 150) thinks we should therefore not only practise metacognition but also 'a *metaphysicality* of not believing everything we feel or sense bodily'.

My position on working with body posture is that patients should **experience and reflect on their posture**, so that from inner experience, in an act of self-validation, they can understand the momentary or lasting meaning of their posture. The therapist can use categories such as those of character structure theory as a hypothetical guideline. However they do not offer any diagnostic certainties. As therapists we should not fall into the trap of interpreting the messages of the body in a facile manner. No bodily communication can simply be reduced to a literal or allegorical meaning. Its significance is only revealed in the context of the patient's biography, their momentary condition, their situation and the relationship in which it is communicated. Bereft of this context, gestures, facial expressions and posture make almost no sense (Heller, 2012, pp. 600–6). Therefore, understanding the language of the body needs careful clarification of its context.

Important
The assertion that 'the body never lies' is a tempting but deceptive slogan. Body expression is ambiguous. We can only understand its meaning in context.

For recognising emotions, posture is less unequivocal than facial expressions. If we show an evaluator videos of embodied emotions, they will tend to mistake pride and even anxiety for joy. Our recognition of despair, fear or pride by means of posture is poor (Wallbott, 1998, p. 889; Section 10.4). However it is also possible for the impression made on us by someone's posture to override that made by facial expression. In an experiment, Meeren et al. (2005) put photos of people together so that either both face and body showed the same emotional expression, or else quite opposite ones (anger/fear). When subjects were asked to say what expression the person was showing **in the face**, this was very difficult when the photos were incongruent. When they were just asked about the feeling the person was showing, they tended to follow the impression they had of the body.

Frey (1999) criticises any interpretation of bodily expression, as it is always an impression formation. Therapy though is a quite different situation from that of research, in which a coder has to decide which psychological attribute to assign to a certain bodily expression (Frey, 1999, p. 60). In the mutual communication of therapy, it is not a question of here an expression and there an impression. Rather the diagnosis of expression takes place as an interactive process between two people: a patient shows an expression; the therapist points

out what they have noticed; the patient reacts to this and the therapist offers a possible interpretation, perhaps in a more open form; the patient says something about this and simultaneously their body language changes; the therapist receives new signals; and so on. In body
psychotherapy, the meaning of an expression is not decoded, but discovered in a mutual
process of communication. We explore rather than research meaning. In my ten principles
of body psychotherapeutic practice I talk about *exploring and discovering* (Geuter, 2019).

With this we come back to the actual subject of this section, body expression in the communicative process of therapy. Posture is here a medium through which we can approach
those parts of the self which are not expressed, or even access buried memories. Griffith and
Griffith (1994) give an example:

Clinical example

In a therapy session a patient, who suffers from severe headaches, grasps her head and neck.
She describes how her head feels with the words 'crushing' and 'contorted'. She also says she
longs to be little again. 'I asked what body position she would assume if she followed her
body's lead. She took pillows from the sofa and curled up on the couch, covering herself
with the pillows. I then asked what important stories from her life connected to this body
position. Remaining curled and hidden, she told how as small child she would curl up like
this in a closet after her father would beat her.' (Griffith & Griffith, 1994, p. 37).

In experiments when they assume a certain body posture, subjects tend to remember the
events in which they had the same position in the original situation (Dijkstra et al., 2007). In
clinical work, we can ask a patient to immerse themselves in a certain biographical scene by
taking up the position of the body that they remember as being part of their experience of
this scene. How were they sitting at the table when a parent acted in a certain way? How did
they stand as a child at their own mother's grave? What was the posture of the body when
they asked for something but their voice broke up? The position of the body in the present
helps them to experience the quality of a scene from the past. Also in therapy we can try out
alternative postures when a patient wants to adopt an attitude to past experiences or a current situation more conducive to their present life.

These would be experiments in which the patient consciously assumes a certain posture.
However, usually body posture is an unconscious way of communicating in the therapeutic process. We observe something without knowing whether the patient feels the way we
believe they do from the posture of their body (Krause, 2006, p. 24). Therefore we have to
take posture as one sign among others as a possible source for therapeutic exploration.

Clinical example

A patient is sitting on the edge of her seat. She has turned one half of her body towards me
and the other away from me. Her hair is hanging on the side towards me like a curtain over
her face. During an earlier therapy, she had never once looked at her therapist. Her posture
is a sign of a great shame. In a long process, it becomes clear that with it she is also expressing a deep fear: she sits as if she expects to have to leave at any minute, because she is not
liked. At the same time she turns part of herself towards me, but does not express the most
important part: she would like to be really close to me and to find peace by being held.

In such a situation, if I only react to the patient's words, in which for instance she tells me about her difficulties with her exams, then I only connect with one part of her. With her posture, however, she is telling me something important above and beyond her words.

There can be several reasons for working with body posture. As in the example, it could be that we experience what the patient is expressing or conveying through various channels of communication as incongruent. Her behaviour and her goals diverge from one another, signs of inconsistency – which in Grawe's (2004) consistency theory is a term for the falling apart of psychological processes. This can express itself when, for example, a patient talks about something sad, but remains unmoved physically; then words and demeanour do not fit together. In another example, when there is what I see as a slight misunderstanding about the time of an appointment, they turn away in a gesture of anger, but say that it is no problem; then the affect motor expression of their posture does not fit the situation and the words. Inconsistencies can be an indication of repressed or split off material.

Inconsistencies are more frequent in mental disorders. In a study by Schwab and Krause (1994), patients with functional disorders of the spine showed strong facial activity, those with colitis ulcerosa a significant reduced level (Section 14.4). This correlated with the extent of unspecific affective arousal. Colitis patients showed a reduction in their experience of core affectivity and did not express emotions physically to an appropriate extent. Especially in patients with severe mental disorders, there are massive changes in illustrative gestures. Schizophrenics show an almost complete lack of synchronised body movements. Depressive patients show an increase in adaptive actions, for example rubbing one part of the body on another part to keep tensions in check (Section 6.7).

14.2 MOVEMENT

In studies, movement characteristics tend to indicate less the type of mental disorder and more the severity of the disturbance (Wallbott, 1989). The degree of the movement disorder correlates with the severity of the illness. Caldwell (2015, p. 427) talks of a 'mobility gradient' ranging from complete immobility to complex, unpredictable movements. However, empirically, we have not been able to identify individual characteristics of movement specific to a group of diagnoses (von Arnim et al., 2007). The interrelation between body behaviour and psychopathology is less clear than many clinicians usually believe (Heller, 2012, p. 596).

Lausberg (1998) studied the movement behaviour of patients with anorexia, bulimia and irritable bowel syndrome compared to a control group. Participants in the study had to perform various motion sequences such as running, hopping, stamping, swinging or spinning. There were differences in the way patients moved in comparison with the control group, but not, however, between the various patient groups. Also no movement parameter was found to be characteristic of a certain group of patients. All the patients showed less shifting of weight, less strength and less free flow of movement, a smaller area of movement, a more isolated use of parts of the body and less integration of the lower half of the body. We can read all this as an indication of a body schema disorder and a reduction in expressivity. Studies of patients with anorexia, however, do show a specific movement profile:

- Restricted flow of movement, possibly as an expression of a need for control.
- Isolated movements of parts of the body.
- Avoidance of movements of the whole body, possibly a sign of the disintegration of body experience.
- Immobility of the lower body, possibly a sign of the rejection of sexuality (von Arnim et al., 2007; Lausberg, 2008).

According to a study by Hoelter et al. (2008), anorectic patients also have more difficulties with their sense of balance.

T. Fuchs (2005) describes a phenomenological view of the movement gestalt of depressive and schizophrenic patients. Studies show that schizophrenic patients walk more slowly, have a shorter stride length and walk at an irregular pace (Martin et al., 2022). Patients with a major depression also walk more slowly and move less in the vertical plane (Section 6.7). Walking more quickly and with more up and down movements is a sign of mood improvement (Adolph et al., 2021). Depressive people also show more lateral swaying movements (Michalak et al., 2009). However Heller (2012, pp. 595–8) points out that studies on the motor activity of depressive patients have not produced unequivocal results. Depressive patients do not move less than others generally, but rather with less variety of movement. In addition it has not been proved that they generally have a lower level of activity (Michalak et al., 2022). In a study on the hand movements of depressive patients, Wallbott (1985) found that following inpatient therapy, movements close to the body became more brisk, more agitated, faster and more erratic. Psychotherapy seems to have influenced those qualities of movement that we could describe as the vitality contours (Section 10.5).

Movement is a medium of **emotional expression**, when for instance we jump for joy or stamp our feet in anger; an **expression of mood** (state-like); but also a central and highly individual **expression of self** (trait-like). We recognise people familiar to us by their gait alone, even without seeing their face.

In an experiment, Cutting and Kozlowski (1977) verified this gait recognition by presenting the walking movements of someone subjects had seen before on a screen in the form of light points showing the joints. The walkers were recognised more often than could be expected by chance. The observers were more accurate the more they concentrated on the movements and not on other characteristics. One observer who consciously focused on height had the worst results. For recognising someone, the dynamic movement gestalt was the most important factor. Also having a trained eye was a help. A dancer was best at recognising other people by their walk, because the memory for arm and leg movements is connected to one's own experience of movement (Reed & Farah, 1995).

Micromovements also have a certain style of body behaviour, for instance in the way in which someone freezes. Behnke (1997) calls this 'ghost gestures', because they are hardly noticeable in the shadow of larger movements and says that they contain the hidden choreography of everyday life, in which the body performs even socially prescribed movements in its own individual way. In movement, we simultaneously reveal ourselves to others and experience ourselves in our relationship to ourselves, to other people and to the world: to 'space, time, objects and our fellow human beings' (Stolze, 1959, p. 35).

Clinical example

A patient precedes me up the stairs. I have the impression that today her joints are quite stiff. Her whole way of moving seems different. At first I ask myself whether she is in pain. But then in the therapy room I see her facial expression – she looks like she has retreated into herself. I mention my impression and she says that for the first time she was dreading coming to the session. As she came through the yard, this dread crept over her.

In the last session we had talked about the fact that in all her life she had never had a satisfactory, friendly relationship to another person and that she had no heartfelt connection to anyone. She had also said that she had to keep her distance from me and was afraid the border between us could become blurred. It was clear to her that this was a hot potato and she was very reluctant to talk about it.

A week later I noticed her walk was different. Now she could say that she was afraid of wanting too much and then not being able to let go. Noticing this had put on the brakes – she had to hold back her wishes. In braking her walk, she held herself back. This was visible even before we spoke about it, but without me being able to recognise its significance at first.

In this case we spoke about her movements. Patients can also explore aspects of themselves in movement experiments (Geuter, 2019, pp. 333–7; Sollmann, 1988, pp. 165–8). Small movements can produce large effects. Just minimal bodily changes can sometimes lead to a different experience of self: moving the head up, away from its hanging position, a slight straightening of the spine, tilting the pelvis slightly – all this can create an experience of a different 'stance'. Sollmann (2009) recommends **slow motion experiments** in which the slowness of the movements is emphasised, so that we can consciously become aware of our sensations. In the exercises Sollmann recommends, the muscles are tensed and then released. The goal is not to relax as with progressive muscle relaxation, but to improve awareness through repetition.

Movement is a fundamental **expression of life** (Section 5.2). Through movement in therapy we can help the patient develop a feeling for the agency of their actions and thus a sense of self. Moving helps to promote a sense of aliveness, for instance an experience of sexual lust and vitality through activating the belly and the pelvic areas (Sollmann, 1988, pp. 128–34, 155). The external dynamics of movement changes the inner dynamics. In our work with suicidal patients, movement can help to encourage contact with themselves and with others, which has been blocked (Imus, 2019).

At the University of Heidelberg's psychiatric clinic, Koch et al. (2007) studied the effects of a dance with music, which activated a rhythmic bouncing up and down, on depressive patients. Compared to a movement programme on an exercise machine and to listening to music without moving, the dance was more successful in alleviating the patients' depression. Also in the two movement groups, vitality increased in comparison with the group just listening to music. Severely depressed patients profited more than did those with a lighter form.

SYMBOLIC LANGUAGE

Concentrative Movement Therapy, developed by Stolze, uses movement as a symbolic language for psychological themes. Meaning is discovered through the symbolic character of movements (Stolze, 2006a). However, symbolic language is never unambiguous and so we can only understand its meaning in the context of our knowledge of the patient and their situation. A symbol cannot be recognised in a fixed system because it is itself always moving and being moved (Stolze, 2006, p. 21). In a group, we sense and become aware of the interpersonal meaning of a movement in interaction with other group members (Schreiber-Willnow, 2012, p. 455).

Streeck (2004, pp. 209–13) describes a videotaped sequence in a preliminary interview for therapy, in which the patient sits there with her knees pressed together cautiously, holds on to her backpack on her lap and tentatively opens the zip just a little. Then she pulls out a piece of paper with her eating protocol and pushes it across the table without letting go of it. As a patient with an eating disorder, control is one of her issues. The therapist has to lean quite far forward in order to reach the paper. It is as if in these few seconds, the patient wants to say: 'I find it difficult to open up, so you have to approach me if you want to know anything about me'. The therapist can just take note of this symbolic language. However in body psychotherapeutic treatment they can themselves 'work with and on this body symbolism' by letting the body tell more of its story through it (Stolze, 2006, pp. 21–2). Only by exploring it together with the patient can they discover whether an interpretation, such as in Streeck's example, fits. Stolze gives us an example for such an exploration:

Clinical example

A patient has the problem that he is not able to stick to his opinion even when he feels he is right. His uncertainty makes him sad, sometimes angry. In a certain situation in the therapy group, he notices his anger coming up and moves his right foot spontaneously as if he wants to trample something. Stolze asks him to complete the motion. He finds this difficult, but at the same time sadness and anger well up in him. Stolze notices that not only is he pressing his right leg into the ground, he is also lifting his foot away from it. He suggests that the patient explore both these contradictory movement signals by standing on a footstool with the one leg so as to continue the movement away from the ground. 'So I address the apparent "ambivalence" of the movement and try to intensify it so that Mr. M. can experience it bodily himself' (Stolze, 2006, p. 22). In Stolze's detailed description, the patient explores the ambivalence between pushing and releasing and can feel that he has to make a decision on what to do. By exploring the situation bodily, he experiences being able to step up or down from it and discovering his own point of view according to the situation.

Movement reveals **meaning** that the patient can understand for themselves directly from the situation (Chapter 16). Because of the multi-layered meaning of body behaviour, the therapist cannot know the significance of a spontaneous movement beforehand. Instead it reveals its meaning only when we explore it by developing the movement. As a symbolic act, movement serves as a metaphor that not only tells us of unconscious ambivalences but also shows a way of resolving them. Active movement helps us access unconscious material (Becker, 1989, p. 121). However this is not only the unconscious as understood by Freud, the container of **repressed material**, but also that of Milton Erickson, which **already knows the solution**.

Clinical example

A patient is talking about a difficult decision he has to reach and at the same time moving both his hands rhythmically away from and back to his body in turn. I ask him whether he can feel one of the sides of the argument in each of his hands. He immediately says which hand stands for which side, and then he senses clearly that the right hand is heavy and the left is tingling. Suddenly he knows what to do: 'The side that tingles is where I want to be, that is where my energy is going'. He feels quite clear about it. A sensed movement has given him the answer that was not possible through cognitive assessment of the various factors.

Important
Exploring the implicit language of movement through the body helps us access an explicit understanding of its symbolic content. This expands the space of what is available to our consciousness.

These examples demonstrate an open approach to the signals of movement. This is typical for body psychotherapeutic work with movement; movement is not analysed with the help of concepts, rather it is 'evaluated as to its individual meaning and significance' (Hoehmann-Kost, 2009, p. 23). In body psychotherapy, there are hardly any explicit theories of movement providing a basis for conceptual work.

Motoric fields

The **theory of movement themes** from Boadella (2000) is an exception to this. He speaks of nine motoric fields of which eight are linked in sets of two as polarities:

- In the **flexion field**, the organism contracts for protection, e.g. in the foetal position; in this position, the organism can collect itself.
- Boadella describes movements with which the body expands, stretches, reaches out to the world and straightens up as the **extension field**. He sees the first great expansion as being at birth.

We can work therapeutically with this pair of opposites by, for instance, showing a person who is always moving energetically towards the world as a counterphobic tactic how to experience their fear and their need for protection and self-collecting in a more flexed, contracted position. Another person who is always more in the flexed position needs instead to move more into extension, stretching or opening up.

- The **traction field** stands for movements such as pulling something towards us, above all when we come close to someone through movements of the arms.
- In contrast to this are movements with which we push ourselves back, push something away or create borders. Boadella calls this the **opposition field**.

People who have difficulty keeping things at a distance will also have trouble with pushing or shoving movements. Practising them is important for people who are easily overwhelmed by anxiety or who had no emotional space for themselves as children. Others have to learn to overcome distance. In the pulling movement we are saying 'yes', in the pushing one 'no' to the world outside.

We can explore the relevant movements in interaction. When patients push against another person's hands, this can activate a boundary schema (Langlotz-Weiss, 2019), but it can also satisfy the need to find a response to their own strength. Pulling someone towards oneself activates an approach schema.

- Boadella calls movements rotating the limbs to the inside or the outside (pronation and supination) the **rotation field**. When someone only ever goes straight ahead into confrontation, it could be helpful if they learn in a symbolic sense to rotate from the axis as do Aikido practitioners, who use the momentum of the opponent to let them run into empty space.
- Opposite this is the **canalisation field**: linear, focused and directed movements orientated towards the axis of the body. People who lack this tend to lose themselves easily. Rigid people on the other hand have too much of it.
- The **activation field** includes all vitalising movements such as running, dancing, bouncing.
- The **absorption field** includes passive movements such as being carried or absorbing impressions from the environment, which could balance out an overactive person.

Boadella puts these eight fields into the superordinate category of the **pulsation field**. This means that movement in any of the eight fields pulsates between the respective poles. Pulsation is thus more a generic term for the mobility of the living person. Mobility means that movement in each of the fields can serve to achieve something or to prevent something, desire or defence. Similar to Boadella with the motoric fields, Frank and La Barre (2011) distinguish six fundamental movements: yield, push, reach, grasp, pull, release.

Reich saw free pulsation between contraction and expansion as a sign of vegetative mobility. Movement also occurs as an inner movement of the body (Caldwell, 2015). Some vegetatively controlled processes, such as the expansion and contraction of the heart, take the form of a pulsatory movement.

The categories of the motoric fields give us pointers as to which movement themes we could explore with a patient on the basis of their psychological structure. Indications could be a lack of a certain type of movement or when it is being used too often; in the one case we would explore and develop the forces of the movement itself, in the other of the opposite one. An anxious patient, for example, needs the pushing away, whereas the narcissist uses that as a defence. The hysterical character is comfortable with the detour, which the obsessive lacks. Through prototypical movements, we can address basic psychological themes connected to character structure (Section 13.2).

Movement analysis in dance and movement therapy

Whereas body psychotherapy has been more concerned with body posture and with the symbolism of movement, dance and movement therapy has developed specific concepts for working with movement in psychotherapy. Samaritter and Payne (2016/17) describe shared experiences of movement as the focus of its therapeutic work, and Bender (2020, pp. 198–214) depicts movement analysis as its basic tool. As an approach closely connected to the medium of music, dance and movement therapy has gone through a process of theory development largely separate from other fields of body psychotherapy, although there are great similarities in both theory and methodology (Chapter 2).

Movement analysis models of dance and movement therapy go back to a system of dance notation developed by von Laban (1926; Section 3.2). Von Laban wanted to describe movements, not interpret them (Trautmann-Voigt & Voigt, 2009, p. 132). This is why his system found no direct use in psychotherapy. However it does provide categories for the theories of dance and movement therapy. The categories of the **Laban movement analysis** are:

1. Effort.
2. Shape, taken by the body.
3. Space: how someone moves in space.
4. Body: which parts of the body are being moved and is body weight shifted? (von Arnim et al., 2007).

Von Laban describes effort in the following dimensions:

- Flow: free as opposed to bound.
- Weight: using the weight of the body with or against gravity.
- Space: direct or indirect use of space.
- Time: quick or sustained.

The polarity of these four categories gives us eight effort elements:

- Human beings can open themselves up or close themselves down (flow).
- They can move strongly or gently (weight).
- They can fight or sense (space).
- They can move quickly or slowly (time) (Trautmann-Voigt & Voigt, 2009, p. 133).

The therapeutic task consists of developing an interpretation of a person's condition from these descriptions. To date this has been done mainly in an analogical and associative manner.

Trautmann-Voigt and Zander (2007) propose an elaborated interaction analysis model in which they create people's movement profiles on the basis of 22 movement categories. The profile gives us information on whether a person's movements are contracted or not, whether or not they put a lot of weight into them, with or against gravity, towards or away from the body axis, dominated by the limbs or the torso, more stretched or flexed, cramped or more extended, fast or slow, smooth or fragmented, variable or repetitive, directed or not. The goal is a diagnosis of movement from which we can derive interventional measures (Trautmann-Voigt & Voigt, 2009, p. 150). The appropriate interventions take place in rhythmic action dialogue between therapist and patient (Trautmann-Voigt, 2003). Kuhn (2018, p. 31) presents a dance therapy approach which explores in a meditative process the possibility of equilibrium between the five rhythms of flowing, staccato, chaos, lyrical and stillness.

In a factor analysis of descriptions of hand movements, Wallbott (1985) identified four factors: intensity/strength, tempo/speed, flow (process, quality) and space. The category of tension flow seems to describe on the movement level a characteristic of temperament (Section 11.5). According to Bender (2007, p. 24), the properties of tension flow are the most persistent of all movement patterns, often lasting a whole life.

We can work with Laban's categories by mobilising material on which the patient is fixated or encouraging what they lack. We can help patients whose kinaesphere is narrow

(Section 13.1) to reach out into the room. To help people sense the force of their efforts, Graeff (2000, p. 156) suggests walking against resistance at the pelvis. I do this exercise as follows:

Exercise

The therapist puts their hands on the iliac crests of the patient's hips and the patient pushes the therapist through the room with the strength of their pelvis. The patient should not bend forwards and use the weight of the upper body but keep it in the vertical axis and walk with lightly bended knees. In this way the force of the push comes from the middle. The exercise makes the patient aware of the power of their centre, which can only be invoked through sensing the body. Also the vitality of the legs is connected to that of the upper body. I call this the Gary Cooper exercise, because the movements remind me of those of the sheriff in the last scene of the film 'High Noon'.

Moving in relation

Just like all body communication, movement is also a relational process. It is lived communication. When we share movement, we create relationship (Galbusera et al., 2019). Affective resonance is generated by the coordination of facial expressions, gestures or tone of voice (Muehlhoff, 2015). Movement is contagious and, just like posture, is adopted by our relational partner, altered and fed back. The findings of copious psychological experiments indicate that people automatically and unintentionally adopt the movements, posture and facial expressions of the person they are looking at. They touch their faces or jiggle their feet after their counterparts have done so. Chartrand and Bargh (1999) have called this the **chameleon effect**.

In one of the first psychotherapy studies using film, Charny (1966) found that a movement of so-called mirror image congruence (when one partner moves to the right, the other moves to the left) correlated with positive interpersonal rapport in the conversation, whereas with incongruent posture there was less relatedness. The patterns of body movements in the relationship changed from one moment to the next as did the topics of conversation.

In a therapeutic relationship, movement themes such as symmetry and asymmetry or synchronousness and reciprocity become important for the quality of the relationship (Koole et al., 2020). From the way two people synchronise the position of their bodies in movement, we can predict 70% of the variance in sympathy judgements (Krause, 1992).

Several studies have been done on movement **synchrony** in therapy (Tschacher & Meier, 2022). Ramseyer and Tschacher (2008) recorded a whole course of psychotherapy on video, charted all movements of the participants and compared them to questions on the therapeutic relationship set after each session. The process analysis showed that the more their movements were synchronised, the more satisfied the client was with the therapeutic relationship.

On the basis of an analysis of an individual case, Ramseyer and Tschacher (2016) could also show that the quality of the therapeutic contact correlated with a higher coordination of hand movements.

However, observing interactions over a longer period of time shows that an increase in sychronised movements over the course of therapy can be connected to unproductive sessions or even to a deterioration in the patient's condition (Ramseyer, 2020). This could be due to a motorically visible dependency resulting from a lack of individuation and the failure to develop the capacity for self-regulation. Thus it seems that at the beginning of therapy, it is beneficial when the therapist is attuned to the movements of the patient, but towards the end it is better when they initiate movement (Ramseyer, 2011). To use terms from neuro-linguistic programming (NLP), *pacing* would be more appropriate at the beginning, *leading* at the end.

Research findings are not unambiguous (Prinz et al., 2021). More coordination is not necessarily better (Wiltshire et al., 2020); for instance in one study, head movements correlate with satisfaction about the session, but whole body movements showed the opposite effect (Ramseyer & Tschacher, 2014). Schizophrenic patients generally showed little synchrony (Kupper et al., 2015). In retrospect, juvenile borderline patients on the other hand tended to evaluate therapy more positively when movement was more attuned (Zimmermann et al., 2021). However this was not true of the evaluation of individual sessions. Patients who experienced trauma as children show less synchronisation of movement (Ramseyer et al., 2020), those with interpersonal problems a higher one (Ramseyer 2020). In patients with anxiety, the synchronisation decreases in the course of treatment; in those with depression it increases (Ramseyer, 2020). It is possible that in the former, an initial anxious clinging reflected in the synchrony starts to dissipate, whereas in the latter a vital resonance starts to develop which enables a later synchronisation.

Wiltshire et al. (2020) combine the various findings of these studies so that movement coordination correlates with the outcome of therapy, the synchrony of physiological changes with empathy and those in other areas, such as the voice, with the experience of the therapeutic relationship.

Despite the fact that they have few clinical implications, these studies sharpen our awareness of the significance of body interaction in therapy (Tschacher & Ramseyer, 2017). Simple statements such as that a closer coordination of movements correlates with a good therapy result and increased patient satisfaction are untenable. Rather it appears that a medium level of attunement is an indication of a favourable therapeutic process (Ramseyer, 2020). According to a study by Galbusera et al. (2019), movement synchrony should not be too strong. In an experiment, a high level of synchronisation facilitated positive affects, but reduced the patient's ability to regulate them themselves. A study by Prinz et al. (2021) showed that it also lessened the ability to activate resources. High synchronicity can also signify a static situation. For this reason, one of my body psychotherapy teachers, David Boadella, taught us to interrupt an overly strong attunement. Possibly more important than synchrony is the quality of the transitions from loss of contact to reconnection, often indicated by synchrony and asynchrony; this is the process of rupture and repair described in infant research (cf. Garcia & Di Paolo, 2018).

The studies mentioned focus solely on bodily synchronisation. However in psychotherapy, this is always connected to a dialogue. Here we have no synchronisation independent of an exchange about meanings. On no account should we conclude from the research that we can practise ideal body postures or movements as a technique: sitting one metre away with arms relaxed, moving moderately, creating postural congruence and nodding the head (Merten, 2001, p. 80). Relationship is not a technique. What we should conclude in my opinion is to **observe** both the patient's **involuntary** bodily communication in movement as well as our own, to use these perceptions as information about their condition and that of the relationship and to ask ourselves why things are as they are (cf. Ramseyer, 2022). Being aware of the interpersonal attunement of movements also facilitates emotional regulation (Cohen et al., 2021).

Movements reveal early acquired affect motor schemata (Chapter 12). In an experiment about participating in movements, subjects who were rated as securely attached in the *Adult Attachment Interview* (Section 11.6) tend to move freely, whereas those who were rated more as 'avoidant' tended to move more together with the experts (Feniger-Schaal et al., 2018).

The relationship is often shown as a 'micro-enactment' in small movements where two people react to one another:

> Sometimes it seems as if the way in which patient and therapist interact in their body behaviour, even before having exchanged one word with each other, already reveals how the therapeutic relationship will develop in the subsequent 'exchange of words'. Their non-verbal behaviour in contact with each other seems to present the therapeutic relationship as if on stage in a pantomime.
>
> (Streeck, 2004, p. 119)

Movements accompany verbal communication in a conversation from body to body. In a case analysis, Davis and Hadiks (1990) looked at how changes in posture and facial expression are linked to verbal changes. They coded body language according to whether the client moved towards the therapist, away from them or neutrally. Their findings showed the following:

> as the client shifted from superficial discussion to actively exploring her internal reactions, her bodily positions became increasingly more accessible, open, and oriented toward the therapist.
>
> (Davis & Hadiks, 1990, p. 347)

In a follow-up study, Davis and Hadiks (1994) examined the body language of the therapist. Video analysis showed that therapist and client were constantly changing their positions, moving their heads, gesturing or fidgeting. Body language mirrored the therapeutic relationship. On the part of the therapist, the affective immediacy and the complexity of her remarks correlated with the intensity and complexity of her gestures. More reserved comments were accompanied by less gesticulation. The complex patterns of body communication in time and space led to an experience of being connected (Davis & Hadiks, 1994, p. 403).

The therapeutic relationship is regulated through the language of body movements. Connection or separateness can be created or avoided even without words. By a gesture, the therapist can invite the patient to further self-exploration or rebuff them. Their body language indicates whether they are prepared to engage with the patient with all their personal experience and can create a holding environment – or sometimes not (Davis & Hadiks, 1994). Thus patients can tell from their posture whether a therapist is good for them.

14.3 HAND GESTURES

As mentioned in Section 3.1, Freud (1890) said that nearly all mental states are communicated through the body, especially through the hands. Bodily changes would serve others as reliable signs to infer mental processes and would be trusted more than what is being deliberately said. Hands can express what the mouth fails to say. However Freud understood gestures as messages from the patient about themselves. In this chapter, I look at them above all as a form of communication between people, which is, in the sense of Merleau-Ponty (2012), intercorporeal.

The term gestures is sometimes used for all motoric behavioural expressions of the body. However, I have discussed whole body expression in Sections 14.1 and 14.2 under the headings of posture and movement. Here I am concerned with the expression of the hands. Hand gestures are a universal phenomenon. Even congenitally blind people gesticulate when they speak; sighted people do so even when there is no one to see them (Goldin-Meadow, 1999). In both evolution and the ontogenetic process, gestures predate language. In childhood development, they are important for the acquisition of language (Iverson & Goldin-Meadow, 2009). Gestures help us think. If someone talks about solving a problem and punctuates the tale with suitable hand gestures, then it is more probable that they will continue with this strategy than if they do not (Alibali et al., 1999). Pupils learn maths better when the teacher highlights their explanations with gestures; this is also true of foreign languages (Macedonia & Knoesche, 2011). This research supports what I said in the previous paragraph: gestures co-determine whether what a therapist says reaches the patient. When attempting to communicate an insight, the quality of our message depends on our gestures and our tone of voice (Section 14.5).

Gestures have various **functions**, as do all bodily signals:

- We can point to something (deictic gesture).
- We can give a conventional sign such as tapping the forehead.
- We can clarify something that is otherwise difficult to convey, such as the shape of Denmark.

Gestures regulate interaction, underscore what we are saying or add something to it (Holler, 2011). In psychotherapeutic communication, patients use **iconic gestures** when they find it difficult to express something in words, for example when someone makes a snakelike movement of the hand to describe their present mood. If a patient is lost for words, we can ask them if they can show what they are feeling with a gesture. Therapists too use gestures to describe something or to initiate something, for instance rotating the hand to indicate that the patient should develop a certain thought further (Streeck, 2004, p. 125).

Gestures also have an emotional function. They can express vitality. The study by Wallbott (1985) mentioned in the previous section showed that in the course of therapy, depressive patients increased their use of illustrative hand movements, whereas those directed towards their own bodies decreased. Touching oneself is often a way of calming down when in stress and as such is an instrument for the autoregulation of emotional tension.

For psychotherapy, **involuntary gestures**, also known as **ideomotor signals**, are of great importance. Here we are dealing with movements of the voluntary muscles controlled by the unconscious. When they accompany speech, they can be a sign of hidden connotations (Goldin-Meadow, 2006). There is an example in Chapter 8: a woman talking about her need for affection who simultaneously makes a pushing away gesture with her hand. Verbally she expresses a need, while with her hand she perhaps shows aggression. The gesture contains something unspoken. Studies of split-brain patients suggest that gestures with emotional meaning are generated more by the right hemisphere, and illustrative and pointing gestures more by the left hemisphere (Lausberg et al., 2000). The former are therefore carried out more by the left hand, the latter more by the right.

Gestures also shed light on the people the patient talks about. In a case study, Lausberg and Kryger (2011) showed how the gestures of a patient with depression and anorexia expressed a change in her relationship to her mother. At the beginning of treatment, she would direct her hand towards herself when speaking of her mother; towards the end, however, her attendant gestures were directed to an area away from the body on the left. The gesture marked how the mother was represented psychologically in relation to herself.

In therapy, involuntary gestures that are neither deictic nor conventional must be explored individually if we want to understand them. They are just as personal and dependent on context as are words. When subjects were shown a film without sound and without knowing the context, they understood the gestures very differently from one another; only 1% of all gestures are unambiguous (Heller, 2012, pp. 598–9). We have to explore the meaning of the rest.

Clinical application

In body psychotherapy, we can explore gestures through the body. We can ask patients to pay attention to them; to repeat them consciously; to make them larger or smaller, stronger or weaker; or to suppress them, always observing what happens (Geuter, 2019, pp. 144–50).

In the example from Lausberg and Kryger, based on her gestures they could ask the patient how she would shape the relationship to her mother if she brought her into the room symbolically in the form of an object. How close or far away would she be? At what angle to the patient would she stand or sit? What would the distance feel like, and how would she feel in relation to the mother? Then we could ask whether she wants to change any aspect of the positions, an intervention on the proxemic level. If she did so, then she could consider what the change feels like. Thus, the gesture would lead to active work on the object relationship in which her feelings towards her mother are explored in an enacted spatial and affect motor dialogue, which does not necessarily need a fantasised verbal exchange with the mother.

Even without registering it consciously, the listener notices any gestural information which deviates from verbal expression (Goldin-Meadow, 1999). Bender (2007, p. 219) calls such gestures **shadow movements**, since they accompany communication like a shadow. This includes, for example, a patient pulling the arms of their jumper over their hands, or wringing their hands so as to prevent an emotion coming up. Involuntary gestures can also point to the therapeutic relationship and be signs of transference. In the language of communication science, Hermer (2004, pp. 28–9) describes it as a sender, concealing their true purpose from their own consciousness, but nevertheless giving hidden cues that non-verbally touch off something in the receiver, without the sender being able to reveal their intent.

Clinical example

A patient sits close to me, desperately looking for support. In a positive transference, she conveys that I am so good to her and the best therapist that she can imagine. She would like to be hugged by me and feels like a very small child. At the same time, I notice that during this exchange, one of her hands is fidgeting. It is not clear whether the hand is searching for something or whether it wants to cling to me. I point out this fidgeting to the patient and ask her to let the hand follow its impulses. By addressing the hand directly and not asking her what she thinks the hand wants, I try to put the patient in a position of observing the impulses of the hand instead of controlling them consciously, so that the involuntary process of body behaviour has more of a chance (cf. Geuter, 2019, pp. 146–7). To her and my astonishment, the hand starts to move more and more vigorously until at last she notices that she has the impulse to hit me because I am not only the person she wants to see in me. The liberation of this spontaneous movement reveals the negative transference which was hidden behind the words.

The hand movement was a shadow movement in the Jungian sense, because in that situation it revealed an invisible side of the patient, the shadow. She was ashamed of it. But after the encounter with the shadow, she felt more alive and stronger. The hand spoke first before she could talk about her disappointment and anger.

Clinical studies show that unintentional movements often herald the arrival of new material (Davis & Hadiks, 1990). Also the therapist's gestures can trigger something new. Streeck (2004, pp. 121–2) gives the example of a therapist asking a patient in what direction something was going and at the same time tips his foot. The patient responds by tipping her feet.

14.4 INTERACTION THROUGH FACIAL EXPRESSIONS

People also communicate character attitudes, their present state or their intentions through facial expressions. The 'unconscious expressions which are frozen into the countenance' are a visible 'part of the personality' (Lowen, 1958, p. 107). Everyone knows people whose mouth is turned down sceptically at the corners or whose lips and eyes are in a permanent state of sullen contempt. In this respect, facial expressions are an indication of character (Section 13.2). However in psychotherapy, they are more significant as part of the process of communication. Nowhere else do we recognise the feelings of another person as well as in their facial expressions (Regenbogen et al., 2012, p. 1008). In these and in small movements, such as the lifting of the head, we also show whether we have understood the feelings of our opposite number (Hyniewska & Sato, 2015).

Facial expressions are as universal as gestures. Even children born deaf and blind express laughter, crying or anger in their faces, also signs of affection or embarrassment (Becker, 1989, p. 114). Basic emotions express themselves in the face, as do the core affective components of activation and pleasure, the cognitive processing of information or preparation for action (Russell et al., 2003). Through facial expressions, we regulate whether we want to make contact with someone (Cole, 2001). A receiver evaluates the meaning of facial expressions in their right hemisphere in less than 30 milliseconds (Schore, 2003, p. 71). In experiments, human beings also recognised the animated facial expressions of apes (Taubert et al., 2021).

The inability to recognise emotions in the faces of others can be an indication of a mental disorder or of autism. Psychopathic prison inmates recognise the facial expressions of sadness and joy less easily than do other people (Hastings et al., 2008).

To understand facial signals, the receiver must be able to sense their own facial expressiveness. People who see anger or joy in someone else's face react with changes in muscle action potential (measurable in an EMG (electromyography)) of their own facial muscles involved in such feelings, even when in an experiment the faces were shown to them in a subliminal timeframe, below the level of conscious perception (Dimberg et al., 2000). A masked presentation of emotional facial expressions, which remains unconscious, affects the activity of the amygdala. Even though we are not aware of it, we register the emotional expression in the face of our opposite number and react to it with signs of our own emotional expression. This is an affect motor contagion which infects people unconsciously. If we see a stutterer, our mouth muscles react in an EMG (Berger & Hadley, 1975) To recognise the contagion, we need sensory feedback from our own expressive muscles. People who cannot move their faces because of some disorder have difficulty recognising the emotions of others (Cole, 2001). As Reich said early on, the resonance of our own bodies makes empathy possible.

> Only when we have *sensed* the patient's facial *expression* are we in a position to comprehend it.
> (Reich, 1972, p. 362)

The inner imitation of another person's facial expression, even though it is unconscious, makes it easier for us to understand what it means (Wallbott, 1998b, p. 224). The more empathic someone is, the more easily they can do this. This too has been confirmed in experiments. Empathic people react more strongly with their expressive muscles to angry or happy faces than do unempathic people (Dimberg et al., 2011).

Hennenlotter et al. (2009) denervated the forehead muscles of subjects with botulinum toxin. Then they showed them images of people with angry or sad expressions. They were asked either to just look at or to try and imitate the expressions. If their forehead muscles were locally denervated and they were supposed to imitate the expression, brain activity in the motor cortex showed no change, but activity in the left amygdala, in the hypothalamic area and in the brain stem associated with emotions was reduced. The neuronal, emotion-related activity was therefore dependent on the possibility of facial feedback. This effect appeared however only in the imitation of anger, not in that of sadness. The authors attribute this to the significance of the movement of the eyebrows in anger, where the denervation was more effective. According to these findings, the inability to sense the facial expression of another person in one's own expressive muscles makes it more difficult to empathise.

Bulnes et al. (2019) replicated the design of this study and found the same difference in the perception of anger and of happiness.

However it is not necessary, as the theory of inner simulation supposes, to sense the feeling of another person in the same channel as they do (Chapter 15). Empathy can be cross-modal, as can lack of empathy. Thus when facial expressivity is inhibited, this leads to a reduction in the ability to process the vocalisation of emotions (Hawk et al., 2012).

In therapy, there is intense communication through facial expressions. Several studies have been done on this. Hufnagel et al. (1991) showed that 60% of the variance in statements made by schizophrenics about their own experience could be explained statistically through data on the facial expressions of their opposite number. In healthy people, this sinks to 20%. This means that schizophrenic patients strongly influence the facial reactions of their interaction partners, even when the latter are unaware of it themselves. With panic patients, in contrast, therapists show less emotional facial activity than do patients (Benecke & Krause,

2005), possibly because they tend to counterbalance the arousal of the patients. Patients' issues are mirrored in the face of the therapist. In the initial interview, both patients suffering from a pain disorder and their therapists often have an expression of contempt, which is frequently a corollary of experiences of shame and fear (Merten & Brunnhuber, 2004). This is possibly an expression of a maladaptive relationship pattern or a way of coping with the therapeutic situation. Bernardy et al. (2004) view a similar pattern in patients with fibromyalgia as signs of a struggle for the recognition of their condition.

Dreher et al. (2001) report on an analysis of facial expressions in an interaction where the patient talks of her contempt; however, the feeling does not appear in her face but in that of the therapist, as if she had to induce it so as to experience it. Obviously this is one of the ways in which transference works. Baenninger-Huber and Widmer (1997) give us the following example:

Clinical example

A patient is talking about her feelings of guilt regarding her husband's reproaches. While speaking she presses her lips together and turns her head and her gaze away, as if not able to regulate the feelings coming up. Then she looks hopefully at the therapist and clears her throat. She seems to be expressing the expectation that the therapist will join her in her indignation about her husband.

Now if the therapist did so and said for example 'How can he do such a thing?' then the patient could avoid her pain. With her signals, the patient tries to involve the therapist in a way of dealing with the problem, which would change nothing. Both facial expression and body behaviour are thus expressing not only the feelings of guilt, but also the 'specific coping strategy' (Baenninger-Huber & Widmer, 1997, p. 359). Now it all depends on how the therapist reacts, whether they fall for it and go along with the indignation, or whether they address the pain. Perhaps the effect of provocative therapy methods is linked to radically breaching the expectations of the patient so that they have to find a new strategy by themselves.

Facial expressions and reactions in suicidal patients

Schwartz and Wiggins (1987) studied how far therapists are able to assess the risk of patients who have already attempted suicide of doing so again. The predictions were not very good. However a video analysis showed that in interaction with endangered patients, therapists exhibited considerably more concern.

Heller and Haynal (1997) compared the facial reactions of 17 patients who had attempted suicide to the question of whether they still wished to end their life with those of nine non-suicidal depressives. They did this comparison a year after the recording of the interviews, by which time 5 of the 17 had again attempted suicide. They found no typical facial sign of suicide intent, but in the faces of the re-attempters they found contempt and no signs of grief. In comparison to the other depressives, suicidal patients showed more asymmetrical facial expressions, for instance a smile frozen only on one side of the lips, and less movement of the eye area. The authors speak of inhibited communication.

On the basis of videos, Heller et al. (2001) studied the facial interaction of a psychiatrist with 59 suicidal patients with the help of the *Facial Action Coding System* (Section 10.4). Two years later, they looked at which patients had again attempted suicide. The later risk of suicide could be predicted with a likelihood of 80% from the facial interaction, particularly from the unconscious signs of resonance in the face of the psychiatrist. Donovan et al. (2017, p. 39) highlight the importance of this study, which has unfortunately not yet been replicated.

The facial reactions of the therapist are one of the determinants of the therapy process. According to a study by Merten et al. (1996), on the basis of the facial-affective interaction in the first session, we can predict 36% of the effect of therapy. We can also tell from facial expressions when a therapy is not going well. The indicator is when the facial reactions of patient and therapist are determined by the same lead affect, for example both faces express joy, anger or submissiveness. In therapies which later do well, Rasting and Beutel (2005) found that facial expressions did not correlate. The authors think that in therapies with a negative outcome, the therapists became overly involved in the patients' patterns and so reduced conflict tension in the therapeutic relationship. This process takes place in body communication. A complementary affect attunement is auspicious for therapy, when for instance the patient's face expresses anger and the therapist shows interest, or the patient expresses joy and the therapist an anxious scepticism (Merten et al., 1996). Psychodynamically this means that the therapist absorbs the repressed emotions, or welcomes the affects discernible beyond the defences. For the emotions the patient exhibits are not always those they are experiencing (Dreher et al., 2001).

This does not contradict the findings reported in Section 14.2 that movements synchronised in time reinforce the feeling of connection. There it was a case of attunement on the level of vitality contours, here one of categorical emotions. In affect attunement with a small child, it is also important to resonate with their vitality contours without adopting their emotions.

In the very first sessions in the treatment of patients with a panic disorder, we can observe, on the basis of their facial reactions and those of the therapists, that they are activating the issue of closeness and distance (Benecke & Krause, 2004, p. 257). Patients offer signals of happiness and react with surprise and sadness to the facial expression of irritation and disgust on the part of the therapist. Here successful therapists behave contrary to the patients' offers of relationship patterns. According to studies done by Baenninger-Huber et al. (2004), a mutual smile showed a successful therapeutic resonance; however this must be balanced out by the ability to tolerate conflict tension. Soth (2009) talks about a paradox in the therapeutic relationship: the therapist has to let themselves become involved in the processes which caused the patient's wounds and at the same time keep their distance so as to be able to treat them. To recognise a negative emotion in the patient we must let ourselves be 'infected' physically. However a physiological activation of arousal which is consistently parallel, especially in couples talking about their problems, indicates an unhappy partnership (Levenson, 2003, p. 357).

Eye contact

The eyes are essentially involved in the expression of feelings; 'the eyes transmit feeling more vividly than any spoken word' (Lowen, 1958, p. 366). They also show what connection a person has to the world. Reich had already linked the lack of connection to reality of schizophrenics to their 'typical faraway look of remoteness' (1972, p. 430), which he also recognised as not always present. Splits become visible in the eyes when for instance they have different expressions. This is probably connected to the laterality of the brain hemispheres and the separating of thinking and feeling.

> NLP or neuro-linguistic programming makes use of **lines of vision** connected to inner observation processes, which are most likely also based on hemispheric laterality. When looking back into the past, there is often eye movement upwards and to the left; neurobiologically, thinking about the past calls for activation of the right prefrontal cortex (Kuhl, 2007, p. 78). Thinking about whether a word is appropriate or not is connected more to eye movements downwards and to the left, also connected to an activation of the right prefrontal cortex. The eyes are more likely to move upwards and to the right when the person is constructing something be it a thought or an image, and downwards and to the right when they are sensing something inside.
>   Thus a patient's eye movements can tell us about possible inner processes.

The eyes are a very special organ of communication. In humans, a large part of the white of the eye round the pupil is visible, so that we can follow someone's intentions with the help of their eye movements; this is not possible in other primates (Tomasello et al., 2007). During communication the eyes change; for example the size of the pupils can change (Kret, 2018). When pupil size diminishes, people register a sad expression more easily but not, however, a happy, angry or neutral one (Harrison, et al., 2006). The quality of the gaze, the signs of which are controlled by the autonomic nervous system (Section 7.1), probably regulates the relationship between interaction partners more than any other factor (cf. Geissler, 2009, p. 188). Babies too look for a connection to others through the eyes and are dependent for their wellbeing on the quality of the gaze offered them. Through their eyes, parents transfer their inner world to their children (Cozolino, 2002, p. 176).

Research on interaction through facial expressions in psychotherapy, which encoded the line of vision by the movement of the pupils or a smile by the movements of the muscles, hardly captures the various qualities of the expression of the eyes. We are not really able to measure whether they are imploring, flirty, cool, adoring, warm or cold. We can recognise happiness by the ring muscles of the eyes, but satisfaction can only be seen in the way they shine (Ekman, 2003).

Heisterkamp has shown quite clearly in several examples how important eye contact is for an intrinsic understanding of the relationship in therapy. From an analysis 25 years ago, he vividly remembers the warm-hearted gaze of his analyst (Heisterkamp, 2002, p. 35). From a later analysis he describes how his analyst greeted him, in what was to become an extremely significant moment for him:

> I paused for a moment and noticed that for the first time I was looking into her eyes in a different way. I was looking into lovely blue eyes, which gazed back at me, shining and steady. I noticed how I kept this eye contact for a few seconds longer than usual. In doing so I felt how a hint of a new self-understanding was streaming through me. It was immediately clear: never before had I dared to look like this into the blue eyes of a woman important to me.
>
> (Heisterkamp, 2002, pp. 37–8)

The deep significance of this moment led him to an insight into the quality of his relationships with women: into an existing anxiety and also into a courage generated in that instance. Worm (2007, p. 223) too describes how important the expression of the eyes and the communication through them can be for patients. One patient craved being held and comforted through eye contact. Worm had noticed her large eyes always looking for something.

Clinical application

In therapy we can modulate affects and beliefs with our gaze. When for instance a patient is trapped in an intense negative transference and is convinced that nobody likes them, including me as the therapist, even that I am not at all well disposed towards them, then I can ask them to look directly into my eyes. When they then see my benevolent, warm-hearted gaze, they may notice that they are stuck in a self-destructive belief system, which is possibly a repeat of an early relationship experience. If they can take in this gaze, then they will have an insight in that moment, a moment of understanding, of the difference between an old pattern and a current experience – something which cannot be communicated verbally (Chapter 16).

Eye contact in therapy is also a possible way of calming someone in a state of shock. Asking patients to look at each other, attuning to them and breathing in the same rhythm as they are, helps them to come back from the state of shock to a reality, where they experience another person not exactly sharing their state, but feeling with them. In this context, Aposhyan (2004, p. 258) talks of a circular attunement, using a term from infant research. Eye contact can activate an early experience of a calming parental gaze (Cozolino, 2002, p. 176) and thus create a feeling of safety and attachment. However for some patients, eye contact can be threatening, for example when a schizoid person perceives a continuous gaze as a threat to their inner cohesion (Moser, 2001, p. 53).

Geissler (2009, p. 182) ascribes the special significance of the eyes to the fact that unlike almost all the other sense organs, they are the sender and the receiver of signals in one. This is also true of the skin. Eyes and skin are probably those sense organs with which we communicate most directly and through which we forge the closest contacts. Gaze and touch create the most intimacy in therapy too, and patients are possibly more vulnerable through these channels than through that of the spoken word.

14.5 PROSODY OF THE VOICE

When we speak, we not only transport content with words but with the prosody, the manner and expression of our speech, we also transport moods, feelings or commenting connotations – for example when we use an ironic, bored or scornful tone of voice. Other people perceive this information. Also how what we say is understood depends on the prosody (Friederici, 2002).

A study by Thompson et al. (2012) shows that neurological patients with a congenital deficit in the perception and processing of music are also less able to understand the emotional meaning of spoken sentences; this is because they lack the ability to adequately process the acoustic properties of language, particularly subtle differences in pitch.

The voice has the same attributes as bodily expression in general. We deploy tempo, volume, articulation, rhythm, voice flow, pitch or pauses for various purposes:

- **Semantic:** the sentence 'You did that' becomes a question when we raise the voice towards the end.
- **Iconic:** we use the voice itself as a signal when we draw out a sound on a descending note while breathing out; this expresses that we find something boring.
- **Accentual:** we emphasise a word to underline it.
- **Interactive:** by letting our voice sink we indicate that someone else can speak.
- **Communicative:** through prosody we convey how we are feeling and try to engender feelings and action readiness in others.
- **Social:** for instance the high rising terminal where the voice pitch goes up on the last syllable of a sentence. This is characteristic of young people in the English speaking world and is an indication of belonging (or trying to belong) to a certain community.

For body psychotherapy, the voice is interesting not least because it is connected to the whole body. Over 100 muscles are involved in creating the voice (Eckert & Laver, 1994, p. 6). How the voice sounds depends on whether the muscles are relaxed or tensed up, thus whether we are open or closed up, and on how we are breathing (Section 6.2). Only a flexible thorax can let the feelings of the heart resound in the voice. Muscle tension changes the voice, which sounds constricted when the chest muscles are hard. To be able to speak with total conviction, it must ring true and free. This is not possible with a constricted chest, which renders the voice thin and guttural.

A whispering voice is accompanied by longitudinal tension in the vocal cords and a closure of the glottis. In contrast, in phonation with a good connection to respiration, all the muscles are relaxed (Klasmeyer & Sendlmeier, 1997, p. 107). Then the breathing can flow freely into the voice. A flat toneless voice is caused when the breathing does not produce enough air for the voice. Such phenomena are connected to a person's psychological state. They are not just an expression of it, but are themselves a part of it (Kraemer, 2006, p. 275).

> Sighing, groaning, moaning and loud breathing are prominent vocal characteristics in patients with pain disorders (Helmer et al., 2020).

The voice reveals both a person's *state* and *trait*. Acquired through character as is posture, it is the unmistakeable sound of a person, and in a particular situation it tells us about their momentary condition, their feelings and intentions. The voice can **habitually** sound aggressive or plaintive or it can **currently** sound irritated or brittle. A flat voice can indicate a character chronically suppressing their feelings; a mechanical voice can be the expression of the restricted scope of experience of a schizoid character; an affected voice can be an hysterical attempt to cover up authentic feelings (Boadella, 1987, p. 118). A person's history is also contained in their voice. For instance, a voice can seem childish when someone habitually or spontaneously speaks from a certain age level.

Clinical application

We can ask a patient to speak a sentence quite consciously with a childish or with an adult voice, so as to enliven the corresponding schema mode, to use an expression from schema therapy. We can also invite them to try out various voices and thus encourage new qualities of experience, for example when they try babbling (Hayes & Lillis, 2013).

Clinical example

A patient who feels that his life is hopeless, without joy or meaning, and who complains of a lack of feeling, often speaks with a voice which only comes from the throat. When I point this out, he calls it his 'presentation voice', which he recognises from his professional life. He perceives it as unemotional. In the session, we work with how he can bring the voice from the tone of 'e' in the throat to the more emotional tone of 'a' in the chest. This is not easy, and he notices a constriction in the solar plexus. When I ask how he could expand this, he sees the image of a 'V' formed by the hands in front of his chest. Holding his hands there and making an 'a' sound helps to bring the area more into vibration and awakens memories of more easy-going times in his life.

In the next few months, he finds more connection to himself and to others as his voice becomes deeper and fills out the chest more.

Other tonal spaces can address other emotional states: an 'o' in the abdomen related more to wellbeing, a deep 'u' in the lower belly to becoming calm (Geuter, 2019, p. 98).

A person's current psychological state influences frequency, vocal intensity, vocal energy distribution, tempo and pauses in speech. These vocal parameters show the intensity and valence of a person's expression (Banse & Scherer, 1996). The voice thus indicates mainly a person's core affective state. We can hear in someone's voice whether they are well or not. The tone pitch shows us whether someone is excited, because then the voice goes up.

The voice is less clear-cut in the case of categorical emotions. We can recognise with a certainty of about 50% of the basic emotions through the voice (Banse & Scherer, 1996). In anger, it sounds more like screaming with a distinctive prosody; in grief it is breathy, in joy full of sudden changes (Klasmeyer & Sendlmeier, 1997, p. 123). As for anxiety, both vibration and pitch increase; pitch increases as well in anger or joy, the more expressive feelings, whereas with contempt, boredom or sadness, it tends to sink and speech slows down (Frick, 1985, p. 417). Shame or disgust, however, are hardly recognisable in the voice.

Clinical application

Evidence that in indifference the voice speeds up, but in emotional expression it usually becomes slower is of great interest for psychotherapy. We can make use of this therapeutically by slowing the process down. We could even see the whole therapeutic situation as one in which speaking and other psychological processes are decelerated and which through this alone encourages feeling (Geuter, 2019, p. 41).

According to these findings, allocating voice variations to individual emotions is not very specific. In submissiveness, for instance, the pitch, which depends on the tension in the muscles of the larynx, also goes up. This is the case with various other emotions. Frick (1985, p. 421) thinks that we therefore cannot identify categorical emotions on the basis of volume, pitch, tonal variety and speech tempo. At most, we can recognise them over the course of a longer prosodic contour. Possibly signals such as a higher pitch in the case of anger or joy point more to a core affective arousal than to the emotion itself (Section 10.1). According to Bachorowski and Owren (2003), the most reliable indication the voice gives us is as to the level of arousal.

Clinical application

In therapeutic work with the voice, we are generally modulating core affective arousal. We encourage the vocal expression of anger or joy by first increasing activation, meaning vocal intensity and modulation range. For instance, we suggest to the patient that they try putting more power into the voice and letting the voice try out which tone it wants to make at that moment. In a next step, they could express an actual feeling more with the voice by screaming or shouting with joy. By softening the voice, we can calm a feeling down. Both exercises entail working with the voice in the sense of intra-psychic auto-regulation (Chapter 17).

In the study by Siegman et al. (1990), mentioned in Section 10.1, it was shown that anger can be encouraged by letting the voice get faster or louder. Feedback from the voice activated an increase in blood pressure. In contrast, speaking more slowly led to a decrease in blood pressure and a slower pulse rate. In a questionnaire, patients stated that they regulate emotional states via the voice (Bauer, 2010, p. 41).

The voice can also carry unconscious **connotations**; these are similar to shadow movements (Section 14.3) and are processual indicators of how a patient is experiencing something in that moment. Sometimes patients do not notice the affective tone of their voice; an example is when they speak in an irritated tone with a high pitch and great intensity, but they experience themselves as explaining something quite matter-of-factly. Then it can be of help to ask them to pay attention to the sound of their voice and perhaps to exaggerate it. The same is true with a complaining or a sobbing tone of voice that the patient is not aware of. Then we explore the voice just as we would a gesture, by focussing our awareness on it.

Clinical examples

A patient is speaking in an apprehensive tone of voice about what happened at the weekend. She wraps her arms around herself. Now I could follow what she is saying or I could make a remark: You are talking about all this in a tone of voice which sounds as if you have a weight on your chest. I could also point out the gesture of the arms. Then I shift the focus to the emotional quality of her communication and thus from content to process.

Another patient is talking about the disturbing fantasies she has about her husband. However the disturbing content is not coming over, because she is speaking in a staccato voice which prevents me from sympathising with her. I tell her this. She says she knows this staccato voice. 'It is how I withstand the pressure my husband exerts on me and the stress this causes me. I have to control myself because I am not allowed to be myself'. She has had this feeling since she was a child. While saying this she comes out of the staccato and I suddenly feel connected to her. With her tone of voice she had shown me how she controls her emotions, with the effect that the contact between us was broken, just as it is with her husband.

Ekman (2003) thinks that it is difficult to alter the voice and keep feelings out of it. Lowen goes even further with his view 'that it is possible to diagnose the neurosis of a person from an analysis of his voice' (Lowen, 1977, p. 270). However empirical research does not support this. The relationship between personality and voice and between voice and psychological state are not clear-cut. In forensic research Lowen's (1977, p. 270) assumption that we can use the voice to detect lies has been refuted (Klasmeyer & Sendlmeier, 1997).

> According to a study by Regenbogen et al. (2012) we can most easily empathise with the emotions of another person when the tone of voice and the facial expression are congruent with what they are saying. In an experiment, subjects watched video clips of actors telling a story. The content of the story, facial expressions and prosody were either all emotional or one of them neutral. For example, sad content was narrated in a sad voice but with a neutral facial expression, or neutral content with a disgusted voice and facial expression. When all channels were congruent, 75% of the subjects reacted with emotions corresponding to those presented. When the channels were incongruent, then their reactions were geared for the most part to what was being said. However, this experiment did not include whole-body expression. For therapeutic work, the study does show how helpful it is to confront incongruences and to work towards a congruent self-expression. Then we are more easily able to agree as to the emotional meaning of a particular expression.

The voice not only has the function of expressing or regulating inner states, but also an **intentional function**. With their voice, the speaker means to affect the listener in some way and to communicate their intentions or feelings (Frick, 1985). Children scream so that somebody will come. If nobody comes, they will stop screaming.

Clinical application

    In therapy, we can stimulate the signal function of the voice by letting the patient use their voice to express their feelings or wishes in their fantasy or towards a symbolising object, another member of a therapy group or the therapist as a transference object. In this way they can learn to use their voice to make something happen, and at the same time they can directly experience their own feelings in relationships through their vocal expression.

Listeners, on the other hand, process a voice on the basis of their own previous experiences and their own emotional state and attribute to it properties of the person speaking. Since the person speaking knows the expectations of the listener, personal vocal expression is created in an interactive experience and is modified according to the context. A great deal of research on laughing shows how much it depends on who is present when we laugh and what feedback we get, for instance whether the others are laughing too, or do not react, or even turn away in irritation (Bachorowski & Owren, 2003).

Clinical application

For therapeutic listening, this means that the more we can hold back our own emotional involvement, the better we can focus our attention on the behavioural clues of the patient's expression. It can also mean that we can reinforce a spontaneous expression of the patient by sharing it vocally with them, for instance anger or joy, and thus validating it.

Vocal signals are also transferred to the listener. The voice induces moods even when the listener is unaware of it. When subjects hear an expression of anger, the skin conductance response around the muscles of the eyebrows, with which we express anger, increases; when they hear an expression of satisfaction, then the smile muscles around the eyes are activated (Hietanen et al., 1998). Functional MRI studies show that the prosody of the voice is processed more in the right brain hemisphere, semantics more in the left hemisphere (Mitchell et al., 2003).

Also non-verbal sounds affect the listener. Warren et al. (2006) showed that pre-motor cortical regions, which are active in facial expressions, react to the arousal and valence of vocal expressions, especially when these are loud and positively toned, even when there is no facial activity. Just like vision, the voice seems to activate the mirror neurons (Chapter 15). It is a powerful tool of affective contagion.

In an experiment allegedly about understanding a text, Neumann and Strack (2000) had subjects listen to texts spoken by a slightly sad or by a slightly happy voice. They found that this induced a congruent mood in the subjects. When they repeated the texts, they spontaneously imitated the emotional expression. The authors call this 'contagion through inadvertent imitation'. When asked, the subjects were not aware of having done this. In a variation of the experiment, when they were distracted from their given task, this reduced their understanding of the text, but not the contagion through the mood of the voice. The authors interpret these findings psychologically: noticing another person's emotional expression induces a congruent feeling in us through an automatic connection of perception and behaviour, without us being aware of any connection to that person.

In therapy, not only does the therapist catch the patient's mood through their voice, it also works the other way around: the **prosody of the therapist** influences the patient. Sometimes **how** the therapist sounds can be more important for a patient than **what** they say (Heisterkamp, 2002, p. 24). In a qualitative analysis of a survey of patients, Bauer (2010) found that they based their emotional evaluation of their therapists on their voices. Patients were also aware that the therapists were using their voices to regulate the emotional atmosphere.

Important
When a therapist gives an interpretation it only becomes effective because it is para-verbally embedded in the sound of their voice.

Clinical example

In a sympathetic, not objective, tone of voice I say to a patient: 'And the pain about the loss of your brother comes up again and again.' She says: 'Yes, that's it. And I fall into this black hole again and again.' Then there is a silence in which I only say 'Yes', in a manner which lets the patient know that I have profoundly understood her.

The effect of what is said is created through the tone of voice, which conveys compassion. Boyesen (1987, p. 109) calls this vocalisation on the tragic instead of the trivial level (Geuter, 2019, p. 392). The prosodic element of the encounter emphasises what is said. Without it, there would only be sterile information. However, prosody is only experienced as authentic when it is part of the whole expression of body communication.

With prosody we can also influence emotions through co-regulation. When a patient is crying, then a gentle voice can aid attunement (Kykyri et al., 2017). When a patient is aroused, it can be helpful if the therapist curbs their own arousal audibly in the voice. However, sometimes it is better to reinforce the patient's arousal with our own voice. Depending on what the process demands, we can encourage emotional activation or calm it through the voice.

According to a study by Weiste and Peräkylä (2014), when therapists express a validation of the patient, they maintain their tone of voice, but when they challenge them, there is a break in their prosody.

The prosodic properties of the voices of therapist and patient can synchronise just as do movements, for instance when the speaking tempo of both slows down when they focus on inner processes. Through the voice, moments of meeting can be created which are not possible through the content of the spoken word alone (Stern, 2004).

Important
Prosody, facial expressions, gestures and body movements play a major role in the affective process between patient and therapist and in determining whether the therapy will be beneficial for the patient.

15

Transference and somatic resonance

Interaction in therapy activates the patient's early relationship experiences. We call this transference. Transference takes place in every psychotherapy and we can work with it when it hinders the therapeutic process. However, we can also use it to help the patient become aware of the dysfunctional schemas of experience and behaviour which transference reveals, and to change them.

The concept of transference is an original contribution of psychoanalysis to psychotherapy. There, working with the transference is a central instrument of treatment. In client-centred therapy, however, it is regarded as less important (Rogers, 1951; Watson et al., 1998, p. 10). Gestalt therapy sees this differently (Hartmann-Kottek, 2008, p. 18), as does body psychotherapy. Both have a psychodynamic tradition, as does transactional analysis, seeing the therapeutic relationship as a field of learning for patients (Soth, 2013; Watson et al., 1998, p. 11).

In behavioural therapy, McCullough et al. (2011) have also taken up the idea in their *Cognitive Behavioural Analysis System of Psychotherapy* (CBASP) that emotional experiences with significant others shape expectations, which are then directed at the therapist. Here difficult relationship constellations are explicitly addressed and worked through with the technique of the interpersonal discrimination exercise, in which the patient can then learn to distinguish between experiences in the then and there and those in the here and now (Guhn, et al., 2018).

Body psychotherapy places particular emphasis on how transference appears in the bodily affect motor behaviour and experience of the patient and how, in their somatic resonance, the therapist reacts to them. Thus our understanding of transference and countertransference is also as a reciprocal communication from body to body. In the therapeutic process, we use the resonance of the therapist for exploration and the dialogue of body communication to clarify transference.

In principle, however, I see transference and countertransference in body psychotherapy no differently than in verbal, psychodynamic therapies. Therefore I will only briefly outline the general theory and go more deeply into those aspects which are important for body psychotherapy, such as bodily sensations, enactments and action dialogues in the transference/countertransference process; and the body psychotherapeutic concept of somatic resonance.

DOI: 10.4324/9781003176893-15

15.1 TRANSFERENCE AND COUNTERTRANSFERENCE

According to the critical hypothesis of Makari (1991), Freud introduced the concept of transference because he wanted to explain the fact that female patients were turning the heads of male analysts. As he himself once wrote, he did not think it possible to control the personal affective relationship (Thomae & Kaechele, 2020). One female patient wanted to kiss him, and he avoided this by explaining that he was not who she meant. Pohlen and Bautz-Holzherr (1995, p. 117) describe Freud's 'isolating and distancing of himself from emotional contagion and physical touch' as a reaction formation to the dangers of temptation. Freud neutralised the affect motor communication in therapy and relegated conflicts to the past (Pohlen and Bautz-Holzherr, 1995, p. 123). He interpreted transference as a false connection between earlier events and the present and as resistance against memories, which has to be fought. After Freud, it was Reich who first worked out the importance of negative transference and who actively invited patients to express their negative feelings towards him (Sharaf, 1994, pp. 78–80).

Since these beginnings, our understanding of transference has changed. Thomae and Kaechele (2020) see it as the **activation of unconscious schemata**, which recur in the relationship with the therapist. These schemas are the fallout from old, childhood relationship dynamics. Transference is regarded as a ubiquitous phenomenon, occurring also in non-therapeutic relationships. In therapy, its appearance is facilitated by the fact that the therapist reveals little about themselves personally and provides a safe space in which these distressing patterns can be revealed. From the client's point of view, the purpose of transference is to resubmit as it were outstanding conflicts, traumata or deficit experiences in the here and now, so that they can be worked through and the patient can heal. In transference, therefore, it is not a case of remembering but of reproducing and enacting a habitual relationship pattern that is problematic for the patient's present life. Transference is thus a remake of interaction experiences. It can surface in fantasies, expectations, feelings, desires, movements or postures. Scenes from the past also reproduce themselves in actions. We call this **enactment** (Geuter, 2019, pp. 286–7). When early self-states, stored in implicit memory, show themselves in this way, Ermann (2017, p. 87) calls it procedural transference.

Clinical example

A patient comes for the first time, sits down on a chair, bends over the jacket he has scrunched up on his knees and starts to speak before the therapist has even sat down. As becomes clear, this is one of his problems: he is so occupied with himself that he has difficulty seeing other people as independent beings. This is displayed as if in a pantomime at his first meeting with the therapist (Streeck, 2004, pp. 207–8).

This patient displays a behavioural pattern which is also distressing for him. He demonstrates it through affect motor bodily dialogue in which he blends the therapist out. Thus he enacts his relationship schema in the interaction with her. A relational experiential body psychotherapy pays particular attention to such bodily enactments in which the dynamics of suffering and hurt reveal themselves (Soth, 2019, p. 299).

As in interactional psychoanalysis, transference is, however, seen as something created in mutual interaction by both parties (Bettighofer, 2016, p. 60).

Clinical examples

A patient is irritated by me reaching for my tense trapezius muscle by putting my hand underneath my shirt collar. I am going too far, just as I do when I cross my legs, she says, because then she can look between them. As we talk about this, it comes out that she likes to watch in a sexual way but that she dare not admit it to herself. She would like to show herself as a sexual woman and still have a non-sexual supportive relationship to me. This was not possible with her invasive stepfather, who was roughly the same age I am now. The issue for her is that she is looking for a healthy relationship to compensate for that, but the whole problem was actualised by me putting my hand on my skin underneath my shirt collar.

Another patient talks about a recent session in which I asked her about the apparent tension in her jaw. What she was not able to say at the time was that she left the session with the feeling that I found her ugly – a reaction that has a whole previous history and which she is also aware of when looking in the mirror. My remark had activated the reaction pattern.

Body work and transference

When body psychotherapists work with the body, they are sometimes not aware that each body-related intervention is embedded in a transference process. Early breath and body therapies denied the existence of transference phenomena (von Steinaecker, 1994, p. 7). To some extent, it is still the case that therapists think they are just giving a massage to release tension, without being aware of what determines the effects of treatment: that no negative transference is hindering the process, that the patient can trust the therapist, that the therapist has attuned themselves in the appropriate manner to the patient and can respond to the patient's interpersonal communications. So it may be that someone reacts defensively to touch because it reminds them of the prudery in their family, or, when asked to do a body exercise, feels as if they have to do their homework. Bodily interventions and interactions can trigger hefty transference feelings, experienced in the body, in patients who are traumatised or have a difficult relationship to their body for other reasons. In cases like this, therapeutic work must focus on clarifying the transference feelings.

Clinical examples

A patient prefers not to move around the room because she is afraid of me judging her, even though she believes I do not. Another patient would like to try a vitalising body exercise, but backs away from it because then I might ask him what he feels. When I do that, he is under pressure to deliver something, even though he knows that with me this is completely unnecessary.

This last patient is aware that he finds it difficult to just answer the question of what he is feeling, because he always experiences it as pressure. Other patients, however, might politely accede to the suggestions of the therapist because they want to get good marks (Geissler & Geissler, 2011).

Even when a patient expresses themselves bodily of their own accord, sometimes through the interaction transference can become astonishingly clear:

Clinical example

A patient has complained that in her previous therapy she was left alone with her tremendous anger and her transference of early feelings towards her parents on to her analyst, which is why despite the unresolved anger, she ended the psychoanalysis after four years. In a session with me, she accesses this anger again and starts hitting the foam rubber block. She becomes completely absorbed in this. At the end, as she is standing there panting, I point out a certain movement of her arm. She immediately shouts at me: 'Do you have to comment on everything? Can't you just let something be?' In the next session she tells me that was meant for her parents, but I had induced it through what I did. Her parents were always nagging at her. Her mother was forever touching her to adjust something.

In the session itself, we are silent for about 10 minutes after her shouting at me. She is moved, her chin wobbles and her eyes are shiny; I too feel how close I am to crying. Then she says: 'I didn't mean that. I like you as well'. This is just as it was at home: excruciating, but she liked her parents too. Now she expresses a wish that she has been carrying around with her for months, because she thought it not allowed here: she wants to lean on me. The experience of being able to stay in contact despite her having been so angry has made this moment possible. As she says later, when I held her, she at last felt like a whole person with a cohesive body, a feeling she never had before.

The bodily expression of anger in conjunction with my intervention, which made her even more angry, intensified the negative transference to such an extent that the patient experienced what had not been possible in her psychoanalysis. Through the hefty physical and verbal expression of her feelings, the transference became directly obvious in the here and now (cf. Totton, 2003, p. 129). Such a moment can help the patient to take back the transference, as the patient did on her own initiative. Because of powerful feeling habits and affect motor schemas, transference will not be resolved through this, however. But in the intense experience in the action dialogue, it becomes clear to the patient what is going on inside her and, at the same time, that it is not what she thought it was. An experience with such a strong affective charge engraves itself on consciousness.

In therapy, we should try to investigate the transference systematically (Downing, 1996, pp. 261–83). For the main part this is verbal work, in which we explore what is going on between the patient and the therapist. The goal of this is to become conscious of relationship patterns and to change them. Whereas through the setting psychoanalysis holds transference feelings in abeyance, so that they can unfold and be analysed, in body psychotherapy we actively sound out transference in the here and now (Geuter, 2019, pp. 414–19). An active confrontation helps the patient to relinquish and resolve transference feelings, even if they do not immediately disappear. Transference tends to blossom unresolved if the dialogue is not cultivated.

When we include the body, we deepen this process of exploration and transformation. As therapists, we can consciously activate and investigate transference by creating a process of interaction and being available as the object of transference (Geuter, 2019, pp. 310–12). As an example of such an enactment, I include here a session I have described in detail elsewhere

(Geuter, 2006, pp. 261–2) with a patient in a depressive phase, who was preoccupied with feelings of low self-esteem and failure. She was not able to defend herself against her mother, who was always perfect and on whom she was dependent. Her despair, however, also contained anger, of which she was afraid.

Clinical example

The patient begins by telling me how embarrassing it was for her in the last session where she sat in front of me like a little child. In response to my question about how old she feels today in relation to me, she says that she became younger as she came in and now feels as if she were 10 years old. This image is connected to the idea that she is dependent on what the grown-ups think of her and to a feeling of inferiority. She has to behave reasonably so that people will like her. I suggest that perhaps she has the notion that I too do not like her. Yes, this thought is there too: 'What must he think of me after the last session?' She is in a maternal transference. She remembers the mother saying: 'Come on, girl!' In her fantasy I become huge. She sees me as if I'm taking up half the room and she is sitting shivering in the corner. She often has the feeling of not even being able to stand in front of other people.

I propose that we enact this feeling just as she describes it, so that we can explore it further. She chooses a corner with a bookshelf behind my chair for herself. I walk slowly towards her, filling up the room, and ask her how she perceives me: 'Huge. At the same time I'm getting smaller and smaller. For me only a tiny corner is left'. We take a sounding whether there is a point at which she has the impulse to resist, or whether she will let me breach the boundary of what she feels to be her private sphere. When I am about one and a half metres away she puts her arms up and says: 'That's enough'. We go one step further to test what will happen when someone goes beyond this 'enough' border, which is what she feels her mother did. I walk very slowly towards her until I am at her outstretched arms. She starts to push me away. At the first try, her resistance collapses and she says to herself: 'You're inferior anyway'. I suggest trying it again and push a bit more against her hands. Suddenly a great strength surges up in her and she positively pushes me around the room. Although I am bigger and, as a man, stronger than her, I am not able to hold out against this power. She is completely surprised at how much strength she has.

In the next session, she says that experiencing her real strength was really impressive. At work she remembered it and felt powerful. However she had also noticed how constrained she usually is. The experience, she adds, was all the more vivid and lasting for having been enacted and not just thought through. 'Encouragement through words quickly fizzles out, but the experience has a lasting effect'.

Enacting and exploring the transference feelings enabled the patient to access a hidden part of herself. She discovered the ability to aggressively assert her boundaries which she had not been able to do with her dominating mother until today. In the bodily enactment, she has a moment of understanding in which she experiences the fact that this strength is tied up in the feeling of being small, but is now accessible to her (Chapter 16). She directly experiences her strength in affect motor activity. Thus she discovers a potential affect motor schema different from the familiar depressed-resigned one, which had come to the fore in the transference relationship with me.

Important

If transference is enacted in a bodily action dialogue, the patient experiences it directly and becomes conscious of it more easily.

In body psychotherapy, we can put forward a further concept of transference different from that of psychodynamic therapy, one in which an affect motor state is transferred bodily from one person to another in the actual sense of contagion. In Eutony, a body-work method developed by Gerda Alexander to regulate body tone, this is called **tonus transference** (Sackmann-Schaefer, 1994). For example, parents transfer their inner calm to their baby when they cradle the fretful child in their arms. We also say when a charismatic person enters a room that they transfer their calmness (or some other core affective state) to those around them. In therapy, we sometimes attempt to transfer our own state to the patient, if we want to help them to calm down or to increase their emotional arousal, for instance through our breathing. We then make our own affective state available to them so that they can regulate themselves. This functions mainly through body communication.

Moser (1994) has often spoken of letting a patient 'refuel' by sitting back to back with them. He interprets this as a transference event in the sense that the patient experiences their mother or father at their back. That is one way of looking at it. However we could also see this refuelling as the sacrum of the patient filling up their energy centre at the sacrum of the therapist with the therapist's strength. In Asian medicine, the sacrum is seen as the dorsal centre of energy. This would mean seeing the transference as not merely symbolic. Koch-Lauscher (1994, p. 65) writes about a 'transference effect of the hand' which can communicate 'being-safe'. This is a concept of transference close to the body which means something different from the psychodynamic concept. I just want to mention it here as a thought-provoking idea.

Countertransference

According to Freud's classic concept, countertransference contains all the therapist's blind spots which cloud their perception of the patient (Thomae & Kaechele, 2020). Downing (1996, p. 316) calls this **personal countertransference**. Lowen also accepts this idea of countertransference as an obstacle to therapy (Heinrich, 2001, p. 67).

Paula Heimann had already pointed out in 1950 that the patient unconsciously evokes reactions in the therapist and **this** countertransference is a means of exploring the patient's inner world. Unconscious parts of the self or object representations of the patient come alive in these inner reactions of the therapist. Downing calls this **induced countertransference**. However, by portraying these feelings as creations of the patient alone, Heimann depersonalises them and disregards their joint creation in a reciprocal relationship (Thomae & Kaechele, 2020).

The therapist's feelings, however, are not a reliable source of information about the patient, but rather evidence of a dynamic interactive process (Kuchuck, 2021, pp. 70–1), in which we can attribute neither cause nor effect to either side. Ermann (2017) therefore talks of an intersubjective transference matrix in which countertransference takes place. In relational body psychotherapy, it is seen nowadays as an embodied happening in a mutual process in the therapeutic relationship (Soth, 2005).

Countertransference does not serve to evaluate anything, but to perceive something that can then flow back into the therapeutic work. Keleman (1989) describes the therapist's own reaction as their most important tool in the therapeutic process. The therapist has to tolerate the feelings generated in them by the patient so as to be able to perceive what is going on. When the therapist is brusque because they reject these feelings, this is what we call **countertransference resistance**. In this case the patient triggers a conflict in the therapist, causing them to fend off unpleasant thoughts or emotions. Then the therapist is trapped in personal countertransference.

According to N. Field (1989), countertransference appears in five different modalities: in feelings, fantasies, dreams, action impulses and physical reactions, which seem unconnected to the apparent material dealt with in the session – for example sudden fatigue or sexual arousal. Field calls this last **embodied countertransference**. Heisterkamp gives us a wealth of examples:

> When the therapist begins to breathe shallowly or more deeply; when the pressure in their head increases or decreases; when they are suddenly unable to see clearly or everything goes black; when the pressure in their ears increases and there is dizziness or a ringing in the ears; when they suddenly become tired or wide awake; when the abdomen tenses up or relaxes; when their heart hurts or races or pounds; when they become aware of their guts or their bladder; when they start to perspire or their throat is sore or the skin itches.
>
> (Heisterkamp, 2007, p. 306)

Such bodily reactions are triggered in **projective identification.** Kernberg (1992) says that the patient projects a menacing part of themselves onto the therapist as a defensive measure. They try to create the feeling in the therapist that they do not want to have themselves and then to control or resist the therapist. This is a way of controlling their own feelings, which they encounter as projections in the therapist.

Clinical example

A patient with a narcissistic disorder was rejected by his parents. Possibly he had survived an attempted abortion. One of the ways he copes with his feelings of inferiority and helplessness and his inability to find validation and affection is by rejecting others and feeling superior to them. However he is in denial about this. In therapy, he often engineers a situation in which I feel so helpless that, despite the fact that I basically like him, I have a downright physical impulse to push him away, so as to be liberated from this helplessness. He notices this and accuses me of rejecting him. Once I am ill and in the next session he paces the room angrily and complains that I cancelled the last session because I am too weak to see him. Through his rage, he is trying to control his own weakness, which his fear of rejection activates. By evoking in me his impulse to push others away and at the same time fighting me for it, he can maintain the denial of his own arrogance.

Under the surface, feelings are often outsourced to the therapist and are thus difficult to unravel. Heinrich Racker (2019) has differentiated the reactions open to the therapist:

- They can identify with parts of the patient's self in **concordant countertransference**, or
- In **complementary countertransference**, they can feel those feelings that significant others had or should have had towards the patient, while the patient feels their own feelings towards the corresponding person.

Clinical example

My own strongest embodied complementary countertransference experience was that in all my years working as a therapist, I once fell asleep in a session. We had been working on the patient's fear of abandonment triggered by the death of one of his colleagues. After a moving sequence of work on his anxiety, we were both lying on the floor when it overcame me. I dozed off for a few moments and was instantly ashamed of myself when I woke up. We talked about it. However not until the end of therapy did the patient tell me that precisely this situation had made him very happy; it had been a highlight of the whole therapy. His grandparents had a pub where his mother also worked, and as a little boy he had often been alone in the flat above the pub. He could never be sure when his mother would come for him or whether she would come at all. When I fell asleep he had the feeling of having the power to make someone not go away but having to stay with him, without that person dying. He so wanted to be able to do that with his mother. Consequently I could see my hefty reaction as a form of embodied countertransference, in which, without being aware of it, I fulfilled the deep, hidden wish that the patient had towards his mother. By me falling asleep, the patient had managed to ease his fear of abandonment.

On the bodily level, countertransference appears as **countersensation** (Keleman, 1989). When we have such a sensation, our therapeutic task is to understand what is happening in the body and translate it into images and words. Above all, projective identification is based on the patient inducing bodily sensations in the therapist (Clauer, 2003, p. 97). Action impulses are also a state of the body in which countertransference surfaces. Trautmann-Voigt and Voigt (2009, p. 143) speak about movement impulses in which the therapist absorbs the vitality contours of the patient (Section 10.5). Making use of such embodied reactions as signals requires of the therapist that they tune into the patient from one moment to the next and are as aware as possible of their own inner state.

> Hence working with embodiment in therapy requires therapists to track and consider their own embodied experience as they sit with the client.
>
> (Totton, 2020, p. 70)

With their embodied experience and affect motor reactions, the therapist responds to how the patient is feeling; they communicate visibly with the patient and in turn generate resonance in them. Thus a mutual incorporation evolves which the therapist actively co-creates, as they also bring relationship patterns into the therapy, not least through their bodily behaviour. This is why Grawe (2004) criticises the concept of countertransference, as it suggests that this is always a response to the transference of the patient.

To diagnose countertransference in the therapeutic process, we could ask ourselves the following questions:

- How do I see the patient bodily?
- What impulses do they activate in me?
- Do I perhaps sense in myself impulses or desires that the patient does not want to reveal?
- Do I have bodily reactions of my own which are a possible response to the patient?

Questions like these are directed towards the patient's inner world as well as to the tone and dynamics of the therapeutic relationship:

> What is the *flavour* or *texture* of an encounter … is it soft or hard, heavy or light? What impulse is stirred in us … is it to fight, or to nurture, to push or to pull?
>
> (Staunton, 2002a, p. 2, ellipses in the original)

Clinical example

This is an account of a situation which impressed me deeply, in which right in the first session I experienced a concordant countersensation (Geuter, 2004, p. 110). A patient told me about how he was feeling and I had no sense that he was concealing something. However the more I let myself be affected by him, the stronger became the sensation of a constriction in my throat. In the end I asked him whether he had ever tried to hang himself. He looked at me and said: 'Nobody has ever asked me that'. He had had interviews in a crisis help centre and had also consulted other therapists. Then he told me how on several occasions he had stood on a chair with a noose around his neck, but he had not kicked away the chair.

In bodily sensations, the therapist can also re-live a patient's childhood experiences, for instance when they suddenly feel cold or hungry. Heinl (2000) has compellingly described such intuitive perceptions.

15.2 RESONANCE

Since countertransference takes place pre-eminently in the body, we can understand it as resonance. I agree with Keleman (1989) in preferring this concept. Also because the term resonance expresses the fact that here the therapist is not countertransferring something onto the patient, but is starting to vibrate like the sound box of an instrument. This image also includes the idea that the note is played on the outside, but the sound depends on how the sound box resonates. In physics, resonance means that a vibration curve is transmitted and becomes stronger. To resonate means to co-vibrate.

Important
According to the enactive approach, 'the therapeutic relationship is characterised as a social interaction based on resonance, engagement and mutual responsiveness' (Garcia & Arandia, 2022, p. 13).

Resonance is more than countertransference. Plassmann (2019) sees transference and countertransference as special forms of resonance and reserves these terms for the process in which someone seems to confuse the actual person they are now with persons from earlier life experiences (Plassmann, 2019, p. 162). I include in countertransference also those processes in which the therapist takes on parts of the patient or of people they have relationships with. When nowadays psychoanalysts conflate under countertransference all the therapist's feelings, thoughts, fantasies and impulses, no matter what their origins (Bettighofer, 2016, p. 70), then the specific meaning of the concept is lost.

Resonance can mean that as therapists we absorb the patient's breathing, posture or movements into our own bodies (Griffith & Griffith, 1994, p. 88). It is not just a case of the state of person A being transferred to B, but that through A, B starts to vibrate in their own way (Breyer & Gerner, 2017). However, resonance often also develops as a process in the interaction, a 'joint vibrating' (Stefan, 2020, p. 51), a mutually experienced interaffectivity (De Jaegher, 2015; Mühlhoff, 2015). Then we sense something that is enacted in the in-between space in the moment (Miller, 2015) as atmospheric resonance, even in mutual silence (Breyer & Gerner, 2017).

To achieve this, the therapist has to be attuned to the patient. This brings both of them into the present moment of the relationship (Staunton, 2008) and in turn generates resonance in the patient. 'We are not only sensing, we are also being sensed' (Rolef Ben-Shahar, 2019, p. 348). If the patient feels seen and understood by the therapist then there can be a 'state of resonance ... *in both members of the dyad*' (Schore, 2003, p. 51) and a moment of secure attachment (Plassmann, 2019, p. 85). Attunement affects the person we are attuning to and so encourages a process of healing (Decety & Fotopoulou, 2015).

Heisterkamp (2007, p. 307) uses the term **co-vibration** for this supportive attunement to the patient. We also vibrate bodily and attune ourselves to the patient so as to access the world of their experience (Griffith & Griffith, 1994, p. 90). Bender (2007, p. 29) thinks that empathy is generated when we attune ourselves to a person's flow pattern of tension. Reich used the notion of **vegetative identification** and wrote that we can empathise with the emotions that patients express without words, through involuntary imitation (1972, p. 362).

In therapy, bodily resonance is a **source of understanding** (Shaw, 2003). Phenomenological understanding is always of the self and of the other and thus bodily resonance is based on the perception of the self and of the other (Richter-Mackenstein, 2021). Merleau-Ponty (2012) wrote that we understand others through our lived body, just as we perceive objects through it. Bodies understand one another (Fuchs, 2008b). The body reacts faster than consciousness and so establishes channels of understanding, since an event evokes a matrix of implicit emotional, procedural, cognitive and sensorimotor memories that shape how the event presents itself to consciousness (Cozolino, 2002, pp. 160–1). Through bodily impressions, we realise the messages sent from our relational partner, such as 'Don't touch me, I'm frightened' or 'Help me, I'm totally confused'. In a survey conducted by Shaw (2004) with 90 psychotherapists, all participants stated that they used bodily sensations as information about their patients. However often therapists are not aware of their sensations (see the study on suicidal patients in Section 14.4).

> Working with resonance does not mean that the therapist is permanently focused on their inner sensations. They must pay attention above all to the patient. According to empirical studies, therapists who concentrate too much on their self-experience tend to have less sense of the patient (Caspar, 2001, p. 141). The task is to make use of inner perception to perceive the patient and the interactive process.

Heinrich-Clauer (2008a) uses resonance as a diagnostic tool. She stands left, then right, then in front of, then behind the patient, so as to receive their 'energy pattern' and through it information about their life story. As already said about countertransference, we have however to allow for the fact that resonance is part of an interactional process in which for example the therapist's belief that she can reach a diagnosis in this way can shape the relational pattern, in that the patient is impressed by the therapist and thus tends to accept their opinion as the truth.

In contrast to such a structured approach, the following example shows how in the therapeutic process, resonance discloses an experience that a patient is unable to express in words:

Clinical example

Melissa Griffith describes a patient she could not understand when she spoke about her problems. One day, totally at a loss, she decided to listen to the music of the language and not to the content. In addition she tried to reproduce in herself the patient's bodily state in that moment: 'with rapid and shallow breathing, stiffly leaning forward with a tense body, arms held tight and immobile on the chair'. In this position, the therapist felt 'an awful sensation in my throat, like the bad taste of acid after gagging'. She then said to the patient that she had a peculiar sensation, as if she was going to belch or to be sick without knowing why. She asked her whether the story she was telling made her have similar feelings. The patient looked into her eyes and said: 'That's it! That's exactly how I feel. I want to throw up, but I can't. I feel that way a lot ... I can't throw up and I can't eat'. Then she was crying and asking how the therapist knew this. She replied: 'I didn't know ... I just knew how I felt as I listened and wondered if there was a connection'. Now the patient felt understood (Griffith & Griffith, 1994, p. 89).

To see and understand another person includes experiencing the difference between them and myself (Scheler, 1913, 2015; Zahavi & Rochat, 2015). The therapist can have an awful feeling in their throat, but this does not tell them what this feeling means in the life of the patient. I can comprehend the pain, but this does not show me what the subjective particularity of this pain means for the other person (Zahavi, 2016). We cannot infer from our own sensations what the patient is feeling; we always need to explore the meaning together.

It is especially important when working with victims of trauma that the therapist stays centred in themselves and does not take on the emotional state of the patient (Rothschild, 2002). In a study done by the Irish National Counselling Service, of 35 counsellors who work with adult victims of childhood abuse and neglect, 70% reported often having unexpected bodily reactions during counselling, as well as feelings of disgust and headaches or tearfulness. The extent of such reactions correlated positively with the number of sick days the counsellors took and negatively with the frequency of supervision (Egan & Carr, 2008). Clinical psychologists working with similar patients exhibited muscle tension and drowsiness as the most frequent form of resonance (Booth et al., 2010).

Bodily resonance is not the only source of understanding. Associations, images and fantasies which come up in a session are also important. As therapists, we experience our patients through thoughts, feelings, bodily sensations, motor impulses and images (Geuter, 2019, pp.

74–8). However, body psychotherapy emphasises somatic resonance in particular. Schmitz has described it beautifully:

> A sensitive person feels the restrained rage, aggravation or discomfort of another person not only through their facial expression or other symptoms of body or behaviour, but equally or even more through their own embarrassed, disconcerted or shocked dismay; they become aware of someone's contentment or relaxed openness through the sense of their own heart opening up.
>
> (Schmitz, 1986, p. 89)

Schmitz calls such resonance phenomena mutual incorporation. There can even be moments when the person empathising feels more than the one they are empathising with. If this happens in a therapy session, then the therapist can point something out to the patient that they have not yet access to themselves.

In resonance, therapists are empathising, but are not as deeply moved by the feeling as the person they are reacting to (cf. Schmitz, 2014, p. 83). We can model therapeutic empathy on that of parents towards a child (Ham & Tronick, 2009, p. 4): they sympathise with the child's joy, and sometimes, when this ecstasy needs to be verified, they will jump around and cheer with the child as well. They participate in the child's anger without becoming angry themselves, but when necessary, for example when they have to defend the child against someone else, they do let themselves be infected by the child's anger. Also in developmental psychology, when two people are attuning themselves to one another, this is sometimes described as resonance (Schore, 2001, p. 19).

The concept of resonance not only means that the therapist absorbs something of the patient into their body. It means also empathising or attuning oneself **in the therapeutic process**. In bodily attunement, the therapist implicitly gives something back. In this respect, resonance is part of a two-body communication in which the states and the feelings of the partners are constantly changing in interaction. This bodily dialogue reveals whether the therapist is well attuned to the patient or over- or under-involved (Eberhard-Kaechele, 2019).

Therapists modulate the moods of the patient less by what they do according to their therapeutic methods and much more through facial expressions and gestures. In a study of sessions of behavioural therapy, Flueckiger and Znoj (2009) determined that therapists reinforce positive moods through bodily signals and alleviate tension through calm behaviour. If a patient disguises an emotion, they counteract this with their own emotional expression. These strategies, mediated by the body, were more important for the outcome of the session than what the therapist said.

Process resonance

For relational body psychotherapy, resonance on the processual level is most important, sometimes even more than on the level of psychological content: that we notice the patient's emotional engagement, a faltering or a moment of understanding, an obstacle, a blanking out or a stirring up, and that we attune ourselves to this level. Plassmann (2019, p. 47) has called this **process resonance** in contrast to **affect resonance**. Process resonance means that, for instance, my own attentiveness increases when something of emotional significance to the patient comes up (p. 56). Being attentive on the processual level helps us to evaluate how coherent the regulation process proceeds (p. 240), by noticing whether something is too much or too little for the patient, whether the stress is too much for them, whether they lose contact with their resources, the mentalisation process stalls or communication loses its regulatory rhythm (Plassmann, 2019, p. 256). Such a process awareness is a resource for making decisions about interventions (cf. Auszra et al., 2017, p. 77).

Through process resonance, we can synchronise with the patient. 'The crescendos and decrescendos of the therapist's affective state must be in *resonance* with similar states of crescendos and decrescendos of the patient'; only through this **attunement** can the therapist become the 'regulator of the patient's physiology' (Schore, 2003, p. 48).

In the one situation, we could structure the session more soberly because the patient feels overwhelmed; in another we let ourselves be enveloped by the patient's feelings so as to explore them together, or we could re-parent a part of the patient which is still a child, or we become protective towards one part of the patient behaving destructively, or we let the patient search for the answers themselves, or we give them some advice when it is helpful for them. In this way we regulate the process. Process resonance is **different from empathy**. In empathy, we feel with the patient; in process resonance, we use our perceptions to discover what wants to be heard in the session and to determine in how far the encounter with the emotional material in the session is conducive to psychological growth (Plassmann, 2019, pp. 181, 157). In this regard it is a precondition for transformation processes. This is illustrated in the first clinical example in Chapter 14.

Plassmann (2019, p. 257) calls it **process interpretation** when we reflect on the emotional regulation that occurred in the session, talk about it with the patient and interpret it. Process resonance is not merely reacting, but includes reflecting on what the patient has experienced. However, it is based on our own experience – for this is the language of resonance.

Just as emotional learning and the process of transformation are most likely to occur in a window of tolerance of emotional arousal (Ogden et al., 2006, pp. 26–40), resonance is most likely to occur in a **window of tolerance in the interaction**. The connection between two people is higher when emotional expressivity and interpersonal coordination are moderate and in flow (Nelson et al., 2016). In a dyadic relationship, good experiences are most likely in an atmosphere of calm attentiveness.

Furthermore, resonance can have other **functions in the therapeutic process**:

- Resonance can be a **guide to conflicts** in the patient. For instance, if we have an inner feeling of heaviness and can hardly listen to the patient, this can be a sign that they are avoiding something and have made a detour, whereby they are talking about something not so connected to themselves.
- In resonance, we sense whether an **interaction** in the session is **contentious** by the fact that our own body resists. The body often reacts faster to a relational conflict than does our consciousness and thus is a crucial tool to understanding the relationship (Worm, 2007, p. 230). We sense whether an interaction is **coherent**. Perhaps a patient wants to be held, we can understand it and we want to respond, but then we notice that our own hand hesitates. This is the body revealing an inconsistency which is not conscious yet.
- In resonance, we can get an **inkling** of the patient's **resources** that are not yet accessible. When the therapist feels that the patient's own inner movement in the process is blocked,

then they can offer to explore their sensations and perceptions (Heisterkamp, 2006, p. 284) so that they can connect to their own potential. Drees (1996, p. 73) thinks that when working with patients with severe disorders, such as victims of torture, through mood transference helpful pre-traumatic feelings can emerge intuitively in the therapist as frozen parts of experience that the patient can no longer feel.

- In resonance, we perceive patients' **body talk**. When these hefty states that we have described in Chapter 14 as body talk and which 'may date back to a time when no words were available and psychic trauma could not be distinguished from physical injury … bodily symptoms in the therapist may provide the first clue to understanding' (Field, 1989, p. 519). Then the patient has no other possibility of articulating their distress than to attempt to generate the same feelings in the therapist through a transference communication; the therapist has to realise the patient's pathology in their own bodily sensations, so that they can regulate their disorganised state (Schore, 2003, pp. 29–32).

15.3 EMPATHY AND MIRROR NEURONS

It is difficult to explain resonance phenomena in the context of scientific psychological theory. At the beginning of the 20th century, Theodor Lipps, the German philosopher and experimental psychologist, advocated the idea that we can explain optical illusions through the fact that the observer is in an unconscious process of **Einfuehlung** with the object (Montag et al., 2008). Later on, Gestalt psychology referred to the closure of a gestalt. Einfuehlung was seen as a projection into the world of nature. Freud adopted this term and said that we understand others by putting ourselves in their place (Pigman, 1995). Titchener translated Einfuehlung as **empathy** (Gallese, 2003a). In order to explain **how** we can understand others, Klages said that we imitate them inside ourselves (Section 3.1.1). Psychoanalysis refers to trial identification (Casement, 1991), Jung to intuitive perception (Asendorpf & Wallbott, 1982). For Rogers, empathy is one of the three characteristic attitudes of the therapist crucial to developing a positive relationship, regulating affects and enabling change in inner belief systems (Watson & Greenberg, 2009).

Empirical science has long neglected empathy. However, since the end of the 1990s, when neuroscientists discovered mirror neurons, this has changed dramatically (Decety & Ickes, 2009). Even before this, it had been established that the brain waves of subjects tend to align with each other when they are asked to contact each other mentally, despite the fact that they are physically separated (Grinberg-Zylberbaum & Ramos, 1987; Grinberg-Zylberbaum & Attie, 1997). In a ground-breaking experiment, researchers investigated the brains of monkeys who were reaching for a peanut. Subsequently they charted the brain activity of a monkey watching someone else picking up the peanut. In both cases the same nerve cells fired. They even fired when the nut was hidden behind a screen and the end of the action was invisible to the watching monkey (Umiltà et al., 2001). The watching monkey must have fantasised the continuation of the arm picking up the nut. The nerve cells did what in psychology we could call the completion of an interrupted action gestalt. What is interesting in the context of the notion of resonance is that in their neuronal firing patterns, primates obviously imitate what others **are doing**. Mirror neurons are not activated by objects, but only when other living beings are interacting with objects (Gallese, 2003, p. 522). They react when someone picks up on the intentions of others through their bodily behaviour. Seeing this action activates the same motor areas of the cortex in the viewer that are in action in the animal being observed. Rizzolatti and Sinigaglia (2008) speak of the activation of motor knowledge.

The idea of motor knowledge (Chapter 12) is of great interest here. It means that the mirror neuron system only reacts to those actions that we know from our own actions; we can only anticipate actions that belong to our own motor repertoire. I can only feel with someone else when I know the feeling in myself (Gallese, 2007, p. 661). This is why humans do not have mirror neurons which would react to a dog barking.

> Empathy is deeply grounded in the experience of our lived body, and it is this experience that enables us to directly recognize others not as bodies endowed with a mind but as *persons* like us.
>
> (Gallese, 2003a, p. 176)

We could also say that empathy is based on bodily resonance (Ciaunica, 2019; Dekeyser et al., 2009, p. 113). Shaw (2003) therefore proposes that we refer to **body empathy**.

> The term mirror neurons can easily be misunderstood. These neurons do not mirror. Rather, when we see the actions of others, they are activated in the same way as when we perform those actions. Therefore they react directly (Fuchs & De Jaegher, 2010, p. 205). Perhaps the mirror metaphor is inappropriate. We could call this simultaneous activation of the equivalent cells a form of participation, measurable on a neuronal level, for the monkey who sees the experiment imitates internally what the other does (Hatfield et al., 2009). In addition, the reaction of the mirror neurons of monkeys observing a motor action is unlike a mirror in that it is modulated according to what value the monkey attaches to the action. The mirror neurons react more strongly when the monkey expects a reward (Caggiano et al., 2012). The firing of mirror neurons thus depends on how someone views the context of a situation (Iacoboni et al., 2005). However this was not clear at the time the mirror neurons got their name.

The activity of mirror neurons was first documented for motor actions. That they are also active in picking up emotions was for a long time unproven (Keysers, 2009). However, this does seem to be the case (Bastiaansen et al., 2009; Gallese & Sinigaglia, 2011, p. 135). Using functional magnetic resonance imaging (fMRI), Carr et al. (2003) charted subjects who were observing or imitating the emotional facial expressions of other people. They found that observing an emotional expression activated pre-motor cortical areas in the same way as imitating it. From this they concluded 'that we ground our empathic resonance in the experience of our acting body and the emotions associated with specific movements' (Carr et al., 2003, p. 5502). Observations in MRI make it clear that dancers, who have a large motor repertoire, can better attune themselves to other people (Calvo-Merino et al., 2005).

How exactly emotional resonance is generated on the neuronal level is not yet known. One difference between sensing intentions and emotions is that the first is on the sensorimotor level and the second on the somatosensory and visceral one (Keysers, 2011). Gallese (2013, p. 97) presumes that the neuronal mechanism is similar in both cases.

Motor representations of an action in the brain of the observer only show the action but not the thoughts connected to the reason for this action (Gallese, 2007, p. 662). Kuenzler, (2010, p. 125) points out the limits of this model from a constructivist perspective: since our sensing ability is influenced by our own experiences, sensing someone else's feelings is a construction. Our mirror neurons may be able to fantasise a coming movement, but we can only grasp the reason for it through our own experience. In relation to psychotherapy, this means we understand other people through our bodily resonance, but experiences govern our interpretations. Besides, understanding motor activity is only one of several possible ways of grasping the inner world of another person.

Psychotherapists often refer to the theory of mirror neurons as a validation (e.g. Watson & Greenberg, 2009). However this theory sees the explanation for intersubjectivity only in the brain of the person mirroring and not in the interaction itself. Cells do not make assumptions about others. We make assumptions as **persons** from our own experiences as to what the actions or the emotional expression of another person means. That cells are firing as we do this is just an associated process on the neurophysiological level. Seen phenomenologically, we can account for understanding another person on the basis of the interaction – as a **communicative process** and not as an individual neurophysiological one (Section 7.2). It may be interesting for scientific research to determine the mechanisms through which an intersubjective field is constituted, but in psychotherapy 'what matters most is the direct experience of embodied mutuality' (Totton, 2019, p. 286).

Schilbach et al. (2013) depict the theory of mirror neurons as a spectator theory, because in its research paradigms, one person is watching what another is doing. In social interaction, however, two people are engaged in a mutual encounter. It is not a case of one reacting internally to the other, but rather of the experiences and behaviour of both participants being part of a reciprocal process that is in constant flux. To study this we need a 'second-person neuroscience'. In interaction, new and shared intentions develop and the histories of the participants flow into it; without knowing all this we cannot completely understand an interaction. Studies show that early experiences can stimulate, inhibit or even reverse the activity of mirror neurons (Schilbach et al., 2013, p. 401). Taking this into consideration, a certain hype around the mirror neuron theory within body psychotherapy may be an expression of the fact that resonance is still generally seen from the perspective of a one-person-psychology, in which the therapist gathers information from the patient (Geuter, 2019, p. 401).

Through inner imitation, therapists can be subject to emotional contagion and empathise with what the patient is feeling, but it is better that they do not react within the emotional world of the patient. The studies cited in Section 14.4 show that incongruence in the facial expressions of therapist and patient indicate a better outcome in therapy. Therapeutic empathy does not consist of an inner simulation, but in how we handle our empathy. Unprocessed resonance is not helpful; it is resonance that the therapist has worked through themselves that is healing.

15.4 SIMULATION AND DIRECT PERCEPTION

Gallese and Goldman (1998) call what we used to know as inner imitation **inner bodily simulation** (Chapter 8). Damasio (1994) refers to 'as-if body loops', in which in the brain we run through certain processes on the basis of changes in the body (Section 6.3). The simulation theory of Gallese and Goldman (1998, p. 497) hypothesises that we decode the mental states of other people by reproducing 'resonant states of one's own' in our own bodies and so replicate the other person's perspective. Research findings on resonant muscle innervation support this theory (Section 14.4). 'Embodied simulation' is an implicit functional mechanism and takes place on a pre-reflective, automatic and unconscious level (Gallese, 2007). Gallese (2013) also talks about 'intercorporeity' as the main source of knowledge, borrowing a concept from Merleau-Ponty's phenomenology.

In contrast, the cognitive sciences have long described human beings as deciphering the inner world of another person as if it were a scientific problem (De Jaegher & Di Paolo, 2007, p. 486). According to the theory of mind (see Box in Section 11.2), which Fonagy et al. (2002) draw on for their psychotherapeutic concept of mentalisation, social understanding functions by one person projecting their inner representations onto another.

However, the inner world of other people is not basically separate from our own (Fuchs & De Jaegher, 2010). We do not need to reproduce and develop a model of it, i.e. represent it, in order to understand it. In fact understanding comes about directly in living interaction in the moment through bodily resonance, affect contagion or the coordination of expressive movements. It is part of the interactional, intercorporeal process between participants: 'Their body schemas and body experiences expand and incorporate the perceived body of the other. This creates a dynamic interplay which forms the basis of social understanding' (Fuchs & De Jaegher, 2010, p. 207). In interaction there is a **direct understanding of action** in embodied contact (Hutto, 2010). Phenomenological theory therefore refers to direct social perception (Vincini & Gallagher, 2021). In the research field of social cognition, this view is becoming ever more widespread (Froese & Leavens, 2014).

The simulation theory seeks the explanation for understanding in the individual and not in reciprocity (Gangopadhyay, 2013), unlike the phenomenological theory, which locates it in the interactive communicative process itself. Interactional processes of bodily communication transcend the processes in those involved and lead to participatory sense-making (Section 5.3). According to Doyon and Wehrle (2020), this means the following:

Important
From the perspective of phenomenology, neither simulation nor a theory of mind is necessary for understanding.

Just as I perceive myself directly through the body, so I perceive others through intercorporeality. We only have to make a theory when we cannot experience the other person directly (Dumouchel, 2019). We perceive others because we are engaged with them (McGann, 2014). Empathy is part of the *conditio humana* because we share our lives with each other (De Jaegher, 2015). It is a specific form of human access to other (Stein, 1989).

Comtois et al. (2000, p. 581) think that the therapist can in a certain sense read the patient's thoughts. However, this mind-reading is based on our ability to feel with the patient through our resonating body and to decipher these feelings cognitively. Using resonance consciously is always also a matter of imagination and cognition. However it is not mind-reading.

We sense something as the process unfolds. When a patient becomes sad, we as therapists also become sad, not because we empathise, but because we are also moved by it (Krebs, 2015, pp. 112–24). When pain is only in the body then we may empathise, but we share feelings because they touch us directly. It is only when something does not touch us directly that we may fall back on inner simulation, by fantasising ourselves into the patient's bodily tension and posture with the intention of understanding them.

For clinical work, two aspects are important:

- We can only perceive through resonance what we can sympathise. We need 'a bodily receptivity' (Rolef Ben-Shahar, 2019, p. 348). This is why the therapist must have an intensive self-awareness as a most important tool for their work and as a basis for perceiving the patient (Aposhyan, 2004, p. 146). Only when the therapist is sufficiently open inwardly that they can allow the impressions they gather of the patient to also affect their body will they be able to feel what they are seeing and hearing (Aposhyan, 2004, p. 148). This is an argument for the great importance of self-experience in the training of psychotherapists. One of the ways we train therapists' perception is by teaching them to be aware of their bodies (Aposhyan, 2004, p. 92). The more exactly a therapist can register their own sensations, as well as their posture, gestures and movements, the more they extend their ability to access not only unconscious attitudes and conflicts in relation to patients (Jacobs, 1973), but also to the patients themselves.
- Our inner perceptions are co-sensations but not copies of the patient's sensations. They tell us nothing about the reasons behind them. We cannot get to the truth through them, but only generate a hypothesis for the therapeutic process.

Inexplicable resonance

We have not as yet been able to explain many of the paths by which information is transferred from one person to another. For example, how did I get toothache as a patient came into the therapy room who later told me he had toothache, or why my jaw seized up on the right side and my patient later told me her jaw was tenser on the right than on the left. Perhaps in such cases I unconsciously received bodily signals that however were not connected to movement, as in the experiments with mirror neurons.

But how am I to explain the following incident? After the Christmas holidays, a patient tells me that her last therapy was mainly about her relationship to her mother. I respond that here, it would be about her. Suddenly I have an unfamiliar image: I see a larva with a fat carapace wrapped around it, which will later become a butterfly. In the last session before the holidays, she had spoken of a 'dress with thorns' that she puts on. I tell her about my image. Dumbfounded she looks at me: 'In the holidays I thought a lot about a poem by Goethe in which a butterfly is so drawn to a source of light that it flies towards it even though this could be its last flight'. We had never spoken about a butterfly or larva or a similar image. We cannot mirror the thought of a butterfly in our body language nor in our motor neurons. And I do not believe in mind-reading.

15.5 WORKING WITH RESONANCE

Downing has specified three steps for working with 'induced countertransference', which we can apply to all resonance phenomena:

1. Give some inner space to the physical reactions that occur, let them unfold, sense them and find words for them.
2. Differentiate that possible part of the countertransference which is personal from induced countertransference and then try to develop a hypothesis as to what the resonance reveals about the patient and their life-story.
3. Decide how to work therapeutically with this information (Downing, 1996, pp. 319–24).

Such decisions will vary according to our therapeutic approach. In psychoanalysis there is a method whereby the therapist makes their understanding of somatic resonance available to the patient in symbolic form. As in CBASP, they disclose their emotional reactions so that patients can experience how they affect other people and come to understand how this is related to early relationship experiences (Streeck, 2018; Guhn et al., 2018). Volz-Boers (2007, p. 39) has a sophisticated case study which illustrates this:

Clinical example

In one of her first therapy sessions with a female patient, Volz-Boers as the therapist feels a strong pressure behind the sternum, which extends into the throat and ears and intensifies painfully. Finally the pain turns into a feeling of cramp in the oesophagus; she can hardly think and keeps control of it by consciously breathing deeply in and out of the pelvic floor. A few sessions later, the patient complains of pain in the throat, behind the sternum and in the stomach, and she has the impulse to kick her legs. She talks as she has often done about her nausea and the feeling that her stomach is being inflated. The therapist in response has an image of the patient as a baby being fed through a tube, whose limbs are fixated, so that she resists by kicking. When the patient asks her parents about this, it turns out that she was fed artificially after birth and at times her wrists were in restraints (Volz-Boers, 2007, pp. 47–9).

This example demonstrates the difference between psychoanalytical and body psychotherapeutic work with resonance. Volz-Boers states that she uses the somatic resonance to **name** it (p. 41). She evaluates her own bodily sensations as 'informants for those experiences which the patient has not or not sufficiently mentally represented' (p. 58). She makes these available to the patient so that they become 'analysable' (p. 57). The only technical possibility she considers is to bring the resonance into the patient's field of mentalisation through words.

From the point of view of body psychotherapy, this is just **one** possible way of working with resonance. This technique precludes the patient from discovering for themselves the significance of what they are experiencing by exploring their sensations and images with the aid of the therapist. In this last case, the therapist would let themselves be guided by the image they had as a hypothesis, without putting it into words for the patient. To do this they firstly have to keep the sensations and images that resonate in them to themselves and not immediately make them available for the patient. For example, they could invite the patient to pursue the feeling in the stomach or the kicking impulse and to be aware of all the sensations, action impulses and images that come up. In body psychotherapy, we utilise free association not just with language, but also **free association with the body** (Geuter, 2019, pp. 139–40).

Furthermore, in body psychotherapy we can bring the inner resonance into a moving dialogue: the therapist responds to the movements of the patient with movements of their own and explores their issues with them (Geuter, 2019, pp. 304–12). Appel-Opper (2008) describes this as the living communication of two bodies.

A second limitation of the naming technique is that it alone will not lead anywhere in the case of 'body talk' (Chapter 14), which indicates there is severe inner fragmentation, or which expresses itself in menacing or destructive introjects, such that the patient is not able to verbalise them at all. In these cases, Moser (1993) recommends working with bodily enactments in which the patient can express their suffering without it having to become directly 'analysable' (Volz-Boers). Vogt (2004, p. 49) thinks it necessary to transform difficult background conflicts into clear, manageable scenes. In psychotherapy, it is precisely those people with severe mental disorders who need a form of implicit learning in a safe interpersonal environment (Schore, 2003, pp. 94–5). When the patient can retain a new emotional experience long enough in their short-term memory, then it can be worked on consciously and transferred to long-term memory (p. 106) To facilitate this, the therapist 'must resonate at the deepest layers of his/her personality to be sufficiently available to the patient's developmental and self-regulatory needs' (Schore, 2003, p. 143), which they can only communicate through the medium of body communication.

Generally, the somatic identification of the therapist with the patient in resonance is an involuntary process in which the therapist directly works through the psychological material transferred to them, for instance a feeling of anxiety, and then returns it to the patient in an altered state, for instance as a release of tension (Schmidt-Zimmermann & Marlock, 2011, p. 283). However, this can also be a consciously created inner process as in the following example:

Clinical example

A patient whose dramatic birth experience I have described in Section 11.1 is often not sure whether or not she wants to live, and in her daily life she often lapses into hefty feelings of numbness and states in which she feels as if she is outside her body. Many symptoms come together into a pattern as if she has never incarnated. In sessions as well she tends to disappear into a kind of fog, has a ringing in her ears or her eyes glaze over. These states of hers often affect me too. In view of her condition, it seems to me that it would not be helpful to relive old pain; she needs a way out of it.

In the session I describe here the patient feels as if there is a block of ice in her throat and a rope around her neck. She is familiar with this bodily sensation and so far she has found nothing which helps. To interpret this as being the umbilical cord would be just an idea and of no help. So together we try to find something that could resolve this sensation when it turns up again. The technical work with resonance in this case consists of me assuming her bodily sensation and looking for a solution in my body. As I do this, my heart starts to beat heftily. I tell her this and she says that this is happening to her too. I notice that circular breathing helps to reduce the pressure in my throat and to calm down my heart; I imagine breathing in down the spine at the back, into the pubic bone and breathing out up through the belly and the chest and into the throat. I suggest she experiments with this. However in her the pressure and dizziness get worse through this breathing. So we try imagining breathing in the opposite direction: down the front and up the back. This releases the tension in the throat. A lot more happened in this session; we worked with the dizziness and the fog too. However I have only described one aspect of the whole to show how, as therapists, we can utilise our bodily resonance with the appropriate methods to further the therapeutic process.

With patients such as the one described here, it is possible that the therapist can develop no clear inner image from these powerful bodily sensations and so is not able to name a symbol. Then it can be helpful if they just tell the patient about their somatic resonance (Aposhyan, 2004, p. 93). Eberhard-Kaechele (2009, p. 145) calls this 'selective disclosure'. On the level of therapeutic work on the self, this can function as a way of helping the patient to access a hitherto unknown part of their self-perception; on the relational level, they experience self-efficacy by seeing that they affect the other person.

16

Moments of understanding

When, with the aid of their body experience and the resonance of the therapist, patients can open themselves up more to their present experience, then a certain form of understanding becomes possible. Heisterkamp (2002) has called this moments of understanding (literally: 'presentist understanding', *präsentisches Verstehen*). He uses this term in the framework of a psychoanalysis, which includes body-related action dialogue and which he connects to a working in the here and now that is characteristic of experiential therapies. With moments of understanding, Heisterkamp means, for example, a situation such as the moment described in Section 14.4 where he looks at his therapist and has an immediate awareness of inner transformation.

I think the notion of moments of understanding is eminently suited as a basic concept of experiential body psychotherapy, for phenomenal experience is always an experience in the present moment (Section 5.3). This is how we give a situation meaning. But we can only know whether something is meaningful for us when we feel it. Felt meaning is based on bodily experience in the present moment (Chapter 6). Present does not, however, mean only the range of seconds in which we can for example remember numbers, but an experienced timespan in the now, in which we can focus our attention on a certain situation (Geuter, 2019, p. 67).

A moment of understanding is a direct grasping of what we are experiencing in the relevant moment of the present. This distinguishes it from a verbally communicated understanding, which represents the experience and takes place in retrospect ('*repräsentisches Verstehen*', Heisterkamp, 2005, p. 130). Moments of understanding arise when, for instance, the patient tries something out in an enactment and gains a 'substantiated experiential certainty' (Heisterkamp, 2005, p. 131). Perhaps Reich (1973, p. 313) meant much the same when he wrote that when we work with body expression we do not need to interpret, since the patient has an 'immediate comprehension' of what is going on. Immediate comprehension is the meaning experienced in the moment. Petzold (2003, p. 694) speaks of **vital evidence**, when rational insight, emotional experience, body experience and social significance come together.

An experience of vital evidence makes a transformative learning process possible (Waibel et al., 2009, p. 18). Transformation takes place when a person in a state of embodied self-perception in the 'subjective emotional present' (Fogel, 2009, p. 66) exposes themselves to possible changes. In this respect, moments of understanding are, in terms of systems theory, self-organised **transition** processes in which at a certain point a new quality appears (cf. Haken, 2004; Tschacher, 2004).

DOI: 10.4324/9781003176893-16

Let us look back at the example Volz-Boers (2007) gives in the previous chapter. By telling the patient in words about her image of the baby being fed through a stomach tube, she initiated a retrospective, cognitive, representative understanding of a mainly bodily experience. In a moment of understanding, in contrast, the insight comes from the experience in the patient themselves. The concept of moments of understanding is thus also different from that of **scenic understanding** (Streeck, 2005), as here through the scene the therapist understands something which they then represent to the patient, so that it becomes an insight for them. In moments of understanding, however, it is the patient who understands directly themselves.

Clinical example

A patient who has long struggled with severe depression and sleep problems complains persistently about a deep exhaustion. Yesterday evening he again sat for half an hour on the couch and cried and the night was again terrible, full of nightmares in which he is not coping at work. Tomorrow his wife wants to go with him and the children to a family celebration, but all he wants is peace and quiet, at best just to drive somewhere and do nothing. We talk for a while about the options of going with the family or staying at home alone. Talking about it, however, does not make it clearer.

Then I ask him to go to two places in the room which stand for going with the family and for staying at home. In the first position he starts to cry, there is a tightness in his chest and breathing becomes difficult: 'I can't do it', he says. To his surprise, in the second place, he immediately feels afraid of loneliness. He sees himself as a child sent to his room, excluded. His throat constricts and so does his heart. He thinks about how he has to drink wine when he is alone, as if on auto-pilot. Thus this second place is no solution. Therefore I ask him to look for a third place in the room and see how he feels there. He stands in the middle of the room, where he is also closer to the door than at either of the other places, and folds his arms. Here he is immediately calmer, more confident, more adult. Here is a free space. Being close to the door means for him that he can leave at any time. Images come up of how he could plan the trip to the family celebration as he would want it: segregating himself now and then, going for a walk, leaving the party earlier in the evening and going to bed. He says the sentence: 'I'll do it, but in my own way'.

At the end I ask him to go to a fourth position and from there to look at the other three. He perches on the arm of the chair, from where he can look at the other places from a 'bird's eye view'. It becomes clear to him here that he feels better when he focuses less on his outer and more on his inner peace and quiet, keeps his poise and checks out what is good for him at each moment and sets boundaries without becoming full of guilt and being the rejected child he felt like with his mother.

At first I had thought the solution would be to stay at home, but the patient knew in a moment of understanding that this was a relapse into a childish pattern. It is only in the third position that, from his inner sensations and spontaneously adopted body posture, he can develop an image of how he can step outside the pattern of exhausted suffering without falling into the familiar childish pattern of feeling lonely and guilty. Discovering this, he was in no need of explanations from me as therapist. He had a symbolic experience, which, according to Lawley and Tompkins (2013, p. 47), should not be interpreted but just accepted.

I would like to demonstrate the difference between moments of understanding and the psychoanalytical idea that insight is created by interpretation with an example of Kernberg's, who, confronted with a patient's bodily expression, offers a complex analysis of the transference:

> The therapist notes that the patient is silent, and because of the patient's clenched fists and facial expression, believes that her silence is a defense against her rage toward the doctor. The therapist says, 'I wonder if you are silent and sitting with clenched fists because you are afraid that if you talk, your anger may emerge and hurt one or both of us?'
>
> (Kernberg et al., 1989, p. 60)

Here Kernberg puts his technical means of clarification, confrontation and interpretation into practice. In order to respond without defending against the interpretation or distracting from her resistance, the patient has to think this complex situation through. This may be one of the reasons why, according to various studies, 'patients responded to transference interpretations with increased defensive behaviour' (Grawe, 2004 p. 106). Moments of understanding, however, are not achieved through interpretation but through exploration, in which the patient understands the meaning from their own sensations.

Fantasising how the patient could have arrived at such a moment of understanding in a body psychotherapy session, I imagine the therapist saying: 'Just take a moment to sense your hands' – not 'clenched fists', as that is already close to an interpretation. If the patient says she cannot feel anything, the therapist could ask her to let her awareness move into her hands. Often such a change of focus already has the effect that the patient says: 'Yes, I'm angry!' or something similar. If she says in a factual way that her hands are making fists, without communicating any inner experience, the therapist could ask her to exaggerate what the hands are doing and see how that feels. Or they could ask: 'What would the hands want to do, if you let them have their own way?' Or if the patient had spoken of fists: 'Is there something the fists want to do?' By having her attention directed towards body experience and being invited to express herself bodily, the patient may possibly already be in a moment of understanding of her anger in transference. Kernberg's goal of expanding the realm of self-knowledge through interpretation would be reached without the patient having to deal with his complex train of thought or having to accept an interpretation from somebody else, with whom she is most probably at that moment angry. In addition, the patient is hardly able to evade an experience she has just made herself. This distinguishes it from a verbal insight, which she can always reject later. And as her therapist, I can always come back to what she experienced in that moment.

This body psychotherapeutic invitation requires, however, that the therapist is able to expose themselves to the patient's anger, which can flare up in their bodily expression towards them. Kernberg's analytical techniques, however, allow the therapist to avoid a possible confrontation with the explosiveness of her rage.

In a dialogue based on body experience, moments of understanding occur in which the patient reaches an insight through meaningful experience (Heisterkamp, 2000, p. 311). Here I have an example of a body psychotherapeutic approach illustrating this:

Clinical example

A patient with a severe somatic symptom disorder always comes with pain and tension. He moans on and on about them and moves around all tensed up, saying: 'There's all these aches and pains, I don't know, it all just hurts'. A small intervention, however, changes things: 'You could try out how it feels when you just let your head hang down a little while you speak'. Spontaneously he says: 'I feel a bit sad'.

That was the first time this patient had been able to express a feeling. This was possible because at a certain point his system had changed bodily and he was able to feel this change. This led to a change in self-perception. It became directly clear to him that there was a sadness inside, without us having spoken about it.

The advantage of such a manifest experience in comparison to a cognitive insight is that the patient cannot go back on it. As his therapist, I can remind him that he experienced this sadness himself. Whereas an interpretation goes from the top down, this is a bottom-up insight, from a small change in the body and the awareness resulting from it. It needs no further clarification. It is quite simply there because the patient felt something new.

What Varela et al. wrote about embodied reflection is also true of a moment of understanding: 'reflection is a form of experience itself' which 'can cut the chain of habitual thought patterns and preconceptions' (Varela et al., 1993, p. 27). In moments of understanding, our habitual point of view is changed and we discover something new. Moments of understanding are an **understanding directly out of experience**, a conscious experiencing **of**, not a reflecting back **on** something. In a moment of understanding, we access the immediacy of experience, revealed through itself, but verifiable for its coherence in reflection.

However, to be effective, experience does not even need to be named. Then change occurs in the present moment without a verbally explicit insight:

> Some enactments of conflict situations, whether intentional or occurring spontaneously, may just sink without comment into the unconscious, where they become a living bedrock for future life.
>
> (Moser, 2012, p. 231)

Sometimes talking about it can even detract from such an understanding. We could compare this to grasping a piece of music. If we listen to Beethoven's Fifth, we understand the heroic melodies of the French revolution, or at least we sense the inherent revolutionary power, even if we know nothing of the anti-Napoleonic impetus that Beethoven presumably wove into this music.

As an experiential approach, body psychotherapy subscribes to an ideographic psychology, which understands each human being as having their own individual existence and life history (cf. Thomae, 1968, pp. 12–4) and to which humanistic psychology also adheres (Laengle & Kriz, 2012). In ideographic psychology, understanding is a first-person phenomenon, the point of view of the subject (Section 5.1). A moment of understanding occurs when the subject themselves has the insight and not when someone else creates this insight from outside. This viewpoint is connected to an understanding of the therapeutic relationship characteristic of humanistic psychotherapy (Section 3.7). Where Kernberg sees the therapist as someone who knows things about the patient that they themselves do not yet know and which the therapist then shares with them as an interpretation, experiential body psychotherapy and humanistic psychotherapy see the competence and the task of the therapist as guiding the process of experience so that the patient begins to sense meaning for themselves. In so doing, the patient's own competence and self-knowledge is treated with respect.

Schellenbaum (1992) proposed the idea of a **sensing awareness**. He means that the patient should turn their awareness towards the inside, looking and listening as if they were in a state of waking trance. According to him in this sensing awareness the functional identity of tensions and emotions becomes a felt experience (Schellenbaum, 1992, p. 174; Section 13.1). Schellenbaum also advocates working in the present, whereby the therapist pays attention to 'the strongest sensation, the most fascinating idea, the most effective word and the body part sending out the most urgent signal' (Schellenbaum, 1992, p. 17). When the patient not only talks about but can also sense themselves, then they become more conscious of the present.

Stern (2004) too insists that psychotherapy should concentrate on the phenomenological level of the here and now. He thinks that in contrast to most psychodynamic treatments, with their overhasty search for meaning, it is essential for the therapist to offer the patient a space to discover meaning through a continual deepening of experience. Stern speaks of the lived experience of the **present moment**, which in traditional psychoanalysis is usually deferred in favour of a reconstructing analysis. Stern's idea is very similar to that of moments of understanding; however it is not identical, as he is not familiar with therapeutic work with a sensing awareness or with an enactment directly experienced through the body.

Without mentioning it, Stern adopts the concept of the present moment from Gestalt therapy, but in contrast to the experiential psychotherapy approaches, he does not say how we can explore the momentary state and present experience of the patient. In body psychotherapy, this exploration is based on body experience. When the body is allowed to communicate out of itself, this intuitively creates experiences of living clarity and vital evidence, which are pivotal for change through body psychotherapy work. There then becomes possible what Heisterkamp (2002, p. 46) calls 'implicit transformation experiences'.

17

Self-regulation and life regulation

In the preceding chapter, I have shown how in body psychotherapy patients can understand themselves for themselves. However understanding oneself is not the main goal of therapy, but more a means to attain the more important goal of enabling a person who is suffering to regulate and look after themselves in such a way that they can overcome, alleviate or accept their affliction and live their own best possible life. We call the ability to do this self-regulation, and in the following I will consider how we can understand it theoretically and clinically in body psychotherapy.

Psychotherapy is an aid to help change damaging and debilitating life patterns, to transform a dysfunctional or dysregulated emotionality into a more functional one. If this succeeds, there is a decrease in incongruences. When thinking, feeling, sensing, fantasising and acting all come together as a coherent whole, feelings harmonise with needs and there is recognition of the conditions and potential of a person's own life, then they will experience consistency (Section 6.4).

However a person does not experience consistency for themselves alone, but in the social environment in which they live. Living systems regulate themselves in interchange with the environment, so that part of self-regulation is being able to regulate their relationships to others of their own accord. A person can only really be fulfilled when they are also fulfilled in their relationships. Fulfilment requires the capacity for individual and interactional regulation (Beebe & Lachmann, 2003).

Self-regulation is often thought of in the context of an autonomous self and less so in that of relationships. In psychotherapy, however people are not only interested in themselves alone, but always also in the lives they are living together with others. This is why I have proposed that psychotherapy refers not only to self-regulation but also to life regulation (Geuter, 2019, p. 455). Patients want to feel better in themselves and in their lives and not just to feel but also to live better. In Acceptance and Commitment Therapy, Hayes and Lillis (2013) use phrases such as 'living a life'. In 1931, the psychoanalyst Otto Rank wrote that it is a question of the patient learning to live (Rank, 2006, p. 527).

Facilitating this is a perpetual goal in the process of psychotherapy.

Much about therapy is about recognizing and understanding existing regulatory patterns, supporting underdeveloped resources, and challenging and helping to reformulate defensive strategies.

(Carroll, 2005, p. 28).

DOI: 10.4324/9781003176893-17

Greenberg and Van Balen see three major sources for dysfunctions: the inability to integrate 'aspects of functioning into coherent, harmonious internal relations', 'the inability to symbolize bodily felt constituents of experience' and 'the activation by minimal cues of maladaptive emotions' (Greenberg & Van Balen, 1998, p. 50). When a person loses the ability to cope with tensions, stress or conflicts themselves, then they need help. This is no different than with a physical illness, when the organism is unable to deal with a pathogen, a cellular degeneration or a wound itself. According to this view, psychological suffering consists of the inability to self-regulate.

This is why psychotherapists focus not only on symptoms but above all on the attempts to restore the missing or reduced capacity for self-regulation. Therapeutic change is the change from the pathological to the non-pathological regulation of emotional, cognitive and behavioural processes (Mergenthaler, 2008). In the view of humanistic psychotherapy it also goes beyond this to include the capacity of a human being to live themselves, to gain more freedom of choice and to limit restrictions on experience (Laengle & Kriz, 2012). Someone who can live through crises, hardship and conflict and keep their spirits up needs no therapeutic help.

Self-regulation is seen differently in the various approaches to psychotherapy (Geissler, 2004a):

- **Gestalt therapy** assumes that the organism possesses forces of **self-healing**. Perls saw self-regulation as the possibility of regulating oneself with no coercion from outside, relying on the 'wisdom of the organism' (Yontef & Fuhr, 2005). This notion is similar to that of self-regulation in the Reichian tradition and belongs to an organismic view of life processes (Gremmler-Fuhr, 1999, pp. 375–8). According to Sreckovic (1999, p. 147), in the wake of the human potential movement, the idea of organismic self-regulation mutated into the concept of growth (Section 3.7).
- According to **client-centred psychotherapy**, the therapist creates an environment which stimulates growth and in which the forces of **self-actualisation** can unfold. Rogers (1959) speaks of an inherent motivational and regulatory system possessed by every organism, which serves their maintenance and growth. He calls the tendency towards greater self-realisation the actualisation tendency. Thus for Rogers, it is a question of potentialities.

  The idea of self-actualisation is central to many humanistic therapy approaches (Laengle & Kriz, 2012; Maslow, 1968). In addition to it, Kriz (2011, p. 335) sees the notion of self-regulation as characteristic of **humanistic psychotherapy**.
- In the **SORC model of behavioural therapy** by Kanfer, self-monitoring, self-evaluation and self-reinforcement are all part of self-regulation (Kanfer & Saslow, 1969). In this model of **self-management**, the point is that a person achieves something by working towards goals they have set themselves (Kanfer et al., 2012, pp. 28–9; Chen et al., 2017). Here self-regulation is seen functionally in relation to behaviour and as a means of self-control or self-efficacy (Bandura, 1997). Parfy and Lenz see **self-control** as a special case of self-regulation, in which the 'preference for a long-term plan leading to positive achievement' is secured (Parfy & Lenz, 2009, p. 78). For them, self-control is more conscious and cognitively based. Self-regulation, on the contrary, can be conscious or unconscious (Foerster & Jostmann, 2012).
- In **systemic therapy**, the concept of **self-organisation** is used in the context of a theory of living systems to depict their 'operational closure' and autonomous logic (von Schlippe & Schweitzer, 2003, pp. 51, 68). According to a definition by Heinz von Foerster, the

human being is a so-called 'non-trivial' system: one that is in permanent, self-perpetuating flux and can never be completely comprehended by an observer (von Schlippe & Schweitzer, 2003, p. 55). From this we can develop a therapeutic model whereby systems are activated from outside, so that they then generate change of their own accord, which we can often not foresee (Schiepek, 2004, p. 258).

In body psychotherapy, self-regulation is traditionally seen on the **organismic level** of the autonomic nervous system (Bhat & Carleton, 2015). Neo-Reichian theories see it 'as an intra-psychic, intra-organismic event in response to the environment' (Carroll, 2009, p. 97). This is an attempt to build a bridge between psychology and biology (Carroll, 2012). Carroll (2009) leans the concept theoretically on homeostatic ideas when she defines it as the ability of human beings to maintain or restore balance. In Functional Relaxation, M. Fuchs advocates an organismic, vegetative idea of self-regulation when she sees it as the regulation of the unconscious breathing in the interplay of tension and relaxation (von Arnim, 2009a, p. 124).

Reich used the term **Selbststeuerung** (self-steering) introduced into physiology by the physician Jakob Moleschott at the end of the 19th century. Reich connected this term with the idea of the philosophy of life, of preserving a vital inner nature from the impositions of culture. Thus for him the idea of natural birth or the freedom of development for children were a part of this self-steering (Thielen, 2009b). This **culturally critical idea** is also to be found in Gestalt therapy, when organismic self-regulation is seen as inner self-determination and almost as the opposite pole to dictatorship (Gremmler-Fuhr, 1999). Self-steering/self-regulation was a notion antithetical to external control and alienation, beholden to the enlightenment ideal of liberating people from their 'self-imposed immaturity' as Kant had said (Sections 3.2–3.5). In the late 20th century, however, it became a cultural imperative to render oneself capable of self-realisation through 'the self-regulative mobilisation of body and mind' (Stoff, 2019, p. 101; Section 3.7).

Following the polarity principle introduced by Boadella (2000a), we can understand self-regulation in the Reichian tradition as creating the freedom of living movement, 'a bodily state of free pulsation, not inhibited by contraction' (Totton, 2003, p. 70). Southwell (1988) names its goal as being independent wellbeing. Self-regulation is often seen metaphorically as a river which regulates the flow of water quite naturally (Carroll, 2009). In this image, the task of the therapist is to help the patient to get into their own flow. Eberwein (1996, p. 9) describes body psychotherapy as an attempt to facilitate the client's 'auto-dynamic processes'. This corresponds to the midwife model of therapy: the therapist should create the best possible conditions for the birth of the client's own capacity for self-regulation (Carroll, 2009, p. 91). Boyesen calls this the obstetric method (1987, p. 102). This concept was already used by Socrates, the son of a midwife, as Plato describes it in his Theaetetus. His maieutics – literally the art of birthing – was a method of awakening the wisdom in others through discourse (Werner, 1966, p. 52). Marlock (2015, pp. 161–2) has described body psychotherapy as maieutics.

ALIVENESS

The background of body psychotherapy in the philosophy of life (Chapter 3) implies close links between the concept of self-regulation and that of aliveness. Functional Relaxation sees the goal of therapy in finding one's own natural rhythm (von Arnim, 2009a, p. 129). Boadella (1987) calls a person 'centred' when they are connected to the rhythm of their breathing. In the tradition of the philosophy of life, however, rhythm is a characteristic of the living (Section 3.4). Lowen wants to help people develop 'a new respect for the instinctive forces of life' and discover 'that the body has life of its own life and the capacity to heal itself' (Lowen, 1967, p. 234).

These statements show that body psychotherapy, despite its diverse backgrounds, is concerned with restoring lost aliveness or attaining a vitality which has not been sufficiently developed. I prefer the term aliveness to that of vitality because this last conjures up a societal culture that uses the body as a presentation of youth and vitality in the labour market and in the relationship market. In contrast, the concept of aliveness points to the fact that a person can only be in harmony with themselves as a living subject in an experienced body. If we connect self-regulation with aliveness, then the goal of therapy is not only that the patient can oscillate more freely between two opposite poles, but can also increase the **amplitude of life movements**. Parents do this when they support their children in regulating the tension of emotional arousal, helping them to tolerate more anxiety or to feel more joy.

SELF-ORGANISATION

Occasionally the concept of self-organisation from systemic theory is used in body psychotherapy (e.g. Leye, 2011, p. 313). Geissler (2009, p. 261) uses the terms self-regulation and self-organisation synonymously. I prefer the term self-regulation because it emphasises more the activity and linguistically is closer to emotional regulation.

Self-organisation is a concept from cybernetics, which was initially a theory of control engineering and message transmission (Wiener, 1961), but it also applied ideas about the transfer of information, e.g. the model of feedback loops in technical processes, to living beings. Grawe's (2004) concept of self-organisation is based on this cybernetic idea about feedback processes. Maturana (1975) first used the term organisation for how living organisms do all they can to maintain their inner organisation. This corresponds to the old idea of the survival instinct.

In synergetics (Haken & Schiepek, 2006; Schiepek et al., 2015), the concept of self-organisation stands for a theory of pattern transitions based on physics, in which new coherent structures emerge spontaneously from instability. For instance, relaxation is depicted as a 'biophysical pattern transition' and not as a regulative process. Psychotherapy is seen as a cascade of pattern transitions, as a perpetual sequence of the alternation between stable and unstable states, in which malign structures are replaced by benign ones. Here, the idea of self-organisation is not connected to that of affect regulation.

REGULATION OF ALIVENESS

The concept of self-regulation is based not on physics, but on biological considerations (Kriz, 1999). Self-regulation is understood as a **property of living systems** (Section 5.2). This property generally means that a living system regulates their regulation themselves. This is also known as **self-referentiality**. Autopoietic systems determine for themselves how they incorporate elements of their environment. Only living systems can regenerate and 'heal' themselves out of themselves (Kurtz, 1990).

According to a model of Thompson and Varela (2001), regulatory processes in the body, in sensorimotor coupling with the material world and in intersubjective interaction constitute life. Hence the concept of self-regulation on such a general level includes biological, psychological and social processes (Ryan et al., 1997, p. 717).

The fundamental **biological regulation** of a living being consists in the first place of avoiding a deterioration of their physical state and maintaining basic bodily functions. This takes place on the level of the protoself (Section 6.5) and is a completely unconscious level of bodily self-regulation. This capacity is inherent in the nature of every living being. When in body psychotherapy we help people to better regulate themselves, then we are touching this level. For example, when someone learns to regulate stress more adequately, this leads to an improved balance between the sympathetic and the parasympathetic nervous systems (Section 7.1). From infant research, we know that the level of endogenous opioids increases when the mother is physically present and looking at the child fondly (Schore, 2003, p. 14). If the gaze of a therapist reaches the patient on a level beyond words, this can instigate a psychobiological regulation process.

By working on the level of vegetative, sensorimotor, psychological and social experience, we can trigger various regulative processes. This is why working functionally on the sensorimotor level with a patient's stance can on the one hand awaken feelings of self-esteem and ideas about their own strength, while on the other it can harmonise the breathing. It has an impact on the cognitive and on the vegetative level and on their emotional state. The same is true in the other direction: a thought or a breath can change a person's stance (Section 6.1). When we activate biological processes, this does not mean, however, that we are working therapeutically with biological means on the biological level itself (Section 7.2).

We often hear the notion that with self-regulation we could just follow the inner wisdom or the innate intelligence of the body (e.g. Levine & Macnaughton, 2004, p. 377). I want to be careful here. It is doubtless true that the body has a great capacity for maintaining itself, but not always does it use the right means. The body of an addict knows what it needs without being wise. In therapy, we cannot just trust the body to 'know what is right', when for instance we are encouraging a patient to hyperventilate. Consistency does not just mean trusting only in the knowledge of the body, but in finding consonance between body and mind.

HOMEODYNAMICS

In body psychotherapy, the embedding of the notion of self-regulation in biology harks back to philosophical and physiological ideas. In 1901, the vitalist biologist and philosopher Hans Driesch spoke of 'organic regulation' (Tanner, 1998, p. 166; Section 3.4: item 10), the internist Ferdinand Hoff in 1928 of the 'vegetative regulation' of the blood. In his theory of the organism, presented first in 1934, Goldstein (1995) made only marginal use of the term self-regulation, but demonstrated that of its own accord the organism creates new order from chaotic states (Corsi, 2012). Cannon offered the concept of **homeostasis** as a principle of living systems, and in 1932 published a book with the title *The Wisdom of the Body* (Heller, 212, pp. 200–2). He attributed to the body the capacity for 'organised self-regulation' when it becomes ill through outside factors (Stoff, 2019, p. 93). Following Cannon, stress is now understood as a state into which the body gets when it can no longer establish a homeostatic balance (Fogel, 2009, p. 142). Carroll (2009) describes self-regulation according to the idea of homeostasis, as the ability of a system to maintain or restore equilibrium.

The concept of homeostasis presupposes an 'optimal stationary state', to which the organism should return after some disturbance. The organism is seen as adapting to changing conditions, but not as 'anticipating potentially undesirable trajectories in the organism-environment couplings and regulating the interaction accordingly' (Garcia & Arandia, 2022, p. 9).

We could describe homeostasis as a basic principle of regulating the functional systems of the body, controlled by the brain stem (Fogel, 2009, pp. 50–1). Human beings, however, can regulate their equilibrium through embodied self-awareness much more effectively by, for example, not eating despite feeling greedy, because they notice it would not be good for them (Fogel, 2009, p. 51). Goldstein had already said in 1934 that the organism tends towards optimal behaviour to maintain its inner order in the face of disruption. In this spirit, humanistic psychology sees not the reduction of tension but the movement towards higher levels of equilibrium as specifically human (Buehler & Allen, 1972). Maslow (1968) states that homeostasis means not bringing tension down to zero, but achieving an optimal level of tension. Levine (2010) also regards the concept of homeostasis as too static and speaks of a **dynamic equilibrium**. We find a similar idea in synergetics. According to Haken und Schiepek (2006, p. 260), homeodynamics is characteristic of a healthy self: to combine **stability** with **adaptivity**. A healthy organism strives towards new experiences (Sreckovic, 1999, p. 33). This goes far beyond homeostasis.

In my view, the body psychotherapy theory of self-regulation should include the concept of homeodynamics. Self-regulation is a process independent of any setpoints and consists of the ability to react flexibly, to anticipate change and to be in flux with oneself and the world (Haken & Schiepek, 2006, pp. 67, 247). This is what is meant by adaptivity as distinct from adaptation (Garcia & Arandia, 2022, p. 9).

In the **personality systems interactions theory** (PSI), self-regulation and self-control are two aspects of **self-determination** (Koole at al., 2019; Kuhl et al. 2021). Here the concept of self-regulation refers to the ability to be aware of and to satisfy one's needs. In contrast, self-control means the ability to carry out difficult plans represented in the conscious ego. Self-regulation can be both autonomous and implicit, but self-control is directed at intentional goals (Ryan et al., 1997; Rothermund, 2011). Both together make up self-determination as that level of self-development where a person has reached the highest degree of freedom.

AFFECT REGULATION

From a **clinical perspective**, the concept of self-regulation is mainly used for the regulation of need tensions and emotional states. Here self-regulation means the ability to take care of one's own needs, to maintain a controllable and highly individual level of affective tension and to use one's own emotions as an orientation. Schore (2003, p. 112) regards this affect regulation as the central task of therapy, especially in the case of personality disorders developed early in life.

Important
If we focus on the regulation of affects or emotions, then we can avoid the one-sided biological and monadic understanding attached to the concept of self-regulation. Clinically regulating emotions requires both intra- as well as interpersonal regulation.

In body psychotherapy, the focus is on intrapyschic regulation in perception-oriented schools such as Focusing (Watson et al., 1998, p. 16). Therapy approaches emphasising self-awareness (e.g. Fogel, 2009) assume that consciousness increases of its own accord when the patient can allow autonomic processes in the body to happen and perceives what is happening. Learning to feel what is happening in each moment promotes inner regulation (Van Dixhoorn, 2000, p. 74).

In our view, self-regulation includes the capacity of the body *to reorganize* through expressive movement, reflexes and other involuntary processes such as shaking, crying, laughing … Working with impulse, breath, movement and sensation … are all effective ways of enhancing the client's self-regulation quite directly. They enhance the body's motor sensory feedback loops which can lead to spontaneous rebalancing of the nervous system and a more coherent sense of body-self.

(Carroll, 2009, p. 97; 2005, p. 23)

Empirical studies show that being aware of the body encourages self-regulation (Geuter, 2019, pp. 443–4). The better the awareness, the more psychosomatic patients can perceive their own stress reactions, influence stress situations and allow themselves to feel (Landsman-Dijkstra et al., 2006). In patients with irritable bowel syndrome, there was a decrease in symptoms (Eriksson et al., 2007). Women who have been abused experienced a lessening of the dissociative symptoms as a result of interventions to help them be aware of their bodies in connection with being touched (Price, 2007).

The model of the affective cycle (Section 10.5; Figure 10.1) assumes that self-regulation takes place by letting an emotional cycle run its course until it is finished. In this model, affect regulation is seen as an emotional process, going through an arousal, into an activation and then ideally quietening down. Here self-regulation consists of the sequence perception-expression-calming down-relaxing or digesting. The upward branch can be linked to self-motivation and the downward branch to self-soothing, the two skills of affect regulation regarded as essential to self-development in Kuhl's (1998) PSI theory model. Theoretically, the model also contains the idea of self-healing, since the forces of reorganisation are seen as being available in the living system of the human being. In this clinical perspective on self-regulation, the therapeutic focus is on the patient themselves.

However, in therapy, a patient's affective cycle takes place in relation to a therapist, in which both influence and change each other. Intrapersonal models such as this therefore need to be supplemented by an interpersonal perspective (Thielen, 2009a, p. 43).

Starting from an intersubjective view of psychotherapy, self-regulation is 'always more or less part of a reciprocal regulation process' (Hartmann & Lohmann, 2004, p. 59; Hartmann, 2006). Since a self only exists in connection to the environment, this is not only true of therapy. In the early years of a child's development, affect regulation is consistently interpersonal (Section 11.3). For adults, too, a successful self-regulation is also a regulation in relationships.

As Fogel (2009, pp. 179–82) impressively demonstrates with the aid of video analysis, however, right from the start a baby already possesses its own capacity for regulation. This is true of all elementary, psychobiological regulation processes. But self-regulatory **competence** grows through good interpersonal regulatory experiences and diminishes through bad ones. Thus how the capacity for self-regulation **develops** depends on the quality of external regulation (Ritz-Schulte et al., 2008, p. 51). Through traumatic relationship experiences, even autonomic regulation systems can be derailed (Porsch, 2009, p. 148; Chapter 9 on body memory). Dyadic experiences thus shape affect regulation. Since in the modulation of the child's state, external regulation is transformed into internal regulation, early relationship patterns become regulation patterns (Schore, 2003, pp. 7–12; cf. Section 11.3 – 11.6). Self-regulation is therefore moulded on the interpersonal level, but not created there. Patterns are interiorised, but not the capacity for self-regulation. When the caregiver is able to affectively attune themselves well to the baby, this is because they can sense what the baby is showing **of their own accord** and not just because the infant is interiorising the regulative ability of the caregiver.

Important
Self-regulation is a natural skill, the patterns and extent of which are shaped through interactional experiences.

AUTO-REGULATION AND CO-REGULATION

If we understand the regulation of needs and emotions as self- and interpersonal regulation, then we find two aspects important for therapy: to encourage them on the intrapersonal level through bodily awareness and interpersonally through therapeutic interaction (cf. Carroll, 2009, p. 99). Both aspects are justified because living systems have two characteristics: they strive to maintain themselves in their structure and to interact with the environment (Chapter 5). This indicates the twofold nature of self-regulation as a regulation of life: living states will be optimised, alternating between auto- and co-regulation strategies according to context. Human beings can regulate their emotions and needs for themselves alone as well as in relationships. Both are strategies of self-regulation. The ability to change from one to the other grows out of a secure attachment, according to Schore (2001). Auto-regulation strategies are for instance an essential mode 'when one is processing emotion but not transacting with external social objects' (Schore, 2003, p. 213). In therapy, working with awareness is aimed at auto-regulation, whereas the objective of relational work is co-regulation. In my view, in body psychotherapy theory and practice, we should pay attention to both.

If we do so, then two healing paths come together: healing through self-healing and through healing relationships. Psychotherapy is basically a way to **self-healing in a healing relationship**.

Important
Healing takes place in a process of new regulation, reorganisation and transformation through new auto- and co-regulatory experiences.

Body psychotherapy has long focused on auto-regulatory processes and on self-perception (Geuter, 2009, p. 71), on which current interactional theories in turn place less emphasis. However we should avoid concentrating alone on either the auto-regulatory, intrapsychic model of self-regulation or on the co-regulatory, interpersonal one and address both modes in therapy. In this respect, we need both a one-person as well as a two-person psychology (Geuter, 2019, p. 401; Schore, 2001, p. 42; Chapter 14). Self-regulation is an attribute of both intrapersonal and interpersonal intelligence (Schore, 2001, p. 48; Wehowsky, 2004). Intrapersonally, it is about the ability to become aware of the wealth of micro-signals on the bodily level, and interpersonally about perceiving the quality and form of contact and about corrective emotional experiences. Beebe and Lachmann (2003) describe self-regulation in the sense of auto-regulation and interactive regulation as two sides of the same coin.

In particular, patients who were not able to establish stable patterns of affect regulation in their childhood need to experience and learn new patterns in interaction. Co-regulation comes about by creating a therapeutic relationship in which the therapist makes themselves available to the patient in transference as an early object for the expression of their needs and feelings, in both verbal and bodily communication, and helps the patient to internalise the qualities of affect regulation they experience in this relationship. This strengthens the patient's ability to cope with difficult feelings both in interaction with others and in auto-regulative terms.

To conclude this discussion, I would like to illustrate with the following vignette how interactive and intrapersonal self-regulation are intertwined:

Clinical example

A patient feels that he is at the end of his tether. He is going through strong feelings of loneliness, anxiety, despair and helplessness. He comes to the session with stomach ache, tears running down his face. He has written ten letters to his ex-girlfriend but has sent none. He is searching for someone to hold him. He does not know how to go on.

In the last session, we had talked about how in his current phase a very small boy has emerged, and as a symbol for this little boy he had taken a doll from the therapy room home with him so that he could hold him in his arms. Now he takes out the doll. I ask him what the little boy is looking for. He says he is longing for his mummy.

Now therapeutically we could have the adult take the little boy's hand, working on his strength in everyday life, so that he can find out how life can go on. However my feeling is that it is not a question of knowing how to go on in life, but that he has to find the strength to go through a crisis in which old childhood fears will come up. The decisive scene for him is when at the age of two he was wheeled away from his parents in his bed during an emergency at the hospital and saw them disappearing slowly down the corridor. My idea is that enacting this scene could lead to a new experience.

So now I suggest that he lie down on the floor and surrender himself to this longing for his mummy. I sit down next to him so that if he needs me I can be the mother figure. As soon as he lies down he starts to sob bitterly. I ask him if there are any words for this. He says: 'Mummy, where are you?' and 'I'm going to die'. Then his whole body starts to shake. He grasps my hand and I lean slightly forward so that if necessary he can reach my body. In the role of mother I call him 'My little one'. He clings to me and presses me to him. As I say 'I am here', some anger comes up: 'You're not really there!' This is directed at the mother, who because of a severe chronic depression, was generally not available to him. He feels very afraid of going home after the session and being alone again. At this point we are in the interaction of the child with his mother.

Then his breathing changes, as if he is re-experiencing the croup attack. He wheezes, gasps for breath, but the breathing is becoming stronger. So I say to him 'You'll get through this' – because he has really got through it, only the fear tells him otherwise. I explain that I am speaking to him as his ideal mother, the one he would have needed. A second wave of crying and shivering comes over him, he holds me even more tightly. Then he says 'The fear has gone'. During the 'croup attack', he had felt a new strength and that he would survive. We let this experience come to an end. He is calm and says that now he feels okay about going home.

In this therapy session, an auto-regulative process starts through co-regulation, which lets the patient give in to what he is experiencing. As the therapist, I do not provide him with solutions but offer to accompany him through his fear and his pain. In this way the solution develops out of being held physically, something he had missed in the situation, while he allows himself to experience the fact that he had survived the greatest threat to his life. Now he can transfer this experience to his current crisis: 'I will survive this deep loneliness and this anxiety too, it will pass without me having to know how to tackle it'. This is a self-regulative process made possible by the deepening of the experience.

HEALING

This example shows how in a session, the old order, fear of loss and of dying, can be transformed into a new one in which the patient feels that he can live. This transformation is not produced from outside but is created through an external impulse in an auto-dynamic process. We can describe this with Plassmann (2005, p. 360) as an expression of a 'psychological healing system' that generates of its own accord phase transitions from dysfunctional to functional patterns of order, when we create suitable conditions for it in therapy. If we agree with Plassmann, then 'a bodily representation of emotions' has the strongest effect on inner reorganisation (Plassmann, 2005, p. 364). In my example, this was living through the deepest fear.

Plassmann advocates that psychotherapy again countenances the idea of healing. As defined by Hippocrates, the physician can treat but nature heals (Chapter 3: 'Forebearers'); this takes place in an autopoietic process through the self-regulatory capacity of living beings. This view corresponds to the midwife model of psychotherapy mentioned at the beginning of this chapter. In therapy, we do something for the patients, but they themselves give birth to the new. We disorganise dysfunctional patterns so that the new can develop from the inside (Geuter, 2019, pp. 342–55; Keleman, 1989a). Self-regulation happens when patterns of avoidance, which are beyond voluntary control, are replaced by patterns of approach (Chapter 12). As Plassmann puts it, he has always understood psychotherapy to be trying 'to get a feeling for when something is stalling and when it is healing' (2010, p. 47).

Self-regulation does not only mean providing patients skills, but also experiences. Part of this is letting them be as they are, so that they themselves can let themselves be; this helps them to grow. Linehan (1993) points out that there is a dialectic of doing and not-doing (cf. Geuter, 2000, pp. 115–6). Plassmann (2005) talks of an ambivalence between intervening and biding one's time. If we see self-regulation therapeutically only as a result of interactive regulation, then we emphasise the significance of what the therapist **does**. However it is also crucial that the therapist understands how **to just be there** and so encourage the patient's own auto-regulative skills.

The **emancipatory** idea of self-regulation that I mentioned before also implies that the subject can assert themselves in the face of the unreasonable demands of society and culture. With reference to Kuhl's PSI theory, Wehowsky (2004) differentiates between self-regulation as the 'democratic' variation of self-determination and 'authoritarian' self-**control**, which is usually socially desirable and is becoming increasingly fashionable in therapy too. When Ryan and Deci (2000) depict self-determination as the overriding goal of human needs, then the values of our time are implicit in such a theory. Self-regulation respects our inner voices, one of which is the voice of body awareness. In contrast to a line of thought that wants to control lower functions through higher ones, the approach of body psychotherapy is to stimulate self-regulation in such a way that contact to the body and to feelings enhances intra- and interpersonal intelligence (Marlock, 2009).

18

The contribution of body psychotherapy to integration

With this book I hope to have demonstrated four things:

- That a theoretical consideration of the body and of body experience can enrich psycho-therapeutic understanding and that including the body in clinical work can be helpful for all forms of psychotherapy.
- That a psychological theory of body psychotherapy is possible on the anthropological basis of a theory of the experiencing subject in interaction with the world and that it should be built on this theory.
- That such a theory should include but also transcend the experience-based knowledge and theoretical concepts which have developed in the existing schools.
- That in the chorus of psychotherapy approaches, experiential body psychotherapy is not only heard as a distinctive voice on the basis of its treatment techniques, but also has the power to raise that voice due to its theory .

I hope that after having read this book, you will have a good idea of how this voice sounds.

My attempt to sketch an outline of a general theory of body psychotherapy developed during a process in which I was rethinking therapeutic experiences, the theories which had grown out of them and scientific theories and research findings and trying to develop a synthesis of them all. I was not able to answer all the questions that came up. When, for example, someone speaks of body mind therapy, we should not fall into the trap of thinking that a clinical discipline can answer the question of how to understand the relationship between body and mind. What is more, humans are hypercomplex beings, and we can never conclusively answer the question of what constitutes an individual person, what motivates them, what makes them happy or what lets them suffer. Any answer that we do find brings up new questions. We can only end this by simplifying. If after having read this book you have some answers and many new questions, I would be quite satisfied.

In the introduction, I asked whether body psychotherapy should be absorbed into a 'general psychotherapy' or whether it should assert its autonomy. The breadth of theoretical understanding that I have described in this outline clearly shows that we cannot just integrate body psychotherapy theoretically with a wave of the hand into psychoanalysis or into behavioural therapy, even though there are attempts in both approaches to use its methods. Rather it can enter into a dialectical process of integration with its own clear understanding of psychotherapy, in which something new can develop out of the various psychotherapeutic modalities. Body psychotherapy brings to this integration a perspective that is generally

DOI: 10.4324/9781003176893-18

lacking in other approaches: our understanding of body experience as the foundation for self-experience, the bodily aspects of core processes of affective regulation, the anchoring of memory, the emotions and the schemas of experience and behaviour in the body, the developing of schemas in bodily interaction, the understanding of how human beings communicate implicitly from body to body and the appreciation of therapy as a resonant, embodied encounter. What distinguishes it from other approaches is its 'holistic perspective, oriented toward the systemic wholeness of subjective experience, in which the psychic dimension of human experience and the bodily dimension of lived experience are equally appreciated' (Marlock & Weiss, 2015, p. 11).

In the practice of psychotherapy, integration is a clinical necessity, since no sole treatment model is capable of being equally effective for all problems, disorders and illnesses or for every type of patient (Senf, 2001, p. 35). Most therapists therefore do not use just the one undiluted method (Babl et al., 2016). However, we have to think carefully about how and what we integrate (Soth, 2013). To combine methods in a way that makes sense, we need principles of treatment to orientate ourselves. I have tried to formulate such principles for body psychotherapy (Geuter, 2019).

Combining body psychotherapy with other approaches can only enrich it (Kern, 2019). In individual therapy, no therapist can manage only with body-oriented methods. They have to have learnt how to work verbally to clarify, actualise, resolve problems and express understanding. Without cognitive or relational psychotherapeutic methods such as have been developed in behavioural, psychodynamic, client-centred or systemic therapy, we cannot do appropriate clinical work (Aposhyan, 2004, p. 234). However, in therapy, body psychotherapy methods are one valuable option among others. When it fits, body psychotherapy can be a method custom-made for certain patients.

In their development, the schools of body psychotherapy, provided they have not gone completely their own way off the beaten track, have for a long time closely associated themselves with the traditions of depth psychology. This is true of both the Reichian and the perception-oriented schools. With Reich, body psychotherapy followed the drive model, while with Kurtz it adopted the cognitive turn of psychoanalysis and its concept of information, and today many body psychotherapists are affiliated to relational psychoanalysis (Soth, 2019). Some of them even regard this field as a treatment variation of psychoanalysis or depth psychology. Thus the question is, where can we locate body psychotherapy in the general field of psychotherapeutic orientations?

Since the 1960s, body psychotherapy has inherited much from psychodynamic and from humanistic psychotherapy and has continued to develop within this close connection to both orientations up to and including the present (cf. Soth, 2012, pp. 66–7). This was made possible not least through the fact that many psychoanalysts broke away from Freudian orthodoxy and inclined towards the humanistic approach. When Winnicott understood the true self as a person's potential, striving for development, this conformed with the idea of self-actualisation in humanistic psychotherapy. When Kohut emphasised the importance of self-esteem for the development of a healthy narcissism, this flowed into a similar idea of the therapeutic relationship represented by Rogers: to give the patient unconditional positive regard and so strengthen their self-esteem. When Stern focuses on the importance of the present moment, he introduces the concept of the here and now into psychoanalysis.

Body psychotherapy owes many insights to psychoanalysis, for instance the psychodynamics of psychological conflict or the significance of transference and interaction in therapy. However, in our experiential understanding, we are more at home in the paradigms of humanistic thinking and humanistic experiential psychotherapy, towards which a great many psychoanalysts and behavioural therapists are increasingly leaning.

According to Kriz's (2004; Chapter 2) model, the whole of psychotherapy is based on the four pillars of the cognitive-behavioural, psychodynamic, humanistic and systemic approaches. He sees body psychotherapy as a possible fifth pillar (Chapter 2: box on the basic orientations). Our own theoretical fundament, which today is based on the systems theory of life, enactivism and phenomenology, supports this view.

Several pillars can support one building. Greenberg (2011), the main proponent of Emotion-Focused Therapy, writes that he is more committed to an integrative approach than to therapies with labels. This is just how I feel. However, the one speciality has to be brought to full bloom before it can become an integrated part of a general psychotherapy.

The separation of both body psychotherapy and Gestalt therapy from psychoanalysis was accompanied by a change in discourse: from the Wilhelmine and Victorian principle of drive renunciation to a theory of the free expression of needs and the search for the self. Psychotherapy as a cultural practice is bound to prevailing values. This change corresponded to a shift in values at the time from those of duty and conforming, geared to control, to those of self-development, dedicated to freedom from coercion. In Reichian body psychotherapy in turn, the emphasis moved from achieving health by overturning sexual repression towards coming into emotional contact with oneself.

Today we can assume clinically that it promotes psychological health when a person can live in harmony with their needs. We recognise whether affect motor schemas are helpful by determining whether they are integrated into a person's life in such a way that they serve their needs and those of their fellow humans and whether at the same time they feel coherent to that person. In the sense of a basic humanistic approach, our goal is that of greater inner freedom, alertness and aliveness, so that the person can live their life well or better in their own life world.

This humanistic understanding is linked to the systems theory of life. According to this theory, living systems determine their organisation but are constantly interacting with their environment, and they develop their individuality for themselves in this interaction (Capra & Luisi, 2014, p. 309). In my view, body psychotherapy can and should base itself on this theory of life. Until now, when body psychotherapists used the concept of life, they almost always took a detour into biology, from where in my opinion nobody has ever returned with insights useful for a theory of treatment.

Treatment is always a matter of **experience** and of a **lived life**. The symptoms that patients bring with them are just a part of this. Therapy is an aid to making life more worth living, when through personal problems the value of someone's life has deteriorated to such an extent that they are suffering. We can only understand a symptom when we see it in the context of the lived life of the person suffering from it.

Body psychotherapy is a child of movements critical of culture and society, the attitudes of which to life and to being human flowed into psychotherapy. This brought with it an ethic of emancipation (Barratt, 2010, p. 128), according to which the antidote to alienation is 'listening to the voice of our embodied experience' (Barratt, 2010, p. 175). Part of this ethic is understanding psychotherapy not just as a way of eliminating symptoms, but as a way of helping people to live more in harmony both with themselves and with those fellow humans who are important to them. This is not a luxury beyond the scope of psychotherapy, as it also leads to less suffering and illness, for the art of life is what limits illness (Meyer-Abich, 2010, p. 273). Hippocrates knew this already and saw health as being founded on the life style or life art of the human being. Recovering one's health is of more value both to the individual and to society than just getting rid of symptoms.

The focus of humanistic psychotherapy has always been on bringing emotional material into consciousness, on becoming aware of repressed feelings and accepting them and on tolerating unwanted emotions (Greenberg, 2011). Greenberg talks of owning experiences previously denied. Early on, Laing (1967) criticised that neither psychoanalysis nor behavioural therapy have ever clarified the significance of experience and pointed out that experience is continually undermining theory. To do justice to patients, psychotherapeutic theory has to see human beings as subjects whom experience has shaped and who will only change through experience. This turn towards experience has been going on in the humanistic and body-oriented psychotherapies since the 1960s (Kurtz, 1990). By starting to work with the body, they found a way in which a person could best connect with their experience and become aware of themselves (Weiss, 2015). Through the body, the world of inner experience opens up in a way matched possibly only by inner images. The goal of therapy, however, is not these experiences per se, but the reorganisation of the way in which we make experiences (Kurtz, 1990). This transformation is closely linked to the bodily experience of self:

> until the client has awareness of the muscular sensations and the embodied experience of the self, they will not be able to change old patterns.
>
> (Levine & Macnaughton, 2004, p. 379)

The practice of body psychotherapy, to speak with Marlock, is 'a revitalisation of the self' in a process which 'helps to resolve the emotional immobility, numbness, and dysregulation' (2015, p. 159). Here he harks back to the conceptual tradition of Fritz Perls and Paul Goodman. Both body psychotherapy and Gestalt therapy are concerned not with the cognitive but with the living appropriation of experience by the living subject as a whole. A revitalisation of the self is not possible without revitalising the bodily sense of self. Therapeutic transformation takes place when within this process, someone discovers their hitherto unlived potential. Marlock states that body psychotherapy should lead 'to the embodied and subjectively felt reassimilation of split-off experiences, feelings, and parts of the personality that had to remain suppressed due to characterological compromises' (Marlock, 2015b, p. 93).

It is not easy to abandon our acquired affect motor patterns, which have become second nature to us. But we can succeed in dissolving the limitations imposed by such a life in the restricted confines of these patterns, thereby extending our options.

In their manifesto of humanistic psychotherapy, Bohart et al. (1998) write that psychotherapy is a process of discovery and of finding meaning, a process with an open end. Perls (1976, p. 27) already preferred the term discovering over the psychoanalytical one of uncovering, and in body psychotherapy today, Boadella (2019) and Geuter (2019, pp. 132–3) advocate it. Uncovering means to know what you are looking for. Those who discover engage in a search process in which they do not know beforehand what they will find; at best they can only guess. Psychotherapists often have to deal with vague, indeterminate, irritating phenomena that are not easy to classify (P Fuchs, 2011). This shows the limits of a scientific explanation of what happens in psychotherapy. What people discover is what they do not know, do not want to know or cannot or do not want to feel; or it is what they do not yet know and could have, or already have without knowing. Sometimes what they find is immediately experienced as a subjective certainty. However, such experiences can never be universally valid, but are so only in the here and now of a situation. Thus in practical psychotherapeutic work, we are not dealing with scientific truths, but with 'situational truths' (Husserl, 2012, p. 143).

My intent with this book was to link body psychotherapy with the findings of scientific research. Such findings can be helpful tools for our practical work as therapists, especially in recognising connections. However, no research can explain to us the meaning of a smile, a feeling in contact or the essence of something happening between therapist and patient. Thus it is difficult to articulate the essence of body psychotherapeutic work in scientific language (Stauffer, 2009, p. 144). Eberwein formulated it for the humanistic therapy approaches in general:

> To feel what we have never before dared to feel, to think and remember what we have never before dared to think or remember, to do what we have never before dared to do.
>
> (Eberwein, 2009, p. 184)

I would add: to sense, feel or think something which we could not previously do because we had no access or no capacity.

This essence is what makes body psychotherapy for me as a therapist so interesting, even sometimes exciting. It is forever surprising us with the diversity of life movement. When in a questionnaire I ask my patients what their important experiences in therapy were, they often name a significant moment or a key experience, and almost always this is an affect motor experience, usually in an interaction. And when I made contact with ex-patients for the purposes of this book – even more for the book about the practice of body psychotherapy – to get their permission to use vignettes from their therapy with me, this was also true. Next to the experience of a stable and helpful relationship, it seems that new embodied experiences were a central agent of change: 'what matters most is the direct experience of embodied mutuality' (Totton, 2019, p. 286).

In a survey of empirical psychotherapy research, Wampold (2001) writes that a psychotherapist works most successfully when they are convinced of their therapeutic approach. This connectedness is more helpful than just following the treatment guidelines of a specific method. Allegiance is more important than adherence. This is not only generally true but also on the personal level. In body psychotherapy, we encounter not only what we can express in words, but the whole wealth of expression of a living being and therein of the person themselves. This is enriching for both sides.

Bibliography[1]

Aalberse, M. (2001). Graceful means: Felt gestures and choreographic therapy. In Heller (Ed.) (pp. 101–132).

Aanstoos, C., Serlin, I., & Greening, T. (2000). History of division 32 (humanistic psychology) of the American Psychological Association. In D. Dewsbury (Ed.), *Unification Through Division: Histories of the Divisions of the American Psychological Association* (Vol. V). Washington, DC: American Psychological Association. https://doi .org/10.1037/10356-004.

Ackerman, J. M., Nocera, C. C., & Bargh, J. A. (2010). Incidental haptic sensations influence social judgements and decisions. *Science, 328,* 1712–1715.

Acolin, J. (2019). Towards a clinical theory of embodiment. A model for the conceptualization and treatment of mental illness. In Payne et al. (Eds.) (pp. 40–52).

Adams, F. (2010). Embodied cognition. *Phenomenology and the Cognitive Sciences, 9,* 619–628.

Adamson, L. B., & Frick, J. E. (2003). The still face: A history of a shared experimental paradigm. *Infancy, 4,* 451–473.

Adler, R. H., Herrmann, J. M., Koehle, K., Schonecke, O. W., von Uexkuell, Th., & Wesiack, W. (Eds.) (1996). *Psychosomatische Medizin [Psychosomatic Medicine]* (5th ed.). Munich: Urban & Schwarzenberg.

Adolph, D., Tschacher, W., Niemeyer, H., & Michalak, J. (2021). Gait patterns and mood in everyday life: A comparison between depressed patients and non-depressed controls. *Cognitive Therapy and Research.* https://doi.org/10.1007 /s10608-021-10215-7.

Aggarwal, A., Cutts, T. F., Abell, T. L., Cardoso, S., Familoni, B., Bremer, J., & Karas, J. (1994). Predominant symptoms in irritable bowel syndrome correlate with specific autonomic nervous system abnormalities. *Gastroenterology, 106,* 945–950.

Aho, J., & Aho, K. (2008). *Body Matters: A Phenomenology of Sickness, Disease, and Illness.* Lanham Lexington.

Ainsworth, M. D. S., Blehat, M. C., Walters, E., & Wall, S. (1978). *Patterns of Attachment. A Psychological Study of the Strange Situation.* Hillsdale: Erlbaum.

Albani, C., Blaser, G., Geyer, M., & Kaechele, H. (1999). Die „Control-Master" Theorie – Eine kognitiv orientierte psychoanalytische Behandlungstheorie von Joseph Weiss [The "Control-Mastery" theory - A cognitively oriented psychoanalytic treatment theory by Joseph Weiss]. *Forum der Psychoanalyse [Forum of Psychoanalysis], 15,* 224–236.

Alexander, F. (1950). *Psychosomatic Medicine. Its Principles and Applications.* New York: Norton.

Alibali, M. W., Bassok, M., Solomon, K. O., Syc, S. E., & Goldin-Meadow, S. (1999). Illuminating mental representations through speech and gesture. *Psychological Science, 10,* 327–333.

Allport, G. W. (1960). The open system in personality theory. *The Journal of Abnormal and Social Psychology, 61,* 301–310.

Altmeyer, M., & Thomae, H. (Ed.) (2006). *Die vernetzte Seele. Die intersubjektive Wende in der Psychoanalyse [The Networked Psyche. The Intersubjective Turn in Psychoanalysis].* Stuttgart: Klett-Cotta.

Ambadar, Z., Schooler, J. W., & Cohn, J. F. (2005). Deciphering the enigmatic face. The importance of facial dynamics in interpreting subtle facial expressions. *Psychological Science, 16,* 403–410.

Amen, D. (1998). *Change Your Brain, Change your Lilfe.* New York: Three Rivers Press.

Anagnostopoulou, L. (2015). Vertical grounding. The body in the world and the self in the body. In Marlock et al. (Eds.) (pp. 684–691).

---

1 If more than one article is listed in this bibliography from an anthology, reference is made to the respective anthology in the bibliography for the sake of brevity. If there are more than two editors, only the first is listed.

Anderson, F. S. (2008). *Bodies in Treatment. The Unspoken Dimension.* New York, London: Routledge.

Ansermet, F., & Magistretti, P. (2007). *Biology of Freedom. Neural Plasticity, Experience, and the Unconscious.* New York: Other Press.

Anzieu, D. (2016). *The Skin-Ego.* London: Routledge.

Aposhyan, S. (2004). *Body-Mind Psychotherapy. Principles, Techniques, and Practical Application.* New York: Norton.

Appel-Opper, J. (2008). Relational living body to living body communication. *The British Journal of Psychotherapy Integration, 5,* 49–56.

Appel-Opper, J. (2011). Relationale Körper-zu-Körper-Kommunikation in der Psychotherapie [Relational body-to-body-communication in psychotherapy]. *Psychoanalyse & Koerper [Psychoanalysis & Body], 10*(18), 65–71.

Appel-Opper, J. (2018). Relationale körperliche Prozesse in Psychotherapie und Supervision [Relational bodily processes in psychotherapy and supervision]. In Thielen et al. (Eds.) (pp. 313–323).

Arbeitskreis, O. P. D. (Ed.) (2007). *Operationalisierte psychodynamische Diagnostik OPD-2 [Operationalised Psychodynamic Diagnostic OPD-2]* (2nd ed.). Bern: Huber.

Arnim, A. von (1994). Funktionelle Entspannung [Functional relaxation]. *Fundamenta Psychiatrica, 8,* 196–203.

Arnim, A. von (1998). Funktionelle Entspannung als Therapie bei Autodestruktion [Functional relaxation as therapy for autodestruction]. In J. Wiesse & P. Joraschky (Eds.), *Psychoanalyse und Koerper [Psychoanalysis and the Body]* (pp. 27–51). Goettingen: Vandenhoeck & Ruprecht.

Arnim, A. von (2009). Spielregeln fürs Leben: FE und Selbstregulation [Rules for life: FE and self-regulation]. In Herholz et al. (Eds.) (pp. 23–27).

Arnim, A. von (2009a). Funktionelle Entspannung [Functional relaxation]. In Thielen (Ed.) (pp. 123–134).

Arnim, A. von (2017). Der weibliche Körper: Heimat oder Kriegsschauplatz [The female body - Home or theatre of war]. In Krueger-Kirn & Schroeter (Eds.) (pp. 105–129).

Arnim, A. von, & Joraschky, P. (2009). Körperbildskulpturtest bei Fibromyalgiepatienten [Body image sculpture test for fibromyalgia patients]. In Joraschky et al. (Eds.) (pp. 192–200).

Arnim, A. von, Joraschky P., & Lausberg, H. (2007). Körperbild-Diagnostik [Body image diagnostics]. In Geissler & Heisterkamp (Eds.) (pp. 165–196).

Arnim, A. von, Lahmann, C., & Johnen, R. (Eds.) (2022). *Subjektive Anatomie. Theorie und Praxis körperbezogener Psychotherapie [Subjective Anatomy. Theory and Practice of Body-Based Psychotherapy]* (3rd ed.). Stuttgart: Schattauer.

Arps-Aubert, E. von (2012). *Das Arbeitskonzept von Elsa Gindler (1885–1961) dargestellt im Rahmen der Gymnastik der Reformpädagogik [The Working Concept of Elsa Gindler (1885-1961) Presented in the Context of the Gymnastics of Reform Pedagogy].* Hamburg: Dr. Kovač.

Asendorpf, J. (2004). *Psychologie der Persönlichkeit [Psychology of Personality]* (3rd ed.). Berlin: Springer.

Asendorpf, J., & Wallbott, H. G. (1982). Contributions of the German "expression psychology" to nonverbal communication research. Part I: Theories and concepts. *Journal of Nonverbal Behavior, 6,* 135–147.

Assmann, S., Borkenhagen, A., & Arnim, A. von (2010). Körperbilddiagnostik [Body image diagnostics]. *Psychotherapeutenjournal [Psychotherapists Journal], 9,* 261–270.

ASPS (2018). *ASPS National Clearinghouse of Plastic Surgery. Procedural Statistics: 2018 Plastic Surgery Statistics Report.* https://plasticsurgery.org. Retrieved December 29, 2021.

Atkinson, A. P., Dittrich, W. H., Gemmell, A. J., & Young, A. W. (2004). Emotion perception from dynamic and static body expressions in point-light and full-light displays. *Perception, 33,* 717–746.

Atzil-Slonim, D., & Tschacher, W. (2020). Dynamic dyadic processes in psychotherapy: Introduction to a special section. *Psychotherapy Research, 30,* 555–557.

Auszra, L., Herrmann, I. R., & Greenberg, L. S. (2017). *Emotionsfokussierte Therapie. Ein Praxismanual [Emotion-Focused Therapy. A Practice Manual].* Goettingen: Hogrefe.

Aviezer, H., Trope, Y., & Todorov, A. (2012). Body cues, not facial expressions, discriminate between intense positive and negative emotions. *Science, 338,* 1225–1229.

Babl, A. Grosse Holtforth, M., Heer, S., Lin, M., Staehli, A., Holstein, D., Belz, M., Egenolf, Y., Frischknecht, E., Ramseyer, F., Regli, D., Schmied, E., Flueckiger, C., Brodbeck, J., Berger, T., & Caspar, F. (2016). Psychotherapy integration under scrutiny: Investigating the impact of integrating emotion-focused components into a CBT-based approach: A study protocol of a randomized controlled trial. *BMC Psychiatry, 16,* 423. https://doi.org/10.1186/s12888-016-1136-7.

Bachmann, J., Zabicki, A., Munzert, J., & Krueger, B. (2020). Emotional expressivity of the observer mediates recognition of affective states from human body movements. *Cognition and Emotion, 34*(7), 1370–1381.

Bachorowski, J., & Owren, M. J. (2003). Sounds of emotion. Production and perception of affect-related vocal acoustics. *Annals of the New York Academy of Sciences, 1000,* 244–265.

Badenoch, B. (2008). *Being a Brain-Wise Therapist.* New York: Norton.

Bader, J.-P., Buehler, J., Endrass, J., Klipstein, A., & Hell, D. (1999). Muskelkraft und Gangcharakteristika depressiver Menschen [Muscle strength and gait characteristics of depressed people]. *Nervenarzt [Neurologist], 70,* 613–619.

Baker, E. (1967). *Man in the Trap.* New York: MacMillan.

Balint, M. (1984). *The Basic Fault. Therapeutic Aspects of Regression*. London: Routledge.

Bandura, A. (1997). *Self Efficacy: The Exercise of Control*. New York: W. H. Freeman.

Baenninger-Huber, E., & Widmer, C. (1997). Affektive Beziehungsmuster [Affective relational patterns]. *Psychotherapeut [Psychotherapist]*, *42*, 356–361.

Baenninger-Huber, E., Juen, B., & Peham, D. (2004). Die Rolle des Lächelns in der Psychotherapie [The function of smiling in psychotherapy]. In Hermer & Klinzing (Eds.) (pp. 157–176).

Banse, R., & Scherer, K. R. (1996). Acoustic profiles in vocal emotion expression. *Journal of Personality and Social Psychology*, *3*, 614–636.

Bargh, J. A., & Shalev, I. (2012). The substitutability of physical and social warmth in daily life. *Emotion*, *12*, 154–162.

Barlow, J. (2001 September). Contemporary somatic psychotherapy: Towards an integrated theory of 'body' psychotherapy [conference lecture]. 8th European Conference on Body Psychotherapy, Egmond Aan Zee, Netherlands.

Barnard, K. E., & Brazelton, T. B. (Eds.) (1990). *Touch: The Foundation of Experience*. Madison: International Universities Press.

Barnow, S. (2012). Emotionsregulation und Psychopathologie [Emotion regulation and psychopathology]. *Psychologische Rundschau [Psychological Review]* *63*, 111–124.

Barratt, B. B. (2010). *The Emergence of Somatic Psychology and Bodymind Therapy*. Houndmills: Palgrave Macmillan.

Barsaglini, A., Sartori, G., Benetti, S., Pettersson-Yeo, W., & Mechelli, A. (2014). The effects of psychotherapy on brain function: A systematic and critical review. *Progress in Neurobiology*, *114*, 1–14.

Barsalou, L. W., Niedenthal, P. M., Barbey, A. K., & Ruppert, J. A. (2003). Social embodiment. In B. H. Ross (Ed.), *The Psychology of Learning and Motivation* (pp. 43–92). Amsterdam: Academic Press.

Barsalou, L. W., Simmons, W. K., Barbey, A., & Wilson, C. D. (2003a). Grounding conceptual knowledge in modality-specific systems. *Trends in Cognitive Sciences*, *7*, 84–91.

Barthelmaes, M., Kesberg, R., Hermann, A., & Keller, J. (2022). Five reasons to cry—FRC: A taxonomy for common antecedents of emotional crying. *Motivation and Emotion*, *46*, 404–427.

Bartholomew, U., & Herholz, I. (2019). Functional relaxation in psychosomatic medicine. In Payne et al. (Eds.) (pp. 266–272).

Bassall, N., & Heller, M. C. (2015). The Norwegian tradition of body psychotherapy: A golden age in Oslo. In Marlock et al. (Eds.) (pp. 62–70).

Bastiaansen, J. A., Thioux, M., & Keysers, C. (2009). Evidence for mirror systems in emotions. *Philosophical Transactions of the Royal Society B: Biological Sciences*, *364*, 2391–2404.

Bateson, G. (2002). *Mind and Nature. A Necessary Unity*. New York: Hampton Press.

Bauer, S. (2010). Die Bedeutung von Stimme und Stimmklang im psychotherapeutischen Prozess aus der Sicht der Patienten und Patientinnen [The importance of voice and voice tone in the psychotherapeutic process from the patients' perspective]. *Psychoanalyse & Koerper [Psychoanalysis & Body]*, *9*(17), 27–50.

Baumann, Z. (2000). *Liquid Modernity*. Cambridge, UK: Polity Press.

Baxa, G.-L., Essen, C., & Kreszmeier, A. H. (Eds.) (2002). *Verkörperungen. Systemische Aufstellungen, Körperarbeit und Ritual [Embodiments. Systemic Constellations, Bodywork and Ritual]*. Heidelberg: Auer.

Bechara, A., & Naqvi, N. (2004). Listening to your heart: Interoceptive awareness as a gateway to feeling. *Nature Neuroscience*, *7*, 102–103.

Bechara, A., Damasio, H., Tranel, D., & Damasio, A. R. (2005). The Iowa Gambling Task and the somatic marker hypothesis: Some questions and answers. *Trends in Cognitive Sciences*, *9*, 159–162.

Becker, H. (1989). *Konzentrative Bewegungstherapie. Integrationsversuch von Körperlichkeit und Handeln in den psychoanalytischen Prozess [Concentrative Movement Therapy. An Attempt to Integrate Corporeality and Action into the Psychoanalytic Process]*. Stuttgart: Thieme.

Becker, H. (2010). Konzentrative Bewegungstherapie [Concentrative movement therapy]. In Mueller-Braunschweig & Stiller (Eds.) (pp. 127–136).

Beckermann, A. (1996). Eigenschafts-Physikalismus [Property physicalism]. *Zeitschrift für philosophische Forschung [Journal for Philosophical Research]*, *50*, 3–25.

Beckmann, N., Baumann, P., Herpertz, S., Trojan, J., & Diers, M. (2020). How the unconscious mind controls body movements: Body schema distortion in Anorexia nervosa. *International Journal of Eating Disorders*, *54*. https://doi.org/10.1002/eat.23451.

Bédécarrats, A., Chen, S., Pearce, K., Cai, D., & Glanzman, D. L. (2018). RNA from trained aplysia can induce an epigenetic engram for long-term sensitization in untrained aplysia. *eNeuro*, May–June; *5*(3). https://doi.org/10.1523/ENEURO.0038-18.2018.

Beebe, B. (2000). Coconstructing mother-infant distress: The microsynchrony of maternal impingement and infant avoidance in the face-to-face-encounter. *Psychoanalytic Inquiry*, *20*, 421–440.

Beebe, B. (2004). Faces in relation. A case study. *Psychoanalytic Dialogues*, *14*(1), 1–51.

Beebe, B., & Lachmann, F. M. (1994). Representation and Internalization in Infancy: Three Principles of Salience. *Psychoanalytic Psychology*, *11*, 127–165.

Beebe, B., & Lachmann, F. M. (2002). *Infant Research and Adult Treatment*. Hillsdale, NJ: The Analytic Press.

Beebe, B., & Lachmann, F. (2003). The relational turn in psychoanalysis. A dyadic systems view from infant research. *Contemporary Psychoanalysis, 39,* 379–409.

Behnke, E. (1997). Ghost gestures: Phenomenological investigations of bodily micromovements and their intercorporeal implications. *Human Studies, 20,* 181–201.

Bender, S. (2007). *Die psychophysische Bedeutung der Bewegung. Ein Handbuch der Laban Bewegungsanalyse und des Kestenberg Movement Profiles [The Psychophysical Meaning of Movement. A Handbook of Laban Movement Analysis and the Kestenberg Movement Profile]*. Berlin: Logos.

Bender, S. (2020). *Grundlagen der Tanztherapie. Geschichte, Menschenbild, Methoden [Foundations of Dance Therapy. History, Image of Man, Methods]*. Giessen: Psychosozial.

Benecke, C., & Dammann, G. (2004). Nonverbales Verhalten von Patientinnen mit Borderline-Persönlichkeitsstörung [Nonverbal behaviour of patients with borderline personality disorder]. In Hermer & Klinzing (Eds.) (pp. 261–272).

Benecke, C., & Krause, R. (2004). Nonverbale Kommunikation in der Psychotherapie von Angststörungen [Nonverbal communication in psychotherapy with anxiety disorders]. In Hermer & Klinzing (Eds.) (pp. 249–260).

Benecke, C., & Krause, R. (2005). Initiales mimisch-affektives Verhalten und Behandlungszufriedenheit in der Psychotherapie von Patientinnen mit Panikstörungen [Initial mimic-affective behaviour and treatment satisfaction in the psychotherapy of female patients with panic disorders]. *Zeitschrift für Psychosomatische Medizin und Psychotherapie [Journal for Psychosomatic Medicine and Psychotherapy], 51,* 346–359.

Bentzen, M. (2015). Shapes of experience. Neuroscience, developmental psychology, and somatic character. In Marlock et al. (Eds.) (pp. 277–300).

Bentzen, M., Jarlnaes, E., & Levine, P. (2004). The body self in psychotherapy: A psychomotoric approach to developmental psychology. In Macnaughton (Ed.) (pp. 51–70).

Berbalk, H. H., & Young, J. E. (2009). Schematherapie [Schema therapy]. In Margraf & Schneider (Eds.) (pp. 645–667).

Berceli, D. (2005). *Trauma Releasing Exercises (TRE). A Revolutinary New Method for Stress/Trauma Recovery*. Charleston, SC: BookSurge Publishing.

Bercik, P., Denou, E., Collins, J., Jackson, W., Lu, J., Jury, J., Deng, Y., Blennerhassett, P., Macri, J., McCoy, K. D., Verdu, E. F., & Collins, S. M. (2011). The intestinal microbiota affect central levels of brain-derived neurotropic factor and behavior in mice. *Gastroentorology, 141,* 599–609.

Berger, S. M., & Hadley, S. W. (1975). Some effects of a model's performance on an observer's electromyographic activity. *American Journal of Psychology, 88,* 263–276.

Bergson, H. (1911). *Matter and Memory*. London: George Allen and Unwin.

Bergson, H. (1946). *The Creative Mind. An Introduction into Metaphysics*. New York: The Philosophical Library.

Bergson, H. (1950). *Time and Free Will. An Essay on the Immediate Data of Consciousness* (6th impr.). London: George Allen & Unwin.

Berking, M. (2017). *Training emotionaler Kompetenzen [Emotional Skills Training]* (4th ed.). Berlin: Springer.

Bermpohl, F. (2009). Funktion und Dysfunktion phänomenalen Erlebens [Function and dysfunction of phenomenal experience]. In Jung & Heilinger (Eds.) (pp. 365–384).

Bermúdez, J. L. (2014). Bodily awareness and self-consciousness. In Gallagher (Ed.) (pp. 157–179).

Bermúdez, J. L., Marcel, A., & Eilan, N. (Eds.) (1998). *The Body and the Self*. Cambridge: MIT Press.

Bernardy, K., Kirsch, A., & Beneke, C. (2004). Mimisch-affektives Verhalten von Fibromyalgie-Patientinnen im Tiefenpsychologischen Interview: Erste Ergebnisse [Mimic-affective behaviour of fibromyalgia patients in the depth psychological interview: First results]. In R. Sandweg (Ed.), *Chronischer Schmerz und Zivilisation. Organstörungen, psychische Prozesse und gesellschaftliche Bedingtheiten [Chronic Pain and Civilisation. Organ Disorders, Psychological Processes and Social Conditions]* (pp. 33–48). Goettingen: Vandenhoeck & Ruprecht.

Berne, E. (1964). *Games People Play: The Basic Handbook of Transactional Analyses*. New York: Ballantine Books.

Bernhardt, P. (2004). Individuation, mutual connection, and the body's resources: An interview with Lisbeth Marcher. In Macnaughton (Ed.) (pp. 93–106).

Bernhardt, P. (2004a). The art of following structure: Exploring the roots of the Bodynamic system: An interview with Lisbeth Marcher. In Macnaughton (Ed.) (pp. 107–130).

Bernhardt, P., Bentzen, M., & Isaacs, J. (2004). Waking the body ego, Part 1: Core concepts and principles. In Macnaughton (Ed.) (pp. 131–160).

Bernhardt, P., Bentzen, M., & Isaacs, J. (2004a). Waking the body ego, Part 2: Psychomotor development and character structure. In Macnaughton (Ed.) (pp. 161–204).

Berntson, G. G., Sarter, M., & Cacioppo, J. T. (2003). Ascending visceral regulation of cortical affective information processing. *European Journal of Neuroscience, 18,* 2103–2109.

Bertalanffy, L. v. (1950). The theory of open systems in physics and biology. *Science, 111,* 23–29.

Bette, K.-H. (1989). *Körperspuren. Zur Semantik und Paradoxie moderner Körperlichkeit [Body Traces. On the Semantics and Paradox of Modern Corporeality]*. Berlin: de Gruyter.

Bettighofer, S. (2016). *Übertragung und Gegenübertragung im therapeutischen Prozess [Transference and Countertransference in the Therapeutic Process]* (5th ed.). Stuttgart: Kohlhammer.

Beutel, M. E. (2002). Neurowissenschaften und Psychotherapie. Neuere Entwicklungen, Methoden und Ergebnisse [Neuroscience and psychotherapy. Recent developments, methods and results]. *Psychotherapeut [Psychotherapist]*, *47*, 1–10.

Beutel, M. E. (2009). Vom Nutzen der bisherigen neurobiologischen Forschung für die Praxis der Psychotherapie [On the benefits of existing neurobiological research for the practice of psychotherapy]. *Psychotherapeutenjournal [Psychotherapists Journal]*, *8*, 384–392.

Bhat, D., & Carleton, J. (2015). The role of the autonomic nerve system. In Marlock et al. (Eds.) (pp. 615–632).

Binder, E. (2020). Stress und Epigenetik [Stress and epigenetics]. In Egle et al. (Eds.) (pp. 139–146).

Bischkopf, J. (2009). Emotionen in der Psychotherapie – Ergebnisse empirischer Psychotherapieforschung und ihre Umsetzung in der Emotionsfokussierten Therapie [Emotions in psychotherapy - Results of empirical psychotherapy research and their implementation in emotion-focused therapy]. In R. Esterbauer & S. Rinofner-Kreidl (Eds.), *Emotionen im Spannungsfeld von Phänomenologie und Wissenschaften [Emotions in the Conflicting Fields of Phenomenology and the Sciences]* (pp. 95–110). Frankfurt: Peter Lang.

Bishop, P. (2019). *Ludwig Klages and the Philosophy of Life. A Vitalist Toolkit*. London: Routledge.

Bizzari, V. (2018). A phenomenological approach to psychopathologies: An embodied proposal. *Intercultural Philosophy Journal*, *1*, 132–156.

Blanke, O., & Metzinger, T. (2009). Full-body illusions and minimal phenomenal selfhood. *Trends in Cognitive Sciences*, *13*, 7–13 (also in Fuchs et al., 2010, S. 21–35).

Bloch, E. (1979). *Erbschaft dieser Zeit [Inheritance of this Time]*. Frankfurt: Suhrkamp.

Bloch, S., Lemeignan, M., & Aguilera, N. (1991). Specific respiratory patterns distinguish among human basic emotions. *International Journal of Psychophysiology*, *11*, 141–154.

Blohm, F. (2015). Tagträume, konkrete Utopien und das "Prinzip Hoffnung". Ernst Blochs vergessener Beitrag zur Psychoanalyse [Daydreams, concrete utopias and the "principle of hope". Ernst Bloch's forgotten contribution to psychoanalysis]. *Psychosozial [Psychosocial]*, *38*(4) (No. 142), 85–99.

Blomeyer, R. (1981). Die Wiederentdeckung des Leibes und die Psychotherapie [The rediscovery of the body and psychotherapy]. In P.-M. Pflueger (Ed.), *Die Wiederentdeckung des Leibes [The Rediscovery of the Body]* (pp. 9–22). Fellbach: Bonz.

Bloom, K. (2006). *The Embodied Self. Movement and Psychoanalysis*. London: Karnac.

Blumenthal, J. A., Babyak, M. A., Doraiswamy, P. M., Watkins, L., Hoffman, B. M., Barbour, K. A., Herman, S., Craighead, W. E., Brosse, A. L., Waugh, R., Hinderliter, A., & Sherwood, A. (2007). Exercise and pharmacotherapy in the treatment of Major Depressive Disorder. *Psychosomatic Medicine*, *69*, 587–596.

Blunk, R. (2006). Neuropsychologie für Psychotherapeutinnen [Neuropsychology for psychotherapists]. In Schmidt (Ed.) (pp. 41–52).

Boadella, D. (1973). *Wilhelm Reich. The Evolution of His Work*. London: Vision Press.

Boadella, D. (1977). Maps of character. Part I. Energy and character. *The Journal of Bioenergetic Research*, *8*(2), 39–51.

Boadella, D. (1978). Maps of character. Part II. Energy and character. *The Journal of Bioenergetic Research*, *9*(2), 19–34.

Boadella, D. (1987). *Lifestreams. An Introduction to Biosynthesis*. London: Routledge & Kegan Paul.

Boadella, D. (1994). Styles of breathing in Reichian therapy. In B. H. Timmons & R. Ley (Eds.), *Behavioral and Psychological Approaches to Breathing Disorders* (pp. 233–242). Boston: Springer.

Boadella, D. (1995). Emotionen in der Körperpsychotherapie [Emotions in Body Psychotherapy]. In H. Petzold (Ed.), *Die Wiederentdeckung des Gefühls. Emotionen in der Psychotherapie und die menschliche Entwicklung [The Rediscovery of Feelings. Emotions in Psychotherapy and the Human Development]* (pp. 519–547). Paderborn: Junfermann.

Boadella, D. (1996). Emotionen in der Körperpsychotherapie [Emotions in body psychotherapy]. *Energie & Charakter [Energy & Character]*, *27*(13), 2–25.

Boadella, D. (1996a). Stress und Charakterstruktur [Stress and character structure]. In D. Hoffmann-Axthelm (Ed.), *Der Körper in der Psychotherapie [The Body in Psychotherapy]* (pp. 36–89). Basel: Schwabe.

Boadella, D. (1998). Embryologie und Therapie [Embryology and therapy]. *International Journal of Prenatal and Perinatal Psychology and Medicine*, *10*, 65–88.

Boadella, D. (2000). Shape flow and postures of the soul: The biosynthesis concept of the motoric fields. *Energy & Character*, *30*/2, 7–17.

Boadella, D. (2000a). Polarity and character. *Energy & Character*, *31*/2, 7–16.

Boadella, D. (2002). Die Erweckung der Sensibilität und die Wiederentdeckung der Motilität. Psycho-physikalische Synthese als Grundlage der Körperpsychotherapie: Das 100-jährige Vermächtnis von Pierre Janet (1859–1947) [The awakening of sensibility and the rediscovery of motility. Psycho-physical synthesis as the basis of body psychotherapy: The 100-year legacy of Pierre Janet (1859-1947)]. *Psychotherapie Forum [Psychotherapy Forum]*, *10*, 13–21.

Boadella, D. (2019). Four forms of knowledge in biosynthesis therapy. In Payne et al. (Eds.) (pp. 291–297).

Bocian, B. (2007). *Fritz Perls in Berlin 1893–1933*. Wuppertal: Peter Hammer.

Bock, J., Helmeke, C., Ovtscharoff, W., Gruss, M., & Braun, K. (2003). Frühkindliche emotionale Erfahrungen beeinflussen die funktionelle Entwicklung des Gehirns [Early emotional experiences influence the functional development of the brain]. *Neuroforum*, *9*(2), 15–20.

Bockrath, F., Boschert, B., & Franke, E. (Ed.) (2008). *Körperliche Erkenntnis. Formen reflexiver Erfahrung [Bodily Cognition. Forms of Reflexive Experience]*. Bielefeld: Transcript.

Boden, M. A. (1999). Is metabolism necessary? *British Journal for the Philosophy of Science, 50,* 231–248.

Boeckh, A. (2019). *Die dialogische Struktur des Selbst. Perspektiven einer relationalen und emotionsorientierten Gestalttherapie [The Dialogical Structure of the Self. Perspectives of a Relational and Emotion-Oriented Gestalt Therapy]*. Giessen: Psychosozial.

Boehme, G. (2003). *Leibsein als Aufgabe. Leibphilosophie in pragmatischer Hinsicht [Being a Body as a Task. Body Philosophy in Pragmatic Terms]*. Kusterdingen: Die graue Edition.

Boehme, G. (2020). *Leib. Die Natur, die wir selbst sind [Body. The Nature We Ourselves Are]*. Frankfurt: Suhrkamp.

Bohart, A. C. (1993). Experiencing: The basis of psychotherapy. *Journal of Psychotherapy Integration, 3,* 51–67.

Bohart, A. C., O'Hara, M., & Leitner, L. M. (1998). Empirically violated treatments: Disenfranchisement of Humanistic and other psychotherapies. *Psychotherapy Research, 8,* 141–157.

Bohne, M. (2008). *Einführung in die Praxis der Energetischen Psychotherapie [Introduction to the Practice of Energetic Psychotherapy]*. Heidelberg: Carl Auer.

Bohne, M. (2012). Bitte klopfen! [Please tap!]. *Kommunikation & Seminar [Communication & Seminar], 3,* 20–23.

Bohne, M. (2019). Vom energetischen Paradigma zur Prozess- und Embodimentfokussierten Psychologie (PEP) [From the energy paradigm to process and embodiment focused psychology]. In M. Bohne (Ed.), *Klopfen mit PEP. Prozess- und Embodimentfokussierte Psychologie in Therapie und Coaching [Tapping with PEP: Process and embodiment focused psychology in therapy and coaching]* (pp. 25–131). Heidelberg: Carl Auer.

Bohne, M., Ohler, M., Schmidt, G., & Trenkle, B. (Eds.) (2016). *Reden reicht nicht!? Bifokal-multisensorische Interventionsstrategien für Therapie und Beratung [Talking is not Enough!? Bifocal-Multisensory Intervention Strategies for Therapy and Counselling]*. Heidelberg: Carl Auer.

Bolis, D., & Schilbach, L. (2018) Observing and participating in social interactions: Action perception and action control across the autistic spectrum. *Developmental Cognitive Neuroscience, 29,* 168–175.

Bolis, D., & Schilbach, L. (2018a). 'I interact therefore I am': The self as a historical product of dialectical attunement. *Topoi, 39,* 521–534.

Bolis, D., Balsters, J., Wenderoth, N., Becchio, C., & Schilbach, L. (2017). Beyond autism: Introducing the dialectical misattunement hypothesis and a Bayesian account of intersubjectivity. *Psychopathology, 50,* 355–372.

Bolm, T. (2015). *Mentalisierungsbasierte Therapie [Mentalisation Based Therapy]*. Munich: Reinhardt.

Bongard, J., Zykov, V., & Lipson, H. (2006). Resilient machines through continuous self-modeling. *Science, 314,* 1118–1121.

Boone, R. T., & Cunningham, J. G. (2001). Children's expression of emotional meaning in music through expressive body movement. *Journal of Nonverbal Behavior, 25,* 21–41.

Booth, A., Trimble, T., & Egan, J. (2010). Body-centred counter-transference in a sample of Irish clinical psychologists. *The Irish Psychologist, 36*(12), 284–289.

Boritz, T. Z., Angus, L., Monette, G., Hollis-Walker, L., & Warwar, S. (2011). Narrative and emotion integration in psychotherapy: Investigating the relationship between autobiographical memory specificity and expressed emotional arousal in brief emotion-focused and client-centred treatments of depression. *Psychotherapy Research, 21,* 16–26.

Borkenhagen, A. (2011). Die Inszenierung des Selbst mit dem Skalpell [The staging of the self with the scalpel]. In M. R. Mueller, H.-G. Soeffner & A. Sonnenmoser (Eds.), *Körper Haben. Die symbolische Formung der Person [To Have a Body. The Symbolic Shaping of the Person]* (pp. 60–69). Weilerswist: Velbrueck Wissenschaft.

Bornemann, B., & Singer, T. (2017). Taking time to feel your body: Steady increases in heartbeat perception accuracy and decreases in alexithymia over 9 months of contemplative training. *Psychophysiology, 54,* 469–482.

Botvinick, M., & Cohen, J. D. (1998). Rubber hand 'feels' what eyes see. *Nature, 391,* 756.

Boulanger, J. L., Hayes, S. C., & Pistorello, J. (2010). Experiential avoidance as a functional contextual concept. In A. M. Kring & D. M. Sloan (Eds.), *Emotional Regulation and Psychopathology* (pp. 107–136). New York: Guilford.

Bourdieu, P. (1984). *Distinction. A Social Critique of the Judgement of Taste*. Cambridge, MA: Harvard University Press.

Boyesen, G. (1982). A personalidade primária [The primary personality]. *Cadernos de Psicologia Biodinâmica [Notebooks of Biodynamic Psychology], 3,* 7–12.

Boyesen, G. (1987). *Über den Körper die Seele heilen. Biodynamische Psychologie und Psychotherapie. Eine Einführung [Healing the Soul Through the Body. Biodynamic Psychology and Psychotherapy. An Introduction]*. Munich: Koesel.

Boyesen, G., & Boyesen, M.-L. (1980). The biodynamic theory of neurosis. *Journal of Biodynamic Psychology, 1*(1), 56–71.

Boyesen, G., & Boyesen, M. L. (1987). *Biodynamik des Lebens. Die Gerda-Boyesen-Methode [Biodynamics of Life. The Gerda-Boyesen-Method]*. Essen: Synthesis.

Boyesen, G., Leudesdorff, C., & Santner, C. (1995). *Von der Lust am Heilen. Quintessenz meines Lebens [The Desire to Heal. Quintessence of my Life]*. Munich: Koesel.

Bradley, M., Cuthbert, B. N., & Lang, P. J. (1993). Pictures as prepulse: Attention and emotion in startle modification. *Psychophysiology, 30*, 541–545.

Braehler, E. (Ed.) (1995). *Körpererleben. Ein subjektiver Ausdruck von Leib und Seele. Beiträge zur psychosomatischen Medizin [Body Experience. A Subjective Expression of Body and Mind. Contributions to Psychosomatic Medicine]*. (2nd ed.). Giessen: Psychosozial.

Braehler, E. (1995a). Körpererleben – Ein vernachlässigter Aspekt der Medizin [Body experience – A neglected aspect of medicine]. In Braehler (Ed.) (pp. 3–18).

Braten, S. (1988). Dialogic mind: The infant and the adult in protoconversation. In M. Carvallo (Ed.), *Nature, Cognition and System* (pp. 187–205). Dordrecht: Kluwer.

Braun, M. G. (2015). *Der Einsatz von Körperpsychotherapie an deutschen Kliniken für Psychosomatik: Eine repräsentative Querschnitterhebung [The Use of Body Psychotherapy in German Psychosomatic Clinics: A Representative Cross-Sectional Survey]*. Regensburg: Hochschulschrift der Universitaet Regensburg (Dissertation) [University publication of the University of Regensburg]. https://doi.org/10.5283/epub.31980.

Bravo, J. A., Forsythe, P., Chew, M. V., Escaravage, E., Savignac, H. M., Dinan, T. G., Bienenstock, J., & Cryan, J. F. (2011). Ingestion of Lactobacillus strain regulates emotional behavior and central GABA receptor expression in a mouse via the vagus nerve. *Proceedings of the National Academy of Sciences, 108*, 16050–16055.

Bremner, G., & Slater, A. (Eds.) (2003). *Theories of Infant Development*. Malden: Blackwell.

Brensing, K. (2013). *Persönlichkeitsrechte für Tiere. Die nächste Stufe der moralischen Evolution [Personality Rights for Animals. The Next Stage of Moral Evolution]*. Freiburg: Herder.

Breuer, J., & Freud, S. (1895). *Studien über Hysterie*. Leipzig: Deuticke [engl.: Studies on Hysteria. New York: Basic Books, 2006].

Breyer, T., & Gerner, A. (2017). Resonanz und Interaktion: Eine philosophische Annäherung anhand zweier Proben [Resonance and interaction: A philosophical approach based on two examples]. In Breyer et al. (Eds.) (pp. 33–46).

Breyer, T., Buchholz, M. B., Hamburger, A., Pfaender, S., & Schumann, E. (Eds.) (2017). *Resonanz Rhythmus Synchronisierung. Interaktionen in Alltag, Therapie und Kunst [Resonance Rhythm Synchronisation. Interactions in Everyday Life, Therapy and Arts]*. Bielefeld: Transcript.

Briñol, P., Petty, R. E., & Wagner, B. (2009). Body posture effects on self-evaluation: A self-validation approach. *European Journal of Social Psychology, 39*, 1053–1064.

Broeckling, U. (2015). *The Entrepreneurial Self: Fabricating a New Type of Subject*. Los Angeles: Sage Publications.

Brooks, C. V. W. (1986). *Sensory Awareness. The Rediscovery of Experiencing through Workshops with Charlotte Selver*. Great Neck: Felix Morrow.

Brosch, T., & Scherer, K. R. (2009). Das Komponenten-Prozess-Modell: Ein integratives Emotionsmodell [The component process model: An integrative emotion model]. In V. Brandstaetter & J. H. Otto (Eds.), *Handbuch der Allgemeinen Psychologie: Motivation und Emotion [Handbook of General Psychology: Motivation and Emotion]* (pp. 446–456). Goettingen: Hogrefe.

Broschmann, D., & Fuchs, T. (2020). Zwischenleiblichkeit in der psychodynamischen Psychotherapie. Ansatz zu einem verkörperten Verständnis von Intersubjektivität [Intercorporeality in psychodynamic psychotherapy. Approach to an embodied understanding of intersubjectivity]. *Forum der Psychoanalyse [Forum of Psychoanalysis], 36*, 459–475.

Brown, M. (1990). *The Healing Touch: Introduction to Organismic Psychotherapy*. Mendocino: LifeRhythm.

Bucci, W. (2001). Pathways of emotional communication. *Psychoanalytic Inquiry, 21*, 40–70.

Bucci, W. (2011). The interplay of subsymbolic and symbolic processes: It takes two to tango – But who knows the steps, Who's the leader? The choreography of the psychoanalytic interchange. *Psychoanalytic Dialogues, 21*, 45–54.

Buchheim, P., Cierpka, M., & Seifert, T. (Eds.) (1992). *Liebe und Psychotherapie: Der Körper in der Psychotherapie: Weiterbildungsforschung [Love and Psychotherapy: The Body in Psychotherapy: Advanced Training Research]*. Berlin: Springer.

Buchheim, A., Viviani, R., Kessler, H., Kaechele, H., Cierpka, M., Roth, G., George, C., Kernberg, O. F., Bruns, G., & Taubner, S. (2012). Neuronale Veränderungen bei chronisch depressiven Patienten während psychoanalytischer Psychotherapie [Neuronal changes in chronically depressed patients during psychoanalytic psychotherapy]. *Psychotherapeut [Psychotherapist], 57*, 219–226.

Buehler, C. (1974). Vorwort [Preface]. In Petzold (Ed.) (pp. 8–9).

Buehler, C. (1979). Humanistic psychology as a personal experience. *Journal of Humanistic Psychology, 19*, 5–22.

Buehler, C., & Allen, M. (1972). *Introduction to Humanistic Psychology*. Monterey: Brooks/Cole Publishing.

Buehler, K. (1934). *Sprachtheorie. Die Darstellungsform der Sprache [Theory of language: The presentation form of the language]*. Jena: Fischer.

Buentig, W. (1992). Die Entfaltung der Beziehung in der Körperpsychotherapie [The unfolding of relationship in body psychotherapy]. In P. Buchheim et al. (Eds.) (pp. 172–188).

Buentig, W. E. (2015). The work of Wilhelm Reich. Part 1: Reich, Freud and character. In Marlock et al. (Eds.) (pp. 47–61).

Buergy, M. (2019). Phenomenology of obsessive-compulsive disorder: A methodologically structured overview. *Psychopathology, 52*, 174–183.

Bugental, J. F. T. (1964). The third force in psychology. *Journal of Humanistic Psychology, 4*, 19–26.

Bulnes, L. C., Mariën, P., Vandekerckhove, M., & Cleeremans, A. (2019). The effects of Botulinum toxin on the detection of gradual changes in facial emotion. *Scientific Reports, 9*, 11734. https://doi.org/10.1038/s41598-019-48275-1.

Bunkan, B. (1991). Das Zwerchfell: Zwischen Körper und Emotion [The diaphragm – Between body and emotion]. *Energie & Charakter [Energy & Character], 22*(3), 26–30.

Buongiorno, F. (2019). From the extended mind to the digitally extended self: A phenomenological critique. *Aisthesis, 12*, 61–68.

Busch, B. (2020). Discourse, emotions and embodiment. In A. De Fina & A. Georgakopoulou (Eds.), *The Cambridge Handbook of Discourse Studies* (pp. 327–349). Cambridge, MA: Cambridge University Press.

Butler, J. E. (2007). Drive to the human respiratory muscles. *Respiratory Physiology & Neurobiology, 159*, 115–126.

Butterworth, G. (1998). An ecological perspective on the origins of self. In Bermúdez et al. (Eds.) (pp. 87–105).

Caggiano, V., Fogassi, L., Rizzolatti, G., Casile, A., Giese, M. A., & Thier, P. (2012). Mirror neurons encode the subjective value of an observed action. *Proceedings of the National Academy of Science, 109*, 11848–11853.

Caldwell, C. (1997). The somatic umbrella. In C. Caldwell (Ed.), *Getting in Touch. The Guide to New Body-Centered Therapies* (pp. 7–28). Wheaton: Quest Books.

Caldwell, C. (2012). Sensation, movement, and emotion. Explicit procedures for implicit memories. In S. Koch et al. (Eds.) (pp. 255–265).

Caldwell, C. (2015). Movement as and in psychotherapy. In Marlock et al. (Eds.) (pp. 426–435).

Caldwell, C. (2018). *Bodyfulness. Somatic Practices for Presence, Empowerment, and Waking Up in This Life*. Boulder: Shambhala.

Calvo-Merino, B., Glaser, D. E., Grèzes, J., Passingham, R. E., & Haggard, P. (2005). Action observation and acquired motor skills: An fMRI study with expert dancers. *Cerebral Cortex, 15*, 1243–1249.

Cameron, O. G. (2001). Interoception: The inside story: A model for psychosomatic processes. *Psychosomatic Medicine, 63*, 697–710.

Campbell, J. (2014). Personal identity. In Gallagher (Ed.) (pp. 339–351).

Cantieni, B. (2006). Wie gesundes Embodiment selbst gemacht wird [How healthy embodiment is made by oneself]. In Storch et al. (Eds.) (pp. 101–125).

Cao, R., Yang, X., Luo, J., Wang, P., Meng, F., Xia, M., He, Y., Zhao, T., & Li, Z. (2021). The effects of cognitive behavioral therapy on the whole brain structural connectome in unmedicated patients with obsessive-compulsive disorder. *Progress in Neuro-Psychopharmacology and Biological Psychiatry, 104*. https://doi.org/10.1016/j.pnpbp.2020.110037.

Cappas, N. M., Andres-Hyman, R., & Davidson, L. (2005). What psychotherapists can begin to learn from neuroscience: Seven principles of a brain-based psychotherapy. *Psychotherapy: Theory, Research, Practice, Training, 42*, 374–383.

Capra, F. (1982). *The Turning Point. Science, Society, and the Rising Culture*. Toronto: Bantam Books.

Capra, F., & Luisi, L. (2014). *The Systems View of Life. A Unifying Vision*. New York: Cambridge University Press.

Carle, L. (2002). Das Energiekonzept in der Bioenergetischen Analyse und Therapie [The energy concept in bioenergetic analysis and therapy]. In Koemeda-Lutz (Ed.) (pp. 151–182).

Carr, L., Iacoboni, M., Dubeau, M.-C., Mazziotta, J., & Lenzi, G. L. (2003). Neural mechanisms of empathy in humans: A relay from neural systems for imitation to limbic areas. *Proceedings of the National Academy of Sciences, 100*, 5497–5502.

Carroll, R. (2002). Biodynamic massage in psychotherapy: Re-integrating, re-owning and re-associating through the body. In Staunton (Ed.) (pp. 78–100).

Carroll, R. (2005). Neuroscience and the 'law of the self'. The autonomic nervous system updated, re-mapped and in relationship. In Totton (Ed.) (pp. 13–29).

Carroll, R. (2006). A new era for psychotherapy: Panksepp's affect model in the context of neuroscience and its implications for contemporary psychotherapy practice. In Corrigall et al. (Eds.) (pp. 50–62).

Carroll, R. (2009). Self-regulation: An evolving concept at the heart of body psychotherapy. In Hartley (Ed.) (pp. 89–105).

Carroll, R. (2012). At the border between chaos and order: What psychotherapy and neuroscience have in common. In C. Young (Ed.), *About the Science of Body Psychotherapy* (pp. 3–26). Stow, Galashiels: Body Psychotherapy Publications.

Carryer, J. R., & Greenberg, L. S. (2010). Optimal levels of meotional arousal in experiential therapy of depression. *Journal of Consulting and Clinical Psychology, 78*, 190–199.

Casement, P. J. (1991). *Learning from the Patient*. New York: The Guilford Press.

Caspar, F. (2001). Die innere Welt des Psychotherapeuten: Schemata und Emotionen, Ratio und Intuition [The inner world of the psychotherapist: Schemata and emotions, ratio and intuition]. In Cierpka & Buchheim (Eds.) (pp. 139–152).

Cassam, Q. (2014). The embodied self. In Gallagher (Eds.) (pp. 139–156).

Castiello, U., Becchio, C., Zoia, S., Nelini, C., Sartori, L., Blason, L., D'Ottavio, G., Bulgheroni, M., & Gallese, V. (2010). Wired to be social: The ontogeny of human interaction. *PloS ONE, 5*, e13199. https://doi.org/10.1371/journal.pone .0013199.

Cavell, M. (2006). Subjektivität, Intersubjektivität und die Frage der Realität in der Psychoanalyse [Subjectivity, intersubjectivity, and the question of reality in psychoanasis]. In Altmeyer & Thomae (Ed.) pp. 178–200).

Caysa, V. (2008). Körperliche Intelligenz als empraktische Körpererinnerung [Bodily intelligence as empractical body memory]. In Bockrath et al. (Eds.) (pp. 73–85).

Chaffin, M., Hanson, R., Saunders, B. E., Nichols, T., Barnett, D., Zeanah, C., Berliner, L., Egeland, B., Newman, E., Lyon, T., Letourneau, E., & Miller-Perrin, C. (2006). Report of the APSAC task force on attachment therapy, reactive attachment disorder, and attachment problems. *Child Maltreatment, 11*, 76–89.

Chalmers, D. J. (1995). Facing up to the problem of consciousness. *Journal of Consciousness Studies, 2*(3), 200–219.

Chamberlain, D. B. (1997). Neuere Forschungsergebnisse aus der Beobachtung vorgeburtlichen Verhaltens [Recent research findings from the observation of prenatal behaviour]. In L. Janus & S. Haibach (Eds.), *Seelisches Erleben vor und während der Geburt [Mental Experience Before and During Birth]* (pp. 23–37). Neu-Isenburg: LinguaMed.

Charny, E. J. (1966). Psychosomatic manifestations of rapport in psychotherapy. *Psychosomatic Medicine, 28*, 305–315.

Chartrand, T. L., & Bargh, J. A. (1999). The chameleon effect: The perception-behavior link and social interaction. *Journal of Personality and Social Psychology, 76*, 893–910.

Chemero, A. (2011). *Radical Embodied Cognitive Science.* Cambridge: MIT Press.

Chen, J. A., Fearey, E., & Smith, R. E. (2017). "That which is measured improves": A theoretical and empirical review of self-monitoring in self-management and adaptive behavior change. *Journal of Behavior Therapy and Mental Health, 1*(4). https://doi.org/10.14302/issn.2474-9273.jbtm-16-1180.

Cheney, D. (2019). Gravity and the development of the (body) self in dance movement psychotherapy. In Payne et al. (Eds.) (pp. 117–124).

Chesler, A., Szczot, M., Bharucha-Goebel, D., Čeko, M., Donkervoort, S., Laubacher, C., Hayes, L. H., Alter, K., Zampieri, C., Stanley, C., Innes, A. M., Mah, J. K., Grosmann, C. M., Bradley, N., Nguyen, D., Foley, A. R., Le Pichon, C. E., & Boennemann, C. G. (2016). The role of PIEZO2 in human mechanosensation. *The New England Journal of Medicine, 375*, 1355–1364.

Chiel, H. J., & Beer, R. D. (1997). The brain has a body: Adaptive behavior emerges from interactions of nervous system, body and environment. *Trends in Neurosciences, 20*, 553–557.

Chiel, H. J., Ting, L. H., Ekeberg, Ö., & Hartmann, M. J. Z. (2009). The brain and its body: Motor control and sensing in a biomechanical context. *The Journal of Neuroscience, 29*, 12807–12814.

Choifer, A. (2018). A new understanding of the first-person and third-person perspectives. *Philosophical Papers, 47*, 1–39.

Ciaunica, A. (2019). The 'Meeting of Bodies': Empathy and basic forms of shared experiences. *Topoi, 38*, 185–195.

Cierpka, M., & Buchheim, P. (Eds.) (2001). *Psychodynamische Konzepte [Psychodynamic Concepts].* Berlin: Springer.

Clark, A. (1999). An embodied cognitive science? *Trends in Cognitive Sciences, 3*, 345–351.

Clark, A., & Chalmers, D. (1998). The extended mind. *Analysis, 58*, 10–23.

Clauer, J. (2003). Von der projektiven Identifikation zur verkörperten Gegenübertragung [From projective identification to embodied countertransference]. *Psychotherapie Forum [Psychotherapy Forum], 11*, 92–100.

Cocks, G. (1997). *Psychotherapy in the Third Reich.* The Göring Institute (2nd ed.). New Brunswick: Transaction Publishers.

Cocks, G. (2019). Johannes Heinrich Schultz oder vom steten Bemühen um entspannte Leistungsfähigkeit [Johannes Heinrich Schultz or the constant effort for relaxed performance]. In Geisthoevel & Hitzer (Eds.) (pp. 155–165).

Code, L. (2014). Self, subjectivity, and the instituted social imaginary. In Gallagher (Ed.) (pp. 715–737).

Coello, Y., & Fischer, M. H. (Eds.) (2016). *Foundations of Embodied Cognition: Perceptual and Emotional Embodiment.* London: Routledge.

Cohen, K., Ramseyer, F. T., Tal, S., & Zilcha-Mano, S. (2021). Nonverbal synchrony and the alliance in psychotherapy for Major Depression: Disentangling state-like and trait-like effects. *Clinical Psychological Science, 9*, 634–648.

Cole, J. (2001). Empathy needs a face. *Journal of Consciousness Studies, 8*, 51–68.

Cole, J. (2016). *Losing Touch: A Man Without His Body.* Oxford, GB: Oxford University Press.

Colombetti, G. (2014). *The Feeling Body. Affective Science Meets the Enactive Mind.* Cambridge, MA: The MIT Press.

Colombetti, G. (2017). Enactive affectivity, extended. *Topoi, 36*, 445–455.

Comtois, K. A., Chochran, B. N., & Linehan, M. (2000). Die verhaltenstherapeutische Behandlung der Borderline-Persönlichkeitsstörungen [The behaviour therapy treatment of borderline personality disorder]. In Kernberg et al. (Eds.) (pp. 573–594).

Cornell, W. F. (2015). Entering the erotic field. Sexuality in body-centered psychotherapy. In Marlock et al. (Eds.) (pp. 692–700).

Cornell, W. F. (2015). *Somatic Experience in Psychoanalysis and Psychotherapy. In the Expressive Language of the Living.* London: Routledge.

Cornell, W. F. (2016). The analyst's body at work: Utilizing touch and sensory experience in psychoanalytic psychotherapies. *Psychoanalytic Perspectives, 13*, 168–185.

Corrigall, J., Payne, H., & Wilkinson, H. (Eds.) (2006). *About a Body. Working with the Embodied Mind in Psychotherapy*. London: Routledge.

Corsi, L. (2012). Organismic self-regulation in Kurt Goldstein's holistic approach. *International Body Psychotherapy Journal, 11*, 57–65.

Cozolino, L. (2002). *The Neuroscience of Psychotherapy. Building and Rebuilding the Human Brain*. New York: Norton.

Craig, A. D. (2002). How do you feel? Interoception: The sense of the physiological condition of the body. *Nature Reviews Neuroscience, 3*, 655–666.

Craig, A. D. (2003). Interoception: The sense of the physiological condition of the body. *Current Opinion in Neurobiology, 13*, 500–505.

Craig, A. D. (2008). Interoception and emotion. A neuroanatomical perspective. In M. Lewis, J. M. Haviland-Jones & L. Feldman Barrett (Eds.), *Handbook of Emotions* (pp. 272–288). New York: The Guilford Press.

Cramer, P. (2000). Defense mechanisms in psychology today: Further processes for adaptation. *American Psychologist, 55*, 637–646.

Critchley, H. D. (2009). Psychophysiology of neural, cognitive and affective integration: fMRI and autonomic indicants. *International Journal of Psychophysiology, 73*, 88–94.

Critchley, H. D., Mathias, C. J., & Dolan, R. J. (2001). Neuroanatomical basis for first- and second-order representations of bodily states. *Nature Neuroscience, 4*, 207–212.

Critchley, H. D., Wiens, S., Rotshtein, P., Öhman, A., & Dolan, R. J. (2004). Neural systems supporting interoceptive awareness. *Nature Neuroscience, 7*, 189–195.

Crook, J. (1987). The nature of conscious awareness. In C. Blackmore & S. Greenfield (Eds.), *Mindwaves: Thougts on Intelligence, Identity and Consciousness* (pp. 383–402). Oxford: Basil Blackwell.

Csordas, T. (1990). Embodiment as a paradigm for anthropology. *Ethos, 18*, 5–47.

Cutting, J. E., & Kozlowski, L. T. (1977). Recognizing friends by their walk: Gait perception without familiarity cues. *Bulletin of the Psychonomic Society, 9*, 353–356.

Csikszentmihalyi, M. (1998). *Finding Flow: The Psychology of Engagement with Everyday Life*. New York: Basic Books.

Czetczok, H. (2010). Die Feldenkrais-Methode [The Feldenkrais method]. In Mueller-Braunschweig & Stiller (Eds.) (pp. 137–156).

Dael, N., Mortillaro, M., & Scherer, K. R. (2012). Emotion expression in body action and posture. *Emotion, 12*, 1085–1101.

Dael, N., Goudbeck, M., & Scherer, K. R. (2013). Perceived gesture dynamics in nonverbal expression of emotion. *Perception, 42*, 642–657.

Dahmer, H. (1982). Sándor Ferenczi – Sein Beitrag zur Psychoanalyse [Sándor Ferenczi – His contribution to psychoanalysis]. In D. Eicke (Ed.), *Tiefenpsychologie, Vol. 1: Sigmund Freud – Leben und Werk [Depth Psychology, Vol. 1: Sigmund Freud - Life and Work]* (pp. 161–190). Weinheim: Beltz.

Dalgleish, T. (2004). The emotional brain. *Nature Reviews Neuroscience, 5*, 582–589.

Damasio, A. R. (1994). *Descartes Error. Emotion, Reason, and the Human Brain*. New York: G. P. Putnam's Son.

Damasio, A. R. (1999). *The Feeling of What Happens. Body and Emotion in the Making of Consciousness*. New York: Harcourt & Brace.

Damasio, A. R. (2004). *Looking for Spinoza. Joy, Sorrow and the Feeling Brain*. London: Vintage Books.

Damasio, A. R. (2012). *Self Comes to Mind. Constructing the Conscious Brain*. London: Vintage Books.

Damasio, A. R., Grabowski, T. J., Bechara, A., Damasio, H., Ponto, L., Parvizi, J., & Hichwa, R. D. (2000). Subcortical and cortical brain activity during the feeling of self-generated emotions. *Nature Neuroscience, 3*, 1049–1056.

Damhorst, K. (2006). Sinneswahrnehmung [Sensory perception]. In Schmidt (Eds.) (pp. 92–97).

Dana, D. (2018). *The Polyvagal Theory in Therapy. Engaging the Rhythm of Regulation*. New York: Norton.

David, N., Newen, A., & Vogeley, K. (2008). The "sense of agency" and its underlying cognitive and neural mechanisms. *Consciousness and Cognition, 17*, 523–534.

Davis, W. (2020). *Funktionale Analyse. Grundlagen und Anwendungen in der Körperpsychotherapie [Functional Analysis. Fundamentals and Applications in Body Psychotherapy]*. Giessen: Psychosozial.

Davis, M., & Hadiks, D. (1990). Nonverbal behavior and client state changes during psychotherapy. *Journal of Clinical Psychology, 46*, 340–351.

Davis, M., & Hadiks, D. (1994). Nonverbal aspects of therapist attunement. *Journal of Clinical Psychology, 50*, 393–405.

Decety, J., & Fotopoulou, A. (2015). Why empathy has a beneficial impact on others in medicine: Unifying theories. *Frontiers in Behavioral Neuroscience, 8*, 457. https://doi.org/10.3389/fnbeh.2014.00457.

Decety, J., & Ickes, W. (Eds.) (2009). *The Social Neuroscience of Empathy*. Cambridge, MA: The MIT Press.

De Clerck, V. (2008). Körper, Beziehung und Übertragung: Die drei Dimensionen der Bioenergetischen Analyse [Body, relationship and transference: The three dimensions of bioenergetic analysis]. In Heinrich-Clauer (Eds.) (pp. 179–203).

de Haan, S. (2010). Comment: The minimal self is a social self. In Fuchs et al. (Eds.) (pp. 12–18).

de Haan, S. (2020). An enactive approach to psychiatry. *Philosophy, Psychiatry, & Psychology, 27*, 3–25.

De Jaegher, H. (2013). Embodiment and sense-making in autism. *Frontiers in Integrative Neuroscience, 7*, 15. https://doi.org/10.3389/fnint.2013.00015.

De Jaegher, H. (2015). How we affect each other. Michel Henry's 'pathos-with' and the enactive approach to intersubjectivity. *Journal of Consciousness Studies, 22*, 112–132.

De Jaegher, H. (2018). The intersubjective turn. In A. Newen, L. De Bruin & S. Gallagher (Eds.), *The Oxford Handbook of Cognition: Embodied, Embedded, Enactive and Extended* (pp. 453–468). Oxford: Oxford University Press.

De Jaegher, H., & Di Paolo, E. (2007). Participatory sense making: An enactive approach to social cognition. *Phenomenology and Cognitive Sciences, 6*, 485–507.

De Jaegher, H., & Di Paolo (2013). Enactivism is not interactionism. *Frontiers in Human Neuroscience, 6*, 345. https://doi.org/10.3389/fnhum.2012.00345.

De Jaegher, H., Pieper, B., Clénin, D., & Fuchs, T. (2017). Grasping intersubjectivity: An invitation to embody social interaction research. *Phenomenology and the Cognitive Sciences, 16*, 491–523.

Dekeyser, M., Elliott, R., & Leijssen, M. (2009). Empathy in psychotherapy: Dialogue and embodied understanding. In Decety & Ickes (Eds.) (pp. 113–124).

Depraz, N. (2008). The rainbow of emotions: At the crossroads of neurobiology and phenomenology. *Continental Philosophy Review, 41*, 237–259.

De Preester, H. (2007). The deep bodily origins of the subjective perspective: Models and their problems. *Consciousness and Cognition, 16*, 604–618.

De Preester, H., & Tsakiris, M. (2009). Body-extension versus body-incorporation: Is there a need for a body-model? *Phenomenology and the Cognitive Sciences, 8*, 307–319.

Dethlefsen, T., & Dahlke, R. (2016). *The Healing Power of Illness: Understanding What Your Symptoms Are Telling You.* Boulder: Sentient Publications (first edition in German 1983).

Deutscher Werkbund e.V. (Ed.) (1986). *Schock und Schöpfung. Jugendästhetik im 20. Jahrhundert [Shock and Creation. Youth Aesthetics in the 20th Century].* Neuwied: Luchterhand.

Diamond, J., (1979). *Your Body Doesn't Lie: How to Increase Your Life Energy Through Behavioral Kinesiology.* New York: Warner Books.

Dietrich, S. (1995). *Atemrhythmus und Psychotherapie. Ein Beitrag zur Geschichte der Psychosomatik und ihrer Therapien [Breathing Rhythm and Psychotherapy. A Contribution to the History of Psychosomatics and Its Therapies].* Unpubl. Med. Diss., University of Bonn (published 2014, Homburg: VAS-Verlag).

Dijkstra, K., Kaschak, M. P., & Zwaan, R. A. (2007). Body posture facilitates retrieval of autobiographical memories. *Cognition, 102*, 139–149.

Dilthey, W. (1924). Ideen über eine beschreibende und zergliedernde Psychologie [Ideas on a descriptive and dissecting psychology]. In *Gesammelte Schriften [Collected Writings], Vol. 5* (pp. 139–240). Leipzig: Teuber.

Dilthey, W. (2002). *The Formation of the Historical World in the Human Sciences.* Princeton: Princeton University Press.

Di Mascio, A., Boyd, R. W., & Greenblatt, M. (1957). Physiological correlates of tension and antagonism during psychotherapy: A study of interpersonal physiology. *Psychosomatic Medicine, 19*, 99–104.

Dimberg, U., Thunberg, M., & Elmehed, K. (2000). Unconscious facial reactions to emotional facial expressions. *Psychological Science, 11*, 86–89.

Dimberg, U., Andréasson, P., & Thunberg, M. (2011). Emotional empathy and facial reactions to facial expressions. *Journal of Psychophysiology, 25*, 26–31.

Di Paolo, E., & De Jaegher, H. (2012). The interactive brain hypothesis. *Frontiers in Human Neuroscience, 6*, 163. https://doi.org/10.3389/fnhum.2012.00163.

Di Paolo, E., & De Jaegher, H. (2015). Toward an embodied science of intersubjectivity: Widening the scope of social understanding research. *Frontiers in Psychology, 6*, 234. https://doi.org/10.3389/fpsyg.2015.00234.

Di Paolo, E., & Thompson, E. (2014). The enactive approach. In Shapiro (Ed.) (pp. 68–78).

Dixhoorn, J. van (2000). Body awareness and levels of self-regulation. In K. T. Kaku (Ed.), *Meditation as Health Promotion* (pp. S. 65–80). Delft: Eburon.

Dixhoorn, J. van (2008). Whole-body breathing. *Biofeedback, 36*, 54–58.

Doering-Seipel, E. (1996). *Stimmung und Körperhaltung. Eine experimentelle Studie [Mood and Body Posture. An Experimental Study].* Weinheim: Beltz.

Donald, M. (2001). *A Mind So Rare: The Evolution of Human Consciousness.* New York: Norton.

Donovan, J. M., Osborn, K. A. R., & Rice, S. (2017). *Paraverbal Communication in Psychotherapy. Beyond the Words.* New York, London: Rowman & Littlefield.

Dornes, M. (1993). *Der kompetente Säugling. Die präverbale Entwicklung des Menschen [The Competent Infant. The Preverbal Development of the Human Being].* Frankfurt: Fischer.

Dornes, M. (1997). *Die frühe Kindheit. Entwicklungspsychologie der ersten Lebensjahre [Early Infancy. Developmental Psychology of the First Years of Life].* Frankfurt: Fischer.

Dornes, M. (2000). *Die emotionale Welt des Kindes [The Emotional World of the Infant].* Frankfurt: Fischer.

Dornes, M. (2002). Der virtuelle Andere. Aspekte vorsprachlicher Intersubjektivität [The virtual other. Aspects of preverbal intersubjectivity]. *Forum der Psychoanalyse [Forum of Psychoanalysis]*, *18*, 303–331.

Downing, G. (1973). *The Massage Book*. Guildford: Wildwood House.

Downing, G. (1996). *Körper und Wort in der Psychotherapie [Body and Word in Psychotherapy]*. Munich: Koesel.

Downing, G. (2000). Emotion theory reconsidered. In M. Wrathall & J Malpass (Eds.), *Heidegger, Coping, and Cognitive Science* (pp. 245–270). Cambridge, MA: MIT Press.

Downing, G. (2004). Emotion, body and parent-infant-interaction. In J. Nadel & D. Muir (Eds.), *Emotional Development. Recent Research Advances* (pp. S. 429–449). Oxford: Oxford University Press.

Downing, G. (2007). Unbehagliche Anfänge. Wie man Psychotherapie mit schwierigen Patienten in Gang setzen kann [Uneasy beginnings. How to get psychotherapy going with difficult patients]. In Geissler & Heisterkamp (Eds.) (pp. 555–581).

Downing, G. (2011). Uneasy beginnings: Getting psychotherapy underway with the difficult patient. *Self-Psychology. European Journal for Psychoanalytic Therapy and Research*, *44/45*, 207–233.

Downing, G. (2015). Early interaction and the body: Clinical implications. In Marlock et al. (Eds.) (pp. 305–321).

Doyon, M., & Wehrle, M. (2020). Body. In D. De Santis, B. C. Hopkins & C. Majolino (Eds.), *The Routledge Handbook of Phenomenology and Phenomenological Philosophy* (pp. 123–137). London: Routledge.

Draaisma, D. (2004). *Why Life Speeds Up as You Get Older. How Memory Shapes our Past*. Cambridge, MA: Cambridge University Press.

Drees, A. (1996). *Folter: Opfer, Täter, Therapeuten. Neue Konzepte der psychotherapeutischen Behandlung von Gewaltopfern [Torture: Victims, Perpetrators, Therapists. New Concepts of Psychotherapeutic Treatment for Victims of Violence]*. Giessen: Psychosozial.

Dreher, M., Mengele, U., & Krause, R. (2001). Affective indicators of the psychotherapeutic process: An empirical case study. *Psychotherapy Research*, *11*, 99–117.

Dreitzel, H. P. (2021). *Human Interaction and Emotional Awareness in Gestalt Therapy. Exploring the Phenomenology of Contacting and Feeling*. New York: Routledge.

Dror, O. E. (2019). Emotionen und der physiologische Körper [Emotions and the physiological body]. In Geisthoevel & Hitzer (Eds.) (pp. 74–88).

Dumouchel, P. (2019). Embodiment: The Ecology of Mind. *Philosophies*, *4*(2), 12. https://doi.org/10.3390/philosophies4020012.

Dunkel, R. M. (2004). *Das Kreuz mit dem Kreuz. Rückenschmerzen psychosomatisch verstehen und behandeln [The Trouble with Back Pain. Understanding and Treating Back Pain Psychosomatically]*. Munich: Reinhardt.

Dupont, J. (1988). Vorwort [Preface]. In Ferenczi (Ed.) (pp. 11–31).

Duus, P. (1983). *Neurologisch-topische Diagnostik [Neurological-topical diagnostics]*. Stuttgart: Thieme.

Eberhard-Kaechele, M. (2009). Von der Katharsis über die Kontrolle zur Ko-Regulation: Rückblick und Ausblick auf die Förderung der Affektregulation in der Tanztherapie [From catharsis to control to co-regulation: Review and training on the promotion of affect regulation in dance therapy]. In S. Trautmann-Voigt & B. Voigt (Eds.) *Affektregulation und Sinnfindung in der Psychotherapie [Affect Regulation and Finding Meaning in Psychotherapy]* (pp. 115–151). Giessen: Psychosozial.

Eberhard-Kaechele, M. (2019). A developmental taxonomy of interaction modalities in dance movement therapy. In Payne et al. (Eds.) (pp. 81–94).

Eberwein, W. (1996). *Biodynamik. ZEN in der Kunst der Körperpsychotherapie [Biodynamics. ZEN in the Art of Body Psychotherapy]*. Paderborn: Junfermann.

Eberwein, W. (2009). *Humanistische Psychotherapie. Quellen, Therapien und Techniken [Humanistic Psychotherapy. Sources, Therapies, and Techniques]*. Stuttgart: Thieme.

Eberwein, W. (2012). Humanistische Psychotherapie. Unterstützung von selbstregulativen Prozessen und Potenzialentfaltung [Humanistic psychotherapy. Support of self-regulatory processes and development of potential]. *Deutsches Aerzteblatt PP [German Medical Journal – PP]*, *11*, 505–506.

Eberwein, W., & Thielen, M. (Eds.). *Humanistische Psychotherapie. Theorien, Methoden, Wirksamkeit [Humanistic psychotherapy: Theories, methods, effectiveness]*. Giessen: Psychosozial.

Ebrecht, A. (1992). *Das individuelle Ganze. Zum Psychologismus der Lebensphilosophie [The Individual Whole. On the Psychologism of the Philosophy of Life]*. Stuttgart: Metzlersche Verlagsbuchhandlung.

Ecker, W., Kuper, J., & Goenner, S. (2014). Incompleteness as a link between obsessive-compulsive personality traits and specific symptom dimensions of obsessive-compulsive disorder. *Clinical Psychology & Psychotherapy*, *21*, 394–402.

Eckert, H., & Laver, J. (1994). *Menschen und ihre Stimmen. Aspekte der vokalen Kommunikation [People and Their Voice. Aspects of Vocal Communication]*. Weinheim: Beltz.

Edelman, G. M. (1992). *Bright Air, Brilliant Fire: On the Matter of the Mind*. New York: Basic Books.

Edmiston, E. E., Wang, F., Mazure, C. M., Guiney, J., Sinha, R., Mayes, L. C., & Blumberg, H. P. (2011). Corticostriatal-limbic gray matter morphology in adolescents with self-reported exposure to childhood maltreatment. *Archives of Pediatrics & Adolescent Medicine*, *165*, 1069–1077.

Egan, J., & Carr, A. (2008). Body-centred countertransference in female trauma therapists. *Éisteacht, 8*(1), 24–27.

Egle, U. T., Hoffmann, S. O., & Joraschky, P. (Eds.) (1997). *Sexueller Missbrauch, Misshandlung, Vernachlässigung [Sexual Abuse, Maltreatment, Neglect]*. Stuttgart: Schattauer.

Egle, U. T., Franz, M., Joraschky, P., Lampe, A., Seiffge-Krenke, I., & Cierpka, M. (2016). Gesundheitliche Langzeitfolgen psychosozialer Belastungen in der Kindheit – Ein Update [Long-term health consequences of psychosocial stress in childhood - An update]. *Bundesgesundheitsblatt - Gesundheitsforschung - Gesundheitsschutz [Bundesgesundheitsblatt - Health Research - Health Protection], 59*, 1247–1254.

Egle, U. T., Heim, C., Strauss, B., & von Kaenel, R. (Eds.) (2020). *Psychosomatik – Neurobiologisch fundiert und evidenzbasiert. Ein Lehr- und Handbuch [Psychosomatics - Neurobiologically Grounded and Evidence-Based. A Training and Handbook]*. Stuttgart: Kohlhammer.

Egle, U. T., Heim, C., Strauss, B., & von Kaenel, R. (2020a). Das bio-psycho-soziale Krankheitsmodell – Revisited [The biopsychosocial model of illnesses - revisited]. In Egle et al. (Eds.) (pp. 39–48).

Ehrenberg, A. (2010). *The Weariness of the Self: Diagnosing the History of Depression in the Contemporary Age*. Montreal: McGill-Queen's University Press.

Ehrenfried, L. (1991). Körperliche Erziehung zum seelischen Gleichgewicht [Corporeal education to mental balance]. In P. Zeitler (Ed.), *Erinnerungen an Elsa Gindler [Memories of Elsa Gindler]* (pp. 34–37). Munich: Uni-Druck.

Ehrensperger, T. (2010). Bioenergetische Analyse [Bioenergetic analysis]. In Mueller-Braunschweig & Stiller (Eds.) (pp. S. 107–126).

Ehrlich, K. B., Ross, K. M., Chen, E., & Miller, G. E. (2016). Testing the biological embedding hypothesis: Is early life adversity associated with a later proinflammatory phenotype? *Development and Psychopathology, 28*(4Pt2), 1273–1283.

Eiden, B. (2002). Application of post-Reichian body psychotherapy: A Chiron perspective. In Staunton (Ed.) (pp. 27–55).

Eiden, B. (2009). The roots and the development of the Chiron approach. In Hartley (Ed.) (pp. 13–30).

Eilan, N., Marcel, A., & Bermúdez, J. L. (1998). Self-consiousness and the body: An interdisciplinary introduction. In Bermúdez et al. (Eds.) (pp. 1–28).

Eisman, J. (2015). Hakomi character theory. In Weiss et al. (Eds.) (pp. 76–90).

Ekerholt, K. (Ed.) (2010). *Aspects of Psychiatric and Psychosomatic Physiotherapy*. Oslo: Oslo University College.

Ekerholt, K., & Bergland, A. (2008). Breathing: A sign of life and a unique area for reflection and action. *Physical Therapy, 88*, 832–840.

Ekman, P. (2003). *Emotions Revealed: Understanding Faces and Feelings*. London: Weidenfeld & Nicolson.

Ekman, P., Levenson, R. W., & Friesen, W. V. (1983). Autonomic nervous system activity distinguishes among emotions. *Science, 221*, 1208–1210.

Elias, N. (2000). *The Civilizing Process: Sociogenetic and Psychogenetic Investigations*. Oxford: Blackwell.

Ellenberger, H. F. (1970). *The Discovery of the Unconscious. The History and Evolution of Dynamic Psychiatry*. New York: Basic Books.

Elliott, R., Greenberg, L. S., Watson, J., Timulak, L., & Freire, E. (2013). Research on humanistic-experiential psychotherapies. In M. J. Lambert (Ed.), *Bergin and Garfield's Handbook of Psychotherapy and Behavior Change* (6th ed.) (pp. 495–538). Hoboken: Wiley.

Emrich, H. (2007). *Identität als Prozess [Identity as Process]*. Wuerzburg: Koenigshausen und Neumann.

Engel, G. E. (1977). The need for a new medical model. *Science, 196*, 129–136.

Engelkamp, J., & Zimmer, H. D. (2006). *Lehrbuch der Kognitiven Psychologie [Textbook of Cognitive Psychoology]*. Goettingen: Hogrefe.

Eriksson, E. M., Moeller, I. E., Soederberg, R. H., Eriksson, H. T., & Kurlberg, G. K. (2007). Body awareness therapy: A new strategy for relief of symptoms in irritable bowel syndrome patients. *World Journal of Gastroenterology, 13*, 3206–3214.

Ermann, M. (1994). Sándor Ferenczis Aufbruch und Scheitern. Sein Umgang mit der Regression aus heutiger Sicht [Sándor Ferenczi's start and failure. His approach to regression from today's perspective]. *Psyche, 48*, 706–719.

Ermann, M. (2004). *Psychosomatische Medizin und Psychotherapie. Ein Lehrbuch auf psychoanalytischer Grundlage [Psychosomatic Medicine and Psychotherapy. A Psychoanalytical Textbook]* (4th ed.). Stuttgart: Kohlhammer.

Ermann, M. (2017). *Der Andere in der Psychoanalyse. Die intersubjektive Wende [The Other in Psychotherapy. The Intersubjective Turn]* (2nd ed.). Stuttgart: Kohlhammer.

Erskine, R. G. (2014). Nonverbal stories: The body in psychotherapy. *International Journal of Integrative Psychotherapy, 5*, 21–33.

Fallend, K. (1988). *Wilhelm Reich in Wien. Psychoanalyse und Politik [Wilhelm Reich in Vienna. Psychoanalysis and Politics]*. Wien: Geyer.

Feldenkrais, M. (2005). Body and Mature Behavior: A Study of Anxiety, Sex, Gravitation, and Learning. Berkeley, CA: Frog Books.

Feldman Barrett, L. (2017). *How Emotions Are Made. The Secret Life of the Brain*. Boston, New York: Houghton Mifflin Harcourt.

Feldman Barrett, L., & Russell, J. A. (1998). Independence and bipolartiy in the structure of current affects. *Journal of Personality and Social Psychology, 74,* 967–984.

Feldman Barrett, L., & Russell, J. A. (1999). The structure of current affect: Controversies and emerging consensus. *Current Directions in Psychological Science, 8,* 10–14.

Feldman Barrett, L., Quigley, K. S., Bliss-Moreau, E., & Aronson, K. R. (2004). Interoceptive sensitivity and self-reports of emotional experience. *Journal of Personality and Social Psychology, 87,* 684–697.

Felitti, V. J., Andra, R. F., Nordenberg, D., Williamson, D. F., Spitz, A. M., Edwards, V., Koss, M. P., & Marks, J. S. (1998). Relationship of childhood abuse and household dysfunction to many of the leading causes of death in adults. The Adverse Childhood Experiences (ACE) Study. *American Journal of Preventive Medicine, 14,* 245–258.

Fellmann, F. (1982). *Phänomenologie und Expressionismus [Phenomenology and Expressionism].* Freiburg: Karl Alber.

Fellmann, F. (1996). Lebensphilosophie [Philosophy of Life]. In F. Fellmann (Ed.), *Geschichte der Philosophie im 19. Jahrhundert [History of Philosophy in the 19th Century]* (pp. 269–349). Reinbek: Rowohlt.

Fenichel, O. (1927/1985). Über organlibidinöse Begleiterscheinungen der Triebabwehr [On organlibidinous accompanying symptoms of the drive defence]. In O. Fenichel (Ed.), *Aufsätze [Essays]* (Vol. 1, pp. 116–137). Frankfurt: Ullstein.

Fenichel, O. (1935/1985). Zur Theorie der psychoanalytischen Technik [On the theory of psychoanalytic technique]. In O. Fenichel (Ed.), *Aufsätze [Essays]* (Vol. 1, pp. 325–344). Franfurt: Ullstein.

Fenichel, O. (2015). *Psychoanalyse und Gymnastik [Psychoanalysis and Gymnastics].* Ed. by J. Reichmayr. Giessen: Psychosozial.

Feniger-Schaal, R., Hart, Y., Lotan, N., Koren-Karie, N., & Noy, L. (2018). The body speaks: Using mirror game to link attachment and non-verbal behavior. *Frontiers in Psychology.* https://doi.org/10.3389/fpsyg.2018.01560.

Ferenczi, S. (1925). Zur Psychoanalyse der Sexualgewohnheiten [On the psychoanalysis of sexual habits]. In Ferenczi, 1982, (Vol. 2, pp. 147–181).

Ferenczi, S. (1926). Kontraindikationen der aktiven psychoanalytischen Technik [Contraindications to the active psychoanalytic technique]. In Ferenczi, 1982 (Vol. 2, pp. 182–193).

Ferenczi, S. (1928). Die Elastizität der psychoanalytischen Technik [The elasticity of psychoanalytic technique]. In Ferenczi, 1982, (Vol. 2, pp. 237–250).

Ferenczi, S. (1930). Relaxationsprinzip und Neokatharsis [Relaxation principle and catharsis]. In Ferenczi, 1982, (Vol. 2, pp. 257–273).

Ferenczi, S. (1931). Kinderanalysen mit Erwachsenen [Child analyses with adults]. In Ferenczi, 1982, (Vol. 2, pp. 274–289).

Ferenczi, S. (1933). Sprachverwirrung zwischen den Erwachsenen und dem Kind [Language confusion between the adults and the child]. In Ferenczi, 1982, (Vol. 2, pp. 303–313).

Ferenczi, S. (1982). *Schriften zur Psychoanalyse (2 Vol.) [Writings on Psychoanalysis].* Frankfurt: Fischer.

Ferenczi, S. (1988). *Ohne Sympathie keine Heilung. Das klinische Tagebuch von 1932.* Frankfurt: Fischer (engl.: The Clinical Diary of Sándor Ferenczi. Cambridge, MA: Harvard University Press, 1995).

Fernald, P. S. (2000). Carl Rogers: Body-centered counselor. *Journal of Counseling and Development, 78,* 172–179.

Fernández-Dols, J.-M., Sánchez, F., Carrera, P., & Ruiz-Belda, M.-A. (1997). Are spontaneous expressions and emotions linked? An experimental test of coherence. *Journal of Nonverbal Behavior, 21,* 163–177.

Fernandez-Duque, D., Evans, J., Christian, C., & Hodges, S. D. (2017). Superfluous neuroscience information makes explanations of psychological phenomena more appealing. *Journal of Cognitive Neuroscience, 27,* 926–944.

Ferri, G., & Cimini, G. (2012). *Psicopatologia e Carattere. L'analisi Reichiana. La psicoanalisi nel corpo ed il corpo in psicoanalisi [Psychopathology and Character. The Reichian Analysis. Psychoanalysis in the Body and the Body in Psychoanalysis].* Rom: Alpes Italia.

Feuchtwanger, L. (1998). *Erfolg [Success].* Berlin: Aufbau-Verlag.

Fiedler, I. (2004). Tanztherapie in Berlin [Dance therapy in Berlin]. In Mueller (Ed.) (pp. 167–181).

Fiedler, P. (2000). *Integrative Psychotherapie bei Persönlichkeitsstörungen [Integrative Psychotherapy for Personality Disorders].* Goettingen: Hogrefe.

Fiedler, P. (Ed.) (2018). *Varianten psychotherapeutischer Beziehung. Transdiagnostische Befunde, Konzepte, Perspektiven [Variations of Psychotherapeutic Relationship. Transdiagnostic Findings, Concepts, Perspectives]* Lengerich: Pabst Science Publishers.

Field, N. (1989). Listening with the body: An exploration in the countertransference. *British Journal of Psychotherapy, 5,* 512–522.

Field, T. (2012). Relationships as regulators. *Psychology, 3,* 467–479.

Field, T., Hernandez-Reif, M., Diego, M., Feijo, L., Vera, Y., Gil, K., & Sanders, C. (2007). Still-face and separation effects on depressed mother-infant interactions. *Infant Mental Health Journal, 28,* 314–323.

Fischer, K. (2000). Psychomotorik und kindliche Entwicklung: Metatheoretische Perspektiven [Psychomotricity and child development: Metatheoretical perspectives]. *Motorik [Motoricity], 23,* 22–26.

Fischer, K., & Kemmann-Huber, E. (1999). *Der bewusste zugelassene Atem. Theorie und Praxis der Atemlehre [The Conscious Allowed Breath. Theory and Practice of Breath Teaching].* Munich: Urban & Fischer.

Fischer, M. (2008). Kommunikation, Mobilisation, Dissoziation: Psychotherapeutisches Arbeiten mit dem Autonomen Nervensystem und seinen drei grundlegenden Modi zur Stressregulation [Communication, mobilization, dissociation: Working with the autonomous nervous system and it's three basic modes of stressregulation in psychotherapy]. In R. Jenny & Y. Traber (Eds.), *Wo beginnt Heilung? Kritische Ansätze in der Therapie somatoformer Störungen [Where begins healing? Critical approaches in the treatment of somatoform disorders]* (pp. 49–90). Berlin: Weißensee.

Fischer, M. (2016). Persönlichkeitsmodell der Integrativen Körperpsychotherapie IBP [Personality model of Integrative Body Psychotherapy IBP]. In Kaul & Fischer (Eds.) (pp. 112–115).

Fischer, U. (2011). *Der viszeral assoziierte Schulterschmerz. Subjektive Perspektiven und diagnostische Vorgehensweisen aus Sicht von Osteopathen [Visceral Associated Shoulder Pain. Subjective Perspectives and Diagnostic Procedures from the Perspective of Osteopaths.].* Unpubl. Master's thesis, Centre for Chinese medicine and complementary medicine, Donau University, Krems.

Fliegel, S. (1994). *Verhaltenstherapeutische Standardmethoden [Standard Behavioural Therapy Methods].* Weinheim: Beltz.

Flueckiger, C., & Znoj, H. (2009). Zur Funktion der nonverbalen Stimmungsmodulation des Therapeuten für den Therapieprozess und Sitzungserfolg. Eine Pilotstudie [On the function of the therapist's non-verbal mood modulation for the therapy process and session success. A pilot study]. *Zeitschrift für Klinische Psychologie und Psychotherapie [Journal for Clinical Psychology and Psychotherapy], 38,* 4–12.

Fodor, J. (1975). *The Language of Thought.* New York: Crowell Press.

Foer, J. (2011). *Moonwalking with Einstein.* New York: The Penguin Press.

Foerster, J. (2003). The influence of approach and avoidance motor actions on food intake. *European Journal of Social Psychology, 33,* 339–350.

Foerster, J., & Jostmann, N. B. (2012). What is automatic self-regulation? *Zeitschrift für Psychologie [Journal for Psychology], 220,* 147–156.

Fogel, A. (2003). Remembering infancy: Accessing our earlist experiences. In Bremner & Slater (Eds.) (pp. S. 204–230).

Fogel, A. (2009). *The Psychophysiology of Self-Awareness. Rediscovering the Lost Art of Body Sense.* New York: Norton.

Folberth, W., Heim, G., Blohmke, M., & Huber, W. (1987). Spektrale Untersuchungen der menschlichen Wärmestrahlung bei Patienten mit chronischen Nierenerkrankungen [Spectral studies of human thermal radiation in patients with chronic kidney disease]. *Nieren- und Hochdruckkrankheiten [Kidney and High Pressure Diseases], 16,* 368–373.

Fonagy, P., & Target, M. (2007). The rooting of the mind in the body: New links between attachment theory and psychoanalytic thought. *Journal of the American Psychoanalytic Association, 55,* 411–456.

Fonagy, P., Gergely, G., Jurist, E. J., & Target, M. (2002). *Affect Regulation, Mentalization, and the Development of the Self.* New York: Other Press.

Fosha, D. (2001). The dyadic regulation of affect. *Journal of Clinical Psychoogy, 57,* 227–242.

Fox, N. (1998). Temperament and regulation of emotion in the first years of life. *Pediatrics, 102*(5 Supplement), 1230–1235.

Francis, D. D., Diorio, J., Liu, D., & Meaney, M. J. (1999). Nongenomic transmission across generations of maternal behavior and stress responses in the rat. *Science, 286,* 1155–1158.

Frank, M. (1994). Vorwort [Preface]. In M. Frank (Ed.), *Analytische Theorien des Selbstbewusstseins [Analytical Theories of Self-Consciousness]* (pp. 7–34). Frankfurt: Suhrkamp.

Frank, R. (2001). *Body of Awareness. A Somatic and Developmental Approach to Psychotherapy.* Cambridge, MA.: Gestalt Press.

Frank, R. (2005). Developmental somatic psychotherapy. In Totton (Ed.) (pp. 115–127).

Frank, R., & La Barre, F. (2011). *The First Year and the Rest of Your Life. Movement, Development, and Psychotherapeutic Change.* New York: Routledge.

Frazzetto, G. (2013). *How we feel. What Neuroscience Can and Can't Tell Us about Our Emotions.* London: Doubleday.

Fredrickson, B. L. (1998). What good are positive emotions? *Review of General Psychology, 2,* 300–319.

Freud, S. [1890] (1953). *Psychical (or Mental) Treatment. Standard Edition* (Vol. 7, pp. 281–302). London: Hogarth Press.

Freud, S. (1915). *The Unconscious. Standard Edition* (Vol. 14, pp. 159–190). London: Hogarth Press.

Freud, S. (1923). *The Ego and the Id. Standard Edition* (Vol. 19, pp. 1–66). London: Hogarth Press.

Freud, S. (1940). An outline of psychoanalysis. *The International Journal of Psychoanalysis, 21,* 27–84.

Frey, S. (1999). *Die Macht des Bildes. Der Einfluss der nonverbalen Kommunikation auf Kultur und Politik [The Power of the Image. The Influence of Non-Verbal Communication on Culture and Politics].* Bern: Huber.

Freyer, T., Klöppel, S., Tuescher, O., Kordon, A., Zurowski, B., Kuelz, A. K., Specka, O., Glauche, V., & Voderholze, U. (2011). Frontostriatal activation in patients with obsessive–compulsive disorder before and after cognitive behavioral therapy. *Psychological Medicine, 41,* 207–216.

Frick, R. W. (1985). Communicating emotion: The role of prosodic features. *Psychological Bulletin, 97,* 412–429.

Friederici, A. D. (2002). Towards a neural basis of auditory sentence processing. *Trends in Cognitive Sciences, 6,* 78–84.

Friedman, R., & Elliot, A. (2008). The effect of arm crossing on persistence and performance. *European Journal of Social Psychology, 38*, 449–461.

Fries, E. (2008). Die biologische Programmierung von späterer Gesundheit und Krankheit durch Erlebnisse in der Kindheit [Biological programming of later health by childhood experiences]. *Report Psychologie [Report Psychology], 33*, 472–483.

Frijda, N. H. (1986). *The Emotions.* Cambridge, MA: Cambridge University Press.

Frijda, N. H. (1996). Gesetze der Emotionen [Laws of emtions]. *Zeitschrift für psychosomatische Medizin und Psychoanalyse [Journal for Psychosomatic Medicine and Psychoanalysis], 42*, 205–221.

Froese, T. (2011). From adaptive behavior to human cognition: A review of Enaction. *Adaptive Behavior, 20*, 209–221.

Froese, T., & Fuchs, T. (2012). The extended body: A case study in the neurophenomenology of social interaction. *Phenomenology and the Cognitive Sciences, 11*, 205–235.

Froese, T., & Leavens, D. A. (2014). The direct perception hypothesis: Perceiving the intention of another's action hinders its precise imitation. *Frontiers in Psychology.* https://doi.org/10.3389/fpsyg.2014.00065.

Froese, T., & Ziemke, T. (2009). Enactive artificial intelligence: Investigating the systemic organization of life and mind. *Artificial Intelligence, 173*, 466–500.

Fromm, E. (1976). *To Have or to Be?* New York: Harper & Row.

Fromm, E. (2020). *Wissenschaft vom Menschen. Ein Lesebuch [Science of the human being].* Giessen: Psychosozial.

Fuchs, M. (1989). *Funktionelle Entspannung. Theorie und Praxis einer organismischen Entspannung über den rhythmisierten Atem [Functional Relaxation. Theory and Practice of Organismic Relaxation Through Rhythmic Breathing].* Stuttgart: Hippokrates.

Fuchs, P. (2010). *Das System Selbst. Eine Studie zur Frage: Wer liebt wen, wenn jemand sagt: „Ich liebe Dich!"? [The System of the Self. A Study on the Question: Who Loves Whom When Someone Says: "I love You!"?].* Weilerswist: Velbrueck.

Fuchs, P. (2011). *Die Verwaltung der vagen Dinge. Gespräche zur Zukunft der Psychotherapie [The Management of Vague Things. Conversations on the Future of Psychotherapy].* Heidelberg: Carl Auer.

Fuchs, T. (2000). *Leib, Raum, Person. Entwurf einer phänomenologischen Anthropologie [Body, Space, Person. Outline of a Phenomenological Anthropology].* Stuttgart: Klett-Cotta.

Fuchs, T. (2005). Corporealized and disembodied minds. A phenomenological view of the body in melancholia and schizophrenia. *Philosophy, Psychiatry & Psychology, 12*, 95–107.

Fuchs, T. (2006). Gibt es eine leibliche Persönlichkeitsstruktur? Ein phänomenologisch-psychodynamischer Ansatz [Is there a bodily personality structure? A phenomenological-psychodynamic approach]. *Psychodynamische Psychotherapie [Psychodynamic Psychotherapy], 5*, 109–117.

Fuchs, T. (2007). Fragmented selves. Temporality and identity in borderline personality disorders. *Psychopathology, 40*, 379–387.

Fuchs, T. (2008). *Leib und Lebenswelt. Neue philosophisch-psychiatrische Essays [Body and Lifeworld. New Philosophical-Psychiatric Essays].* Kusterdingen: Die graue Edition.

Fuchs, T. (2008a). Psychotherapie und Neurobiologie: Ein neuer Dialog [Psychotherapy and neurobiology. A new dialogue]. In Wollschlaeger (Ed.) (pp. 119–132).

Fuchs, T. (2008b). Phänomenologische Spurensuche in der psychiatrischen Diagnostik [Phenomenological search for traces in psychiatric diagnostics]. In Wollschlaeger (Ed.) (pp. 55–68).

Fuchs, T. (2009). Leibgedächtnis und Lebensgeschichte [Body memory and life history]. *Existenzanalyse [Existential Analysis], 26*(2), 46–52.

Fuchs, T. (2016). Intercorporeality and interaffectivity. *Phenomenology and Mind, 11*, 194–209.

Fuchs, T. (2017). *Ecology of the Brain. The Phenomenology and Biology of the Embodied Mind.* Oxford: Oxford University Press.

Fuchs, T. (2017a). Self across time: The diachronic unity of bodily existence. *Phenomenology and the Cognitive Sciences, 16*, 291–315.

Fuchs, T. (2019). The interactive phenomenal field and the life space: A sketch of an ecological concept of psychotherapy. *Psychopathology, 52*, 67–74.

Fuchs, T. (2020). The circularity of the embodied mind. *Frontiers in Psychology, 11*, 1707. https://doi.org/10.3389/fpsyg.2020.01707.

Fuchs, T. (2020a). Selbsterleben und Selbststörungen [Self-experience and self-disorders]. In T. Fuchs & T. Breyer (Eds.), *Selbst und Selbststörungen [Self and Self-Disorders]* (pp. 31–65). Freiburg: Karl Alber.

Fuchs, T. (2020b). Verkörperte Emotionen und ihre Regulation [Embodied emotions and their regulation]. In S. Barnow (Ed.), *Handbuch Emotionsregulation [Handbook of Emotion Regulation]* (pp. 19–28). Berlin: Springer.

Fuchs, T. (2020c). *Verteidigung des Menschen. Grundfragen einer verkörperten Anthropologie [Defending the Human Being. Basic Questions of an Embodied Anthropology].* Frankfurt: Suhrkamp.

Fuchs, T. (2022). The disappearing body: Anorexia as a conflict of embodiment. *Eating and Weight Disorders, 27*, 109–117. https://doi.org/10.1007/s40519-021-01122-7.

Fuchs, T., & De Jaegher, H. (2010). Non-representational intersubjectivity. In Fuchs et al. (Eds.) (pp. 203–215).

Fuchs, T., & Koch, S. C. (2014). Embodied affectivity: On moving and being moved. *Frontiers in Psychology*. https://doi.org/10.3389/fpsyg.2014.00508.

Fuchs, T., & Roehricht, F. (2017). Schizophrenia and intersubjectivity: An embodied and enactive approach to psychopathology and psychotherapy. *Philosophy, Psychiatry, and Psychology, 24*, 127–142.

Fuchs, T., & Vogeley, K. (2016). Selbsterleben und Selbststörungen [Self-experience and self-disorders]. In S. Herpertz, F. Caspar & K. Lieb (Eds.), *Psychotherapie. Funktions- und störungsorientiertes Vorgehen [Psychotherapy. Function- and Disorder-Oriented Approach]*. (pp. 119–136). Munich: Elsevier.

Fuchs, T., Sattel, H. C., & Henningsen, P. (Eds.) (2010). *The Embodied Self. Dimensions, Coherence and Disorders.* Stuttgart: Schattauer.

Fuckert, D. (1999). Persönlichkeitsentwicklung, Trauma und Sexualität in der Nachfolge der Schule Wilhelm Reichs. Ein integratives körperpsychotherapeutisches Modell [Personality development, trauma and sexuality in the succession of Wilhelm Reich's school. An integrative body-psychotherapeutic model]. *Persönlichkeitsstörungen – Theorie und Therapie [Personality Disorders – Theory and Therapy], 3*, 132–155.

Fuckert, D. (2002). Traumazentrierte Psychotherapie in der Nachfolge Wilhelm Reichs. Ein integratives körpertherapeutisches Modell [Trauma-centred psychotherapy in the wake of Wilhelm Reich. An integrative body-therapeutic model]. In U. Sachsse, I. Oezkan & A. Streeck-Fischer (Eds.), *Traumatherapie – Was ist erfolgreich? [Trauma Therapy – What is Effective?]* (pp. 83–112). Goettingen: Vandenhoeck & Ruprecht.

Fuhr, R., Sreckovic, M., & Gremmler-Fuhr, M. (Eds.) (1999). *Handbuch der Gestalttherapie [Handbook of Gestalt Therapy]*. Goettingen: Hogrefe.

Fusaroli, R., Demuru, P., & Borghi, A. M. (2012). The intersubjectivity of embodiment. *Journal of Cognitive Semiotics, 4*, 1–5. https://doi.org/10.1515/cogsem.2009.4.1.1.

Fusaroli, R., Bjørndahl, J. S., Roepstorff, A., & Tylén, K. (2016). A heart for interaction: Shared physiological dynamics and behavioral coordination in a collective, creative construction task. *Journal of Experimental Psychology: Human Perception and Performance, 42*(9), 1297–1310.

Gadamer, H. (2010). *Wahrheit und Methode. Grundzüge einer philosophischen Hermeneutik (=CW Vol. 1)*. Tuebingen: Mohr Siebeck (engl.: Truth and Method. London: Bloomsbury, 2013).

Gaensbauer, T. J. (2002). Representations of trauma in infancy: Clinical and theoretical implications for the understanding of early memory. *Infant Mental Health Journal, 23*, 259–277.

Galbusera, L., & Fellin, L. (2014). The intersubjective endeavor of psychopathology research: Methodological reflections on a second-person perspective approach. *Frontiers in Psychology, 5*, 1150. https://doi.org/10.3389/fpsyg.2014.01150.

Galbusera, L., Finn, M. T. M., Tschacher, W., & Kyselo, M. (2019). Interpersonal synchrony feels good but impedes self-regulation of affect. *Scientific Reports, 9*, 14691. https://doi.org/10.1038/s41598-019-50960-0.

Gallagher, S. (2000). Philosophical conceptions of the self: Implications for cognitive science. *Trends in Cognitive Sciences, 4*, 14–21.

Gallagher, S. (2003). Neurophenomenological research on embodied experience. In C.-F. Cheung, I. Chvatik, I. Copoeru, L. Embree, J. Iribarne & H. R. Sepp (Eds.), *Essays in Celebration of the Founding of the Organisation of Phenomenological Organiziations*, No. 41. Retrieved October 11, 2022, from https://www.researchgate.net/publication/242728627.

Gallagher, S. (2005). *How the Body Shapes the Mind*. New York: Oxford University Press.

Gallagher, S. (2005a). Metzinger's matrix: Living the virtual life with a real body. *Psyche: An Interdisciplinary Journal of Research on Consciousness, 11*. Retrieved October 11, 2022, from http://journalpsyche.org.

Gallagher, S. (2008). Intersubjectivity in perception. *Continental Philosophy Review, 41*, 163–178.

Gallagher, S. (Ed.) (2014). *The Oxford Handbook of the Self*. Oxford: Oxford University Press.

Gallagher, S. (2014a). Introduction: A diversity of selves. In Gallagher (Ed.) (pp. 1–29).

Gallagher, S. (2014b). Phenomenology and embodied cognition. In Shapiro (Ed.) (pp. 9–18).

Gallagher S. (2018). Decentering the brain: Embodied cognition and the critique of neurocentrism and narrow-minded philosophy of mind. *Constructivist Foundations, 14*(1), 8–21. Retrieved Oktober 11, 2022, from https://ro.uow.edu.au/lhapapers/3784.

Gallagher, S. (2019). Precis: Enactivist interventions. *Philosophical Studies, 176*, 803–806.

Gallagher, S. (2020). Enactivism, causality, and therapy. *Philosophy, Psychiatry, & Psychology, 27*, 27–28.

Gallagher, S. (2021). The 4Es and the 4As (affect, agency, affordance, autonomy) in the meshed architecture of social cognition. In Robinson & Thomas (Eds.) (pp. 357–379).

Gallagher, S., & Bower, M. (2014). Making enactivism even more embodied. *Avant, 5*, 232–247.

Gallagher, S., & Hutto, D. D. (2008). Understanding others through primary interaction and narrative practice. In J. Zlatev, T. P. Racine, C. Sinha, & E. Itkonen (Hg.), *The shared mind: Perspectives on intersubjectivity* (pp. 17–38). Amsterdam: John Benjamins Publishing Company.

Gallagher, S., & Hutto, D. (2019). Narratives in embodied therapeutic practice: Getting the story straight. In Payne et al. (Eds.) (pp. 28–39).

Gallagher, S., Hutto, D., Slaby, J., & Cole, J. (2013). The brain as part of an enactive system. *Behavioral and Brain Sciences, 36*(4), 421–422.

Gallese, V. (2003). The manifold nature of interpersonal relations: The quest for a common mechanism. *Philosophical Transactions of the Royal Society, 358*, 517–528.

Gallese, V. (2003a). The roots of empathy: The shared manifold hypothesis and the neural basis for intersubjectivity. *Psychopathology, 36*, 171–180.

Gallese, V. (2007). Before and below 'theory of mind': Embodied simulation and the neural correlates of social cognition. *Philosophical Transactions of the Royal Society, 362*, 659–669.

Gallese, V. (2013). Den Körper im Gehirn finden. Konzeptionelle Überlegungen zu den Spiegelneuronen [Finding the body in the brain. Conceptual reflections on mirror neurons]. In Leuzinger-Bohleber et al. (Eds.) (pp. 75–112).

Gallese, V., & Goldman, A. (1998). Mirror neurons and the simulation theory of mind-reading. *Trends in Cognitive Sciences, 2*, 493–501.

Gallese, V., & Sinigaglia, C. (2010). The bodily self as power for action. *Neuropsychologia, 48*, 746–755.

Gallese, V., & Sinigaglia, C. (2011). How the body in action shapes the self. *Journal of Consciousness Studies, 18*, 117–143.

Gallo, F. (2000). *Energy Diagnostic and Treatment Methods.* New York: Norton.

Gallup, G. G., Anderson, J. R., & Platek, S. M. (2014). Self-recognition. In Gallagher (Ed.) (pp. 80–110).

Galuska, J., & Galuska, D. (2006). Körperpsychotherapie im Spektrum der Strukturniveaus [Body psychotherapy in the spectrum of structural levels]. In Marlock & Weiss (Eds.) (pp. 585–597).

Gangopadhyay, N. (2013). Introduction: Embodiment and empathy, current debates in social cognition. *Topoi, 33*, 117–127. https://doi.org/10.1007/s11245-013-9199-2.

Gapp, K., Jawaid, A., Sarkies, P., Bohacek, J., Pelczar, P., Prados, J., Farinelli, L., Miska, E., & Mansuy, I. M. (2014). Implication of sperm RNAs in transgenerational inheritance of the effects of early trauma in mice. *Nature Neuroscience, 17*, 667–669.

Garcia, E., & Arandia, I. R. (2022). Enactive and simondonian reflections on mental disorders. *Frontiers in Psychology, 13*, 938105. https://doi.org/10.3389/fpsyg.2022.938105.

Garcia, E., & Di Paolo, E. A. (2018). Embodied coordination and psychotherapeutic outcome: Beyond direct mappings. *Frontiers in Psychology, 9*, 125. https://doi.org/10.3389/fpsyg.2018.01257.

Garcia, E., Di Paolo, E. A., & De Jaegher, H. (2022). Embodiment in online psychotherapy: A qualitative study. *Psychology and Psychotherapy. Theory, Research and Practice, 95*, 191–211.

Gard, T., Hoelzel, B. K., Sack, A. T., Hempel, H., Lazar, S. W., Vaitl, D., & Ott, U. (2012). Pain attenuation through mindfulness is associated with decreased cognitive control and increased sensory processing in the brain. *Cerebral Cortex, 22*, 2692–2702.

Garvey, A., & Fogel, A. (2008). Emotions and communication as a dynamic developmental system. *Espaciotiempo, 2*, 62–73.

Gassmann, D. (2010). Allgemeine Wirkfaktoren und körperorientiertes Vorgehen [General working factors and body-oriented approach]. In Kuenzler et al. (Eds.) (pp. 335–347).

Gay, P. (2001). *Weimar Culture. The Outsider as Insider.* New York: Norton.

Gebauer, G. (2008). Das Sprachspielkonzept und der Sport [The language game concept and sports]. In Bockrath et al. (Eds.) (pp. 41–52).

Geissler, C., & Geissler, P. (2011). Die Behandlung der angstgestörten Patientin B. aus der Perspektive der Analytischen Körperpsychotherapie [The treatment of the anxiety-disordered patient B. from the perspective of analytical body psychotherapy]. In Roehricht (Ed.) (pp. 138–143).

Geissler, P. (1996). *Neue Entwicklungen in der Bioenergetischen Analyse. Materialien zur analytischen körperbezogenen Psychotherapie [New Developments in Bioenergetic Analysis. Materials on Analytical Body-Related Psychotherapy].* Frankfurt: Peter Lang.

Geissler, P. (Ed.) (2004). *Was ist Selbstregulation? Eine Standortbestimmung [What is Self-Regulation? Where Do We Stand].* Giessen: Psychosozial.

Geissler, P. (2004a). Erste Gedanken zur Einführung in das Thema [First thoughts on the introduction to the topic]. In Geissler (Ed.) (pp. 9–19).

Geissler, P. (Ed.) (2005). *Nonverbale Interaktion in der Psychotherapie [Nonverbal Interaction in Psychotherapy].* Giessen: Psychosozial.

Geissler, P. (2007). Entwicklungspsychologisch relevante Konzepte im Überblick [An overview of relevant concepts of developmental psychology]. In Geissler& Heisterkamp (Eds.) (pp. 99–164).

Geissler, P. (2009). *Analytische Körperpsychotherapie. Eine Bestandsaufnahme [Analytical Body Psychotherapy. A Survey of the State of the Art].* Giessen: Psychosozial.

Geissler, P. (2014). Intersubjektivität in der Körperpsychotherapie [Intersubjectivity in body psychotherapy]. In P. Potthoff & S. Wollnik (Eds.), *Die Begegnung der Subjekte. Die intersubjektiv-relationale Perspektive in Psychoanalyse und Psychotherapie [The Encounter of Subjects. The Intersubjective-Relational Perspective in Psychoanalysis and Psychotherapy]* (pp. 169–188). Giessen: Psychosozial.

Geissler, P. (2017). *Psychodynamische Körperpsychotherapie [Psychodynamic Body Psychotherapy]*. Goettingen: Vandenhoeck & Ruprecht.

Geissler, P., & Heisterkamp, G. (Eds.) (2007). *Psychoanalyse der Lebensbewegungen. Zum körperlichen Geschehen in der psychoanalytischen Therapie. Ein Lehrbuch [Psychoanalysis of Life Movements. On Bodily Processes in Psychoanalytic Therapy. A Textbook]*. Wien: Springer.

Geisthoevel, A., & Hitzer, B. (Eds.) (2019). *Auf der Suche nach einer anderen Medizin. Psychosomatik im 20. Jahrhundert [In Search of a Different Medicine. Psychosomatics in the 20th Century]*. Frankfurt: Suhrkamp.

Gendlin, E. (1961). Experiencing. A variable in the process of psychotherapeutic change. *American Journal of Psychotherapy*, 15, 233–245.

Gendlin, E. (1988). Carl Rogers (1902–1987). *American Psychologist*, 43, 127–128.

Gendlin, E. (1993). Die umfassende Rolle des Körpergefühls im Denken und Sprechen [The comprehensive role of body sensation in thinking and speaking]. *Deutsche Zeitschrift für Philosophie [German Journal for Philosophy]*, 4, 693–706.

Gendlin, E. (1996). *Focusing Oriented Psychotherapy. A Manual of the Experiental Method*. New York: The Guilford Press.

Gendlin, E. (1997). *Experiencing and the Creation of Meaning* (2nd ed.). Evanston: Northwestern University Press.

Gendlin, E. (2016). *Ein Prozess-Modell [A Process Model]*. Freiburg: Karl Alber.

Gendlin, E. T., & Hendricks-Gendlin, M. N. (2015). The bodily 'felt sense' as a ground for body psychotherapies. In Marlock et al. (Eds.) (pp. 248–254).

Gergen, K. J. (2014). The social construction of self. In Gallagher (Ed.) (pp. 633–653).

Gerhardt, J., & Sweetnam, A. (2001). The intersubjective turn in psychoanalysis: A comparison of contemporary theorists: Part 2: Christopher Bollas. *Psychoanalytic Dialogues*, 11, 43–92.

Gerhardt, J., Sweetnam, A., & Borton, L. (2000). The intersubjective turn in psychoanalysis: A comparison of contemporary theorists: Part 1: Jessica Benjamin. *Psychoanalytic Dialogues*, 10, 5–42.

Gershon, M. (1998). *The Second Brain: The Scientific Basis of Gut Instinct and a Groundbreaking New Understanding of Nervous Disorders of the Stomach and Intestines*. New York: HarperCollins.

Geuter, U. (1986). Zeit der Krisen. Die Jugend in der deutschen Literatur um 1900 [Time of crises. Youth in German literature around 1900]. In G. Juettemann (Ed.), *Die Geschichtlichkeit des Seelischen [The Historicity of The Psyche]* (pp. 209–236). Weinheim: PVU Beltz.

Geuter, U. (1992). *The Professionalization of Psychology in Nazi Germany*. New York: Cambridge University Press.

Geuter, U. (1994). The whole and the community: Scientific and political reasoning in the holistic psychology of Felix Krueger. In M. Renneberg & M. Walker (Eds), *Science, Technology, and National Socialism* (pp. 197–223). Cambridge, UK: Cambridge University Press.

Geuter, U. (1996). Körperbilder und Körpertechniken in der Psychotherapie [Body images and body techniques in psychotherapy]. *Psychotherapeut [Psychotherapist]*, 41, 99–106.

Geuter, U. (2000). Wege zum Körper. Zur Geschichte und Theorie des körperbezogenen Ansatzes in der Psychotherapie [On the history and theory of the body-centred approach in psychotherapy]. *Krankengymnastik. Zeitschrift für Physiotherapeuten [Physiotherapy. Journal for Physiotherapists]*, 52, 1175–1183 & 1346–1351 (also in *Energie & Charakter* [Energy & Character], 31, 2000, 103–126).

Geuter, U. (2000a). Historischer Abriss zur Entwicklung der körperorientierten Psychotherapie [Historical outline of the development of body-oriented psychotherapy]. In Roehricht (pp. 53–74).

Geuter, U. (2002). Wie man sich verändern kann [How you can change]. *Psychologie heute [Psychology Today]*, 29(H. 11), 42–49.

Geuter, U. (2004). Körperpsychotherapie und Erfahrung. Zur Geschichte, wissenschaftlichen Fundierung und Anerkennung einer psychotherapeutischen Methode [Body psychotherapy and experience. On the history, scientific foundation and recognition of a psychotherapeutic method]. *Report Psychologie [Report Psychology]*, 29(H. 2), 98–111.

Geuter, U. (2004a). Die Anfänge der Körperpsychotherapie in Berlin [The beginnings of body psychotherapy in Berlin]. In Mueller (Ed.) (pp. 167–181).

Geuter, U. (2006). Körperpsychotherapie. Der körperbezogene Ansatz im neueren wissenschaftlichen Diskurs der Psychotherapie [The body-related approach in the recent scientific discourse of psychotherapy]. *Psychotherapeutenjournal [Psychotherapist Journal]*, 5(2), 116–122, & (3), 258–264.

Geuter, U. (2009). Emotionsregulation und Emotionserkundung in der Körperpsychotherapie [Emotion regulation and emotion exploration in body psychotherapy]. In Thielen (Ed.) (pp. 69–94).

Geuter, U. (2012). Book Review: Forms of vitality. Exploring dynamic experience in psychology, arts, psychotherapy, and development, by Daniel Stern. *Body, Movement and Dance in Psychotherapy*, 7, 235–239.

Geuter, U. (2015). The history and scope of body psychotherapy. In Marlock et al. (Eds.) (pp. 22–39).

Geuter, U. (2016). Body psychotherapy: Experiencing the body, experiencing the self. *International Body Psychotherapy Journal*, 15, 6–19.

Geuter, U. (2018). Selbst und Struktur. Zum klinischen Verständnis kindlicher Entwicklung in der Körperpsychotherapie [Self and structure. On the clinical understanding of child development in body psychotherapy]. In Thielen et al. (Eds.) (pp. 47–66).

Geuter, U. (2019). *Praxis Körperpsychotherapie. 10 Prinzipien der Arbeit im therapeutischen Prozess [Body Psychotherapy Practice. 10 Principles of Working in the Therapeutic Process].* Berlin, Heidelberg: Springer.

Geuter, U. (2019a). Emotional regulation in body psychotherapy. In Payne et al. (Eds.) (pp. 315–324).

Geuter, U., & Schrauth, N. (1997). Wilhelm Reich, der Körper und die Psychotherapie [Wilhelm Reich, the body and psychotherapy]. In K. Fallend & B. Nitzschke (Eds.), Der 'Fall' Wilhelm Reich. Beiträge zum Verhältnis von Psychoanalyse und Politik [The 'Case' of Wilhelm Reich. Contributions to the Relationship Between Psychoanalysis and Politics] (pp. 190–222). Frankfurt: Suhrkamp (New edition Psychosozial-Verlag, 2002).

Geuter, U., & Schrauth, N. (2001). Emotionen und Emotionsabwehr als Körperprozess [Emotions and emotion defence as a body process]. *Psychotherapie Forum [Psychotherapy Forum], 9,* 4–19.

Geuter, U., & Schrauth, N. (2015). The role of the body in emotional defense processes: Body psychotherapy and emotional theory. In Marlock et al. (Eds.) (pp. 543–552).

Geuter, U., Heller, M. C., & Weaver, J. O. (2010). Elsa Gindler and her influence on Wilhelm Reich and body psychotherapy. *Body, Movement and Dance in Psychotherapy, 5,* 59–73.

Ghin, M. (2005). What a self could be. *Psyche, 11,* 1–10 https://journalpsyche.org/files/0xaade.pdf.

Gibbs, R. (2006). *Embodiment and Cognitive Science.* Cambridge, MA: Cambridge University Press.

Gibson, J. (1979). *The Ecological Approach to Visual Perception.* Boston: Houghton-Mifflin.

Giefer, M. (2019). Georg Groddeck oder der "wilde" Versuch, das Es psychodynamisch zu behandeln [Georg Groddeck or the "wild" attempt to treat the id psychodynamically]. In Geisthoevel & Hitzer (Eds.) (pp. 102–112).

Gigerenzer, G. (2007). *Bauchentscheidungen. Die Intelligenz des Unbewussten und die Macht der Intuition.* Munich: Bertelsmann [engl.: Gut Feelings: The Intelligence of the Unconscious. London: Penguin Books, 2008].

Gilbert, A. R. (1951). Recent German theories of stratification of personality. *The Journal of Psychology, 31,* 3–19.

Gilbert, A. R. (1973). Bringing the history of personality theories up to date: German theories of personality stratification. *Journal of the History of the Behavioral Sciences, 9,* 102–114.

Gilbert, P., Gilbert, J., & Irons, C. (2004). Life events, entrapments and arrested anger in depression. *Journal of Affective Disorders, 79,* 149–160.

Gillie, B. L., Vasey, M. W., & Thayer, J. F. (2014). Heart rate variability predicts control over memory retrieval. *Psychological Science, 25,* 458–465.

Gindler, E. (1926). Die Gymnastik des Berufsmenschen [The gymnastics of the working people]. *Gymnastik [Gymnastics], 1,* 82–89 (reprinted in Ludwig, 2002, pp. 83–93).

Gindler, E. (1931). [No title - Lecture] Generalversammlung des Deutschen Gymnastikbundes [General assembly of the German Gymnastics Federation]. In Ludwig (Ed.) (2002, pp. 95–125).

Giummarra, M. J., Gibson, S. J., Georgiou-Karistianis, N., & Bradshaw, J. L. (2008). Mechanisms underlying embodiment, disembodiment and loss of embodiment. *Neuroscience and Biobehavioral Reviews, 32,* 143–160.

Glas, G. (2020). An enactive approach to anxiety and anxiety disorders. *Philosophy, Psychiatry & Psychology, 27,* 35–50. https://doi.org/10.1353/ppp.2020.0005.

Glenberg, A. (2010). Embodiment as a unifying perspective for psychology. *Wiley Interdisciplinary Reviews. Cognitive Science, 1,* 586–596.

Glenberg, A. M., & Kaschak, M. P. (2002). Grounding language in action. *Psychonomic Bulletin & Review, 9,* 558–565.

Glenn, M. (2015). Prenatal and perinatal psychology: Vital foundations of body psychotherapy. In Marlock et al. (Eds.) (pp. 332–344).

Goldin-Meadow, S. (1999). The role of gesture in communication and thinking. *Trends in Cognitive Sciences, 3,* 419–429.

Goldin-Meadow, S. (2006). Talking and thinking with our hands. *Current Directions in Psychological Science, 15,* 34–39.

Goldin-Meadow, S. (2015). Gesture as a window onto communicative abilities: Implications for diagnosis and intervention. *Perspectives on Language and Education, 22*(2), 50–60.

Goldsmith, H. H., & Campos, J. J. (1982). Toward a theory of infant temperament. In R. N. Emde & R. J. Harmon (Eds.), *The Development of Attachment and Affiliative Systems* (pp. 161–193). New York: Plenum Press.

Goldstein, K. (1931). Das psycho-physische Problem in seiner Bedeutung für ärztliches Handeln [The psycho-physical problem in its significance for medical action]. *Therapie der Gegenwart. Medizinisch-chirurgische Rundschau für praktische Aerzte [Therapy of The Present. Medical-Surgical Review for General Practitioners], 33,* 1–11.

Goldstein, K. (1995). *The Organism. A Holistic Approach to Biology.* New York: Zone Books.

Goodill, S. W., Raeke, J., & Koch, S. (2013). Sich ausweitend, aufsteigend, voranschreitend. Entwicklungen in medizinischer Tanztherapie und Ausbildung [Expanding, ascending, progressing. Developments in medical dance therapy and training]. *Koerper - tanz - bewegung [Body - Dance - Movement], 1,* 66–73.

Oliveira, C. (2005). Bewusstseinszentrierte Körperpsychotherapie – Angewandte Neurobiologie? [Consciousness-centred body psychotherapy - Applied neurobiology?] In Sulz et al. (Eds.) (pp. 105–198).

Gottwald, C. (2007). Von Neurobiologie inspirierte Erweiterung der psychodynamischen Praxeologie durch bewusstseinszentrierte Körperpsychotherapie [Neurobiology-inspired extension of psychodynamic praxeology through consciousness-centred body psychotherapy]. *Psychotherapie Forum [Psychotherapy Forum]*, *15*, 73–77.

Gottwald, C. (2015). Neurobiological perspectives on body psychotherapy. In Marlock et al. (Eds.) (pp. 126–147).

Graeff, C. (2000). *Konzentrative Bewegungstherapie in der Praxis [Concentrative Movement Therapy in Practice]* (3rd ed.). Stuttgart: Hippokrates.

Grassmann, H. (2019). Die Strukturelle Körpertherapie und das Wechselspiel zwischen Faszien, Nervensystem und Psyche [Structural body therapy and the interplay between fascia, nervous system and psyche]. *Trauma - Zeitschrift für Psychotraumatologie und ihre Anwendungen [Trauma. Journal for Psychotraumatology and it's Applications]*, *17*, 50–60.

Graumann, C. F. (1980). Psychologie - Humanistisch oder human? [Psychology – Humanistic or human?] In U. Voelker (Ed.), *Humanistische Psychologie. Ansätze einer lebensnahen Wissenschaft vom Menschen [Humanistic Psychology. Approaches to a Lifelike Science of the Human Being]* (pp. 39–51). Weinheim: Beltz.

Graumann, C. F., & Métraux, A. (1977). Die phänomenologische Orientierung in der Psychologie [The phenomenological orientation in psychology]. In K. A. Schneewind (Ed.), *Wissenschaftstheoretische Grundlagen der Psychologie [Scientific-Theoretical Foundations of Psychology]* (pp. 27–53). Munich: Reinhardt.

Graven, S. N., & Browne, J. V. (2008). Sensory development in the fetus, neonate, and infant: Introduction and overview. *Newborn and Infant Nursing Reviews*, *8*, 169–172.

Grawe, K. (1995). Grundriss einer Allgemeinen Psychotherapie [Outline of General Psychotherapy]. *Psychotherapeut [Psychotherapist]*, *40*, 130–145.

Grawe, K. (2004). *Psychological Therapy*. Goettingen: Hogrefe & Huber.

Grawe, K. (2007). *Neuropsychotherapy. How the Neurosciences Inform Effective Psychotherapy*. Mahwah: Lawrence Erlbaum Associates.

Greenberg, L. S. (2004). Emotion-focused therapy. *Clinical Psychology and Psychotherapy*, *11*, 3–16.

Greenberg, L. S. (2011). *Emotion-Focused Therapy*. Washington, DC: American Psychological Association.

Greenberg, L. S. (2021). *Changing Emotion with Emotion: A Practitioner's Guide*. Washington, DC: American Psychological Association.

Greenberg, L. S., & Bischkopf, J. (2007). Anger in psychotherapy: To express or not to express? That is the question. In T. A. Cavell & K. T. Malcom (Eds.), *Anger, Aggression, and Interventions for Interpersonal Violence* (pp. 165–183). Mahwah: Lawrence Erlbaum.

Greenberg, L., & Pascual-Leone, J. (2001). A dialectical constructivist view of the creation of personal meaning. *Journal of Constructivist Psychology*, *14*, 165–186.

Greenberg, L. S., & Paivio, S. C. (1997). *Working with the Emotions in Psychotherapy*. New York: Guilford Press.

Greenberg, L. S., & Safran, J. D. (1989). Emotion in psychotherapy. *American Psychologist*, *44*, 19–29.

Greenberg, L. S., & Van Balen, R. (1998). The theory of experience-centered therapies. In Greenberg et al. (Eds.) (pp. 28–57).

Greenberg, L. S., Watson, J. C., & Lietaer, G. (Eds.) (1998). *Handbook of Experiential Psychotherapy*. New York: The Guilford Press.

Greene, D. (2013). Expanding the dialogue: Exploring contributions from energy medicine. *International Body Psychotherapy Journal*, *12*, 56–73.

Gremmler-Fuhr, M. (1999). Grundkonzepte und Modelle der Gestalttherapie [Basic concepts and models in Gestalt therapy]. In Fuhr et al. (Eds.) (pp. 344–392).

Griffith, J. L., & Griffith, M. E. (1994). *The Body Speaks: Therapeutic Dialogues for Mind-Body Problems*. New York: Basic Books.

Grinberg-Zylberbaum, J., & Attie, L. B. (1997). Ideas about a new psychophysiology of consciousness: The syntergic theory. *Journal of Mind & Behavior*, *18*, 443–458.

Grinberg-Zylberbaum, J., & Ramos, J. (1987). Patterns of interhemispheric correlation during human communication, *International Journal of Neuroscience*, *36*, 1–2, 41–53.

Groddeck, G. (1931). Massage [Massage]. In Kretschmer & Cimbal (Eds.) (pp. 51–55).

Groddeck, G. (1992). *Schicksal, das bin ich selbst [Destiny, That is Myself]*. Frankfurt: Limes.

Grof, S. (1985). *Beyond the Brain. Birth, Death and Transcendence in Psychiatry*. Albany: The State University of New York Press.

Grof, S. (1988). *The Adventure of Self-Discovery. Dimensions of Consciousness and New Perspectives in Psychotherapy and Inner Exploration*. Albany: State University of New York Press.

Grosse Holtforth, M., & Grawe, K. (2004). Inkongruenz und Fallkonzeption in der Psychologischen Therapie [Incongruence and case conception in psychological therapy]. *Verhaltenstherapie & psychosoziale Praxis [Behaviour Therapy & Psychosocial Practice]*, *36*(1), 9–21.

Grossmann, K. (2000). Verstrickung, Vermeidung, Desorganisation: Psychische Inkohärenzen als Folge von Trennung und Verlust [Enmeshment, avoidance, disorganisation: Psychological incoherence as a consequence of separation and loss]. In L. Opher-Kohn, J. Pfaefflin & B. Sonntag (Eds.), *Das Ende der Sprachlosigkeit? [The End of Speechlessnes?]* (pp. 85–111). Giessen: Psychosozial.

Grossmann, K. E., Grossmann, K., Winter, M., & Zimmermann, P. (2002). Attachment relationships and appraisal of partnership: From early experience of sensitive support to later relationship representation. In L. Pulkkinen & A. Caspi (Eds.), *Paths to Successful Development: Personality in the Life Course* (pp. 73–105). New York: Cambridge University Press.

Grunwald, M. (2012). Das Sinnessystem Haut und sein Beitrag zur Körper-Grenzerfahrung [The sensory system skin and its contribution to the body-boundary experience]. In Schmidt & Schetsche (Eds.) (pp. 29–54).

Gruzelier, J. H. (2002). A review of the impact of hypnosis, relaxation, guided imagery and individual differences on aspects of immunity and health. *Stress, 5*, 147–163.

Guendel, H., Greiner, A., Ceballos-Baumann, A. O., von Rad, M., Foerstl, H., & Jahn, T. (2002). Erhöhte sympathische Grundaktivität bei hoch- versus niedrig-alexithymen Patienten mit spasmodischem Tortikollis [Increased baseline sympathetic activity in high- versus low-alexithymic patients with spasmodic torticollis]. *Psychotherapie, Psychosomatik, Medizinische Psychologie [Psychotherapy, Psychosomatics, Medical Psychology], 52*, 461–468.

Guenther, H. (1990). Geschichtlicher Abriss der deutschen Rhythmusbewegung [Historical outline of the German rhythm movement]. In E. Bannmueller & P. Roethig (Eds.), *Grundlagen und Perspektiven ästhetischer und rhythmischer Bewegungserziehung [Foundations and Perspectives of Aesthetic and Rhythmic Movement Education]* (pp. 13–49). Stuttgart: Klett.

Gugnowska, K., Novembre, G., Kohler, N., Villringer, A., Keller, P. E., & Sammler, D. (2022). Endogenous sources of interbrain synchrony in duetting pianists. *Cerebral Cortex, 32*, 4110–4127. https://doi.org/10.1093/cercor/bhab469.

Gugutzer, R. (2002). *Leib, Körper und Identität. Eine phänomenologisch-soziologische Untersuchung zur personalen Identität [Soma, Body and Identity. A Phenomenological-Sociological Investigation into Personal Identity]*. Wiesbaden: Westdeutscher Verlag.

Gugutzer, R. (2004). *Soziologie des Körpers [Sociology of The Body]*. Bielefeld: Transcript.

Gugutzer, R. (2006). Der body turn in der Soziologie. Eine programmatische Einführung [The body turn in sociology. A programmatic introduction]. In R. Gugutzer (Ed.), *Body Turn. Perspektiven der Soziologie des Körpers und des Sports [Body Turn. Perspectives on the Sociology of the Body and Sport]* (pp. 9–53). Bielefeld: Transcript.

Guhn, A., Koehler, S., & Brakemeier, E.-L. (2018). Phasen- oder Übertragungsorientierung? Die therapeutische Beziehungsgestaltung in der IPT und im CBASP [Phase or transference orientation? The therapeutic relationship in IPT and CBASP]. In Fiedler (Ed.) (pp. 213–229).

Gumpp, A. M., Boeck, C., Behnke, A., Bach, A. M., Ramo-Fernández, L., Welz, T., Guendel, H., Kolassa, I.-T., & Karabatsiakis, A. (2020). Childhood maltreatment is associated with changes in mitochondrial bioenergetics in maternal, but not in neonatal immune cells. *Proceedings of the National Academy of Sciences, 117*(40), 24778–24784. https://doi.org/10.1073/pnas.2005885117.

Haag, M. (2018). Hell-Dunkel-Versuche [Light-dark experiments]. *Rundbrief Nr. 16 der Heinrich Jacoby Elsa Gindler Stiftung [Newsletter No. 16 of the Heinrich Jacoby Elsa Gindler Foundation]*, 6–11.

Haas, R. (1993). Die Erfassung des Raumverhaltens und -erlebens bei psychisch Kranken [The recording of spatial behaviour and experience in mentally ill people]. In Hoelter (Ed.) (pp. 94–108).

Habermas, J. (1987) *Knowledge and Human Interests. Cambridge*. UK: Polity Press (German: Erkenntnis und Interesse. Frankfurt: Suhrkamp, 1969).

Habermas, T. (1990). *Heisshunger. Historische Bedingungen der Bulimia nervosa [Cravings. Historical Conditions of Bulimia Nervosa]*. Frankfurt: Fischer.

Habermas, T. (1994). *Zur Geschichte der Magersucht. Eine medizinpsychologische Rekonstruktion [On the History of Anorexia. A Medical-Psychological Reconstruction]*. Frankfurt: Fischer.

Haken, H. (2004). Ist der Mensch ein dynamisches System [Is the human being a dynamic system]? In von Schlippe & Kriz (Eds.) (pp. 68–77).

Haken, H., & Schiepek, G. (2006). *Synergetik in der Psychologie. Selbstorganisation verstehen und gestalten [Synergetics in Psychology. Understanding and Shaping Self-Organisation]*. Goettingen: Hogrefe.

Ham, J., & Tronick, E. (2009). Relational psychophysiology: Lessons from mother-infant physiology research on dyadically expanded states of consciousness. *Psychotherapy Research, 19*, 619–632.

Hamel, L. M., Moulder, R., Albrecht, T. L., Boker, S., Eggly, S., & Penner, L. A. (2018). Nonverbal synchrony as a behavioural marker of patient and physician race-related attitudes and a predictor of outcomes in oncology interactions: Protocol for a secondary analysis of video-recorded cancer treatment discussions. *BMJ Open*, Dec 4; 8(12), e023648. https://doi.org/10.1136/bmjopen-2018-023648.

Hanna, T. (1986). What is Somatics? *Somatics: Magazine: Journal of the Bodily Arts and Sciences, 5*, 4. Retrieved April, 30, 2020, from https://somatics.org/library/htl-wis1.

Hanna, T. (2004). *Somatics: Reawakening the mind's control of movement, flexibility, and health*. Cambridge, MA: Da Capo Press.

Harms, T. (2000). *Auf die Welt gekommen: Die neuen Baby-Therapien [Coming into the World: The New Baby Therapies]*. Berlin: Leutner.

Harms, T. (2008). *Emotionelle Erste Hilfe [Emotional First Help]*. Berlin: Leutner.

Harms, T. (2013 June 1). *Wilhelm Reich und das Zentrum für Orgonomische Säuglingsforschung (OIRC) [Wilhelm Reich and the Orgonomic Infant Research Centre (OIRC)]* [conference lecture]. Annual Convention of the Wilhelm-Reich-Society, Berlin, Deutschland.

Harms, T. (2017). Die Funktion des Orgasmus – 90 Jahre danach. Die Sexualtheorien Wilhelm Reichs und ihre Relevanz für die moderne Körperpsychotherapie [The function of the orgasm - 90 years later. The sexual theories of Wilhelm Reich and their relevance for modern body psychotherapy]. In Harms & Thielen (Eds.) (pp. 13–48).

Harms, T., & Thielen, M. (Eds.) (2017). *Körperpsychotherapie und Sexualität. Grundlagen, Perspektiven und Praxis [Body Psychotherapy and Sexuality. Foundations, Perspectives and Practice]*. Giessen: Psychosozial.

Harrington, A. (1996). *Reenchanted Science: Holism in German Culture from Wilhelm II to Hitler*. Princeton: Princeton University Press.

Harrison, N., Singer, T., Rotshtein, P., Dolan, R., & Critchley, H. (2006). Pupilary contagion: Central mechanisms engaged in sadness processing. *Social Cognitive and Affective Neuroscience. 1*, 5–17. https://doi.org/10.1093/scan/nsl006.

Hartley, L. (1995). *Wisdom of the Body Moving. An Introduction to Body-Mind Centering*. Berkeley: North Atlantic Books.

Hartley, L. (Ed.) (2009). *Contemporary Body Psychotherapy. The Chiron Approach*. London: Routledge.

Hartley, L. (2009a). Introduction. In Hartley (Ed.) (pp. 1–7).

Hartmann, H.-P. (2006). Ein selbstpsychologischer Blick auf die Selbstregulation [A self psychological view on self regulation]. *Psychosozial [Psychosocial], 29*(106), 19–32.

Hartmann, H.-P., & Lohmann, K. (2004). Selbstregulation [Self-regulation]. In Geissler (Ed.) (pp. 41–65).

Hartmann, S., & Belsky, J. (2018). Prenatal programming of postnatal plasticity revisited – And extended. *Development and Psychopathology, 30*, 825–842.

Hartmann-Kottek, L. (2008). *Gestalttherapie [Gestalt Therapy]*. Heidelberg: Springer.

Hartmann-Kottek, L., & Kriz, J. (2005). Humanistische Verfahren und ihr Kontext [Humanistic approaches and their context]. *Psychotherapie im Dialog [Psychotherapy in Dialogue], 6*, 112–116.

Hastings, M. E., Tangney, J. P., & Stuewig, J. (2008). Psychopathy and identification of facial expressions of emotion. *Personality and Individual Differences, 44*, 1474–1483.

Hatfield, E., Rapson, R. L., & Le, Y.-C. L. (2009). Emotional contagion and empathy. In Decety & Ickes (Eds.) (pp. 19–30).

Hauke, G., & Kritikos, A. (2018). *Embodiment in Psychotherapy: A Practitioner's Guide*. Cham: Springer.

Hausmann, B., & Neddermeyer, R. (1996). *Bewegt Sein. Integrative Bewegungs- und Leibtherapie in der Praxis [Being Moved. Integrative Movement and Body Therapy in Practice]*. Paderborn: Junfermann.

Hawk, S. T., Fischer, A. H., & Van Kleef, G. A. (2012). Face the noise: Embodied responses to nonverbal vocalizations of discrete emotions. *Journal of Personality and Social Psychology, 102*, 796–814.

Hayes, S. C. (2004). Acceptance and committment therapy and the new behavior therapies: Mindfulness, acceptance, and relationship. In S. C. Hayes, V. M. Folette & M. M. Linehan (Eds.), *Mindfulness and Acceptance. Expanding the Cognitive-Behavioral Tradition* (pp. 1–29). New York: The Guilford Press.

Hayes, S. C., & Lillis, J. (2013). *Acceptance and Commitment-Therapy*. Washington, DC: American Psychological Association.

Hayes, S. C., Strosahl, K., & Wilson, K. G. (1999). *Acceptance and Commitment Therapy: An Experiential Approach to Behavior Change: The Process and Practice of Mindful Change*. New York: Guilford.

Haynal, A. (2000). *Die Technik-Debatte in der Psychoanalyse [The Debate on Technique in Psychoanalysis]* Giessen: Psychosozial.

Heedt, T. (2020). Somatoforme Störungsbilder und der Nutzen körperzentrierter Psychotherapien [Somatoform disorders and the benefits of body-centred psychotherapies]. *Koerper – tanz – bewegung [Body – Dance – Movement], 8*, 3–15.

Hehlmann, W. (1963). *Geschichte der Psychologie [History of Psychology]*. Stuttgart: Kroener.

Heidegger, M. (1962). *Being and Time*. Oxford: Blackwell Publishers.

Heilinger, J.-C., & Jung, M. (2009). Funktionen des Erlebens. Neue Perspektiven des qualitativen Bewusstseins [Functions of Experience. New perspectives of qualitative consciousness]. In Jung & Heilinger (Eds.) (pp. 1–37).

Heilmann, C. M. (2009). *Körpersprache richtig verstehen und einsetzen [Understanding and using body language correctly]*. Munich: Reinhardt.

Heim, C. M., Mayberg, H. S., Mletzko, T., Nemeroff, C. B., & Pruessner, J. C. (2013). Decreased cortical representation of genital somatosensory field after childhood sexual abuse. *American Journal of Psychiatry, 170*, 616–623.

Heim, C., Dammering, F., & Entringer, S. (2020). Frühe Programmierung von Gesundheit und Krankheit [Early programming of health and disease]. In Egle et al. (Eds.) (pp. 185–192).

Heiner, B. T. (2008). Guest editor's introduction. The recorporealization of cognition in phenomenology and cognitive science. *Continental Philosophy Review, 41*, 115–126.

Heinl, P. (2000). The infant voice in adult speech: The transmission of information about the first year of life in adult communication. *International Journal of Prenatal and Perinatal Psychology and Medicine, 12*, 155–166.

Heinl, P. (2001). *Splintered Innocence. An intuitive approach to treating war trauma.* Hove: Brunner-Routledge.

Heinrich, V. (2001). Übertragungs- und Gegenübertragungsbeziehung in der Körperpsychotherapie [Transference and countertransference relation in body psychotherapy]. *Psychotherapie Forum [Psychotherapy Forum], 9*, 62–70.

Heinrich-Clauer, V. (Ed.) (2008). *Handbuch Bioenergetische Analyse [Handbook of Bioenergetic Analysis].* Giessen: Psychosozial.

Heinrich-Clauer, V. (2008a). Therapeuten als Resonanzkörper. Welche Saiten geraten in Schwingung [Therapists as resonating bodies. Which strings start to vibrate]? In Heinrich-Clauer (Ed.) (pp. 161–178).

Heisterkamp, G. (1993). *Heilsame Berührungen. Praxis leibfundierter analytischer Psychotherapie [Healing Touch. Practice of Body-Based Analytical Psychotherapy].* Munich: Pfeiffer.

Heisterkamp, G. (1999). Zur Freude in der analytischen Psychotherapie [On happiness in analytical psychotherapy]. *Psyche, 53*, 1247–1265.

Heisterkamp, G. (2000). Die leibliche Dimension in psychodynamischen Psychotherapien [The somatic dimension in psychodynamic psychotherapies]. In C. Reimer & U. Rueger (Eds.), *Psychodynamische Psychotherapien [Psychodynamic Psychotherapies]* (pp. 295–320). Berlin: Springer.

Heisterkamp, G. (2002). *Basales Verstehen. Handlungsdialoge in Psychotherapie und Psychoanalyse [Basic Understanding. Action dialogues in psychotherapy and psychoanalysis].* Stuttgart: Pfeiffer.

Heisterkamp, G. (2004). Enactments. Basale Formen des Verstehens [Enactments. Basic forms of understanding]. *Psychoanalyse & Koerper [Psychoanalysis & Body], 3*(5), 103–130.

Heisterkamp, G. (2005). Unmittelbare Wirkungszusammenhänge in der Psychotherapie [Direct ways of change in psychotherapy]. In Geissler (Ed.) (pp. 117–139).

Heisterkamp, G. (2006). Selbst und Körper [Self and body]. In Marlock & Weiss (Eds.) (pp. 281–289).

Heisterkamp, G. (2007). Praxis der Analyse seelischer Lebensbewegungen [Practice of the analysis of mental life movements]. In Geissler & Heisterkamp (Eds.) (pp. 299–340).

Heisterkamp, G. (2010). Analytische Körperpsychotherapie [Analytical body psychotherapy]. In Mueller-Braunschweig & Stiller (Eds.) (pp. 87–105).

Heitkemper, M., Burr, R. L., Jarrett, M., Hertig, V., Lustyk, M. K., & Bond, E. F. (1998). Evidence for autonomic nervous system imbalance in women with irritable bowel syndrome. *Digestive Diseases and Sciences, 43*, 2093–2098.

Helfaer, P. M. (2011). The somatic-energetic point of view: Towards a bioenergetic character analysis. *The USA Body Psychotherapy Journal, 10*, 79–90.

Heller, M. (1997). Posture as an interface between biology and culture. In U. Segerstråle & P. Molnár (Eds.), *Nonverbal Communication. Where Nature Meets Culture* (pp. 245–262). Mahwah: Lawrence Erlbaum.

Heller, M. (Ed.) (2001). *The Flesh of the Soul: The Body we Work with.* Bern: Peter Lang.

Heller, M. (2007). The golden age of body psychotherapy in Oslo I: From gymnastics to psychoanalysis. *Body, Movement and Dance in Psychotherapy, 2*, 5–16.

Heller, M. (2009). Die dynamische Körperhaltung eines psychoanalytischen Prozesses [The dynamic posture of a psychoanalytic process]. Part 2. *Psychoanalyse & Koerper [Psychanalysis & Body], 8*(14), 51–67.

Heller, M. (with G. Westland) (2011). The system of the dimensions of the organism (SDO): A common vocabulary for body psychotherapy. *Body, Movement and Dance in Psychotherapy, 6*, 43–56.

Heller, M. (2012). *Body Psychotherapy: History, Concepts, Methods.* New York: Norton.

Heller, M., & Haynal, V. (1997). Depression and suicide faces. In P. Ekman & E. L. Rosenberg (Eds.), *What the Face Reveals* (pp. 339–407). Oxford: Oxford University Press.

Heller, M., Haynal-Reymond, V., Haynal, A., & Archinard, M. (2001). Can faces reveal suicide attempt risks? In Heller (Ed.) (pp. 231–256).

Helmer, L. M. L., Weijenberg, R. A. F., de Vries, R., Achterberg, W. P., Lautenbacher, S., Sampson, E. L., & Lobbezoo, F. (2020). Crying out in pain: A systematic review into the validity of vocalization as an indicator for pain. *European Journal of Pain, 24*. 1703–1715.

Hendricks, G. (1995). *Conscious Breathing.* New York: Bantam Books.

Hendricks, G., & Hendricks, K. (1993). *At the Speed of Light: A New Approach to Personal Change Through Body-Centered Therapy.* New York: Bantam Books.

Hendricks, M. N. (1986). Experiencing level as a therapeutic variable. *Person-Centered Review, 1*, 141–162.

Henley, N. M. (1977). *Body Politics. Power, Sex, and Nonverbal Communication.* Englewood Cliffs: Prentice Hall.

Hennenlotter, A., Dresel, C., Castrop, F., Ceballos Baumann, A. O., Wohlschlaeger, A. M., & Haslinger, B. (2009). The link between facial feedback and neural activity within central circuitries of emotion: New insights from Botulinum toxin-induced denervation of frown muscles. *Cerebral Cortex, 19*, 537–542.

Henningsen, P. (2002). Körper und psychische Struktur: Anmerkungen zur Psychosomatik der Psyche [Body and psychic structure: Notes on the psychosomatics of the psyche]. In G. Rudolf, T. Grande & P. Henningsen (Eds.), *Die Struktur der Persönlichkeit [The Structure of Personality]* (pp. 132–143). Stuttgart: Schattauer.

Henry, A., & Thompson, E. (2014). Witnissing from here: Self-Awareness from a bodily versus embodied perspective. In Gallagher (Ed.) (pp. 228–249).

Herbert, B. M., & Pollatos, O. (2008). Interozeptive Sensitivität, Gefühle und Verhaltensregulation [Interoceptive sensitivity, emotions and behaviour regulation]. *Zeitschrift für Neuropsychologie [Journal for Neuropsychology], 19*, 125–137.

Herholz, I., Johnen, R., & Schweitzer, D. (Eds.) (2009). *Funktionelle Entspannung. Das Praxisbuch [Functional Relaxation. The Practice Book].* Stuttgart: Schattauer.

Hermans, H. J. M. (2001). The dialogical self: Toward a theory of personal and cultural positioning. *Culture & Psychology, 7*, 243–281.

Hermans, H. J. M. (2014). The dialogical self: A process of positioning in space and time. In Gallagher (Ed.) (pp. 654–680).

Hermer, M. (2004). Stille Begegnungen [Silent Encounters]. In Hermer & Klinzing (Eds.) (pp. 9–54).

Hermer, M., & Klinzing, H. G. (Eds.) (2004). *Nonverbale Prozesse in der Psychotherapie [Nonverbal Processes in Psychotherapy].* Tuebingen: dgvt-verlag.

Herrmann, C. S., Pauen, M., Rieger, J. W., & Schicktanz, S. (Eds.) (2005). *Bewusstsein. Philosophie, Neurowissenschaften, Ethik [Consciousness. Philosophy, Neuroscience, Ethics].* Munich: Fink.

Hertenstein, M. J., Keltner, D., App, B., Bulleit, B. A., & Jaskolka, A. R. (2006). Touch communicates distinct emotions. *Emotion, 6*, 528–533.

Herzog, T. (2017). Humanistisch-Existenzielle Perspektiven der Zwangsstörung. Existenzanalyse, Psychodrama und Personzentrierte Psychotherapie im Dialog [Humanistic-existential perspectives on obsessive-compulsive disorder. Existential analysis, psychodrama and person-centred psychotherapy in dialogue]. *Existenzanalyse [Existential Analysis], 34*(1), 54–61.

Heyer, G. R. (1931). Die Behandlung des Seelischen vom Körper aus [The treatment of the mind starting from the body]. In Kretschmer & Cimbal (Eds.) (pp. 1–9).

Heyer, G. R. (1932). *Der Organismus der Seele [The Organism of the Mind].* Munich: Lehmanns.

Hiergeist, A., Manook, A., Gessner, A., Rupprecht, R., & Baghai, T. C. (2020). Untersuchung des Dickdarm-Mikrobioms in der klinischen Forschung [Investigation of the colon microbiome in clinical research]. *Nervenheilkunde [Neurology], 39*, 10–18.

Hietanen, J. K., Surakka, V., & Linnankoski, I. (1998). Facial electromyographic responses to vocal affect expressions. *Psychophysiology, 35*, 530–536.

Hietanen, J. K., Glerean, E., Hari, R., & Nummenmaa, L. (2016). Bodily maps of emotions across child development. *Developmental Science, 19*(6), 1111–1118. https://doi.org/10.1111/desc.12389.

Hillman, C. H., Hisao-Wecksler, E. T., & Rosengren, K. S. (2005). Postural and eye-blink indices of the defensive startle reflex. *International Journal of Psychophysiology, 55*, 45–49.

Ho, R. (2019). Embodiment of space in relation to the self and others in psychotherapy. In Payne et al. (Eds.) (pp. 232–240).

Hochauf, R. (1999). Imaginative Psychotherapie bei frühtraumatisierten Patienten [Imaginative psychotherapy for early traumatised patients]. *International Journal of Prenatal and Perinatal Psychology and Medicine, 11*, 503–517.

Hochauf, R. (2001). Der Umgang mit traumabezogenen Beziehungserfahrungen [Dealing with trauma-related relationship experiences]. In U. Bahrke & W. Rosendahl (Eds.), *Psychotraumatologie und Katathym-imaginative Psychotherapie [Psychotraumatology and Catathym-Imaginative Psychotherapy]* (pp. 47–55). Lengerich: Pabst.

Hochauf, R. (2006). Zur Spezifik pränataler Traumatisierungen und deren Bearbeitung in der Therapie erwachsener Personen [On the specificity of prenatal traumatisation and its treatment in adult therapy]. In Krens & Krens (Eds.) (pp. 126–143).

Hochauf, R. (2008). Der Körper als „Leitsymptomträger" [The body as a "leading symptom carrier"]. In Vogt (Ed.) (pp. 177–196).

Hochschild, A. R. (1996). Soziologie der Emotionen als eine Methode der Erkenntnis – Am Beispiel der Liebe [Sociology of emotions as a method of knowledge - The example of love]. *Zeitschrift für psychosomatische Medizin und Psychoanalyse [Journal for Psychosomatic Medicine and Psychoanalysis], 42*, 222–234.

Hoehmann-Kost, A. (2009). Der komplexe Bewegungsbegriff [The complex concept of movement]. In Waibel & Jakob-Krieger (Eds.) (pp. 21–25).

Hoelter, G. (Ed.) (1993). *Mototherapie mit Erwachsenen [Mototherapy with Adults].* Schorndorf: Hofmann.

Hoelter, G. (1993a). Ansätze zu einer Methodik der Mototherapie [Approaches to a methodology of mototherapy]. In Hoelter (Ed.) (pp. 52–80).

Hoelter, G. (2002). Spuren vom Übersinnlichen zum Sinnlichen. Franz Schönberger im Spiegel ausgewählter Bewegungskulturen des 20. Jahrhunderts [Traces from the supernatural to the sensual. Franz Schönberger in the mirror of selected movement cultures of the 20th century]. In A.K. Paedagogik (Ed.), *Vom Wert der Kooperation. Gedanken zu Bildung und Erziehung [On the Value of Cooperation. Thoughts on Literacy and Education]* (pp. 173–187). Frankfurt: Peter Lang.

Hoelter, G. (2011). *Bewegungstherapie bei psychischen Erkrankungen: Grundlagen und Anwendung [Movement Therapy for Mental Illness: Fundamentals and Application].* Cologne: Deutscher Aerzteverlag.

Hoelter, G., Troska, S., & Beudels, W. (2008). Körper- und bewegungsbezogenes Verhalten und Erleben von anorektischen jungen Frauen – Ausgewählte Befunde zur Gleichgewichtsregulation und zum Körpererleben [Body and movement-related behaviour and experience of anorexic young women - Selected findings on balance regulation and body experience]. In Joraschky et al. (Eds.) (pp. 89–107).

Hoffmann, S. O. (1996). *Charakter und Neurose [Character and Neurosis]* (2nd ed.). Frankfurt: Suhrkamp.

Hofmann, S. G., & Weinberger, J. (2007). The art and science of psychotherapy: An introduction. In S. G. Hofmann & J. Weingerber (Eds.), *The Art and Science of Psychotherapy* (pp. XVII–XIX). New York: Routledge.

Holler, J. (2011). Verhaltenskoordination, Mimikry und sprachbegleitende Gestik in der Interaktion [Behavioural coordination, mimicry and speech-accompanying gestures in interaction]. *Psychotherapie-Wissenschaft [Psychotherapy Science], 1*, 23–31.

Holodynski, M. (2004). The miniaturization of expression in the development of emotional self-regulation. *Developmental Psychology, 40*, 16–28.

Holodynski, M. (2009). Milestones and mechanisms of emotional development. In B. Roettger-Roessler & H. J. Markowitsch (Eds.), *Emotions as Bio-cultural Processes* (pp. 139–163). New York: Springer.

Hopper, J. W., Spinazzola, J., Simpson, W. B., & van der Kolk, B. (2006). Preliminary evidence of parasympathetic influence on basal heart rate in posttraumatic stress disorder. *Journal of Psychosomatic Research, 60*, 83–90.

Horovitz, M. J. (1991). *Person Schemas and Maladaptive Interpersonal Patterns.* Chicago: Chicago University Press.

Horsthemke, B. (2018). A critical view on transgenerational epigenetic inheritance in humans. *Nature Communications, 9*, 2973. https://doi.org/10.1038/s41467-018-05445-5.

Hortelano, X. S. (2015). Vegetotherapy with psychosomatic disorders. Functionalism in practice. In Marlock et al. (Eds.) (pp. 748–755).

Horvath, A. O., Del Re, A. C., Flueckiger C., & Symonds, D. (2011). Alliance in individual psychotherapy. *Psychotherapy, 48*, 9–16.

Huber, C., Hauke, W., Ruppert, S., & Zaudig, M. (2005). Verhaltenstherapie und Körpertherapie: Eine Effektivitätsstudie an psychosomatischen Patienten [Behavioural therapy and body therapy: An effectiveness study on psychosomatic patients]. In Sulz et al. (Eds.) (pp. 69–101).

Huber, R. (2000). Annas Geschichte. Beziehungsaufträge der Eltern an das ungeborene Kind [Anna's story. Relationship mandates of the parents to the unborn child]. In Levend & Janus (Ed.) (pp. 100–111).

Huether, G. (2003). Die Auswirkungen traumatischer Erfahrungen im Kindesalter auf die Hirnentwicklung [The effects of traumatic experiences in childhood on brain development]. In L. Koch-Kneidl & J Wiesse (Eds.), *Entwicklung nach früher Traumatisierung [Development After Early Traumatisation]* (pp. 25–38). Goettingen: Vandenhoeck & Ruprecht.

Huether, G. (2005). Mein Körper – Das bin doch ich… Neurobiologische Argumente für den Einsatz körperorientierter Verfahren in der Psychotherapie [My body - That's me… Neurobiological arguments for the use of body-oriented methods in psychotherapy]. *Psychoanalyse & Koerper [Psychoanalysis & Body], 4*(7), 7–23.

Huether, G. (2006). Wie Embodiment neurobiologisch erklärt werden kann [How embodiment can be explained neurobiologically]. In Storch et al. (Eds.) (pp. 73–97).

Huether, G. (2009). Die Auswirkungen traumatischer Erfahrungen im Kindesalter auf die Hirnentwicklung [The impacts of traumatic experiences on brain development]. In K.-H. Brisch & T. Hellbruegge (Eds.), *Bindung und Trauma. Risiken und Schutzfaktoren für die Entwicklung von Kindern [Attachment and trauma: Perils and protecting factors for the development of children]* (pp. 94–104). Stuttgart: Klett-Cotta.

Huether, G. (2010). *Neurobiologie: Umdenken, umfühlen oder umhandeln [Neurobiology: Rethinking, refeeling or reacting]?* In Kuenzler et al. (Eds.) (pp. 115–119).

Huether, G., & Sachsse, R. (2007). Angst- und stressbedingte Störungen. Auf dem Weg zu einer neurobiologisch fundierten Psychotherapie [Anxiety and stress-related disorders. Towards a neurobiologically based psychotherapy]. *Psychotherapeut [Psychotherapist], 52*, 166–179.

Huether, G., Doering, S., Rueger, U., Ruether, E., & Schuessler, G. (1999). The stress-reaction process and the adaptive modification and reorganization of neuronal networks. *Psychiatry Research, 87*, 83–95.

Hufnagel, H., Steimer-Krause, E., & Krause, R. (1991). Mimisches Verhalten und Erleben bei schizophrenen Patienten und Gesunden [Mimic behaviour and experience in schizophrenic patients and healthy persons]. *Zeitschrift für Klinische Psychologie [Journal for Clinical Psychology], 20*, 356–370.

Huizink, A. (2000). *Prenatal Stress and Its Effect on Infant Development.* Unpubl. Med. Diss., University of Utrecht.

Husserl, E. (2012). *Die Krisis der europäischen Wissenschaften und die transzendentale Phänomenologie.* Hamburg: Felix Meiner (engl.: The Crisis of European Sciences and Transcendental Phenomenology. Evanston, IL: Northwestern University Press, 1970).

Hutterer, R. (1998). *Das Paradigma der Humanistischen Psychologie. Entwicklung, Ideengeschichte und Produktivität [The Paradigm of Humanistic Psychology. Development, History of Ideas, and Productivity].* Wien: Springer.

Hutto, D. D. (2010). Radical enactivism and narrative practice. Implications for psychopathology. In Fuchs et al. (Eds.) (pp. 43–66).

Hutto, D. D. (2011). Enactivism: Why be radical? In H. Bredekamp & J. M. Krois (Eds.), *Sehen und Handeln [Seeing and Acting]* (pp. 21–44). Berlin: Akademie Verlag.

Hutto, D. D. (2013). Psychology unified: From folk psychology to radical enactivism. *Review of General Psychology*, *17*, 174–178.

Hutto, D. D., & Myin, E. (2013). *Radicalizing Enactivism. Basic Minds without Content*. Cambridge, MA: MIT Press.

Huttunen, M. O., & Niskanen, P. (1978). Prenatal loss of father and psychiatric disorders. *Archives of General Psychiatry*, *35*, 429–431.

Hyniewska, S., & Sato, W. (2015). Facial feedback affects valence judgments of dynamic and static emotional expressions. *Frontiers in Psychology*, *6*, 291. https://doi.org/10.3389/fpsyg.2015.00291.

Iacoboni, M., Molnar-Szakacs, I., Gallese, V., Buccino, G., Mazziotta, J. C., & Rizzolatti, G. (2005). Grasping the intentions of others with one's own mirror neuron system. *PloS Biology*, *3*(3): e79. https://doi.org/10.1371/journal.pbio.0030079.

Imus, S. D. (2019). Interrupted rhythms: Dance/movement therapy's contributions to suicide prevention. In Payne et al. (Eds.) (pp. 135–146).

Insel, T. R., & Young, L. J. (2001). The neurobiology of attachment. *Nature Reviews Neuroscience*, *2*, 129–136.

Israel, A., & Reissmann, B. (2008). *Früh in der Welt. Das Erleben des Frühgeborenen und seiner Eltern auf der neonatologischen Intensivstation [Early in the World. The Experience of the Premature Baby and His Parents in the Neonatal Intensive Care Unit]*. Frankfurt: Brandes & Apsel.

Iverson, J. M., & Goldin-Meadow, S. (2009). Gesture paves the way for language development. *Psychological Science*, *16*, 367–371.

Jacob, G., & Arntz, A. (2014). Schematherapie [Schema Therapy]. Goettingen: Hogrefe.

Jacobs, T. J. (1973). Posture, gesture, and movement in the analyst: Cues to interpretation and countertransference. *Journal of the American Psychoanalytic Association*, *21*, 77–92.

Jacobs, T. J. (2001). On unconscious communications and covert enactments: Some reflections on their role in the analytic situation. *Psychoanalytic Inquiry*, *21*, 4–23.

Jacobson, E. (2011). Structural integration, an alternative method of manual therapy and sensorimotor education. *The Journal of Alternative and Complementary Medicine*, *17*, 891–899.

Jaeger, S., & Staeuble, I. (1978). *Die gesellschaftliche Genese der Psychologie [The Social Genesis of Psychology]*. Frankfurt: Campus.

Jaenig, W. (1980). Das vegetative Nervensystem [The vegetative nerve system]. In R. F. Schmidt & G. Thews (Eds.), *Physiologie des Menschen [Physiology of Man]* (pp. 118–157). Berlin: Springer.

Jaenig, W. (2006). Wie beeinflusst das Gehirn den Darm und der Darm das Gehirn [How does the brain influence the gut and the gut influence the brain?]? *Forschende Komplementärmedizin, [Researching Complementary Medicine]*, *13*, 245–146.

Jahn, E. B. (2016). Embodied Emotional Master (EEM): Mit Selbstmodifikation von der Einsicht zur Handlung [Embodied Emotional Master (EEM): With self-modification from insight to action]. In Bohne et al. (Eds.) (pp. 119–152).

Jahn, E. B. (2018). Embodiment in group therapy: From IQ to WeQ: Together we are stronger! In Hauke & Kritikos (Eds.) (pp. 339–370).

James, W. (1932). A study of the expression of bodily posture. *The Journal of General Psychology*, *7*, 405–437.

James, W. (1994). The physical basis of emotion. *Psychological Review*, *101*, 205–210 (Reprint from 1894).

Janov, A. (1971). *The Anatomy of Mental Illness*. New York: G. P. Putnam's Son.

Jarlnaes, E., & Luytelaar, J. van (2004). The therapeutic power of peak experiences: Embodying Maslow's old concept. In Macnaughton (Ed.) (pp. 241–262).

Jaynes, J. (1976). *The Origin of Consciousness in the Breakdown of the Bicameral Mind*. Boston: Houghton Mifflin.

Jeschke, C. (1990). Isadora Duncan in ihrer Zeit [Isadora Duncan and her time]. *Tanz aktuell, Beilage Tanzgeschichten [Dance Updating. Supplement Histories of Dance]*, *10*, 25–35.

Johnen, R. (2010). Funktionelle Entspannung [Functional relaxation]. In Mueller-Braunschweig & Stiller (Eds.) (pp. 61–85).

Johnson, D. H. (2000). Intricate tactile sensitivity. A key variable in Western integrative bodywork. In E. A. Mayer & C. B. Saper (Eds.), *The Biological Basis for Mind Body Interactions* (pp. 479–490). Amsterdam: Elsevier.

Johnson, D. H. (2015). The primacy of experiential practices in body psychotherapy. In Marlock et al. (Eds.) (pp. 117–125).

Johnson, D. H. (Ed.) (2018). *Diverse Bodies, Diverse Practices. Toward an Inclusive Somatics*. Berkeley: North Atlantic Books.

Johnson, M. (2007). *The Meaning of the Body. Aesthetics of Human Understanding*. Chicago: The University of Chicago Press.

Johnson, R. (2014). Contacting gender. *Gestalt Review*, *18*, 80–95.

Johnson, R. (2015). Grasping and transforming the embodied experience of oppression. *International Body Psychotherapy Journal*, *14*, 80–95.

Johnson, R. (2019). Oppression and embodiment in psychotherapy. In Payne et al. (Eds.) (pp. 351–359).

Johnson, S. M. (1985). *Characterological Transformation: The Hard Work Miracle*. London: W. W. Norton & Company.

Johnstone, A. A. (2012). The deep bodily roots of emotion. *Husserl Studies*, *28*, 179–200.

Jonas, H. (2001). *The Phenomenon of Life: Toward a Philosophical Biology*. Evanston: Northwestern University Press.

Joraschky, P. (1995). Das Körperschema und das Körper-Selbst [Body schema and body self]. In Braehler (Ed.) (pp. 34–49).

Joraschky, P. (1997). Die Auswirkungen von Vernachlässigung, Misshandlung, Missbrauch auf Selbstwert und Körperbild [The effects of neglect, maltreatment, abuse on self-esteem and body image]. In Egle et al. (Eds.) (pp. 117–130).

Joraschky, P., & Poehlmann, K. (2008). Theorien zum Körpererleben und ihre Bedeutung für das Körpererleben von Patienten mit Essstörungen [Theories of body experience and their significance for the body experience of patients with eating disorders]. In Joraschky et al. (Eds.) (pp. 25–33).

Joraschky, P., & Poehlmann, K. (2014). Schatten im Körperbild. Die Bedeutung von Traumatisierungen und strukturellen Störungen [Shadows in the body image. The significance of traumatisation and structural disorders]. *Psychodynamische Psychotherapie [Psychodynamic Psychotherapy], 13,* 27–40.

Joraschky, P., Arnim, A. von, Loew, T., & Tritt, K. (2002). Körperpsychotherapie bei somatoformen Störungen [Body psychotherapy for somatoform disorders]. In B. Strauss (Ed.), *Psychotherapie bei körperlichen Erkrankungen [Psychotherapy of Somatic Illnesses]* (pp. 81–95). *Jahrbuch der medizinischen Psychologie [Yearbook of Medical Psychology], 21.* Goettingen: Hogrefe.

Joraschky, P., Lausberg, H., & Poehlmann, K. (Eds.) (2008). *Körperorientierte Diagnostik und Psychotherapie bei Essstörungen [Body Oriented Diagnostics and Psychotherapy of Eating Disorders].* Giessen: Psychosozial Verlag.

Joraschky, P., Loew, T., & Roehricht, F. (Eds.) (2009). *Körpererleben und Körperbild. Ein* Handbuch zur Diagnostik [Body experience and body image. A diagnostic manual]. Stuttgart: Schattauer.

Jordan, J. S., & Ghin, M. (2006). (Proto-)consciousness as a contextually emergent property of self-sustaining systems. *Mind & Matter, 4,* 45–68.

Jung, C. G. (1928/1969). On psychic energy. In *Collected Works, Vol. 8 Structure & Dynamics of the Psyche* (pp. 3–66). Princeton: Princeton University Press.

Jung, C. G. (1971). *The Spiritual Problem of Modern Man. Collected Works, Vol. 10, § 148-196.* Princeton: Princeton University Press.

Jung, M., & Heilinger, J.-C. (Eds.) (2009). *Funktionen des Erlebens. Neue Perspektiven des qualitativen Bewusstseins [Functions of Experiencing. New Perspectives of Qualitative Consciousness].* Berlin: De Gruyter.

Just, M. A., Cherkassky, V. L., Aryal, S., & Mitchell, T. M. (2010). A neurosemantic theory of concrete noun representation based on the underlying brain codes. *PLoS ONE, 5*(1), e8622. https://doi.org/10.1371/journal.pone .0008622.

Kabat-Zinn, J. (2017). *Mindfulness-Based Stress Reduction: The MBSR Program for Enhancing Health and Vitality.* Novato: New World Library.

Kaji, M. (2019). The importance of subtle movement and stillnes in Japanese dance movement therapy. A comparison with the Japanese tradtional performing art of 'Noh'. In Payne et al. (Eds.) (pp. 224–231).

Kalawski, J. (2020). The Alba Method and the science of emotions. *Integrative Psychological & Behavioral Science, 54*(4), 903–919. https://doi.org/10.1007/s12124-020-09525-4. PMID: 32212066.

Kaletsch, M., Krueger, B., Pilgramm, S., Stark, R., Lis, S., Gallhofer, B., Zentgraf, K., Munzert, J., & Sammer, G. (2014). Borderline personality disorder is associated with lower confidence in perception of emotional body movements. *Frontiers in Psychology, 5,* 1262. https://doi.org/10.3389/fpsyg.2014.01262.

Kamper, D., & Wulf, C. (1982). Die Parabel der Wiederkehr [The parable of return]. In D. Kamper & C. Wulf (Eds.), *Die Wiederkehr des Körpers [The Return of the Body]* (pp. 9–21). Frankfurt: Suhrkamp.

Kanakogi, Y., Miyazaki, M., Takahashi, H., Yamamoto, H., Kobayashi, T., & Hiraki, K. (2022). Third-party punishment by preverbal infants. *Nature Human Behaviour, 6,* 1234–1242.

Kandel, E. R. (1998). A new intellectual framework for psychiatry. *American Journal of Psychiatry, 155,* 457–469.

Kandel, E. R. (1999). Biology and the future of psychoanalysis: A new intellectual framework for psychiatry revisited. *American Journal of Psychiatry, 156,* 505–524.

Kanfer, F. H., Reinecker, H., Schmelzer, D. (2012). *Selbstmanagement-Therapie, Ein Lehrbuch für die klinische Praxis [Self-Management Therapy. A Textbook for Clinical Practice]* (5th ed.). Berlin, Heidelberg: Springer.

Kanfer, F. H., & Saslow, G. (1969). Behavioral diagnosis. In C. M. Franks (Ed.), *Behavior Therapy: Appraisal and Status* (pp. 417–444). New York: McGraw-Hill.

Kant, I. (1966/1787). *Kritik der reinen Vernunft.* Stuttgart: Reclam [engl.: Critique of Pure Reason. Penguin, 2007].

Kaplan-Solms, K., & Solms, M. (2000). *Clinical Studies in Neuro-Psychoanalysis.* Madison: International Universites Press.

Karch, S., Heinzel, S., Pogarell, O., & Schiepek, G. (2012). Neurobiologische Grundlagen psychotherapeutischer Verfahren [Neurobiological foundations of psychotherapeutic methods]. *Psychotherapeut [Psychotherapist], 57,* 204–212.

Karen, R. (1998). *Becoming Attached: First Relationships and How They Shape Our Capacity to Love.* Oxford: Oxford University Press.

Kaul, E., & Fischer, M. (Eds.) (2016). *Einführung in die Integrative Körperpsychotherapie IBP (Integrative Body Psychotherapy) [Integrative Body Psychotherapy. An Introduction].* Bern: Hogrefe.

Keleman, S. (1985). *Emotional Anatomy. The Structure of Experience*. Berkeley: Center Press...

Keleman, S. (1989). *Bonding. A Somatic Emotional Approach to Transference*. Berkeley: Center Press.

Keleman, S. (1989a). *Patterns of Distress*. Berkeley: Center Press.

Keleman, S. (2015). The maturation of the somatic self. In Marlock et al. (Eds.) (pp. 230–236).

Kelley, C. R. (1976). New techniques in vision improvement. In D. Boadella (Ed.), *In the Wake of Reich* (pp. 351–381). London: Conventure.

Kelley, C. R. (2004). *Life Force: The Creative Process in Man and in Nature*. Bloomington: Trafford On-Demand Publishers.

Kepner, J. (1993). *Body Process. A Gestalt Approach to Working with the Body in Psychotherapy*. New York: Routledge.

Kern, E. (2014). *Personzentrierte Körperpsychotherapie [Person Centred Body Psychotherapy]*. Munich: Reinhardt.

Kern, E. (2019). Bezug auf Wissenschaftlichkeit oder auf ein Menschenbild als Basis für Körperpsychotherapie [Reference to scientificity or to a conception of the human being the basis for body psychotherapy]? *Koerper – tanz – bewegung [Body – Dance – Movement]*, 7, 169–172.

Kernberg, O. (1976). *Object Relations Theory and Clinical Psychoanalysis*. New York: Jason Aronson.

Kernberg, O. (1992). *Aggression in Personality Disorders and Perversions*. New Haven: Yale University Press.

Kernberg, O. (2000). Borderline-Persönlichkeitsorganisation und Klassifikation der Persönlichkeitsstörungen [Borderline personality organization and classification of personality disorders]. In Kernberg et al. (Eds.) (pp. 45–56).

Kernberg, O. (2006). Neue Überlegungen zur Frage der Identität [New considerations on the question of identity]. In Remmel et al. (Eds.) (pp. 3–21).

Kernberg, O., Selzer, M., Koenigsberg, H., Carr, A., & Appelbaum, A. (1989). *Psychodynamic Psychotherapy of Borderline Patients*. New York: Basic Books.

Kernberg, O., Dulz, B., & Sachsse, U. (Eds.) (2000). *Handbuch der Borderline-Störungen [Handbook of Borderline Disorders]*. Stuttgart: Schattauer.

Kestenberg Amighi, J., Loman, S., Lewis, P., & Sossin, M. (1999). *The Meaning of Movement. Developmental and Clinical Perspectives of the Kestenberg Movement Profile*. New York: Routledge.

Keysers, C. (2009). Mirror neurons. *Current Biology*, 19, R971–R973.

Keysers, C. (2011). *The Empathic Brain. How the Discovery of Mirror Neurons Changes Our Understanding of Human Nature*. Ebook: Social Brain Press.

Kiersky, S., & Beebe, B. (1994). The reconstruction of early nonverbal relatedness in the treatment of difficult patients. *Psychoanalytic Dialogues*, 4, 389–408.

Kimmel, M., Irran, C., & Luger, M. A. (2015). Bodywork as systemic and inter-enactive competence: Participatory process management in Feldenkrais® Method and Zen Shiatsu. *Frontiers in Psychology*, 5, 1424. https://doi.org/10.3389/fpsyg.2014.01424.

Kitayama, S., Mesquita, B., & Karasawa, M. (2006). Cultural affordances and emotional experience: Socially engaging and disengaging emotions in Japan and the United States. *Journal of Personality and Social Psychology*, 91(5), 890–903.

Klages, L. (1926). *Die Grundlagen der Charakterkunde [The Foundations of Characterology]*. Leipzig: Barth.

Klages, L. (1937). *Der Mensch und das Leben [Man and Life]*. Jena: Diederichs.

Klasmeyer, G., & Sendlmeier, W. F. (1997). The classification of different phonation types in emotional and neutral speech. *Forensic Linguistics*, 4, 104–124.

Klatt, F. (1922). *Die schöpferische Pause [The Creative Pause]*. Jena: Diederichs.

Klein, G. (2005). Das Theater des Körpers. Zur Performanz des Körperlichen [The theater of the body. On the performance of the physical]. In Schroer (Ed.) (pp. 73–91).

Kleinbub, J. R. (2017). State of the art of interpersonal physiology in psychotherapy: A systematic review. *Frontiers in Psychology*, 8, 2053. https://doi.org/10.3389/fpsyg.2017.02053.

Kleinman, A. (2012). The art of medicine. Culture, bereavement, and psychiatry. *The Lancet*, 379, 608–609.

Klengel, T., Mehta, D., Anacker, C., Rex-Haffner, M., Pruessner, J. C., Pariante, C. M., Pace, T., Mercer, K. B., Mayberg, H. S., Bradley, B., Nemeroff, C. B., Holsboer, F., Heim, C. M., Ressler, K. J., Rein, T., & Binder, E. B. (2013). Allele-specific FKBP5 DNA demethylation mediates gene–childhood trauma interactions. *Nature Neuroscience*, 16, 33–41.

Klopstech, A. (2005). Stellen die Neurowissenschaften die Psychotherapie vom Kopf auf die Füsse? [Are the neurosciences turning psychotherapy from head to toe?] *Psychoanalyse & Koerper [Psychoanalysis & Body]*, 4, (7), 69–108.

Klopstech, A. (2009). So which body is it? The concepts of the body in psychotherapy. *Bioenergetic Analysis*, 19, 11–30.

Knop, A., & Heim, C. (2020). Psychoendokrinologie [Psycho-endocrinology]. In Egle et al. (Eds.) (pp. 78–92).

Knopf, M., Goertz, C., & Kolling, T. (2011). Entwicklung des Gedächtnisses bei Säuglingen und Kleinkindern [The development of memory in infants]. *Psychologische Rundschau [Psychological Review]*, 62, 85–92.

Koch, S. C. (2006). Interdisciplinary embodiment approaches. Implications for the creative arts therapies. In S. C. Koch & I. Braeuninger (Eds.), *Advances in Dance/ Movement Therapy. Theoretical Perspectives and Empirical Findings* (pp. 17–28). Berlin: Logos.

Koch, S. C. (2011). *Embodiment: Der Einfluss von Eigenbewegung auf Affekt, Einstellung und Kognition [Embodiment. The Impact of Self-Movement on Affect, Attitudes, and Cognition].* Berlin: Logos.

Koch, S. C., & Fischman, D. (2014). Enaktive Tanztherapie. Systemtheoretische Ansätze in den Bewegungstherapien [Enactive dance therapy. Systems views in movement therapies]. *Koerper – tanz – bewegung [Body – Dance – Movement], 2,* 3–11.

Koch, S. C., Morlinghaus, K., & Fuchs, T. (2007). The joy dance. Specific effects of a single dance intervention on psychiatric patients with depression. *The Arts in Psychotherapy, 34,* 340–349.

Koch, S., Holland, R. W., Hengstler, M., & van Knippenberg, A. (2009). Body locomotion as regulatory process. Stepping backward enhances cognitive control. *Psychological Science, 20,* 549–550.

Koch, S. C., Fuchs, T., & Summa, M. (Eds.) (2012). *Body Memory, Metaphor and Movement.* Amsterdam: John Benjamins.

Koch-Lauscher, I. (1994). Übertragung? Gedanken zum Tagungsthema [Transference? Thoughts on the conference topic]. In Steinaecker (Ed.) (pp. 61–67).

Koehler, L. (1990). Neuere Ergebnisse der Kleinkindforschung. Ihre Bedeutung für die Psychoanalyse [Recent results of infant research. Their significance for psychoanalysis]. *Forum der Psychoanalyse [Forum of Psychoanalysis], 6,* 32–51.

Koelbl, C. (2010). Die Psychologie der kulturhistorischen Schule als konkrete Psychologie [The psychology of the cultural-historical school as concrete psychology]. In G. Juettemann & W. Mack (Eds.), *Konkrete Psychologie. Die Gestaltungsanalyse der Handlungswelt [Concrete Psychology. The Structural Analysis of the World of Action]* (pp. 150–161). Lengerich: Pabst.

Koemeda-Lutz, M. (Ed.) (2002). *Körperpsychotherapie – Bioenergetische Konzepte im Wandel [Body Psychotherapy. Changing Concepts in Bioenergetics].* Basel: Schwabe.

Koemeda-Lutz, M. (2002a). Ein psychosomatisches Persönlichkeitsmodell: Charakterstrukturen [Character structures. A psychosomatic personality model]. In Koemeda-Lutz (Ed.) (pp. 117–137).

Koemeda-Lutz, M. (2012). Integrating brain, mind, and body: Clinical and therapeutic implications of neuroscience. *Bioenergetic Analysis, 22,* 57–77.

Koemeda-Lutz, M., & Gutzat, R. (2022). Energie: Ein universelles Wirkprinzip [Energy. A universal change mechanism]. *Koerper – tanz – bewegung [Body – dance - movement], 10* (1), 14–21.

Koemeda-Lutz, M., & Steinmann, H. (2004). Implikationen neurobiologischer Forschungsergebnisse für die Körperpsychotherapie unter spezieller Berücksichtigung der Affekte [Implications of neurobiological reserach findings for body psychotherapy with special considerations of affects]. *Psychotherapie Forum [Psychotherapy Forum], 12,* 88–97.

Koenig, K. (2004). *Charakter, Persönlichkeit und Persönlichkeitsstörung [Character, Personality, and Personality Disorder].* Stuttgart: Klett-Cotta.

Koenig, W. (1981). Zur Neuformulierung der psychoanalytischen Metapsychologie: Vom Energie-Modell zum Informationskonzept [Reformulating psychoanalytic meta-psychology: From the energy model to the information concept]. In W. Mertens (Ed.), *Neue Perspektiven der Psychoanalyse [New Perspectives in Psychoanalysis]* (pp. 83–123). Stuttgart: Kohlhammer.

Koerner, A., Topolinski, S., & Strack, S. (2015). Routes to embodiment. *Frontiers in Psychology,* 02. July 2015. https://doi.org/10.3389/fpsyg.2015.00940.

Koeth, A. (2013). Der Körper als Speicher und als Kompass [The body as memory and compass]. *Koerper – tanz – bewegung [Body – Dance – Movement], 1,* 59–65 & 120–126.

Koeth, A. (2014). Muss sich die ambulante Körperpsychotherapie verstecken [Does outpatient body psychotherapy have to hide]? *Psychodynamische Psychotherapie [Psychodynamic Psychotherapy], 13,* 9–14.

Kogan, G. (Ed.) (1980). *Your Body Works. A Guide to Health Energy and Balance.* Berkeley: And/Or Press.

Kohut, H. (1971). *The Analysis of the Self. A Systematic Approach to the Psychoanalytic Treatment of Narcissistic Personality Disorders.* New York: International University Press.

Kolbe, C. (2019). Wie fühlt sich das an? Verständnis und Bedeutung von Emotionen in der Humanistischen Psychotherapie [How does that feel? Understanding and meaning of emotions in humanistic psychotherapy]. In Thielen & Eberwein (Eds.) (pp. 109–119).

Konzag, T. A., Klose, S., Bandemer-Greulich, U., Fikentscher, E., & Bahrke, U. (2006). Stationäre körperbezogene Psychotherapie bei Anorexia und Bulimia nervosa [Inpatient body related psychotherapy in anorexia and bulimia nervosa]. *Psychotherapeut [Psychotherapist], 51,* 35–42.

Koole, S. L., & Rothermund, K. (2011). "I feel better but I don't know why": The psychology of implicit emotion regulation. *Cognition and Emotion, 25,* 389–399.

Koole, S. L., Schlinkert, C., Maldei, T., & Baumann, N. (2019). Becoming who you are: An integrative review of self-determination theory and personality systems interactions theory. *Journal of Personality, 87,* 15–36.

Koole, S. L., Atzil-Slonim, D., Butler, E., Dikker, S., Tschacher, W., & Wilderjans, T. (2020). In sync with your shrink: Grounding psychotherapy in interpersonal synchrony. In J. P. Forgas, W. D. Crano & K. Fiedler (Eds.), *Applications of Social Psychology. How Social Psychology Can Contribute to the Solution of Real World Problems* (pp. 161–184). New York: Routledge.

Korischek, C. (2020). Die Methode des "gereinigten Herzens" oder der Körper der Psychotherapeutin als Diagnoseinstrument. Eine Reise in die Welt des Chanmi Qigong [The method of the "purified heart" or the psychotherapist's body as a diagnostic tool. A journey into the world of Chanmi Qigong]. *Psychoanalyse & Koerper [Psychoanalysis & Body]*, No. 36, *19*(1), 21–45.

Korn, E. (1963). Das neue Lebensgefühl in der Gymnastik [The new attitude to life in gymnastics]. In E. Korn, O. Suppert & K. Vogl (Eds.), *Die Jugendbewegung. Welt und Wirkung [The Youth Movement. It's World and Influence]* (pp. 101–119). Duesseldorf: Diederichs.

Kozlowska, K. (2005). Healing the disembodied mind: Contemporary models of conversion disorder. *Harvard Review of Psychiatry, 13*, 1–13.

Kraemer, S. (2006). Die 'Rehabilitierung der Stimme'. Über die Oralität hinaus [The rehabilitation of the voice. Beyond orality]. In D. Kolesch & S. Kraemer (Eds.), *Stimme [Voice]* (pp. 269–295). Frankfurt: Suhrkamp.

Kramar, M., & Alim, K. (2021). Encoding memory in tube diameter hierarchy of living flow network. *Proceedings of the National Academy of Sciences*, March 9, 118(10), e2007815118. https://doi.org/10.1073/pnas.2007815118.

Kramer, R. (2019). *The Birth of Relationship Therapy. Carl Rogers meets Otto Rank.* Giessen: Psychosozial.

Krause, R. (1992). Die Zweierbeziehung als Grundlage der psychoanalytischen Therapie [The relationship of the two as the basis of psychoanalytic psychotherapy]. *Psyche, 46*, 588–612.

Krause, R. (1996). Emotion als Mittler zwischen Individuum und Umwelt [Emotion as a mediator between the individual and the environment]. In Adler et al. (Eds.) (pp. 252–261).

Krause, R. (1997). *Allgemeine psychoanalytische Krankheitslehre [General Psychoanalytic Theory of Disorders]. Vol. 1: Grundlagen [Foundations].* Stuttgart: Kohlhammer.

Krause, R. (1998). *Allgemeine psychoanalytische Krankheitslehre [General Psychoanalytic Theory of Disorders]. Vol. 2: Modelle [Models].* Stuttgart: Kohlhammer.

Krause, R. (2006). Emotionen, Gefühle, Affekte – Ihre Bedeutung für die seelische Regulierung [Emotions, feelings, affects: Their significance for mental regulation]. In Remmel et al. (Eds.) (pp. 22–44).

Krebs, A. (2015). *Zwischen Ich und Du. Eine dialogische Philosophie der Liebe [Between I and You. A Dialogic Philosophy of Love].* Frankfurt: Suhrkamp.

Krens, I., & Krens, H. (Eds.) (2005). *Grundlagen einer vorgeburtlichen Psychologie [Foundations of Prenatal Psychology].* Goettingen: Vandenhoeck & Ruprecht.

Krens, I., & Krens, H. (Eds.) (2006). *Risikofaktor Mutterleib. Zur Psychotherapie vorgeburtlicher Bindungsstörungen und Traumata [Risk Factor Womb. On the Psychotherapy of Prenatal Attachment Disorders and Traumata].* Goettingen: Vandenhoeck & Ruprecht.

Kret, M. E. (2018). The role of pupil size in communication. Is there room for learning? *Cognition and Emotion, 32*, 1139–1145.

Kretschmer, E., & Cimbal, W. (Eds.) (1931). *Bericht über den VI. Allgemeinen Ärztlichen Kongress für Psychotherapie in Dresden [Report on the 6th General Medical Congress for Psychotherapy in Dresden].* Leipzig: Hirzel.

Kripal, J. (2007). *Esalen. America and the Religion of No Religion.* Chicago: Chicago University Press.

Kriz, J. (1999). *Systemtheorie für Psychotherapeuten, Psychologen und Mediziner [Systems Theory for Psychotherapists, Psychologists, and Physicians].* Wien: Facultas.

Kriz, J. (2001). *Grundkonzepte der Psychotherapie [Basic Concepts of Psychotherapy]* (5th ed.; 7th ed. 2014). Weinheim: Beltz.

Kriz, J. (2004). Wissenschaftliche Grundlagen: Denkmodelle [Scientific foundations: Models of thought]. In W. Senf & M. Broda (Eds.), *Praxis der Psychotherapie [The Practice of Psychotherapy]* (3rd ed.) (pp. 18–24). Stuttgart: Thieme.

Kriz, J. (2004a). Personzentrierte Systemtheorie – Grundfragen und Kernaspekte [Person centred systems theory – Basic questions and core aspects]. In von Schlippe & Kriz (Eds.) (pp. 13–67).

Kriz, J. (2009). Vielfalt in der Psychotherapie: Das Vier-Säulen-Modell. Plädoyer, die internationale und stationäre Verfahrenspluralität auch in deutschen Praxen wieder zuzulassen [The four-columns-model. Plea to allow international and inpatient plurality of methods back into German outpatient practice]. *VPP aktuell [VPP Newsworthy], 6*, 3–5.

Kriz, J. (2010). Systemtheorie als eine Metatheorie zur Integration psychotherapeutischer Ansätze [Systems theory as meta-theory for integrating psychotherapeutic approaches]. *Psychotherapie im Dialog [Psychotherapy in Dialogue], 11*, 28–34.

Kriz, J. (2011). „Humanistische Psychotherapie" als Verfahren. Ein Plädoyer für die Übernahme eines einheitlichen Begriffs [„Humanistic psychotherapy" as an approach. A plea for using a single concept]. *Psychotherapeutenjournal [Psychotherapists Journal], 10*, 332–338.

Kriz, J. (2017). *Subjekt und Lebenswelt. Personzentrierte Systemtheorie für Psychotherapie, Beratung und Coaching [The person and it's life-world: Person-centred systems theory for psychotherapy, counseling, and coaching].* Goettingen: Vandenhoeck & Ruprecht.

Krizan, H. (1992). Atemtherapie [Breath therapy]. In P. Buchheim et al. (Eds.) (pp. 203–216).

Krohs, U., & Toepfer, G. (Eds.) (2005). *Philosophie der Biologie [Philosophy of Biology].* Frankfurt: Suhrkamp.

Krueger, J. (2019). Enactivism, other minds, and mental disorders. *Synthese*. https://doi.org/10.1007/s11229-019-02133 -9.

Krueger, J., & Colombetti, G. (2018). Affective affordances and psychopathology. *Discipline Filosofiche [Philosophical Disciplines]*, *2*, 221–247.

Krueger-Kirn, H., & Schroeter, B. (Eds.) (2017). *Verkörperungen von Weiblichkeit. Gendersensible Betrachtungen körperpsychotherapeutischer Prozesse [Embodiment of Femininity. Gender Sensitive Views on Body Psychotherapeutic Processes]*. Giessen: Psychosozial.

Kuchuck, S. (2021). *The Relational Revolution in Psychoanalysis and Psychotherapy*. London: Confer Books.

Kuechenhoff, J. (2003). Körperbild und psychische Struktur – Zur Erfassung des Körpererlebens in der psychodynamischen Diagnostik [Body image and psychic structure – Understanding body experience in psychodanymic diagnostics]. *Zeitschrift für psychosomatische Medizin und Psychotherapie [Journal for Psychosomatic Medicine and Psychotherapy]*, *49*, 175–194.

Kuechenhoff, J. (2008). Den Körper verstehen – Psychoanalytische Annäherungen [Understanding the body – Psychoanalytic approaches]. In J. Kuechenhoff & K. Wiegerling (Eds.), *Leib und Körper [Lived Body and Physical Body]* (pp. 72–131). Goettingen: Vandenhoeck & Ruprecht.

Kuechenhoff, J. (2009). Das Körpererleben bei Schmerzpatienten und Gesunden: Eine Vergleichsuntersuchung mit der Repertory-Grid-Methode [Body experience in pain patients. A comparative study with the repertory grid method]. In Joraschky et al. (Eds.) (pp. 171–181).

Kuenzler, A. (2006). Ressourcen und körperzentrierte Psychotherapie [Ressources and body centred psychotherapy]. *Psychotherapie [Psychotherapy]*, *11*, 165–170.

Kuenzler, A. (2010). Neurokörperpsychotherapie [Neuro-body-psychotherapy]? In Kuenzler et al. (Eds.) (pp. 121–136).

Kuenzler, A., Boettcher, C., Hartmann, R., & Nussbaum, M.-H. (Eds.) (2010). *Körperzentrierte Psychotherapie im Dialog. Grundlagen, Anwendungen, Integration. Der IKP-Ansatz von Yvonne Maurer [Body Centred Psychotherapy in Dialogue. Foundations, Applications, Integration. The IKP-Approach of Yvonne Maurer]*. Heidelberg: Springer.

Kuhl, J. (1998). Wille und Persönlichkeit: Funktionsanalyse der Selbststeuerung [Will and personality. A functional analysis of self regulation]. *Psychologische Rundschau [Psychological Review]*, *49*, 61–77.

Kuhl, J. (2007). Psychologie des Selbstseins [The psychology of being a self]. In J. Kuhl & A. Luckner (Eds.), *Freies Selbstsein. Authentizität und Regression [Being a Free Self. Authenticity and Regression]* (pp. 49–81). Goettingen: Vandenhoeck & Ruprecht.

Kuhl, J. (2019). Wie funktioniert das Selbst [How works the self]? In S. Rietmann & P. Deing (Eds.), *Psychologie der Selbststeuerung [The Psychology of Self-Regulation]* (pp. 45–62). Cham: Springer.

Kuhl, J., Quirin, M., & Koole, S. L. (2015). Being someone: A neuropsychological model of the integrative self. *Social and Personality Psychology Compass*, *9*, 115–132.

Kuhl, J., Quirin, M., & Koole, S. R. (2021). The functional architecture of human motivation: Personality systems interactions theory. In A. J. Elliot (Ed.), *Advances in Motivation Science (Vol. 8)* (pp. 1–62). London: Elsevier Academic Press.

Kuhn, R. J. (2018). Fieldwork: Seeking balance through the 5rhythms. In D. H. Johnson (Ed.) (pp. 21–44).

Kupper, Z., Ramseyer, F., Hoffmann, H., & Tschacher, W. (2015). Nonverbal synchrony in social interactions of patients with schizophrenia indicates socio-communicative deficits. *Plos One*, *10*(12): e0145882. https://doi.org/10.1371/journal.pone.0145882.

Kurtz, R. (1983). *Hakomi Therapy*. Boulder: Hakomi Institute.

Kurtz, R. (1990). *Body Centered Psychotherapy. The Hakomi Method*. Mendocino: Life Rhythm.

Kurzt, R. (2015). Bodily expression and experience in body psychotherapy. In Marlock et al. (Eds.) (pp. 411–418)

Kurtz, R., & Prestera, H. (1976). *The Body Reveals: An Illustrated Guide to Psychology of the Body*. New York: Harper & Row.

Kutas, M., & Federmeier, K. D. (1998). Minding the body. *Psychophysiology*, *35*, 135–150.

Kykyri, V.-L., Tourunen, A., Wahlström, J., Kaartinen, J., Penttonen, M., & Seikkula, J. (2017). Soft prosody and embodied attunement in therapeutic interaction: A multimethod case study of a moment of change. *Journal of Constructivist Psychology*, *30*, 211–234.

Kyselo, M. (2013). Enaktivismus [Enactivism]. In A. Stephan & S. Walter (Eds.), *Handbuch Kognitionswissenschaft [Handbook of Cognitive Sciences]* (pp. 197–201). Stuttgart: J. B. Metzler.

Kyselo, M. (2014). The body social: An enactive approach to the self. *Frontiers in Psychology*, *5*, 986. https://doi.org/10.3389/fpsyg.2014.00986.

Laban, R. von (1926). *Gymnastik und Tanz [Gymnastics and Dance]*. Oldenburg: Stalling.

Laengle, A., & Kriz, J. (2012). The renewal of humanism in European psychotherapy: Developments and applications. *Psychotherapy*, *49*, 430–436.

Laing, R. D. (1967). *The Politics of Experience*.New York: Ballantine.

Lakoff, G., & Johnson, M. (1999). *Philosophy in the Flesh: The Embodied Mind and Its Challenge to Western Thought*. New York: Basic Books

Lamme, V. A. F. (2003). Why visual attention and awareness are different. *Trends in Cognitive Sciences*, *7*, 12–18.

Lammers, C.-H. (2007). *Emotionsbezogene Psychotherapie [Emotion Related Psychotherapy]*. Stuttgart: Schattauer.

Landsman-Dijkstra, J. J. A., van Wijck, R., & Groothoff, J. W. (2006). The long-term lasting effects on self-efficacy, attribution style, expression of emotions and quality of life of a body awareness program for chronic a-specific psychosomatic symptoms. *Patient Education and Counseling, 60*, 66–79.

Lang, P. J. (1995). The emotion probe. Studies of motivation and attention. *American Psychologist, 50*, 372–385.

Lange, D., Leye, M., & Loew, T. H. (2006). Phänomenologie in der Körperpsychotherapie [Phenomenology in body psychotherapy]. In Marlock & Weiss (Eds.) (pp. 450–454).

Langlotz-Weis, M. (2019). *Körperorientierte Verhaltenstherapie [Body-Oriented Behaviour Therapy]*. Munich: Reinhardt.

Larsen, R. J., & Diener, E. (1992). Promises and problems with the circumplex model of emotion. In M. Clark (Ed.), *Review of Personality and Social Psychology: Vol. 13. Emotion* (pp. 25–29). Thousand Oaks, CA: Sage.

Laska, B. (1981). *Wilhelm Reich in Selbstzeugnissen und Bilddokumenten [Wilhelm Reich in Self-Testimonies and Pictorial Documents]*. Reinbek: Rowohlt.

Laubichler, M. D. (2005). Systemtheoretische Organismuskonzeptionen [Systems theory concepts of organism]. In Krohs & Toepfer (Eds.) (pp. 109–124).

Lausberg, H. (1998). Does movement behavior have differential diagnostic potential? Discussion of a controlled study on patients with anorexia nervosa and bulimia. *American Journal of Dance Therapy, 20*, 85–99.

Lausberg, H. (2008). Bewegungsdiagnostik und -therapie in der Behandlung von Körperbild-Störungen bei Patienten/innen mit Essstörungen [Movement diagnostics and therapy in the treatment of body image disorders in patients with eating disorders]. In Joraschky et al. (Eds.) (pp. 109–127).

Lausberg, H. (2009). Bewegungsanalyse in der Diagnostik von Körperschema- und Körperbildstörungen [Movement analysis in the diagnosis of body schema and body image disorders]. In Joraschky et al. (Eds.) (pp. 125–133).

Lausberg, H., & Kryger, M. (2011). Gestisches Verhalten als Indikator therapeutischer Prozesse in der verbalen Psychotherapie: Zur Funktion der Selbstberührungen und zur Repräsentation von Objektbeziehungen in gestischen Darstellungen [Gestural behaviour as an indicator of therapeutic processes in verbal psychotherapy: On the function of self-touch and the representation of object relations in gestural representations]. *Psychotherapie-Wissenschaft [Psychotherapy Science], 1*, 41–55.

Lausberg, H., Davis, M., & Rothenhaeusler, A. (2000). Hemispheric specialization in spontaneous gesticulation in a patient with callosal disconnection. *Neuropsychologia, 38*, 1654–1663.

Lawley, J., & Tompkins, P. (2013). *Metaphors in Mind. Transformation through Symbolic Modelling*. s. l.: The Developing Company Press.

Lazarus, R. S. (1982). Thoughts on the relations between emotion and cognition. *American Psychologist, 37*, 1019–1024.

LeDoux, J. (1996). *The Emotional Brain. The Mysterious Underpinnings of Emotional Life*. New York: Simon and Schuster.

LeDoux, J. (2002). *Synaptic Self. How Our Brains Become Who We Are*. New York: Viking Penguin.

Legrand, D. (2007). Subjectivity and the body: Introducing basic forms of self-consciousness. *Consciousness and Cognition, 16*, 577–582.

Legrand, D. (2010). Subjective and physical dimensions of bodily self-consciousness, and their dis-integration in anorexia nervosa. *Neuropsychologia, 48*, 726–737.

Leitan, N. D., & Murray, G. (2014). The mind–body relationship in psychotherapy: Grounded cognition as an explanatory framework. *Frontiers in Psychology, 5*(5), 472. https://doi.org/10.3389/fpsyg.2014.00472.

Leuzinger-Bohleber, M. (2001). „…und dann – mit einem Male – war die Erinnerung da…" (Proust). Aus dem interdisziplinären Dialog zwischen Psychoanalyse und Cognitive Science zum Gedächtnis ["…and then - all at once - the memory was there…" (Proust). From the interdisciplinary dialogue between psychoanalysis and cognitive science on memory]. In Cierpka & Buchheim (Eds.) (pp. 99–123).

Leuzinger-Bohleber, M. (2015). The relevance of the embodiment concept for psychoanalysis. In M. Leuzinger-Bohleber (Ed.), *Finding the Body in the Mind. Embodied Memories, Trauma, and Depression* (pp. 33–48). London: Routledge.

Leuzinger-Bohleber, M., & Pfeifer, R. (2013). Embodiment: Den Körper in der Seele entdecken: Ein altes Problem und ein revolutionäres Konzept [Embodiment: Discovering the body in the soul: An old problem and a revolutionary concept]. In Leuzinger-Bohleber et al. (Eds.) (pp. 14–35).

Leuzinger-Bohleber, M., & Pfeifer, R. (2013a). Psychoanalyse und Embodied Cognitive Science in Zeiten revolutionären Umdenkens [Psychoanalysis and embodied cognitive sciences in times of revolutionary rethinking]. In Leuzinger-Bohleber et al. (Eds.) (pp. 39–74).

Leuzinger-Bohleber, M., Emde, R. N., & Pfeifer, R. (Eds.) (2013). *Embodiment. Ein innovatives Konzept für Entwicklungsforschung und Psychoanalyse [Embodiment. An Innovative Concept for Developmental Research and Psychoanalysis]*. Goettingen: Vandenhoeck & Ruprecht.

Levend, H., & Janus, L. (Eds.) (2000). *Drum hab ich kein Gesicht. Kinder aus unerwünschten Schwangerschaften [That's Why I Don't Have Face. Children From Unwanted Pregnancies]*. Wuerzburg: Echter.

Levenson, R. W. (1999). The Intrapersonal Functions of Emotion. *Cognition and Emotion, 13*, 481–504.

Levenson, R. W. (2003). Blood, sweat, and fears. The autonomic architecture of emotion. *Annals of the New York Academy of Sciences, 1000*, 348–366.

Levine, P. (1997). *Waking the Tiger. Healing Trauma.* Berkeley: North Atlantic Books

Levine, P. (2010). *In an Unspoken Voice. How the Body Releases Trauma and Restores Goodness.* Berkeley: North Atlantic Books.

Levine, P. A., & Macnaughton, I. (2004). Breath and Consciousness: Reconsidering the Viability of Breathwork in Psychological and Spiritual Interventions in Human Development. In Macnaughton (Ed.) (pp. 367–393).

Lewis, M. D. (2000). Emotional self-organization at three time scales. In M. D. Lewis & I. Granic (Eds.), *Emotion, Development, and Self-Organization: Dynamic Systems Approaches to Emotional Development* (pp. 37–69). Cambridge, MA: Cambridge University Press.

Leye, M. (2011). Fallbeispiele störungsspezifischer, stationärer (kombinierte Einzel- und Gruppenpsychotherapie) Psychotherapie mit der Methode „Funktionelle Entspannung" [Case studies of disorder-specific, inpatient (combined individual and group psychotherapy) psychotherapy with the "Functional Relaxation" method]. In Roehricht (Ed.) (pp. 297–321).

Lichtenberg, J. D. (1989). *Psychoanalysis and Motivation.* Hillsdale: The Analytic Press.

Lichtenberg, J. D., Lachmann, F. M., & Fosshage, J. L. (2001). *Self and Motivational Systems. Towards A Theory of Psychoanalytic Technique.* London: Routledge.

Lincoln, T. M., Schulze, L., & Renneberg, B. (2022). The role of emotion regulation in the characterization, development and treatment of psychopathology. *Nature Reviews Psychology.* https://doi.org/10.1038/s44159-022-00040-4.

Linden, D. E. (2006). How psychotherapy changes the brain: The contribution of functional neuroimaging. *Molecular Psychiatry, 11*, 528–538.

Linehan, M. (1993). *Cognitive-Behavioral Treatment of Borderline Personality Disorder.* New York: The Guilford Press.

Linse, U. (1986). Die Freiluftkultur der Wandervögel [The outdoor culture of the Wandervogel]. In Deutscher Werkbund (Eds.) (pp. 398–406).

Linse, U. (1998). Das „natürliche" Leben: Die Lebensreform [The ‚natural' life: The life reform]. In R. van Duelmen (Ed.), *Erfindung des Menschen. Schöpfungsträume und Körperbilder 1500-2000 [Invention of the Human Being. Dreams of Creation and Images of the Body 1500–2000]* (pp. 435–457). Wien: Boehlau.

Liss, J. (2001). *Maps of Experience.* In Heller (Eds.) (pp. 173–186).

Liss, J., & Stupiggia, M. (1994). *La Terapia Biosistemica: Un Approccio Originale Al Trattamento Psico-Corporeo Della Sofferenza Emotiva [Biosystemic Therapy. An Independent Approach to Psychophysical Treatment of Emotional Suffering].* Milan: F. Angeli.

Lowe, R., & Laeng-Gilliatt (Eds.) (2007). *Reclaiming Vitality and Presence. Sensory Awareness as a Practice for Life. The Teachings of Charlotte Selver and Charles V. W. Brooks.* Berkeley: North Atlantic Books.

Lowen, A. (1958). *The Language of the Body.* New York: Grune and Stratton.

Lowen, A. (1967). *The Betrayal of the Body.* New York: The Macmillan Company.

Lowen, A. (1977). *Bioenergetics: The Revolutionary Therapy That Uses the Language of the Body to Heal the Problems of the Mind.* Harmondsworth: Penguin.

Lowen, A. (2013). *The Spirituality of the Body.* Shelburne: The Alexander Lowen Foundation.

Lowen, A., & Lowen, L. (2012). *The Way to Vibrant Health: A Manual of Bioenergetic Exercises: 100 Innovative and Powerful Exercises.* Shelburne: The Alexander Lowen Foundation.

Ludwig, S. (2002). *Elsa Gindler – Von ihrem Leben und Wirken. 'Wahrnehmen, was wir empfinden' [Elsa Gindler – About Her Life and Work. 'Perceiving What We Feel'].* Hamburg: Hans Christians.

Lundy, B. L., Jones, N. A., Field, T., Nearing, G., Davalos, M., Pietro, P., Schanberg, S., & Kuhn, C. (1999). Prenatal depression effects on neonates. *Infant Behavior & Development, 22*, 119–129.

Lutz, C. (1982). The domain of emotion words on Ifaluk. *American Ethnologist, 9*, 113–128.

Luyten, P., van Houdenhove, B., Lemma, A., Target, M., & Fonagy, P. (2012). A mentalization-based approach to the understanding and treatment of functional somatic disorders. *Psychoanalytic Psychotherapy, 26*, 121–140.

Lyons, N., Michaelsen, M. M., Graser, J., Bundschuh-Mueller, K., Esch, T., & Michalak, J. (2021). Bodily experience in depression: Using focusing as a new interview technique. *Psychopathology.* https://doi.org/10.1159/000514128.

Lyons-Ruth, K. (1998). Implicit relational knowing: Its role in development and psychoanalytic treatment. *Infant Mental Health Journal, 19*, 282–289.

Ma, B., Wasiliewski, R.v., Lindenmaier, W., & Dittmar, K. E. J. (2007). Immunohistochemical study of the blood and lymphatic vasculature and the innervation of mouse gut and gut-associated lymphoid tissue. *Anatomia, Histologia, Embryologia, 36*, 62–74.

Maaz, H.-J. (2001). Integration des Körpers in eine analytische Psychotherapie [Integration of the body in analytical psychotherapy]. In H. Maaz & A. H. Krueger (Eds.), *Integration des Körpers in die analytische Psychotherapie [Integration of the Body in Analytical Psychotherapy]* (pp. 16–27). Lengerich: Pabst.

Maaz, H.-J. (2008). Zur Integration des Körpers in tiefenpsychologisch fundierte analytische Psychotherapie [On the integration of the body in depth-psychologically based analytical psychotherapy]. In Vogt (Ed.) (pp. 220–230).

Macedonia, M., & Knoesche, T. R. (2011). Body in mind: How gestures empower foreign language learning. *Mind, Brain, and Education, 5*, 196–211.

MacLean, P. (1974). *A Triune Concept of the Brain and Behaviour.* Buffalo: University of Toronto Press.

Macnaughton, I. (Ed.) (2004). *Body, Breath and Consciousness. A Somatics Anthology.* Berkeley: North Atlantic Books.

Macnaughton, I. (with P. A. Levine). (2015). The role of the breath in mind-body psychotherapy. In Marlock et al. (Eds.) (pp. 633–643).

Maier, S. E., Hardy, C. J., & Jolesz, F. A. (1994). Brain and cerebrospinal fluid motion: Real-time quantification with M-mode MR imaging. *Radiology, 193*, 477–483.

Makari, G. (1991). German philosophy, Freud, and the riddle of the woman. *Journal of the American Psychoanalytic Association, 39*, 183–213.

Ma-Kellams, C., Blascovich, J., & McCall, C. (2012). Culture and the body: East–West differences in visceral perception. *Journal of Personality and Social Psychology, 102*(4), 718–728.

Malkemus, S. A., & Smith, J. F. (2021). Sexual disembodiment: Sexual energy, trauma, and the body. *Journal of Humanistic Psychology.* https://doi.org/10.1177/0022167821996144.

Manian, N., & Bornstein, M. H. (2009). Dynamics of emotion regulation in infants of clinically depressed and nondepressed mothers. *Journal of Child Psychology and Psychiatry, 50*, 1410–1418.

Mannhart, R., & Backhaus, S. (1993). *Reich und Bergson. Die lebensphilosophischen Wurzeln der Körpertherapie [Reich and Bergson. Life Philosophical Sources of Body Therapy].* Unpubl. Diploma Thesis, Psychological Institute, Free University of Berlin.

Marcel, G. (1976). *Being and Having: An Existentialist Diary.* Gloucester: Harper & Row.

Marcher, L., & Fich, S. (2010). *Body Encyclopedia. A Guide to the Psychological Functions of the Muscular System.* Berkeley: North Atlantic Books.

Margraf, J., & Schneider, S. (Eds.) (2009). *Lehrbuch der Verhaltenstherapie. Bd. 1: Grundlagen, Diagnostik, Verfahren, Rahmenbedingungen [Textbook of Behaviour Therapy. Vol. 1. Foundations, Diagnostics, Method, Parameters]* (3rd ed.). Heidelberg: Springer.

Markowitsch, H.-J. (2005). *Dem Gedächtnis auf der Spur. Vom Erinnern und Vergessen [On the Trail of Memory. On Remembering and Forgetting]* (2nd ed.). Darmstadt: Wissenschaftliche Buchgesellschaft.

Markus, H. T., & Kitayama, S. (1991). Culture and the self: Implications for cognition, emotion, and motivation. *Psychological Review, 98*, 224–253.

Marlock, G. (Ed.) (1993). *Weder Körper noch Geist. Einführung in die Unitive Körperpsychotherapie [Neither Body nor Mind. Introduction to Unitive Body Psychotherapy].* Oldenburg: Transform.

Marlock, G. (1993a). Überlegungen zu einem humanwissenschaftlichen Verständnis der Körperpsychotherapie [Reflections on a human-scientific understanding of body psychotherapy]. In Marlock (Ed.) (pp. 14–24).

Marlock, G. (2009). Versuch über Selbsregulation [An attempt at self-regulation]. In M. Thielen (Ed.) (pp. 19–33).

Marlock, G. (2010). Sinnliche Selbstreflexivität. Zum Arbeitsmodus der Körperpsychotherapie [Sensory self-reflexivity. On the working model of body psychotherapy]. In Mueller-Braunschweig & Stiller (Eds.) (pp. 47–57).

Marlock, G. (2015). Body psychotherapy as a revitalization of the self: A depth-psychological and phenomenological-existential perspective. In G. Marlock et al. (Eds.) (pp. 148–162).

Marlock, G. (2015a). Sensory self-reflexivity: Therapeutic action in body psychotherapy. In G. Marlock et al. (Eds.) (pp. 392–401).

Marlock, G. (2015b). Body psychotherapy as a major tradition of modern depth psychology. In G. Marlock et al. (Eds.) (pp. 83–101).

Marlock, G., & Weiss, H. (Eds.) (2006). *Handbuch der Körperpsychotherapie [Handbook of Body Psychotherapy].* Stuttgart: Schattauer.

Marlock, G., & Weiss, H. (2006a). Nachwort [Epilogue]. In Marlock & Weiss (Eds.) (pp. 953–954).

Marlock, G., & Weiss, C. (2015). Preface: The field of body psychotherapy. In Marlock et al. (Eds.) (pp. 1–17)

Marlock, G., Weiss, H., Young, C., & Soth, M. (Eds.) (2015). *The Handbook of Body Psychotherapy and Somatic Psychology.* Berkeley: North Atlantic Books.

Marmeleira, J., & Duarte Santos, G. (2019). Do not neglect the body and action: The emergence of embodiment approaches to understanding human development. *Perceptual and Motor Skills, 126*, 410–455.

Martin, E. (1998). Die neue Kultur der Gesundheit. Soziale Geschlechtsidentität und das Immunsystem in Amerika [The new culture of health. Social gender identity and the immune system in America]. In Sarasin & Tanner (Eds.) (pp. 508–525).

Martin, L. I., Harlow, T. F., & Strack, F. (1992). The role of bodily sensations in the evaluation of social events. *Personality and Social Psychology Bulletin, 18*, 412–419.

Martin, L., Stein, K., Kubera, K., Troje, N. F., & Fuchs, T. (2022). Movement markers of schizophrenia: A detailed analysis of patients' gait patterns. *European Archives of Psychiatry and Clinical Neuroscience*, April 1. https://doi.org/10.1007/s00406-022-01402-y.

Maslow, A. H. (1959). Critique of self-actualization: I. Some dangers of being-cognition. *Journal of Individual Psychology, 15*, 24–32.

Maslow, A. H. (1967). A theory of metamotivation: The biological rooting of the value-life. *Journal of Humanistic Psychology, 7,* 93–127.

Maslow, A. H. (1968). *Toward a Psychology of Being* (2nd ed.). New York: Van Nostrand.

Maturana, H. R. (1975). The organization of the living: A theory of the living organization. *The International Journal of Man-Machine Studies, 7,* 313–332.

Maturana, H. R., & Varela, F. J. (1992). *The Tree of Knowledge. The Biological Roots of Human Understanding.* Boston/London: Shambhala.

Maurer, Y. (1993). *Körperzentrierte Psychotherapie. Ganzheitlich orientierte Behandlungskonzepte und Therapiebeispiele [Body-Centred Psychotherapy. Holistically Oriented Treatment Concepts and Therapy Examples]* (2nd ed.). Stuttgart: Hippokrates.

Maurer, Y. (1999). *Der ganzheitliche Ansatz in der Psychotherapie [The Holistic Approach in Psychotherapy].* Wien: Springer.

Maurer, Y. (2001). *Atemtherapie in der therapeutischen Praxis [Breath Therapy in Therapeutic Practice].* Uelzen: ML-Verlag.

Maurer, Y. (2010). Von der Psychotherapie zur Körperzentrierten Psychotherapie [From psychotherapy to body-centred psychotherapy]. In Kuenzler et al. (Eds.) (pp. 1–15).

Maurer-Groeli, Y. (2004). Neurophysiologische Hintergründe für ganzheitliches psychotherapeutisches Arbeiten mit spezieller Berücksichtigung von Gedächtnis, Körpergedächtnis und Ressourcen [Neurophysiological backgrounds for holistic psychotherapeutic work with special consideration of memory, body memory and resources]. *Psychotherapie Forum [Psychotherapy Forum], 12,* 98–103.

McCullough, J. P., Lord, B. D., Martin, A. M., Conley, K. A., Schramm, E., & Klein, D. N. (2011). The significant other history: An interpersonal-emotional history procedure used with the early-onset chronically depressed patient. *The American Journal of Psychotherapy, 65* (3), 225–248.

McEwen, B. S. (2003). Early life influences on life-long patterns of behavior and health. *Mental Retardation and Developmental Disabilities Research Reviews, 9,* 149–154.

McEwen, B. S. (2007). Physiology and neurobiology of stress and adaptation: Central role of the brain. *Physiological Reviews, 87,* 873–904.

McGann, M. (2014). Enacting a social ecology: Radically embodied intersubjectivity. *Frontiers in Psychology, 5,* 1321. https://doi.org/10.3389/fpsyg.2014.01321.

McGann, M., De Jaegher, H. D., & Di Paolo, E. (2013). Enaction and psychology. *Review of General Psychology, 17,* 203–209.

McGowan, P. O., Sasaki, A., D'Alessio, A. C., Dymov, S., Labonté, B., Szyf, M., Turecki, G., & Meaney, M. J. (2009). Epigenetic regulation of the glucocorticoid receptor in human brain associates with childhood abuse. *Nature Neuroscience, 12,* 342–348.

McLaughlin, J. T. (1991). Clinical and theoretical aspects of enactment. *Journal of the American Psychoanalytic Association, 39,* 595–614.

McNeely, D. A. (1987). *Touching. Body Therapy and Depth Psychology.* Toronto: Inner City Books.

Mecacci, L. (2013). Solomon V. Shereshevsky: The great Russian mnemonist. *Cortex, 2013, 49,* 2260–2263.

Medina, J., & Coslett, H. B. (2010). From maps to form to space: Touch and the body schema. *Neuropsychologia, 48,* 645–654.

Meeren, H., Heijnsbergen, C. van, & de Gelder, B. (2005). Rapid perceptual integration of facial expression and emotional body language. *Proceedings of the National Academy of Sciences, 102,* 16518–16523.

Mehling, W.-E. (2010). Atemtherapie: Grundlagen, Wirkungsweisen, Interventionsstudien [Breath therapy. Foundations, impact modes, intervention studies]. In Mueller-Braunschweig & Stiller (Eds.) (pp. 157–173).

Mehling, W.-E., Gopisetty, V., Daubenmier, J., Price, C., Hecht, F. M., & Stewart, A. (2009). Body awareness: Construct and self-report measures. *Plos One, 4*(5), e5614, S. 1–18. https://doi.org/10.1371/journal.pone.0005614.

Mehr, S. A., Singh, M., Knox, D., Ketter, D. M., Pickens-Jones, D., Atwood, S., Lucas, C., Jacoby, N., Egner, A., Hopkins, E., Howard, R., Hartshorne, J., Jennings, M., Simson, J., Bainbridge, C., Pinker, S., O'Donnel, T., Krasnow, M., & Glowacki, L. (2019). Universality and diversity in human song. *Science, 336,* 6468. https://doi.org/10.1126/science.aax0868.

Mei, S. van der, Petzold, H. G., & Bosscher, R. (1997). Runningtherapie, Stress, Depression: Ein übungszentrierter Ansatz in der Integrativen leib- und bewegungsorientierten Psychotherapie [Running therapy, stress, depression: An exercise-centred approach in integrative body- and movement-oriented psychotherapy]. *Integrative Therapie [Integrative Therapy], 3,* 374–428.

Meier, B. P., & Robinson, M. D. (2006). Does "feeling down" mean seeing down? Depressive symptoms and vertical selective attention. *Journal of Research in Personality, 40,* 451–461.

Meinlschmidt, G., & Tegethoff, M. (2017). Psychotherapie: Quo vadis [Psychotherapy: Quo vadis]? *Fortschritte der Neurologie und Psychiatrie [Progresses in Neurology and Psychiatry], 85,* 479–494.

Meltzoff, A. N., & Moore, M. K. (1994). Imitation, memory, and the representation of persons. *Infant Behavior and Development, 17,* 83–99.

Melzer, A., Shafir, T., & Tsachor, R. P. (2019). How do we recognize emotion from movement? Specific motor components contribute to the recognition of each emotion. *Frontiers in Psychology*, July 3. https://doi.org/10.3389/fpsyg.2019.01389.

Menary, R. (2014). Our glassy essence: The fallible self in pragmatist thought. In Gallagher (Eds.) (pp. 609–632).

Mergenthaler, E. (1996). Emotion-abstraction patterns in verbatim protocols: A new way of describing psychotherapeutic processes. *Journal of Consulting and Clinical Psychology, 64*, 1306–1315.

Mergenthaler, E. (2008). Resonating minds: A school independent theoretical conception and its empirical application to psychotherapeutic processes. *Psychotherapy Research, 18*, 109–126.

Merleau-Ponty, M. (1994). *Keime der Vernunft. Vorlesungen an der Sorbonne 1949–52 [Germs of Reason. Lectures at the Sorbonne 1949–52]*. Munich: Fink.

Merleau-Ponty, M. (2012). *Phenomoenology of Perception*. Abingdon: Routledge.

Merritt, M. (2015). Thinking-is-moving: Dance, agency, and a radically enactive mind. *Phenomenology and the Cognitive Sciences, 14*, 95–110.

Merten, J. (2001). *Beziehungsregulation in Psychotherapien. Maladaptive Beziehungsmuster und der therapeutische Prozess [Relationship Regulation in Psychotherapies. Maladaptive Relationship Patterns and the Therapeutic Process]*. Stuttgart: Kohlhammer.

Merten, J., & Brunnhuber, S. (2004). Facial expression and experience of emotions in psychodynamic interviews with patients suffering from a pain disorder. Indicators of disorders in self- and relationship regulation in the involuntary facial expression of emotions. *Psychopathology, 37*, 266–271.

Merten, J., Anstadt, T., Ullrich, B., Krause, R., & Buchheim, P. (1996). Emotional experience and facial behavior during the psychotherapeutic process and its relation to treatment outcome: A pilot study. *Psychotherapy Research, 6*, 198–212.

Messer, D. (2003). Processes of development in early communication. In Bremner & Slater (Eds.) (pp. 284–316).

Métraux, A., & Graumann, C. F. (Eds.) (1975). *Versuche über Erfahrung [Attempts About Experience]*. Bern: Huber.

Metzinger, T. (2005). Die Selbstmodell-Theorie der Subjektivität: Eine Kurzdarstellung in sechs Schritten [The selfmodel theory of subjectivity. A short description in six steps]. In Herrmann et al. (Eds.) (pp. 242–269).

Metzinger, T. (2010). *The Ego Tunnel: The Science of the Mind and the Myth of the Self*. New York: Basic Books.

Metzinger, T. (2013). The self-model theory of subjectivity. Retrieved October 4, 2013, from www.scholarpedia.org/article/Self_models.

Meyer, E. (2019). Body psychotherapy in Australia. *International Body Psychotherapy Journal, 18*, 230–236.

Meyer, J.-E. (1961). Konzentrative Entspannungsübungen nach Elsa Gindler und ihre Grundlagen [Concentrative relaxation practices according to Elsa Gindler and their basics]. In Stolze (Ed.) (Vol. 2002, pp. 50–59).

Meyer, V. (2001). Körperorientierte Psychotherapie und die frühkindliche Basis des sexuellen Erlebens [Body-oriented psychotherapy and the early childhood basis of sexual experience]. *Psychotherapie im Dialog [Psychotherapy in Dialogue], 2*, 277–283.

Meyer, V. (2009). Der Körper als ein Führer durch das Tal der Tränen [The body as a guide through the valley of tears]. *Psychotherapeut [Psychotherapist], 54*, 139–144.

Meyer-Abich, K. M. (2010). *Was es bedeutet, gesund zu sein. Philosophie der Medizin [What it Means to be Healthy. Philosophy of Medicine]*. Munich: Carl Hanser.

Micali, S. (2019). *Negative Zukunft. Eine phänomenologische Analyse der Angst [Negative future. A phenomenological analysis of anxiety]*. In T. Fuchs & T. Breyer (Eds.), *Selbst und Selbststörungen [Self and SelfDisorders]* (pp. 123–148). Freiburg: Karl Alber.

Michalak, J., Troje, N. F., Fischer, J., Vollmar, P., Heidenreich, T., & Schulte, D. (2009). Embodiment of sadness and depression: Gait patterns associated with dysphoric mood. *Psychosomatic Medicine, 71*, 580–587.

Michalak, J., Mischnat, J., & Teismann, T. (2014). Sitting posture makes a difference: Embodiment effects on depressive memory bias. *Clinical Psychology & Psychotherapy, 21*, 519–524.

Michalak, J., Lyons, N., & Heidenreich, T. (2019). The evidence for basic assumptions of dance movement therapy and body psychotherapy related to findings from embodiment research. In Payne et al. (Eds.) (pp. 53–65).

Michalak, J., Niemeyer, H., Tschacher, W., Baumann, N., Zhang, X. C., & Adolph, D. (2022). Subjective and objective measures of activity in depressed and non-depressed individuals in everyday life. *Journal of Experimental Psychopathology, 13*, 1–8.

Michalak, J., Aranmolate, L., Bonn, A., Grandin, K., Schleip, R., Schmiedtke, J., Quassowsky, S., & Teismann, T. (2022a). Myofascial tissue and depression. *Cognitive Therapy and Research, 46*, 560–572.

Middendorf, I. (1995). *Der Erfahrbare Atem. Eine Atemlehre [The Experiential Breath. A Breath Theory]*. Paderborn: Junfermann.

Milch, W., & Berliner, B. (2005). Auf den Spuren der Selbstwerdung [On the traces of becoming oneself]. In Krens & Krens (Eds.) (pp. 134–149).

Miller, A. (1980). *The Drama of the Gifted Child: The Search for the True Self*. New York: Harper & Row.

Miller, A. L., McDonough, S. C., Rosenblum, K. L., & Sameroff, A. J. (2002). Emotion Regulation in Context: Situational Effects on Infant and Caregiver Behavior. *Infancy, 3*, 403–433.

Miller, J. A. (2010). Alexander Lowen (1910–2008): Reflections on his life. *Body, Movement and Dance in Psychotherapy*, 5, 197–202.

Miller, V. (2015). Resonance as a social phenomenon. *Sociological Research Online, 20*, 58–70. https://doi.org/10.5153/sro.3557.

Mitchell, R. L. C., Elliott, R., Barry, M., Cruttenden, A., & Woodruff, P. W. R. (2003). The neural response to emotional prosody, as revealed by functional magnetic resonance imaging. *Neuropsychologia, 41*, 1410–1421.

Moeller, A., Soendergaard, H. P., & Helstroem, L. (2017). Tonic immmobility during sexual assault: A common reaction predicting post-traumatic stress disorder and severe depression. *Acta Obstetricia et Gynecologica Scandinavica, 96*, 932–938.

Monsen, J. T., & Monsen, K. (1999). Affects and affect consciousness: A psychotherapy model integrating Silvan Tomkins's affect- and script theory within the framework of self psychology. In A. Goldberg (Ed.), *Progress in Self Psychology* (pp. 287–306). Hillsdale: The Analytic Press.

Montag, C., Gallinat, J., & Heinz, A. (2008). Theodor Lipps and the concept of empathy: 1851–1914. *American Journal of Psychiatry, 165*, 1261.

Montagu, A. (1971). *Touching: The Human Significance of the Skin*. New York: Columbia University Press.

Monteiro, D. A., Taylor, E. W., Sartori, M. R., Cruz, A. L., Antin, F. T., & Leite, C. A. C. (2018). Cardiorespiratory interactions previously identified as mammalian are present in the primitive lungfish. *Science Advances, 4*(2). https://doi.org/10.1126/sciadv.aaq0800.

Moore, G. A., Cohn, J., & Campbell, S. (2001). Infant affective responses to mother's still face at 6 months differentially predict externalizing and internalizing behaviors. *Developmental Psychology, 37*, 706–714.

Moscovici, H. K. (1991). *Vor Freude tanzen, vor Jammer halb in Stücke gehen. Pionierinnen der Körpertherapie [Dancing for Joy, Half in Pieces From Lamentation. Pioneers of Body Therapy]*. Hamburg: Luchterhand.

Moser, T. (1987). *Der Psychoanalytiker als sprechende Attrappe. Eine Streitschrift [The Psychoanalyst as a Speaking Dummy. A Polemic]*. Frankfurt: Suhrkamp.

Moser, T. (1989). *Körpertherapeutische Phantasien. Psychoanalytische Fallgeschichten neu betrachtet [BodyTherapeutic Fantasies. Psychoanalytic Case Historries Revisited]*. Frankfurt: Suhrkamp.

Moser, T. (1992). *Stundenbuch. Protokolle aus der Körperpsychotherapie [Book of Hours. Protocols From Body Psychotherapy]*. Frankfurt: Suhrkamp.

Moser, T. (1993). *Der Erlöser der Mutter auf dem Weg zu sich selbst. Eine Körperpsychotherapie [The Mother's Redeemer on The Way to Himself. A Body Psychotherapy]*. Frankfurt: Suhrkamp.

Moser, T. (1994). *Ödipus in Panik und Triumph. Eine Körperpsychotherapie [Oedipus in Panic and Triumph. A Body Psychotherapy]*. Frankfurt: Suhrkamp.

Moser, T. (2001). *Berührung auf der Couch. Formen der analytischen Körperpsychotherapie [Touching on The Couch. Forms of Analytical Body Psychotherapy]*. Frankfurt: Suhrkamp.

Moser, T. (2012). Psychotherapie und Körperkontakt [Psychotherapy and body contact]. In Schmidt & Schetsche (Eds.) (pp. 219–235).

Moser, T., & Pesso, A. (1991). *Strukturen des Unbewussten. Protokolle und Kommentare [Structures of the Unconscious. Protocols and Comments]*. Stuttgart: Klett-Cotta.

Muehlhoff, R. (2015). Affective resonance and social interaction. *Phenomenology and the Cognitive Sciences, 14*, 1001–1019.

Muehlleitner, E. (2008). *Ich: Fenichel. Das Leben eines Psychoanalytikers im 20. Jahrhundert [I: Fenichel. The Life of a Psychoanalyst in the 20th Century]*. Vienna: Paul Zsolnay.

Mueller, T. (Ed.) (2004). *Psychotherapie und Körperarbeit in Berlin. Geschichte und Praktiken der Etablierung [Psychotherapy and Body Work in Berlin. History and Practices of Their Establishment]*. Husum: Matthiesen Verlag.

Mueller, T. (2004a). Zur Etablierung der Psychoanalyse in Berlin [On establishing psychoanalysis in Berlin]. In Mueller (Ed.) (pp. 53–95).

Mueller-Braunschweig, H. (1997). Zur gegenwärtigen Situation der körperbezogenen Psychotherapie [On the current situation of body related psychotherapy]. *Psychotherapeut [Psychotherapist], 42*, 132–144.

Mueller-Braunschweig, H. (1998). Zur Funktion extraverbaler Psychotherapieformen in der Behandlung frühtraumatisierter Patienten [On the function of extraverbal forms of psychotherapy in the treatment of early traumatised patients]. In R. Vandieken, E. Haeckl & D. Mattke (Eds.), *Was tut sich in der stationären Psychotherapie? Standorte und Entwicklungen [What is Happening in Inpatient Psychotherapy? Facilities and Developments]* (pp. 201–220). Giessen: Psychosozial.

Mueller-Braunschweig, H., & Stiller, N. (Eds.) (2010). *Körperorientierte Psychotherapie. Methoden, Anwendungen, Grundlagen [Body Oriented Psychotherapy. Methods, Applications, Foundations]*. Heidelberg: Springer.

Mueller-Hofer, B., Geiser, C., Juchli, E., & Laireiter, A.-R. (2003). Klientenzentrierte Körperpsychotherapie (GFK-Methode): Ergebnisse einer Praxisevaluation [Client-centred body psychotherapy (GFK method): Results of a practice evaluation]. *Psychotherapie Forum [Psychotherapy Forum], 11*, 80–91.

Muir, D. W. (2002). Adult communication with infants through touch: The forgotten sense. *Human Development, 45*, 95–99.

Mullan, K. (2014). Somatics: Investigating the common ground of western body–mind disciplines. *Body Movement and Dance in Psychotherapy, 9*(4), 253–265.

Mullan, K. (2016). Harmonic gymnastics and somatics: A genealogy of ideas. Currents: *Journal of the Body-Mind Centering Association, 1,* 16–28.

Mullan, K. J. (2017). Somatics herstories: Tracing Elsa Gindler's educational antecedents Hade Kallmeyer and Genevieve Stebbins. *Journal of Dance and Somatic Practices, 9,* 159–178.

Museum der Dinge (n.d.). *Hochfrequenz-Strahlapparat Energos [High-frequency Radiation Apparatus Energos].* Retrieved October 18, 2022, from https://dingpflege.museumderdinge.de/pflegedinge/hochfrequenz-strahlapparat-energos/.

Museum fuer Energiegeschichte (n.d.) *Medizin ohne Medikamente. Die Anfänge der Elektromedizin [Medicine Without Medications. The Early Days of Energy Medicine].* Retrieved May 18, 2010, from www.energiegeschichte.de/ContentFiles/Museum/Downloads/Sammelblatt_Medizin.pdf.

Musial, F., Haeuser, W., Langhorst, J., Dobos, G., & Enck, P. (2008). Psychophysiology of visceral pain in IBS and health. *Journal of Psychosomatic Research, 64,* 589–597.

Myin, E., & Hutto, D. D. (2009). Enacting is enough. *Psyche, 15,* 24–30. http://www.theassc.org/files/assc/2575.pdf.

Nagel, T. (1974). What is it like to be a bat?. *The Philosophical Review, 83*(4), 435–450.

Nagler, N. (2003). Die paranoide Rufmordkampagne gegen Sándor Ferenczi und seinen Entwurf zu einer ganzheitlichen Psychoanalyse [The paranoid character assassination campaign against Sándor Ferenczi and his outline for a holistic psychoanalysis]. *Integrative Therapie [Integrative Therapy], 29,* 235–249.

Nathanielsz, P. W. (1999). *Life in the Womb: The Origin of Health and Disease.* Ithaca: Promethean Press.

Nelson, A. A., Grahe, J. E., & Ramseyer, F. (2016). Interacting in flow: An analysis of rapport-based behavior as optimal experience. *SAGE Open,* Dec. 1. https://doi.org/10.1177/2158244016684173.

Nelson, J., Klumparendt, A., Doebler, P., & Ehring, T. (2017). Childhood maltreatment and characteristics of adult depression: Meta-analysis. *British Journal of Psychiatry, 210* (2), 96–104.

Neumann, R., & Strack, F. (2000). „Mood contagion": The automatic transfer of mood between persons. *Journal of Personality and Social Psychology, 79,* 211–223.

Newen, A. (2013). *Philosophie des Geistes. Eine Einführung [Philosophy of the Mind. An Introduction].* Munich: Beck.

NICE (2008). *Schizophrenia. Core Interventions in the Treatment and Management of Schizophrenia in Adults in Primary and Secondary Care (Update).* National Collaborating Centre for Mental Health. Commissioned by the National Institute for Health and Clinical Excellence. Retrieved. December 16, 2008, from http://www.nice.org.uk/nicemedia/pdf/SchizophreniaUpdateFullGuidelineDraft%20ForConsultation.pdf.

Nicely, P., Tamis-LeMonda, C. S., & Grolnick, W. S. (1999). Maternal responsiveness to infant affect: Stability and prediction. *Infant Behavior & Development, 22,* 103–117.

Niedenthal, P. M., Brauer, M., Halberstadt, J. B., & Innes-Ker, Å. H. (2001). When did her smile drop? Facial mimicry and the influences of emotional state on the detection of change in emotional expression. *Cognition and Emotion, 15,* 853–864.

Niedenthal, P. M., Barsalou, L. W., Ric, F., & Krauth-Gruber, S. (2005). Embodiment in the acquisition and use of emotion knowledge. In L. Feldman Barrett, P. M. Niedenthal & P. Winkielman (Eds.), *Emotion and Consciousness* (pp. 21–50). New York: The Guilford Press.

Niedenthal, P. M., Barsalou, L. W., Winkielman, P., Krauth-Gruber, S., & Ric, F. (2005a). Embodiment in attitudes, social perception, and emotion. *Personality and Social Psychology Review, 9,* 184–211.

Nietzsche, F. (2006). *Thus Spoke Zarathustra.* Cambridge, UK: Cambridge University Press.

Nietzsche, F. (1980). Unzeitgemässe Betrachtungen [Untimely reflections]. In F. Nietzsche, *Werke I [Collected Works]* (pp. 135–434). Frankfurt: UIlstein.

Nijenhuis, E. R. S. (2004). *Somatoform Dissociation: Phenomena, Measurement, & Theoretical Issues.* New York: Norton.

Nijenhuis, E. (2016). *Die Trauma-Trinität: Ignoranz – Fragilität – Kontrolle. Die Entwicklung des Traumabegriffs/Traumabedingte Dissoziation: Konzept und Fakten [The Trauma Trinity: Ignorance - Fragility - Control. The Development of the Trauma Concept/Trauma-Induced Dissociation: Concept and Facts].* Goettingen: Vandenhoeck & Ruprecht.

Nitschke, A. (1990). Der Kult der Bewegung. Turnen, Rhythmik und neue Tänze [The cult of movement. Gymnastics, rhythmics and new dances]. In A. Nitschke, G. Ritter, D. Peukert & R. von Bruch (Eds.), *Jahrhundertwende. Der Aufbruch in die Moderne 1880–1930. [Turn of the Century. The Dawn of Modernity 1880–1930]* (Vol. 1, pp. 258–285). Reinbek: Rowohlt.

Nitzschke, B. (1989). Freud und die akademische Psychologie. Einleitende Bemerkungen zu einer historischen Kontroverse [Freud and academic psychology. Introductory remarks on a historical controversy]. In B. Nitzschke (Ed.), *Freud und die akademische Psychologie [Freud and Academic Psychology]* (pp. 2–21). Munich: Psychologie-Verlags-Union.

Nitzschke, B. (1998). *Aufbruch nach Inner-Afrika. Essays über Sigmund Freud und die Wurzeln der Psychoanalyse [Departure for Inner Africa. Essays on Sigmund Freud and the Roots of Psychoanalysis].* Goettingen: Vandenhoeck & Ruprecht.

Noah, T., Schul, Y., & Mayo, R. (2018). When both the original study and its failed replication are correct: Feeling observed eliminates the facial-feedback effect. *Journal of Personality and Social Psychology, 114*(5), 657–664.

Noble, E. (1996). *Having Twins. A Parent's Guide to Pregnancy, Birth, and Early Childhood.* New York: Gardners Book.

Noë, A. (2010). *Out of Our Heads. Why You Are Not Your Brain, and Other Lessons from the Biology of Consciousness.* New York: Hill and Wang.

Noë, A. (2021). The enactive approach: A briefer statement, with some remarks on "radical enactivism". *Phenomenology and the Cognitive Sciences, 20,* 957–970.

Northoff, G., Boeker, H., & Bogerts, B. (2006). Subjektives Erleben und neuronale Integration im Gehirn: *Benötigen wir eine Erste-Person-Neurowissenschaft [Subjective Experience and Neural Integration in the Brain: Do We Need a First-person Neuroscience?]? Fortschritte der Neurologie und Psychiatrie [Progresses in Neurology and Psychiatry], 74,* 627–633.

Nummenmaa, L., Glerean, E., Hari, R., & Hietanen, J. K. (2014). Bodily maps of emotions. *Proceedings of the National Academy of Sciences, 111,* 646–651.

Oeberst, A., Wachendoerfer, M. M., Imhoff, R., & Blank, H. (2021). Rich false memories of autobiographical events can be reversed. *Proceedings of the National Academy of Sciences, 118*(13) e2026447118. https://doi.org/10.1073/pnas.2026447118.

Ogden, P., Minton, K., & Pain, C. (2006). *Trauma and the Body. A Sensorimotor Approach to Psychotherapy.* New York, London: Norton.

Olbrich, D. (2004). Kreativtherapie in der psychosomatischen Rehabilitation [Creative therapy in psychosomatic rehabilitation]. *Psychotherapeut [Psychotherapist], 49,* 67–70.

Oliveira, B. S., Zunzunegui, M. V., Quinlan, J., Fahmi, H., Tu, M. T., & Guerra, R. O. (2016). Systematic review of the association between chronic social stress and telomere length: A life course perspective. *Ageing Research Reviews, 26,* 37–52.

Ollars, L. (2005). Challenges of the way towards a common ground of body psychotherapy: Body psychotherapy versus the established areas of psychology. *European Association of Body Psychotherapy,* Newsletter, Spring, 27–37.

Orbach, S. (2004). The John Bowlby Memorial Lecture 2003. The body in clinical practice. Part one: There is no such thing as a body; Part two: When touch comes to therapy. In White (Ed.) (pp. 17–34 & 35–47).

O'Shaughnessy, B. (1998). Proprioception and the body image. In Bermúdez et al. (Eds.) (pp. 175–203).

Osietzki, M. (1998). Körpermaschinen und Dampfmaschinen. Vom Wandel der Physiologie und des Körpers unter dem Einfluss von Industrialisierung und Thermodynamik [Body machines and steam engines. On the transformation of physiology and the body under the influence of industrialisation and thermodynamics.]. In Sarasin & Tanner (Eds.) (pp. 313–346).

O'Toole, M. S., Bovbjerg, D. H., Renna, M. E., Lekander, M., Mennin, D. S., & Zachariae, R. (2018). Effects of psychological interventions on systemic levels of inflammatory biomarkers in humans: A systematic review and meta-analysis. *Brain, Behavior, and Immunity, 74,* 68–78.

Paananen, K., Vaununmaa, R., Holma, J., Tourunen, A., Kykyri, V.-L., Tastasishvili, V., Kaartinen, J., Penttonen, M., & Seikkula, J. (2018). Electrodermal activity in couple therapy for intimate partner violence. *Contemporary Family Therapy, 40,* 138–152.

Paar, G. H., Hagen, C.v., Kriebel, R., & Woerz, T. (1999). Genese und Prognose psychosomatischer Störungen [Origins and prognosis of psychosomatic disorders]. In R. Oerter, C. V. Hagen, G. Roeper & G. Noam (Eds.), *Klinische Entwicklungspsychologie [Clinical Developmental Psychology]* (pp. 299–313). Weinheim: Beltz.

Paggio, P., & Navarretta, C. (2013). Head movements, facial expressions and feedback in conversations: Empirical evidence from Danish multimodal data. *Journal on Multimodal User Interfaces, 7*(1–2), 29–37.

Palumbo, R., Marraccini, M. F., Weyandt, L. L., Wilder-Smith, O., McGee, H. A., Liu, S., & Goodwin, M. S. (2016). Interpersonal autonomic physiology: A systematic review of the literature. *Personality and Social Psychology Review, 21,* 99–141.

Panksepp, J. (1998). *Affective Neuroscience. The Foundations of Human and Animal Emotions.* Oxford: Oxford University Press.

Panksepp, J. (2001). The long-term psychobiological consequences of infant emotions: Prescriptions for the twenty-first century. *Infant Mental Health Journal, 22,* 132–173.

Panksepp, J. (2006). Examples of application of the affective neuroscience strategy to clinical issues. In Corrigall et al. (Eds.) (pp. 33–49).

Panksepp, J., Normansell, L., Herman, B., Bishop, P., & Crepeau, L. (1988). Neural and neurochemical control of the separation distress call. In J. D. Newman (Ed.), *The Physiological Control of Mammalian Vocalization* (pp. 263–299). New York: Plenum Press.

Papoušek, M. (1994). *Vom ersten Schrei zum ersten Wort. Anfänge der Sprachentwicklung in der vorsprachlichen Kommunikation [From the First Cry to the First Word. Beginnings of Language Development in Pre-Language Communication].* Bern: Huber.

Parfit, D. (2014). The unimportance of identity. In Gallagher (Ed.) (pp. 419–441).

Parfy, E., & Lenz, G. (2009). Menschenbild [Image of the human being]. In Margraf & Schneider (Eds.) (pp. 64–82).

Parnas, J., & Sass, L. A. (2010). The spectrum of Schizophrenia. In Fuchs et al. (Eds.) (pp. 227–244).

Parnas, J., & Sass, L. A. (2014). The structure of self-consciousness in schizophrenia. In Gallagher (Ed.) (pp. 521–546).

Parsons, L. M., Gabrieli, J., Phelps, E., & Gazzaniga, M. (1998). Cerebrally lateralized mental representations of hand shape and movement. *The Journal of Neuroscience, 18*, 6539–6548.

Pauen, M. (2007). Keine Kränkung, keine Krise. Warum die Neurowissenschaften unser Selbstverständnis nicht revidieren [No grievance, no crisis. Why neuroscience does not revise our self concept]. In A. Holderegger, B. Sitter-Liver & C. W. Hess (Eds.), *Hirnforschung und Menschenbild [Brain Research and Image of the Human Being]* (pp. 41–53). Basel: Schwabe.

Pauly, P. J. (2005). The political structure of the brain: Cerebral localization in Bismarckian Germany. *Electroneurobiologia, 14*, 25–32.

Payne, H. (2006). The body as container and expresser. Authentic Movement groups in the development of wellbeing in our bodymindspirit. In Corrigall et al. (Eds.) (pp. 162–180).

Payne, H., Koch, S., Tantia, J., & Fuchs, T. (Eds.) (2019). *The Routledge International Handboook of Embodied Perspectives in Psychotherapy. Approaches from Dance Movement and Body Psychotherapies.* London: Routledge.

Payne, H., Koch, S., Tantia, J., & Fuchs, T. (2019a). Introduction to embodied perspectives in psychotherapy. In Payne et al. (Eds.) (pp. 1–14).

Pecher, D., Zeelenberg, R., & Barsalou, L. W. (2004). Sensorimotor simulations underlie conceptual representations: Modality-specific effects of prior activation. *Psychonomic Bulletin and Review, 11*, 164–167.

Pechtl, C., & Nagele, J. (2019). Grundlagen der Bioenergetischen Analyse [Foundations of bioenergetic analysis]. In Schwenk & Pechtl (Eds.) (pp. 15–24).

Pechtl, C., & Trotz, R. (2019). Zentrale Begrifflichkeiten [Central concepts]. In Schwenk & Pechtl (Eds.) (pp. 25–47).

Peglau, A. (2013). *Unpolitische Wissenschaft? Wilhelm Reich und die Psychoanalyse im Nationalsozialismus [Unpolitical Science? Wilhelm Reich and Psychoanalysis in National Socialism].* Giessen: Psychosozial.

Perlitz, V., Cotuk, B., Schiepek, G., Sen, A., Haberstock, S., Schmidt-Schoenbein, H., Petzold, E. R., & Flatten, G. (2004). *Synergetik der hypnoiden relaxation* [Synergetics of hypnoid relaxation]. *Psychotherapie, Psychosomatik, Medizinische Psychologie [Psychotherapy, Psychosomatics, Medical Psychology], 54*, 250–258.

Perls, F. S. (1976). *Gestalt Therapy Verbatim.* New York: Bantam.

Perls, F. S. (1981). *In and Out of the Garbage Pail.* New York: Bantam Books.

Perls, F. S., Hefferline, R. E., & Goodman, P. (1980). *Gestalt Therapy: Excitement and Growth in the Human Personality.* New York: Bantam Book.

Pert, C. (1999). *Molecules of Emotion: The Science Behind Mind-Body Medicine.* New York: Scribner.

Pesso, A. (1973). *Experience in Action: A Psychomotor Psychology.* New York: New York University Press.

Pesso, A. (1997). PBSP: Pesso Boyden system psychomotor. In Caldwell (Ed.) (pp. 117–152).

Pesso, A. (2015). "When is now? When is now?" Corrective experiences: With whom? When? And where? In Marlock et al. (Eds.) (pp. 436–443).

Peter, B. (2001). Geschichte der Hypnose in Deutschland [History of hypnosis in Germany]. In Revenstorf & Peter (Eds.) (pp. 697–737).

Peterson, F., & Jung, C. G. (1907). Psycho-physical investigations with the galvanometer and pneumograph in normal and insane individuals. *Brain. A Journal of Neurology, 30*, 153–218.

Petzold, H. (Ed.) (1974). *Psychotherapie & Körperdynamik. Verfahren psycho-physischer Bewegungs – und Körpertherapie [Psychotherapy and Body Dynamics. Approaches of Psychophysical Movement and Body Therapy]* (6th ed. 1988). Paderborn: Junfermann.

Petzold, H. (Ed.) (1977). *Die neuen Körpertherapien [The New Body Therapies]* (4th ed. 1985). Paderborn: Junfermann.

Petzold, H. (1984). Der Schrei in der Therapie [The scream in therapy]. In U. Sollmann (Ed.), *Bioenergetische Analyse [Bioenergetic Analysis]* (pp. 79–98). Essen: Synthesis.

Petzold, H. (Ed.) (1986). *Leiblichkeit. Philosophische, gesellschaftliche und therapeutische Perspektiven [Corporeality. Philosophical, Social and Therapeutic Perspectives].* Paderborn: Junfermann.

Petzold, H. (1986a). Vorwort [Preface]. In Petzold (Ed.) (pp. S. 9–11).

Petzold, H. (2000). Body narratives: Traumatische und Posttraumatische Erfahrungen aus Sicht der Integrativen Therapie [Body narratives: Traumatic and post-traumatic experiences from the perspective of Integrative Therapy]. *Energie & Charakter [Energy & Character], 21*, 45–64 & 22, 26–43.

Petzold, H. (2003). *Integrative Therapie [Integrative Therapy]* (Vol. 1–3) (2nd ed.). Paderborn: Junfermann.

Petzold, H. (2006). Der „informierte Leib": „embodied and embedded": Ein Metakonzept für die Leibtherapie [The "informed body": "embodied and embedded": A meta-concept for body therapy]. In Marlock & Weiss (Eds.) (pp. 100–118).

Petzold, H. (2007). „Hot seat?" Ein problematischer Begriff [„Hot seat?" A problematic concept]. *Polyloge*, No. 2. www.fpi-publikation.de/polyloge.

Petzold, H. (2009). Der „Informierte Leib" [The ‚informed body']. In Waibel & Jakob-Krieger (Eds.) (pp. 27–44).

Petzold, H. (Eds.) (2012). *Die Menschenbilder in der Psychotherapie: Interdisziplinäre Perspektiven und die Modelle der Therapieschulen [Images of the Human Being in Psychotherapy: Interdisciplinary Perspectives and the Models of the Schools of Therapy].* Wien: Krammer.

Petzold, H., & Berger, A. (1980). Integrative movement therapy. In Kogan (Ed.) (pp. 49–56).

Pfeifer, R., & Bongard, J. (2007). *How the Body Shapes the Way We Think: A New View of Intelligence.* Cambridge: MIT.

Pfeifer, R., Lungarella, M., & Iida, F. (2007). Self-organization, embodiment, and biologically inspired robotics. *Science, 318,* 1088–1093.

Pfeiffer, A. (2022). *Emotionale Erinnerung: Klopfen als Schlüssel für Lösungen. Neurowissenschaftliche Wirkhypothesen der Klopftechniken [Emotional Memory: Tapping as a Key to Solutions. Neuroscientific Impact Hypotheses of Tapping Techniques].* Heidelberg: Carl Auer.

Pfeiffer, W. M. (1987). Der Widerstand in der Sicht der klientenzentrierten Psychotherapie [Resistance in the perspective of client-centred psychotherapy]. *GwG-Zeitschrift [GwG-Journal], 18*(66), 55–62.

Piaget, J. (2001). *The Psychology of Intelligence.* London: Routledge.

Piaget, J., & Inhelder, B. (2000). *The Psychology of the Child.* New York: Basic Books.

Pierrakos, J. (1987). *Core Energetics: Developing the Capacity to Love and Heal.* Mendocino: LifeRhythm.

Pigman, G. W. (1995). Freud and the history of empathy. *The International Journal of Psychoanalysis, 76,* 237–256.

Pilates, J. H., & Miller, W. J. (1945). *Return to Life Through Contrology.* New York: Augustin.

Piontelli, A. (1992). *From Fetus to Child.* London: Routledge.

Plassmann, R. (2005). Selbstorganisation und Heilung [Self organization and healing]. In Geissler (Ed.) (pp. 357–385).

Plassmann, R. (2010). Kann man Heilungsprozesse hören und fühlen? Die musikalischen Eigenschaften mentaler Transformationsprozesse [Can healing processes be heard and felt? The musical properties of mental transformation processes]. *Psychoanalyse & Koerper [Psychoanalysis & Body], 9*(16), 43–59.

Plassmann, R. (2011). *Selbstorganisation. Über Heilungsprozesse in der Psychotherapie [Self-Organization. Healing Processes in Psychotherapy].* Giessen: Psychosozial.

Plassmann, R. (2016). *Körper sein und Körper haben. Zum Verhältnis von Körper, Leib und Psyche am Beispiel von Kopfschmerzen, selbstverletzendem Verhalten und artifiziellen Krankheiten [Being a Body and Having a Body. On the Relationship between Body, Lived Body and Psyche using the Example of Headaches, Self-Injurious Behaviour and Artificial Diseases].* Giessen: Psychosozial.

Plassmann, R. (2019). *Psychotherapie der Emotionen. Die Bedeutung von Emotionen für die Entstehung und Behandlung von Krankheiten [Psychotherapy of the Emotions. The Importance of Emotions for the Development and Treatment of Diseases].* Giessen: Psychosozial.

Plassmann, R. (2021). *Das gefühlte Selbst. Emotionen und seelisches Wachstum in der Psychotherapie [The Felt Self. Emotions and Mental Growth in Psychotherapy].* Giessen: Psychosozial.

Plessner, H. (1975). *Die Stufen des Organischen und der Mensch.* Berlin: de Gruyter [engl.: Levels of Organic Life and the Human: An Introduction to Philosophical Anthropology. New York: Fordham University Press, 2019].

Poettgen-Havekost, G. (2007). Die Traumatisierung als erstarrte Lebensbewegung [Traumatisation as a frozen life movement]. In Geissler & Heisterkamp (Eds.) (pp. 239–258).

Pohl, H. (2010). *Unerklärliche Beschwerden? Chronische Schmerzen und andere Leiden körpertherapeutisch verstehen und behandeln [Unexplained Complaints? Understanding and Treating Chronic Pain and Other Conditions with Body Therapy].* Munich: Knaur.

Pohlen, M., & Bautz-Holzherr, M. (1995). *Psychoanalyse: Das Ende einer Deutungsmacht [Psychoanalysis: The End of a Power of Interpretation].* Reinbek: Rowohlt.

Polenz, S. von (1994). *Und er bewegt sich doch. Ketzerisches zur Körperabstinenz der Psychoanalyse [And Yet It Moves. Heresies on the Abstinence from the Body in Psychoanalysis].* Frankfurt: Suhrkamp.

Pollani, E. (2016). Hypnose-Ego-state-therapie-Eye movement integration: Drei wirkungsvolle Behandlungsmöglichkeiten in der Traumatherapie [Hypnosis-Ego-state therapy-Eye movement integration: Three effective treatment options in trauma therapy]. In Bohne et al. (Eds.) (pp. 153–170).

Pollatos, O., Traut-Mattausch, E., Schroeder, H., & Schandry, R. (2007). Interoceptive awareness mediates the relationship between anxiety and the intensity of unpleasant feelings. *Journal of Anxiety Disorders, 21,* 931–943.

Porges, S. (2009). Reciprocal influences between body and brain in the perception and expression of affect: A polyvagal perspective. In D. Fosha, D. J. Siegel & M. F. Solomon (Eds.), *The Healing Power of Emotion. Affective Neuroscience, Development, & Clinical Practice* (pp. 27–54). New York: Norton.

Porges, S. (2011). *The Polyvagal Theory: Neurophysiological Foundations of Emotions, Attachment, Communication, and Self-Regulation.* New York: Norton.

Porsch, U. (2009). Spaltungsphänomene und symbolische Verdichtungen von Beziehungserfahrungen im Körperorgan [Splitting phenomena and symbolic condensations of relational experiences in the body organ]. In Joraschky et al. (Eds.) (pp. 135–151).

Portmann, A. (1951). *Biologische Fragmente zu einer Lehre vom Menschen [Biological Fragments to a Doctrine of Man].* Basel: Schwabe.

Povinelli, D. J., & Preuss, T. M. (1995). Theory of mind: Evolutionary history of a cognitive specialization. *Trends in Neurosciences, 18*, 418–424.

Prehn-Kristensen, A., Wiesner, C., Bergmann, T. O., Wolff, S., Jansen, O., Mehdorn, H. M., Ferstl, R., & Pause, B. M. (2009). Induction of empathy by the smell of anxiety, *PLoS One, 4*(6), e5987. https://doi.org/10.1371/journal.pone.0005987.

Price, C. (2007). Dissociation reduction in body therapy during sexual abuse recovery. *Complementary Therapies in Clinical Practice, 13*, 116–128.

Prinz, J. J. (2004). *Gut Reactions. A Perceptual Theory of Emotion*. Oxford, New York: Oxford University Press.

Prinz, J., Boyle, K., Ramseyer, F., Kabus, W., Bar-Kalifa, E., & Lutz, W. (2021). Within and between associations of nonverbal synchrony in relation to Grawe's general mechanisms of change. *Clinical Psychology & Psychotherapy, 28*, 159–168.

Prinz, W. (2016). *Selbst im Spiegel. Die soziale Konstruktion von Subjektivität [Self in the Mirror. The Social Construction of Subjectivity]*. Frankfurt: Suhrkamp.

Probst, M., Knapen, J., Poot, G., & Vancampfort, D. (2010). Psychomotor therapy and psychiatry: What's in a name? *The Open Complementary Medicine Journal, 2*, 105–113.

Racker, H. (2019). *Transference and Countertransference*. London: Routledge.

Ramseyer, F. (2011). Nonverbal synchrony in psychotherapy: Embodiment at the level of the dyad. In W. Tschacher & C. Bergomi (Eds.), *The Implications of Embodiment: Cognition and Communication* (pp. 193–207). Exeter: Imprint Academic.

Ramseyer F. (2020). Exploring the evolution of nonverbal synchrony in psychotherapy: The idiographic perspective provides a different picture. *Psychotherapy Research, 30*, 622–634.

Ramseyer, F. (2022). iCAST: Ein praktisches Modell für die Integration nonverbaler Signale in die Psychotherapie [iCAST: A practical model for the integration of non-verbal signals in psychotherapy]. *Psychotherapie [Psychotherapy]*. https://doi.org/10.1007s00278-022-00618-6.

Ramseyer, F., & Tschacher, W. (2008). Synchrony in dyadic psychotherapy sessions. In S. Vrobel, O. E. Roessler & T. Marks-Tarlow (Eds.), *Simultaneity: Temporal Structures and Observer Perspectives* (pp. 329–347). Singapore: World Scientific.

Ramseyer, F., & Tschacher, W. (2014). Nonverbal synchrony of head- and body movement in psychotherapy: Different signals have different associations with outcome. *Frontiers in Psychology*. https://doi.org/10.3389/fpsyg.2014.00979.

Ramseyer, F., & Tschacher, W. (2016). Movement coordination in psychotherapy: Synchrony of hand movements is associated with session outcome. A single case study. *Nonlinear Dynamics, Psychology, and Life Sciences, 20*, 145–166.

Ramseyer, F., Ebert, A., Roser, P., Edel, M.-A., Tschacher, W., & Bruene, M. (2020). Exploring nonverbal synchrony in borderline personality disorder: A double-blind placebo-controlled study using oxytocin. *British Journal of Clinical Psychology, 59*, 186–207.

Rand, M. L. (2004). Experiencing: A memoir. *The USA Body Psychotherapy Journal, 3*, 69–74.

Ranganathan, V. K., Siemionow, V., Liu, J. Z., Sahgal, V., & Yue, G. H. (2004). From mental power to muscle power: Gaining strength by using the mind. *Neuropsychologia, 42*, 944–956.

Rank, O. (1926). *Die analytische Situation. Illustriert an der Traumdeutungstechnik [The analytical situation. Illustrated by the dream interpretation technique]*. Leipzig: Franz Deuticke (quoted after reprint in Rank, 2006).

Rank, O. (1929). *Technik der Psychoanalyse II. Die analytische Reaktion in ihren konstruktiven Elementen [Technique of Psychoanalysis II. The Analytical Response in its Constructive Elements]*. Leipzig: Franz Deuticke (quoted after reprint in Rank, 2006).

Rank, O. (1931). *Technik der Psychoanalyse III. Die Analyse des Analytikers und seiner Rolle in der Gesamtsituation* [Technique of Psychoanalysis III. The Analysis of the Analyst and His Role in the Global Situation]. Leipzig: Franz Deuticke (quoted after reprint in Rank, 2006).

Rank, O. (2006). *Technik der Psychoanalyse [Technique of Psychoanalysis] Vol. I–III*. Giessen: Psychosozial.

Ras, M. de (1986). „Wenn der Körper restlos rhythmisch ist und hemmungslos innerviert..." ["When the body is completely rhythmic and innervates without restraint..."]. In Deutscher Werkbund (Ed.) (pp. 412–416).

Rasting, M., & Beutel, M. E. (2005). Dyadic affective interaction patterns in the intake interview as a predictor of outcome. *Psychotherapy Research, 15*, 188–198.

Redcay, E., & Schilbach, L. (2019). Using second-person neuroscience to elucidate the mechanisms of social interaction. *Nature Reviews Neuroscience, 20*, 495–505.

Reddemann, L. (2004). *Psychodynamisch Imaginative Traumatherapie. PITT: Das Manual [Psychodynamic Imaginative Trauma Therapy. PITT: The Manual]*. Stuttgart: Pfeiffer.

Reddemann, L., & Sachsse, U. (2000). Traumazentrierte Psychotherapie der chronifizierten, komplexen Posttraumatischen Belastungsstörung vom Phänotyp der Borderline-Persönlichkeitsstörungen [Trauma-centred psychotherapy of chronic, complex post-traumatic stress disorder of the borderline personality disorder phenotype]. In Kernberg et al. (Eds.) (pp. 555–571).

Reddy, V. (2008). *How Infants Know Minds*. Cambridge, MA: Harvard University Press.

Reed, C. L., & Farah, M. J. (1995). The psychological reality of the body schema: A test with normal participants. *Journal of Experimental Psychology, 21*, 334–343.

Reed, C. L., & McIntosh, D. N. (2008). The social dance: On-line body perception in the context of others. In R. L. Klatzky, M. Behrmann & B. MacWhinney (Eds.), *Embodiment, Ego-space, and Action* (pp. 79–111). Hillsdale: Erlbaum.

Reed, C. L., McGoldrick, J. E., Shackelford, J. R., & Fidopiastis, C. M. (2004). Are human bodies represented differently from other objects? Experience shapes object representations. *Visual Cognition, 11*, 523–550.

Regenbogen, C., Schneider, D. A., Finkelmeyer, A., Kohn, N., Derntl, B., Kellermann, T., Gur, R. E., Schneider, F., & Habel, U. (2012). The differential contribution of facial expressions, prosody, and speech content to empathy. *Cognition and Emotion, 26*, 995–1014.

Reich, W. (1923/1977). Zur Trieb-Energetik [On the energetics of drive]. In Reich, (Vol. 1977, pp. 153–167).

Reich, W. (1925). Weitere Bemerkungen über die therapeutische Bedeutung der Genitallibido [Further remarks on the significance of genital libido]. In Reich, (Vol. 1977, pp. 208–230).

Reich, W. (1927/1980). *Genitality in the Theory and Therapy of Neurosis*. New York: Farrar, Straus and Giroux.

Reich, W. (1948). *Listen, Little Man*. New York: The Noonday Press (quoted from http://www.listenlittleman.com/).

Reich, W. (1953). *The Murder of Christ. Vol. One of the Emotional Plague of Mankind*. New York: Simon and Schuster.

Reich, W. (1972). *Character Analysis*. New York: Farrar, Strauss and Giroux (1st ed. in German 1933, 2nd 1944, 3rd 1948).

Reich, W., (1973). *The Function of the Orgasm*. New York: Farrar, Strauss and Giroux.

Reich, W. (1974). *The Impulsive Character and Other Writings*. New York: New American Library. (1st ed.: The Impulsive Character in German 1925).

Reich, W. (1977). *Frühe Schriften 1 [Early Writings 1]*. Cologne: Kiepenheuer & Witsch.

Reich, W. (1994). *Beyond Psychology. Letters and Journals 1934–1939*. New York: Farrar, Strauss and Giroux.

Reinert, T. (1997). „Ja, hab' ich ein Lebensrecht?" Widerspiegelungen eines überlebten Abtreibungsversuches in der Therapie einer Borderline-Patientin ["Yes, do I have a right to live?" Reflections of a survived abortion attempt in the therapy of a borderline patient]. *International Journal of Prenatal and Perinatal Psychology and Medicine, 9*, 475–494.

Reinert, T. (2004). *Therapie an der Grenze: Die Borderline-Persönlichkeit [Therapy at the Border: The Borderline Personality]*. Stuttgart: Pfeiffer bei Klett Cotta.

Reisenzein, R. (1994). Pleasure-arousal theory and the intensity of emotions. *Journal of Personality and Social Psychology, 67*, 525–539.

Remmel, A., Kernberg, O. F., Vollmoeller, W., & Strauss, B. (Eds.) (2006). *Handbuch Körper und Persönlichkeit. Entwicklungspsychologie, Neurobiologie und Therapie von Persönlichkeitsstörungen [Handbook Body and Personality. Developmental Psychology, Neurobiology and Therapy of Personality Disorders]*. Stuttgart: Schattauer.

Remus, U. (2008). Miriam Goldberg: Philosophin des Augenblicks [Miriam Goldberg: Philosopher of the Moment]. *Heinrich Jacoby-Elsa Gindler-Stiftung, Rundbrief [Heinrich Jacoby-Elsa Gindler Foundation, Newsletter]* No. 10, 25–27 http://www.jgstiftung.de/sites/default/files/Rundbrief_10.pdf.

Revenstorf, D. (2000). Nutzung des Affekts in der Psychotherapie [Using the affect in psychotherapy]. In Sulz & Lenz (Eds.) (pp. 191–215).

Revenstorf, D. (2001). Nutzung der Beziehung in der Hypnotherapie [Using the relationship in hypnotherapy]. In Revenstorf & Peter (Eds.) (pp. 53–75).

Revenstorf, D. (2013). Körperpsychotherapie und die Integration in die Psychotherapie [Body psychotherapy and the integration in psychotherapy]. In Thielen (Ed.) (pp. 177–189).

Revenstorf, D., & Peter, B. (Eds.) (2001). *Hypnose in Psychotherapie, Psychosomatik und Medizin. Manual für die Praxis [Hypnosis in Psychotherapy, Psychosomatics and Medicine. Practitioner's Manual]*. Berlin: Springer.

Richter, M. (2019). *Psychotherapie zwischen Neurowissenschaften und Kunst der Begegnung [Psychotherapy between Neuroscience and the Art of Encounter]*. Giessen: Psychosozial.

Richter-Mackenstein, J. (2021). Zwischenleiblichkeit und vegetative Identifikation [Intercorporeality and vegetative identification]. *Koerper – tanz – bewegung [Body – Dance – Movement], 9*, 114–127.

Riemann, F. (1972). *Grundformen der Angst* (7th ed.). Munich: Reinhardt [engl.: Anxiety. Using Depth Psychology to Find a Balance in Your Life. Munich: Reinhardt, 2009].

Rifkin, J. (2009). *The Empathic Civilization. The Race to Global Consciousness in a World in Crisis*. New York: Jeremy P.Tarcher/Penguin.

Riskind, J. H., & Gotay, C. C. (1982). Physical posture: Could it have regulatory or feedback effects on motivation and emotion? *Motivation and Emotion, 6*, 273–298.

Riskind, J. H., Schrader, S. W., & Loya, J. M. (2021). Embodiment in clinical disorders and treatment. In Robinson & Thomas (Eds.) (pp. 499–523).

Rispoli, L. (1993). *Psicologia Funzionale del Sé: Organizzazione, Sviluppo e Patologia dei Processi Psicocorporei (Functional Psychology of the Self: Organisation, Development and Pathology of Psychophysical Processes)*. Rom: Astrolabio.

Rispoli, L. (2006). Funktionalismus und Körperpsychotherapie [Functionalism and body psychotherapy]. In Marlock & Weiss (Eds.) (pp. 636–645).

Ritz-Schulte, G., Schmidt, P., & Kuhl, J. (2008). *Persönlichkeitsorientierte Psychotherapie [Person-Oriented Psychotherapy]*. Goettingen: Hogrefe.

Rizzolatti, G., & Sinigaglia, C. (2008). *Mirrors in The Brain: How Our Minds Share Actions and Emotions.* Oxford: Oxford University Press.

Rizzolatti, G., Fadiga, L., Fogassi, L., & Gallese, V. (1997). The space around us. *Science, 277*, 190–191.

Robinson, M. D., & Thomas, L. E. (Eds.) (2021). *Handbook of Embodied Psychology: Thinking, Feeling, and Acting.* Cham: Springer.

Robles-De-La-Torre, G. (2006). The importance of the sense of touch in virtual and real environments. *IEEE Multimedia, 13*(3), 24–30. Retrieved March 17, 2010, from www.roblesdelatorre.com/gabriel/GR-IEEE-MM-2006 .pdf.

Rochat, P. (2003). Emerging co-awareness. In Bremner & Slater (Eds.) (pp. 258–283).

Rochat, P. (2014). What is it like to be a newborn? In Gallagher (Ed.) (pp. 57–79).

Roediger, H. L. (1990). Implicit memory. Retention without remembering. *American Psychologist, 45*, 1043–1056.

Roediger, H. R., & Abel, M. (2022). The double-edge sword of memory retrieval. *Nature Reviews Psychology, 1*, 708–720.

Roehricht, F. (2000). *Körperorientierte Psychotherapie psychischer Störungen [Body Oriented Psychotherapy of Psychic Disorders]*. Goettingen: Hogrefe.

Roehricht, F. (2002). Klinische Körperpsychotherapie. Systematisierungsansätze und Standortbestimmung [Clinical body psychotherapy. Systematising approaches and positioning. Practice]. *Praxis Klinische Verhaltensmedizin und Rehabilitation [Practice Clinical Behaviour Medicine and Rehabilitation], 59*, 182–189.

Roehricht, F. (2009). Body oriented psychotherapy. The state of the art in empirical research and evidence-based practice: A clinical perspective. *Body, Movement and Dance in Psychotherapy, 4*, 135–156.

Roehricht, F. (2009a). Das Körperbild im Spannungsfeld von Sprache und Erleben: Terminologische Überlegungen [The body image in the field of tension between language and experience: Terminological considerations]. In Joraschky et al. (Eds.) (pp. 25–34).

Roehricht, F. (2009b). Ansätze und Methoden zur Untersuchung des Körpererlebens: Eine Übersicht [Approaches and methods for the study of body experience: An overview]. In Joraschky et al. (Eds.) (pp. 35–52).

Roehricht, F. (Ed.) (2011). *Störungsspezifische Konzepte in der Körperpsychotherapie [Disorder-Specific Concepts in Body Psychotherapy]*. Giessen: Psychosozial.

Roehricht, F. (2011a). Leibgedächtnis und Körper-Ich: Zwei zentrale Bezugspunkte in der störungsspezifischen körperorientierten Psychotherapie [Corporeal memory and body ego: Two central points of reference in disorder-specific body-oriented psychotherapy]. *Psychologie in Österreich [Psychology in Austria], 31*, 239–248.

Roehricht, F. (2011b). Körperpsychotherapie [Body psychotherapy]. In R. H. Adler, W. Herzog, P. Joraschky, K. Köhle, W. Langewitz, W. Söllner & W. Wesiack (Eds.), *Psychosomatische Medizin. Theoretische Modelle und klinische Praxis [Psychosomatic Medicine. Theoretical Models and Clinical Practice]* (7th ed.) (pp. 476–484). Munich: Urban & Fischer.

Roehricht, F. (2011c). Das theoretische Modell und die therapeutischen Prinzipien/Mechanismen einer integrativen Körperpsychotherapie (KPT) bei somatoformen Störungen [The theoretical model and therapeutic principles/ mechanisms of integrative body psychotherapy (BPT) for somatoform disorders]. *Psychotherapie-Wissenschaft [Psychotherapy Science], 1*, 41–49.

Roehricht, F. (2015). Body oriented psychotherapy for the treatment of severe mental disorders. *Body, Movement and Dance in Psychotherapy, 10*, 51–67.

Roehricht, F. (2015a). The relevance of body related features and processes for diagnostics and clinical formulation in body psychotherapy. In Marlock et al. (Eds.) (pp. 532–542).

Roehricht, F. (2021). Psychoanalysis and body psychotherapy: An exploration of their relational and embodied common ground. *International Forum of Psychoanalysis*, https://doi.org/10.1080/0803706X.2021.1959638.

Roehricht, F., & Geuter, U. (2020). Klinische Körperpsychotherapie [Clinical body psychotherapy]. In Egle et al. (Eds.) (pp. 735–742).

Roehricht, F., & Priebe, S. (2006). Effect of body-oriented psychological therapy on negative symptoms in schizophrenia: A randomized controlled trial. *Psychological Medicine, 36*, 669–678.

Roehricht, F., Beyer, W., & Priebe, S. (2002). Störungen des Körpererlebens bei akuten Angsterkrankungen und Depressionen: Neurotizismus oder Somatisierung [Disturbances of body experience in acute anxiety disorders and depression: Neuroticism or somatisation]? *Psychotherapie, Psychosomatik, Medizinische Psychologie [Psychotherapy, Psychosomatics, Medical Psychology], 52*, 205–213.

Roehricht, F., Seidler, K.-P., Joraschky, P., Borkenhagen, A., Lausberg, H., Lemche, E., Loew, T., Porsch, U., Schreiber-Willnow, K., & Tritt, K. (2005). Konsensuspapier zur terminologischen Abgrenzung von Teilaspekten des Körpererlebens in Forschung und Praxis [Consensus paper on the terminological classification of partial aspects of body experience in research and practice]. *Psychotherapie, Psychosomatik, Medizinische Psychologie [Psychotherapy, Psychosomatics, Medical Psychology], 55*, 183–190.

Roehricht, F., Gallagher, S., Geuter, U., & Hutto, D. (2014). Embodied cognition and body psychotherapy: The construction of new therapeutic environments. *Sensoria: A Journal of Mind, Brain, and Culture, 10*, 11–20.

Rogers, C. (1951). *Client-Centered Therapy: Its Current Practice, Implications, and Theory.* Boston: Houghton Mifflin.

Rogers, C. (1959). A theory of therapy, personality and interpersonal relationships as developed in the client-centered framework. In S. Koch (Ed.), *Psychology: A Study of a Science. Vol. 3: Formulations of the Person and the Social Context* (pp. 184–256). New York: McGraw-Hill.

Rogers, C. (1975). Client-centered therapy. In A. M. Freedman, H. I. Kaplan & B. J. Sadock (Eds.), *Comprehensive Textbook of Psychiatry, Vol. II* (pp. 1831–1843). Baltimore: Williams & Wilkins.

Rogers, C. R., & Wood, J. K. (1974). Client-centered theory: Carl Rogers. In A. Burton (Ed.), *Operational Theories of Personality* (pp. 211–258). New York: Brunner/Mazel.

Rolef Ben-Shahar, A. (2014). *Touching the Relational Edge. Body Psychotherapy.* London: Karnac.

Rolef Ben-Shahar, A. (2019). Being moved to tears. Somatic and motoric aspects of self-disclosure. In Payne et al. (Eds.) (pp. 342–350).

Rosen, M., & Brenner, S. (1991). *The Rosen Method of Movement.* Berkeley, CA: North Atlantic Books.

Rosenberg, J. L., & Morse, B. K. (2015). Segmental holding patterns of the body-mind. In Marlock et al. (Eds.) (pp. 666–674).

Rosenberg, J. L., Rand, M. L., & Asay, D. (1985). *Body, Self & Soul - Sustaining Integration.* Atlanta: Humanics Limited.

Roth, G. (2001). *Fühlen, Denken, Handeln. Wie das Gehirn unser Verhalten steuert [Feeling, Thinking, Acting. How the Brain Controls Our Behaviour].* Frankfurt: Suhrkamp.

Roth, G. (2004). Das Verhältnis von bewusster und unbewusster Verhaltenssteuerung [The relationship between conscious and unconscious behavioural control]. *Psychotherapie Forum [Psychotherapy Forum], 12*, 59–70.

Roth, G. (2007). *Persönlichkeit, Entscheidung und Verhalten [Personality, Decision, Behaviour].* Stuttgart: Klett-Cotta.

Roth, G. (2009). *Aus Sicht des Gehirns [From the Point of View of the Brain].* Frankfurt: Suhrkamp.

Roth, M. (2000). Körperbild-Struktur bei chronisch kranken Jugendlichen [Body image structure in chronically ill adolescents]. *Zeitschrift für Gesundheitspsychologie [Journal for Health Psychology], 8*, 8–17.

Rothbart, M. K., & Hwang, J. (2005). Temperament and the development of competence and motivation. In A. J. Elliot & C. S. Dweck (Eds.), *Handbook of Competence and Motivation* (pp. 167–184). New York: Guilford Press.

Rothe, K. (2014). The gymnastics of thought: Elsa Gindler's networks of knowledge. In L. Cull & A. Lagaay (Eds.), *Encounters in Performance Philosophy* (pp. 197–219). London: Palgrave Macmillan.

Rothermund, K. (2011). Selbstregulation statt Selbstkontrolle: Intentionalität, Affekt und Kognition als Teamgefährten im Dienste der Handlungssteuerung [Self-regulation instead of self-control: Intentionality, affect and cognition as team mates in the service of action control]. *Psychologische Rundschau [Psychological Review], 62*, 167–173.

Rothschild, B. (2000). *The Body Remembers: The Psychophyisology of Trauma and Trauma Treatment.* New York: Norton.

Rothschild, B. (2002). Understanding dangers of empathy. *Psychotherapy Networker,* July/August. Retrieved July 26, 2022, from www.somatictraumatherapy.com/dangers-of-empathy/.

Rowan, J. (1987). Primal integration therapy. *Self & Society, 15*(2), 73–79.

Rudolf, G. (2000). *Psychotherapeutische Medizin und Psychosomatik. Ein einführendes Lehrbuch auf psychodynamischer Grundlage [Psychotherapeutic Medicine and Psychosomatics. An Introductory Textbook on a Psychodynamic Basis].* Stuttgart: Thieme.

Rudolf, G. (2006). *Strukturbezogene Psychotherapie. Leitfaden zur psychodynamischen Therapie struktureller Störungen [Structural Psychotherapy. Guide to the Psychodynamic Therapy of Structural Disorders]* (2nd ed.). Stuttgart: Schattauer.

Rudolf, G. (2018). Strukturbezogene Psychotherapie [Structural psychotherapy]. In Fiedler (Ed.) (pp. 63–81).

Ruegg, J. C. (2006). *Gehirn, Psyche und Körper. Neurobiologie von Psychosomatik und Psychotherapie [Brain, Psyche and Body. Neurobiology of Psychosomatics and Psychotherapy]* (3rd ed.). Stuttgart: Schattauer.

Russell, J. A. (1994). Is there universal recognition of emotion from facial expression? A review of cross-cultural studies. *Psychological Bulletin, 115*, 102–141.

Russell, J. A. (2003). Core affect and the psychological construction of emotion. *Psychological Review, 110*, 145–172.

Russell, J. A., Bachorowski, J.-A., & Fernández-Dols, J.-M. (2003). Facial and vocal expressions of emotion. *Annual Review of Psychology, 54*, 329–349.

Russelman, G. (1988). Der Energiebegriff in der Bioenergetik. Eine kritische Abhandlung [The concept of energy in bioenergetics. A critical treatise]. *Integrative Therapie [Integrative Therapy], 1*, 4–39.

Ryan, R. M., & Deci, E. L. (2000). Self-determination theory and the facilitation of intrinsic motivation, social development, and well-being. *American Psychologist, 55*, 68–78.

Ryan, R. M., Kuhl, J., & Deci, E. L. (1997). Nature and autonomy: An organizational view of social and neurobiological aspects of self-regulation in behavior and development. *Development and Psychopathology, 9*, 701–728.

Sachsse, U., & Roth, G. (2008). Die Integration neurobiologischer und psychoanalytischer Ergebnisse in der Behandlung Traumatisierter [The integration of neurobiological and psychoanalytical findings in the treatment of traumatised persons]. In M. Leuzinger-Bohleber, G. Roth & A. Buchheim (Eds.), *Psychoanalyse, Neurobiologie, Trauma [Psychoanalysis, Neurobiology, Trauma]* (pp. 69–99). Stuttgart: Schattauer.

Sackmann-Schaefer, K. (1994). Tonusübertragung [Tonus transfer]. In Steinaecker (Ed.) (pp. 99–106).

Sacks, O. (1985). *The Man Who Mistook His Wife for a Hat and Other Clinical Tales.* New York: Summit Books.

Sacks, O. (1993). *A Leg to Stand On.* New York: Harper Collins Publishers.

Sacks, O. (1995). *An Anthropologist on Mars. Seven Paradoxical Tales.* New York: A. A. Knopf.

Sacks, O. (1997). *The Island of the Colorblind.* New York: A. A. Knopf.

Salisch, M. von, & Kunzmann, U. (2005). Emotionale Entwicklung über die Lebensspanne [Emotional development across the lifespan]. In J. Asendorpf (Ed.), *Enzyklopädie der Psychologie. Themenbereich C: Theorie und Forschung. Serie 5: Entwicklungspsychologie, Bd. 3: Soziale, emotionale und Persönlichkeitsentwicklung [Encyclopaedia of Psychology. Subject area C: Theory and research. Series 5: Developmental Psychology, Vol. 3: Social, Emotional and Personality Development]* (pp. 259–334), Goettingen: Hogrefe.

Salovey, P., Rothman, A., Detweiler, J., & Steward, W. (2000). Emotional states and physical health. *American Psychologist, 55,* 110–121.

Samaritter, R., & Payne, H. (2016/17). Being moved: Kinaesthetic reciprocities in psychotherapeutic interaction and the development of enactive intersubjectivity. *European Psychotherapy, 13,* 50–65.

Sander, D., Grandjean, D., & Scherer, K. (2005). A systems approach to appraisal mechanisms in emotion. *Neural Networks, 18,* 317–352.

Sarasin, P., & Tanner, J. (Eds.) (1998). *Physiologie und industrielle Gesellschaft [Physiology and Industrial Society].* Frankfurt: Suhrkamp.

Sartory, A. (2015). The main variants of character theory in the field of body psychotherapy. In Marlock et al. (Eds.) (pp. 301–304).

Sauer, M., & Emmerich, S. (2017). Chronischer Schmerz nach Trauma: Ein Phänomen des leiblich Unbewussten [Chronic pain after trauma: A phenomenon of the bodily unconscious]. *Trauma: Zeitschrift für Psychotraumatologie und ihre Anwendungen [Trauma: Journal for Psychotraumatology and its Applications], 15,* 24–37.

Schacter, D. L. (2001). *The Seven Sins of Memory: How the Mind Forgets and Remembers.* New York: Houghton Mifflin.

Schaechinger, H., & Finke, J. B. (2020). Psychophysiologie und Autonomes Nervensystem [Psychophysiology and autonomic nervous system]. In Egle et al. (Eds.) (pp. 93–104).

Schaible, H.-G. (2006). Zur Innervation des Darms [On the innervation of the intestine]. *Forschende Komplementärmedizin [Complementary Medicine Research], 13,* 244–245.

Schaible, M. (2009). Biodynamic massage as a body therapy and as a tool in body psychotherapy. In Hartley (Ed.) (pp. 31–45).

Schakel, L., Veldhuijzen, D. S., Crompvoets, P. I., Bosch, J. A., Cohen, S., van Middendorp, H., Joosten, S. A., Ottenhoff, T. H. M., Visser, L. G., & Evers, A. W. M. (2019). Effectiveness of stress-reducing interventions on the response to challenges to the immune system: A meta-analytic review. *Psychotherapy and Psychosomatics, 88,* 274–286.

Schatz, D. S. (2002). Klassifikation des Körpererlebens und körperpsychotherapeutische Hauptströmungen [Classification of body experience and main streams of body psychotherapy]. *Psychotherapeut [Psychotherapist], 47,* 77–82.

Schechter, D. S., & Serpa, S. R. (2013). Affektive Kommunikation traumatisierter Mütter mit ihren Kleinkindern [Affective communication of traumatised mothers with their infants]. In Leuzinger-Bohleber et al. (Eds.) (pp. 230–263).

Scheele, D., Striepens, N., Guentuerkuen, O., Deutschlaender, S., Maier, W., Kendrick, K. M., & Hurlemann, R. (2012). Oxytocin modulates social distance between males and females. *The Journal of Neuroscience, 32,* 16074–16079.

Scheff, T. (1983). *Catharsis in Healing, Ritual, and Drama.* Berkeley: University of California Press.

Scheler, M. (1913/²1923/2015). *Wesen und Formen der Sympathie.* Paderborn: Aischines (engl.: The Nature of Sympathy. London, New York: Routledge, 2008).

Scheler, M. (1966). *Die Stellung des Menschen im Kosmos.* Bern: Francke (engl.: The Human Place in the Cosmos. Evanston, IL; Northwestern University Press, 2009).

Schellenbaum, P. (1992). *Nimm deine Couch und geh [Take Your Couch and Go]!* Munich: Koesel.

Scherer, K. R. (2009). Emotions are emergent processes: They require a dynamic computational architecture. *Philosophical Transactions of the Royal Society, 364,* 3459–3474.

Schiepek, G. (2004). Synergetisches Prozessmanagement: Ein Beitrag zu Theorie und Praxis der Psychotherapie [Synergetic process management: A contribution to the theory and practice of psychotherapy]. In von Schlippe & Kriz (Eds.) (pp. 252–268).

Schiepek, G., Heinzel, S., Karch, S., Ploederl, M., & Strunk, G. (2015). Synergetics in psychology: Patterns and pattern transitions in human change processes. In A. Pelster & G. Wunner (Eds.), *Selforganization in Complex Systems: The Past, Present, and Future of Synergetics* (pp. 181–208). Bern: Springer.

Schilbach, L., Timmermans, B., Reddy, V., Costall, A., Bente, G., Schlicht, T., & Vogeley, K. (2013). Toward a second-person neuroscience. *Behavioral and Brain Sciences, 36,* 393–414.

Schindler, P. (2002). Geschichte und Entwicklung der Bioenergetischen Analyse [History and development of bioenergetic analysis]. In Koemeda-Lutz (Ed.) (pp. 27–47).

Schlippe, A. von, & Kriz, W. C. (Eds.) (2004). *Personzentrierung und Systemtheorie. Perspektiven für psychotherapeutisches Handeln [Person-centredness and Systems Theory. Perspectives for Psychotherapeutic Acting].* Goettingen: Vandenhoeck & Ruprecht.

Schlippe, A. von, & Kriz, W. C. (2004a). Vorwort [Preface]. In von Schlippe & Kriz (Eds.) (pp. 7–12).

Schlippe, A. von, & Schweitzer, J. (2003). *Lehrbuch der systemischen Therapie und Beratung [Textbook of Systemic Therapy and Counselling]* (9th ed.). Goettingen: Vandenhoeck & Ruprecht.

Schmidt, E. (Ed.) (2006). *Lehrbuch Konzentrative Bewegungstherapie. Grundlagen und klinische Anwendung [Textbook Concentrative Movement Therapy. Foundations and Clinical Applications]*. Stuttgart: Schattauer.

Schmidt, E. (2006a). Zur Bedeutung des Körperbildes [On the importance of body image]. In Schmidt (Ed.) (pp. 3–20).

Schmidt, P. (2020). Störungen des Selbst in der Borderline-Persönlichkeit. Der Zusammenhang von Affekt und Identitätserleben [Disorders of the self in the borderline personality. The connection between affect and identity experience]. In T. Fuchs & T. Breyer (Eds.), *Selbst und Selbststörungen [Self and Self-Disorders]* (pp. 165–193). Freiburg: Karl Alber.

Schmidt, R.-B., & Schetsche, M. (Eds.) (2012). *Körperkontakt. Interdisziplinäre Erkundungen [Body Contact. Interdisciplinary Explorations]*. Giessen: Psychosozial.

Schmidt, R.-B., & Schetsche, M. (2012a). Körperkontakte: Eine vergessene Wirklichkeit [Body contact: A forgotten reality]? In Schmidt & Schetsche (Eds.) (pp. 7–26).

Schmidtner, A. K., & Neumann, I. D. (2020). Präklinische Einblicke in das Zusammenspiel von Mikrobiota und Verhalten [Preclinical insights into the interplay of microbiota and behaviour]. *Nervenheilkunde [Neural Medicine]*, 39, 19–25.

Schmidt-Zimmermann, I. (2010 October 30). Considerations on a contemporary body psychotherapy [Conference lecture]. 12th Congress of the European Association of Body Psychotherapy, Vienna, Austria.

Schmidt-Zimmermann, I., & Marlock, G. (2011). Behandlung einer Borderline-Persönlichkeitsstörung mit Unitiver Körperpsychotherapie [Treatment of borderline personality disorder with unitive body psychotherapy]. In Roehricht (Ed.) (pp. 276–290).

Schmidt-Zimmermann, I., & Marlock, G. (2011a). Unitive KPT bei Depressionen [Unitive body psychotherapy for depression]. In Roehricht (Ed.) (pp. 93–107).

Schmitter-Boeckelmann, A. (2013). Körperpsychotherapeutische Interventionen in der Arbeit mit komplex traumatisierten Kindern und Jugendlichen [Body-psychotherapeutic interventions in the work with complexly traumatised children and adolescents]. In Thielen (Ed.) (pp. 321–334).

Schmitz, H. (1986). Phänomenologie der Leiblichkeit [Phenomenology of corporeality]. In Petzold (Ed.) (pp. 71–106).

Schmitz, H. (1992). *Leib und Gefühl. Materialien zu einer philosophischen Therapeutik [Body and Feeling. Elements of a Philosophical Therapeutics]* (2nd ed.). Paderborn: Junfermann.

Schmitz, H. (1992a). *Was bleibt vom Philosophen Ludwig Klages [What remains of philosopher Ludwig Klages]*? In Hammer (Ed.) (pp. 14–22).

Schmitz, H. (2014). *Kurze Einführung in die Neue Phänomenologie [A Short Introduction into New Phenomenology]*. Freiburg: Karl Alber.

Schmitz, U. (2006). Raum und Zeit [Space and time]. In Schmidt (Ed.) (pp. 89–92).

Schneider, K. J., & Laengle, A. (2012). The renewal of humanism in psychotherapy: A roundtable discussion. *Psychotherapy*, 49, 427–429.

Schoenberger, F. (1992). Bobath-Konzept und Gindler-Arbeit. Wurzeln der Arbeit Berta Bobaths in der Gymnastikbewegung der 20er Jahre [Bobath concept and Gindler work. Roots of Berta Bobath's work in the gymnastics movement of the 1920s]. *Krankengymnastik [Physical Therapy]*, 44, 408–420.

Schore, A. N. (2001). Effects of a secure attachment relationship on right brain development, affect regulation, and infant mental health. *Infant Mental Health Journal*, 22, 7–66.

Schore, A. N. (2003). *Affect Regulation and the Repair of the Self*. New York: Norton.

Schramme, T. (2005). Psychische Krankheit in wissenschaftlicher und lebensweltlicher Perspektive [Mental illness in a scientific and lifeworld perspective]. In Herrmann et al. (Eds.) (pp. 383–406).

Schrauth, N. (2001). *Körperpsychotherapie und Psychoanalyse [Body Psychotherapy and Psychoanalysis]*. Berlin: Leutner.

Schrauth, N. (2006). Körperpsychotherapie und das vegetative Nervensystem [Body psychotherapy and the vegetative nervous system]. In Marlock & Weiss (Eds.) (pp. 658–666).

Schreiber-Willnow, K. (2000). *Körper-, Selbst- und Gruppenerleben in der stationären Konzentrativen Bewegungstherapie [Body, Self and Group Experience in Inpatient Concentrative Movement Therapy]*. Giessen: Psychosozial.

Schreiber-Willnow, K. (2012). Körperpsychotherapeutische Gruppen [Body psychotherapy in groups]. In B. Strauss & D. Mattke (Eds.), *Gruppenpsychotherapie [Group Psychotherapy]* (pp. 449–461). Berlin: Springer.

Schreiber-Willnow, K. (2013). Die Entwicklung der körperorientierten Gruppentherapie im Osten und im Westen: Am Beispiel der Konzentrativen Bewegungstherapie [The development of body-oriented group therapy in the East and the West: The example of concentrative movement therapy]. In Thielen (Ed.) (pp. 31–40).

Schreiber-Willnow, K., & Seidler, K.-P. (2013). Therapy goals and treatment results in body psychotherapy: Experience with the Concentrative Movement Therapy evaluation form. *Body, Movement and Dance in Psychotherapy*, 4, 254–269.

Schrenker, L. (2008). *Pesso-Therapie: Das Wissen zur Heilung liegt in uns [Pesso Therapy: The Knowledge for Healing Lies Within Us]*. Stuttgart: Klett-Cotta.

Schroer, M. (Ed.) (2005). *Soziologie des Körpers [Sociology of the Body]*. Frankfurt: Suhrkamp.

Schroer, M. (2005a). Zur Soziologie des Körpers [On the sociology of the body]. In Schroer (Ed.) (pp. 7–47).

Schroeter, B. (2013). Gesellschaft, Körper, Zeitgeist [Society, body, zeitgeist]. In Thielen (Ed.) (pp. 191–196).

Schubert, A. (2009). *Das Körperbild. Die Körperskulptur als modulare Methodik in Diagnostik und Therapie [The Body Image. Body Sculpture as a Modular Methodology in Diagnostics and Therapy]*. Stuttgart: Klett Cotta.

Schubert, C. (2015). *Psychoneuroimmunologie und Psychotherapie [Psychoneuroimmunology and Psychotherapy]* (2nd ed.). Stuttgart: Schattauer.

Schubert, C. (2019). *Was uns krank macht, was uns heilt. Aufbruch in eine neue Medizin [What Makes Us Sick, What Cures Us. The Dawn of a New Medicine]* (6th ed.). Munderfing: Fischer & Gann.

Schubert, C. (2020). Psychoimmunologie [Psychoimmunology]. In Egle et al. (Eds.) (pp. 105–121).

Schubert, T. W., & Koole, S. L. (2009). The embodied self: Making a fist enhances men's power-related self-conceptions. *Journal of Experimental Social Psychology*, 45, 828–834.

Schultz-Hencke, H. (1940). *Der gehemmte Mensch [The Inhibited Human Being]*. Leipzig: Thieme.

Schultz-Venrath, U. (1996). Ernst Simmel (1882–1947): Ein Pionier der Psychotherapeutischen Medizin [Ernst Simmel (1882–1947): A pioneer of psychotherapeutic medicine]. *Psychotherapeut [Psychotherapist]*, 41, 107–115.

Schultz-Venrath, U. (2021). *Mentalisieren des Körpers [Mentalisation of the Body]*. Stuttgart: Klett-Cotta.

Schultz-Venrath, U., & Hermanns, L. (2019). Ernst Simmel oder die Psycho-Klinik der Zukunft [Ernst Simmel or the psycho clinic of the future]. In Geisthövel & Hitzer (Eds.) (pp. 124–132).

Schultz-Zehden, W. (1995). *Das Auge: Spiegel der Seele [The Eye: Mirror of the Soul]*. Munich: dtv.

Schulz von Thun, F. (1981). *Miteinander reden 1: Störungen und Klärungen. Allgemeine Psychologie der Kommunikation [Talking to Each Other 1: Disruptions and Clarifications. General Psychology of Communication]*. Reinbek: Rowohlt.

Schulze, G. (2005). *Die Erlebnisgesellschaft: Kultursoziologie der Gegenwart [The Experience Society: Contemporary Cultural Sociology]*. Frankfurt: Campus.

Schwab, F., & Krause, R. (1994). Über das Verhältnis von körperlichen und mentalen emotionalen Abläufen bei verschiedenen psychosomatischen Krankheitsbildern] On the relationship between physical and mental emotional processes in various psychosomatic disease patterns]. *Psychotherapie, Psychosomatik, Medizinische Psychologie [Psychotherapy, Psychosomatics, Medical Psychology]*, 44, 308–315.

Schwartz, M. A., & Wiggins, O. P. (1987). Typifications: The first step for clinical diagnosis in psychiatry. *Journal of Nervous and Mental Disease*, 175, 65–77.

Schwenk, R., & Pechtl, C. (Eds.) (2019). *Körper im Dialog. Theorie und Anwendungsfelder der Bioenergetischen Analyse [Body in Dialogiue. Theory and Fields of Application of Bioenergetic Analysis]*. Giessen: Psychosozial.

Scott, C. L., Harris, R. J., & Rothe, A. R. (2001). Embodied cognition through improvisation improves memory for a dramatic monologue. *Discourse Processes*, 31, 293–305.

Seewald, J. (1991). Von der Psychomotorik zur Motologie. Über den Prozess der Verwissenschaftlichung einer „Meisterlehre" [From psychomotricity to motology. On the process of scientification of a „master teaching"]. *Motorik [Motoricity]*, 14, 3–16.

Seewald, J. (2002). Psychomotorische Vorläufer in der Geschichte der Rhythmus- und Gymnastikbewegung [Psychomotor precursors in the history of the rhythm and gymnastics movement]. *Motorik [Motoricity]*, 25, 26–33.

Segal, Z. V., Williams, J. M. G., & Teasdale, J. D. (2012). *Mindfulness-Based Cognitive Therapy for Depression: A New Approach to Preventing Relapse*. New York: Guilford Press.

Seiffge-Krenke, I. (2000). „Annäherer" und „Vermeider": Die langfristigen Auswirkungen bestimmter Coping-Stile auf depressive Symptome ["Approachers" and "Avoiders": The long-term effects of certain coping styles on depressive symptoms]. *Zeitschrift für Medizinische Psychologie [Journal for Medical Psychology]*, 9, 53–61.

Senf, W. (2001). Integrativer Ansatz in der tiefenpsychologisch fundierten Psychotherapie [Integrative approach in depth psychology-based psychotherapy]. In Cierpka & Buchheim (Eds.) (pp. 33–38).

Senf, W., & Broda, M. (Eds.) (1996). *Praxis der Psychotherapie. Ein integratives Lehrbuch für Psychoanalyse und Verhaltenstherapie [Practice of Psychotherapy. An Integrative Textbook for Psychoanalysis and Behavioural Therapy]*. Stuttgart: Thieme.

Senf, W., & Broda, M. (1996a). Was ist Psychotherapie? Versuch einer Definition [What is psychotherapy? Attempt at a definition]. In Senf & Broda (Eds.) (pp. 2–5).

Senna, I., Maravita, A., Bolognini, N., & Parise, C. V. (2014). The marble-hand illusion. *Plos One*, 9(3). https://doi.org/10.1371/journal.pone.0091688.

Sennett, R. (2000). *The Corrosion of Character: The Personal Consequences of Work in the New Capitalism*. New York: Norton.

Shapiro, F. (1995). *Eye Movement Desensitization and Reprocessing: Basic Principles, Protocols, and Procedures*. New York: Guilford.

Shapiro, L. (Ed.) (2014). *The Routledge Handbook of Embodied Cognition*. Abingdon: Routledge.

Sharaf, M. (1994). *Fury on Earth. A Biography of Wilhelm Reich*. Lebanon: Da Capo Press.

Shaw, P., Eckstrand, K., Sharp, W., Blumenthal, J., Lerch, J. P., Greenstein, D., Clasen, L., Evans, A., Giedd, J., & Rapoport, J. L. (2007). Attention-deficit/hyperactivity disorder is characterized by a delay in cortical maturation. *Proceedings of the National Academy of Sciences, 104*, 19649–19654.

Shaw, R. (2003). *The Embodied Psychotherapist. The Therapist's Body Story*. Hove: Brunner-Routledge.

Shaw, R. (2004). The embodied psychotherapist: An exploration of the therapists' somatic phenomena within the therapeutic encounter. *Psychotherapy Research, 14*, 271–288.

Sheets-Johnstone, M. (1999). Emotion and movement. A beginning empirical-phenomenological analysis of their relationship. *Journal of Consciousness Studies, 6*, 259–277.

Sheets-Johnstone, M. (2009). *The Corporeal Turn: An Interdisciplinary Reader*. Exeter: Imprint Academic.

Sheets-Johnstone, M. (2010). Kinesthetic experience: Understanding movement inside and out. *Body, Movement and Dance in Psychotherapy, 5*, 111–127.

Sheets-Johnstone, M. (2017). Moving in concert. *Choros: International Dance Journal, 6*, 1–19.

Sheets-Johnstone, M. (2019). If the body is part of our discourse, why not let it speak? Five critical perspectives. In N. Depraz, & A. J. Steinbock (Eds.), *Surprise: An Emotion?* (pp. 83–95). Cham: Springer.

Shirtcliff, E. A., Coe, C. L., & Pollak, S. D. (2009). Early childhood stress is associated with elevated antibody levels to Herpes Simplex Virus Type 1. *Proceedings of the National Academy of Sciences, 106*, 2963–2967.

Siegel, D. (1999). *The Developing Mind. How Relationships and the Brain Interact to Shape Who We Are*. New York: Guilford Press.

Siegman, A. W., Anderson, R. A., & Berger, T. (1990). The angry voice: Its effects on the experience of anger and cardiovascular reactivity. *Psychosomatic Medicine, 52*, 631–643.

Silva, G. da (1990). Borborygmi as markers of psychic work during the analytic session. *International Journal of Psychoanalysis, 71*, 641–659.

Simmel, E. (1993). *Psychoanalyse und ihre Anwendungen. Ausgewählte Schriften [Psychoanalysis and its Application. Selected Writings]*. Frankfurt: Fischer.

Sinding, C. (1998). Vitalismus oder Mechanismus? Die Auseinandersetzungen um die forschungsleitenden Paradigmata in der Physiologie [Vitalism or mechanism? The disputes about the paradigms guiding research in physiology]. In Sarasin & Tanner (Eds.) (pp. 76–98).

Slavin, J. H., & Rahmani, M. (2016). Slow dancing: Mind, body, and sexuality in a new relational psychoanalysis. *Psychoanalytic Perspectives, 13*, 152–167.

Sletvold, J. (2014). *The Embodied Analyst. From Freud and Reich to Relationality*. London: Routledge.

Slunecko, T, & Wieser, M. (2014). Cultural psychology. In T. Teo (Ed.), *Encyclopedia of Critical Psychology*. (pp. 347–352) New York: Springer.

Smith, E. W. L., Clance, P. R., & Imes, S. (Eds.) (1998). *Touch in Psychotherapy. Theory, Research, and Practice*. New York: The Guilford Press.

Smith, M. E. (2005). Bilateral hippocampal volume reduction in adults with post-traumatic stress disorder: A meta-analysis of structural MRI studies. *Hippocampus, 15*, 798–807.

Snowdon, P. F. (1998). Persons, animals, and bodies. In Bermúdez et al. (Eds.) (pp. 71–86).

Solbakken, O. A., Hansen, R. S., Havik, O. E., & Monsen, J. T. (2012). Affect integration as a predictor of change: Affect consciousness and treatment response in open-ended psychotherapy. *Psychotherapy Research, 22*, 656–672.

Sollmann, U. (1988). *Bioenergetik in der Praxis [Bioenergetics in Practice]*. Reinbek: Rowohlt.

Sollmann, U. (2009). Zeitlupenbewegung (Slow-motion-movement SMM) [Slow motion movement]. In Thielen (Ed.) (pp. 105–113).

Sonne, J. C. (1996). Interpreting the dread of being aborted in therapy. *Internationale Zeitschrift für Prä- und Perinatale Medizin und Psychologie [International Journal of Pre- and Perinatal Medicine and Psychology], 8*, 317–339.

Sonntag, M. (1988). *Die Seele als Politikum. Psychologie und die Produktion des Individuums [The Psyche as a Political Issue. Psychology and the Production of the Individual]*. Berlin: D. Reimer.

Sonntag, M. (2008). Mentalitäten des Nicht-Erwägens. Zu einigen Aspekten der homerischen Kultur [Mentalities of not considering. On some aspects of Homeric culture]. In G. Juettemann (Ed.), *Suchprozesse der Seele. Die Psychologie des Erwägens [Search Processes of the Psyche. The Psychology of Considering]* (pp. 33–45). Goettingen: Vandenhoeck & Ruprecht.

Soth, M. (2005). Embodied countertransference. In Totton (Ed.) (pp. 40–55).

Soth, M. (2009). From humanistic holism via the 'integrative project' towards integral-relational body psychotherapy. In Hartley (Ed.) (pp. 64–88).

Soth, M. (2012). Current body psychotherapy: An integral-relational approach for the 21st century? In Young (Ed.) (pp. 55–68).

Soth, M. (2013). We are all relational, but are some more relational than others? Completing the paradigm shift towards relationality. *Transactional Analysis Journal, 43*(2),122–137.

Soth, M. (2015). The use of body psychotherapy in the context of group therapy. In Marlock et al. (Eds.) (pp. 816–833).

Soth, M. (2019). The relational turn in body psychotherapy. In Payne et al. (Eds.) (pp. 298–314).

Southwell, C. (1988). The Gerda Boyesen method: Biodynamic therapy. In J. Rowan & W. Dryden (Eds.), *Innovative Therapy in Britain* (pp. 179 –201). Philadelphia: Open University Press.

Spangler, G., & Grossmann, K. (1995). Zwanzig Jahre Bindungsforschung in Bielefeld und Regensburg [Twenty years of attachment research in Bielefeld and Regensburg]. In G. Spangler & P. Zimmermann (Eds.), *Die Bindungstheorie. Grundlagen, Forschung und Anwendung [Attachment Theory. Foundations, Research, Applicatin]* (pp. 50–63). Stuttgart: Klett-Cotta.

Spangler, G., Grossmann, K. E., & Schieche, M. (2002). Psychobiologische Grundlagen der Organisation des Bindungsverhaltenssystems im Kleinkindalter [Psychobiological foundations of the organisation of the attachment behaviour system in infancy]. *Psychologie in Erziehung und Unterricht [Psychology in Education and Teaching]*, *49*, 102–120.

Spinazzola, J., van der Kolk, B., & Ford, J. D. (2018). When nowhere is safe: Interpersonal trauma and attachment adversity as antecedents of posttraumatic stress disorder and developmental trauma disorder. *Journal of Traumatic Stress*, *31*, 631–642.

Spremberg, A. (2018). Depression and psychosis: Perspectives on the body, enactivism, and psychotherapy. *InterCultural Philosophy*, *1*, 83–106.

Sreckovic, M. (1999). Geschichte und Entwicklung der Gestalttherapie [History and development of Gestalt therapy]. In Fuhr et al. (Eds.) (pp. 15–178).

Stack, D. M., & Muir, D. W. (1992). Adult tactile stimulation during face-to-face interactions modulates five-month-olds' affect and attention. *Child Development*, *63*, 1509–1525.

Staemmler, F.-M. (2017). *Relationalität in der Gestalttherapie: Kontakt und Verbundenheit [Relationality in Gestalt therapy: Contact and Connectedness]*. Gevelsberg: Ehp.

Starobinski, J. (1987). *Kleine Geschichte des Körpergefühls [A Brief History of Body Feeling]*. Konstanz: Universitaetsverlag.

Stattman, J. (1989). *Creative Trance*. Amsterdam: International Academy for Bodytherapy.

Stattman, J. (1993). Organische Übertragung [Organic transference]. In Marlock (Ed.) (pp. 31–48).

Stauffer, K. (2009). The use of neuroscience in body psychotherapy: Theoretical and clinically relevant aspects. In Hartley (Ed.) (pp. 138–150).

Staunton, T. (Ed.) (2002). *Body Psychotherapy*. London: Routledge.

Staunton, T. (2002a). Introduction. In Staunton (Ed.) (pp. 1–6).

Staunton, T. (2008). Finding a relational home for the body. *British Journal for Psychotherapy Integration*, *5*, 21–25.

Stauss, K., & Fritzsche, K. (2006). Psychodynamische Kurzzeittherapie mit erlebnisaktivierenden Interventionen [Psychodynamic short-term therapy with experience-activating interventions]. *Psychotherapeut [Psychotherapist]*, *51*, 214–222.

Stebbins, G. (1893). *Dynamic Breathing and Harmonic Gymnastics. A Complete System of Psychical, Aesthetic and Physical Culture*. New York: Edgar Werner.

Stefan, R. (2020). Zukunftsentwürfe des Leibes. Integrative Psychotherapiewissenschaft und kognitive Neurowissenschaften im 21. Jahrhundert [Future Models of the Body. Integrative Psychotherapy Science and Cognitive Neuroscience in the 21st Century]. Wiesbaden: Springer.

Stein, E. (1989). *On the Problem of Empathy*. Washington, DC: ICS Publications.

Steinaecker, K. von (Ed.) (1994). *Der eigene und der fremde Körper. Übertragungsphänomene in der Atem- und Leibpädagogik [One's Own Body and the Body of Others. Transference Phenomena in Breath and Body Pedagogy]*. Berlin: Lit Europe.

Steinaecker, K. von (2000). *Luftsprünge. Anfänge moderner Körpertherapien [Jumping in The Air. Beginnings of Modern Body Therapies]*. Munich: Urban & Fischer.

Steinaecker, K. von (2010). Atem- und Leibtherapie. Geschichte, Therapiekonzepte, Anwendung [Breath and body therapy. History, therapy concepts, application]. In Mueller-Braunschweig & Stiller (Eds.) (pp. 173–194).

Stepper, S., & Strack, F. (1993). Proprioceptive determinants of emotional and nonemotional feelings. *Journal of Personality and Social Psychology*, *64*, 211–220.

Stern, D. (1985). *The Interpersonal World of the Infant*. New York: Basic Books.

Stern, D. (1995). *The Motherhood Constellation*. New York: Basic Books.

Stern, D. (2004). *The Present Moment in Psychotherapy and Everyday Life*. New York: Norton.

Stern, D. (2010). *Forms of Vitality. Exploring Dynamic Experience in Psychology, the Arts, Psychotherapy, and Development*. Oxford: Oxford University Press.

Stern, D., Bruschweiler-Stern, N., Harrison, A. M., Lyons-Ruth, K., Morgan, A. C., Nahum, J. P., Sander, L., & Tronick, E. Z. (1998). The process of therapeutic change involving implicit knowledge: Some implications of developmental observations for adult psychotherapy. *Infant Mental Health Journal*, *19*, 300–308.

Stern, E. (1952). *Lebenskonflikte als Krankheitsursachen [Life Conflicts as Causes of Disease]*. Zurich: Rascher.

Stern, W. (1927). [Selbstdarstellung] [Selfportrayal]. In R. Schmidt (Ed.), *Die Philosophie der Gegenwart in Selbstdarstellungen [Contemporary Philosophy in Self-Portrayals]* Vol. 6 (pp. 1–56). Leipzig: Meiner.

Stern, W. (1930). *Studien zur Personwissenschaft. I. Teil: Personalistik als Wissenschaft [Studies in Person Science. Part I: Personalistics as a Science]*. Leipzig: Barth.

Stewart, J., Gapenne, O., & Di Paolo, E. A. (Eds.) (2010). *Enaction. Toward a New Paradigm for Cognitive Science*. Cambridge, MA: MIT-Press.

Stewart, J., Gapenne, O., & Di Paolo, E. A. (2010a). Introduction. In Stewart, Gapenne & Di Paolo (Eds.) (pp. VII–XVII).

Stoerig, H. J. (1969). *Kleine Weltgeschichte der Philosophie [A Short World History of Philosophy]*, Vol. 2. Frankfurt: Fischer.

Stoff, H. (2019). Endokrine Psychosomatik oder der Versuch, Hormon- und Psychotherapie zu verbinden [Endocrine psychosomatics or the attempt to combine hormone- and psychotherapy]. In Geisthövel & Hitzer (Eds.) (pp. 89–101).

Stolze, H. (1959). Zur Bedeutung von Erspüren und Bewegen für die Psychotherapie [On the importance of sensing and moving for psychotherapy]. In Stolze (Ed.) (2002) (pp. 28–38).

Stolze, H. (1983). Concentrative Movement Therapy. *The Charlotte Selver Foundation Bulletin: The Work After Elsa Gindler, 11*, 9–15.

Stolze, H. (Ed.) (2002). *Konzentrative Bewegungstherapie. Grundlagen und Erfahrungen [Concentrative Movement Therapy. Foundations and Experiences]* (3rd ed.). Berlin: Springer.

Stolze, H. (2006). Symbol – Symbolik – Symbolisieren [Symbol – Symbolism – Symbolising]. In Schmidt (Ed.) (pp. 21–26).

Stolze, H. (2006a). Bewegen – Besinnen – Begreifen – Bedeuten: Symbolisieren in der Körperpsychotherapie [Moving - Reflecting - Grasping - Signifying: Symbolising in body psychotherapy]. In Marlock & Weiss (Eds.) (pp. 442–449).

Storch, M. (2002). Die Bedeutung neurowissenschaftlicher Forschungsansätze für die psychotherapeutische Praxis. Teil I: Theorie [The significance of neuroscientific research approaches for psychotherapeutic practice. Part I: Theory]. *Psychotherapie [Psychotherapy], 7*, 281–294.

Storch, M. (2003). Die Bedeutung neurobiologischer Forschung für die psychotherapeutische Praxis. Teil II: Praxis: Das Zürcher Ressourcen Modell (ZRM) [The importance of neurobiological research for psychotherapeutic practice. Part II - Practice: The Zurich Resource Model (ZRM)]. *Psychotherapie [Psychotherapy], 8*, 11–29.

Storch, M. (2006). Wie Embodiment in der Psychologie erforscht wurde [How embodiment was explored in psychology]. In Storch et al. (Eds.) (pp. 35–72).

Storch, M., Cantieni, B., Huether, G., & Tschacher, W. (2006). *Embodiment. Die Wechselwirkung von Körper und Psyche verstehen und nutzen [Embodiment. Understanding and Using the Interaction of Body and Psyche]*. Bern: Huber.

Strack, F., Martin, L. L., & Stepper, S. (1988). Inhibiting and facilitating conditions of the human smile: A nonobtrusive test of the facial feedback hypothesis. *Journal of Personality and Social Psychololgy, 54*, 768–77.

Straub, J. (2019). *Das optimierte Selbst. Kompetenzimperative und Steigerungstechnologien in der Optimierungsgesellschaft. Ausgewählte Schriften [The Optimised Self. Competence Imperatives and Enhancement Technologies in the Optimisation Society. Selected Writings]*. Giessen: Psychosozial.

Strauss, B., & Schwark, B. (2007). Die Bindungstheorie und ihre Relevanz für die Psychotherapie [Attachment theory and it's relevance for psychotherapy]. *Psychotherapeut [Psychotherapist], 52*, 405–425.

Strawson, G. (2014). The minimal subject. In Gallagher (Ed.) (pp. 253–278).

Streeck, U. (2004). *Auf den ersten Blick. Psychotherapeutische Beziehungen unter dem Mikroskop [At First Glance. Psychotherapeutic Relationships under the Microscope]*. Stuttgart: Klett-Cotta.

Streeck, U. (2005). Erzählen und Interaktion im psychotherapeutischen Dialog [Narrative and interaction in psychotherapeutic dialogue]. In Geissler (Ed.) (pp. 33–49).

Streeck, U. (2013). Implizites Beziehungswissen [Implicit relatonal knowledge]. *Psychotherapeut [Psychotherapist], 58*, 143–151.

Streeck, U. (2018). Die "antwortende" therapeutische Beziehung. Zur psychoanalytisch-interaktionellen Methode [The "responding" therapeutic relationship. On the psychoanalytical-interactional method]. In Fiedler (Ed.) (pp. 51–62).

Stumm, G. (2000). Psychotherapie [Psychotherapy]. In G. Stumm & A. Pritz (Eds.), *Wörterbuch der Psychotherapie [Dictionary of Psychotherapy]* (pp. 569–570). Wien: Springer.

Stupiggia, M. (2019). Traumatic dis-embodiment. Effects of trauma on body perception and body image. In Payne et al. (Eds.) (pp. 389–396).

Sugamura, G., Takase, H., Haruki, Y., & Koshikawa, F. (2007 August). Bodyfulness and posture: It's concept and some empirical support [Poster presentation]. 65th Convention of the International Council of Psychologists, San Diego, CA.

Sugamura, G., Takase, H., Haruki, Y., & Koshikawa, F. (2008 Juli). Expanded and upright postures can reduce depressive mood [Poster presentation]. 29th International Congress of Psychology, Berlin, Deutschland.

Sugamura, G., Shiraishi, S., & Higuchi, R. (2009 May). The 'gaze-down' stance elicits negative mood states [Poster presentation]. 21st Annual Convention of the Association for Psychological Science, San Francisco, CA.

Sugimoto, K., Matsui, K., Iijima, Y., Akakabe, Y., Muramoto, S., Ozawa, R., Uefune, M., Sasaki, R., Alamgir, K. M., Akitake, S., Nobuke, T., Galis, I., Aoki, K., Shibata, D., & Takabayashi, J. (2014). Intake and transformation to a glycoside of (Z)-3-hexenol from infested neighbors reveals a mode of plant odor reception and defense. *Proceedings of the National Academy of Sciences*, 111, 7144–7149.

Sulz, S. K. D. (2005). Gehirn, Emotion und Körper [Brain, emotion, and body]. In Sulz et al. (Eds.) (pp. 3–23).

Sulz, S. K. D. (2015). Cognitive behavioral therapists discover the body. In Marlock et al. (Eds.) (pp. 883–890).

Sulz, S. K. D. (2021). *Mit Gefühlen umgehen. Praxis der Emotionsregulation in der Psychotherapie [Dealing with Feelings. Practice of Emotion Regulation in Psychotherapy]*. Giessen: Psychosozial.

Sulz, S. K. D., & Lenz, G. (Eds.) (2000). *Von der Kognition zur Emotion. Psychotherapie mit Gefühlen [From Cognition to Emotion. Psychotherapy with Feelings]*. Munich: CIP-Medien.

Sulz, S. K. D., Schrenker, L., & Schricker, C. (Eds.) (2005). *Die Psychotherapie entdeckt den Körper. Oder: Keine Psychotherapie ohne Körperarbeit [Psychotherapy Discovers the Body. Or: No Psychotherapy without Bodywork]?* Munich: CIP-Medien.

Synofzik, M., Vosgerau, G., & Newen, A. (2008). I move, therefore I am: A new theoretical framework to investigate agency and ownership. *Consciousness and Cognition*, 17, 411–424.

Tameling, A., & Sachsse, U. (1996). Symptomkomplex, Traumaprävalenz und Körperbild von psychisch Kranken mit selbstverletzendem Verhalten (SVV) [Symptom complex, trauma prevalence and body image of mentally ill people with self-harming behaviour]. *Psychotherapie, Psychosomatik, Medizinische Psychologie [Psychotherapy, Psychosomatics, Medical Psychology]*, 46, 61–67.

Tanner, J. (1998). „Weisheit des Körpers" und soziale Homöostase. Physiologie und das Konzept der Selbstregulation ["Wisdom of the body" and social homeostasis. Physiology and the concept of self-regulation]. In Sarasin & Tanner (Eds.) (pp. 129–169).

Tantia, J. (2019). Having a body and moving your body: Distinguishing somatic psychotherapy from dance/movement therapy. In Payne et al. (Eds.) (pp. 66–75).

Tassinary, L. G. & Cacioppo, J. T. (1992). Unobservable facial action and emotion. *Psychological Science*, 3, 28–33.

Taubert, N., Stettler, M., Siebert, R., Spadacenta, S., Sting, L., Dicke, P., Thier, P., & Giese, M. A. (2021). Shape-invariant encoding of dynamic facial expressions in human perception. *eLife*, 10, e61197. https://doi.org/10.7554/eLife.61197.

Teegen, F. (1986). Verstärkte Atmung und seelisches Erleben [Forced breathing and mental experience]. In Petzold (Ed.) (pp. 499–545).

Teegen. (1994). *Körperbotschaften. Selbstwahrnehmung in Bildern [Body Messages. Self-Perception in Pictures]*. Reinbek: Rowohlt.

Theilemann, S. (2018). *Harald Schultz-Hencke und die Freideutsche Jugendbewegung. Biografie bis 1921 und die Geschichte einer Bewegung [Harald Schultz-Hencke and the Free German Youth Movement. Biography until 1921 and the History of a Movement]*. Giessen: Psychosozial.

Thelen, E. (2000). Grounded in the world: Developmental origins of the embodied mind. *Infancy*, 1, 3–28.

Thelen, E., & Smith, L. (1994). *A Dynamic Systems Approach to the Development of Cognition and Action*. Cambridge, MA: MIT Press.

Thielen, M. (Ed.) (2009). *Körper – Gefühl – Denken. Körperpsychotherapie und Selbstregulation [Body - Feeling - Thinking. Body Psychotherapy and Self-Regulation]*. Giessen: Psychosozial.

Thielen, M. (2009a). Selbstregulationskonzepte in der Körperpsychotherapie [Concepts of self-regulation in body psychotherapy]. In Thielen (Ed.) (pp. 35–52).

Thielen, M. (2009b). Säuglingsforschung – Selbstregulation – Körperpsychotherapie [Infant research – self-regulation – body psychotherapy]. In Thielen (Ed.) (pp. 187–208).

Thielen, M. (Ed.) (2013). *Körper – Gruppe – Gesellschaft. Neue Entwicklungen in der Körperpsychotherapie [Body – Group – Society. New Developments in Body Psychotherapy]*. Giessen: Psychosozial.

Thielen, M. (2013a). Der Körper im Feld der Gruppe. Charakteristika der Körpergruppenpsychotherapie [The body in the field of the group. Features of body group psychotherapy]. In Thielen (Ed.) (pp. 41–66).

Thielen, M. (2013b). Neue Entwicklungen in der Wissenschaft und ihre Bedeutung für die körperpsychotherapeutische Praxis. Säuglingsforschung – Mikropraktiken – Körperpsychotherapeutische Praxis [New developments in science and their significance for body psychotherapy practice. Infant Research - Micropractices - Body psychotherapeutic practice]. In Thielen (Ed.) (pp. 309–318).

Thielen, M. (2014). Körperpsychotherapie heute. Theorie – Praxis – Anwendungsbereiche [Body psychotherapy today. Theory - practice - areas of application]. In Eberwein & Thielen (pp. 113–133).

Thielen, M., & Eberwein, W. (Eds.) (2019). *Fühlen und Erleben in der Humanistischen Psychotherapie [Feeling and experiencing in humanistic psychotherapy]*. Giessen: Psychosozial.

Thielen, M., von Arnim, A., & Willach-Holzapfel, A. (Eds.) (2018). *Lebenszyklen: Körperrhythmen. Körperpsychotherapie über die Lebensspanne [Life Cycles: Body Rhythms. Body Psychotherapy Across The Lifespan]*. Giessen: Psychosozial.

Thomae, H. (1968). *Das Individuum und seine Welt. Eine Persönlichkeitstheorie [The Individual and Their World. A Theory of Personality]*. Goettingen: Hogrefe.

Thomae, H., & Kaechele, H. (2020). *Psychoanalytic Therapy. Principles and Practice. Vol. 1: Principles*. Giessen: Psychosozial.

Thompson, E. (2010). *Mind in Life. Biology, Phenomenology, and the Sciences of Mind.* Cambridge, MA: Harvard University Press.

Thompson, E., & Varela, F. J. (2001). Radical embodiment: Neural dynamics and consciousness. *Trends in Cognitive Sciences, 5,* 418–425.

Thompson, W. F., Marin, M. M., & Stewart, L. (2012). Reduced sensitivity to emotional prosody in congenital amusia rekindles the musical protolanguage hypothesis. *Proceedings of the National Academy of Sciences, 109,* 19027–19032.

Thornquist, E. (2010). Psychomotor physiotherapy: Principles, perspectives, and potentials. In Ekerholt (Ed.) (pp. 203–215).

Thornquist, E., & Bunkan, B. H. (1991). *What is Psychomotor Therapy?* Oslo: Norwegian University Press.

Tietke, M. (2011). *Yoga im Nationalsozialismus. Konzepte, Kontraste, Konsequenzen [Yoga in National Socialism. Concepts, Contrasts, Consequences].* Kiel: Ludwig.

Toepfer, G. (2005). *Der Begriff des Lebens [The concept of life].* In Krohs & Toepfer (Eds.) (pp. 157–174).

Tomasello, M., Carpenter, M., Call, J., Behne, T., & Moll, H. (2005). Understanding and sharing intentions: The origins of cultural cognition. *Behavioral and Brain Sciences, 28,* 675–691.

Tomasello, M., Hare, B., Lehmann, H., & Call, J. (2007). Reliance on head versus eyes in the gaze following of great apes and human infants: The cooperative eye hypothesis. *Journal of Human Evolution, 52,* 314–320. https://doi.org/10 .1016/j.jhevol.2006.10.001.

Tonella, G. (2000). The interactive self. *The Clinical Journal of Bioenergetic Analysis, 11,* 25–59.

Totton, N. (2002). Foreign bodies: Recovering the history of body psychotherapy. In Staunton (Ed.) (pp. 7–26).

Totton, N. (2002a). The future for body psychotherapy. In Staunton (Ed.) (pp. 202–224).

Totton, N. (2003). *Body Psychotherapy. An Introduction.* Maidenhead: Open University Press.

Totton, N. (Ed.) (2005). *New Dimensions in Body Psychotherapy.* Maidenhead: Open University Press.

Totton, N. (2015). *Embodied Relating. The Ground of Psychotherapy.* London: Karnac.

Totton, N. (2019). Embodied relational therapy. In Payne et al. (Eds.) (pp. 283–290).

Totton, N. (2020). *Body Psychotherapy for the 21st Century.* London: Confer Books.

Totton, N., & Priestman, A. (2012). Embodiment & relationship: Two halves of one whole. In Young (Ed.) (pp. 35–53).

Tourunen, A., Kykyri, V.-L., Kaartinen, J., Penttonen, M., & Seikkula, J. (2016). Sympathetic nervous system synchrony in couple therapy. *Journal of Marital and Family Therapy, 42,* 383–395.

Tracy, J. L., & Robins, R. W. (2004). Show your pride. Evidence for a discrete emotion expression. *Psychological Science, 15,* 194–197.

Traue, H. C. (1998). *Emotion und Gesundheit. Die psychobiologische Regulation durch Hemmungen [Emotion and Health. The Psychobiological Regulation through Inhibitions].* Heidelberg: Spektrum.

Trautmann-Voigt, S. (2003). Tanztherapie. Zum aktuellen Diskussionsstand in Deutschland [Dance therapy. On the current state of discussion in Germany]. *Psychotherapeut [Psychotherapist], 48,* 215–229.

Trautmann-Voigt, S. (2006). Tanztherapie. Zwischen künstlerischem Ausdruck und psychotherapeutischem Verfahren [Dance therapy. Between artistic expression and psychotherapeutic method]. *Psychodynamische Psychotherapie [Psychodynamic Psychotherapy], 5,* 40–53.

Trautmann-Voigt, S. (2015). Dance therapy. In Marlock et al. (Eds.) (pp. 849–863).

Trautmann-Voigt, S., & Voigt, B. (Eds.) (1996). *Bewegte Augenblicke im Leben des Säuglings – Und welche therapeutischen Konsequenzen? Verbindung von Säuglingsforschung und Psychotherapie mit Körper-Bewegung-Tanz [Moving Moments in the Life of the Infant - and What Therapeutic Consequences? Linking Infant Research and Psychotherapy with Body-Movement-Dance].* Cologne: Claus Richter.

Trautmann-Voigt, S., & Voigt, B. (Eds.) (1998). *Bewegung ins Unbewusste. Beiträge zur Säuglingsforschung und analytischen KörperPsychotherapie [Movement into the Unconscious. Contributions to Infant Research and Analytic Body Psychotherapy].* Frankfurt: Brandes & Apsel.

Trautmann-Voigt, S., & Voigt, B. (Eds.) (2007). *Körper und Kunst in der Psychotraumatologie. Methodenintegrative Therapie [Body and Art in Psychotraumatology. Method Integrative Therapy].* Stuttgart: Schattauer.

Trautmann-Voigt, S., & Voigt, B. (2009). *Grammatik der Körpersprache. Körpersignale in Psychotherapie und Coaching entschlüsseln und nutzen [Grammar of Body Language. Decoding and Using Body Signals in Psychotherapy and Coaching].* Stuttgart: Schattauer.

Trautmann-Voigt, S., & Voigt, B. (2010). Körpertherapeutische Interventionen im tiefenpsychologischen Setting. Was bewegt die Bewegung im therapeutischen Kontakt [Body therapy interventions in the depth psychology setting. What moves movement in therapeutic contact]? In W. Wöller & J. Kruse (Eds.), *Tiefenpsychologisch fundierte Psychotherapie. Basisbuch und Praxisleitfaden [Depth Psychologically Based Psychotherapy. Basic Book and Practice Guide]* (3rd ed.) (pp. 455–466). Stuttgart: Schattauer.

Trautmann-Voigt, S., & Zander, D. (2007). Interaktionsanalyse des Körperverhaltens – Entwicklung eines Instruments zur Bewegungsanalyse [Interaction analysis of body behaviour - Development of a movement analysis tool]. In Trautmann-Voigt & Voigt (Eds.) (pp. 189–219).

Tretter, F., & Gruenhut, C. (2010). *Ist das Gehirn der Geist? Grundfragen der Neurophilosophie [Is the Brain the Mind? Basic Questions of Neurophilosophy].* Goettingen: Hogrefe.

Trevarthen, C. (2001). Intrinsic motives for companionship in understanding: Their origin, development, and significance for infant mental health. *Infant Mental Health Journal, 22*, 95–131.

Trevarthen, C. (2003). Neuroscience and intrinsic psychodynamics: Current knowledge and potential for therapy. In J. Corrigall & H. Wilkinson (Eds.), *Revolutionary Connections: Psychotherapy and Neuroscience* (pp. 53–78). London: Karnak.

Trevarthen, C. (2004). Intimate contact from birth. How we know one another by touch, voice, and expression in movement. In White (Ed.) (pp. 1–15).

Trevarthen, C. (2012). Embodied human intersubjectivity: Imaginative agency, to share meaning. *Journal of Cognitive Semiotics, 4*, 6–56. https://doi.org/10.1515/cogsem.2012.4.1.6.

Trevarthen, C., & Aitken, K. J. (2001). Infant intersubjectivity: Research, theory, and clinical application. *Journal of Child Psychology and Psychiatry, 42*, 3–48.

Troesken, A. K., & Grawe, K. (2004). Inkongruenzerleben aufgrund brachliegender und fehlender Ressourcen: Die Rolle von Ressourcenpotentialen und Ressourcenrealisierung für die psychologische Therapie [Incongruent experience due to idle and missing resources: The role of resource potentials and resource realisation for psychological therapy]. *Verhaltenstherapie & psychosoziale Praxis [Behaviour Therapy and Psychosocial Practice], 36*(1), 51–62.

Tronick, E. (1989). Emotions and emotional communication in infants. *American Psychologist, 44*, 112–119.

Tronick, E. (1998). Dyadically expanded states of consciousness and the process of therapeutic change. *Infant Mental Health Journal, 19*, 290–299.

Trotz, R. (2019). Der Körper erinnert sich: Traumaverarbeitung [The body remembers: Trauma processing]. In Schwenk & Pechtl (Eds.) (pp. 135–151).

Tsakiris, M. (2014). The sense of body ownership. In Gallagher (Ed.) (pp. 180–203).

Tsakiris, M., Prabhu, G., & Haggard, P. (2006). Having a body versus moving your body: How agency structures body-ownership. *Consiousness and Cognition, 15*, 423–432.

Tschacher, W. (2004). Kognitive Selbstorganisation als theoretische Grundlage eines personzentrierten Ansatzes [Cognitive self-organisation as the theoretical basis of a person-centred approach]. In von Schlippe & Kriz (Eds.) (pp. 78–101).

Tschacher, W. (2006). Wie Embodiment zum Thema wurde [How embodiment became a topic]. In Storch et al. (Eds.) (pp. 11–34).

Tschacher, W., & Meier, D. (2020). Physiological synchrony in psychotherapy sessions. *Psychotherapy Research, 30*, 558–573.

Tschacher, W., & Meier, D. (2022). Embodiment in der therapeutischen Kommunikation [Embodiment in therapeutic communication]. *Psychotherapie [Psychotherapy].* https://doi.org/10.1007/s00278-022-00616-8.

Tschacher, W., & Ramseyer, F. (2017). Synchronie in dyadischer Interaktion: Verkörperte Kommunikation in Psychotherapie, Beratung, Paargesprächen [Synchronicity in dyadic interaction: Embodied communication in psychotherapy, counselling, couple conversations]. In Breyer et al. (Eds.) (pp. 319–334).

Tschacher, W., & Storch, M. (2012). Die Bedeutung von Embodiment für Psychologie und Psychotherapie [The significance of embodiment for psychology and psychotherapy]. *Psychotherapie [Psychotherapy], 17*, 259–267.

Tschacher, W., & Storch, M. (2017). Grundlagen des Embodiment-Ansatzes in den Humanwissenschaften [Foundations of the embodiment-approach in the humanities]. *Motorik [Motoricity], 40*, 118–126.

Tschuschke, V. (2020). Kastriert sich die Psychoonkologie selbst? Zur Kritik der Forschung in Psychoonkologie und Psychotherapie – Warum wir andere wissenschaftliche Paradigmen benötigen [Is psychooncology castrating itself? On the critique of research in psychooncology and psychotherapy: Why we need other scientific paradigms]. In C. Schuber & M. Singer (Eds.), *Das Unsichtbare hinter dem Sichtbaren. Gesundheit und Krankheit neu denken [The Invisible Behind the Visible. Rethinking Health and Disease]* (pp. 109–138). Norderstedt: Books on Demand.

Tucker, M., & Ellis, R. (1998). On the relations between seen objects and components of potential actions. *Journal of Experimental Psychology: Human Perception and Performance, 24*, 830–846.

Uexkuell, J. von (2010). *A Foray into the Worlds of Animals and Humans.* Minneapolis: University of Minnesota Press (first published in German in 1956).

Uexkuell, T. von (2001). Körper-Sein, Körper-Haben – Der Hintergrund des Dualismus in der Medizin [Being a body – Having a body- The background of dualism in medicine]. *Psychotherapie, Psychosomatik, Medizinische Psychologie [Psychotherapy, Psychosomatics, Medical Psychology], 51*, 128–133.

Uexkuell, T. von, & Wesiack, W. (1996). Wissenschaftstheorie: Ein bio-psycho-soziales Modell [Philosophy of science: A bio-psycho-social model]. In Adler et al. (Eds.) (pp. 13–52).

Uhlemann, C. (2006). Beeinflussbarkeit funktioneller Darmstörungen über die Körperdecke: Naturheilkundliche Konzepte [Influencing functional intestinal disorders via the body surface: Naturopathic concepts]. *Forschende Komplementärmedizin [Complementary Medicine Research], 13*, 249–250.

Umiltà, M. A., Kohler, E., Gallese, V., Fogassi, L., Fadiga, L., Keysers, C., & Rizzolatti, G. (2001). I know what you are doing. A neurophysiological study. *Neuron, 31*, 155–165.

Unfried, N. (2006). Pränatale Traumata und ihre Bearbeitung in der Kindertherapie [Prenatal traumata and their treatment in child therapy]. In Krens & Krens (Eds.) (pp. 187–202).

Uvnaes-Moberg, K. (1998). Oxytocin may mediate the benefits of positive social interaction and emotions. *Psychoneuroendocrinology, 23*, 819–835.

van Alphen, F. (2014). Tango and enactivism. First steps in exploring the dynamics and experience of interaction. *Integrative Psychological and Behavioral Science, 48*, 322–331.

Van den Bergh, B. R. H. (1990). The influence of maternal emotions during pregnancy on fetal and neonatal behavior. *Pre- and Peri-Natal Psychology, 5*, 119–130.

van der Kolk, B. (1994). The body keeps the score: Approaches to the psychobiology of posttraumatic stress disorder. *Harvard Review of Psychiatry, 1*(5), 253–265.

van der Kolk, B. (2006). Clinical implications of neuroscience research in PTSD. *Annals of the New York Academy of Science, 1071*, 277–293.

van der Kolk, B. (2011). Foreword. In S. Porges, *The Polyvagal Theory: Neurophysiological Foundations of Emotions, Attachment, Communication, and Self-Regulation* (pp. 9–16). New York: Norton.

van der Kolk, B. (2014). *The Body Keeps the Score. Brain, Mind, and Body in the Healing of Trauma.* New York: Viking.

van der Kolk, B., McFarlane, A., & Weisaeth, L. (Eds.) (1996). *Traumatic Stress. The Effects of Overwhelming Experience on Mind, Body and Society.* New York: Guilford.

Varela, F. J., Thompson, E., & Rosch, E. (1993). *The Embodied Mind. Cognitive Science and Human Experience* (rev. ed. 2017). Cambridge, MA: MIT Press.

Varela, F., Lachaux, J.-P., Rodriguez, E., & Martinerie, J. (2001). The brainweb: Phase synchronization and large-scale integration. *Nature Reviews Neuroscience, 2*, 229–239.

Veenstra, L., Schneider, I. K., & Koole, S. L. (2017). Embodied mood regulation: The impact of body posture on mood recovery, negative thoughts, and mood-congruent recall. *Cognition and Emotion, 31*, 1361–1376.

Velden, M. (2007). *Psychosomatik [Psychosomatics].* Goettingen: Vandenhoeck & Ruprecht.

Velden, M. (2013). *Hirntod einer Idee. Die Erblichkeit der Intelligenz [Brain Death of an Idea. The Inheritance of Intelligence].* Goettingen: Vandenhoeck & Ruprecht.

Velmans, M. (2007). Where experiences are: Dualist, physicalist, enactive and reflexive accounts of phenomenal consciousness. *Phenomenology and the Cognitive Sciences, 6*, 547–563.

Vickhoff, B., Malmgren, H., Åstroem, R., Nyberg, G., Ekström, S-R., Engwall, M., Snygg, J., Nilsson, M., & Joernsten, R. (2013). Music structure determines heart rate variability of singers. *Frontiers in Psychology.* https://doi.org/10.3389/fpsyg.2013.00334.

Vidal, F., & Ortega, F. (2017). *Being Brains: Making the Cerebral Subject.* New York: Fordham University Press.

Vignemont, F. de (2010). Body schema and body image: Pros and cons. *Neuropsychologia, 48*, 669–680.

Vincini, S., & Gallagher, S. (2021). Developmental phenomenology: Examples from social cognition. *Continental Philosophy Review, 54*, 183–199.

Vogeley, K., & Gallagher, S. (2014). Self in the brain. In Gallagher (Ed.) (pp. 111–136).

Vogt, R. (2004). *Beseelbare Therapieobjekte. Strukturelle Handlungsinszenierungen in einer körper- und traumaorientierten Psychotherapie [Soul-like Therapy Objects. Structural Enactments of Action in a Body- and Trauma-oriented Psychotherapy].* Giessen: Psychosozial.

Vogt, R. (Ed.) (2008). *Koerperpotenziale in der traumaorientierten Psychotherapie. Aktuelle Trends in körperorientierter Psychotraumatologie, Hirnforschung und Bewegungswissenschaften [Body Potentials in Trauma-Oriented Psychotherapy. Current Trends in Body-Oriented Psychotraumatology, Brain Research and Movement Sciences].* Giessen: Psychosozial.

Voigt, B., & Trautmann-Voigt, S. (2001). Tiefenpsychologische Aspekte der Körpertherapie und der Tanztherapie [Depth psychological aspects of body therapy and dance therapy]. *Psychotherapeut [Psychotherapist], 46*, 60–74.

Volz-Boers, U. (2007). Psychoanalyse mit Leib und Seele: Körperliche Gegenübertragung als Zugang zu nicht symbolisierter Erfahrung und neuer Repräsentationsbildung [Psychoanalysis with body and soul: Bodily countertransference as access to non-symbolised experience and new representation formation]. In Geissler & Heisterkamp (Eds.) (pp. 39–58).

Votsmeier, A. (1995). Gestalt-Therapie und die 'Organismische Theorie': Der Einfluss Kurt Goldsteins [Gestalt therapy and "organismic theory": The influence of Kurt Goldstein]. *Gestalttherapie [Gestalt Therapy], 1*, 2–16.

Wachtel, P. L. (2014). An integrative relational point of view. *Psychotherapy, 51*, 342–349.

Wagenmakers, E.-J., Beek, T., Dijkhoff, L., & Gronau, Q. F. (2016). Registered replication report: Strack, Martin, & Stepper (1988). *Perspectives on Psychological Science, 11*(6), 917–928.

Wahida, A., Mueller, M., Hiergeist, A., Popper, B., Steiger, K., Branca, C. et al. (2021). XIAP restrains TNF-driven intestinal inflammation and dysbiosis by promoting appropriate immune responses of Paneth and dendritic cells. *Science Immunology, 6*, eabf7235. https://doi.org/10.1126/sciimmunol.abf7235.

Waibel, M. J., & Jakob-Krieger, C. (Eds.) (2009). *Integrative Bewegungstherapie. Störungsspezifische und ressourcenorientierte Praxis [Integrative Movement Therapy. Disorder-specific and Resource-oriented Practice].* Stuttgart: Schattauer.

Waibel, M. J., Petzold, H. G., Orth, I., & Jakob-Krieger, C. (2009). Grundlegende Konzepte der Integrativen Leib- und Bewegungstherapie (IBT) [Basic concepts of Integrative Body and Movement Therapy (IBT)]. In Waibel & Jakob-Krieger (Eds.) (pp. 1–20).

Waldenfels, B. (2008). The role of the lived-body in feeling. *Continental Philosophy Review, 41,* 127–142.

Walker, W. (1996). *Abenteuer Kommunikation. Bateson, Perls, Satir, Erickson und die Anfänge des Neurolinguistischen Programmierens (NLP) [The Adventure of Communication. Bateson, Perls, Satir, Erickson and the beginnings of Neurolinguistic Programming (NLP)].* Stuttgart: Klett-Cotta.

Wallbott, H. G. (1985). Hand movement quality: A neglected aspect of nonverbal behavior in clinical judgment and person perception. *Journal of Clinical Psychology, 41,* 345–359.

Wallbott, H. G. (1989). Movement quality canges in psychopathological disorders. In B. Kirkcaldy (Ed.), *Normalities and Abnormalities in Human Movement* (pp. 128–146). Basel: Karger.

Wallbott, H. G. (1998). Bodily expression of emotion. *European Journal of Social Psychology, 28,* 879–896.

Wallbott, H. G. (1998a). Ausdruck von Emotionen in Körperbewegungen und Körperhaltungen [The expression of emotions in body movements and body postures]. In C. Schmauser & T. Noll (Eds.), *Körperbewegungen und ihre Bedeutung [Body Movements and Their Meaning]* (pp. 121–135). Berlin: Berlin Verlag.

Wallbott, H. G. (1998b). Decoding emotions from facial expression: Recent developments and findings. *European Review of Social Psychology, 9,* 191–232.

Wallin, D. J. (2007). *Attachment in Psychotherapy.* New York: The Guilford Press.

Walther, A., Mackens-Kiani, A., Eder, J., Herbig, M., Herold, C., Kirschbaum, C., Guck, J., Wittwer, L. D., Beesdo-Baum, K., & Kraeter, M. (2022). Depressive disorders are associated with increased peripheral blood cell deformability: A cross-sectional case-control study (Mood-Morph). *Translational Psychiatry, 12,* 150. https://doi.org/10.1038/s41398-022-01911-3.

Walusinski, O. (2006). Yawning: Unsuspected avenue for a better understanding of arousal and interoception. *Medical Hypotheses, 67,* 6–14.

Wampold, B. E. (2001). *The Great Psychotherapy Debate. Models, Methods, and Findings.* New York: Routledge.

Warren, J. E., Sauter, D. A., Eisner, F., Wiland, J., Dresner, M., Wise, R., Rosen, S., & Scott, S. (2006). Positive emotions preferentially engage an auditory-motor „mirror" system. *The Journal of Neuroscience, 26,* 13067–13075.

Watson, J. C., & Greenberg, L. S. (2009). Empathic resonance: A neuroscience perspective. In Decety & Ickes (Eds.) (pp. 125–137).

Watson, J. C., Greenberg, L. S., & Lietaer, G. (1998). The experiential paradigm unfolding: Relationship and experiencing in therapy. In Greenberg et al. (Eds.) (pp. 3–27).

Weaver, J. O. (2015). The influence of Elsa Gindler. In Marlock et al. (Eds.) (pp. S. 40–46).

Weaver, I. C. G., Cervoni, N., Champagne, F. A., D'Alessio, A. C., Sharma, S., Seckl, J. R., Dymov, S., Szyf, M., & Meaney, M. J. (2004). Epigenetic programming by maternal behavior. *Nature Neuroscience, 7,* 847–854.

Wedemeyer-Kolwe, B. (2004). *„Der neue Mensch". Körperkultur im Kaiserreich und in der Weimarer Republik [„The New Man". Physical Culture in the Empire and the Weimar Republic].* Wuerzburg: Koenigshausen & Neumann.

Wegscheider, H. (2020). *Dialog und Intersubjektivität in der Gestalttherapie. Von der jüdischen Tradition und der Dialogphilosophie zu relationalen Entwicklungen in Psychoanalyse und Gestalttherapie [Dialogue and Intersubjectivity in Gestalt Therapy. From the Jewish Tradition and the Philosophy of Dialogue to Relational Developments in Psychoanalysis and Gestalt Therapy].* Gevelsberg: Ehp.

Wehowsky, A. (1994). Atem-Dialoge. Muster des Atmens als Muster der sozialen Bindung [Breath dialogues. Patterns of breathing as patterns of social bonding]. In Steinaecker (Ed.) (pp. 107–117).

Wehowsky, A. (2004). Zum Kompetenzkompass der Selbststeuerung [On the competence compass of self-regulation]. In. Geissler (Ed.) (pp. 153–177).

Wehowsky, A. (2006). Wirkprinzipien der Körperpsychotherapie [Change mechanisms in body psychotherapy]. In Marlock & Weiss (Eds.) (pp. 188–201).

Wehowsky, A. (2015). The concept of energy in body psychotherapy. In Marlock et al. (Eds.) (pp. 163–175).

Wehowsky, A. (2015a). Affective-motor schemata. In Marlock et al. (Eds.) (pp. 322–331).

Weiher, S. (2012). *Der Körper als Letztfundierung. Gesundheit und Wohlbefinden systemtheoretisch beobachtet [The Body as the Ultimate Foundation. Health and Well-Being as Observed by Systems Theory].* Heidelberg: Carl Auer.

Weinberg, K. M., & Tronick, E. Z. (1996). Infant affective reactions to the resumption of maternal interaction after the still-face. *Child Development, 67,* 905–914.

Weinberger, D. A., & Davidson, M. N. (1994). Styles of inhibiting emotional expression: Distinguishing repressive coping from impression management. *Journal of Personality, 62,* 587–613.

Weiss, H. (2015). The experiencing body. In Marlock et al. (Eds.) (pp. 419–425).

Weiss, H., & Daye, M. (2019). The art of bottom-up processing. Mindfulness, meaning and self-compassion in body psychotherapy. In Payne et al. (Eds.) (pp. 273–282).

Weiss, H., Harrer, M. E., & Dietz, T. (2010). *Das Achtsamkeitsbuch [The Mindfulness Book]*. Stuttgart: Klett Cotta.

Weiss, H., Johanson, G., & Monda, L. (Eds.) (2015). *Hakomi Mindfulness-Centered Somatic Psychotherapy. A Comprehensive Guide to Theory and Practice*. New York: Norton.

Weiss, S. J. (1990). Parental touching: Correlates of a child's body concept and body sentiment. In Barnard & Brazelton (Eds.) (pp. 425–459).

Weiste, E., & Peraekylae, A. (2014). Prosody and empathic communication in psychotherapy interaction. *Psychotherapy Research, 24*, 687–701.

Weizsaecker, V. von (1997). Der Gestaltkreis [The Gestalt cycle]. In Weizsaecker (Ed.), *Gesammelte Schriften [Collected Works]* (Vol. 4, pp. 77–337). Frankfurt: Suhrkamp.

Weller, L., Weller, A., & Roizman, S. (1999). Human menstrual synchrony in families and among close friends: Examining the importance of mutual exposure. *Journal of Comparative Psychology, 113*, 261–268.

Wells, G. L., & Petty, R. E. (1980). The effects of overt head movements on persuasion: Compatibiblity and incompatibility of responses. *Basic and Applied Social Psychology, 3*, 219–230.

Welzer, H. (2002). *Das kommunikative Gedächtnis. Eine Theorie der Erinnerung [Communicative Memory. A Theory of Remembering]*. Munich: Beck.

Welzer, H., & Markowitsch, H. J. (2005). Towards a bio-psycho-social model of autobiographic memory. *Memory, 1*, 63–78.

Werner, C. (1966). *Die Philosophie der Griechen [The Philosophy of the Greek]*. Freiburg: Herder.

Westland, G. (2015). *Verbal and Non-Verbal Communication in Psychotherapy*. New York: Norton.

Westland, G. (2019). Relating through the body. Self, other and the wider world. In Payne et al. (Eds.) (pp. 255–265).

White, K. (Ed.) (2004). *Touch. Attachment, and the Body. The Jown Bowlby Memorial Conference Monograph 2003*. London: Karnac.

White, K. (2004a). Introduction to the John Bowlby memorial conference 2003. Touch: Attachment and the body. In ds (Ed.) (pp. XXIII–XXV).

White, K. (Ed.) (2014). *Talking Bodies. How Do We Integrate Working with the Body in Psychotherapy from an Attachment and Relational Perspective?* London: Karnac.

Wienands, A. (2014). Körperorientierte systemische Therapie [Bodyoriented systemic therapy]. In A. Wienands (Ed.), *System und Körper. Der Körper als Ressource in der systemischen Praxis [System and Body. The Body as a Resource in Systemic Practice]* (pp. 107–121). Goettingen: Vandenhoeck & Ruprecht.

Wiener, D. J. (Ed.) (1999). *Beyond Talk Therapy. Using Movement and Expressive Techniques in Clinical Practice*. Washington, DC: American Psychological Association.

Wiener, J. (1994). Looking out and looking in: Some reflections on 'body talk' in the consulting room. *Journal of Analytical Psychology, 39*, 331–350.

Wiener, N. (1961). *Cybernetics or Control and Communication in the Animal and the Machine* (2nd ed.). Cambridge, MA: The MIT Press.

Wiens, S. (2005). Interoception in emotional experience. *Current Opinion in Neurology, 18*, 442–447.

Wildt, A. (2001). Gefühle als Atmosphären. Schmitz' Gefühlstheorie, ozeanische Erfahrungen und tiefenpsychologische Psychotherapien [Feelings as atmospheres. Schmitz's theory of feelings, oceanic experiences and depth psychological psychotherapies]. *Logos, 7*, 464–505.

Wilkes, C., Kydd, R., Sagar, M., & Broadbent, E. (2017). Upright posture improves affect and fatigue in people with depressive symptoms. *Journal of Behavior Therapy and Experimental Psychiatry, 54*, 143–149.

Will, H. (1987). *Georg Groddeck. Die Geburt der Psychosomatik [Georg Groddeck. The Birth of Psychosomatics]*. Munich: dtv.

Williams, M., Teasdale, J., Segal, Z., & Kabat-Zinn, J. (2007). *The Mindful Way Through Depression. Freeing Yourself from Chronic Unhappiness*. New York: Guilford.

Willke, E. (1986). Tanztherapie. Zur Verwendung des Mediums Tanz in der Psychotherapie [Dance therapy. On the use of the medium of dance in psychotherapy]. In Petzold (Ed.) (pp. 465–498).

Wilson, M. (2002). Six views of embodied cognition. *Psychonomic Bulletin and Review, 9*, 625–636.

Wiltshire, T. J., Philipsen, J. S., Trasmundi, S. B., Jensen, T. W., & Steffensen, S. V. (2020). Interpersonal coordination dynamics in psychotherapy: A systematic review. *Cognitive Therapy and Research, 44*(4), 752–773.

Winkielman, P., Niedenthal, P. M., & Oberman, L. (2008). The embodied emotional mind. In G. R. Semin & E. R. Smith (Eds.), *Embodied Grounding* (pp. 263–288). Cambridge, New York: Cambridge University Press.

Winnicott, D. (1965). *The Maturational Process and the Facilitating Environment: Studies in the Theory of Emotional Development*. London: The Hogarth Press.

Winterhoff-Spurk, P. (2005). *Kalte Herzen. Wie das Fernsehen unseren Charakter formt [Cold Hearts. How Television Shapes our Character]*. Stuttgart: Klett-Cotta.

Wittgenstein, L. (1967). *Philosophische Untersuchungen. Frankfurt: Suhrkamp [engl.: Philosophical Investigations*. Chichester, UK: Wiley-Blackwell, 2009].

Wobbe, E. (1992). Die Gymnastik. Entwicklung der Bewegung bis zur Rhythmischen Gymnastik und deren Einfluss auf den Ausdruckstanz [Gymnastics. Development of movement up to rhythmic gymnastics and its influence on expressive dance]. In G. Oberzauber-Schueller (Ed.), *Ausdruckstanz. Eine mitteleuropäische Bewegung der ersten Hälfte des 20. Jahrhunderts [Expressive Dance. A Central European Movement of the First Half of the 20th Century]* (pp. 25–33). Wilhelmshaven: Heinrichshofen.

Wolf, B. (2010). *Körperpsychotherapie studieren. Entwurf eines universitären Curriculums nach dem Vorbild US-amerikanischer Studiengänge [Studying Body Psychotherapy. Draft of a University Curriculum Modelled after US Courses of Study].* Saarbruecken: Suedwestdeutscher Verlag fuer Hochschulschriften.

Wolf, E. S. (1998). *Treating the Self. Elements of Clinical Self Psychology.* New York: The Guilford Press.

Wollny, R. (2012). Ich werde berührt, ich berühre. Körperkontakte aus bewegungswissenschaftlicher Sicht [I am touched, I touch. Body contact from the perspective of movement science]. In Schmidt & Schetsche (Eds.) (pp. 55–76).

Wollschlaeger, M. (Ed.) (2008). *Hirn – Herz – Seele – Schmerz. Psychotherapie zwischen Neurowissenschaften und Geisteswissenschaften [Brain - Heart - Soul - Pain. Psychotherapy between Neuroscience and the Humanities].* Tuebingen: DGVT-Verlag.

Worm, G. (1998). Zum Umgang mit Übertragung in einer analytischen Körperpsychotherapie. In P. Geissler (Ed.), *Analytische Körperpsychotherapie in der Praxis* (pp. S. 69–82). Munich: Pfeiffer.

Worm, G. (2007). Zum Umgang mit Handlungsdialogen in der therapeutischen Beziehung [Dealing with transference in analytical body psychotherapy]. In Geissler & Heisterkamp (Eds.) (pp. 211–238).

Worm, G. (2007a). "Der Körper lügt nicht" – ? Zur Widerstandsanalyse in der körperlichen Interaktion ["The body never lies" - ? On resistance analysis in bodily interaction]. In Geissler & Heisterkamp (Eds.) (pp. 259–289).

Wubben, M. J. J., De Cremer, D., & van Dijk, E. (2012). Is pride a prosocial emotion? Interpersonal effects of authentic and hubristic pride. *Cognition and Emotion, 26,* 1084–1097.

Wundt, W. (1911). *Grundriss der Psychologie [Outline of Psychology]* (10th ed.). Leipzig: Engelmann.

Yalom, I. (1995). *The Theory and Practice of Group Psychotherapy.* New York: Basic Books.

Yontef, G. M. (1993). *Awareness, Dialogue and Process.* Highland: Gestalt Journal Press.

Yontef, G. M., & Fuhr, R. (2005). Gestalt therapy theory of change. In A. L. Woldt & S. M. Toman (Eds.), *Gestalt Therapy: History, Theory, and Practice* (pp. 81–100). Los Angeles: Sage Publications.

Yontef, G., & Schulz, F. (2016). Dialogue and experiment. *British Gestalt Journal, 25,* 9–21.

Young, C. (2002). The memory of the flesh: The family body in somatic psychology. *Body & Society, 8*(3), 25–47.

Young, C. (Ed.) (2012). *About Relational Body Psychotherapy.* Stow, Galashiels: Body Psychotherapy Publications.

Young, C. (2015). Heart, heart feelings, and heart symptoms. In Marlock et al. (Eds.) (pp. 644–651).

Young, C. (2015a). The work of Wilhelm Reich, Part 2. Reich in Norway and America. In Marlock et al. (Eds.) (pp. 71–82).

Young, C. (2015b). Risks within body psychotherapy. In Marlock et al. (Eds.) (pp. 587–593).

Young, C., & Heller, M. (2000). The scientific 'what!' of psychotherapy: Psychotherapy is a craft, not a science! *International Journal of Psychotherapy, 5,* 113–131.

Young, J. E., Klosko, J. S., & Weishaar, M. E. (2006). *Schema Therapy. A Practitioners Guide.* New York: Guilford Press.

Young, L. (1992). Sexual abuse and the problem of embodiment. *Child Abuse & Neglect, 16,* 89–100.

Zahavi, D. (1994). Husserl's phenomenology of the body. *Études Phénoménologiques, 10*(19), 63–84.

Zahavi, D. (2007). *Phänomenologie für Einsteiger [Phenomenology for Novices].* Paderborn: Fink.

Zahavi, D. (2008). *Subjectivity and Selfhood. Investigating the First-Person Perspective.* Cambridge, MA: MIT Press.

Zahavi, D. (2010). Minimal self and narrative self. A distinction in need of refinement. In Fuchs et al. (Eds.) (pp. 3–11).

Zahavi, D. (2016). *Self and Other. Exploring Subjectivity, Empathy, and Shame.* Oxford: Oxford University Press.

Zahavi, D., & Rochat, P. (2015). Empathy≠sharing: Perspectives from phenomenology and developmental psychology. *Consciousness and Cognition, 36,* 543–553.

Zajonc, R. B. (1984). On the primacy of affect. *American Psychologist, 39,* 117–123.

Zanotta, S. (2018). *Wieder ganz werden. Traumaheilung mit Ego-State-Therapie und Körperwissen [Becoming Whole Again. Trauma Healing with Ego-State Therapy and Body Knowledge].* Heidelberg: Carl Auer.

Zatti, A., & Zarbo, C. (2015). Embodied and exbodied mind in clinical psychology. A proposal for a psycho-social interpretation of mental disorders. *Frontiers in Psychology, 5.* 1593. https://doi.org/10.3389/fpsyg.2015.00236.

Zhang, T.-Y., Bagot, R., Parent, C., Nesbitt, C., Bredy, T. W., Caldji, C., Fish, E., Ansiman, H., Szyf, M., & Meaney, M. J. (2006). Maternal programming of defensive responses through sustained effects on gene expression. *Biological Psychology, 73,* 72–89.

Zimmermann, R. Fürer, L., Kleinbub, J. R., Ramseyer, F. T., Huetten, R., Steppan, M., & Schmeck, K. (2021). Movement synchrony in the psychotherapy of adolescents with borderline personality pathology: A dyadic trait marker for resilience? *Frontiers in Psychology, 12,* 660516. https://doi.org/10.3389/fpsyg.2021.660516.

Zinck, A. (2008). Self-referential emotions. *Consciousness and Cognition, 17,* 496–505.

Zinck, A., & Newen, A. (2008). Classifying emotions: A developmental account. *Synthese, 161,* 1–25.

Zubek, J. P., Aftanas, M., Kovach, K., Wilgosh L., & Winocur, G. (1963). Effect of severe immobilization of the body on intellectual and perceptual processes. *Canadian Journal of Psychology, 17,* 118–133.

Zwaan, R. A., Stanfield, R. A., & Yaxley, R. H. (2002). Language comprehenders mentally represent the shape of objects. *Psychological Science, 13,* 168–171.

Subject Index

Name Index

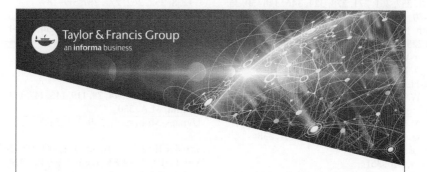